THE CONSUMER'S WORLD

ECONOMIC ISSUES AND MONEY MANAGEMENT

SECOND EDITION

E. Thomas Garman

Department of Management, Housing, and Family Development
Virginia Polytechnic Institute and State University

Sidney W. Eckert

Chairman, Department of Business Education &.
Office Administration
Delta State University

Gregg Division

McGraw-Hill Book Company

New York St. Louis Dallas San Francisco Auckland Bogotá
Düsseldorf Johannesburg London Madrid Mexico Montreal
New Delhi Panama Paris São Paulo Singapore Sydney Tokyo Toronto

E. THOMAS GARMAN has taught consumer economics and family finance courses on the high school, college, and university levels in Colorado, Utah, Texas, Illinois, and Virginia. He holds an Ed.D. from Texas Tech University. Among his activities in consumer education, he has served as president of the national professional association, the American Council on Consumer Interests.

SIDNEY W. ECKERT has taught consumer education courses in Illinois, Minnesota, and Mississippi in secondary schools, colleges, and universities. His Ph.D. is from the University of Minnesota. He is actively involved in promoting the interests of consumers and consumer education, and has served as president of the Mississippi Consumers Association.

Library of Congress Cataloging in Publication Data
Garman, E Thomas.
  The consumer's world—economic issues and money management : resource.

  Includes index.
  1. Consumer education.   I. Eckert, Sidney W.,
joint author.   II. Title.
TX335.G36   1978   640.73   78-21309
ISBN 0-07-022878-7

1 2 3 4 5 6 7 8 9 0   DODO   7 8 5 4 3 2 1 0 9

The editors for this book were Gail Smith and Alice V. Manning, the art and design coordinator was Tracy A. Glasner, the designer was Blaise Zito Associates, Inc., the cover artist was Elizabeth Thayer, the art supervisor was George T. Resch, and the production supervisors were May E. Konopka and Laurence Charnow. It was set in Times Roman by Bi-Comp, Inc.
Printed and bound by R.R. Donnelly & Sons Company.

Contents

Contents

Unit 3 Consumer Planning for the Future

The objective of *The Consumer's World* is to help people become more informed and better consumers. One cannot become an effective citizen/consumer without becoming more fully aware of factual information, developing favorable attitudes and a personal code of ethics, and making a commitment to helping to effect positive changes in the American marketplace. Informed consumers make wise decisions in the marketplace. These decisions ultimately raise the consumers' individual levels of living while also contributing to improvement in the morality of the marketplace.

Such an objective combined with a multidisciplinary strategy throughout *The Consumer's World* provides for an effective and appropriate educational program. This approach can be effective in such courses as consumer economics, personal finance, family finance, consumer finance, home and family living, money management, consumer issues, consumer problems, and consumer education.

The opening chapter highlights the basic consumer problems that are to be examined in depth. In all chapters students are given a distinct feeling for their involvement as consumers. Their attitudes and ability to critically analyze are challenged. The marketplace, its functions, and its reliance on consumer satisfaction are subsequently discussed. A special effort is made to introduce basic economic concepts and to explore the consumer's economic environment. And at every opportunity a strong emphasis is placed on the responsibilities of consumers.

The resource book is organized around three areas of consumer impact—consumers themselves, their effectiveness in the marketplace, and their preparation for the future. Each chapter opens with relevant problems confronting consumers, frequently using anecdotes and examples to gain and hold interest. A logical examination of the topic then follows which is written from the point of view of the student. We have accepted the challenge to write an interesting text which the student will read thoroughly. Hence, the style of writing is crisp and concise, anecdotes are appropriate, and cartoons are used to incisively illustrate selected points. A closing section, "Points of View and Problems to Think About," stresses important present and emerging issues and problems for consumers to consider. End-of-chapter study aids include a vocabulary checkup, a review of essential ideas dealt with in the chapter, and issues for analysis.

The Consumer's World is a challenge. It is controversial. It is informative. It is factual. It is honest. We believe such an approach will make the reader a far better informed consumer who in turn will help shape a continually improving consumer's world.

A separate *Practicum* accompanies the resource text. The *Practicum* is designed to serve the student first as a self-study device, and second as an opportunity to draw upon knowledge and experience to solve problems. It contains performance objective statements that give dimension and meaning to the resource text. Self-check exercises help the students estimate their readiness to proceed with the chapter activities. The heart of the *Practicum* is its full range of problems, incidents, projects, and cases that engage the students in various simulated or real consumer roles requiring them to apply their own values and judgments.

An *Instructor's Manual* is also available. It contains teaching suggestions, course management guidance, numerous related readings, learning enrichment ideas, and test questions.

We wish to acknowledge our appreciation to those who contributed to the development of the second edition of *The Consumer's World*. We thank the thousands of students all across the country and their teachers who have offered comments and suggestions based upon the first edition. Much appreciation is also extended to reviewers of various parts of the manuscript during its development, including Drs. Al Pender and David Graf of Northern Illinois University, Dr. John Burton of The University of Utah, and Dr. William L. Johnston of Oklahoma State University. We also wish to extend our appreciation to doctoral student Bobby H. Sharp of Virginia Polytechnic Institute and State University for researching text material, and to secretaries Charlene Jones of Delta State University and Gail Heikkenen of Virginia Polytechnic Institute and State University, who did the final processing and typing of the manuscript.

Responsibility for the final content, errors, or omissions rests with the authors, of course.

We think you'll like this second edition a lot!

E. T. Garman
S. W. Eckert

Foreword

A Nation of Consumers

Senator Charles H. Percy

We are a nation of over 220 million consumers. As consumers our demands are relatively modest. We ask for protection of our legal rights and the prevention of unfair or deceptive trade practices. We seek adequate product information, labels, and warnings; fair advertising, promotion, and sale practices; and the preservation of a free and informed choice in a competitive market.

As one who has spent over 25 years with a major American corporation, I can attest to the fact that what is good for the consumer is not only good for American business, it is *best* for business. Not surprisingly, most businesspeople are acutely aware of this and build their businesses on the philosophy that the product or service they produce is worthy of public acceptance. The corollary to this is, of course, that if a product or service proves unfit for the purpose intended, if it is unsafe or defective or its marketing deceptive, then those facts should be writ large so that an informed consuming public can make more rational decisions.

The Consumer's World represents a major breakthrough in communicating to the public the essence of what consumerism is all about as well as the larger implications of the consumer movement in the United States today. In the most graphic detail, the authors have assembled example after example of disregard of consumer interests by certain corporations in this country, large and small, and neglect of consumer interests by government bureaucracies at all levels.

When all is said and done, this carefully documented work constitutes a primer for avoiding the empty warranties and guarantees, the deceptive packaging, the unfair pricing and bait and switch merchandising, the misleading advertising, and the anti-competitive conduct which we find, to our dismay, in all too many facets of our daily activity.

If instances of corporate, industry, and governmental irresponsibility are to be weeded out, then the consumer needs to be better taught to spot and deal with such conduct. If we are to separate out those few firms which act without regard for their customers from the overwhelming majority that do, it is through an education process that this can be accomplished. *The Consumer's World* provides the kind of instructive and sometimes common-sense cautions which will aid immeasurably in furthering informed and responsible consumer behavior. And in so doing, it should, in turn, have a positive effect on promoting more forthright remedial action by those companies and those industries whose good name and reputations are indelibly tarnished because of the indecencies of the few.

It is high time that we as a society say "ENOUGH" to ineffective flu vaccines, rancid food, filth-laden warehouses, squalor and inhumane treatment in nursing homes, and diseased blood used in transfusions. "ENOUGH" to leaded paint that kills children, to carbon monoxide that poisons auto passengers, to clothes that flare into flame, to contaminated roasts, to chicken wings pocked with tumors. "ENOUGH" to unfair property taxes, insurance inequities, and the erosion due to inflation of the purchasing power of all consumers.

Messrs. Garman and Eckert document many of these problems and more. They have immersed themselves fully in the fight for consumer protection and in so doing have stormed the battlements for quality in goods and services, fairness in advertising and promotion, and honesty in the marketplace.

I personally believe that the consumer movement, of which this book now becomes an important part, represents a yearning, felt by all of us, for an improved quality of life—for an America that works again, for an America that cares again, and for people, products, corporations, institutions, and a philosophy that support this society rather than embitter it or tear it apart.

If we are to achieve that and do away with one-sided lobbying for loopholes and secret deals that sell out the consumer, we need a more informed and aroused public. Such information and cause for arousal is contained in the pages that follow. Perhaps the end result will be an affirmation of the interest of the many over the interest of the few and a realization that our society works best when a broader public interest overshadows narrow special interests.

Foreword

Consumer Education

Esther Peterson

Special Assistant to the President for Consumer Affairs

One of the primary goals of the American education system has always been to teach people the skills and knowledge they need to earn a living. Our schools do a very credible job of teaching people how to make money. But that is only half the task. It is just as important to teach people how to spend money.

Fortunately, in the last few years educators have begun to realize that teaching people how to spend is important. This recognition, coupled with a new awareness of the increasingly complex and technological character of our marketplace, has added importance to a vital yet controversial discipline—consumer education.

Consumer education is an active study specialty which develops sound purchasing skills and provides a wealth of knowledge to help people make more intelligent marketplace and life-style decisions throughout their lives. It will help you gain the tools you will need to survive and prosper in the marketplace.

You may find the material covered by this book useful immediately. Or, if you are living at home, some of it may seem unimportant right now. However, in any case, you will find it of great practical value in the future. When you have to decide which car to buy, which life insurance policy will best provide for your family, or whether to buy or rent a home, consumer education skills will be very useful in helping you examine the options.

Consumers must learn to vote their dollars effectively in their own best interests. As our society becomes more and more complex, it becomes more difficult to gather, study, and analyze all the various options available. Not only must consumers learn to read the fine print, they must know what the fine print means and how it compares with the alternatives.

Consumers must also remember that the best choice for their next-door neighbors may not necessarily be best for them. Each consumer is an individual, with individual wants, needs, and desires. They should learn to weigh all the possibilities and make the choices best suited to them as individuals.

Furthermore, while people must learn how to protect their health, safety, and pocketbooks, they must also understand how government actions affect their lives. They must realize that while they can buy energy-efficient appliances and conserve energy in their homes, their utility bills are affected by rate decisions of state and local utility boards and by federal legislation; these rates will never reflect their needs unless they get involved.

Consumers must learn how the decision-making process works in order to influence it. Once they understand the intricacies of government, citizens can become more involved in the formation of public policy. By becoming more effective as consumers, people become more effective as citizens, improving our political system and reducing dissatisfaction with government and the marketplace.

You as consumers must let your voices be heard on issues that are important to you. Our health, safety, and economic well-being can be enhanced only if each of us acts as a watchdog over not only the marketplace, but also the laws and statutes that regulate it.

The Dilemma
of the Consumer

THE PROBLEMS

Today's American consumer faces a dilemma. How does he or she make choices about buying in a market that provides only poor opportunities for making wise decisions? How does one find answers to such questions as these:

"Which brand of mouthwash shall I buy?"

"How much down payment do I need for a house?"

"Which tires should I buy?"

"The bank turned down my loan. Where else can I borrow money?"

"Where should I invest money for retirement?"

Simple answers to these questions are unavailable, and the reasons for this are many: (1) Fraudulence, deception, and misrepresentation characterize every area of consumer interest. (2) Inequities, or unfair advantages, exist for many consumers. (3) Marketplace complexities often overwhelm consumers. (4) Consumers feel helpless in many dealings, and often assistance is not around when it is needed most. (5) Ignorance, or lack of sufficient buying knowledge, is common with many consumers. (6) Apathy, or a "why get involved" attitude, is typical of many consumers.

Let us examine these consumer questions more closely. For example, when deciding which brand of mouthwash to buy, are consumers aware of some of the propagandistic terms associated with mouthwashes? Consider the words "medicinal" and "deodorizing." Fraud! Deception! Misrepresentation!

The Food and Drug Administration (FDA) reports that commercial, over-the-counter mouthwashes have no medicinal value whatsoever. Nor are they strong enough to have a long-lasting effect upon mouth odor. For a mouthwash to be truly effective either as a medicine or as a deodorant, it would have to be so strong that it would be illegal because it would damage delicate mouth tissues. Cold water is just as good for cleansing the mouth, or a solution of one-half teaspoon of baking soda to a half glass of water may be preferable to those who like that "tingling feeling."

Certain inequities can be observed when a consumer decides to buy a home. The required down payment on a $60,000 house can vary from $300 to $15,000, depending on the type of financing. Many potential homeowners have not served

1

in the Armed Forces and therefore cannot qualify for minimum-down-payment financing through the Veterans Administration. And strangely enough, low-down-payment financing may not be available through the Federal Housing Administration if the combined income of both husband and an employed wife is too low. The government, in the case of housing, may have inadvertently created inequities.

Wise buying decisions are almost impossible to make when consumers buy items such as tires. Factors to consider include tire size, driving habits, prices, manufacturer, warranty, quality, and the numerous synthetics used to make tires. Then there are the various types and prices of tires that can fit a given automobile. "First-line" tires from one store may be "second-line" tires at the next. So then one must compare nylon, rayon, beaded, belted, bias-belted, elliptic, 4-ply rated, 2-ply, 24-month guarantee, 20,000-mile guarantee, $39.95 per tire, and $62.50 per tire! The marketplace leaves consumers very confused indeed when they are buying new tires, yet a poor decision can cost money and perhaps even lives.

The question of where to invest money for retirement suggests that consumers have a definite lack of knowledge of investments. Are government savings bonds a good investment? Will real estate provide a "nest egg" for the future? What type of public bonds have the highest yield? Are second mortgages a good investment? Insurance? Annuities? What about the stock market? Serious study, counseling, and planning are needed to develop an investment program, and they should begin long before retirement age.

These types of problems are commonplace, and we will consider them further in this chapter. *Fraud and deception* exist, but hopefully the consumer can learn to avoid them. *Inequities* also exist, but with effort the consumer may be able to eliminate many of them. The *overwhelmingness* of the marketplace, too, can be minimized if one has knowledge to help

in making decisions. So also can the *helplessness* of the consumer, which is less formidable than it seems if one knows where to turn. The underlying problem of consumer *ignorance* shows the importance of consumer education. And finally, consumer *apathy* can be understood, reversed, and turned into a more positive action effort.

FRAUD, DECEPTION, AND MISREPRESENTATION

The uninformed and trusting American consumer is easy prey for the fraudulent and deceptive practices of dishonest businesses and individuals. If only 5 percent of the businesses in the United States are dishonest, that still adds up to approximately 260,000 companies. If we include the thousands of individuals who continually practice fraud and deception, dishonesty in the marketplace has got to be displayed in capital letters.

The principle of competition might suggest that unfair businesses will eventually be forced out of operation by honest ones, as it stands to reason that if people find out who the honest ones are and buy only from them, the dishonest ones will be eliminated. After all, consumers who were once "taken" should not fall for the same deception again. Nonetheless, dishonest business people have more than 220 million American shoppers to choose from and therefore do not need repeat customers—although the sad fact is that they often get them.

A formal education is no proof against fraudulent or deceptive practices, as the following example shows. A college senior was approached by a life insurance salesperson who interested the student in a policy. The salesperson then asked the student to sign an application form, stating that there was a $10 application fee that would be refunded if the student later decided he did not want the coverage. The following week the student decided not to accept the policy after all. He wrote the company and asked them to refund his $10. They replied that the fee was not refundable, as was clearly stated on the original application form.

Fraud? Perhaps, but if this case were taken to court it would be a lost cause. True, the student obviously did not read the application thoroughly, but equally obviously he was misled by the insurance salesperson.

The courts have been hesitant to try to define fraud precisely. This is because such a definition would only invite the dishonest to find equally precise—and legal—loopholes. Legally, *fraud* is considered to be a deliberate deception that the plaintiff-buyer relies upon as being true. But the buyer must prove deceitful intentions, and such proof is usually not available. Court decisions and other government actions do help by stopping thousands of fraudulent practices every year. For instance, almost all shady operators do some business by mail, and federal mail-fraud statutes can be used to prosecute these cases. Nevertheless, legal loopholes and problems of enforcement permit millions of consumers to be deceived daily.

One instance of consumer fraud and deception is an example of "bait and switch" that involved Sears, Roebuck and Company. Sears had advertised a portable zigzag sewing machine (which sewed on buttons and made buttonholes, monograms, etc.) for a nationwide sale price of $58 (the "bait"). However, people inquiring about the sewing machine were told by Sears salespersons across the country that the machine was noisy, was hard to adjust, did not sew buttonholes well, etc. Others were told the warranty on this machine was not as good as the one on the more expensive models or that there would be a long wait for delivery for the machine on sale. The customers were then encouraged to buy higher-priced sewing machines (the "switch"). The Federal Trade Commission (FTC) investigated these sales and got a consent order from the company to refrain from such a deceptive practice.

Another case of deception concerns the husband of the late Mrs. Lois Barker, who received a C.O.D. parcel addressed to his wife shortly after her death. This being a very emotional time for Mr. Barker, he could not possibly return something that his late wife had apparently ordered. After paying the $17 bill, he opened the parcel to find a cheap plastic trinket box, certainly not worth more than 59 cents and not an item that his wife would have ordered at all. Mr. Barker had clearly fallen into an unordered merchandise trap.

Even presumably worthwhile charitable organizations' efforts to help others can be fraudulent or deceptive. Take the case of Phillip Gordon, a professional fund-raising consultant, who established "The United Fireman Fund." This organization was supposedly developed to help the widows of firemen killed in the line of duty. After two years $120,000 had been raised. Of this, $90,000 was paid to Mr. Gordon and the remainder was divided between actual widows and the executive director of the fund (again, Gordon).

No idea or business practice is ignored by those who want to deceive or misrepresent. Sincere efforts toward self-improvement frequently go astray because of the deceptive practices of others. For example, Mary Jane Price, single and slightly overweight, saw an advertisement for exercise lessons at a local health spa that were guaranteed to "tone up sagging muscles so that life can be an exciting adventure again." A free physical fitness analysis was offered. Mary Jane visited the health spa. While there she was weighed, measured, and photographed. The instructor said that with a little work she could be a "new person." In dreamy excitement, Mary Jane signed a contract for 1 year of weekly sessions for $400. After a few weeks she realized that she could just as easily continue the exercise program on her own, but the $400 was nonrefundable. At the end of the year the instructor took new measurements and photographs to show her the improvement she had made. Since Mary Jane had already decided to

There's no charge for the options—mind you, the car's extra.

Courtesy of Edd Uluschak.

end the sessions, she did not buy the bargain offer for additional sessions. She saw through the plan and didn't want to get "bitten" twice. The first "bite" of $400 had been large enough.

All too frequently, incidents involving the selling of goods or services to consumers are not actually considered fraud. Such cases, which fall just short of fraud in the eyes of the law, are often considered *deceptive practices*. The way in which the product or service is being offered to the unknowing consumer is deceptive because it does not tell the whole truth. *Misrepresentation* is often a problem, too, since this includes a false statement of fact made innocently and without any intent to deceive. Honest business practices, together with honest consumers, would eliminate most forms of fraud, deception, or deliberate misrepresentation. Unfortunately, those who disregard these ethical or moral practices are only too numerous.

Misrepresentation can be illustrated by those "freebies" which can create problems for the unwary consumer. A classic example is the merchant who advertised that a 48-piece set of stainless steel flatware would be included *free* when a couple bought a 120-piece set of dinnerware. Bob and Lou Guthrie thought they were really getting a bargain when they made this purchase. Later Lou priced similar sets of flatware and dinnerware separately

and found that the price they had paid for the dinnerware had been marked up to include the cost of the flatware. They still had the merchandise, but they were disappointed to find that they had purchased it under such false pretenses.

Hasty decisions and ignorance can make one a victim of misrepresentation or deceptive practices without one realizing it. For example, Marilyn Day answered the doorbell one morning to find a handsome young man wishing to show her samples from a set of encyclopedias. She invited him in, and he explained to her the fine quality of the books. He pointed out the many uses that he was sure her intelligent children would find for the encyclopedias. Along with the books, she would receive a dictionary and five yearly supplements to the set. This offer was for a limited time only. Becoming more and more convinced, Mrs. Day asked the salesman a few questions about himself. He claimed to be working his way through college and really needed customers. This was the clincher. Mrs. Day could not resist the deal and the opportunity to help him. She signed a contract for the books. Mrs. Day had had no intention of buying encyclopedias and had not discussed the matter with her children.

In the months to come, Mrs. Day found that her children used the encyclopedias provided by their school instead of the ones at home just about every time they needed them. Later, when the first yearly supplement arrived, she was billed $20 for the book. In comparing prices paid by a neighbor, she found she had paid $200 more than the set was actually worth. Making such a hasty and uninformed purchase was truly a mistake, but it is very typical.

More outright fraudulent schemes appear almost daily in the American marketplace. The *Ponzi scheme* was promoted by Robert Johnson, operating as Ridge Associates, which had to do with wine imports. Johnson claimed to have a business purchasing "industrial wine" for use in manufacturing salad dressing and other wine byproducts. Many consumers were led to invest in this scheme by promises of 30 to 100 percent profits in only 6 months. Some of the investments were as great as $250,000. The investors were encouraged not to collect their money when due, but to let their profits accumulate. Johnson, it turned out, was not in this business at all, as "industrial wine" does not exist. He had kept the scheme going by paying off investors who wanted out of the deal with money from new and present investors. It wasn't long before the whole scheme fell through.

The so-called "con artist" has risen to new heights in the *bank examiner* scheme used on John Bowman. During a routine visit to his bank, he was approached by a man who claimed to be an undercover bank examiner. The man quietly asked Bowman to withdraw a sum of money from a certain teller, as they suspected the teller of withholding funds. The "examiner" reminded Bowman to be very secretive. The man sat in the lobby while Bowman withdrew $1000 from his savings account. He then returned to the "examiner" to have the money counted. The "examiner" took the money and wrote a receipt for it. He thanked Bowman for helping in the investigation and told him to return to the bank the next day. When Bowman tried to cash the receipt, a bank official told him there had been no such investigation and the receipt was invalid. He had lost the money completely.

Almost as old as time, the *pigeon drop* is so obvious, so exploited, and yet it still seems to work on the gullible, ignorant, and unassuming consumer. It is generally tried on the elderly—and frequently works.

Take the case of a 75-year-old widow in Roanoke, Virginia. The widow lost $1000 of her savings in a pigeon drop involving two young women. She felt the situation was too embarrassing to report. But two weeks later she received a telephone call from a man who said he was a member of the police department. He reported that the two women had been found and were in custody. He further said that it would cost $5000 to "make sure" that the women were convicted. Two men later arrived at her home to escort her to city hall to "confront the two women in custody." On the way, they stopped for her to withdraw the money from her bank and gave her a large envelope in which to put it. One of the men held the envelope on the way to city hall.

After entering the building, the two men told the widow to take the envelope and "see Lt. Robinson on the second floor" while they checked on another case in the courtroom on the main floor. The widow climbed the stairs in search of "Lt. Robinson," only to discover that there was no such person. When she looked into the envelope, she found that the "officer" had switched envelopes, leaving her with cut-up pieces of blank paper. She hurried back downstairs, but of course the two thieves had fled. The widow had become the victim of a "double drop," an added twist to the pigeon drop.

The generous American public also falls prey to charity rackets. Letters are sometimes received stating, "This deserving group needs your contribution, no matter how small." Or, "Won't you give just $5 to help?" These statements deserve close attention, particularly when the charities are not known to the consumer. Postal inspectors stopped one large fund-raising firm that sought contributions to find a cure for a crippling disease. Of the $22 million contributed over the years, $11 million was discovered to be earmarked for salaries and expenses. Furthermore, there had been illegal kickbacks to the officers of the charity.

One final instance of the gullibility of Americans can be seen in this ludicrous example. Many consumers rushed $10 for a mail-order product guaranteed to "kill flies dead." In return, they got a small mallet and a block of wood. The accompanying instructions stated that all the buyer had to do was catch the flies first!

Fraudulent practices, deceptions, and misrepresentation are, unfortunately, a characteristic of the American market system. Such practices as short-weighing produce and meats; short-measuring gasoline; offering outrageous land deals; luring consumers into expensive contests; offering them overpriced sewing kits and cookware; making them the victim of surgical frauds, mislabeled drugs, and insurance swindles are only a few of the more common fraudulent practices. And only 25 to 30 percent of them are stopped.

Present and pending legislation combined with effective investigative agencies could save consumers billions of dollars annually. But government alone cannot eliminate the problem. The consumer must learn to take care. *Caveat emptor*—"let the buyer beware."

CONSUMER INEQUITIES

The words *injustice* and *unfairness* may seem inappropriate outside of legal surroundings, but these words do apply to everyday consumer affairs. A more frequently used term, however, is *inequity*. Consumer inequities exist in many forms, although too often the consumer is unaware of them. Evidence of these inequities can be seen in routine purchasing problems, some of which are noted below.

A housing inequity case is that of Larry and Betty Wright, a black couple from Seattle, Washington, who tried to rent an apartment. Larry saw an advertisement in the local newspaper, called the number listed, and asked what the rent would be. He was told it was $250 per month, utilities included. Larry

asked the man to hold the apartment until he and his wife could get there to put down a deposit.

Upon arriving at the apartment building, the Wrights were greeted by a Mrs. Solomon. Larry described the phone call and repeated the rental price as quoted, only to be told that there must have been some mistake. The rent was $290 plus utilities, and the apartment was already promised to another couple. Mr. Wright then confronted Mr. Solomon, who had just come to the door. Mr. Solomon denied any telephone conversation. The inequity in such a situation is clear.

The following case shows inequity in our tax system. From January 1 to April 15 many of us work on our income tax forms. However, many other taxpayers do not bother with such a task; they turn it over to attorneys, accountants, or tax specialists. Of course, they pay for this service. Let us see where the inequity lies in this case. As a specific example, take Randall Fredling, a garage mechanic from Omaha, who goes to the local Internal Revenue Service office every year for help with his taxes. This service is free to Mr. Fredling; it is all he can afford. On the other hand, Cedric Byron, a sales manager at a large department store in the same city, goes to a tax accountant and pays a fee of $100. In the final analysis, Mr. Fredling pays a net tax of $1900 based on a salary of $14,900 including standard deductions and six exemptions. Mr. Byron ends up paying a net tax of only $950 based on a salary of $42,000. For those who can afford it, a tax specialist can uncover *every* legal loophole and can substantially reduce the tax liability.

Although most investors must cope with a general inequity—rich versus poor—other inequities also exist. To illustrate, a middle-aged couple in San Antonio, Texas, reevaluated their financial position. They decided to take advantage of the rising interest rates on certain types of short-term investments. George and Ethel Sager wanted to invest in 180-day Treasury bills, which at the time paid a very high interest rate. Mr. Sager talked to a

Courtesy of Edd Uluschak.

woman at the local bank about investing $6000 in Treasury bills. Under normal circumstances, no problems would exist; however, a new regulation had been established in Washington that prevented the banker from processing Sager's request. The new regulation stated that only amounts of at least $10,000 could be invested in Treasury bills. The Sagers concluded that the investment paying a high return was only for the extremely rich. They found it hard to believe that such an inequity had actually been authorized by the United States government.

The consumer who invests in the stock market faces another inequity. Mr. Max Bordley of New York City saw a chart showing the commission rates charged by his broker. He discovered that the small investor pays a proportionately higher commission rate than the large investor. And his broker charges a minimum fixed fee of $20 for any purchase transaction. Mr. Bordley felt that this was unfair especially since he wanted to invest only $400.

Inequities also appear as one looks at the food purchasing practices of a low-income consumer from Denver, Colorado. When Mr. Richard Jackson goes grocery shopping, he can spend only a small amount of money, and this for essentials. While on a shopping trip to the supermarket. Mr. Jackson noticed a sale of apples. They regularly sold for 42 cents a pound, but on this particular day they were marked 3 pounds for 99 cents—a considerable savings. But Mr. Jackson could not afford more than a pound. An inequity in income prevented him from taking advantage of the sale.

As shown by the several cases thus far, inequities do not single out any particular group of consumers. Conversely, no group can escape all the inequities that do exist. For example, a large supermarket advertised a big once-a-year savings on canned vegetables. Mrs. Hattie O'Connor from Elko, Nevada, an invalid widow with a meager income, looked at the advertisement regretfully since she had no way of getting to the store by herself and she hated to impose on friends. She usually bought her groceries at a small neighborhood shop because they made free deliveries. She

The number of similar but not identical products in different package sizes can be overwhelming to consumers looking for the best buy. (*Guy Debaud*)

also realized that the grocery prices at her regular shop were much higher than those at the supermarket. Mrs. O'Connor was penalized because she was unable to get to the supermarket.

A rather simple but strange inequity was found by Jack Collins of Atlanta, Georgia, when he was buying cat food. He picked up a 6-ounce can of Pert-All Tuna for cats, and noticed the following information on the label: crude protein, minimum 22 percent; crude fat, minimum 2 percent; crude fibre, maximum 1 percent; ash, maximum 2 percent, and moisture, maximum 74 percent. It was the first time Jack had seen percentages of such ingredients printed on the label. To compare a like product for human consumption, Jack examined a 6-ounce can of tuna and studied the label, "Packed in vegetable oil. Seasoned with vegetable broth and salt." There was a conspicuous absence of the percentages of the ingredients.

What is true with deceptions, misrepresentations, and fraud, is also true with inequities: Consumers need to be aware of the areas in

which they are being taken advantage of, knowingly or unknowingly. After that, it still takes time, patience, effort, and sometimes even money to find a possible cure.

OVERWHELMINGNESS

A major characteristic of the consumer's world is its *overwhelmingness*—its sheer size. More than 220 million consumers make billions of daily buying decisions involving more than 13 million businesses; the economy produces a gross national product (GNP) of well over $2 trillion annually. Equally overwhelming to the individual consumer is the specific area where buying decisions are made: the supermarket, the department store, the service station, and so on. Perhaps we can get a better perspective by looking at some of these specific areas.

The neighborhood supermarket probably has between 9000 and 10,000 items for the consumer to choose from. Each aisle can provide a challenge, as shown by the following cases. Mary Metcalf wanted a change, and she also wanted to save money. She decided to stop eating bacon and eggs every morning and instead went shopping for dry cereal. She discovered that one entire aisle contained cereals, and that there were more than 40 brands. Also, the sizes of the boxes were unbelievable: 6½ ounces, 7 ounces, 10 ounces, 10¾ ounces, 14 ounces, 14¾ ounces, 22 ounces, 28½ ounces, and 1½ pounds. Ms. Metcalf wondered why two boxes appeared to be the same size when upon closer inspection she found that they contained 10 and 10¾ ounces, respectively. The prices ranged from 39 to 97 cents, so Mary decided to compare the brands. Kellogg's Corn Flakes in one size sold for 41 cents and a comparable size by Post sold for 37 cents. Three other brands of corn flakes were marked 39, 42, and 53 cents, but the 53-cent brand was sugar-coated. To compare sugar-coated cereals she would have had to examine several other brands farther down the aisle. The overwhelmed Ms. Metcalf remembered the commercial on television, gave up, and decided to settle for the sugar-coated frosted flakes!

It was the soft-drink aisle that was a real surprise for John Gilliam. He was having a bridge game at his home that afternoon and he needed soft drinks. When he tried to choose a cola drink, he noticed Pepsi, Coke, Royal Crown, and four other brands. The sizes ranged from 6½ to 64 ounces. He saw 6-packs, 8-packs, 12-packs, returnable bottles, nonreturnable bottles, and cans. Mr. Gilliam finally settled on a brand; then he began to compare prices. He examined the 6-pack of 10-ounce bottles at $1.79, the 8-pack of 12-ounce bottles at $1.95, the 6-pack of 10-ounce cans at $1.49, the 28-ounce "quart size" bottle at 65 cents, and the 64-ounce bottle at $1.35. After spending 10 minutes determining the price per ounce for each type of container with his hand calculator, he bought what he thought was the best buy—$1.95 for the 8-pack of 12-ounce cans (calculated at $0.0203 per ounce).

The variety of supermarket products is appreciated by consumers, but the misleading package sizes, the large number of competing brands, and the absence of uniform unit pricing are *not* appreciated!

The size of the new car market had never bothered Lenora Calloway. She always bought Chrysler products, and this particular year she went shopping for another new automobile. She found that the Chrysler Corporation manufactures almost 100 model variations, and that choosing one brand was only the first of her many decisions. After selecting a medium-sized Chrysler, Ms. Calloway was faced with these additional choices: eight cylinders, a big engine with top horsepower, a smaller V-8 engine, or a six-cylinder size engine, power or regular steering, automatic or regular transmission (or "four on the floor"), power or regular brakes, regular or vinyl roof, and two doors or four. Also, should she buy air conditioning, power seats, radio, power windows, special gearing for extra traction, or whitewall tires? Ms. Calloway finally drove away with a "fully loaded" new car.

These extras are heavily suggested in the advertisements. In addition, advertising continually states that "This is the year that you *deserve* a new car." All in all, the consumers' world of automobiles is a confusing and pressured one.

Taxes are another overwhelming aspect of the American way of life, as a thumbnail sketch of the life of Bill Pace points out. When Bill was born in Detroit, his father paid $2 for a copy of Bill's birth certificate. When Bill received his first bicycle, his father took him to the local police station and together they bought a bicycle license. As a teenager Bill worked at various summer jobs and found that he had to pay federal income taxes and Social Security taxes. While in college, Bill bought a used car and paid a sales tax, a registration fee, a title fee, and a license-plate tax.

When a distant relative died and left him some money, he learned about inheritance taxes. After graduation, Bill got a job and discovered the city income tax. Later, he became dissatisfied and decided to open his own retail business with part of his inheritance. He had to buy business permits and licenses from the local government and from the state. During that year, Bill also married and paid $8 for a license. Shortly after, he paid $10 for his dog's license!

The Paces paid many other taxes. On their new home they paid property taxes to the state, county, and local governments. They had to pay state income tax, as well as various business taxes. Bill's father gave the newlyweds a gift of several thousand dollars, and Bill learned about gift taxes. Then Bill decided to buy a foreign sports car. He was shocked to discover the hundreds of dollars of import duties (taxes) that were hidden in the price of the automobile. Bill also found out that he had to buy an annual city motor vehicle sticker (tax) for the windshield. A business trip out West showed Bill the excise taxes that were part of airline ticket prices. And upon his return, Bill discovered that his community had just passed a special property tax assessment to finance a new fire station!

The ever-increasing list of taxes, the

Courtesy of Edd Uluschak.

numerous and complicated forms that must be filled out, and the increasing amounts that consumers pay in taxes every year is truly overwhelming.

In today's complex society, the field of services is also overwhelming in two ways. First, many services are essential. Even the poor cannot do without them. Second, the costs of almost all services are rising at a phenomenal rate. A brief look at the experience of two families shows some of the overwhelming aspects of services.

Len Stewart and his family live near the downtown section of Cleveland. A steady income is a problem for the Stewarts because Len's work is seasonal. He does not own a car, so he must use public transportation when he cannot walk the distance. The Stewart's apartment costs $240 a month plus utilities. Their oldest son, Len, Jr., wears glasses and, because of a leg injury, must visit his doctor once a week for therapy. The family rarely eats out. Len was planning on repainting their apartment, but recently his mother died after 3 weeks of hospitalization, and the money is no longer available.

Bob Johnson and his young family live in a suburb of San Diego. They own their home and Bob drives into the city each day to his office job. Bob's wife is active socially and has her hair done every week. They occasionally dine out on weekends. Their youngest daughter is learning to play the piano, and she also wears braces on her teeth. The Johnsons hope to fly to Hawaii this summer for a vacation.

The Stewarts and the Johnsons have different levels of living but their reliance upon services is similar, and both families accept these services as essential. A study of the Consumer Price Index shows that over the past 5 years the cost of glasses for the Stewarts' son rose 36 percent. Restaurant meals cost them 36 percent more, doctor's office visits 54 percent more, and a hospital room 126 percent more. Also, the cost of repainting a room rose 59 percent.

The Johnsons have not fared any better. Over the same 5 years, the parking fee for Mr. Johnson's car rose 32 percent. Beauty shop costs rose 29 percent, property taxes jumped 42 percent, babysitting charges rose 42 percent, piano lessons rose 30 percent, and the cost of orthodontics rose more than 40 percent. The plane fare for the Johnson's vacation has risen only about 17 percent, so if they can keep their budget in order they may be able to afford their visit to Hawaii.

CONSUMER HELPLESSNESS

Faced with the need to buy or rent a house, use credit, manage consumer services, and buy goods of all types, most consumers have come to believe that problems are inevitable. When faced with perplexing alternatives, consumers often do not know where to go for help; they face numerous situations in which they feel helpless. Let us illustrate this point with a few cases.

After having rented a third-floor apartment in a midwestern city for 8 years for which he paid $125 a month rent, Mr. Roosevelt James felt that buying a house would be more practical in the long run. Mr. James found a desirable single-family house, contacted the seller, and arranged to see the house. He loved it, but his dream of buying it was shattered when he was told it would cost $55,000 with a 25 percent down payment, using conventional financing. Neither the total cost of the home nor the amount of monthly payments were a problem, but a $13,750 down payment was out of the question. Then the seller turned to Mr. James and said, "On the other hand, I could sell this property to you on contract for only 10 percent down. The interest rate, of course, would be higher." Because he wanted the house, Mr. James had little choice.

Another case in point is that of Ron and Alice Cambridge from New York City. The Cambridges had too many debts for their income and wanted to consolidate them. Then Ron saw a newspaper ad for a loan company that offered a financial planning service as well as loans. The Cambridges met with Mr. Ron Conty at the loan company and discussed their plight. Mr. Conty assured them that he had a plan that would solve their problems.

"Of course," he added, "we do charge a small fee for helping you straighten out your finances. Since you need $4000 to consolidate your debts, our fee is $400. To make it easier for you we will just add in this amount for a total of $4400 plus interest." Mr. and Mrs. Cambridge were unhappy about the fee, but what could they do?

Buying and using services frequently places consumers in a helpless situation. To illustrate, after a severe cold-weather spell in the Twin City area of Minnesota, Charlie Jacobsen received a bill for heat for his home. The bill covered only 1 month, and Mr. Jacobsen was shocked at the amount. He looked in his files for past heating bills and concluded that the bill was about $50 too high. He then called the utility company to see if an error had been made. After Mr. Jacobsen explained the situation, a Mr. Littler of the utility company said, "There is no error. The bill was high because of the cold weather." Mr. Jacobsen then asked Mr. Littler about other utility companies from which he could purchase cheaper services. "There are no other companies authorized to handle natural gas in the area," Mr. Littler stated. "You have to use our gas or convert to some other form of heating. I'm sorry." This did not leave much choice for Mr. Jacobsen.

Buying tires can really "tire" one out if one experiences problems similar to those of a college professor in Terre Haute. A shopping trip made to investigate tires ended up with Professor John Gentry feeling most confused. All the brand names, the tread designs, the sizes, the various chemical compositions, and the complex pricing system contributed to his confusion. Even the salesperson could not explain the differences. Evidently, the professor concluded, there is no quality standardization in the tire industry.

CONSUMER IGNORANCE

Added to the list of problems confronting the consumer is that of ignorance. *Ignorance* in this context is based upon Webster's definition—"resulting from or showing lack of knowledge or awareness of *particular* things" (italics added). Used this way, the term is not derogatory but refers to the limited knowledge any consumer has on some particular topic, no matter how high that consumer's intelligence or how extensive that consumer's schooling. Let us look at some eye-opening examples.

Consumers buy homes only a few times in a lifetime at most, and ignorance in this area can be very costly. For example, Bruce Linden from Memphis decided to buy a house priced at $61,000. He agreed to pay $6100 down on the contract and to pay $469.76 per month for 25 years. Mr. Linden did not fully understand the rate of interest he would pay over 25 years. The interest was 9 percent per year—for a total cost of $140,978 over the full term! And, more important, Mr. Linden was buying a home on *contract* rather than by mortgage. He did not know that this meant that the house did not have to be appraised for the loan, and that the title would not pass to him until all the payments were made. Furthermore, Mr. Linden later discovered from a knowledgeable friend that his $61,000 house probably had an appraised value of only $54,000 or about $7000 less than the purchase price. His ignorance was truly expensive.

A similar problem in credit involves consumer ignorance about sources of credit. Ms. Sally Toms, mechanic for a local Ford dealership, found herself short of cash near the end of December. Her Christmas expenses left her in need of about $200 until the next payday. A nearby consumer finance company advertised "payday loans" as their specialty. Ms. Toms borrowed the $200 and in January repaid the loan plus an $8 service charge. Had she known, she could have borrowed the money from the Ford Employees Credit Union at 1.5 percent per month on the unpaid balance, which would have cost her only $3.00 instead of $8.00.

The field of savings and investments is so broad that no one person can be an expert in the entire area. However, average consumers need a working knowledge of the field if they are going to put their money to work.

One consumer, Al Pender, deposited $1000 in his savings account, which earned 4½ per-

cent interest annually, compounded quarterly. Al did not realize that, only a block away, the Lincoln Federal Savings and Loan Association was paying 5 percent interest annually, compounded monthly. After only 1 year this difference might seem small; the bank interest would amount to $45.76, while the savings and loan interest would total $51.76. However, if the $1000 was left on deposit for 10 years the compounded interest would amount to $564.38 and $647.01, respectively—a difference of over $80.

Consumer ignorance when buying insurance is pointedly illustrated by this example of poor judgment shown by one consumer. A young married man, Les Russell, with one child, felt that he could not afford health insurance. A group health policy available through his employer would have cost Les $58.40 a month for total family coverage, but he did not take it. For almost 3 years, he prided himself on saving money. Suddenly, tragedy struck. His wife became seriously ill with a kidney infection and was hospitalized for several weeks. Further complications developed, and surgery was necessary. The bills amounted to $26,975. Was what happened to the Russell family a result of unsound judgment, or was it just plain ignorance?

The problems of buying are compounded by consumer ignorance about product labeling. Let us consider two shoppers in a San Antonio supermarket. Sandra Willett, a newlywed, pushed her grocery cart up the detergent aisle. First she was fascinated by the number of detergents, then she became confused. In the box size she wanted, the prices ranged from 99 cents to $1.69, and the labeling did not help at all—"Whiter than white," "Brighter than white," "Cleaner than white," and so on. There was no concrete, useful information. Although Ms. Willett was college educated, she realized that she was totally ignorant about something as supposedly simple as buying detergents.

Over in the next aisle, Jack Pearson was studying labels on cans of spaghetti. One can read "meatballs with spaghetti" and was priced at 89 cents for a 15¼-ounce can. Another read "spaghetti with meatballs" and was priced at 69 cents for a 15½ ounce can. Mr. Pearson wondered why there was a difference in price for virtually the same size can of what seemed to be the same ingredients. He finally bought the one for 69 cents. Mr. Pearson did not know that food manufacturers are generally required to list the heaviest ingredient *first* on the label. Through his ignorance, Jack Pearson bought more spaghetti than he did meatballs.

Knowing what labels actually mean may seem unimportant, but consumers often make poor choices because of their ignorance. On a daily basis, this ignorance can be serious—not only financially, but nutritionally. To lack information or to be misinformed temporarily is one thing, but to continue through life doing nothing about it can be destructive.

CONSUMER APATHY

A final dilemma is consumer apathy. *Apathy* as defined in the dictionary is "absence or lack of interest or concern; an alarming degree of listlessness and indifference." This definition aptly describes the "unconcern" and "I don't care" attitude frequently displayed by many consumers.

Consumers are faced with numerous problems in the marketplace, and in many cases they are harmed physically, mentally, or financially. Apathetic consumers make no effort whatsoever to eliminate these problems and right the wrongs in the economy. Essentially apathy is a flagrant indifference to one's responsibility as a consumer, and it must be eliminated. Let us look at some incidents that will help to understand the effect of consumer apathy.

Ms. Anita Webb, from Georgia, purchased some egg noodles from a supermarket one day. That evening she opened one bag when preparing the evening meal and noticed small bugs among the noodles. She gasped, and immediately closed the bag. She examined another bag; it also had small bugs.

Her menu for the evening meal was abruptly changed.

Ms. Webb did not bother to contact the store about the incident but instead just threw the packages away. Ms. Webb's apathy here did not reduce or eliminate the problem. Had she talked to the store manager about the bugs, perhaps other consumers would not have suffered the nuisance she did. Retailers, manufacturers, and food processors need to know about these unpredictable incidents. Ms. Webb as an apathetic consumer was hardly a helpful source.

Or take the case of Bill Black from Seattle, who purchased a new suit at a local store. When he got home and made a more careful inspection of the garment, he found a flaw in the seam. Mr. Black fumed for a few minutes, but then convinced himself that nothing could be done about it, since he had not reported the flaw when he bought the suit. He did absolutely nothing. He just didn't want to be bothered and felt uncomfortable about reporting the incident. He decided to wear the suit, flaw and all. Mr. Black was truly an apathetic consumer.

Jane Allerson took her automobile into a Chevrolet dealership garage for minor repairs. The repairs were estimated to cost about $35. When Jane returned later in the day for her car, she was given a repair bill of $95. When she asked about the difference, she was told that other problems had been discovered that needed repair. Jane paid the bill by check.

After returning to her office, she carefully read the itemized statement showing the repairs to her car. She noticed several items and terms that she did not understand; furthermore, she did nothing about having them explained. Jane was afraid the mechanic would think her "stupid" about these items, and this would be too embarrassing. Because of her vanity, she joined the ranks of apathetic consumers. Consequently, she may have paid more than she should, and she remained ignorant about the items in question.

Consumer apathy also seems to occur in the area of household utilities. Normally one would think that a water bill would not be of much concern to anyone. However, Ms. Paula Crawford of Jackson, Mississippi, received a water bill in December for $45 for 1 month. Ms. Crawford realized that the bill was very high for that period. In fact, it was three times as high as her highest bill during the summer months. And during the summer she had watered her grass and garden almost daily.

Ms. Crawford mentioned the high bill to a friend of hers, who thought it needed explanation, but Ms. Crawford really did not want to get involved. She felt she would be accusing water department personnel of making an error, and that would hurt their feelings. It would be too embarrassing for her as well. So Ms. Crawford sent a check for $45 to the water department and forgot the entire incident.

In these cases, consumer apathy was apparent. Also, consumers paid money for products or services that were not properly provided. Yet each apathetic consumer rationalized the behavior of not questioning, reporting, or getting involved due to personal vanity or embarrassment.

Action of some kind, between business, consumers, and government will help solve problems. Consumer apathy must certainly be reduced or even eliminated. It must be replaced by interest, enthusiasm, questions, concern, involvement, action, and responsibility on the part of the consumer.

THE DILEMMA CONFRONTED

The dilemma of the consumer was earlier identified as being centered in the American marketplace. It is there that the consumer must make choices about buying in a setting that does not provide good opportunities for making those choices. It is true that the marketplace does have its problems with deceptions, frauds, and inequities, and that it is also a place where consumers sometimes feel overwhelmed and helpless. But the marketplace is not the sole contributor to the problem.

Consumers must look to themselves to solve the problem. Ignorance and apathetic behavior in certain areas contribute unnecessarily to their dilemmas. Much information is available, although too often it is not effectively used because many consumers do not want to "get involved." The *real* problem for consumers comes when they try to make decisions on something they know very little about. They must become informed. They must then "act" when they are dissatisfied in the marketplace.

To counter this problem, consumers must be prepared to analyze how they can effectively go about buying, and how the free enterprise system operates. They need to understand their role in the American marketplace, their rights and responsibilities, how the system works, and the economic principles that govern it. They need to be better informed about buying goods and services, about managing and planning money, and about the economic understandings that underlie decision making. Finally, consumers must bear the responsibility of acting, reacting, or just plain speaking out to help correct consumer problems that affect them directly or indirectly.

CHAPTER ACTIVITIES

Checkup on Consumer Terms and Concepts

Fraudulent practice	Caveat emptor
Bait and switch	Inequities
Deceptive practices	Overwhelmingness
Misrepresentation	Helplessness
Ponzi scheme	Ignorance
Pigeon drop	Consumer apathy

Review of Essentials
1. How many businesses are operated in a manner to deceive and purposely practice fraud?
2. What relationship does a formal education have to immunity from fraudulent practices?
3. Why is it that consumers can be easy

prey for fraudulent and deceptive practices in society?

4. Why are probably only 25 to 30 percent of fraudulent practices, deceptions, and misrepresentations stopped?

5. What is the primary difference in the labeling of pet foods and human foods?

6. About the size of the U.S. marketplace: How many consumers are there? How many businesses are there? How many items are available to choose from in a typical grocery store?

7. How is it that the pigeon drop and the Ponzi scheme can be successful fraudulent practices in our society today?

8. How is it possible that one person can earn a significantly higher salary than another and yet pay a much lower income tax on his salary?

9. With the rising costs of selected consumer services, identify some that have increased in price the least; the most.

10. Which type of home financing commonly requires the larger down payment, conventional financing or contract financing? Why?

11. What sort of problems arise for consumers as a result of their ignorance and apathy?

Issues for Analysis

1. To what degree should consumers become involved with consumer problems in the marketplace? When should they get involved?

2. Businesses are frequently charged with causing consumer problems in the marketplace. Discuss whether this charge is correct.

3. The role of government, particularly at the federal level, is that of being a watchdog, regulating activities, and trying to eliminate problems in the marketplace. However, it is said that these government regulations can contribute to consumer problems. Discuss the pros and cons of government regulation.

2

Functioning in the American Marketplace

THE PROBLEMS

Often the resources available in the economy are being sought by many—government, business, and consumers. Demand is far outpacing supply in mined ores, oil products, and other energy products. In addition, the responsibility of who shall *allocate* the various resources for use becomes another problem. For consumers who may benefit or not depending on who, how, and what resources shall be allocated, this problem is very important.

Many consumers do not understand the economic system by which the American marketplace functions. High prices, high unemployment, scarce commodities, product embargoes, and other recurring problems are part of the current system. However, they are not necessarily inherent in the system. The system is basically sound, but problems have developed as a result of internal, external, business, government, and individual influences and interactions in the marketplace. What corrective action can be taken and who shall effectively administer this corrective action are two questions that remain unanswered. That in itself presents still another problem.

Should government be a watchdog over the marketplace? What should be the role of government in society? How far should its regulatory powers extend? As laws are enacted by the Congress for the benefit of society, it may turn out that they are too restrictive for free business operations and the free *economic voting* of consumers. Society must monitor the amount and degree of government regulatory actions. But determining who shall do it, and how effective and equitable the monitoring should be, is yet another problem.

Business must assume greater responsibility for the manufacture and merchandising of products. Safe, healthful, and clean products and services should be the aim of all businesses. Government *should not have to* set the guidelines for the quality of products or services being sold in the marketplace. High standards *should* be established by businesses themselves. It is businesses' responsibility to operate in the marketplace fairly and in a nondeceptive fashion. But, full acceptance of this responsibility by business is difficult.

Consumers must become more responsible if they are to function effectively in

Courtesy of Edd Uluschak.

the marketplace. If a questionably safe lawnmower is manufactured, consumers can either accept or reject it by what they do. If they buy, they accept; if not, they do not accept. Essentially the consumer has cast an *economic vote* for or against the product by this action. Also, if they think a product is unsafe, consumers should notify persons or agencies to correct the problem. This is a consumer responsibility. Furthermore, it is the consumer's right to speak out to all concerned about products or services being sold in the marketplace. A problem exists, however, in getting consumers to exercise their rights and responsibilities effectively.

Consumers, businesses, and governments (federal, state, and local) have problems related to and affecting each other. A closer look at the American marketplace will give you a better understanding of its characteristics, help you see how we satisfy our economic goals in the system, and give you a clearer perception of accurate economic voting.

HOW THE AMERICAN MARKET SYSTEM FUNCTIONS

To work effectively, the American market system must depend on the cooperative efforts of several components. These include businesses, governments at all levels, and millions of consumers throughout the country. All together they determine *what, how, how much,* and *for whom* goods and services are produced.

Resources

The central economic problem in the American market system is satisfying *unlimited wants* with *limited resources*. People's wants are unlimited; they are variable and changing. It is impossible to satisfy all of them with limited resources; therefore, priorities must be established.

Types of Resources. We are limited in material availability (such as natural resources:

Harmony in Productivity

1. Take some natural resources
2. Add some labor
3. Add some machinery and equipment (capital)
4. Mix together with management
5. Moderate mixture with regulation and control for safety, health, morals, and general welfare
6. Output = Productivity = prosperity and well-being for consumers and business

FIGURE 2-1   The relationship of production factors to output

coal, oil, ore), quantity (of both natural and synthetic resources), quality (such as availability of only low-grade ores), and technical skill and money for investment (for further development). The task of the economic system is to try to determine the best combinations of the various resources involved. Consideration must be given to how much is to be produced, and for whom. It all comes back to the fundamental laws of supply and demand—business will usually supply goods that are demanded by the public at a reasonable price.

All factors of production are resources insofar as the economy is concerned, and all are subject to fluctuation. Figure 2-1 graphically illustrates how these factors of production work together toward efficiency in productivity.

Resource Availability.   The amounts of resources available remain reasonably stable or decline, but the population keeps growing. Sooner or later the amounts of the various resources available will fall behind the population growth. This will result in a lower level of living unless, as we hope, advanced technology, the production of synthetic raw materials, the development of skills, research, accumulation of capital, and general initiative can increase the supply of resources faster than the population increases.

Factors for Allocating.   The supply and demand for resources are two factors which contribute much to the allocation decisions of the market. If a great deal of one resource is needed to make a particular product, the allocation of that resource will be different from the allocation of one used in smaller amounts. The high demand for petroleum for making plastics is different from the demand for salt for use in canneries.

Consumers continually demand products through their purchases. As the demand for products increases, the manufacturer will try to supply more. As manufacturers need more resources, the market prices help decide who will get these resources. As a resource in demand becomes more scarce, the price normally rises. Therefore, higher prices ultimately place a restriction on allocation, and "allocation priorities" are established. Prices thus reach a point where demand for a resource is roughly equal to supply.

Energy is of utmost importance in the economy today because it is a high-priority item. Energy-producing resources are in short supply in America. To buy these resources (oil, for example) from other countries is very expensive; consequently, the costs will rise and become too high for many to afford. In such cases, priorities are established not only by prices but also by public policies on the national level. Conversely, if buying power is low (people have little money to spend for a resource), regardless of availability, that resource will not be used because there is no *demand*.

Circular Flow and the Production and Distribution Functions

Obviously, the factors involved in production make a major contribution to the American market system. Another important component is distribution to the final consumer. As the produced goods are moved from manufacturer to consumer, money moves from the consumer to the manufacturer.

Figure 2-2 shows how goods and payment for them move among the various sectors of the American economy. Together, the production and distribution processes give us a picture of the basic functions in the economy. Another term that describes the economic activity of both consumers and businesses is *circular flow*.

Of major importance in understanding the concept of circular flow is seeing how each factor depends on the others. Business depends on individuals to do work; individuals depend on business to employ them; consumers depend on business for goods and services; business depends on consumers to buy. All must work together. The money flow from consumers to businesses in payment for the produced goods and from businesses to consumers in payment for labor services is also part of the circular flow. None of the parts can stand alone; where one stops, another starts. Or, in other cases, while one goes on, another goes on at the same time.

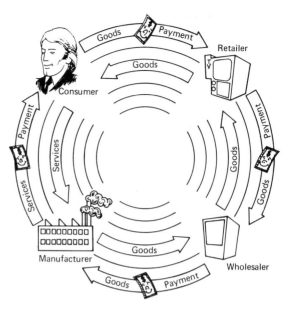

FIGURE 2-2   Circular flow

The Producer to Consumer Flow

Another type of flow which is important to consumers is that of getting goods to them from the manufacturer. There are several different ways of doing this, called *channels of distribution*. The channel used to get goods from the producer to the consumer can be either *direct* or *indirect*. Figure 2-3 illustrates the channels of distribution commonly used in the marketplace.

For the most part the particular channel used depends on the convenience or service the consumer wants. For example, it is more convenient to buy shoes locally than to order them directly from a manufacturer or to travel to the nearest wholesaler. Also, it is more convenient and less costly for a manufacturer to sell to a few hundred wholesalers than to several thousand retailers. And service on appliances, for example, can be provided more quickly and effectively by a local retailer than by a manufacturer or wholesaler. In the marketplace the consumer chooses among the available channels of distribution when buying any product or service.

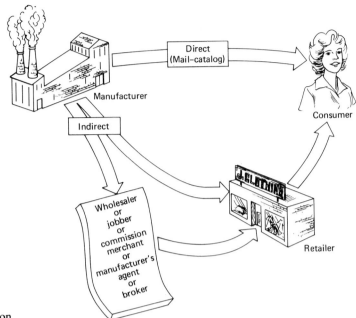

FIGURE 2-3   Channels of distribution

THE ECONOMIC GOALS OF AMERICAN SOCIETY

All of us, individuals and groups, are affected by what are known as the *economic goals* of American society. The six basic goals—freedom, efficiency, growth, stability, security, and justice—are discussed below.

Freedom

Certain rights and freedoms are given us by the Constitution and the Bill of Rights. Few of us, however, think about the economic freedoms these provide. Freedom of choice in buying, or its counterpart—the freedom to reject—is a basic right.

Essentially, freedom of choice gives citizens such rights as deciding what kind of house to live in, what goods to buy, what papers and books to read, and how to manage their towns and cities. Furthermore, businesspeople, merchants, producers, or manufacturers have the freedom to decide on the nature and method of operation of the business, such as when and where to advertise and how to market the goods.

Consumers and businesses must cooperate. If both are to do well, their freedoms—or choices—must be protected. That is, the consumer must be given choices and information about them. A consumer who then chooses unwisely must be prepared to accept the consequences.

Efficiency

In 1940 it cost about $40 to take a train from New York to Detroit, and the trip took 12 hours. A factory worker had to work for about 54 hours to pay for that train ride. Today, a similar trip by airplane would cost about $62 and would take only about an hour. Furthermore, today's factory worker could pay for such a trip with only about 10 hours' work—certainly an increase in efficiency!

Other examples of efficiency are found in living comforts: in the heating and cooling of homes, the preparation—such as freezing—of food, and the wide distribution of products that has made shopping nationwide as easy as shopping at one huge local market. It is through the combined efforts of the producers, workers, and consumers, that efficiency has improved in the last several decades. And the consumer's freedom of choice, when exercised, leads producers to aim for even greater efficiency.

Growth

Most Americans enjoy getting ahead. The same is true of the economy as a whole. A *gross national product* (GNP) of $750 billion in 1966, of $1700 billion in 1976, and of an estimated $2500 billion in 1982 certainly indicates healthy growth in the economy, even allowing for inflation. The GNP is the total value of all goods and services produced in 1 year. *Inflation* is a rapid price increase that reduces consumer buying power. A rise in personal income from $584 billion in 1966 to $1386 billion in 1976 gives proof of economic growth for consumers, too—consumers realized about a 137 percent increase in personal income between 1966 and 1976. Even after inflation, the "real increase" was a significant percentage.

The GNP has generally been accepted as *the* measure of growth in the economy and the level of living. Another measure, recently developed and currently being advocated as a better measure of the *quality of life*, is called the *Net Economic Welfare* (NEW). Nobel prize–winning economist Paul A. Samuelson has strongly advocated this new concept. The basis for it was first developed by two Yale economists, William Nordhaus and James Tobin. They called it the *Measure of Economic Welfare* (MEW).

Actually, NEW (or MEW) also takes into consideration the effects of leisure, household work, pollution, and "urban disamenities." For example, workers may reject overtime because they would rather have more free time than more money to spend. This value judgment would show up in NEW as a plus, but not in the GNP, which counts only money spent. Or moving from a small town to a big city might mean a higher salary (part of GNP) but also a longer commuting time, more noise, and generally more hectic surroundings (not part of GNP). Such urban characteristics show up as minuses in NEW.

The quality of life in America is important, but at the same time it is very hard for economists to measure. Regardless of how growth is measured, it is a fundamental goal for both society and individuals, since it brings with it overall economic progress and an improved level of living.

Stability

The government tries in various ways to produce stability and growth in the economy. It uses both *monetary* policies (the regulation of money and credit by the Federal Reserve Board) and *fiscal* policies (the adjustment of federal taxes and government spending). The government tries to look for and correct any imbalances, such as inflation, deflation, and unemployment. Both business people and consumers look to the federal government to help maintain economic stability.

Security

Linus, of Charlie Brown fame, clings to a blanket for his security. Children look to their parents for security. Adults seek financial security through having a steady job and earning a good income.

Security is an important goal for both individuals and society. For the individual, a job is a most basic form of security. For the nation, a sound national defense program provides one form of security, and government-subsidized work and welfare programs provide other forms. Regardless of its form, economic security is essential to us all. We work for an economy and a government that provide security.

Justice

Economic justice (distribution of wealth in a fair and equitable manner) is a basic American goal. And economic injustices affect our spending as well as our earning. We cannot abandon the goal of economic justice because of short-run injustices. And complain as some do, voters generally do not want to replace our economic system with another, even though in many ways "free enterprise" can lead to injustices. When one considers the alternatives, the system is still good.

The main problem is that as we try to get rid of one injustice, we often create others. Isn't it fair and just to guarantee all workers at least a minimum wage? Yes? No? But what if some small merchants cannot pay such wages and have to go out of business? Is then another injustice created? And if all were to be paid a minimum wage, who would pay for (be taxed for?) the unemployment income for people who could not find work? Perhaps whether a situation is considered equitable and just depends on who is evaluating it and from what point of view.

COMPARING ECONOMIC GOALS AND SYSTEMS

All countries in the world are similar in one way. Each country must solve a basic economic problem—how to satisfy ever-increasing wants with limited resources. Each society must respond to the following questions: What shall be produced? How shall it be produced? How shall it be distributed? The problem is the same; only the approach to solving the problem is different in each society. Basic systems or approaches used throughout the world today include *centralized authority* and *shared authority*.

Centralized Authority
Under this system nearly all the decisions on production are made by one person or group. Generally there is government ownership of most resources used by industry. The decisions on what to produce, how to produce it, and how goods will be distributed are made by this central body. Decisions are largely collective; under this system there is little or no *free enterprise* (freedom to begin and own a business) where individual decisions are essential.

Communism, for example, is a central authority economic system. This system seeks effort from each according to ability, and gives goods to each according to needs. Equal social well-being for all is sought as a goal, and indi-

viduality is permitted only when it agrees with the central authority.

Shared Authority
Most economic systems today deviate to a degree from a pure centralized authority system. In many, decisions are made partly by an authoritarian leader or group, and partly by the market.

In the Soviet Union most economic decisions are made by the central authority, with only a small portion left for the free market. In other countries, fewer decisions are made by the central authority and more are made by individuals in the market.

An economic system that reflects a lesser degree of centralized authority than communism is *socialism*. Essentially, under this system a little more individual effort is sought, and consequently the goals include incentives for individuals. Also, most of the central authority decisions are those that will result in social benefit to all.

As currently practiced in some parts of the world, *capitalism* encourages more private ownership of land and goods. It strives for individual initiative in using resources and in purchasing consumer goods. The system asks for effort from each according to needs and abilities, and provides goods to each according to earnings and most basic needs. The goals include individual satisfaction, opportunity, and freedom of choice.

Varying degrees of shared authority are found in Sweden, Great Britain, and the United States. In Sweden many major industries or services are run by a central authority; others are run by individuals. Great Britain has some centralized operations for the benefit of all—medical help, for example. But there is greater participation in private enterprise by individuals for personal or company profit. In both these countries the decisions made by the central authority can be watched by the people. Those persons or groups in authority can be removed from office (by elections) if most people disagree too often with their decisions.

The United States at present has perhaps the least degree of central authority. Basic economic decisions are generally made in the marketplace. What, how, and how much shall be produced will largely depend on the purchases and the use of products and services by consumers, business people, and government. Fewer societal and economically beneficial decisions are made by elected leaders. Centralized authority comes mainly in the form of government regulations to watch for and guard against the illegal or improper acts of a few. Ultimately these regulations benefit the public in the marketplace.

Consumer buying decisions are flexible under shared authority and somewhat restricted under centralized authority. Yet in shared authority systems there are varying degrees of centralized decision making and individual incentive and initiative. A right to be heard and to complain is available under capitalism but is more restricted under others. Decisions as to what shall be produced are largely made by consumers under capitalism, but are almost always made by the government under centralized authority systems. The consumers in each economic system must adjust to their own society's economic goals.

CHARACTERISTICS OF THE AMERICAN MARKETPLACE

"Moneymongers," "exploiters," "cheaters," and "persuaders" are a few of the negative terms that some people use to describe the American marketplace. It is unfortunate that conditions have developed that lead people to use such terms, even if they are sometimes true. Regardless of what various people say about different aspects of the American marketplace, there are certain fundamental concepts that describe it fairly well.

The Market System

A *market-oriented* system is probably the best way to label the system in the United States today. Essentially, it has five major factors: private property, free enterprise, profit motivation, competition, and supply and demand.

Private Property. Along with free enterprise and competition, Americans also have incentives and the right to buy and own personal and business property. The right to own property is guaranteed by law in this country, as is the right to maintain and improve that property as one wants. But, again, the government serves as the "watchful eye." If the property is not taken care of properly—if the use made of it has a bad effect on the health, welfare, or safety of others—the government tries to step in.

Free Enterprise. Free enterprise lets an American produce anything, governed only by restrictions in the public interest and for general welfare. Those who persevere and work hard can benefit from free enterprise. However, the government does stop people from engaging in such activities as printing their own money(!) or maintaining unsanitary and unhealthy food operations.

Certain obligations normally are placed on the entrepreneur. Taxes have to be paid on the operation. Certain licenses have to be bought. To some, such obligations seem too prohibitive. However, when we look at the highly controlled economic systems—socialism and communism—free enterprise, even with its restrictions, seems quite acceptable.

There are three basic operational arrangements used by businesses, and they are the single proprietorship, the partnership, and the corporation.

The *single proprietorship* is essentially business with one owner. It may be almost any type of business. The owner invests the capital, makes the decisions, operates the business (with hired help if needed), takes all the profits, and suffers all the losses. Typically, single proprietorships are small businesses, but there are some large businesses operating today under this arrangement.

Partnerships must have two or more owners. In other respects, a partnership is like a single proprietorship. The owners agree by a legally binding contract to operate a business for a specified purpose. The partners usually agree on operational aspects of the business to reach their goals. Often different partners contribute different things to the partnership. One partner may bring a large investment; another, accounting expertise; and still another, manufacturing or selling expertise. Thus the partnership will benefit from the special contributions of each partner toward the common business goal.

A *corporation* is perhaps the most complicated of the three business arrangements. It is formed by selling stock (for capital acquisition) to at least three or more persons who become the initial stockholders. The stockholders are the corporation's owners, even if they own only one share. A corporation is a separate legal entity, or person. If it loses money, the stockholders are not responsible for the loss. They can lose only the amount they paid for their stock. A board of directors is elected by the stockholders, and the officers of the corporation are appointed by the board of directors and charged with the day-to-day operations of the firm. Thus, the officers of a corporation are similar to partners and proprietors in that they must operate the firm on a regular daily basis. Potentially the corporation will attract the most owners. For example, a corporation with 50,000 shares of stock authorized and sold could conceivably have several thousand owners.

Naturally, there are advantages and disadvantages of each of the three arrangements. It will, however, be the responsibility of those who choose to go into business to evaluate the pros and cons and decide which is best for their operation. All types of business arrangements exist, some large and some small. Some will fail and some will succeed. But one outstanding feature of the free enterprise system is that one has the right to fail as well as to succeed.

Profit Motivation. The desire for profit instills energy, gives added incentive to work harder, and encourages people to take risks in developing new products and services or improving old ones.

The desire for *profit*, that income left after paying all one's expenses, can be either positive or negative. When it is positive it can have a tremendous effect on one's personal wealth and lead to increased national development and productivity. When it is negative (selfish), it can lead to exploitation of consumers, businesses, and even governments, and to major national problems.

Profit is healthy for both business and individuals, as it not only rewards them for their efforts but provides money for future investment, resulting in overall economic growth. However, some people don't see profits in this way. All too often the "man or woman on the street" does not understand the profit earned by firms. A recent survey of fairly large firms showed that the profit after taxes ranged from 2 to 10 percent. Yet the average consumer, when asked how much profit companies earn, often estimates 25 to 35 percent.

Profit has a purpose in our American business system. When one learns more about this purpose, profit motivation can be better brought into focus. This purpose includes (1) payment for taking business risks; (2) payment for money invested in capital improvement; and (3) payment for a job well done and a reward for genius, invention, or knowhow. Profits therefore serve a worthwhile purpose; they instill desire, motivation, and incentive. Perhaps the real problem is not profits in and of themselves, but excessive profits, and who decides what is excessive is another problem.

Without the "profit" motive, what with all the risks, investments, worries, and frustrations, few firms would enter the business world. Profit can be a catalyst, a driving force, and a necessary ingredient leading people to enter a business and succeed.

Consumers also, as stockholders, can enjoy the benefits of the profit motive of a business firm by investing money. The benefits ultimately would be the dividends paid to the stockholders based on the profits earned.

Essentially, the average citizen can understand and accept profits *per se*. However, the profit motive should not become a selfish motive for the company officials and owners. And it should not become a goal for a few at the expense of individuals, customers, and other businesses. If such practices should dominate business operations, it is time to take a careful look and perhaps seek action through the regulatory bodies both in government and business. It is important to understand that these regulatory forces are not meant to stop profit making. They do, however, serve to moderate it, and to keep competition alive.

Competition. The American marketplace affords tremendous opportunities for one to succeed in operating a business, but another ingredient, *competition*, means that a business must be operated effectively and efficiently if it is to survive. Competition allows those persons engaged in similar businesses to compete for customers, primarily on the basis of price, quality, and service. For example, one manufacturer may "build a better mousetrap." If so, the competitors may lose customers unless they charge less for their so-so mousetraps. On the other hand, one of the competitors may build an "even better" mousetrap and attract almost all the customers. In this way, competition helps to keep quality up, prices down, and reasonable quantities produced.

Monopoly stems from imperfect competition that results in circumstances in which customers can buy a product or service from only a small number of firms. This imperfect competition involves one or more sellers who are able to gain relatively complete control over the price at which to sell and the quantity of the product to be produced. Thus, under monopolistic conditions, one or a few firms effectively control one part of the marketplace.

In the market-oriented economy of the United States, there are government regulations that try to maintain competition and free enterprise and to prevent monopolies. And when there is a monopoly, the government usually steps in and tries to restore competition.

One legal kind of monopoly is a *natural monopoly*. In this case, the government gives one business the legal right to operate as a monopoly when it feels this is in the public interest or for the general welfare. Public utilities are often legal monopolies.

The American economy thus has some government regulation, but it tries as much as possible to operate with open competition among businesses. Therefore, the American economy can be described as a *mixed economy,* since *it is not* perfectly competitive.

Supply and Demand. An important functional characteristic of the free enterprise system is the relationship of supply and demand in the marketplace. Essentially, the two groups closely associated with the supply/demand relationship are the producers (supply) and the consumers (demand). What must be determined in the marketplace under the free enterprise system is *how much* to produce and at *what price* to sell the products being produced. There is continual bargaining between producers and consumers in the marketplace. Ultimately, barring extreme controls or market restrictions, the price that consumers are willing to pay for goods will be the same as that at which producers are willing to produce and sell.

To illustrate what happens, one can look more closely at supply/demand relationships by looking at demand and supply schedules. A *demand schedule* can be set up for any product selected, for example sweaters. The quantity of sweaters demanded by consumers in any given location will depend on such variables as price, income, taste, styles, and substitutes (like jackets). But assuming that all these variables except price are held constant for a given area or time, a demand schedule can be set up that will show what consumers would buy (*demand*) at various prices. The demand schedule would appear as shown in Table 2-1. This demand schedule can then be arranged to show the relationship between price and quan-

TABLE 2-1

Illustrative Demand Schedule
for Sweaters

Quantity Demanded	Price
2	$22.00
4	20.00
6	18.00
8	16.00
10	14.00
12	12.00
14	11.00
16	10.00
18	9.00

TABLE 2-2

Illustrative Supply Schedule
for Sweaters

Quantity Supplied	Price
18	$22.00
16	20.00
14	18.00
12	16.00
10	14.00
8	12.00
6	11.00
4	10.00
2	9.00

tity, and the end result will be a *demand curve*, as shown in Figure 2-4.

As can be seen from both the demand schedule and the demand curve, the quantity demanded will increase as the price is decreased. If any or all the other variables were changed, the demand schedule would be different. Obviously, therefore, many factors will affect how a demand schedule appears in reality.

If we look at the same product (sweaters) from the standpoint of supply (what producers are willing to supply at any given time and place), variables will again have to be considered. These variables include price, raw materials costs, labor costs, capital investment, government and union controls, and profit sought.

Assuming that all these variables are held constant except price, a *supply schedule* can be constructed. It would be as shown in Table 2-2. And, as with the demand schedule, a *supply curve* can result. This supply curve is shown in Figure 2-5. One can see from either

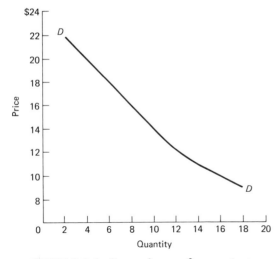

FIGURE 2-4   Demand curve for sweaters

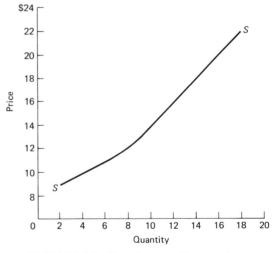

FIGURE 2-5   Supply curve for sweaters

the supply schedule or the supply curve that producers are willing to produce more sweaters when they will get more money for each. When other variables in addition to price change, the supply schedule will be altogether different.

A continual problem is getting demanders (consumers) and suppliers (producers) to agree on quantities produced and prices paid with which they will both be satisfied. This agreement, when it comes, is referred to on a graph as an *equilibrium point E*. This equality relationship is shown in Figure 2-6 by using the two curves (demand and supply) on the same set of vertical and horizontal axes—price and quantity.

As can be seen from Figure 2-6, the point of equilibrium comes at a price of $14.00 and a quantity of 10. And looking further, it can be seen that if the producers were to suggest a price of $20.00, the consumers would be willing to buy only four at that price. Consumers would tend to buy alternatives (light jackets, vests, coats, etc.) until the producers were willing to lower the price. Through the interaction of the producers and consumers in the market system, gradually the price would come down until it was agreeable to both groups.

A reverse action would tend to occur if the price consumers were willing to pay was only $9.00. At that price the quantity demanded would be high (18). But producers would be willing to produce only two sweaters. With so few sweaters supplied for such a heavy demand, the price would go upward, since some consumers would be willing to offer more dollars for a few sweaters. Thus, the price would tend to be forced back to a point where the supply of sweaters would equal the demand for sweaters. Again interaction between producer and consumer as they vie for and achieve a position of supply and demand satisfaction is inherent in the free market.

The Role of Business

An integral part of the marketplace is the business sector. Businesses, governments, and

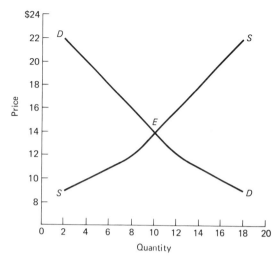

FIGURE 2-6 Demand and supply curves for sweaters

consumers must work together, and each must perform their function as best they can. Business' role includes regulatory responsibility, pace setting, and self-policing. Ultimately, business is accountable to itself, to the government, and to consumers.

Regulatory Responsibility. It seems that all too often business owners and managers, and also the public, look to government for regulatory guidelines and enforcement. This should *not* be the case in a market-directed economy. Government regulation, needed to help monitor problems in the marketplace, should be used only as a last resort when other avenues have been tried and failed.

Businesses can take on more regulatory responsibility than they have done. For example, if businesses are making unsafe products, why is it necessary for the Consumer Product Safety Commission to issue regulations requiring businesses to notify the government that the product as tested is unsafe? Could it be that some business owners do not care? Or, why is it necessary for the federal government to require businesses to stop most air and water pollution? Can business officials not see that sometimes their manufacturing processes are polluting the air and water unnecessarily?

In essence, businesses must take on the responsibility of checking their own operations for quality and safety. They must anticipate environmental problems resulting from manufacturing processes and not wait for a government agency to tell them. The problems exist continually, but up to now too many businesses have shirked their responsibility of self-regulation. In fact, if business does not do a better job of regulating itself, more will be done by government. Does business want more government regulation as part of the American free enterprise system?

Setting the Pace. Former President Gerald Ford once vetoed a bill which would have authorized $160 million in research money for developing an electric car. The idea seemed plausible in view of the energy problem in the country. But President Ford said in his veto message, "While government can play an important role in exploring particular phases of electric vehicle feasibility, it must be recognized that private industry already has substantial experience and interest in the development of practical electric transportation."

Did Henry Ford use government-funded research to help design and develop his first combustion engine vehicle? Hardly. He saw a need, had an idea and knowhow, and pursued the development with vigor as a private businessperson. He set the pace. President Ford probably was right. It is the responsibility of private industry in a market-directed economy to be the leaders and set the pace, and not allow the government to do too much of the planning and research. Private industry is well aware of the energy problem and the need to develop an electric car or a noncombustion engine of some kind. Businesses need to lead, not follow, in the free enterprise system.

To help decide how to set examples, what to manufacture, or the quantities to establish, business officials need to listen to their employees and to the public. Pitney Bowes, Inc., a manufacturer of mail processing equipment, for several years has held "jobholder meetings" similar to stockholder meetings. The main purpose is to give all employees a chance to ask questions of management, to get information, and to offer suggestions. In addition, it is the policy of Pitney Bowes that all questions and suggestions will be given an acceptable response either on the spot or in writing. In this way management is setting the pace for seeking help from and giving information to its employees. So long as the communication lines are left open between employees and management, there is less need to seek help from outside sources.

Self-Policing. "Set your sights high and work diligently to achieve them," a successful businessman told a group of high school students. The businessman was describing his philosophy about designing, developing, manufacturing, and promoting a product that he had started within business. Specifically, his statement was aimed at ensuring product quality.

Business must police itself on the quality of the products and/or services it supplies to customers. Several companies have taken major steps in recent years to improve their self-policing. Many of these companies have established a consumer affairs department within their organizations. These departments try to help customers who have complaints about a product or service, to deal with problems about the company, and to provide information to the public. The feedback these departments provide can help management improve quality control for the product or service. Therefore, self-policing comes about with the help of a business's customers.

Peter Drucker, a well-known management authority and consultant, advises top management to get out and see and hear for themselves what is going on in their business. Further, he warns that not to do this is to ignore their business, their customers, and their general business responsibility in society. What better way is there for the president of General Motors, for example, to find out what is going on in auto dealerships throughout the

country than to visit some of these
dealerships? He needs to talk to the managers,
the salespersons, and particularly the customers. This information would be first-hand and
not "laundered" several times through several management levels.

Richard Ferris, president of United Airlines, often talks to his customers on United
flights to get their comments on airline service.
And these customer conversations are purposely insulated from airline managers,
supervisors, or employees to get the plain
truth. In fact, Mr. Ferris will often ride coach.
He says that if he doesn't ride "back there,"
he doesn't know what is going on.

Self-policing is being done by many
businesses. More needs to be done, however,
so that management knows more about what's
going on in the marketplace with their product
or service. Then if errors are made, product
quality is lowered, or service is too slow,
these can be corrected quickly. And finally, if
businesses monitor themselves, there is less
need for government policing through regulations and legislation.

Accountability. Accountability is not a new
idea. It is, however, getting a new emphasis.
The public is becoming more concerned about
inflation, air and water pollution, and the quality of products and services. They want to hold
someone accountable—why not business?
Businesses are involved directly and indirectly
in making and distributing products and services that can cause economic or other problems in the marketplace.

If a toy bought for a child for her birthday
does not work, who should answer? If a food
product is contaminated during processing,
who should answer? When pollution results
from the manufacture of chemical products,
and the residue is poured into rivers and lakes
and the air knowingly and willingly, who
should answer? Business must be held accountable for these infractions of both product
and service.

A renewed age of accountability is upon us.
Many persons are in effect "grading" all as-

pects of the economy—business, government,
politics, regulatory agencies, and others. In
one survey people were asked to rate various
aspects of our economy on a scale of 1 (poor)
to 7 (excellent), as shown in Table 2-3. Although the ratings covered a number of institutions, the items of particular interest to us
would be those that are classified as business
or business-related. As can be noted, there is
quite a range, and few were given a very high
rating.

This is just one way of measuring the accountability of business. To others a good
profit or customer service is a way of showing
accountability. And to yet others, for
businesses to be willing to accept criticism or
suggestions and to act in response shows
accountability.

Because of this accountability, the president of Lone Star Brewing samples the product daily. He consumes from three to five bottles of Lone Star Beer each day at various
places to check on the quality. He is an example of one who knows he is accountable and is
doing something about it in a constructive
way. Other corporate executives representing
Pizza Hut, Howard Johnsons, Sonesta International Hotels, Cole National Shop, Southern Airways, Montgomery Ward and Co., and
Stop and Shop have been spot-checking to find
out what is going on "in the field" with their
products and/or services.

No matter how businesses are held accountable or what they are held accountable
for, such accountability needs to continue.
Business accountability for deeds and misdeeds is a must to help ensure quality in the
marketplace.

The Role of the Federal Government

At times the federal government steps in to
regulate the market system. Under our Constitution, it tries through a system of checks
and balances to make the dishonest honest and
to make the irresponsible more responsible. In
addition, it participates very widely in the
economy, through its fiscal and monetary

policies, to try to uphold the ideals and goals of our American form of government and market-directed economy.

Fiscal Policy.   Using *fiscal policies* the government can affect economic activity through its own spending, and through raising or lowering taxes. These policies affect both consumers and businesses. For example, if there is too great a money supply and rising consumer demand, increased spending and higher prices (an inflationary situation) usually result. The government, using its fiscal policy tools, could then raise taxes. If taxes are raised, less money is available to spend. (We assume here, that the taxes collected would not be immediately spent by the government.)

To capsule the fiscal policy as exercised by

TABLE 2-3

How Americans Judge Basic Institutions

Using a scale of 1 (poor) to 7 (excellent), here is the way those surveyed rank industries, professions and institutions for:

Honesty, Dependability, and Integrity	Average Rating	Ability to "Get Things Done"	Average Rating
1. Banks	5.00	1. Banks	5.06
2. Small businesses	4.62	2. Television	4.81
3. Organized religion	4.57	3. Medical profession	4.78
4. Medical profession	4.49	4. Newspapers	4.74
5. Educators	4.31	5. Radio	4.71
6. Supreme Court	4.27	6. Advertising agencies	4.70
7. Radio	4.13	7. Large businesses	4.61
8. Newspapers	3.94	8. Business executives	4.45
9. Magazines	3.90	9. Magazines	4.37
10. U.S. military	3.89	10. Small businesses	4.28
11. Business executives	3.68	11. Labor-union leaders	4.23
12. Television	3.67	12. U.S. military	4.21
13. Local governments	3.59	13. Organized religion	4.09
14. Legal profession	3.50	14. Legal profession	4.07
15. State governments	3.40	15. Supreme Court	3.98
16. Large businesses	3.38	16. Educators	3.88
16. Senate	3.38	17. Local governments	3.60
18. The White House	3.34	18. State governments	3.42
19. House of Representatives	3.29	19. Democratic Party	3.22
20. Advertising agencies	3.21	20. The White House	3.17
21. Regulatory agencies	3.20	20. Senate	3.17
22. Democratic Party	3.17	22. Regulatory agencies	3.14
23. Republican Party	2.93	23. House of Representatives	3.05
24. Labor-union leaders	2.72	24. Republican Party	2.93
25. Federal bureaucracy	2.63	25. Politicians	2.58
26. Politicians	2.33	26. Federal bureaucracy	2.57

Source: U.S. News and World Report, September 13, 1976, p. 41.

Economic Problem	Prescribed Fiscal Policy	Possible Reaction	Normal Effect
Slowing down of the economy, little spending	Increase government spending, reduce federal taxes, or both	Greater spending by consumers and business, more money made available	More jobs created, increased spending power, greater confidence in business and government
Inflation	Decrease spending, increase taxes	Reduce consumer and business spending, less money available	Reduced net pay for consumer and business spending, cutback in consumer and business spending, decreased demand for goods, gradual reduction in prices

the federal government, an action-reaction economic chain as adapted from J. C. Penney Co. would appear as shown above.

All in all, the efforts made by the government in its role as overseer of the economy are made with good intentions. On occasion, of course, there are disagreements over these policies. Still, the actions taken are for the good of the public and the country.

Monetary Policy. Monetary tools include raising or lowering the *discount rate,* the interest rate at which banks can borrow money from the federal reserve banks; adjusting the *reserve requirement ratio,* the percentage of deposits that banks must hold as money reserves as security for deposits held for its customers; and *open market operations,* buying and selling government securities. These powers, along with others, are used to increase or decrease the flow of money.

In summary, government monetary policy used to develop an economic action could be as shown below.

Another factor which increases or decreases the money flow is the *multiplier principle.* The multiplier principle reinforces the fiscal and monetary policies of the government as well as private spending. What happens is that with earnings, part will be used for consumption and part for saving. The part which is used for consumption will be a second person's earnings. This second person will also use part for consumption and part for savings.

Economic Problem	Prescribed Monetary Policy	Possible Reaction	Normal Effect
Inflation	Tighten money supply, reduce bank reserves	Interest rates increase, less money available	Money is scarce, reduced borrowing, reduced spending, decreased demand for goods, general slowdown in economy
High unemployment	Increase bank reserves, buy back government securities	Increase in economic activity, lower interest rates	Economy strengthened, more loans are made, more money is made available to spend, more jobs are created as spending is increased

The pattern will be repeated several times, and the amount of earnings with which the cycle began will be increased or multiplied many times. (See Table 2-4.)

As can be seen from the figures in Table 2-4, the final amount earned is about 10 times the original amount. The same is true with the consumption and savings amounts. At this 10/90 percent savings/consumption ratio, the multiplier will be 10. The multiplier is determined by dividing 1 by the savings rate. To illustrate, if one has a savings rate of 10 percent ($^1/_{10}$ of 100 percent) of income, 1 divided by $^1/_{10}$ equals 10. If the savings rate was 25 percent (100 percent divided by 25 percent equals $^1/_4$), the multiplier would be 1 divided by $^1/_4$, or 4. One should also realize that a decrease in consumption (increase in savings) could result in a much larger decrease in the flow of funds in the economy.

Regulatory Processes. The federal government's role in the economy is largely one of regulation. Through various agencies, departments, Congress, and the executive levels, the government tries to regulate some aspects of the economy.

Frequent questions asked are: "How much regulation is good?" "Does the government overregulate?" "Is regulation administered fairly to all groups in the economy?" Several government agencies have been criticized for offering preferential treatment to the industries they are supposed to regulate instead of acting more in the "public interest." For example, the Interstate Commerce Commission (ICC), the Civil Aeronautics Board, (CAB), and the Federal Communications Commissions (FCC) are often called "client-oriented" agencies, since they tend to protect the industries rather than regulate them. Many other government agencies reach, to some extent, almost every phase of business and touch the lives of every consumer indirectly and sometimes directly through their regulatory powers.

The sometimes overwhelming regulatory processes are often staggeringly inefficient. For example,

- It costs about half as much to fly between San Francisco and Los Angeles (397 miles intrastate) than between Chicago and Minneapolis (429 miles) or Washington and New York (234 miles) (interstate federally regulated rates).
- The ICC will not allow interstate truckers to carry shipments on return trips.

TABLE 2-4

Multiplier Principle Illustrated

Earnings Step	Earnings*	Consumption/90%	Savings/10%
1	$ 10,000.00	$ 9,000.00	$ 1,000.00
2	9,000.00	8,100.00	900.00
3	8,100.00	7,290.00	810.00
4	7,290.00	6,561.00	729.00
5	6,561.00	5,904.90	656.10
6	5,904.90	5,314.41	590.49
All other steps	53,144.10	47,829.69	5,314.41
Accumulated totals	$100,000.00	$90,000.00	$10,000.00

* Consumption spending by one becomes earnings of another.

- A small TV station has to supply 45 pounds of documents to the FCC when applying for license renewal.

On the other hand, there are regulations that protect and aid the consumer, which are very important and under less criticism. Mary Bennett Peterson in her book *The Regulated Consumer* classified government regulation as benign on one end of a continuum and interventionistic at the other. *Benign* regulation is designed to be neutral or helpful to all in our society. Traffic laws, safety regulations, and pollution standards of all types are examples of benign regulation. *Interventionistic* regulation distorts the free market and all too often interrupts the process of supply and demand. In her view, interventionistic regulation almost always protects business rather than the consumer.

Coincidentally, many of the government agencies that enforce regulations to protect consumers are headed by persons who have been employed in the industry they are now charged with regulating. Knowledge about an industry may be helpful to an agency's director and staff, but the end result often seems to be favoritism toward that industry. The reverse occurs too where the staff leave high government positions and go to work for the industries they formerly regulated at high salaries. President Jimmy Carter has tried very hard to eliminate such favoritism by requiring as a minimum that all high government officials sign a contract which states that they will not go to work for the industries they have directly regulated for at least 2 years after leaving office.

Regulatory reform is an important issue in many areas. Excessive regulation, no regulation, overly time-consuming regulation, high costs of regulation, and special-interest-group–serving regulation are mounting concerns of all.

For example, why should a transportation rate case referred to the Interstate Commerce Commission take 18 months for a ruling? Or

why should a price-fixing investigation by the Department of Energy take from 4 to 14 years? These are just a few cases in which rulings coming from the regulatory agencies take a large amount of time. Are these agencies so overwhelmed that they cannot regulate effectively? Are they trying to regulate so specifically that their efforts inhibit business operation? Are these agencies so swamped that it becomes too costly to operate effectively? These and other questions on the minds and lips of many Americans are being answered with some type of regulatory reform. President Carter's general reorganization of the federal government bureaucracy and "zero-based budgeting" approach demands more accountability of purpose and cost than in the past.

Bureaucratic Syndrome. There are twelve Cabinet departments; 44 independent federal agencies; over 1200 national advisory boards, commissions, councils, and committees; countless offices and bureaus; more than 1000 aid programs at the state and local levels; 228 health programs; 156 income-security programs; and so on. This represents bureaucracy; it further represents the "tip of the iceberg" in the bureaucratic syndrome in the country. As one congressional aide stated recently, after several weeks of concentrated investigation, many of the bureau activities remain hidden. Unfortunately, about one-third of the federal government expenditures are permanent authorizations and are "rubber stamped" yearly rather than seriously reviewed. The "oversight" function of Congress is intended to watch over the effectiveness of the many thousands of programs. But there are so many commissions, boards, committees, etc., that it is extremely difficult to keep track of them all, let alone carefully monitor and evaluate the need, effectiveness, and cost of each.

Senator Edmund Muskie of Maine, Chairman of the Senate Budget Committee, was quoted recently as saying "Government inefficiency is becoming today's number one villain.'' Senator Muskie and a group of over 30 senators have sponsored legislation in an effort to curb government inefficiency. Essentially it is a bureaucracy-cutting bill that would force Congress to review all federal programs every 4 years. If a program is renewed, fine; if not, it is eliminated. In addition, these senators recommend grouping together several overlapping and duplicated programs; operation on a zero-based review principle (each dollar spent is to be justified, rather than accepting the original yearly appropriation without question as a base and increasing it); that the government ''watchdog'' agencies themselves name inactive or duplicate programs for review and possible elimination by Congress. Of course, skeptics feel that such idealistic efforts to streamline the government bureaucracy are utopian; ''Overwhelming, not feasible, and staggering beyond human imagination'' is one such comment. But pragmatists are joining idealists, and government reform *is* going on.

Inefficiency, high costs of government operation, scandals among officials, and ''other shenanigans'' are both causes and effects of the bureaucratic syndrome in the American economy. Corporate political contributions to some members of Congress (not to mention former President Richard Nixon and Vice President Spiro Agnew) tend to buy influence and gain government favors. Falsified or extravagant ''official trips'' by certain members of Congress and sex scandals like those involving Representatives Wayne Hays of Ohio and Wilbur Mills of Arkansas are, unfortunately, known practices of some government officials. Each of these activities involves spending of government funds and results in a loss of confidence in our government leaders. On the ''Honesty, Dependability, and Integrity'' rating in Table 2-3, the Senate, White House, and House of Representatives ranked far down the list.

But what can be done to wipe out these activities that appear to be inherent in the ''system''? Members of Congress have been shouting misconduct and calling for disciplinary action and reform since the early 1960s with the investigations of Bobby Baker (who was secretary to the Senate majority leader), Representative Adam Clayton Powell of New York, and Senator Thomas Dodd of Connecticut, but with little result. Both the Senate Committee on Standards and Conduct and the House Committee on Standards of Official Conduct have done very little to investigate and discipline their members for alleged and otherwise obvious improprieties.

The House Committee had never investigated a member of the House since its formation 8 years earlier until it began a conflict of interest charge against Representative Robert L. F. Sikes of Florida in 1976 and subsequently found him guilty. He got a ''light rap on the knuckles.'' Similar inactivity has been the pattern for the Senate Committee. Critics of these two committees have said that instead of looking for wrongdoing, by doing nothing these committees have actually ended up hiding improprieties.

These cases of activities and alleged misconduct of members of Congress and other government officials are not the complete picture. They do, however, give an indication of possible misdeeds that warrant further investigation by independent groups. Such misdeeds continue to contribute to high cost of government operation, inefficiency, and possibly irregularities in congressional voting and high government influence on legislation and regulations. Consumers need not accept these activities and practices as inherent in the bureaucracy that is part of the American marketplace. This image of the bureaucratic syndrome can be a thing of the past if elected officials are allowed to work toward a better government system.

Monopoly Revisited

It has been over 80 years since the Sherman Antitrust Act was passed—in 1890—to stop the formation of large monopolies in the United States. However, during the last 20 years there have been thousands of mergers as well as enormous growth for some individual businesses, and these have resulted in a tremendous concentration of business power in America. Therefore, there has been renewed thinking about what constitutes a monopoly and what the Sherman Act is all about.

A Need for Reform. Ralph Nader, a widely respected national consumer advocate, reported in one of his studies that these new "monopolies" are costing the consumer over $15 billion a year. One of Nader's investigators, Mark J. Green, who conducted the study as a background for his book *The Closed Enterprise System,* further reported that if these monopolies were broken up, prices could be reduced by 25 percent or more; that monopolies and oligopolies (a few firms dominating a product market) cost the consumer nearly $60 billion a year in lost output of goods and services; that business people have gone to jail for criminal price fixing only three times in the 80 years that the antitrust laws have been in effect; and that 200 companies control two-thirds of all American manufacturing assets.

Thus, big business has been under fire for its monopolistic practices. Antitrust suits have been filed in federal district courts against Goodyear Tire & Rubber Co., Firestone Tire & Rubber Co., Uniroyal, Inc., B. F. Goodrich Co., and General Tire and Rubber Co. They are accused of conspiring to fix prices, thus controlling the supplying of tires to bus companies. Another filed antitrust case involved several major airplane manufacturers, who were charged with eliminating competition in research and development through illegal patent pooling and cross-licensing agreements by the Manufacturers Aircraft Association Incorporated and its members, allegedly in violation of the Sherman Antitrust Act.

A major scandal in antitrust investigations involved the International Telephone and Telegraph Company (ITT). It was alleged that ITT donated huge sums of money to political parties. Highly paid lobbyists wooed the executives of the *conglomerate* (a company resulting from mergers between firms not competing directly, but often complementing each other and creating a source of large economic power) to provide these donations. ITT allegedly exploited the consumer by charging higher prices.

The following case is unusual because one business instead of the government brought the charges. Litton Industries, Inc. has filed a $100 million antitrust suit against another business, AT&T. Litton charged it had been restricted in competition in making, selling, and distributing specialized telephone equipment as a result of the illegal pressure tactics of AT&T on political and regulatory bodies. In its charges, Litton claimed AT&T controlled over 98 percent of the telephone terminal equipment in the United States.

In continued efforts to reduce or eliminate potential or real monopolistic operations, some diversified cooperatives, milk cooperatives, community cooperatives, and fruit and vegetable cooperatives are also being investigated. Some may be operating in violation of antitrust laws even though they can legally operate outside the laws because of exceptions made to the Sherman Antitrust Act. Some cooperatives tend to dominate the market for their products. For example, the almond growers cooperative has approximately 75 percent of this country's market; Ocean Spray Cranberries has over 80 percent of the market for cranberries; and the Sunkist growers in California have about 85 percent of the lemon market. If the antitrust laws are good for business, then perhaps large, market-dominating cooperatives need to be looked at in the same light as large corporations. Market domination restricts trade and prevents competition no matter who is doing it. These cooperative operations should at least trigger renewed study and investigation by antitrust officials.

Economies of Scale. There are two kinds of production costs, fixed and variable. *Fixed costs* are those that do not change no matter how many units (each specific manufactured item) are produced. *Variable costs* are the additional costs for each unit produced. Large firms typically can increase production

Because fixed costs do not depend on the number of items produced, firms that can produce large quantities of goods can produce them more cheaply. This allows the large company to charge lower prices, but it may also drive smaller, less efficient companies out of the market and give the large company monopoly power. (*Kenneth Karp*)

amounts. The fixed costs are then divided among more units of production. Consequently, unit costs for large firms decrease. Most small firms cannot afford as high a production rate as can the large firms, and so the small firm cannot reduce its unit costs as much. This practice of large firms developing lower unit costs of production than those of small firms is called *economies of scale*. In and of itself, the practice of economies of scale is good.

Large firms can also reduce their unit costs through specialization, improved equipment, technological research, improved distribution strategies, or by maintaining greater stability in their finances and operation. Small firms usually cannot do as much because of their smaller size and smaller financial capacity.

This continued effort to decrease unit costs is a primary driving force for all firms involved in production, as lower costs make possible lower prices and probably greater sales for the company. Because of the economies of scale,

competition, the tremendous size of some firms, and other factors, in the long run many small firms are squeezed out of the market. They are underpriced and/or out-serviced by the larger firms. Once the smaller firm is squeezed out, the large firm can capture a larger share of the market. In such cases, the larger firms thus legally gain a monopolistic or oligopolistic share of an industry or market. In such cases, the firm can gradually increase its selling prices. Since the unit costs remain the same or are further reduced, the firm can make a much larger profit than when it was competing with other firms.

Furthermore, a tendency toward monopolizing an industry or market does not have to be overt or flagrant in the economy. It can be subtle and gradual, yet end by wiping out most of the competition. Being "big" is not bad and normally results from being efficient and highly competitive. But when it becomes apparent that smaller businesses are being smothered by the large ones, by whatever means, it is time to take a hard look at antitrust laws and strengthen, broaden, and revise them to keep competition alive in America.

Divestiture Actions. In 1974 the U.S. Justice Department brought an antitrust suit against AT&T. The Justice Department began action aimed at breaking up AT&T to restore competition in the telecommunications industries. AT&T, Western Electric (a manufacturing subsidiary), and Bell Laboratories (a research arm co-owned by AT&T and Western Electric) were all charged with conspiring to monopolize the communications industry; the case will be in court at least 10 years.

To indicate its dominance of the market, it was observed that the Bell network services 82 percent of the nation's telephones; over 1700 independent telephone companies handle the remaining 18 percent. Over 90 percent of all interstate phone calls in the country are handled totally or partially by the Bell system. The firm is so large and controls so many patents that other small companies find it impossible to expand and compete with AT&T.

A company spokesperson for AT&T contends that if the breakup should come about, telephone service would get worse and the cost would be higher. The spokesperson goes on to say that if the Bell system is not allowed to operate as it is, it can't begin to operate efficiently. Naturally, there are two sides to the divestiture question. Some people are promoting divestiture, and others are firmly against it.

The National Association of Manufacturers (NAM) and the oil companies in the country are firmly against divestitures. The NAM has said "that efforts to break up the oil industry is part of a popular, but misguided, 'big is bad' syndrome." Undoubtedly, those who are against divestiture also stand to lose as a result.

One oil company executive speaking about divestiture has indicated that oil company divestiture could have some terrible repercussions: (1) reduce energy investments by 50 percent, (2) increase unemployment, (3) reduce United States personal income, and (4) by 1985 reduce energy production significantly. These and other statements sound alarming and may tend to sway those who waver on the divestiture issue. But, of course, these comments are representative of biased opinions.

Recent activities of several oil companies, however, have given ammunition for the oil company critics. The oil company image has been badly tarnished since their profits have grown so large in the last few years. Corporate officials argue that they need larger profits to pay for research for new oil sources: Indeed energy research is needed, but that is not the whole story.

Several oil companies have decided to put these high profits to uses other than oil research. Mobil, for example, has bought a controlling interest in the Montgomery Ward Company and the Container Corporation of America. Atlantic Richfield has bought the major copper producer, Anaconda. Most oil companies have decided to diversify into closely allied energy areas, such as coal and uranium. But this "horizontal diversification"

may raise problems later as these oil companies face antitrust battles because of their domination of "energy industries." Many oil companies may be faced with other "energy industry" divestiture actions in later years as a result.

Active efforts in favor of divestiture are limited to a relatively few individuals and certain members of Congress. One person, Harold Williams, a millionaire businessman, sees and supports the divestiture concept. At one time, however, he was a nonsupporter. Divestiture legislation proposes to monitor monopolistic power through profit levels, price competition, and industry concentration. This is exactly what the legislation should do, according to Williams.

Williams and others have been recruiting the financial support of 30,000 American Citizens for Energy Action. Its current goal is to prepare a "Divestiture Factbook" to counter actions from the opposition such as the National Association of Manufacturers and others. Williams has stated, "I want to prevent the energy future from being determined at the Houston Oil Club, by using divestiture as a lever to force oil companies to make public more information on resources." Currently about a half million dollars has been raised to finance a Washington office for this lobbying group.

In spite of all these efforts, it must be remembered that divestiture cases take many years in the courts. And too, it appears unlikely that AT&T, for instance, will divest itself of one or more of its divisions because of years of delayed investigation. The same can be said for divestiture action against oil companies or other large corporations. One suit against IBM has been in court in New York since 1975. In the first year alone, the company filed more than a million pages of documents—and the end is not in sight.

Price Fixing. The dairy industry, by law given special consideration in regard to prices, is indirectly authorized to fix prices at some level. This authorization is given by the federal government. At one time an imbalance in milk-product production and consumption, price wars, milk strikes, and violence hit the dairy industry and this was the impetus for government action. The federal government set minimum prices that most dairy and cheese makers had to pay for raw milk. The dairy industry has changed markedly since these special regulations were enacted. But the federal laws that regulate milk prices have essentially remained the same.

In effect, the federal government has caused a decline in milk consumption by setting up and approving these minimum price levels. It has literally made milk purchases cost too much for those who need them most. Currently, it costs the government over $700 million a year to regulate the dairy industry. This is a bit too much for informed taxpayers and consumers to absorb for outright "legalized price fixing."

An old form of price fixing was fair-trade laws. Congressional legislation banning fair-trade regulations in the marketplace took effect in 1976. This ended an era of legalized price fixing in more than 30 states which had passed their own fair-trade laws in the 1930s. Although fair-trade price fixing has been outlawed, there is still occasional evidence of illegal price-fixing attempts. Some manufacturers have refused to sell to retailers who lower their prices too much. And those manufacturers who dominate a large segment of the market can get by with this "price blackmail" at least for several months.

Harold Rotenberg, president of Creative Merchandising and a strong enemy of fair-trade laws, has frequently criticized these restrictive distribution actions. Supply was definitely a problem, according to Rotenberg. Many discount stores in particular were refused merchandise by manufacturers because they were accused of selling at "cut-rate prices."

A spokesperson from Naum Brothers, a discount chain based in Rochester, New York, has also revealed efforts to monitor prices by manufacturers. For example, several manufacturers, including Texas Instruments, had two lines of products—one for department stores at one price and another for discount stores at another price. In both cases the products to be offered for sale by the retailer were the same. These actions may not be illegal yet, but they are certainly unethical.

Some retailers, however, have been able to get around such practices by buying in other ways. One way is to buy "at the bootlegger"—buying from someone who supposedly is getting the item for his or her own use. And so it goes, one unethical practice breeds another. This will continue at least until these price discrimination practices become illegal. Even then they will end only if the guilty are properly charged, prosecuted, convicted, and sentenced.

Strengthening Antitrust Laws. A major effort to break up monopoly and oligopoly power in the United States came in the form of legislation originally introduced into the Senate by the late Senator Philip A. Hart. The bill would establish an Industrial Reorganization Commission and give it some tough new monopoly-busting powers during its recommended 15-year life. The Commission would give its primary attention to seven major industries: chemicals and drugs, electronic computing and communication equipment, electrical machinery and equipment, energy, iron and steel, motor vehicles, and nonferrous metals. These industries appear to be the ones with the greatest impact on the total economy. Basically the proposed legislation would update and strengthen many of the provisions of the Sherman Antitrust Act and plug its loopholes.

In a more recent effort to strengthen antitrust-law enforcement, Donald I. Baker, assistant attorney general for antitrust laws, has proposed treating antitrust violators as felons. Price fixers or other antitrust violators, suggests Baker, should be treated as common criminals. This hard line on antitrust crimes is supported by several, including President Carter and Vice President Mondale, as a way to help preserve honesty and integrity in business.

There is a serious lag problem in the prosecution and conviction of antitrust violators compared with other "white-collar" crimes. In a recent year, average sentences for certain white-collar crimes were: security fraud, 45.7 months in prison; forged security transportation, 45.4 months; bank embezzlement, 22.6 months, and income tax fraud, 15.4 months imprisonment. But the 75 persons convicted of purely antitrust violations drew a combined *total* of 2½ months imprisonment.

In 1974 price fixing and other serious violations of the Sherman Antitrust Act became felonies instead of misdemeanors through amendments to strengthen the law. These acts are punishable by up to 3 years in jail and fines up to $100,000 for individuals, and up to $1 million for corporations. More recently, the Antitrust Improvement Act of 1976 was passed. It strengthened antitrust laws in three ways: (1) It gave states power to enforce antitrust laws and sue for damage; (2) it broadens the powers of the Justice Department Antitrust Division in conducting civil investigations; and (3) parties to large mergers would be required to give the Justice Department Antitrust Division and the FTC advance notice.

Involving Consumers. Antitrust violations need to be attended to by all who suspect them. The U.S. Department of Justice is the primary responsible government agency to notify of violations. However, other persons or agencies at a more local level can be contacted as needed.

At the state level consumers can contact the state attorney general, their state representative, or the public utilities commission to report violations or suspected violations of antitrust laws. On the federal level consumers can contact either the Antitrust Division of the Justice Department or the Federal Trade Commission in Washington, D.C., or any of their field offices.

To help consumers and business people spot possible antitrust violations, the following signs were offered by the U.S. Department of Justice in one of their pamphlets, *Antitrust Enforcement and the Consumer:*

> *A consumer should keep an eye out for tell-tale signs. For instance:*
>
> - *if there are large price changes involving more than one seller of a highly similar product, particularly if the price changes are of equal amount and occur at the same time;*
> - *if competing sellers have identical pricing of the same or similar products, and if prices among competing sellers seem to move in the same direction at the same time;*
> - *if a seller ever tells a consumer "Oh no, we don't sell in that area; so-and-so is the only firm that sells in that area, according to our agreement."*

If the signs are there, consumers and business people alike should report them to the appropriate government agency.

It becomes increasingly apparent that consumers need to be vitally aware of the characteristics of the economy. Where there is gradual growth of conglomerates and the oligopolistic and monopolistic characteristics of big business, consumers need to be alert. This is especially true because evidence shows that higher prices result from illegal price fixing and elimination of competition.

Unfortunately, the Justice Department and the Federal Trade Commission have low budgets for antitrust enforcement. This is in contrast to the high salaries of the giant corporations' lobbyists and their many lawyers. The continued efforts of giant corporations to merge seem to have given the interests of consumers the lowest priority. But small businesses, corporations, and giant businesses alike all need consumers in order to exist.

Special Interest Groups

The influence of special interest groups in the marketplace is not exactly "penny ante." Altogether, billions of dollars are allocated and spent. State governments, city governments, political groups, corporations, industry, lobbyists, and consumers too are involved in the influencing processes.

State Government. Many state governments have influenced the marketplace indirectly through various pieces of legislation. Fair-trade laws, very popular and necessary during the Depression-ridden 1930s, were first repealed by many state legislative bodies. Later, Congress repealed fair-trade laws nationally. These states took the initiative and set the pace first. A question is often raised: Would the federal government have taken such action had the states not set the pace?

However, not all actions taken by state agencies can be regarded as positive. For example, more than 20 states prohibit the substitution of a less expensive drug for a brand-name drug even when the consumer asks for it. Also, because of state laws forbidding advertising of prices of such items as eyeglasses and hearing aids, many elderly persons—most on fixed incomes—are unable to get the lowest price.

State licensing laws sometimes restrain competition. This is particularly true in the building and trade areas. What can happen is that in order to keep competition out of the trade or industry, state licensing boards refuse to issue licenses to newcomers to the trade by setting artificially high or "unreasonable" standards, sometimes even quotas. Consequently, new competition is kept out and those already licensed can continue to charge what they want.

At one time in Florida 100 percent of those who took general contractor exams failed, and of course no license could be issued to anyone who did not pass the exam. However, it was such a clear rip-off that pressure was placed on the examining board to regrade the exams. They did, and 88 percent passed. But this kind of licensing "hokus pokus" still continues in many states.

Although licensing is necessary to keep out the unqualified, the unskilled, or the incompetent, it can be carried to extremes. According to a Justice Department report, more than 20 states license midwives, nearly 20 license bug exterminators, about 12 license well-diggers, and the State of Hawaii protects a few by licensing tattoo artists. A difficult question to resolve in each case is: Does licensing protect the consumer from the incompetents, or does it protect the occupation from competition?

The traditional professionals—doctors, dentists, and lawyers—also are guilty of restraining competition to a considerable degree. Medical boards in some states block competition by refusing to recognize medical licenses granted by other states. Recently, many of those doctors and dentists who have been "locked out" have organized to fight this unfair denial.

And people can be prepared to pay a higher price for ear piercing if some state medical boards have their way. These boards are pressuring legislators to pass state laws allowing only doctors to pierce ears—at a price three times as high as the current charge. Would such action protect the health of consumers, or would it fatten the pockets of doctors?

In one county in Virginia the property title search fee is uniform—$50,000 home value, $500 search fee. The fee seems disproportionately high, since the search usually takes only a few hours in the courthouse record room. If a struggling young lawyer wanted to charge a smaller fee, say $200, the state bar association probably could put much pressure on him for violating the lawyer's code of ethics.

In California two young attorneys set up a legal clinic to handle uncontested divorces for $100. The state bar association brought action against them for "moral turpitude and dishonesty." Excessive fees seem to be the norm with many legal activities. $1200 for a will, $2000 for a divorce, or over $3000 to probate an estate for a poor person are examples of some state bar association dictates. The U.S. Supreme Court has ruled that such price fixing is in fact an attempt to restrain trade. Thus more competition is coming to the professions.

It is common practice in some states to buy from the lowest bidder within the state rather than accepting a much lower bid from outside the state! Also, state utility commissions dictate the so-called excessive prices of electricity, gas, water, insurance, transportation, and telephones.

Guilty as charged should be the verdict for many state governments and agencies. In some ways, they have become unethical, immoral, discriminatory, and unprofessional. One thing is sure: Some laws and regulations that supposedly protect the consumer from *harm* are, in fact, rip-offs. Laws that eliminate competition or fix prices at the expense of the consumer are highly questionable.

Cities. Cities can also have considerable impact toward influencing the marketplace. For example, city governments license certain occupational groups to monitor who shall or shall not practice a trade within the city limits.

Local building permits dictate which construction company shall build new homes within a city and which shall not. One may also question whether city governments should only accept bids for construction of city buildings, streets, highways, parks, etc., from contractors within the city, regardless of costs. Out-of-city bidders frequently offer comparable construction at a much lower cost. Consequently, these city officials are not using city funds efficiently. The consumer ultimately pays for this preferential treatment through higher taxes.

Poverty pleas by large cities—New York City is a prime example—to the federal government for "bail-out" loans is influential as it spurs congressional action. The consumer in the marketplace is continually affected by such actions.

Politics. Ever since "Watergate" the public has become more sensitive to political clout in the marketplace. "Laundered money," "under-the-table" payments, "payoffs" for favors, "kickbacks," and illegal corporate contributions to campaign funds have been quite common in recent years. Regardless of how the money reaches the hands of politicians at all levels—federal, state, and local—there always seem to be some strings attached. The string is usually a favor of some kind.

A $5000 campaign contribution may result in a major highway being built very close to a restaurant, thus boosting the contributor's business; another $20,000 contribution could help block legislation to close certain tax loopholes; a $500-a-month "kickback" might sway the issuing of government contracts to a certain builder.

A recent report by Common Cause, a national lobbying group for consumers, indicated that over $90 million was spent by Senate and House candidates seeking election. Nearly half of this amount was contributed by various groups and individuals. Heavy donations by large groups included business groups, over $2 million; health groups, more than $1.5 million; labor groups, nearly $3 million; and special interest groups, over $12.5 million. Why have these groups given money to politicians or political campaigns? Could it be that they hope their contributions will influence activity in the marketplace through voting in the local councils, state legislatures, or Congress? Or is this simply "humanitarian" gift-giving for the preservation of mankind, the love of country, and to help out a friend?

The Federal Election Commission and the Congress have allowed large and small companies to help finance politics. Corporations can use fund-raising organizations called PACs (*political action committees*) to solicit funds from employees at all levels as well as from stockholders. These funds can later be given to candidates for federal offices. Top management in these corporations usually decides who shall get the donated funds. Some PAC-sponsoring corporations include U.S.

Steel, Xerox, General Electric, Lockheed Aircraft, Texaco, Weyerhaeuser, Coca Cola, and Georgia-Pacific. Although each company's PACs cannot give more than $5000 to one candidate, this still appears to foster influence in the marketplace. This is because many firms establish many PACs.

Even in small towns indiscriminate "influence peddling" is evident. One elected official, who is also a lawyer, in a small town in the South approves or disapproves the use of government-owned parcels of land and charges a fee accordingly. Furthermore, licenses of many types coincidentally are approved through his law office. This person literally dictates what shall or shall not be in the community.

And this influence continues in many small cities and towns. As shameful as these actions are, they are more shameful because they are in effect condoned by public ignorance and/or apathy.

Lobbyists. Attempts to influence political figures and their votes are allowed and needed at all levels of government. Problems result, however, when too much money is spent for lobbying or when "payoffs," "kickbacks," or bribery become part of this lobbying process.

Well-paid lobbyists backed by large corporations or industries seem more often than not to get the political action they want. In fact, these actions are frequently so important to an industry that the lobbyists may "pull out all the stops" to get the vote. They will "wine and dine" and provide other favors to political figures. In addition, they may make large financial contributions to the campaign funds of politicians. In some cases money may even be paid to a legislator or a member of Congress through some circuitous route to avoid discovery.

Millions of dollars are spent annually by corporation or industry lobbyists to influence decisions. By contrast, lobbyists for consumer groups must often operate on an extremely low budget—a "closet" for an office, taking a bus to formal hearings, and walking to a congressional office to state a position or provide testimony.

SATISFYING OUR ECONOMIC GOALS IN THE SYSTEM

The American market system may not be considered the best by some critics, but it is the best we have at present and it does work. In view of this, let us see how one can satisfy one's economic goals within the system through personal economic activities and economic voting in the American marketplace.

Consumers are, by definition, involved in economic activities. The activities in the marketplace are earning, spending, borrowing, saving, investing, and utilizing.

Earning
A basic economic activity for most individuals is earning. Usually it is essential for survival. Consumer goods cost money, and for most people money comes from work. *Aggregate personal income* in the United States will probably amount to more than $1.4 trillion in 1979 and may reach $1.9 trillion in 1982—a healthy amount of economic activity by anyone's standards.

Spending
Nearly 80 percent of the total individual earnings is spent on personal items. Spending is obviously necessary to supply both tangible wants (food, transportation, clothing, shelter) and intangible wants (entertainment, recreation)—and this spending, amounting to many billions, again indicates a healthy amount of consumer activity.

Borrowing
Many consumers must at some time borrow. In a recent year, Americans borrowed over $173 billion which was classified as installment credit. More than $84 billion, or about 49 percent of this installment credit, was borrowed from commercial banks. And approximately

Courtesy of Edd Uluschak.

"Guess what dear? This is the last payment on all last year's Christmas shopping!"

$17 billion, or about 10 percent, was in the form of installment credit extended by retail stores.

Saving

In 1978, *aggregate personal savings* amounted to about $98 billion; it is expected to rise to about $130 billion by 1982. This amounts to about 7 percent of aggregate personal income. By saving, people spend less now in order to spend more later. In addition, giving up spending now may allow one to enjoy future earnings, perhaps in the form of interest.

Investing

For consumers, investing is using current earnings to increase future income. With investing, though, go certain risks that are not part of other personal economic activities. Individual investing forms a significant part of the total investment in business or government, and it is therefore a vital part of all personal economic activities. As with savings,

however, it does mean sacrificing current needs and wants for potential future income.

Utilizing

Another personal economic activity very important in the lifestyle of the consumer is utilizing. When applied to personal economic activities, utilizing means using earnings and goods and services effectively.

Utilizing, however, is more importantly applied to effective *time management.* In this context it simply means how effectively a person spends limited time. Many activities, projects, work, school, and relaxation compete for this scarce commodity. Individuals must evaluate the time they spend on selected activities in terms of the benefits they get. In effect, *opportunity costs* (that which is given up as a result of using time for something else) are an important consideration. A person who uses time for a particular activity (beneficial or not) must realize that the time spent can no longer be used for something else. Time is irrecoverable, and therefore its utilization must be planned for carefully by consumers.

Voting in the American Marketplace

Voting in the usual sense of the word often means the selecting of a political candidate by the people. Used in another way, people "vote" for a product or service by spending money for it and thus accepting that product or service. Not voting for—or not buying—the product means rejecting it.

How an Economic Vote Is Cast. Actually, everybody who buys goods or services has already voted. For example, Tom and Bridgette Towner of St. Louis were looking at some notebooks and other supplies in a college bookstore. After careful comparisons of the products they were going to buy, they cast their economic vote by making a choice: They bought.

Comparing, looking, and eventually making a choice also means understanding general economic concepts. A primary concept in economic voting is *opportunity cost,* sometimes called *alternative cost.* This is the "cost" of giving up one product or service when another is purchased or used. A person who spends $6000 in savings for a new automobile gets the car and gives up the cash. That person also gives up an expensive vacation and gives up other kinds of cars.

One important aspect of economic voting is not voting. When a person casts an economic vote for one product, this is also a vote against others. One may vote for a particular product for a number of reasons. Nonetheless, if a vote is cast for a dishwasher from a certain store, for example, based solely on price, the fact remains that some manufacturers and retailers did not get a vote. Those whose prices were too high according to the wants of the consumer did not get the vote. In effect, a vote for the product and the store at the right price was at the same time a vote against similar products and stores that did not meet the price criterion. Other bases (quality, service, size) used for casting a vote for a product or store

will have the same voting/not-voting result when purchases are made.

Advertising as an Influence. Advertising is considered a great influence on economic voting. It is large-scale. It bombards consumers in every way possible from the minute business card to the Goodyear blimp. Newspapers, magazines, radio, television, transit and bus-car ads, billboards, and posters of various kinds reach out to voice the advertisers' messages. In 1977 over $33 billion was spent on advertising. This is, of course, designed to get the consumer to buy particular products or services. To put it more bluntly, advertising makes every possible legal effort to influence consumers to buy.

The consumer often views advertising as a way of *becoming informed,* while the seller views it as a way of *informing and influencing or persuading* the buyer. Consumers, manufacturers, retailers, advertising agencies, and government regulatory agencies continually defend their ideas on the purposes of advertising. And on it goes.

There appears to be, however, a basic conflict in regard to advertising. Words such as "informative," "interesting," "enlightening," "awareness," or "factual" may describe one viewer's reaction to advertising. On the other hand, words like "false," "deceptive," "misleading," "manipulative," or "exaggerated" may be another viewer's reaction to the same ads. But all these words could at various times correctly describe certain types of advertising.

Advertising is by no means pure. Corporations, government regulatory agencies, and advertising agencies realize that problems, half-truths, and illegalities exist. But what is more important is that the consumer recognize these problems, illegalities, and half-truths in advertising, since they influence choice making.

Advertising, of course, is helpful. It does provide a wealth of information. But much advertising today has gone well beyond the bounds of supplying information. In a study made by Stephen Greyser of the Harvard Business School, approximately 2700 business people gave their views on advertising. Most agreed that (1) the public intelligence is insulted and advertising has become irritating; (2) a true picture of the product is not presented; (3) a poor representation of real-life people is shown; (4) ads unnecessarily influence and persuade people—particularly children—to buy things they do not need; (5) excessive amounts of money are being spent on advertising. These comments were made by business people who understand what business, including advertising, is all about.

Consumers often rely on advertising to aid them in wise buying instead of seeing it as an effort to change their economic vote. Through the combined efforts of advertising people and *motivational research* experts (people who study why consumers buy what they buy), behavior patterns of consumer buying are researched and studied carefully. Advertising then capitalizes on these patterns to gain economic votes.

Not all advertising need have a negative connotation. The self-regulatory "watchdog" of the advertising industry is the National Advertising Division (NAD) of the Council of Better Business Bureaus. It takes advertisers to task for misleading or otherwise deceptive ads. For example, Electrolux ran an ad that said, "Stated simply, the Finest Vacuum Cleaner in the World." NAD asked for proof of the claim. Electrolux could not produce it, so the ad was dropped. On the other hand, Pam Vegetable Spray, which claimed "it cuts the cost of pan-frying by two-thirds compared with cooking oil," came through with a vote of approval by NAD. Research data presented to NAD backed up the claims by Pam.

So what is the answer to the conflict of advertising purposes? Eliminating advertising would hardly be an apt choice. Not only would the over $33 billion that is spent on it be lost, but the subsequent purchases of goods and services would drop sharply. This drop would be largely because of a lack of buying information the consumer gets from advertising.

Perhaps the solution is better policing of advertising by advertising agencies, businesses, governments, and consumers. *Corrective* (to correct false or misleading ads), *counter* (to present an opposing view of products or services), and *substantiative* (to corroborate claims made in ads) advertising could be used to bring about a more equitable balance in what advertising should or should not do. More accurate information would be available, and more accurate choice making and economic voting would probably result. Ultimately the realistic practice of an "advertising code of ethics" in which more honest, straightforward, factual information is given may be the solution.

Values and other Influences upon Economic Voting. Individual *values* obviously vary, and these values influence the economic votes cast. Consider Bill Fraser and Carla Hill, who worked in the same office of a major insurance company in Memphis but had very different feelings about cars. Bill bought a Mercedes-Benz because of its quality; Carla bought a Chevrolet Chevette because of its low price. The effect of both these sets of values is felt in the American marketplace. *Customs and habits,* such as some religious, ethnic, social, or income characteristics that restrict certain types of purchases, also influence economic voting.

Economic voting also can be influenced by *fashions* or *fads.* When styles change, such as in men's clothing, an economic vote is often cast for a product largely because of fashion. For example, Charles Gregg of New Orleans purchased an entire new wardrobe of trousers, shirts, and new suits with shoes to match. Fashion was the primary influence.

Consumers are also influenced in their economic voting by *inflation* (a steady rise in prices accompanied by a decrease in the value of the dollar). Often people will not buy if the price is too high. Instead, they wait for the price to go down, or they choose another product. For example, if beef prices were significantly higher than those of most other kinds of meat, many shoppers would cast their votes for those other kinds of meat. Unfortunately, individuals become less flexible in their voting when it comes to necessities such as food. Even so, the direction of the voting is still influenced by inflation.

Having three cars, three television sets, and a backyard swimming pool are essential for some people. And the reason often given is to maintain a certain social level in the community. Casting an economic vote for a particular product is often based upon "keeping up with the Joneses" rather than price, quality, or purpose of that product. In effect the rationale for voting has been influenced by *societal expectations* rather than common sense, need, or effective decision and choice making. Simply put, it is *conspicuous consumption*.

Whether the reason for voting for a certain product or service is psychological, physical, social, or something else each person has to judge its effectiveness and satisfaction. One person's wise decision or choice of a product or service may be another's folly.

Accurate Economic Voting. To cast an economic vote to begin with, an individual must need or want the product or service. It is, of course, of critical importance to have basic information about these goods or services, and to compare one with another. Hopefully, this careful buying results in casting an *accurate* vote, as dollars spent on a product tell the manufacturer to continue producing more.

Accurate economic voting may not necessarily mean that effective decision making has taken place, however, and vice versa. For example, Jack Smith may decide to buy a motorbike instead of overhauling an inefficiently operating furnace in his home. He may have done effective comparison shopping and made a good choice on the motorbike. But the question is: Did he make a wise decision to buy the motorbike in the first place?

Ultimately accurate economic voting reflects intelligent consumer behavior in the marketplace. Conversely, an inaccurate vote endorses inferior products and services and will result in continued problems such as consumer helplessness, misrepresentation, and inequities.

POINTS OF VIEW AND PROBLEMS TO THINK ABOUT

Despite all that has been done in the American marketplace, much more is needed to ensure harmony between consumers, businesses, and governments. One of the major undertakings of all sectors should be to identify the important problems affecting all, to arrive at some set of priorities, and to begin taking affirmative action.

A typical problem facing the consumer and business is that of quality versus quantity in the production of consumer goods. When consumers want more, more, more, it is extremely difficult for manufacturers to meet the demand without modifying their production standards. Should the emphasis on quantity necessarily mean a reduction of quality?

Over $33 billion a year is being spent on advertising. Advertising itself is not bad, but the way the consumer is being bombarded with it is disturbing, especially when much of it is misleading. Advertising agencies should try to provide basic, reliable product and service information. Perhaps ad agencies, in addition to the advertisers, should be held liable for any inaccurate statements.

Just as properly handled advertising is basically healthy for an economy, so is competition. Competition promotes quality. The problem is that today there are too many restrictions on open and free competition. Through mergers and oligopolistic operations, many corporations have turned Americans away from free competition. A few large firms must not be allowed to dominate an industry, even though *they say* it is in the consumer's interest and that it provides lower prices, larger quantities, and sometimes improved quality. Through the decades it has been proven that this is not the case. A realistic, free, and competitive economy will accomplish the goals of our nation for all people when economic activity is not limited to a relatively small number of large corporations. Furthermore, where competition exists, the economic voting of the American people serves as a check-and-balance system. An economic vote for a product or a service is a vote to stay in business. When there is a lack of competition, the vote may be cast because of a lack of choice.

Also, the role of government needs to be reaffirmed as an aid to the consumer. Laws have been passed to give government the power to act when there is evidence of monopoly formation, illegal price fixing, bribery, kickbacks, or conflicts of interest. But what should be the role of government in regard to the oligopolistic operations of certain major industries in the country? For example, Ford, Chrysler, General Motors, and American Motors control virtually all U.S. automobile manufacturing. General Foods, General Mills, and Kellogg handle over 90 percent of the cereal processing in the country. Recent legislation has been passed to help prevent harmful mergers, but what about the operations of those companies that ignore regulation and use all means available to get around the law?

The government must do what it can to control the large firms, and it must have the power to enforce the laws that are passed. Also, effort and money must be provided to counter the skillful work of the powerful lobbyists and lawyers who act on behalf of businesses. There seems to be no limit to the amount of money made available to business lobbyists to help those with special interests (all of which is tax deductible). Although lobbyists do provide valuable information, they can be extremely biased and overbearing at times.

Furthermore, the country seems overrun with "white-collar" crime. Stiff and deserved prosecution just does not happen to those who cheat on taxes; pad expense accounts; get kickbacks on building contracts; commit bribery; offer contracts only to friends, local businesses, or relatives regardless of costs; hire "female workers" for personal gratification at government expense; make secret

political contributions; extend gifts to members of Congress for favors; and so on. These moral and legal violations must be checked. When one reads about and observes the behavior of some corporate officials, some ranking government employees, and some members of Congress, it makes the immorality and decadence of Watergate seem like a Sunday School picnic. Americans *themselves* must lead the way for a higher standard of marketplace morality.

And, too, are consumers and the rank-and-file employees guiltless? Certainly not. Thousands of consumers shoplift, intentionally buy products and then return them for refunds claiming the wrong size or color after using them, occasionally take a few supplies or samples home from work, refuse to tell clerks when they have been given too much change, or cheat on their income tax.

America can be improved; morality can be raised. The public, private, and government sectors can all contribute to improve conditions and morality in the marketplace and the political system. Enlightened people in government can help bring about change. Business people with renewed vigor and refreshing ideas and practices can offer more. But the *more knowledgeable consumer* can offer the most with improved and responsible behavior in the marketplace.

In the American economy, the problems must be identified and isolated, and well-thought-out solutions must be found. Consumers, businesses, and governments must do more than coexist in the American marketplace.

CHAPTER ACTIVITIES

Checkup on Consumer Terms and Concepts

Circular flow	Centralized economic
Economic freedom	system
Economic growth	Decentralized
and stability	economic system
Economic security	Shared economic
Economic justice	system

Free enterprise
  system
Imperfect
  competition
Monopoly
Oligopoly

Multiplier principle
Inflation
Economies of scale
Divestiture
Economic voting

Review of Essentials

1. What are the six basic goals of American society?
2. Describe the two aggregate measures used to measure economic growth in the American economy.
3. Economic injustices exist in the American economy. Identify one such injustice and suggest how it might be corrected.
4. Explain the basic differences between a centralized economic system and a decentralized economic system.
5. What purposes does competition serve within the American marketplace and for consumers?
6. Why would the American economic system be identified more realistically as a "shared economy"?
7. What two policies are used by the federal government to help control the money supply and other economic activity? Distinguish between the two.
8. Identify the two personal economic activities which contribute to the multiplier principle and explain how it works.
9. Describe recent incidents that seem to indicate that greater controls are needed to restrain monopolistic or oligopolistic business operations in this country.
10. The "circular flow" is frequently used to label much of the economic activity in the American marketplace. Explain how the flow works and why it is called circular.
11. Identify ways in which the American marketplace has diminished morally. Who and what have been the primary causes?

Issues for Analysis

1. The primary economic systems—centralized, decentralized, and shared—are frequently talked about in terms of good or evil. Should these systems necessarily be viewed on this basis? Can the economic foundation of these systems be considered apart from the political structure? Must any country accept an economic system "wholly" or can it combine several systems into one?
2. What should the role of government be in the American economy? Should it have very direct controls, or should it merely serve as a quiet watchdog and "bark" occasionally to let the businesses know it is around when they tend to stray?
3. What purpose should advertising serve, and should greater restraints be placed on it?
4. What should the role of business be in the economy? What freedoms should it have? Restrictions? How should business be held accountable?

The Changing Role
of the Consumer

3

THE PROBLEMS

Poverty, tenement housing, inequities in income and welfare rights, municipal corruption, unsafe working conditions, deceptive selling practices, hazardous toys, price fixing, unwholesome food, pollution . . . Are these yesterday's problems or today's?

These and other similar examples suggest clearly that the life of the consumer is no "bed of roses." There are frauds and deceptions, inequities, overwhelming conditions, apathy—and often the consumer feels helpless, and actually is helpless, although greater knowledge could help.

But the marketplace is changing, and consequently the role of the consumer is changing, too. The consumer's voice is being heard more clearly with each passing decade.

CONSUMERS OF YESTERDAY

Change has, of course, been part of the history of America, not to mention the world. With each passing era, the role of the individual consumer has changed significantly. Historically, the consumer movement can be looked at in five periods: (1) before the 1890s; (2) from the 1890s to 1929 (early consumer movement); (3) from 1929 through the 1950s (renewed consumer interest); (4) the 1960s (consumerism); and (5) today. Let us consider briefly the first three of these periods.

Before the 1890s

Our ancestors lived a highly individualistic life. They wanted freedom and independence, and were extremely self-reliant. They were basically self-sustaining, cooperative, and giving, yet the welfare of consumers depended in part upon the honesty and buying skill of the few local shopkeepers. Most goods had no trademarks and few had brand names. The wise consumer "knew the merchandise" and tried to avoid shoddy products, but had almost no protection against merchants who raised prices needlessly, and could do little to stop frauds such as misbranding and adulteration. But toward the end of the century, the effects of a rapidly growing society changed the role of the consumer.

Industrialization, along with the growth in population, brought about 40 percent of the people to the cities. A nationwide system of railroads served the economic needs of those who had moved into urban areas, but the congestion also led to "urban poverty, tenement housing, immigrant ghettos, municipal corruption, hazardous working conditions, sweat shops, child labor and a variety of consumer problems."[1] To fight these problems, people banded together. The numerous reform organizations included those concerned with political change. The populists and progressives promoted economic and social changes; volunteer groups of "do-gooders" concerned themselves with local issues; and newly created unions sought equity for people of the working class.

The 1890s through the 1920s

The years from the 1890s through the 1920s can be called the early consumer movement. It provided many of the foundations for today's consumer activities. The first Consumers' League was formed in 1891 in New York City.

In 1899, the National Consumers' League (which is still active today) was founded, and soon branch offices were established in twenty states.

A feeling for the times can be seen in typical newspaper headlines:

STANDARD OIL "TRUST" SUCCEEDS THROUGH BRIBERY, GRAFT, FRAUD, VIOLENCE, AND THE DESTRUCTION OF COMPETITION

AGRICULTURE DEPARTMENT DOCUMENTS 1400 PAGES OF FOOD ADULTERATION

FORMALDEHYDE USED AS FOOD PRESERVATIVE

GROUPS OPPOSE FOOD AND DRUG LEGISLATION, INCLUDING AMERICAN MEDICAL ASSOCIATION

"THE JUNGLE" MAKES COUNTRY SICK!

[1] Robert O. Herrmann, *The Consumer Movement in Historical Perspective* (University Park, Pa.: The Pennsylvania State University, Department of Agricultural Economics and Rural Sociology, 1970), p. 1.

Upton Sinclair's book provides an exposé of the working conditions in the Chicago meat packing houses. "These rats were nuisances, and the packers would put poisoned bread out for them and they would die, and then rats, bread and meat go into the hoppers together. . . . Men, who walked in the tank rooms full of steam . . . fell into the vats; and when they were fished out, there was never enough of them to be worth exhibiting—sometimes they would be overlooked for days, till all but the bones of them had gone out to the world as Durham's Pure Leaf Lard!"

PRESIDENT ROOSEVELT INVESTIGATES FOODS

PURE FOOD AND DRUG LAW PASSES CONGRESS

CHICAGO HOUSEWIVES LEAGUE FORMED TO CHECK SANITARY CONDITIONS IN FOOD STORES

U.S. ENTERS WORLD WAR

Patriotic fever, wartime shortages, and postwar readjustments then diverted much attention from consumer problems, although consumer incomes rose during the early 1920s. More and newer products appeared for sale, and advertising budgets exceeded $3 billion annually, a level not reached again until 1947. Buyers were confused by the growing array of products, and it is no wonder that the book by Stuart Chase and F. J. Schlink, *Your Money's Worth*, became a bestseller in 1927. It attacked most advertising and called for scientific product standards. Consumers' Research, Inc., was formed by Schlink in 1929, as were a number of other product-testing laboratories, some of which were run by department stores and trade associations.

From 1929 through the 1950s

Because of a variety of circumstances, consumer interest was renewed from 1929 through the 1950s. Early on, the Great Depression of the 1930s came; typical headlines that tell about the times:

ONE-THIRD OF LABOR FORCE UNEMPLOYED

BARGAIN SALES OF PRE-DEPRESSION MERCHANDISE

CONSUMERS SHOULD BEWARE OF SHODDY MERCHANDISE

IS ADVERTISING RESPONSIBLE FOR THE WASTEFUL PROLIFERATION OF BRANDS AND COSTING CONSUMERS MORE?

"WEAR IT OUT, USE IT UP, MAKE IT DO!"—NEW CONSUMER SLOGAN

CONSUMER ADVISORY BOARD (CAB) TO ADVISE GOVERNMENT

CAB DECLARED UNCONSTITUTIONAL

The U.S. Supreme Court declared the Consumer Advisory Board unconstitutional as it was set up through the National Industrial Recovery Act of 1933. During the past two years more than 100 local consumer councils were organized. . . .

PICKETING DETROIT HOUSEWIVES FORCE MEAT PRICES TO ROLL BACK 20 PERCENT

EMPLOYEES ON STRIKE AT CONSUMERS' RESEARCH, INC.

NEW TESTING GROUP ORGANIZED—CONSUMERS UNION, INC.

PURE FOOD AND DRUG LAW NOW OUTDATED

NEW SULPHA WONDER DRUG KILLS NEARLY 100 PEOPLE

IMPROVED FOOD AND DRUG LAW PASSES CONGRESS

The next postwar period saw strong economic growth and rising consumer incomes. Magazine circulation for *Consumer Reports* grew to almost a half million by 1950. In 1956,

the National Association of Consumers, a small consumer interest group, quietly disappeared in a merger with the Council on Consumer Information. Grass-roots issues were not numerous, but the increased use of installment credit and the buying of new homes and new durable products did provide some incentive for including consumer education courses in the schools. Then Russia's first Sputnik, in 1957, rapidly turned attention away from such "life-adjustment" courses. The curriculum instead began to emphasize science and mathematics.

Some consumer issues still caught the headlines, however, such as those brought out by Vance Packard in *The Hidden Persuaders,* in which he argued that the public was being manipulated by advertisers. But generally speaking, the relative prosperity of the 1950s, the McCarthyism campaign against "Communists," and the interest in space and national defense kept things rather quiet on the consumer front.

CONSUMERISM AND RESPONSES

The beginnings of the fourth era of consumer interest during the 1960s, which some call consumerism, saw Americans developing a greater social conscience. They were more open to self-criticism regarding social and economic problems, many of which were of deep concern to all consumers. Rachel Carson's *The Silent Spring* (1962, environment), Michael Harrington's *The Other America* (1962, poverty), Jessica Mitford's *The American Way of Death* (1963, funerals), David Caplovitz's *The Poor Pay More* (1963, poverty and credit), Maurine Neuberger's *Smoke Screen: Tobacco and the Public Welfare* (1963, cigarettes), and Richard Harris's *The Real Voice* (1964, drug safety) all became best-selling books. The nation was becoming more aware.

In 1962, John F. Kennedy presented the *first* presidential message to Congress that was directed at consumer concerns. He asked for legislative action and new programs in several areas. The most important aspect, however, was the now famous Consumer Bill of Rights: (1) the right to safety, (2) the right to be informed, (3) the right to choose, and (4) the right to be heard. This message became a springboard for a new surge of interest in consumer concerns.

The thalidomide drug scandal (which resulted in over 20,000 deformed babies being born around the world, although few in the United States), the Kefauver-Harris drug hearings, the establishment of a Consumer Advisory Council to President Kennedy's Council of Economic Advisors, the numerous best-selling books, and an awakened public interest kept consumer problems in the news.

In January of 1964, President Johnson created a new White House position, Special Assistant for Consumer Affairs. He appointed Esther Peterson to this post. With White House visibility, consumer concerns became front-page news. In February of 1964, Johnson sent a consumer message to Congress urging passage of twelve new laws. The liberal landslide in the 1964 election gave strength to those calling for reforms.

In 1966, Ralph Nader's book *Unsafe at Any Speed* became a best seller after it was revealed that General Motors had investigated Nader's background in an attempt to discredit both the man and his book. The resulting controversy led to an apology by the chairman of the board of General Motors during congressional hearings, which were televised before a nationwide audience, and passage of the National Traffic and Motor Vehicle Safety Act later that year.

Consumerism of the sixties also saw housewives boycotting supermarkets because of high meat prices; exposés in the form of books, news articles, and radio and television programs; organization of local consumer-action groups; a flurry of legislative action on national and state levels; scandals concerning foods, fabrics, drugs, credit, and product safety; further presidential support by Lyndon B. Johnson and Richard M. Nixon through more consumer messages; introduction of consumer education courses into many public schools; an increased media interest in consumer issues as news; and a general broadening of support for consumer concerns. In 1968, the Consumer Federation of America was formed. It lobbied for consumers in Washington, D.C., primarily on issues of national concern. Its strength came from the nearly 200 other consumer organizations which were members. The "ism" in consumerism became appropriate as once-quiet consumers organized and spoke out on a wide spectrum of issues. Active leaders were almost militant in promoting the needed equality for consumers.

Government Response to Consumerism

During the 1960s, local, state, and federal legislation was the traditional government response to consumer problems. If a problem arose, it seemed logical to write a new law, start a special agency, and/or create a commission to study the matter and make recommendations. In addition, the existing and newly created organizations tried to do a better job. By the end of the decade, there were almost fifty complaint departments in the federal agencies and more than 225 county and city consumer offices.

Consumers were later to discover that putting laws on the books is one thing and enforcing them is another. In spite of that realization, several states and localities passed strict laws and regulations to protect consumers: civil and criminal penalties against offenders, injunctions against unethical merchants, licensing of business services (such as television and automobile repairs), required posting of octane ratings for gasoline, prohibition of pyramid sales promotions and "little FTC acts" making it unlawful to use fraud, deception, or false pretense in the sale or advertising of any merchandise. Other states and localities banned advertising any items when sufficient quantities were not readily available. They also prohibited *wage garnishment* clauses in contracts (which permit employers to withhold part of an employee's wages and pay them directly to the lending agency), and eliminated *confession of judgment* clauses in legal contracts (where the consumer-borrower agrees in advance to let the plaintiff's lawyer plead the consumer guilty in court without even notice of such legal action should the consumer fall behind in an installment credit contract).

The federal legislative rush to protect consumers resulted in more than 150 bills being proposed—many for political reasons only. As a result, fewer than twenty of the bills were passed. Many major pieces of legislation were never acted upon, and enforcement of laws written was typically very weak. Nevertheless, on the legislative front the "consumerism decade" made tremendous progress compared with earlier years.

Business Response to Consumerism

The social consciousness of the early 1960s, rising incomes of consumers, and higher expectations of quality (suggested primarily through advertising) were signs that could have been used to predict the "consumerism" of that decade. Inflation, beginning in the mid-1960s, and rising unemployment, combined with the louder voices of consumer advocates, finally convinced business that consumerism was a force to be reckoned with. How did business respond?

In the early 1960s, "ignore them and they will go away" had been a typical response. But during the mid-sixties, *caveat emptor*—let the buyer beware—changed to *caveat venditor*—let the seller beware! Fear was the reason. Some businesspersons said, "Fight the consumerists! Save our free enterprise system!" But others went along with the demands of consumers when it did not cost them too much money. Comparatively few, especially during the late sixties, actually looked upon the consumer movement as an opportunity; those who did sought the help of consumers, knowing that this was where they could expect improvement of their public relations and also better sales.

The typical business response to government regulation, and really the consumer issues of the sixties, was concisely stated by the editors of *Business Week* in September of 1969:

> *Deny everything.* Nearly everyone goes through a phase of shock when hallowed business practices are questioned, and this is the automatic response.
>
> *Blame wrongdoing on the small marginal companies.* In any industry where fragmentation and ease of entry are the rule, the argument is popular that the major companies are blameless, but that the small outfits must cut corners to survive.
>
> *Discredit the critics.* "Hell," says one Congressional staff man, "I've had publishers worried about circulation sales investigation down here peddling stuff on the Communist nature of consumerism based on 1942 documents."
>
> *Hire a public relations person.* A big campaign to modify public opinion is alluring. But, as one PR man says, "there's no sense in a PR campaign if you have nothing to say."
>
> *Defang the legislation.* Trade associations and Washington law firms are specialists in this, and it is often effective, at least for a while. It worked for the tobacco industry in 1965. It also worked in respect to the Truth-in-Packaging Law.
>
> *Launch a fact-finding committee* to find out whether anything really needs to be improved in the way the company does business. The food industry is deeply involved in this now.
>
> *Actually do something,* whether you think you are guilty or innocent.

PRECIPITATING AND SUSTAINING INTERESTS OF CONSUMERS

The *consumer interest* is multidimensional. Consumers have so many different points of view that the term almost defies definition. Consumer advocate and attorney James Turner, however, has illustrated one major aspect of the consumer interest. Using price and quality as factors, one can readily see that the *consumer interest* is to obtain goods and services of the highest quality at the lowest possible prices. The *business interest*, on the other hand, is to sell the lowest cost products at the highest possible prices. The *public interest*, hence, is clearly distinguishable from the consumer interest; it involves selling goods and services of fair quality at fair prices. The broad interests of consumers encompass much more than just price and quality, and some discussion of the history of consumer movements may give us insights into the term. In addition, we can gain some understanding of the factors that make consumer movements successful.

Economic Conditions

When we have high unemployment and/or rising prices, consumers begin to feel the pressure. They become acutely interested in what happens to their dollars; they get upset; they organize. The inflationary period of the early 1900s helped give rise to the union movement. The Depression of the 1930s brought consumer education courses into the schools, and forced the federal government to legislate unemployment programs, pass Social Security laws, and establish the Securities and Exchange Commission (SEC). Also, the consumer voice was recognized for the first time in government through the Consumer Advisory Board. Inflation in the 1960s and 1970s helped provide the impetus for welfare reforms, a call for a guaranteed minimum income, and price controls on such things as health care.

Scandals

Print media during the 1800s, radio during the 1920s and 1930s, television in the late 40s and 50s, and all mass media in more recent years have provided a ready outlet for scandals. Best-selling books, journalistic muckraking exposes, and stories by investigative reporters quickly gain and hold the attention of consumers. This helps to sustain consumer movements.

Without media attention, scandals would have little or no impact. The moral feelings of the country were shocked and outraged by Sinclair's *The Jungle*, which exposed the scandalous conditions of the meat-packing plants and led to food and drug legislation. Chase and Schlink's book *Your Money's Worth* resulted in the formation of several product-testing organizations. The liquid form of a drug called Elixir Sulfanilamide killed nearly 100 persons and this, in part, resulted in improved drug and food legislation in 1938. A similar drug scandal concerned thalidomide, which caused birth defects in thousands of babies and led to further drug amendments in the 1960s.

Ralph Nader's book *Unsafe at Any Speed* did not sell well at all until the televised congressional hearings disclosed the scandalous investigation of him by General Motors. The publicity made him something of a folk hero and helped to pass major automobile safety legislation later that year. Illegal corporate contributions to political campaigns in the 1970s led to ethics legislation and limits on such contributions.

Charismatic People

Certain people have a magnetic quality. They receive attention because of their particular leadership styles. These leaders can be found in all areas of human life (both good and bad—remember Hitler!). Throughout each consumer era a few individuals have inspired others to listen and to act. People followed Theodore Roosevelt; when, as president, he called for food and drug legislation, the country responded. Schlink's writings led to the formation of Consumer's Research, Inc., which published its findings in a periodical (now called *Consumers' Research Magazine*) to which thousands subscribed.

John F. Kennedy also had a charismatic personality and his famous Consumer Bill of Rights heralded a new era of consumer interest. Partially because of her flair for dramatics, Betty Furness, acting as President Lyndon Johnson's Special Assistant for Con-

"My goodness, Mr. Merry-weather, we certainly *did* make a boo-boo with that prescription of yours!"

sumer Affairs, attracted considerable interest when she spoke out on consumer problems. According to a recent Harris survey, Ralph Nader is looked upon with high esteem by more than two-thirds of the population.

Other charismatic leaders include personalities in government, including Senators William Proxmire, Charles Percy, Henry Jackson, and Edward Kennedy, and Congress members Charles Vanik and Benjamin Rosenthal. President Jimmy Carter has some charisma, too. In fact, he once said he wants to challenge Ralph Nader as the country's leading spokesperson for consumers.

Government Organizations

Federal, state, and local government organizations have much to do with promoting the consumer interest. They have the power, after all, to propose and/or enforce laws and regulations. In the 1890s, for example, Dr. Harvey W. Wiley of the Department of Agriculture got excellent news coverage when he dramatized the food adulteration problem. He created a "poison squad" of twelve men who were fed adulterants common to the diet of most Americans. None died, although some became ill, but the overuse of adulterated foods was publicized.

During the 1920s, the Antitrust Division of the Federal Trade Commission was responsible for vigorous enforcement of the laws as well as the breaking up of business *trusts* which illegally conspired to fix prices. The drug thalidomide did not deform many children in *this* country, but only because of the active efforts of the Food and Drug Administration in the early 1960s. In the 1970s, the Consumer Product Safety Commission made headlines by prohibiting the sale of flammable sleepwear for children. Legal aid attorneys across the country regularly file lawsuits on behalf of the disadvantaged. And the president's Special Assistant for Consumer Affairs testifies at congressional hearings and speaks out on consumer issues.

As noted, Congress has its charismatic leaders, but it also has many committees and subcommittees. They do not necessarily make laws, but they hold frequent hearings on consumer concerns, and these are well publicized. It is usually good politics to be pro-consumer, and such government committees provide quite a forum for promoting consumer interests.

State and local governments actively sustain consumer interests in a number of ways. In almost every state, the attorney general now actively represents consumers. In most states, the representation consists of a full staff of lawyers and paraprofessionals, such as the Illinois Attorney General's Consumer Fraud Division. Large cities and counties also often maintain consumer affairs offices; New York City's program is considered one of the best. The expertise and effectiveness of the more than 600 such government organizations continue to grow.

Private Organizations

A wide variety of private organizations has helped to sustain interest in consumer matters. In 1891, a New York City action group "white listed" shops that treated employees fairly. This group encouraged patronage of those businesses that "paid fair minimum wages, had reasonable working hours, and de-

cent sanitary conditions." By 1903, the National Consumer's League had 64 branch offices in twenty states. Today's largest consumer-action group, the Consumer Federation of America (CFA), represents approximately 200 local and state organizations. It lobbies in Washington, D.C. on behalf of all consumers. Although the size of its professional staff is limited, the voice of CFA is being heard increasingly. Every state today has a consumer-action group organized on a statewide basis. Examples of particularly strong organizations are those in California and Ohio. Some cities or neighborhoods are well organized, too; the local Hyde Park (Chicago) cooperative, for example, is a very active group. Complaint handling and arbitration organizations exist also. Two of the most respected include the Major Appliance Consumer Action Panel (MACAP) and the dozens of AUTOCAPS (Automobile Consumer Action Panels) in cities across the country.

Other effective, privately organized groups include the numerous "Nader's Raiders" people. Perhaps Nader's strongest catalysts are the Center for the Study of Responsive Law, Public Citizen, Senior Citizens, and the Student Public Interest Research Groups. Consumers Union, Inc., publishes the widely read product-testing *Consumer Reports,* while also actively supporting various consumer concerns.

The list of present-day groups representing some form of consumer interest is quite long and includes many unions, chambers of commerce, cooperatives, credit unions, and better business bureaus. The National Consumers League, the Family Finance Association, the National Council of Better Business Bureaus, and the Cooperative League of the United States are some of the largest organizations. The American Council on Consumer Interests, successor to the Council on Consumer Information, is a professional association for those in the consumer field, and it works in an information-exchange capacity. The Society for Consumer Affairs Professionals in Business (SOCAP) serves a similar function for those who work in business. The variety of private organizations attests to the interest in sustaining and strengthening the consumer movement (see Appendix).

TODAY'S CONSUMER MOVEMENT

The current era of consumer interest is one that has matured and become organized. Most of the big issues concerning quality of life have been addressed in recent years, issues such as credit, food and drugs, product safety, and warranty protection. In addition, it is now recognized that "passing a law" does not solve the problems. Thus, today's consumer movement is primarily concerned with improving the effectiveness of existing laws and the organizations that protect consumers. Yet it continues to research and lobby for more legislation in the remaining areas of considerable consumer concern.

The seller/consumer conflict will always remain because of the fundamental differences in motivation. However, today's consumer movement has seen a maturing of these relationships, too. To simply accuse is no longer the norm. Cooperation is now becoming a mutually satisfactory course of action.

One illustration is the consumer action panels in various industries. In the automobile industry, AUTOCAPS hear consumer complaints and arbitrate differences between auto dealers (and in some communities auto repairers as well) and consumers. In many cities across the country, both industry people and consumer representatives judge cases brought before them for action. Such cooperation resolves many consumer complaints on a voluntary basis and thus avoids either government regulation or legal action. Self-regulation has its strengths, but it has weaknesses, too, and therefore cannot address all the issues of concern.

Issues of interest to consumers are in the headlines every day. And the consumer movement is responding in its attempts to resolve them. Any listing of "issues for action" is subject to considerable debate. However,

there is general agreement that (1) consumers need to strengthen their powers, (2) there are several critical issues of concern to all, and (3) many big issues will be debated during the coming years. These three points are further discussed below.

Strengthening of Consumer Powers

There could be many ways to strengthen the role of consumers in the balance of power between sellers and consumers; the aim would be to prevent as well as solve consumer problems. Suggestions could range from reactionary to radical.

Six moderate and realistic proposals are given here.

1. *Expand the powers of existing regulatory agencies.* This, along with increased funding and personnel, would make the government role in consumer protection more effective. For example, is it asking too much to demand that the Food and Drug Administration guarantee pure foods and drugs when it does not have the authority to demand "pre-market clearance" for many products? Prescription drugs are checked for safety, but over-the-counter drugs are not, and neither are many foods. The FDA tries to protect consumers against economic fraud and health hazards, and to research new health and drug products. But it has very limited funds—about $1 per person per year. There are more than 100,000 manufacturing, processing, and warehouse establishments to inspect, and the FDA staff of 6000 people (less than one-fourth of whom are inspectors) is woefully inadequate. The FDA does have the power to seize unsafe products and to prosecute offenders, but it needs a more adequate inspection staff to stop dangerous products before they reach the marketplace. Other federal, state, and local government regulatory agencies have similar problems.

2. *Create a powerful consumer-protection agency* on the federal level which could

Reprinted with permission from CHANGING TIMES Magazine, © Kiplinger Washington Editors, Inc.

"Mine's tasty beef by-products. What's yours?"

coordinate the efforts of all these numerous agencies and departments attempting to serve consumers; this is of critical importance. The agency needs to be independent with the authority to represent consumer interest(s) before the federal regulatory agencies and the courts. In addition, such an agency needs the authority to seek information from businesses (not trade secrets) that would help to identify areas of potential or real abuse. Creating a "paper" consumer protection agency without such powers would be a symbolic gesture and a step forward but would have little long-term importance.

Concerning the need for a powerful consumer protection agency, President Carter has said that "its purpose will be to plead the consumer's case within the government . . . to improve the way rules, regulations, and decisions are made and carried out, rather than issuing new rules itself . . . and aid in the fight against inflation by monitoring governmental actions that unnecessarily raise costs for consumers."

3. *Provide for increased use of class action lawsuits* on both the federal *and* state

levels. These lawsuits are generally aimed at price fixers who are in apparent violation of antitrust laws. They permit members of a common class, such as consumers, to band together to seek joint redress of their grievance. Many states prohibit such lawsuits, and recent U.S. Supreme Court rulings have greatly inhibited the filing of federal court cases; therefore, few class action lawsuits are being filed. To keep markets free and competitive, it takes more than just the Justice Department to file such lawsuits; consumers have the keenest interest in fair pricing, and the leverage of civil suits is needed to help police the market. One illustration of a limitation is that even if you can prove that you were the victim of a price-fixing conspiracy, you cannot recover damages unless you dealt *directly* with the fixer. Thus, if some television manufacturers fix prices, you can't sue them if you bought the products through a retailer or wholesaler.

4. *Encourage counteradvertising and corrective advertising. Counteradvertising* is a way to rebut claims made by advertisers. It involves giving groups, such as consumers, free and/or paid-for broadcasting time to respond to advertising that stressed just one side of a controversial issue. This concept began when the American Cancer Society received permission from the Federal Communications Commission to show advertisements against smoking which rebutted the then permitted cigarette commercials. Now, such nonsmoking commercials are run as "public service announcements." Counteradvertisements, if permitted, could tell the "other side of the story" on such things as pain relievers saying how effective they are, oil companies reporting how much they are doing for the environment, and many commercials that are silent about negative aspects of a product, such as liquor, whole-life insurance, and automobiles.

Corrective advertising is remedial in concept. It is meant to take away the unfair advantage that an advertiser may gain by running unfair advertisements and also to serve as a deterrent to future deception. Corrective advertisements have on occasion been ordered by the Federal Trade Commission as part of agreements with companies that have allegedly run deceptive advertisements. The intent is to "tell the truth" and thus restore the competitive situation to what it was before the advertisements were originally run. Profile Bread, for example, explained in a corrective ad that the reason why Profile Bread has fewer calories is "because it was sliced thinner." Further, Listerine was ordered by the U.S. Supreme Court to run ads saying that "contrary to prior advertising, Listerine will not help prevent colds or sore throats or lessen their severity."

5. *Encourage use of a deceptive sales injunctive power* by various regulatory agencies on the federal and state levels. Typical government weapons against deceptions include *cease and desist* orders and *consent agreements.* In a *consent agreement,* a company and the government agree that a particular practice (probably deceptive or illegal) will not be carried on by the company in the future. The company does not admit it has done anything wrong; it only agrees not to do that practice in the future. Consent agreements usually accompany *cease and desist* orders, which are formal orders by government agencies, such as the FTC, telling companies to stop doing something. Since most such orders are not really punitive, consent agreements are often signed. Sometimes the government and the company involved cannot agree, that is, the firm will not sign a consent agreement. In such cases, the case goes to the courts for resolution. When a company selling a product like Listerine (Warner-Lambert) is ordered to run this explicit sentence in their corrective adver-

tisements, "Listerine will not help prevent colds or sore throats or lessen their severity," the legal battle begins, runs on for several years and frequently ends up at the U.S. Supreme Court.

A deceptive sales injunctive power could stop many deceptive and fraudulent sales practices. (*Injunctions* are court orders stopping a particular practice on either a temporary or permanent basis.) The Federal Trade Commission already has such authority but rarely uses it. Most state agencies do not have such powers. Encouraging use of a deceptive sales injunctive power would stop deceptions *now* and litigate later.

6. *Encourage public participation in regulatory proceedings.* Too often on both the federal and state levels, there is little input from consumers on issues of concern to them. Why is that? A recent study of the appointment calendars of 39 regulatory commissioners on the federal level showed that they had 10 times as many meetings with industry representatives as they had with consumer representatives. In another study of the Food and Drug Administration alone, it was found that "less than 45 percent of the adjudicatory proceedings of the FDA had public interest groups participate." Therefore, consumer groups want legislation that will permit broader participation and representation of consumers and small businesses who normally cannot afford to participate in agency and court proceedings. What they want is reimbursement for reasonable attorney and expert witness fees and related expenses. Some federal agencies already have limited funds for such purposes— to hear "a point of view that normally would not be represented." However, this is rare on the federal level and nonexistent on the state level.

Critical Issues of Concern to All
Several consumer problems exist for Americans that can be righted by legislation and/or

effective enforcement. Nine issues—unranked—are reviewed below.

1. *Strengthening the weaknesses of earlier legislation*—both federal and state—could go far to protect the consumer more fully. The Truth-in-Lending law, the Flammable Fabrics Act amendments, the Fair Packaging and Labeling Act, and the law establishing the Consumer Product Safety Commission are just some of the federal laws that need strengthening. For example, the Fair Packaging and Labeling Act of 1966 is supposed to regulate the packaging and labeling of consumer goods to see that there are uniform standards for packages that allow fair comparison by consumers. Why then is it still almost impossible to compare breakfast cereals, olives, and many other food products? Why does one brand of instant mashed potatoes provide four "large" servings of 2 ounces while the next brand's "large" servings are only 1½ ounces? More efforts are needed to provide "differential" benefits to those segments of our population who need them (like the nondiscrimination provisions of the Equal Credit Opportunity Act).

2. *No-fault automobile insurance* that meets or exceeds national standards seems imperative. Why should approximately one-third of all accident victims never receive one penny in compensation for their injuries simply because they were unable to *prove* which driver was at fault? Why should automobile insurance premiums for young drivers in urban communities cost $2500 or more? This large sum frequently forces them not to purchase any coverage at all. Why should it take 5 years in many areas for an automobile liability lawsuit even to get in front of a judge and jury? No-fault automobile insurance is no panacea, but with acceptable minimum standards in all states, it could greatly help all consumers by reducing many of these inequities. Assurance of prompt and adequate benefits for accident victims or their survivors is sorely needed.

3. *National health insurance* with coverage that would at least include catastrophic illnesses is now being demanded as a basic right. Since the Medicare program began paying for kidney dialysis treatments for thousands of patients several years ago, many Americans have expressed a desire for more and broader government protection in the area of health care. The poor and the elderly suffer much more illness than the average American, but it is the middle-income family whose finances are often completely wiped out by a major illness when they do not have sufficient health insurance. Preventive medicine plans have been operating in selected areas of the United States for many years and have resulted in better medical care for participants—often with a one-fourth or greater reduction in total costs. The primary question is, is good health care a basic right of Americans? If so, should any consumer hesitate to obtain medical care because of worries about how to pay for it?

4. *Arbitration courts* to mediate the differences between customers and businesses are needed on the neighborhood level. This would be more than just a reform of small claims courts. These new courts would also tighten supervision of the trade associations that have voluntarily established regional or national arbitration panels whose decisions are usually binding upon members. Two good examples of the latter are the Cleaning Dyers Institute in New York City and the Major Appliance Consumer Action Panel.

As effective as these groups are, they do not go far enough on the local level. Millions of consumers with complaints don't bother to complain at all, others complain but don't receive satisfaction from the retailer or manufacturer, and most don't even know about arbitration panels. Complaining people are typically well educated and have above-average incomes—hardly the average person in most neighborhoods.

Economic remedial justice at the neighborhood level could be developed, perhaps in cooperation with the American Arbitration Association, businesses, and consumer groups. One advantage for working people would be that claims could be settled at night and on weekends. An additional and important function of such a neighborhood activity would be to serve as a consumer information center.

5. *Unconscionable and unfair contracts* should be eliminated. When a contract is unduly—and obviously—burdensome to one of the parties, it should be held to be unconscionable, even if part of the fault is poor judgment or ignorance. Such a contract can also, in the long run, be against the best interest of the business. For example, when a "hard-sell" magazine or encyclopedia salesperson knowingly sells to a family with a very low income and therefore little hope of being able to meet payments, is it fair? When a consumer gives up the right to a legal defense because of a clause in small print *(confession of judgment)* on the back of a contract, is it unconscionable? When a family misses payments for a television set, and all the other furniture they bought and paid for on installments from the same store is repossessed because of an *add-on* clause written into the credit agreement, is it fair? Are clauses of this nature in anyone's best interest?

6. *Quality standards* are needed wherever possible and feasible for various types of products, including such food items as produce and manufactured items like automobile tires. Quality standards would make the choice-making process easier for consumers while at the same time promoting competition in the marketplace.

7. *Product testing information* from federal and state governments is not readily available to consumers. Governments often have criteria they use when making comparisons and purchases. If these were publicized, it would help consumers buy more intelligently. Government agencies often collect information about performance, construction, and effectiveness—just the kind of information consumers need.

8. *Federal chartering for large corporations* would reshape the privileges and responsibilities of the nation's giant businesses. More than half of the largest corporations in America were organized under the laws of Delaware more than 60 years ago. No other state or court system anywhere gives as many privileges to corporate officers and directors and absolves them of as many responsibilities, and the impact of these supercorporations upon society has increased tremendously. Required federal chartering for large businesses would rewrite the "constitutional laws" under which each operates. Should there be provisions concerning pollution responsibilities? Restrictions against conflicts of interest of officers? Restrictions on *interlocking directorships* (serving on more than one board of directors in the same industry) among corporations and banks? Should explicit antimonopoly standards be written to promote competition and "consumer sovereignty?"

9. *Ecological pollution* of our planet will not be solved by half-hearted efforts of members of Congress, state legislators, consumers, or businesspersons. Water, air, solid waste, and noise pollution will require the concerted efforts of all citizens. The research of the broad-based organization of concerned citizens called Common Cause, as well as innumerable private and government studies, has clearly shown the disruption in chemical balances that the 4 billion inhabitants of "spaceship earth" have caused. When will all waterways be protected? What technology is required and what standards are necessary to dispose of solid refuse and other waste? What can be done to reduce the 163 mil-

lion tons of smoke and noxious fumes pouring annually into the atmosphere? What should we do about establishing noise-pollution standards?

ECONOMIC IDEOLOGY AND INTERPRETATION OF CONSUMER ISSUES

Consumer protection proposals are both numerous and controversial. And the major reason for the controversy is that the American people differ in their economic ideologies. There are three basic economic ideologies today: (1) the neoclassical belief system, (2) the managerial belief system, and (3) the liberal-Galbraithian belief system.[2] Each has its own set of beliefs about the structure of our economy, about how the companies in the United States behave, and about the effects of that behavior upon consumers. Additionally, each ideology includes beliefs about the best ways to remedy consumer problems and whether certain things are in fact consumer concerns. Figure 3-1 summarizes the basic views of three economic belief systems.

Neoclassical Belief System
The neoclassical belief system holds that our economy is, or should be, basically a free enterprise competitive system. They see the economy as governed by vigorous competition based primarily upon price. The role of the consumer is that of an intelligent shopper who is basically immune to manipulation by advertising and other forms of persuasion. Consumers cast their "dollar votes" for the products and services they really need. Their power over the marketplace is called "consumer sovereignty."

The neoclassicist believes that there are few

[2] The substance of this discussion is taken with permission from Robert O. Herrmann, "Relating Economic Ideologies to Consumer Protection: A Suggested Unit in Consumer Education," *Business Education World,* (September–October 1977), pp. 13–15.

consumer problems other than frauds, deceptions, and unsafe products. The way to resolve these consumer problems is through individual lawsuits by those affected. Government controls and regulations are considered ineffective, unwanted, and an interference with the free competitive marketplace. Individual rights and freedom of choice are paramount in weighing the costs and benefits of any proposal. Thus, passive restraint systems like air bags in automobiles and open dating for food products would be seriously challenged, as the neoclassicist believes that the self-correcting forces of the marketplace will offer such devices or information when the public dollars demand it. Advocates of the neoclassical belief system include Nobel prize–winning economist Milton Friedman and a number of conservative businesspersons and politicians.

Managerial Belief System
The managerial belief system emphasizes the important role of the professional manager in today's corporations. It recognizes that the economy is dominated by large corporations and that competition is based upon many things other than price. Crucial to this system of thinking is the belief that corporate managers serve responsibly (almost as trustees) and in the interest of workers, shareholders, and consumers. The corporate manager has a high degree of social conscience which helps protect consumers. Of great importance is the recognition that advertising does affect consumers by stimulating demand, which in turn ensures a high level of overall economic activity.

The role of government is primarily to help maintain a high level of economic activity. That some government actions are needed to protect consumers is acknowledged; those against misleading advertising are an example. But the managerial belief system holds that the best protection for consumers comes from corporate competition and the corporate managers' sense of responsibility. Consequently, businesses should be self-regulatory and gov-

	Neoclassical	Managerial	Liberal-Galbraithian
How competitive is our economy?	Highly competitive.	Highly competitive, even though it is dominated by large firms.	Dominated by monopolies and oligopolies.
How do firms compete with each other?	Prices.	Prices, product features, advertising, services.	Advertising, minor differences in product design and services.
What keeps the behavior of individual firms in line?	Competition of other firms for customers.	Competition of other firms for customers, managers' sense of responsibility to workers, shareholders, consumers.	Nothing except firm's desire for security and stable growth.
What is the role of consumers in the economy?	Intelligent shoppers who guide the market by casting their "dollar votes" for products they prefer.	Generally intelligent shoppers who can be manipulated by advertising, spenders who influence level of overall economic activity.	Buyers whose wants and beliefs are manipulated by advertising and other techniques so as to maintain a high level of spending.
What kinds of problems do consumers have?	Fraud and deception, unsafe products.	Misleading advertising, difficulties in obtaining redress.	A variety of problems arising from unchecked corporate power: excessive prices, unsafe products, difficulty in obtaining redress.
How can these consumer problems best be remedied?	Legal action by individual consumer affected.	Business self-regulation, improved systems of complaint handling.	Government regulation.
What should be the role of government in regulating the economy?	Minimal, so as not to interfere with competition.	Removing barriers to competition, maintaining a high level of economic activity.	Antitrust action and strengthened government regulation (Nader). Government regulation of large corporations and controls over their prices (Galbraith).

Source: Adapted from Joseph R. Monsen, Jr., *Modern American Capitalism: Ideologies and Issues.* Boston: Houghton Mifflin, 1963.

FIGURE 3-1 Comparing the basic views of three economic belief systems

ernment should work toward removing barriers to competition. One of the biggest supporters of the managerial belief system is *Fortune* magazine.

Liberal-Galbraithian Belief System

This system has its roots in the reform tradition of the turn of the century and the liberal reform movement of the 1960s. The economy is perceived as being dominated by monop-

olies, oligopolies, and shared monopolies. Corporations work with little competition to serve their own ends, which are security and continued growth. Economist John Kenneth Galbraith has elaborated on this liberal belief system and labels such corporations as "the planning system" which exercises great control over consumers and government as well. The remainder of the economy is viewed by Galbraith in much the same way as by the neoclassicists; he calls the remaining small firms "the market system."

Consumers are not viewed as the dominant force in the economy, since advertising effectively shapes their values and beliefs to accommodate the needs of the planning system. Consumer problems arise from unchecked corporate power. These problems include excessive prices, unsafe products, and difficulty in seeking redress.

Ralph Nader's perception of the economy stems from this belief system. Similarly, many of the proposals from active consumer organizations to resolve consumer problems come from the liberal-Galbraithian belief system. Nader and his followers prescribe stronger antitrust actions, strict government regulation of corporate activities to discourage irresponsible actions (pollution) and encourage responsible ones (safer products), and much more access to information so that consumers can act more intelligently in the marketplace. Further, consumers need government protection because of the complexities and technologies in the marketplace today.

Galbraith perceives the economy much as Nader does but offers different solutions to the problems. Antitrust action, he says, is of little value, since "a government cannot proclaim half of the economic system illegal." Instead, Galbraith suggests price controls as one method of controlling the power of large firms. Further, government must break the grip of the planning system, with Congress being a much stronger representative of the public interest. Otherwise, attempts to regulate such immense corporate power will be blunted and, as he believes often happens now, actually serve the needs of the planning system.

Support for Consumer Protection Proposals

Reaction to consumer protection proposals varies widely given the diverse opinions held by Americans. The widest support would very likely go to proposals that would make product information available, provided that it is low in cost, reaches many consumers, comes basically from business, and involves a minimum of government involvement. Information, *per se*, encourages competition and more and better products—a goal valued by all three belief systems.

Antitrust proposals receive the least support. Nader would favor such actions, but Galbraith would prefer price controls. Those of the managerial belief system would not favor antitrust activities if they would reduce the effectiveness of the corporate manager. The neoclassicists, of course, would fear any kind of government intrusion. Proposals for safety-related concerns receive mixed support, since those in the managerial belief system and the Liberal-Galbraithian belief system agree with government involvement, while the neoclassicists do not.

Moreover, the attitudes of Americans vary widely because of their basic economic ideological beliefs. To successfully effect change—get new consumer protection proposals accepted—will require an appreciation of these views and strong efforts to win enough support. Some recently passed and proposed consumer protection legislation and regulations are shown in Table 3–1. One could easily analyze which economic ideology is likely to support or oppose such legislation.

CONSUMER RIGHTS, RESPONSIBILITIES, AND REDRESS

The American marketplace is complex, and many of its influences directly affect consumer behavior. In view of this, certain basic rights, responsibilities, and methods of redress need to be well understood by consumers.

Rights of Consumers

In recent years, consumer rights have been taken for granted. Further, these rights have often been abused by businesses that assume that most consumers are not aware of their rights. Unfortunately, they are often correct. A study by researchers at the University of Texas, reported in the *Journal of Marketing*, found that "with few exceptions, the rich, the poor, the public, and attorneys knew little

"You can say what you like, but I think the consumer game is fascinating."

Reprinted with permission from CHANGING TIMES Magazine, © Kiplinger Washington Editors, Inc.

about their rights as consumers." No income group scored over 39.4 percent correct on a test of knowledge of rights. Most consumers are not aware of their rights. Yet if consumers want to function effectively in the American marketplace, they must know their rights and exercise their responsibilities, and must seek redress when any such rights are violated. The legal rights of consumers are examined below along with their moral and ethical rights.

Legal Rights.   A person who purchases a new clothes dryer that does not work properly has the right to get the problem corrected. The person has a legal right to have the dryer fixed to work properly. If it is not fixed, the consumer should be able to get another dryer or get his or her money back.

Should a merchant not respond to requests to have such products replaced, the consumer can bring legal action to get his or her money back. In effect, the consumer has a legal right to buy products that operate properly. Also, the merchant has a legal obligation not to knowingly sell products that are working improperly.

Consumers also buy services of various kinds and have a legal right to get quality ser-

TABLE 3–1

Recent and Proposed Consumer Protection Legislations and Rulings

Year Passed	Law or Regulation	Major Provisions
Proposed Legislation		
—	Consumer Cooperative Act	To facilitate the establishment of consumer cooperatives for buying directly and in quantity from producers.
—	Public Participation Act	To provide funds to reimburse costs and expenses of persons testifying before regulatory agencies, such as consumers and owners of small businesses.
—	National No-Fault Automobile Insurance Act	To provide for a comprehensive automobile insurance program in which accident victims' personal-injury expenses are paid by their own insurance companies, regardless of who is at fault; sets minimum federal standards.

TABLE 3–1 (Continued)

Year Passed	Law or Regulation	Major Provisions
—	National Health Insurance Act	To provide for a comprehensive national health insurance program (combining private and social funding) for all Americans.
—	Class Action Lawsuit Act	To facilitate joint redress through the courts when groups of consumers have common grievances.
—	Consumer Protection Agency Act	To provide for a formal consolidation of existing federal consumer offices and to provide advocates to present the positions of consumer interests in federal decision making; includes authority to appeal cases to the courts.
—	Drug Regulation Reform Act	To get new "breakthrough" drugs on the market sooner and to give more information on the risks and benefits of all drugs.

Recent Legislation and Regulations

Year Passed	Law or Regulation	Major Provisions
1978	Co-op Bank Bill	Authorizes creation of a federal bank to make loans to consumer cooperatives set up to provide everything from health care to food.
1978	National Energy Act	To formalize a national energy policy directed at encouraging conservation of resources; provides for general tax incentives and penalties, promotes research on alternative energy sources, and phases out price regulation of oil and natural gas.
1977	Creation of Department of Energy	Creates a new executive department to consolidate existing energy programs and to coordinate a national energy policy.
1977	Emergency Natural Gas Act	Empowers president and Federal Power Commission to authorize emergency transportation and deliveries of natural gas during periods of shortage in certain locales.
1977	Hearing Aid Regulation	Requires medical examinations prior to hearing aid purchases, but permits waiver of the examination.
1977	Fair Debt Collection Practices Act	Restricts unfair techniques used by debt collectors.
1976	Health Professions Educational Assistance Act	Restricts the recruiting of alien interns and residents by hospitals.
1976	National Consumer Health Information and Health Promotion Act	Authorizes grants to develop health information programs. Expands program to control venereal diseases. Extends HEW & CPSC lead-based paint poisoning programs.
1976	Toxic Substances Control Act	Regulates commerce and protects human health and the environment by requiring testing and necessary use restrictions on certain chemical substances.
1976	Cosmetic Labeling Ruling	Requires ingredient listing on cosmetic labels, excluding "trade secrets," as ordered by the FDA.
1976	Consumer Leasing Act	Requires detailed disclosures of terms and cost by companies leasing certain merchandise.
1976	Medical Devices Amendments	Expands FDA's authority to regulate the marketing of certain medical devices.
1976	Holder-in-Due-Course Ruling	Preserves rights of consumers regarding undelivered, damaged, or incorrect goods when the credit contract is held by a third party, as ordered by the FTC.
1975	Metric Conversion Bill	Provides for voluntary switchover by American industry to the metric system, and establishes a metric conversion board to coordinate the U.S. effort.

TABLE 3–1 (Continued)

Year Passed	Law or Regulation	Major Provisions
1975	Auto Recall Repair Law	Requires tire, auto, and replacement part makers to offer refund, replacement, or refund options on defective products.
1975	Energy Policy and Conservation Act	Requires energy efficiency labels on various home appliances. Specifies mandatory fuel economy standards for autos. Gives president conditional fuel rationing powers.
1975	Emergency Housing Act	Authorizes temporary assistance to help defray mortgage payments on homes owned by temporarily unemployed or underemployed persons.
1975	Home Mortgage Disclosure Act	Requires mortgage lenders above a prescribed size to disclose where they make their mortgage loans.
1975	Consumer Goods Pricing Act	Repeals "fair-trade" laws in states which still had them.
1975	Equal Credit Opportunity Act	Prohibits creditors from discriminating against consumers on the basis of race, sex, age, etc., and from applying inconsistent standards in granting credit.
1974	Real Estate Settlement Procedures Act	Provides uniform disclosures of the costs involved in closing real estate transactions.
1974	Privacy Act	Gives individuals right of access to information on file about them. Restricts federal agency distribution of mailing lists.
1974	Employee Retirement Income Security Act	Establishes standards of conduct for administrators of pension plans. Establishes funding, participation, and vesting requirements.
1974	Fair Credit Billing Act	Assists consumers in resolving credit disputes. Protects against credit card liabilities for defective products.
1974	Education Amendments of 1974	Creates Office of Consumers' Education in the Office of Education and establishes grant program for public consumer education programs.
1974	Magnuson-Moss Warranty-FTC Improvement Act	Authorizes FTC to set rules under which manufacturer must disclose terms and conditions of warranties given on products costing more than $5.
1974	Safe Drinking Water Act	Amends Public Health Service Act by adding Title XIV, assuring that the public is provided with safe drinking water.
1974	Housing and Community Development Act	Establishes a program of community development block grants. Directs the establishment of federal construction and safety standards for mobile homes.
1974	Transportation Safety Act	Improves protections afforded the public against risks connected with the transportation of hazardous materials.
1974	National Mass Transportation Assistance Act	Increases federal assistance to mass transportation systems.
1973	Trans-Alaska Pipeline Authorization and FTC Improvements Act	Expands FTC power to seek temporary restraining orders and preliminary injunctions, and raises maximum fines for violation of FTC orders.
1973	Health Maintenance Organization Act	Amends Public Health Service Act regarding the establishment and expansion of Health Maintenance Organizations (HMOs).
1973	Emergency Petroleum Act	Authorizes and requires president of U.S. to allocate refined petroleum products to deal with existing or imminent shortages and dislocations in the national distribution system which jeopardize public health, safety, and welfare.
1972	Consumer Product Safety Act	Creates the Consumer Product Safety Commission (CPSC), and transfers to it the enforcement of the Flammable

TABLE 3–1 (Continued)

Year Passed	Law or Regulation	Major Provisions
		Fabrics Act, Federal Hazardous Substances Act, and Poison Prevention Packaging Act.
1972	Noise Control Act	Establishes control of noise detrimental to the human environment. Authorizes the establishment of federal noise standards.
1972	Drug Listing Act	Requires drug manufacturers and processors to provide the FDA with a list of all their products in commercial distribution. Requires over-the-counter (OTC) drug manufacturers to submit lists of active ingredients in their products.
1972	Motor Vehicle Information and Cost Savings Act	Establishes bumper standards, specifies that tampering with odometers will be a federal offense, and permits similar regulations to be issued.
1970	Poison Prevention Packaging Act	Authorizes the establishment of standards for child-resistant packaging of hazardous substances.
1970	Fair Credit Reporting Act	Restricts access to credit files by unauthorized persons, and specifies procedures for correcting inaccurate information in files.
1970	Amendments to the Truth in Lending Act	Prohibits distribution of unauthorized credit cards. Establishes a $50 limitation on cardholder liability for unauthorized card use.
1970	Rail Passenger Service Act	Establishes and provides financial assistance for a national rail passenger system (AMTRAK).
1970	Egg Products Inspection Act	Establishes standards for USDA inspection of certain egg products in interstate and foreign commerce.
1970	Occupational Safety and Health Act	Provides for the establishment and enforcement of standards for safe and healthful working conditions.

vice. If one is charged $8.00 for dry cleaning services, it is understood that the cleaning will be done properly. The proprietor has a legal obligation to stand by the quality of the work. If the clothing is not cleaned properly, either it should be processed again or the money should be refunded. If neither occurs, the consumer has a right to bring legal action. Consumers must be aware of these legal rights and know when and how to exercise them properly.

Moral and Ethical Rights. Consumers also have moral and ethical rights in the marketplace. The problem is, however, that more often than not these rights are not automatically provided. Moral and ethical rights include:

- Being treated as equals in the marketplace.
- Being given an opportunity to practice intelligent comparison shopping without interference.
- Being treated courteously by merchants when shopping for goods or services even though a purchase may not be made.
- Being provided equal access to products and services available for sale.
- Being assured of honesty from merchants in each transaction.
- A warranty that products manufactured are safe for all expected purposes.
- Fair treatment by sellers of products and services regardless of economic, political, religious, racial, or ethnic factors.

President John F. Kennedy was the first president to formally proclaim *consumer rights*. His rights have never been deemed legal rights. Therefore, they are classified as moral or ethical rights. The rights as President Kennedy set them down in 1962 are

- The right to safety
- The right to be informed
- The right to choose
- The right to be heard

President Lyndon B. Johnson expanded these rights by calling for a special consumer protection program. It included consumer aid in the areas of health and safety, auto insurance, repairs, warranties, guarantees, and deceptive sales practices. Some of Johnson's proposals have been enacted by Congress and consequently have become legal rights. Others will be discussed and debated in subsequent congressional sessions.

President Richard M. Nixon, in a special message to Congress, reconfirmed the rights of consumers with these words:

> *Consumerism in the America of the seventies means that we have adopted the concept of "buyers rights." The buyer in America today has the right to make an intelligent choice . . . has the right to accurate information . . . has the right to health and safety . . . has the right to register his dissatisfaction, to provide greater personal freedom for individuals as well as better business to everyone in trade.*

President Gerald R. Ford put his stamp of approval on the four rights stated by Kennedy and added another very important one. Ford stated, as a fifth right, that all consumers should have the "right to consumer education." President Jimmy Carter during his first 3 months in office delivered two major addresses in support of the rights of consumers and called for passage of specific consumer protection legislation.

It is reassuring that the last several presidents have acknowledged the dilemmas of consumers and have supported their moral and ethical rights. But isn't it ironic that our society all too frequently has to depend on local ordinances and state or federal laws and regulations to implement these moral and ethical rights? How pleasant it would be if merchants, manufacturers, and consumers could recapture morality in the American marketplace by practicing and living with moral and ethical rights more and relying less upon legal rights. But, reality suggests otherwise—there is usually a need to legally implement aspects of the rights.

Responsibilities of Consumers

All too often the consumer is quick to indict a businessperson for denying rights. But consumers also too often fail to exercise proper judgment and restraint. A shoe that does not fit properly may not be the fault of the salesperson or the merchant; the fault may lie with the manufacturer and mass production operations. But an impatient, irresponsible consumer may take out anger on the local salesperson and thus impose on the salesperson's rights as an individual. It is each individual's responsibility to maintain perspective with his or her dissatisfaction.

In addition, consumers themselves must be aware of their rights (legal as well as moral and ethical), and must know what to do when these have been denied. This brings into the picture consumer responsibilities. Without them, the rights are worthless. Consumer responsibilities include getting satisfaction, understanding legal agreements, and other specific responsibilities related to consumer rights.

Getting Satisfaction. With each consumer right goes certain responsibilities, as can be seen from the shopping experience of Mrs. John Burnion of Cleveland, Ohio. Mrs. Burnion purchased a new dress for which she paid $90. She seemed very pleased with her choice until her husband pointed to a crooked seam that she had not noticed. Mr. Burnion suggested that she return the dress and get her money back. She refused, saying, "It is such a minor flaw that I doubt if anyone will ever notice it. And it's such a bother to return a dress."

Mrs. Burnion did not carry out one of her important responsibilities as a consumer. She paid for a dress with a flaw. Yet the dress was not advertised and priced as a "second." Very likely the salesperson did not intend to sell the flawed dress to Mrs. Burnion, thinking that she might be an irresponsible consumer. It was probably just an oversight. The real problem is that Mrs. Burnion did not *get satisfaction* for her $90. Consumers have a responsibility to get satisfaction for their money. If all consumers were like Mrs. Burnion, there would probably be more laxness than there is now in the quality of goods and services produced.

One excellent way to achieve satisfaction for money paid is through comparison shopping. Consumers must look for the *best buy* when buying products or services. This means selecting what best suits their values, needs, and personal preferences. By comparison shopping for price, quality, and performance, consumers perform a service for themselves. Of considerable importance is that they are also telling the merchant and producer, through their economic votes, that they are or are not satisfied with the choices available.

Understanding Legal Agreements. Another major consumer responsibility is to understand and read contracts before signing them. Perhaps one of the greatest abuses of responsibility lies in consumers not being informed about legal documents that they sign.

One of the rights previously cited was the right to be informed. In regard to legal agreements, this right implies that the consumer will read an agreement and, if he or she does not fully understand it, will ask questions. How else can one be informed and know what the consequences of signing will be?

Undeniably, "legalese" is annoying for the average consumer, but it need not be. If an individual should come across an especially difficult agreement, he or she should just ask what it means. The person providing the contract can give insight into what it means; so can a knowledgeable friend, or even an attor-

ney. For those without enough money, there are local legal aid service agencies in many communities to help them interpret and understand contracts. If people will just ask for help, many problems can be avoided. Keep in mind that it is important to refuse such statements as, "It's a standard contract; you don't have to read it all," or "Just sign here; I'll fill it in later to save time," or "If you sign now the price will be reduced 10 percent, but if you wait until tomorrow it will be back to the regular price." Such pressure is a clear signal that something is wrong.

Some tips when it comes to legal transactions include: (1) Read and understand before you sign; (2) make sure all blank spaces are filled in first; (3) have the agreement satisfactorily explained if you do not understand it fully; (4) if you find the explanation unsatisfactory, consult a reliable attorney before you complete the transaction; (5) do not allow yourself to be hurried; and (6) above all, do not let emotion override your basic knowledge and common sense. Be as informed as you can about legal transactions before you act.

Other Specific Responsibilities Related to Consumer Rights. Consumers who fulfill their responsibilities perform a most important function in the American economy—accurate economic voting. There are, of course, no guarantees to solving problems, however. If a consumer is responsible and complains about inferior merchandise or service, the problem may not be immediately solved. But this will certainly be a start toward getting the problem corrected. On the other hand, those consumers who do not do anything at all are irresponsible.

Each consumer must take the initiative. Esther Peterson, President Carter's Special Assistant for Consumer Affairs, fully supports this concept of citizen participation, as she states in the preface to this book. One must act and not wait for a problem to go away or for someone else to do it. Also, remember that not all consumers stand up for their rights. So one person who does probably really represents the voices and concerns of 50 or perhaps 100 others, and that is an added and important responsibility for each of us. Moreover, a citizen who fails to carry out his or her responsibilities as a consumer is, in effect, denying fellow citizens the benefit of his or her opinion.

Listed below are several specific responsibilities that are related to consumer rights.

Regarding the right to safety, consumers should:

- Assume personal responsibility for normal precautions when using any product.
- Read and heed warning labels.
- Examine merchandise for safety features before buying.
- Read and follow care and use instructions carefully.
- Inform retailers, manufacturers, business organizations, and government agencies when a product does not perform as claimed.

Regarding the right to be informed, consumers should:

- Seek out accurate information about products and services.
- Read advertisements carefully.
- Analyze and understand performance claims.
- Keep informed about new products and developments and continue their self-education.
- Ask questions of sellers about products and services when complete information is not available.
- Become more knowledgeable about the characteristics of the American marketplace and the consumer's role in it.

Regarding the right to choose, consumers should:

- Understand their personal motivations for buying certain products and services.
- Select carefully both merchandise and services, weighing many factors.
- Exercise personal judgment in decision making.

- Avoid buying by habit.
- Choose carefully from whom they buy.
- Practice comparison shopping.

Regarding the right to be heard, consumers should:

- Know where to go for help when seeking redress.
- Speak up when errors occur or when quality of products or services is inferior.
- Become informed about and speak up on larger issues that affect the public in general.
- Make suggestions for product improvements.
- Let merchants know about poor selling or merchandising practices (discourteous salespersons, for example), even though they may not have anything directly to do with product quality or price.
- Seek to right wrongs occurring in the marketplace.
- Report favorable incidents to retailers and manufacturers about quality of products, services, and general operation.
- Assist other consumers with their questions or grievances.

There could well be other responsible actions to be taken by consumers; the list is not complete. Having only a few truly responsible consumers carry the load for the many is wrong. We all need to carry our share of consumer responsibilities.

Some persons who are well off financially, for example, might feel that this "responsible consumer" behavior does not apply to them. It has been said that both J. Paul Getty and Howard Hughes, now deceased multimillionaires, "squeezed the lettuce for quality, weighed the 10-pound sack of potatoes for honesty, and counted their change for accuracy to make sure they were satisfied." They, too, were responsible consumers.

Seeking Redress

In a survey of 2500 households about people's experiences with 34 categories of goods and

If you aren't satisfied with the quality or operation of something you buy, you should try to get the store you bought it from to repair or replace it. (*Kenneth Karp*)

services, it was discovered that Americans found something wrong with 28.2 percent of their purchases. The study, conducted by the Center for the Study of Responsive Law, found that the top areas of dissatisfaction were (1) automobile repairs, (2) appliance repairs, (3) mail-order items, (4) household repairs, and (5) toys. Surprisingly, only 32.6 percent of the complaints were reported to the businesses involved and only *1 percent* were reported to a third party, such as a consumer complaint agency. Of those complaints reported to businesses, 36.5 percent resulted in eventual consumer satisfaction.

Food may be inedible, clothing may not fit, an automobile may not function properly, a refrigerator may fail, or a roof may leak. All of these are consumer problems that need some type of corrective action. Redress can be obtained directly, indirectly, by arbitration, or by legal means.

Direct Redress. Perhaps the most important point to keep in mind when seeking redress directly is to start at the bottom and go up. *Direct* redress can involve all persons or businesses who were directly involved in sell-ing, distributing, or manufacturing the prod-

uct. For example, if a refrigerator fails shortly after you buy it, go first to the merchant from whom you bought it. You owe the local merchant the opportunity to correct any problems—and in most cases the remedy will come from the business itself. Still, the merchant may choose to do nothing or "not enough" in the consumer's opinion. When this happens, the consumer needs to know what to do next. Responsible consumers follow the problem until it is resolved!

If consumers do not get satisfaction from the "higher ups" in the local business, there are other direct sources. For example, some wholesaler or regional supplier may have sold the product to the retailer. They can be contacted directly. If that level of complaint does not get a favorable response, go to the next highest level, which in all likelihood will be the manufacturer. More aptly stated, give them each a chance to solve the problem by practicing former President Harry Truman's (and now Jimmy Carter's) slogan, "the buck stops here." Continue to carry complaints to a higher source until you are satisfied. Route A in Figure 3-2 illustrates an appropriate direct route to follow. In addition, "indirect" routes include Route B (local and state groups or

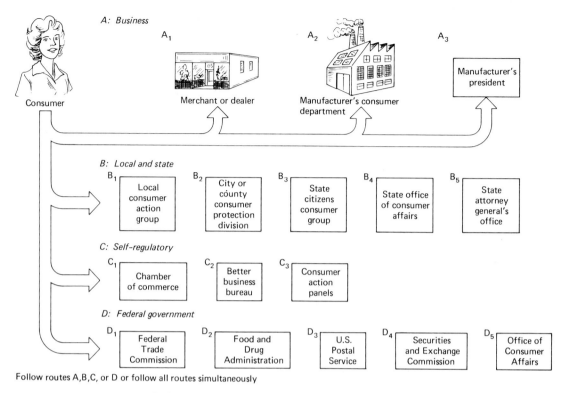

FIGURE 3-2 Recommended complaint procedure

agencies), Route C (self-regulatory groups), and Route D (federal government agencies). Follow all routes at the same time if necessary.

Most complaints are aimed at the manufacturing, merchandising, and service industries. However, governments at all levels perform services in a variety of ways, and they sometimes deserve complaints, too. Consumers pay for these services through taxes and other special assessments. Naturally, if the services are carelessly provided (poor road or highway construction or repair), or not provided (no snow removal), responsible consumers need to complain to the appropriate government agency. The complaint process is the same; only the circumstances are different.

Hopefully the complaining party will get redress at the lowest level possible, but if not, then each successive step is a higher and more responsible level. Reaching out to the highest

possible source to receive redress when all else has failed is the route responsible consumers *must* take.

An interesting and effective direct procedure used by several major manufacturing companies is the *hotline*. The hotline is a special telephone line (toll free) established to encourage consumers to call in about problems concerning products or services. The hotline concept is fine and does reflect genuine concern, but it's a shame that consumers have to call the higher echelons at all. The problems should be solved at the local level. Then, too, most consumer problems would not occur if manufacturers, distributors, and retailers carried out their responsibilities well. A criticism of some hotlines is that they are used to route the consumer right back to the local level—yet if the consumer had been satisfied there in the first place, there would be no reason to use the hotline.

In many large firms, public relations offices in charge of consumer affairs, or offices with some such title, exist as another helpful outlet to consumers. This type of office should reduce the amount of red tape when consumers write for help. A shortcoming is that these offices are sometimes more public relations than consumer-problem oriented.

The direct route to seek redress should be the most frequently used. From the consumer to the retailer to businesses in the middle to the manufacturer is a redress route to follow. A problem remaining for the consumer always will be how far up the chain to go before getting results. The names and addresses of corporate officers for 37,000 companies are listed under "Directors" and "Executives" in *Standard & Poor's Register of Corporations*. Most public libraries have a copy. And, one thing is sure—consumers who make themselves heard when dissatisfied are exercising their rights and fulfilling their responsibilities.

Indirect Redress. There are many indirect sources that the conscientious consumer can turn to. *Indirect sources* do not directly involve the manufacturer, distributor, or seller of the product. Some suggested routes to follow are Routes B, C, and D in Figure 3-2.

On the local level, in many communities the mayor's office has a consumer protection division to handle consumer complaints. In all states and in many communities there are volunteer consumer groups to aid the consumer. Also, the Better Business Bureau, Chamber of Commerce, or city or county attorney and state attorney general can help with complaints or other grievances. Most large city newspapers have established a service column to which people can write about unresolved consumer problems. "Action Please," for example, is a service that runs in the *Memphis Commercial Appeal* which has been very effective in helping consumers.

In some colleges and universities organizations have been formed to help student consumers in particular. Most of the efforts of volunteer student groups have been directed toward educating consumers as a "preventive measure," and they refer problems to other agencies for help. The student Public Interest Research Groups are different, however, in that their own experts investigate the larger consumer problems and seek corrective action.

Every state has some type of volunteer consumer organizations, such as the Illinois Federation of Consumers, the Mississippi Consumers Association, the California Consumers Association, and the Pennsylvania League for Consumer Protection. The state insurance office, department of agriculture, bar association, or medical association can also help when called upon. And, of course, representatives in the state legislature, to a limited degree (depending on their empathy for consumer problems), can provide help to consumers seeking redress.

On the national level, there are agencies such as the Federal Trade Commission, the Food and Drug Administration, the Consumer Product Safety Commission, and the Office of Consumer Affairs, to name a few. These federal agencies were established primarily to help consumers. Numerous other helpful agencies—local, state, federal, and private—are cited in the Appendix.

Results from these indirect sources are usually not as swift as those from the more direct routes. Nonetheless, these indirect sources are alternatives and sometimes offer an even stronger hand to help consumers seeking redress.

Arbitration. Consumer problems that are not solved by the usual direct and indirect sources can often be resolved through arbitration. *Arbitration* is a nonlegal "court of last resort" for consumers who are not satisfied. Binding arbitration is offered through more than 100 of the 143 better business bureaus across the country. In addition, AUTOCAPS handle and resolve complaints between consumers and business in the automobile industry, FICAP those in the furniture industry, and MACAP those in the appliance industry. Others are being formed. (See the Appendix for addresses.)

Most arbitration services are free, but a few charge a small fee of $5 to $10. The process involves a minimum of paperwork. Arbitration requires that both sides to a dispute submit the problem to an arbitrator or arbitration panel. After hearing each side of the dispute, judgment is usually issued on the spot or within 10 days. Consumers win just a little over half the time in arbitration cases. Watch out for precommitment clauses in sales contracts which require arbitration of grievances, because such a clause may also deprive the consumer of the right to sue. Still, the inexpensive process of arbitration usually resolves disputes to everyone's satisfaction. Consumers everywhere owe a debt of gratitude to those persons who serve as arbitrators, since they serve without pay.

Legal Redress. Naturally, all consumers have the right to take legal action against a merchant or manufacturer. However, most consumers *mistakenly* believe that the costs are too high. They think that they must hire a lawyer, pay high court costs, and get extra legal help from other lawyers, making the redress being sought seem quite expensive. And, of course, consumers just do not want to bother with legal means of seeking redress when the legal fees far exceed the amount being sought. But this need not be the case!

One inexpensive process of seeking legal redress of this type is through the *small claims court* (sometimes known as "courts not of record"). These courts were set up in all states to provide effective, economical legal help for cases involving contract breach and other money claims of relatively small amounts, usually under $1000. Some small claims courts are open evenings and weekends, too. Since it is uneconomical for a consumer to bring a regular civil suit for faulty electrical work done by a contractor which originally cost $200, the small claims court provides a realistic and inexpensive alternative.

To start a small claims proceeding, the consumer goes to the appropriate legal city or county office and fills out a short complaint form, similar to the one shown in Figure 3-3. One pays a small fee, around $5 to $10, plus the cost of sending the defendant a summons by registered mail, probably another $1.

Usually a hearing is set 30 days after the filing date. The judge hears both sides of the argument and normally gives the decision at the close of the session. If the defendant fails to appear for the hearing, a default judgment is usually made and the plaintiff/consumer wins. One delaying tactic used by defendants is to telephone the court at the last moment and request a continuance; the unknowing plaintiff/consumer thus shows up twice for the same case and perhaps must take time off from work to do it.

Attorneys are usually allowed in small claims courts, but often they are not used; a sympathetic judge typically helps consumers without an attorney. The purpose of the court is to help decide cases inexpensively and without the formality of the usual courtroom. In the better small claims courts, attorneys for both sides are prohibited.

The procedure is simple, but several points should be made clear. First, the judge may reject the complaint if he or she believes it to be unwarranted. Second, the plaintiff/consumer must show evidence of having tried to resolve the complaint with the defendant. Third, the judge's decision is final for the plaintiff; only the defendant may appeal. Fourth, even if a plaintiff/consumer wins a case, it may involve considerable time and effort with some expense, and there is no guarantee of ultimate redress. Sometimes a second legal action becomes necessary to force the losing defendant to pay the judgment.

Most consumers are not aware of the procedures or low dollar costs involved in small claims court filings. Consequently, consumers do not use them as often as they could. More than three-fourths of the small claims court cases heard are from nonconsumers (retailers,

S.C. _____ 197___

CITY COURT, CITY OF ANY CITY
CIVIL BRANCH, SMALL CLAIMS, ROOM ONE, CITY HALL BLDG., 1ST FLOOR,
Any City, Any State 00000

TO: _____

_____

_____

TAKE NOTICE THAT _____

asks judgment in this Court against you for _____

together with costs, upon the following claim _____

_____

_____

There will be a hearing before the Court upon this claim on _____

19 _____ at _____ o'clock _____ M.. in the Small Claims Part of this Court, held at ANY City Hall. YOU MUST APPEAR to present your defense or to present any claim that you may have against the other party at the hearing described above. IF YOU DO NOT APPEAR IN PERSON OR BY AN ATTORNEY, JUDGMENT WILL BE ENTERED AGAINST YOU, EVEN THOUGH YOU MAY HAVE A DEFENSE.

If your defense or counterclaim is supported by witnesses, account books, receipts or other documents, you must bring them to the hearing.

If you admit the claim but desire time to pay, you must appear personally on the day set for the hearing, state to the court that you require time to pay and show your reason for same.

DATED _____ 19___   _____

Judge/Clerk

NOTE: If you desire a jury trial, you must, before the day set for the hearing, file with the judge or clerk of the court a written demand for a trial by jury. You must also pay to the judge or clerk a jury fee of $6 and file an undertaking in the sum of $50 or deposit such sum in cash to secure the payment of costs that may be awarded against you. You will also be required to make an affidavit specifying the issues of fact which you desire to have tried by a jury stating that such trial is desired and demanded in good faith.

Under the law, the court may award $25 additional costs to the plaintiff if a jury trial is demanded by you and a decision is rendered against you.

FIGURE 3-3   Complaint form

medical services, repair services) seeking to collect from consumers. *They* are familiar with the system and the procedures, so they often use the small claims courts rather than the civil court system when they can. Consumers should become more knowledgeable about the procedures and use the small claims courts when necessary. Plaintiff/consumers typically win more than half the court decisions.

Another method of seeking redress is through class action suits, when these are legally permitted by state law and not inhibited by federal restraints. A *class action* suit is a suit filed on behalf of several or many consumers who have a similar grievance. Several homeowners in a housing development, for instance, could bring a class action suit for a construction infraction by a contractor. The suit would be filed in the name of all who suffered from the violation. Ineffective safety devices on lawn mowers could be handled by a class action suit against the manufacturer by all injured parties, but only if all potential parties to the suit are notified. All those who were injured similarly by the product would benefit from a ruling in favor of the plaintiff. Class action suits usually involve more serious, widespread physical or monetary infractions to many people. They represent an effective legal process for consumers to use when seeking redress.

POINTS OF VIEW AND PROBLEMS TO THINK ABOUT

The thrust of the consumer movement has broadened from single concerns such as safe food, honest labeling, or disclosure of credit rates to the larger problem of ethics. Whether we are in a time of rising incomes and prosperity or of inflation and economic decline, the question of ethics remains paramount. This intangible frame of reference raises at least three questions about any consumer-felt problem: Is what they are doing or not doing ethical? What ecological considerations should there be? And what social costs and consequences will result from action or inaction?

Optimistically, it appears that in the years ahead business will develop a stronger social conscience. It must become more socially responsible if it wants to regain the confidence of the American consumer. Lost confidence has been shown in Harris surveys in recent years. Now, less than 24 percent of Americans are willing to give business positive ratings for bringing better-quality products to the people. And the national Chamber of Commerce has repeatedly expressed concern about the hos-

tile attitude of young consumers—the valued customers of tomorrow—toward business.

A recent president of that association, Edward B. Rust, who is now president of State Farm Companies, said that businesses should stop trying to fight consumer advocate Ralph Nader and join him in improving the quality of goods and services. Such a comment obviously jolted most members of the Chamber of Commerce. Nader, said Rust, "has been described in some quarters as 'an enemy of the system,' but if we were willing to look objectively at his activities, I think we are forced to the conclusion that his commitment is to make the system work. The whole point of Nader—so obvious that it is often overlooked—is his single-minded dedication to making the free enterprise system work as it's supposed to . . . to make marketplace realities of the very virtues that businessmen ascribe to the system." Rust points out that Nader just wants products to live up to their advertising and the reasonable expectations of consumers, and wants people to take their complaints to the proper regulatory agencies rather than taking to the streets in protest. "That kind of activity," said Rust, "suggests a considerable degree of faith in the system and contrasts sharply with the revolutionary who would tear it down." The *Arizona Daily Star* reported that "it could not have been said any better."

A broader view was taken by Leo H. Schoenhofer, board chairman of Marcor (a large holding company): "Believe it or not, what's good for the consumer is not only good for business, it's best for business. Only when the consumer believes his rights are adequately protected will public confidence in, and the health and vigor of, business and the competitive free enterprise system be fully restored."

The response of business to the consumer movement in the years immediately ahead should be relatively positive and responsive; however, several negative approaches are also predictable. Lobbyists will continue to influence legislation in our states' and nation's capitols to weaken consumer efforts. Voluntary codes of ethics of trade associations will become stronger on paper (not too strong or they run the risk of antitrust action), but not nearly so strong in practice. Self-policing business groups like the Chamber of Commerce and the Better Business Bureau will seem to be more favorable to consumer interests, but will remain primarily concerned with public relations.

The realistic concern for ethics as a major goal of the consumer movement was aptly summarized by Virginia Knauer, a former Presidential Special Assistant for Consumer Affairs, when she defined consumerism in a speech in 1972:

> *Consumerism is nothing more and nothing less than a challenge to business to live up to its full potential—to give consumers what is promised, to be honest, to give people a product that will work, and that is reasonably safe, to respond effectively to legitimate complaints, to provide information concerning the relevant quality characteristics of a product, to take into consideration the ecological and environmental ramifications of a company decision, and to return to the basic principle upon which so much of our nation's business was structured— "satisfaction guaranteed, or your money back."*

Many more millions of active consumers will respond to consumer issues in the years to come, if for no other reason than reaction to the widespread public disenchantment about the quality of life. A Harris survey revealed that 44 percent of the public believes that the quality of life has worsened over the past decade. More than seven out of ten individuals were concerned with air and water pollution, the quality of education, conserving energy, privacy rights of individuals, and "making products and services safer." A 72 percent majority felt that "the trouble with most leaders is that they don't understand that people want better quality of almost everything they have rather than more quantity of most things."

Wider involvement in consumer affairs will be seen in a variety of ways. More cooperatives will be established. More tenant unions will be formed. Credit unions will serve more people. More buying groups will be established. Local action organizations will multiply. Volunteers for all types of services will be more available and willing. Government at all levels will hear from consumer-oriented representatives. And statewide and national consumer organizations will grow in strength.

Ruling of state supreme courts will become of greater importance in securing consumer rights, as they traditionally provide more protection than the U.S. Supreme Court. The impact of consumer education both in and out of schools will grow because of the heightened public awareness of and interest in consumer issues.

The result, as with any broad-based and popular grass-roots movement, will be a more sincerely concerned and ethical American consumer, a more responsive electorate, a more responsible marketplace, and a better American society.

CHAPTER ACTIVITIES

Checkup on Consumer Terms and Concepts

Individualistic
  lifestyle
"Do-gooders"
Consumer Advisory
  Board
Economic conditions
Scandals
Charismatic
  leadership
Government
  organizations
Private organizations
Consumer Bill of
  Rights
Buying boycott

Caveat venditor
Independent
  consumer protection
  agency
Class action lawsuit
No-fault insurance
National health
  insurance
Unconscionable
  contracts
Consumer
  responsibilities
Chain of complaining
Consumerism

Review of Essentials

1. What five consumer eras can be identified?
2. What were three major consumer issues before 1960?
3. Describe the causes of the consumerism of the 1960s.
4. List five important pieces of federal legislation that were enacted during the 1970s and their basic provisions.
5. What factors contribute to the success of consumer movements?
6. What is the response of business to consumerism today, and why?
7. Through legislation or any other means, list five ways in which the power of consumers could be increased.
8. Choose three critical issues of the consumer movement of today and describe why you think they are important.
9. Explain how the rights and responsibilities of consumers can work together to improve the American market system.
10. How do direct and indirect routes for seeking redress differ? Give examples of each.
11. What will the consumer movement be like in 1985? Briefly describe how you see it developing.

Issues for Analysis

1. React to Senator Gaylord Nelson's comment that "There is a lack of balance in the consumer's capacity to deal equally with the guy who's got an item to sell."
2. Assume that you are an officer in a very large, well-established, and responsible business. You have been asked to write a publicity release in response to a group of people who were picketing in front of your plant today with signs saying "Stop the pollution," "Products are unsafe," "This company discriminates," and the like. Write a one- or two-page company reaction for the newspapers.
3. In commenting on retail marketing practices in inner-city areas, Robert Pitofsky, a member of the Federal Trade Commission, stated that "there's tremendous exploitation and it's a cause of great frustration among people, the kind of civil fraud that they run into day in and day out where the judicial system seems to throw all its weight on the side of the seller and the collector of debts rather than the purchaser." React to his statement.

4

Using Services

THE PROBLEMS

More than 40 cents of every dollar of take-home pay of the typical American consumer is spent on services. With our high standard of living, we have come to rely increasingly upon these services, but with them have come problems. There are thousands of services, each with its own unique characteristics, and no consumer can gain adequate knowledge of them all. Yet, we still spend thousands of dollars on them each year and the marketplace makes it even more challenging by developing new ones all the time. To top it off, the prices for services keep rising rapidly.

Donald Furster of Dodge City learned a valuable lesson the hard way when he called for a plumber to fix a stopped-up washbasin. Intelligently, he telephoned three different plumbers and asked their hourly rate. He chose the one with the lowest rate per hour, which was $18. Two plumbers came, fixed the drain, smiled, and handed him the bill. The job took only about 20 minutes, but the bill was $43.10. "First of all," the man in charge explained, "*each* of us earns the hourly rate. Now the parts," he continued, "were only $1.10, but the use of our rotojack machine is always $6." Donald reluctantly paid the bill. Fortunately, he was not charged for the "transportation time" for the men to go from the repair shop to his home and back.

That price was cheap compared to the cost of a hospital bed in Detroit, as Brenda and John Robertson found out. They carefully planned their savings and reread their hospitalization insurance policy before becoming the proud parents of a 7-pound, 6-ounce baby daughter. But the charge for the hospital room was $215 per day! And the nursery fee for the baby was another $72 per day. Their hospitalization insurance paid only $65 for Brenda's room, $30 for the baby's room, and hardly anything for the medicines and drugs that were needed. The Robertsons were somewhat pleased that their insurance did pay the physician's fee of $375 for delivery. Their out-of-pocket expenses above what the insurance paid amounted to $972.80. Fortunately, there were no complications other than the large financial one. The policy language was more complicated than they had originally thought.

Doctors, health insurance, tax specialists, education, mass transit, utilities, employment agencies, funerals . . . all these services and thousands more are used by consumers. Since we spend so much time and money on them, perhaps we should become better acquainted with some of the "how's and why's" of using services.

BUYING SERVICES

Less money was spent on services 20 years ago than is spent today. This is primarily because of rising incomes and because new services are being created to help us satisfy whatever new wants society suggests. Nearly 42 percent of the dollars spent are for services. And increased spending on services is predicted for the future. Another reason why more money will go for services in the future is because consumers traditionally continue to buy services regardless of the state of the economy. During recessions consumers rarely cut back on services or *nondurables* (goods lasting less than 1 year); rather, they reduce their spending on *durable* goods.

The Cost of Services
The money spent on services can be examined in two ways. First, on what services are those dollars spent? And second, what is happening to the costs of services? As can be seen from Figure 4-1, nearly one-half of the spending on services goes for housing-related expenses, with medical costs additionally taking up almost one-fourth of each dollar. The costs of almost all services are rising and are expected to continue to rise, as shown in Figure 4-2.

What do these increases mean? Certainly incomes have risen in recent years, but why have there been such large increases in the costs of most services? And what has been the effect of inflation?

Inflation and the Purchasing Power of the Dollar
Inflation, of course, is a larger-than-normal increase in the price of goods and services over a period of time because of too much demand and/or rapidly increasing costs. Prices are

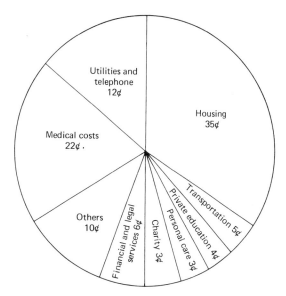

FIGURE 4-1 Of each dollar spent on services . . .

"inflated" since money does not buy as much as it used to. If a person's income goes up as much as the rate of inflation he or she stays even; otherwise purchasing power is lost.

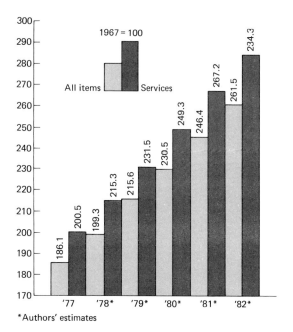

FIGURE 4-2 Consumer price index: cost of services compared with all items

Table 4-1 shows the purchasing power of $1000 decreased by inflation at different rates. If, for example, you put $1000 under your mattress on January 1 of this year, after five years at an inflation rate of 6 percent the value of the money would have dropped to $747. The $1000 could buy only $747 worth of goods and services because prices had increased over the 5 years.

The New Consumer Price Index

A *consumer price index* is a measure of the increases and decreases in our costs of living. It tracks the price changes of a large number of goods and services month after month. With an index, one can get an estimate of the overall changes in the cost of living as well as individual groups and even types of items.

Two consumer price indexes are presently published by the federal government's Bureau of Labor Statistics. The consumer price index (CPI) for urban wage earners and clerical workers is the older of the two. It includes the prices of 398 items typically bought by consumers in 56 cities. By weighting the various items according to their importance in the urban consumer's budget, this "market basket" index shows how costs are changing. Data are collected by about 250 price agents

from about 18,000 retail stores and service establishments and from about 40,000 tenants. The CPI is considered one of the federal government's most accurate and reliable sets of statistics. But, in reality, it is not!

By definition a consumer price index is going to have inaccuracies. This is because the market basket of goods and services must remain consistent over the years in order to compare prices from year to year. Thus, "spaghetti and tomato sauce" shopped for and priced in 1967 should be pretty much the same product in 1977, and so on. Since people's buying habits change over the years (they might buy instant spaghetti sauce, for example) the index becomes inaccurate. The CPI is also criticized for having a built-in inflationary bias. It does not take into account that a higher price might be the result of an increase in the quality of a product; the weighting for various subparts of the index (food versus transportation, for example) are not shifted quickly enough to reflect reality; it does not include income taxes or Social Security payments; and there is considerable doubt as to how relevant the goods and services included in the CPI are to consumers' actual expenditures. Two examples should suffice. To represent *all* small appliances the CPI uses "carpet sweepers"! A "routine urinalysis" represents the many hundreds of different lab tests commonly used today.

Despite these known weaknesses, the consumer price index is widely accepted. Nearly one-half of the American people are directly affected by changes in the CPI. That is because the payments to millions of recipients of Social Security, government employee pensions, food stamps, and other government benefits are tied to changes in the index, as are the earnings of the millions of wage earners whose increases are covered by escalator plans.

The new consumer price index (Urban Household Index) includes not only urban wage earners and clerical workers but also urban households of managers and professionals, retirees, and even the unemployed. Although rural families are not included in the

TABLE 4-1

The Value of the Purchasing Power of $1000 Decreased by Inflation

On Jan. 1	At 3% Annual Inflation	At 6% Annual Inflation	At 10% Annual Inflation
This year	$1000	$1000	$1000
1 year later	971	943	909
2 years later	943	890	826
3 years later	915	840	751
4 years later	888	792	683
5 years later	863	747	621
6 years later	837	705	564
7 years later	813	665	513
8 years later	789	627	467
9 years later	766	592	424
10 years later	744	558	386

broader index, it includes the purchasing patterns of about 80 percent of the population, about twice that of the older CPI. And a new and larger market basket of goods and services is surveyed.

Both indexes are being reported now, since some groups, labor in particular, believe that the broader index understates inflation. Nathaniel Goldfinger, AFL-CIO research director, stated that, "Urban wage earners and clerical workers—low and middle-income families and individuals—spend a certain portion of their income on food. High-salaried people—executives, supervisors, professionals, the upper-income groups generally—spend a much smaller portion of their income on food." After a test period of a few years, if the two indexes come out pretty close to each other, the older CPI will be scrapped. Then only the broad Urban Household Index figures will be used.

Figure 4-2 also shows the increasing costs in the old consumer price index when the base period was 1967. Therefore, 1967 prices represent 100. In 1978 the CPI was 199.3, which meant that it cost $199.30 to buy the same amount of goods and services that cost $100.00 in 1967. As can easily be seen, the cost of services has been climbing much faster than the cost of all items combined.

To determine how increases in the cost of living affect you, first calculate how much of an increase in income (if any) you had during the year. For example, if your income went up last year by 9 percent while the CPI rose 6.1 percent, you had a new increase in your level of living of 2.9 percent in terms of spending power. This is, however, only an approximation at best.

The consumer price indexes give some indication of the "cost of living." Even though the indexes are not perfect, they are useful in trying to show increases in the cost of living.

Standards and Levels of Living
Two concepts closely related to the cost of living are quite important to understand: standards and levels of living. Joseph S. Davis differentiated these terms many years ago. He noted that the *standard of living,* for an individual, a family, or a community, is a "plane or content of living which an individual or group *earnestly seeks and strives to attain,* to maintain if attained, to perserve if threatened, and to regain if lost." (Emphasis added.) The *level of living* is not something striven for but is "*reality experienced* by an individual or group. It is made up of a complex combination of consumption, working conditions, possessions, freedom and 'atmosphere,' and the balance or harmony among them, in relation to needs and felt wants." (Emphasis added.)

By comparing these terms and then thinking about what the consumer price indexes are showing, one can easily see what a misunderstood term "consumer price index" is. A CPI shows part of the reality of the level of living—assuming that it is accurate for you as an individual, which it is not. You are what you are. You have your own lifestyle, values, attitudes, and perceptions about the satisfactions of life. That is your level of living. What you aspire toward is your standard of living. When the television news reporter says the "standard of living" has gone up because of increases in the consumer price index, that is inaccurate. The cost of living figures reflected by a CPI affect both your level of living and your standard of living. But you experience your own level of living and establish your own standard of living.

Comparison Shopping for Services
It is more difficult to comparison shop for services than for consumer goods because services are intangible and qualitative. The price, the length of warranty, and the cost for parts may be quantitative, but that is about all. It is the *quality* of the service that counts. Fortunately, today's communications technology lets consumers comparison shop for services with some degree of confidence. "Let your fingers do the walking" is the slogan of the Yellow Pages of the telephone companies, and that is one of the more important steps in shopping for services. The steps in shopping for services are the same as those for products except for emphasis.

First, the consumer must learn about the service. To purchase from a position of ignorance will guarantee that you will stay there. You do not choose a college without comparing. Nor a physician. And, hopefully, not even an airline. Friends and neighbors can recommend services, but the responsible consumer must seek out actual information *before* beginning to shop. A variety of reading sources is usually available, ranging from specific consumer publications, to periodicals, to encyclopedias.

Second, when you are more informed, you can write down a list of characteristics, or "buying tips" to look for or "questions to ask" when you compare services.

Third, compare two or three places that offer the same service—particularly when it is expensive! It is here that you can easily shop by telephone. Being informed helps you, the consumer, to ask the right kind of questions when you talk to service representatives. An added benefit in comparison shopping is that you often learn a little more by talking to salespeople who are knowledgeable.

Fourth, make an informed decision based upon your values and needs, keeping in mind both rational and emotional motives. Your *best buy* may not be either the least or the most expensive. Your choice will be a personal one involving many factors and hopefully satisfying your wants.

PROFESSIONAL SERVICES

A dictionary definition of a professional is "a person belonging to one of the professions," and, in the adjective form, "of, engaged in, or worthy of the high standards of, a profession." The term can include anyone from athletes to ministers. For our purposes, let us just consider doctors, dentists, and lawyers. These are three of the professions for whom consumers have *high regard,* in whom they tend to place *considerable trust,* of whom they expect the *greatest competence,* and of whom they assume the *highest ethics.*

As with any occupational group, the professions have members with a wide range of ability, wisdom, and competence. We can paraphrase a comment from a Ralph Nader report entitled "One Life—One Physician": Doctors, dentists, and lawyers deal daily with matters of crisis. As a result, their errors in judgment "can certainly create a problem of greater magnitude and consequence than an error in judgment by a plumber." Let us consider these three groups of professionals in greater detail.

Doctors

A medical degree obtained in 1947 still permits a physician to practice today. He or she may be up to date in knowledge and skills or may not be. The doctor's conscience is the major factor in how well qualified he or she has remained. The quality of physicians can be measured in many ways, and it has been in numerous studies.

- A 2-year study of the quality of surgery in ninety-five hospitals in seven states found that nearly half of the postoperative complications and 35 percent of the deaths studied were preventable. The congressional study noted that 78 percent of the "preventable" complications or deaths resulting from medical operations involved the surgeon.
- A Harvard University study reviewed 285,000 operations performed in four metropolitan areas across the country by 2700 physicians and found that too many operations were being performed by doctors who were not specialists in surgery. General practitioners were performing operations for which they might not be qualified, including hysterectomies and removals of appendixes and gall bladders. The researchers found that "31 percent of the doctors who did operations were performing less than 10 a year."
- A study at Children's Hospital in Pittsburgh noted that tonsillectomies declined by 73.8 percent over a 4-year period

"once doctors began taking a closer look at whether each operation really was necessary."

- "Hysterectomies have passed tonsillectomies as the most commonly performed major 'operation' and thousands are done unnecessarily and sometimes for profit," Dr. John Morris, gynecology chief at Yale, and Dr. Kenneth Ryan, obstetrics and gynecology chief at Harvard, reported to a House commerce subcommittee.
- Of 10,000 nurses responding to a survey, 42 percent said "they had seen deaths among patients which they thought had been caused accidentally by doctors." (In fact, 38 percent of the nurses also reported that they would not like to be patients in their own hospitals.)
- In a pilot program with 110,000 New York City employees, which permitted getting a second opinion from another physician, "it was revealed that almost 30 percent of surgery recommendations made by their physician were found to be unwarranted by a second consulting expert."

Dr. Sidney Wolfe, Director of the Washington-based Health Research Group, told the government's Commission on Malpractice that at least 10,000 Americans die annually as a result of 2 million unnecessary operations. Dr. Willard Gaylin of the Institute of Society, Ethics, and the Life Sciences, Hastings-on-Hudson, New York, told a Senate subcommittee that "We should know the types of operations that are being done, by whom and for what purpose." A past president of the American College of Physicians and Surgeons said that "40 percent of the doctors then operating were not qualified to do so." Dr. John Knowles, former general director of Massachusetts General Hospital, summarizes this aspect of physician incompetence: "There are incredible amounts of unnecessary surgery going on, and that can't be tolerated." An "ounce of prevention is worth a pound of cure" and consumers need to be aware of these problems.

Malpractice. The most common basis for malpractice suits is negligence. The physician must consider all possibilities in reaching a diagnosis, get from the patient "informed consent" for surgery or other treatment, and follow up closely afterward. Suing for malpractice is becoming almost commonplace. The American Medical Association reports that one out of every six physicians is sued during his or her professional career. And more than three-fourths of these suits are settled out of court in favor of the consumer. As a result of the 20,000 claims each year and the large awards granted, insurance premiums are skyrocketing. Some specialist physicians are paying $20,000 or more in annual premiums for malpractice insurance. About 11 percent of the bill the consumer pays to the physician goes to pay for malpractice insurance.

One result has been *defensive medicine.* This involves many extra tests and procedures to make the physician more certain of the diagnosis. It is mainly meant to protect the physician from malpractice suits. An American Medical Association survey revealed that "About 75 percent of the physicians in America are currently practicing defensive medicine."

There are other serious problems with physicians. One of these is the shortage of doctors, which is in part being met by foreign-trained doctors. Federal mental health officials estimate that at least 8500 foreign medical graduates are entering the United States each year to practice. One out of every seven doctors practicing today received an M.D. degree abroad! The Health Professions Educational Assistance Act places some curbs on recruiting of alien interns and residents in hospitals, but the whole system would be disrupted if alien physicians were not allowed to practice. Some of these doctors are U.S. citizens trained abroad, but most are not. They often speak English poorly, yet they form most of the staff of many state mental hospitals, prison psychiatric wards, and institutions for the mentally retarded. Their cultural differences compound the problem.

State licensing laws are woefully inadequate. Virtually all doctors can go on practicing all their lives as long as they are not convicted of a crime; even then many still continue to practice. Harming patients, abusing the narcotics license, padding insurance claims, falsifying Medicaid charges (a General Accounting Office four-state study "found such overcharges, or markups, by more than a third" of the physicians they checked), and evading income taxes are all grounds for license revocation. But a doctor in those circumstances can easily move to another state and begin practicing again.

Peer Review. The present peer review system—doctors checking on other doctors—is simply not working. Incompetents are not truly barred from the profession. Doctors seem to be reluctant to turn in fellow members of the profession. The numerous local medical societies are notoriously slow to act on complaints from patients. And the societies have no legal right to reveal the names of members being investigated or disciplined. Expulsion from a medical society results in a stigma (if it becomes known), not revocation of a license. The American Medical Association reports that in a recent year 130 licenses were revoked by legal authorities.

Surprisingly, only 30 percent of the 15 million operations performed each year by general practitioners are done under the supervision of board-certified surgeons or members of the American College of Surgeons. The AMA reports that fewer than 10 percent of today's physicians list themselves as surgeons. The Department of Health, Education and Welfare Secretary's Commission on Medical Malpractice recommended that medical licensing boards require "reregistration" of the competency of all physicians and that states strengthen their laws to revoke licenses.

A strong move toward more effective peer review was made with the appointment of William I. Bauer as head of the nationwide Professional Standards Review Organization (PSRO). Congress authorized this accountability system of peers checking on the quality and appropriateness of health care. However, the PSROs will only check on services performed under federally funded programs. Aetna Life and Casualty, one of the nation's largest health insurers, recently began to offer its 125,000 Washington, D.C., subscribers the opportunity to get another doctor's opinion on suggested surgery without extra charge. Despite the refusal of the D.C. Medical Society to cooperate, Aetna sees it as an effort "to cut health costs by eliminating unneeded surgery."

Ethics and dollars conflict in the medical profession, too. Medical fee-splitting is common in many states; it is illegal in some. This "kickback" approach works when one doctor refers a patient to another doctor. States making this illegal require that doctors bill the patient separately. In some states the law applies also to clinical laboratories. A patient is most often referred to another doctor because of that doctor's expertise and medical judgment, and this is needed. However, referring a patient to the doctor who provides the highest kickback is unethical. Unfortunately, the Internal Revenue Service actually encourages the practice by making the kickback deductible in those states that permit it. A related ethics problem exists when the physician writes a prescription and suggests that the patient get it filled at a certain conveniently located pharmacy, often in the same building. It is only a recommendation, but is it ethical if the physician just happens to own the pharmacy, too?

Competence and ethics are only part of the picture of today's 365,000 practicing doctors. There is a shortage of primary or family physicians in the United States. Rural Americans must often travel 50 to 100 miles to see a doctor. Urban ghettos often have a doctor-population ratio of 1 to 10,000, in contrast to the national average of 1 to 1000 (or 1 to 400 about 50 years ago). The number of family doctors has shrunk to a low of about 80,000. Doubling the output of the medical schools will not solve the problem, since the great majority of graduates prefer to specialize. Aggravating the issue is the fact that doctors must often perform tasks that could easily be handled by paraprofessionals or specially trained nurses, thus releasing the doctors for more needed work.

One very bright spot in the medical field is the voluntary certification by The American Academy of Family Physicians. Passage of the 2-day examination certifies the physician as a specialist qualified "to care for at least 85 percent of one's medical needs." All members must complete 50 hours of approved study through scientific meetings, seminars, and university medical courses every year and take the certification examination again every 6 years. A list of certified physicians can be obtained by writing the organization (1740 West 92nd Street, Kansas City, Missouri 64114).

Dentists

In many ways the profession of the dentist is similar to that of the doctor, and some of the same problems exist: The license to practice lasts a lifetime, incompetence is nearly impossible to prove, and many more dentists are needed than today's 140,000.

Tooth decay is one of the most prevalent diseases in America today. It does not kill, but it hurts and damages. Only about 20 percent of Americans get regular dental treatment; the remaining millions suffer in varying degrees from the effects of poor dental care: inability to eat properly and resulting inadequate diet, headaches, difficulty in speaking, more rapid destruction of bone, and unnecessary stresses on the body's systems.

In the future we may get injections or pills to prevent tooth decay. Even though such predictions have been made every year for the last 20 years, it is beginning to appear that progress in decay prevention is finally being made. In decay treatment already, a chemical called GK-101 is available as a spray to remove decayed tooth material with little or no drilling and virtually no pain.

Today, however, there is another serious problem. The code of ethics of the American Dental Association prevents one dentist from criticizing the work of another! When have you personally heard your current dentist openly criticize the work of your previous dentist?

As reported in the book *Dentistry and Its Victims,* one Virginia woman complained to the Northern Virginia Dental Society that three of her good teeth were pulled instead of the three bad ones. No dentist would testify on her behalf until one professional from a dentistry school consented. But it was too late; the accused dentist had "lost " the x-rays.

The American Dental Association has virtually no machinery to effectively discipline its members (85 percent of all dentists are members), and a wronged consumer's only recourse is a lawsuit. Some dentists, such as those in California, are now subject to limited peer review under a recently established system. Most of the cases heard so far have been arguments between dentists and insurance companies about overcharges or incompetence. With more people buying group dental insurance through employers or unions, the insurance companies have a vested interest in helping to keep costs down and weed out the incompetents. The severity of the problem of incompetence can be noted in one statement of the anonymous author of the aforementioned book: "Of patients coming for initial examinations, the great majority had dental restorations that were below state board licensing standards. A high proportion of this poor work fell so far short of minimum standards as to be disgraceful."

Using Your Doctor or Dentist Effectively. This requires that you know something about your body and consumer health care.

First, take care of yourself. Brush your teeth regularly and effectively. Eat properly, exercise, and avoid or be moderate in using health-damaging products (such as sweets, cigarettes, alcohol, and nonprescription drugs).

Second, ask friends, neighbors, and coworkers to recommend professionals with whom they have had successful experiences. Ask the staff of a local hospital for their suggestions, too. And get recommendations about specialists from general practitioners.

Third, practice preventive medicine. Visit your dentist twice a year and your doctor once every year for checkups (unless you have a particular health problem that needs more attention).

Fourth, talk about costs with your doctor or dentist. If he or she refuses to discuss costs because "it is unprofessional," go elsewhere! At the same time, be prepared to pay a little more for the best. Saving a few dollars on these services may cost you more than just money in the future.

Fifth, ask questions during any visit, whether it is your first or your twentieth. Since you are paying for the time, use it by learning why your doctor or dentist is prescribing something or recommending one procedure instead of another. Your doctor or dentist's time is valuable, but don't be hurried. Be sure you understand the alternatives, benefits, and possible complications. And consider getting an independent consultation or opinion on health matters of particular importance.

Sixth, know what to avoid. There are some dentists who are "x-ray crazy" (since they can make good money taking those pictures), others who would rather fill and refill a decaying tooth over the years instead of doing a thorough job the first time, and still others who want to put braces on teeth because they are slightly crooked (besides fattening the dentist's pocketbook, unnecessary braces tend to weaken the bone and cause additional tooth and gum problems). Unfortunately, tips for spotting weak physicians are not so easily listed, although the "sure cures," "special devices," and other quack-type operations can certainly be avoided by being careful. But three general tips might help: Does your doctor maintain a complete and current medical history on you? Is your doctor in group practice and/or does he or she freely consult with other doctors? And, are you getting better? *If not,* see another doctor.

Lawyers

A study in Missouri about attitudes toward lawyers was reported in Murray Bloom's *The Trouble with Lawyers.* Some of the findings indicated that, in terms of "general reputation," lawyers ranked below bankers, doctors, dentists, and teachers. Almost two-thirds of the people thought lawyers were less than honest and less than truly dedicated to their profession; about 40 percent felt that lawyer's fees were too high; more than two-thirds felt that fees should be based on effort rather than on a "fee-schedule"; more than one-half felt that lawyers created lawsuits unnecessarily; and more than 10 percent of those who used lawyers were solicited for their cases. U.S. Supreme Court Chief Justice Warren Burger made many lawyers angry by saying publicly that 50 percent are not competent to practice in a courtroom. The Internal Revenue Service further reports that 1 in every 10,000 lawyers can be expected to be convicted of a tax violation; the rate for the public as a whole is 1 in every 75,000. Thus, the image of lawyers is not as good as it could be.

The fees charged vary from lawyer to lawyer, city to city, and assignment to assignment. A lawyer may charge $25 to $100 per hour for office work; from $150 to $300 per half day for representing you in court; from $50 to $125 for examining a real-estate title abstract; from $300 to $800 for a title search for a home purchase; from $200 to $600 for administering a small estate; from $50 to $100 for drawing up a simple will; and from $500 to $2500 for *each* spouse for an uncomplicated divorce.

Writing in the *Virginia Law Review,* Fred Rodell said that "while law is supposed to be a device to serve society, a civilized way of helping the wheels go round without too much friction, it is pretty hard to find a group less concerned with serving society and more concerned with serving themselves than the lawyers." Documentation of these charges unfortunately is abundant.

Some of the distinctively negative aspects of the legal profession are obvious. One is "restriction of trade," since only lawyers can act as lawyers. This was changed by the state of Arizona, which amended its constitution to permit real estate brokers to complete their own paperwork without the help of a lawyer. Other states are considering similar changes. Price fixing is a historical practice in every part of the United States where the local bar associations have published "suggested minimum fee schedules." The constitutionality of such price fixing is questionable, as the U.S. Supreme Court has ruled against it.

Similar "fee schedules" and "code of ethics prohibitions against advertising" will probably be ruled unconstitutional for all types of professionals, including doctors, dentists, eye specialists, accountants, engineers, architects, Realtors, pharmacists, and veterinarians. In the Supreme Court ruling on lawyer advertising, only "truthful advertisements concerning the availability and terms of routine legal services" are to be allowed. This ruling permits some advertising, but limits the amount of information attorneys can include. Ads are likely to be limited to fee schedules or other objective data like age, public offices held, and bank references. Another case, expected to be ruled upon by the U.S. Supreme Court, is aimed at promoting the dissemination of more valuable information on the qualifications and abilities of lawyers.

Now it is possible to comparison shop for a less expensive lawyer. However, the similarity of prices in some communities makes one wonder if price fixing is still going on. And there is occasional collusion between lawyers and judges. Conflicts of interest happen every day, too. In Canon 28, the lawyers' code of ethics specifically prohibits them from entering a speculative field from which they might profit, yet abuses occur. The big problem seems to be a lack of concern on the part of either the legal profession or the government about controlling such abuses more adequately.

The Reform Movement. Changes in the legal profession are under way as more people are taking an interest in the operations of the system. Paralegal assistants in some states are allowed to handle many of the routine functions

of lawyers. Small claims courts (often criticized as representing everyone but consumers with small claims) are beginning to change and realize their original purpose and thus prohibit lawyers from initiating claims. The emphasis now is on low-cost legal clinics, arbitration, mediation, conciliation, ombudsmen, and neighborhood tribunals or administrative panels. These are efforts to "delawyer" some disputes. Neighborhood arbitration offices are especially being recommended to handle the numerous "little" injustices in which a question of fact and not of law is to be decided. Another proposal is that tax credits, deductions, or subsidies be given to lawyers or firms that take on public-interest disputes.

Things are changing, and representation is becoming more available to consumers. However, until consumer rights are truly represented in the legal arena, putting pressure on large legal firms to expand their public-interest activities can help. So can organized efforts to improve the government's regulatory agencies. There are also hundreds of local, federally financed Legal Aid Society offices and neighborhood legal service agencies all across the country. Prepaid group legal services are becoming more available now for individual employees of large businesses. Unions are promoting such legal insurance programs as a fringe benefit and therefore more consumers have access to low-cost legal assistance.

INSTITUTIONAL SERVICES

Many institutional services are government services, and several of our recurring questions and problems concern them. The *U.S. Postal Service* keeps raising its rates for stamps, but the Zip code still does not seem to move the mail faster. A test mailing of nearly 800 letters by Associated Press bureaus in six cities showed that 80 percent of the letters without Zip codes got to their destination at least as fast as those that were Zip-coded.

Running the *judicial system* is becoming an increasingly difficult task. One observer commented that there are "interminable delays in civil cases, unconscionable delays in criminal cases, inconsistent and unfair bail impositions . . . overcrowded penal institutions, unremitting pressure on judges and prosecutors to process cases by plea bargaining and . . . the clogging of court calendars with inappropriate or relatively unimportant matters." The *public assistance and welfare services* are virtually bankrupting both our states and major cities to the point where the federal government has had to step in with financial help. The country seems to be losing the battle against poverty in spite of increasing costs (there were more than 25 million aid and welfare recipients last year). And complaints continue to multiply about *city services:* garbage collection, snow removal, street repair, and fire and police protection.

Other important and expensive institutional services also need consumer consideration. The areas of health care, insurance, education, and energy certainly need careful scrutiny.

Costs of Health Care in America

Without question, the United States leads all countries in medical research, technology, and sophisticated medical hardware. In fact, about 10 percent of the federal budget goes for health care. In 1978, the average person spent $780 for health services, or $3120 for a family of four. This is expected to double by 1983. Hospital costs alone have been rising at three times the rate of inflation in the rest of the economy.

So from a financial point of view, health care appears to be both expensive and excellent. However, in spite of the many dollars, our health care delivery system is failing miserably. Rosemary Stevens's statement in *American Medicine and the Public Interest* pinpoints some aspects of the dilemma. "The result is a crisis—overtrained physicians who cannot provide basic care to those who need it most, too many hospitals in some areas, not enough in others, an oversupply of some specialists (most notoriously surgeons) and an undersupply of others, a growing shortage of family physicians." Medical authorities agree

that at least 40 million Americans have no ready access to medical care; many of these are low-income people, but many are also middle-income rural Americans.

Two further indications of the severity of the health care problem are the international comparisons of infant mortality and adult longevity—the United States ranks only fifteenth and twelfth, respectively!

A woman from St. Louis complained recently that "when you come to the hospital you have to bring 2 years' back rent receipts, gas, electric, and wage slips before they even look at your child." In other testimony before a congressional subcommittee, the Citizen's Board of Inquiry into Health Services for Americans reported, "When we visited a county hospital near Portland, Oregon, there was a 6-month wait for appointments at the psychiatric clinic, a 4-month wait at the eye clinic, and a 3-month wait at the hematology and neurology clinics." Consumers using the present health care system are constantly faced with "unavailability of care, delays, neglect, and exorbitant costs."

There are many areas of criticism and controversy concerning the cost and quality of medical care. Some examples can be cited:

- "Unnecessary hospitalizations, construction and maintenance of unneeded beds in hospitals, unnecessary surgery and unnecessary drugs are among the items that add up to $21.5 billion of waste," reports Dr. Sidney Wolfe of the Public Citizens Health Research Group.
- Less than one-half of all children under the age of four are immunized against common childhood diseases.
- At a hospital in Pennsylvania a malfunctioning ventilating system was flooding the operating room with air from an open garbage area, which resulted in postoperative wound infections at five times the normal rate before the problem was discovered and fixed.
- The U.S. government estimates that one

out of every twelve patients who enters a hospital incurs an injury that he or she did not have before coming there in the first place; such accidents seem common.

- Dr. Martin Goldfield of New Jersey's Department of Health reports that 18 percent of the clinical laboratories surveyed performed a simple test for hemoglobin levels in the blood *inadequately*. (The 1967 federal Clinical Laboratories Improvement Act applies only to labs in interstate commerce, or about 6 percent of all labs.)
- In Los Angeles, all 80 resident doctors joined in a lawsuit against Los Angeles County—USC Medical Center charging that patients were being treated in "unsafe, inadequate and unlawful facilities" and that the treatment is "a public nuisance and a serious threat to public health."

Getting to the hospital in an ambulance is particularly important for those injured in highway accidents, yet in many communities funeral directors send hearses because ambulances are not available when needed. The National Academy of Sciences estimates that 80 percent of our ambulances are inadequate in both space and equipment. The Department of Transportation estimates that more than half of them do not have the equipment specified by the standards of the American Council of Surgeons.

The fifth largest state in population, Illinois, has fewer than 2000 private ambulances, according to a study by the Illinois state police superintendent. He found that almost half— 43.9 percent—could not respond to an emergency call in less than 5 minutes, and that nearly 12 percent needed 10 minutes or more. In addition, even though nearly 80 percent of the ambulance personnel had had standard first-aid instruction, more than one-third had not kept their training current. Furthermore, over 60 percent of the ambulances did not even have a resuscitator. And less densely populated states often have more serious problems. A report by the House Interstate and Foreign Commerce Committee notes that 69,000 people die unnecessarily each year because of inadequate care before they can reach a hospital.

The failures of our health care system are caused in part by the lack of an effective use of medical personnel and physical facilities. The field is largely unaffected by competition or the need for cost-cutting innovations. Also, there is a growing subsidization of the health care bill by employer-paid insurance plans and government programs. Since consumers pay only indirectly, they typically are not overly concerned about costs. Coupled with these is an ever-increasing demand for more medical services by a public that wants and needs them.

Government incentives and cost-review committees have made limited progress in reducing medical care costs. Joseph A. Califano, Jr., Health, Education and Welfare secretary, heavily criticized the nation's two largest health groups—the American Medical Association and the American Hospital Association—for resisting attempts by the government to curb rising hospital costs. He stated that, "They have opposed virtually every progressive step in the health care area, every step for the government to become the catalyst and further expand service to the poor and needy."

But cutting hospital costs, for example, is hard because about two-thirds of all funds go for labor costs related to patient care. Two plans seem to offer some hope. (1) If every patient in the United States this year were to go home one day earlier than normal, the savings would be $2.4 billion. Besides making more bed space available, reducing paperwork, and freeing time for other patients, the dollars-and-cents benefit to both the individual and the economy would be tremendous. (2) Many hospital procedures, including various types of surgery, can be handled successfully on an *outpatient* basis, with the patient admitted, treated, and released within a matter of hours. The outpatient cost is about 75 percent less than the inpatient.

Social Security Provides Health Coverage

To most people, Social Security only means retirement benefits. But just as important, Social Security benefits also reach consumers through Medicare, Medicaid, and disability insurance.

Medicare hospital coverage is available to all citizens 65 years of age or older (called Part A) and paid for through various taxes. However, the medical insurance benefits program (called Part B) is optional for today's 25 million senior citizens. Since the Medicare program was started, costs for both the hospitalization coverage and the doctor's fees have risen dramatically. The costs are paid through a part of the Social Security tax, general revenues of the federal and state governments, and monthly premiums charged the elderly (the last is only for Part B). Therefore, the Medicare program is being heavily subsidized by the younger and working tax-paying people.

In contrast to the nearly free medical care for the elderly in most Western European countries, Medicare pays only about 38 percent of the total medical costs for older Americans. Medicare patients have to pay a deductible amount (in excess of $100) before they receive services. A *deductible* clause means that the person pays that much of the cost before the insurance program begins to pay anything.

The Medicare program has loopholes in coverage, too, and many elderly persons buy private insurance to cover what Medicare does not. Examples of items not covered under Medicare are glasses (5 million elderly wear them), dentures (3.5 million have dentures needing replacement or refitting, according to the House Aging Committee's health subcommittee), hearing aids and examinations (another 1.5 million), immunizations, orthopedic shoes, and routine physical checkups. These are not covered in spite of the fact that they are essential to health and well-being. Furthermore, the average older person spends twice as much on health care annually as a younger person.

The *Medicaid* program, which has various names in different states, helps to pay medical expenses of poor people. The federal government provides more than half the total cost, and the individual states pay the rest. It reaches more than 20 million Americans. Hospital and doctor costs are paid according to a schedule of fees. The doctor, for example, either accepts the scheduled fee as "payment in full" or bills the patient for any extra amount. Thus, most Medicaid recipients go to physicians who accept Medicaid as payment in full. The Medicaid program has loopholes or exceptions in coverage similar to those in the Medicare program.

Scandals in Medicare and Medicaid abound. A Senate Finance Committee study revealed that Medicare patients were charged more than others for the same services. There is considerable evidence that some physicians have conducted "gang visits" to hospitals and nursing homes, visiting as many as fifty patients in 2 hours' time and billing Medicare for perhaps $800. According to Senate investigators for the Senate Special Committee on Aging, "as much as one fourth to one half of the dollars going for Medicaid are being drained off by fraud or by poor or unnecessary medical services." U.S. attorney Samuel K. Skinner, who convicted some physicians in kickback schemes, reported that we "have witnessed the greatest ripoff in history as literally millions of dollars in hard-earned and sorely needed tax dollars have been mismanaged, squandered, wasted and stolen from federally funded health programs."

The Senate hearing emphasized that "only 4 percent of the nation's doctors are involved in fraud." But that is a lot of doctors! For example, two chiropractors admitted cheating the government out of $600,000 in their chain of New York City Medicaid clinics. Each was sentenced to 5 years in jail, the stiffest terms to date. One commented that "everyone will be careful for a month or two." Dr. Joseph Ingber further explained that the system encourages them to cheat. It pays for the Medicaid patients less than half of what doctors could get from private patients, "and payments from the government were so slow that they had to sell their bills to agencies at 88 cents on the dollar to get quick cash.''

Doctors and hospitals complain that waits of up to 2 years of payment are not unknown under Medicaid and Medicare. They also complain of burdensome paperwork and red tape. Some doctors insist that they are not allowed to charge their ''usual and customary fees,'' and that they must treat such patients at a financial loss. Finally, all groups complain about the communications problem between the departments of public aid and the state and federal officials. The question remains, when will something be done about these programs?

Disability coverage is a form of health-income protection provided through Social Security. For the working person who becomes totally disabled, this provision is invaluable. An average 30-year-old worker with a spouse and two children could be entitled to perhaps $615 a month, or $7380 a year tax-free if disabled. A young worker disabled before age twenty-four needs credit for only 1½ years of work in the 3 years before the disability starts. In such cases, 6 months must elapse before the benefits start. According to Social Security Administration figures, more than 8 million people are receiving disability or survivors benefits, including 3.8 million children.

Today's Health Insurance

Besides Medicare for the elderly, Medicaid for the needy, and Social Security's disability insurance program, Americans have Workers' Compensation, private health insurance, and a variety of group insurance plans available.

Workers' Compensation and Employer's Liability. These benefits cover about 70 million workers—more than four out of five employees. The major thrust of Workers' Compensation and Employer's Liability is accidental health insurance and disability benefits. Each state has its own regulations concerning what occupations are covered, what benefits are paid, and what the eligibility requirements are. But two points are the same throughout the country: The employer must pay the cost of the premiums, and the accident must have occurred while the employee was working (fault does not need to be proved). Medical expenses up to a certain maximum are paid, and a loss-of-income supplement is provided. However, the supplement is usually around 75 percent of the employee's wages with a maximum weekly payment ranging from $60 in Oklahoma to $358 in Alaska.

Most of the 2.3 million workers who are injured on the job annually do, therefore, have some type of health insurance protection. Although quite limited, the Workers' Compensation and Employer's Liability benefits are becoming more liberal each year. However, other kinds of insurance are generally needed to cover the injuries, accidents, diseases, and illnesses that affect Americans throughout their daily lives. With the rising costs of medical and surgical care, most consumers decide to protect themselves by purchasing some type of private health insurance.

Private Health Insurance. More than 1000 private health insurance companies cover about three-fourths of all Americans to some degree for hospital and surgical benefits.

The major insurance protections are as follows:

1. *Hospitalization* pays for hospital expenses. This usually covers the cost of a semiprivate room, meals, laboratory fees, x-rays, anesthesia, operating-room expenses, certain supplies and medicines, and nursery-room charges for newborn infants. Most companies have a schedule of maximum amounts that will be paid for these expenses. Private insurance companies customarily offer an *indemnification* type of policy. This means that the company reimburses the policyholder for expenses up to the limits of the coverage. Frequently, the policyholder ''signs over'' the benefits, to a hospital for example, and never sees the cash. Some outpatient services are also covered.

2. *Surgical and doctor* pays for doctor's charges. This usually covers the cost of surgery performed at the hospital, in-hospital visits, and minor surgery performed in the doctor's office. There is usually a schedule of amounts that will be paid for these expenses.

3. *Major medical* pays for serious illnesses and accidents not covered by the first two categories above. A prolonged illness can be protected against with major medical coverage; however, $30,000 or $50,000 may be the top amount paid. This coverage involves some degree of *coinsurance* so that the policyholder and the insurance company share the risk. For example, the policyholder may pay 15 percent of all the major bills while the insurance company pays the remaining 85 percent.

It is important to note that each of these three types of coverage commonly has a *deductible* clause. For hospitalization, the insured may have to pay the first $100; for surgical coverage, the first $50; and for major medical, the first $250. After that, the company often pays according to a schedule. If the amount charged is more than the schedule, the consumer must pay the difference.

In buying health insurance, it is essential that you read the actual policy carefully for limitations, exclusions, amounts of deductibles, and future insurability. The wise consumer will definitely want a *guaranteed renewable* policy or one that is *noncancelable*. A person who contracts some chronic or recurrent condition would certainly want to continue to have the protection. Guaranteed renewable provisions permit this, but allow the premiums to rise; noncancelable offers the same protection but also prohibits the company from raising the premium for any individual policyholder.

Other types of commonly available health insurance include:

4. *Accidental death and dismemberment* pays a flat amount for death by accident (less than 1 percent of all deaths) or a specific type of dismemberment, such as loss of one or both hands or one or both feet. Since such accidents are rare, the premium costs are low.

5. *Disability* is similar to Workers' Compensation and Employer's Liability in that it provides an income while one is hospitalized by illness or injury. Such disability income begins *only* a certain number of days or months after the incident. Sometimes benefits do not begin until after Social Security benefits are exhausted. Also, different companies' definitions of "disability" vary considerably and should be clearly understood. Such insurance is available from commercial insurers, but at this point in time it is quite costly, and it discriminates in rates against people who are not gainfully employed. As more people buy such coverage, the inequities will probably be reduced, since the companies will have better loss data upon which to base their rates.

6. *Dental insurance* pays for a limited amount of dental care above certain deductible amounts. Usually the benefits are paid according to scheduled amounts. More than 50 million Americans are covered. This insurance is aimed not so much at catastrophes but at preventing the need for extensive dental work later on.

Blue Cross and Blue Shield. People commonly think of Blue Cross and Blue Shield as insurance companies, but they are not. They just look like insurance companies. They are really nonprofit associations that pay for the hospital and physician expenses of their members. Each of the more than eighty Blue Cross voluntary nonprofit hospitalization plans offers different amounts of protection. They provide coverage for more than 40 percent of the people who have medical insurance. The Blue Shield part of the program only pays for physicians' fees, while Blue Cross pays for hospital costs. Payment is most often for services rendered according to "usual and customary fees'' rather than according to a schedule. Thus, Blue Cross and Blue Shield coverage pays most if not all the typical hospital and physicians' costs, in contrast to many private insurance companies, which use schedules of fees that are quite often lower. A private insurance company may pay ''$80 per day for 120 days,'' while Blue Cross might pay the ''average cost of a semiprivate room'' for the same 120 days—which would be much better coverage, since hospital costs are already over $150 per day and rising. Remember, however, that many private companies also have policies that provide coverage equal to or better than Blue Cross/Blue Shield plans.

Group Insurance. Health insurance sold to large groups of people costs much less than individual policies do. The most obvious reason is that the salesperson's commission is proportionately lower when many people (perhaps working for the same company) are insured. In addition, when groups are large enough, there are enough healthy people covered to share the risks for all concerned. As a rule, consumers should take advantage of any group health insurance available to them. Also, many employers, as a fringe benefit, pay part or all of the premium cost.

Mail-Order Insurance. Insurance policies offered through the mail can be quite misleading. In fact, one consumer spokesperson said that if he wanted to go into ''legalized fraud'' he would start a mail-order insurance company. Deceptions most often include puffery in the advertisements, which is taken away in the small print. One company advertised ''Maximum Policy Benefits for Hospital Care $5,000.'' Upon careful reading, it was discovered that the total amount payable for hospital care in *any one year* shall not exceed $500 per person. Also, many such policies include a provision that, for the first 2 years, *any* claim filed can be denied on the grounds that the insured has a physical condition that existed before the policy began. Some mail-order policies define the term ''hospital'' so

specifically that more than 80 percent of the hospitals in the United States do not qualify.

The low rates offered sometimes go up in later years, but that is not mentioned in the advertising either. More often than not the low rates reflect the small amount of coverage actually provided. The Federal Trade Commission reports that ''Low rates do not guarantee the honesty of the company, and often mean that the company rejects most claims.''

Some mail-order companies might offer limited protection for your needs; however, you should read the policy very carefully. It is extremely important to check with your state insurance commissioner to see if the company is licensed to do business in your state. If it isn't, the commissioner has no control over the company and has absolutely no authority to help you should a difficult situation arise.

Failures of Our Health Delivery System. The private health insurance industry and the government programs in America are riddled with failures and scandals. A partial descriptive listing follows.

- One study reported that out of every $25 collected by doctors, $1 was an overcharge. The National Association of Blue Shield Plans refused to pay 4 percent of the doctors' charges because they were too high. The lower payments were called ''reductions,'' and the savings amounted to $500 million.
- ''Overutilizers''—doctors who pile up unnecessary charges with a battery of diagnostic tests—were refused payment by Blue Shield to the amount of 2.5 percent of the total fees.
- Private insurance policies pay out in benefits only about one-half of what they collect in premiums. Some companies pay out as little as 7 cents on each dollar paid in! In contrast, Blue Cross and Blue Shield plans pay back 90 to 97 cents on the premium dollar.
- Television personalities repeatedly urge you to ''protect your family with this $600 a

month extra cash plan.'' Former Pennsylvania insurance commissioner Herbert S. Denenberg classifies most of these advertisements for mail order indemnity insurance as ''lousy'' and ''nothing short of fraud.''

- Life insurance companies sell two-thirds of all health insurance and write 86 percent of the $22 billion in private policies. Such a stranglehold on the private insurance business is permitted because life insurance companies are exempt from antitrust regulations under the McCarran-Ferguson Act of 1945.
- Rates for similar rooms in comparable hospitals in the same general area can vary by as much as $50 a day.
- Thirty million Americans have no health insurance protection at all.
- In most states, there is little real control over Blue Cross premiums, as they rise automatically to cover costs.
- Testimony before a Senate antitrust committee included the statement that about 30 percent of the people admitted to hospitals need not have been. It was further observed that ''well-trained family physicians can comfortably and effectively care for 85 percent of the usual ordinary illnesses that beset mankind.''
- The health records of some 13 million individuals are kept in a ''secret'' data bank in Boston maintained by the Medical Information Bureau. The computer can flag people who have been ill previously, as well as those currently in poor health, who apply for medical insurance—and 90,000 inquiries come in daily from the 760 insurance companies that have access to the files.

A Call for Reform

Americans are understandably concerned about these health-related problems, and they are making their concern known. The health care system in the United States has its problems, and for the wage earner these problems often translate into dollars. The working person today is confronted with:

1. Increasing Social Security taxes to pay for Medicare.
2. Increasing premiums for private health insurance.
3. Increasing state and local taxes to pay for Medicaid.
4. An increasing share of federal tax dollars going to finance Medicaid and Medicare.
5. Increasing out-of-pocket costs to cover the deductible and coinsurance portions of higher medical charges.
6. Finding medical facilities where appropriate care is offered at reasonable prices.
7. Knowing enough about a doctor's suggested treatment to decide whether to seek a second opinion and/or to follow the treatment at all.

National Health Insurance

The health-care crisis facing this country concerns quantity, quality, and cost. There is a shortage of at least 50,000 family physicians. Urban hospital services have been deteriorating, and fewer urban hospitals are being built. Also, there is a serious shortage of nurses and other hospital workers, and the cost of medical care has been skyrocketing. And, of course, the cost of medical insurance has necessarily gone up. As a result, the idea of national health insurance is becoming a reality. Even the American Medical Association (which fought Medicare with millions of dollars in lobbying and advertising) now favors some kind of national health insurance. The question to be answered next is, how comprehensive a program do we want and can we afford to pay for it?

The Proposals Are Numerous. President Jimmy Carter strongly supports a comprehensive national health insurance program. He stated that, ''The coverage must be universal and mandatory. We must lower the present barriers, in insurance coverage and otherwise, to preventive and primary care—and thus reduce the need for hospitalization.'' A major problem, however, is cost. More than 200 proposals for national health insurance have been introduced in Congress through the years. The most far-reaching has been the Health Security Program sponsored by Senator Edward M. Kennedy and Representative James C. Corman, commonly known as the Kennedy-Corman bill. The insurance would cover *all* hospital care, physicians' services (including physical checkups, immunizations, well-child care, and family planning services), dental care, home health care, psychiatric care, laboratory tests, prescription drugs, medical care in skilled nursing homes, and more. The insurance carrier would be the federal government, not the present-day private commercial insurance companies. All wage earners would pay a 1 percent payroll tax, and employers would contribute 3.5 percent. The remaining funding would come from general federal revenues. Critics of the Kennedy-Corman proposal say that it is too costly, it would totally eliminate the private health industry, and it smacks of "socialized medicine."

The least expensive proposal is the Long-Ribicoff bill, sponsored by Senators Russell Long and Abraham Ribicoff, which would primarily protect Americans against catastrophic health-care costs. Amounts for serious illnesses and accidents above a certain figure, such as $20,000, would be paid for by the federal government, which would contract with private companies to provide the insurance.

Compromise. In a democratic society compromise is often possible. This is especially true in health matters, since most Americans now believe that health care is an inherent right of each individual.

The three basic philosophical approaches to national health insurance include a social-insurance approach, a private-insurance approach, and a combination. President Carter's health-care program is a combination. The President has stated that, "We must phase in the program as rapidly as revenues permit. We must have government reorganization that will end bureaucratic fragmentation that now frustrates any hope for a rational and effective national health policy. This is crucial—it must be done."

Carter's national health insurance will be financed by a combination of employer and employee payroll taxes in addition to general tax revenues. Administration of the program will rest with the private insurance companies, and unless it is shown to be inefficient, that authority will remain with the private sector.

The phasing in of the program may well continue into 1990 to permit modifications of the system as needed. The highest priorities are for catastrophic illnesses and certain forms of emergency, maternal, and child-care coverage. Many existing federal programs, such as Medicaid, will be phased out as broader and more comprehensive coverage becomes available.

Health Maintenance Organizations

Another name for prepaid health care is the more popular term Health Maintenance Organizations (HMOs). The philosophy is group care for a prepaid amount, with the emphasis upon preventive medicine. HMOs are in contrast to the traditional fee-for-service payment plan. Since all expenses are paid for in advance, the consumer is likely to visit the physician more frequently, remain healthier, and avoid hospitalization more often, and the result is lower overall costs.

Regular examinations are encouraged so that problems can be discovered and treated early. A serious health problem costing tens of thousands of dollars will be covered by the same annual fee. Most HMOs also cover dental care, eye examinations, and psychiatric services. Every plan is different, but Table 4-2 shows some comparisons between the three major types of health plans available.

Comparisons between HMO participants and fee-for-service patients show that HMO people have cut their hospital stays by 50 percent. Another study of New York City's Health Insurance Plan (HIP), which serves more than 800,000 members, found that Medicaid patients using HIP had a 14 percent lower mortality rate than those using the fee-for-service system.

The best-known HMO is the Kaiser-Permanente Medical Care Program, which serves more than 3.25 million consumers in California, Colorado, Ohio, Oregon, Washington, and Hawaii. It has 27,000 employees, including 3100 physicians, and operates 26 hospitals and 68 outpatient centers. The average annual cost is about $400 per member or $1400 per family. About 175 other preventive medical groups have been established around the country.

To spur the creation of HMOs, the government passed the Federal HMO Act of 1973. As more recently amended, companies with twenty-five or more employees having current health benefits must give the employees the option of joining an HMO if one is available. The law, however, prohibits the employer from paying the higher costs for an HMO membership.

The approach of each HMO is similar. A member is assigned a doctor of his or her choice upon entering the system, although the member can change doctors later. An important aspect is that regardless of what is wrong, a patient-member can easily be referred to other specialists. Another attraction of the HMO is that of teamwork and "peer re-views," since higher standards of excellence are likely to be set. Some HMOs even offer health education classes. Critics suggest that some skimping on health care might occur in order to keep costs down. Also, since the doctor is sometimes simply assigned to a patient, the result may be impersonal care between a staff of doctors and a patient.

Interestingly, even though more HMO's are being organized, only about 20 percent of those eligible actually join them. It may be the *apparent* higher monthly cost. It could be that many Americans are satisfied with their health-care plans and prefer to wait until illness strikes before worrying about it. Or it could indicate that many people just do not understand what preventive medicine could mean for them. The president of New York's Strang Clinic—Preventive Medicine Institute states that "one out of every seven premature deaths in the United States could be eliminated through preventive medicine."

Education: the Great American Fraud?
In our nation of approximately 220 million people, about 90 million are in the work force

TABLE 4-2

Three Different Health Plans (Group Rates)

	Family's Monthly Premium	Hospital Benefits	Medical Benefits
Health-maintenance organization	$125	No limit on regular hospital costs in semiprivate room; for maternity stay, patient pays first $50.	Unlimited physician care in hospital, office or clinic; patient pays $5 for first house call for each illness.
Blue Cross-Blue Shield	$105	365 days in semiprivate room.	Insurer pays 80 percent of physicians' bills, including lab tests, after patient pays first $100 each year.
Insurance-company indemnity plan	$90	First $1000 of room and board plus 80 percent thereafter; for other hospital expenses, insurer covers 80 percent of cost after the first $25.	Insurer pays 80 percent of medical bills after patient pays first $50 each year.

Courtesy of Edd Uluschak.

Come, come, Arnold—the labor force and marketplace awaits!

and 65 million are enrolled in schools. (Some people, of course, are doing both.) Apparently education is the nation's largest "employer."

Because of the obligatory nature of education ("You must stay in school until you are at least sixteen"; "Dropouts don't make as much money as graduates"; "To be successful you have to go to college"), three predominant values—health, wealth, and security—are ingrained in those who come through the system. These may not be the individual's personal goals, but the educational system is directed toward them. This is a good point for philosophical debate but, for the present, we will concern ourselves with how well our educational system meets our needs.

Elementary and Secondary Schools. These schools apparently do a good job of educating students to be successful in college—that is, the relatively small number of students who go on to obtain college degrees (20 percent). Obviously that number is a minority.

Let us follow the path of a typical group of 100 beginning first grade pupils. On the average, about 70 will graduate from high school. What will happent to the other 30? They wind up in lower-paying jobs, perhaps on welfare, but certainly frustrated with the educational system. Of the graduating 70, about 35 will enter the work force and 35 will go on to some sort of higher education. For the most part, the group entering the work force will not have salable skills, as traditional schools do not emphasize career or vocational education enough. What kind of employment future is in store for them?

The group going on to higher education will go to trade schools, area vocational schools, community colleges, state and private colleges, and universities. Within a year or two, some of them will develop the skills they need to get a job. Of those that choose the 4-year approach, only about one-half will receive a bachelor's degree in 4 years. Dropouts may or may not have developed salable skills; graduates may have the same problem.

This example does not mean that all students should be in vocational education; rather, it is in a way an indictment of a system that continues to fail many of its consumers. Should not every student be permitted to develop his or her own personal capacities to their fullest and at the same time become prepared for a lifetime as an earner and a contributor to society?

Some economic facts about the cost of high-school dropouts were compiled for the Senate Select Committee on Equal Educational Opportunity. It was reported that $237 billion in lifetime income will be lost by the 3.2 million young people who have already dropped out of school. It would have cost about $40 billion to provide adequate schooling for them to graduate, and the taxes on their additional earnings if they had graduated would have amounted to $71 billion. Theoretically, the nation would have gained $31 billion. Then, of course, there is the multiplier effect of the extra dollars that would have been spent had these people had higher earnings. The study further projected that the country would have saved another $3 billion annually in welfare payments and $3 billion through less crime.

Vice President Walter F. Mondale said about this report: "The real costs of inadequate education and the lack of equal educational opportunity in this country are for the most part immeasurable. For the individual, educational failure means a lifetime of lost opportunities. But the effects are visited on the nation as well, for society as a whole also pays for the undereducation of a significant segment of its population."

Overall, we are spending about $150 billion on our education systems, or about 9 percent of the Gross National Product. Spending on public elementary and secondary education goes for about 50 million pupils. Enrollments in recent years have just about leveled off, yet spending rises.

But we still do not have a good educational system with equal opportunity for all. In fact, a study for the U.S. Office of Education revealed that 35 million adult Americans should be classified as "functional illiterates." One critic of education observed that, "When 30 percent of our kids who graduate from high school can't even fill out a simple application for a job and 50 percent of our incoming college freshmen need remedial reading classes, it's time to rethink our entire elementary educational processes."

In Florida, 37 percent of high school juniors failed the state's new functional literacy exam (which covers math and English at the eighth grade level) the first time it was given. After three failures, a senior is given a "certificate of attendance" instead of a diploma. In Chicago, 35 percent of eighth graders failed a similar exam and could not go on to ninth grade without successfully completing summer school. These are efforts to help ensure quality in our nation's educational programs.

College Education. Similar dilemmas occur in college education. Billions are spent each year for the more than 11 million students enrolled at these institutions. The U.S. Census Bureau reported some inequities resulting from the increasing costs of higher education. The data showed that families with low annual incomes sent far fewer of their high-school seniors—only about 20 percent—on to college than did families with higher incomes. The high costs of college are prohibitive in the first place. A similar dilemma exists for many middle-income families, too.

College costs are rising at about 7 percent per year, and more and more students are turning to loans. Approximately one-fourth of today's students are getting government-guaranteed loans to help meet expenses, particularly since some of them are faced with increases of 20 to 30 percent in tuition, fees, and room and board expenses. If loans from relatives and other sources are considered along with grants and scholarships, four out of five of today's college students are receiving some type of outside financial assistance. Of these, about 40 percent receive less than $1000 a year. Hence, students also work and save to help put themselves through school.

Private colleges with costs amounting to $6000 per year are losing students to the public colleges and universities, where expenses are often closer to $2500. Some students also cut costs by attending a junior or community colleges for the first 2 years and/or attending a commuter college, thereby saving the costs of room and board. With leveling enrollments, the nation's 1665 four-year schools now actively compete for students with the more than 1200 two-year junior and community colleges.

People attend college for a variety of reasons, and columnist Tom Braden espouses a widely held view that "A college education ought to have nothing to do with making money. It ought to have to do with understanding, with learning to think in a certain way, with arousing curiosity, with satisfying it, with a perception of values and judging among them. It ought, in short, to have to do with living one's life."

Private Business and Vocational Schools. These educational institutions are serving an increasing number of students each year. There are more than 7000 business and vocational schools "to teach jobs." They train students for hundreds of specific career positions.

Unlike public institutions, private schools must prove themselves if they are to attract more customers and stay in business. The quality of these schools ranges from superior to poor, and one must be very selective in deciding which one to attend. Widespread advertising of free job placement and claims of accreditation for veterans definitely do *not* indicate superiority. Bilking most commonly occurs with the "fly-by-night" schools that talk students into signing noncancelable contracts for large sums of money and then do not provide the services promised. The Accrediting Commission for Business Schools and the National Association of Trade and Technical Schools are the two most reliable sources of information. Also, each state usually has an accrediting agency that can give you information.

Private schools fill an important void in our public educational system, and the better ones truly serve a genuine need. Graduates of good private schools who have done fairly well rarely have trouble finding jobs.

Correspondence Schools. These schools thrive upon those who want to improve their education at home. Such students usually find it most difficult to go somewhere to attend formal classes. The only recognized accrediting agency in this field is the National Home Study Council (NHSC). Any school selling its "education" without such accreditation is probably suspect, although some well-established schools feel that they do not need NHSC's accreditation.

False advertising by gyp schools is just pathetic, and both the Federal Trade Commission and numerous state attorneys general are trying to take action against it. Watch out for such claims as "guaranteed placements," "no previous qualifications needed," "endorsed by prominent public personalities," "glamorous pay for graduates," and "approved for veterans." The Veterans Administration does not approve anything; each state follows its own often loose guidelines as to what constitutes education. Also watch out for firms that want you to sign a noncancelable contract for the whole course. And, keep in mind that most reputable correspondence schools do not send out sales people!

One well-known correspondence school was investigated by author Jessica Mitford and reported in the *Atlantic Monthly* (vol. 226). The inquiry showed that 65,000 students were enrolled in the Famous Writers School under the ''guiding faculty'' of fifteen prominent writers—yet the guiding faculty rarely if ever even saw the work sent in by the students. In fact the teaching faculty numbered 55, or 1181 students per instructor! There were 800 salespersons selling the program for $785 (approximately $900 with interest if it was financed)—or 14 salespersons to every teacher. The key to the financial success of this correspondence school was its high dropout rate—somewhere between 65 and 90 percent.

Energy

The United States is in an era of ''energy shortages with a system of fuel and power regulation so disjointed and inconsistent that it is nearly impossible to respond to problems before they become crises,'' reports Jean Heller of the Associated Press. Many problems confront the energy industries.

The Energy and Ecological Crisis Is Here to Stay. Oil embargoes and cold winters did not cause our energy crisis. Rather, it was due to our consumption surpassing domestic capabilities beginning in the 1940s and 1950s. Events of the 1970s just helped bring the message to the minds of American consumers.

As a nation, we consume twice as much energy per capita as any other industrialized country. In fact, the demand for energy is doubling every 15 years, with the United States presently consuming over 30 percent of the world's power. Yet the world supply of fossil fuels (coal, oil, and gas) is decreasing.

Ecologically, each of the present methods of obtaining and using fossil fuels has harmful effects. Coal burning is worst of all; besides, the strip mining that often accompanies it

gashes and scars hundreds of thousands of acres. Oil use is somewhat cleaner, but the reserves are rapidly being depleted. Even though new sources are being found, at much higher costs, the ecological consequences of oil spills and pipeline breaks can be disastrous. Embargoes by oil-exporting countries that have formed cartels, such as OPEC (Organization of Petroleum Exporting Countries), are an ever-present possibility with dangerous and serious implications. Natural gas is the cleanest of the three, but the costs of exploration have become somewhat prohibitive and the supply will also run out in the not-too-distant future.

Legal Monopolies Exist. In the energy and utility areas, legal monopolies exist because historically it seemed that they were best for the common needs. After all, should a community have one telephone company putting up poles and stringing wires or five competing companies all putting up poles and stringing wires? Similarly, should a community have two power companies, each operating at one-half capacity, or one? Times change, however, and now we are beginning to see that such monopolies have not been serving the country as well as they should.

Yet the monopoly trend is continuing. All possible foreseeable energy sources—including gas, coal, and uranium production—are rapidly being taken over by the oil companies. In other words, ''there will always be an Exxon.'' The federal Department of Energy reports that five oil and gas companies control approximately 62 percent of domestic uranium milling capacity; twelve oil and gas companies control approximately 51 percent of domestic uranium reserves; and fourteen companies control approximately 44 percent of leased coal reserves. A Brookings Institution study in 1975 reported that by 1980 the United States could be self-sufficient in oil if vigorous antitrust action was taken to break up the energy conglomerates. To date, however, the Antitrust Division of the Federal Trade Commission has shown little interest in

Courtesy of Edd Uluschak.

"You'll have to give up smoking, drinking and thinking about the 16 per cent hike in utility rates."

the matter. The monopoly trend is continuing because of a series of regulatory failings.

One company, Westinghouse Electric Corporation, after seeing a 500 percent increase in the price of uranium, sued in federal court. Westinghouse accused twenty-nine major American and foreign companies of violations of the federal antitrust laws (Westinghouse, like any other company or a government, can file suit under the Sherman Antitrust Act). In this case, Westinghouse alleged that "the price rises for uranium resulted from alleged rigged bidding, conspiracies to split up markets, and withholding of uranium except at discriminatorily high prices."

Utility regulations can be characterized as a mixed-up mess of *non*regulation. Natural gas and electric utilities come under the eye of the Department of Energy and the individual states. The oil industry is regulated by the Department of the Interior, by presidential proclamation, and by the state governments. The coal industry is basically not regulated. The federal Department of Energy *tries* to coordi-

nate what is happening. Critics say that rapid rate hikes and scant research efforts could become a thing of the past *if* the various regulatory agencies would strengthen their control over the energy industries.

A Senate study of utilities found the following: (1) most utilities did not give the public enough notice of proposed rate changes; (2) millions of dollars were spent in unnecessary advertising (electric utilities spent 7½ times more on advertising and sales than on research and development); (3) country-club memberships were being counted as a "cost of business," and free telephone service for employees was being subsidized (and paid for by consumers, of course); (4) private deals were being made between utilities and ex-utility employees in state regulatory agencies; (5) there were few professional staff members working for the regulatory agencies; and (6) the public had little or no access to company files that were supposedly available under the Freedom of Information Act. The conclusion was that "much stiffer regulation" is needed.

National Energy Policy. No national energy policy existed before President Carter and the Congress passed comprehensive legislation in 1978. The Department of Energy was created and 113 separate bills were formed into one National Energy Act. In addition to eventual self-sufficiency in energy, the goals President Carter stated for 1985 were:

1. Reduce the annual growth rate in energy consumption from 4.6 to 2.0 percent.
2. Reduce gasoline consumption by 10 percent by encouraging production of smaller, more efficient automobiles.
3. Reduce imports of foreign oil to less than 6 million barrels a day, less than half the amount that we will be importing if we do not conserve.
4. Create a strategic petroleum reserve of 1 billion barrels, which would meet our needs for about 10 months in the event of another embargo.
5. Increase coal production by two-thirds to 1 billion tons annually, and shift industrial consumers to coal instead of gas and oil.
6. Require insulation of all new buildings and 90 percent of all existing homes.
7. Install solar energy devices in 2.5 million homes.

These seven goals, largely endorsed by Congress, are the basis for a national energy policy. Hence, there will be a shift from oil and natural gas to coal in the short run, and eventually to alternative forms of energy in future years. For example, in 1977 nuclear power accounted for 10 percent of our total energy supplies and by 1988 it will probably amount to 20 percent. Conservation is being stressed in order to "stretch out" existing resources. And self-sufficiency is being promoted in two ways: a petroleum reserve and additional research and development funds from the federal government for alternative forms of energy.

Energy Alternatives. Besides the fossil fuels, there are other available or potential sources of energy for future use. Perhaps the most controversial is nuclear power, in particular nuclear fission. But to many, nuclear power seems to be the only viable alternative to meet the projected energy demand for the end of the century.

By the year 2000, nuclear energy could well supply 50 percent of our power demands. However, serious ecological battles are being fought in courts across the land to stop the building of nuclear plants. People are concerned about the increase in water temperature near the nuclear plants, radiation leaks into water and air, and the possibility of a technological failure of the system that cools and protects the operations. The latter would result in a "meltdown." In a *Time* article, M.I.T. physicist Hugh Kendall described what could happen. "The nuclear core would become a molten mass, so hot that it could melt through anything guarding it. Subsequent steam explosions could rupture the outer container, releasing a cloud of radioactivity about two miles wide and 60 miles long. Much of the population in that area would be dead within two weeks."

That type of accident is highly unlikely *but* within the realm of possibility. The type of nuclear plant referred to is a "thermal" or "light water" facility. This common civilian thermal nuclear plant uses low-enriched rods of uranium as a fuel. When the fuel is spent, the fission process leaves a residue of plutonium in the rods. In that form, it is not explosive. It is the next step that presents greater concern—a reprocessing procedure that refines the plutonium. Plutonium is a most potent poison and in its fuel form can be fashioned into a nuclear bomb rather easily. To date, in this country, only the military reprocesses plutonium. This is why there is so much concern about another type of nuclear power plant—the fast breeder reactor. After becoming president, Jimmy Carter placed a moratorium on the building of this type of facility for commercial purposes. A reprocessing plant near Barnwell, South Carolina, and a breeder reactor power plant at Clinch River, Tennessee, have been affected.

The fast breeder reactor plant uses plutonium as a fuel and has the capability of creating *more* plutonium as its waste product. For example, a 2200-pound bundle of uranium will produce about 3000 pounds of plutonium in less than 4 years. That is enough to fuel a fast breeder reactor plant, which itself will generate a still more potent form of plutonium to fuel yet another plant. This is also enough plutonium to produce 100 atomic bombs. A meltdown accident in a breeder reactor would increase the death toll by 10 to 100 times. Even more dangerous is the increased possibility of terrorists obtaining some plutonium if commercial users are allowed to build such plants. The biggest plus for breeder reactors is their lack of dependence upon some other source of fuel—they make their own.

Nuclear fusion is another energy source that offers promise but has yet to be harnessed for peaceful purposes. Hydrogen bombs employ *fusion,* which is the combining of certain atoms to create tremendous amounts of energy; the fuel is hydrogen atoms from water. Nuclear *fission* splits enriched uranium atoms to release heat; this is the principle used in atomic bombs. Although fusion has been researched for more than 30 years, the necessary breakthroughs have not yet developed to permit the safe creation of energy. If and when the technology is developed, fusion will create more energy than fission and have virtually none of the problems with the radiation and wastes that accompany fission.

Solar energy is one of the most promising sources of energy for the future. The Joint Economic Committee of Congress reports that by 1985 solar heat will be the cheapest form of energy to warm homes and water. Once the initial expenses for surface collectors and the transfer system to a storage area have been paid, the lower cost of operation pays for the initial expenses quite rapidly, often in only 8 to 10 years. Improvements in solar technology are expected to reduce this payback period even more.

Windmills are an age-old source of energy which may well make a comeback in the years to come. Some large windmills are already in operation, and scientists have redesigned the blades to increase their efficiency. Two Lock-heed Aircraft Corporation engineers have concluded that up to one-fifth of the nation's energy needs could be met by installing 50,000 giant nonpolluting windmills. Other researchers note that each would cost about $60,000 and that they would pay for themselves in 7 years while remaining operative for 50 years.

Geothermal power is the major source of Iceland's energy and is also used in Italy, New Zealand, Japan, and Mexico. Harnessing the energy from the interior of the earth either as steam or superheated water (as in a geyser), or from heated rocks under the earth's crust could also be a potential source for the United States. Most sites are in the West, however, such as the plant in Santa Rosa, California. One caution is the possibility of sulfur emissions being too high.

All energy alternatives are being pursued for their potential effectiveness, since our fossil fuels are running out. The years ahead will see more "blackouts" and "brownouts" until conservation and alternative forms of energy can be safely and efficiently used.

Consumer Responsibilities and Energy Use
The American consumer already uses twice as much energy as a consumer in the most industrialized Western European countries. The "overuse" and "overconsume" philosophy of the past is hard to slow down, let alone turn around. Yet, conservation is the simplest and most directly responsible method consumers can use to help themselves and their country. The love affair with the large automobiles must come to an end; homes should be insulated to an effective level of efficiency; and consumer decisions in general need to be toward more energy-efficient choices.

It is very important that the consumer voice be heard in energy matters. Future growth patterns and numerous manufacturing decisions are largely determined by the strength of the consumer voice, both as economic voting and as active involvement. For example, when 3300 utility companies request rate increases from the state public utility commissions "to increase profit and attract capital to meet

America's future energy needs, consumers,'' suggests Dennis Pirages of the University of Maryland, ''might start asking 'what needs?' '' Often these needs are projections based upon the rapid growth rates of earlier years, which may not be valid for the future. In sum, perhaps consumers' responsibility in energy matters is really what more and more writers are saying: Bigger and faster is not better because small is beautiful. Our society is already moving in this direction as more people are making the transition in lifestyles from quantity to quality.

With regard to utility companies in particular, there are a few issues that need local input in almost every community. *Flat rates,* which charge a more equal price per unit to *all* users, instead of lower rates to big users are given by only a few utility companies. *Peak load* or *time-of-day* pricing is the idea that charging higher rates when usage is highest will hopefully encourage consumers—industrial as well as family—to reduce consumption at these times. This would result in more overall powerplant efficiency.

The *inverted* rate structure is also being discussed whereby the price of energy would go up as consumption increased. Also, *lifeline* rates are being proposed. This assumes that all customers should have a ''right'' to a certain minimum basic amount of electricity at low rates (such as the first 450 kilowatt-hours), after which the rate reflects the costs. *Fuel adjustment* clauses are somewhat controversial too, especially since they are permitted in more than forty states. These clauses allow companies to automatically pass increased fuel costs to ratepayers without first getting official approval from the public utility commission. How knowledgeable about these concerns are you? Where do you stand on these issues? What actions do you think responsible consumers ought to take?

PERSONAL SERVICES FOR CONSUMERS

We spend our dollars trying to gain some satisfactions for ourselves and others. Some buy many material goods and some buy few, but all of us buy certain personal services. And with personal services, there are some problems that we need to be aware of so that they can be avoided.

Book and Record Clubs

Books, records, cassettes, magazines—almost anything can be bought on a contractual basis. Such sales are made door-to-door or through the mails. This becomes a personal service to consumers, as it seems more convenient to purchase in this manner. Problems abound however.

Traveling crews of youngsters are sometimes duped into selling door-to-door, telling customers that they are ''working their way through college'' or ''working toward earning enough money to support a Dr. Martin Luther King, Jr., school in Alabama.'' Long-term contracts are signed, hefty deposits are required, and subscriptions may or may not arrive. Protection is available under federal law, since consumers have a 3-day *cooling-off period* during which they may cancel the contract *if* they made no appointment in advance. However, door-to-door salespersons often get around this by arranging for the ''sales manager'' to come by later to ''finalize the deal.'' This means, in effect, that the consumer has agreed to an appointment, and thus waives the right to rescind the contract. Most states have their own ''cooling-off'' laws for door-to-door sales, too, some of which offer more protection.

Mail-order clubs can just about drive consumers crazy. Once you join, it is nearly impossible to get off the mailing list. Getting records, books, or tapes from the large mail-order firms frequently involves the *negative-option clause*—that is, remembering to mail in the card saying that you *do not* want the particular selection of the month. If you forget to mail in the card, you get the product. Surely consumers have the responsibility to carefully examine what selections are offered and indicate a choice, but it seems that they are often not given enough time to return the cards, and mail them back only to receive the item anyhow.

Consumers using any negative-option club privileges *must* keep accurate records for their own protection. Furthermore, if something arrives that you did not order (you sent in your negative-option card), simply open the side of the attached envelope and see what was sent. If the wrong item has arrived, carefully reseal the envelope, mark in dark letters on the front "Return to Sender—Refuse to Accept," and make a written record of what happened. Then drop the package back in the mailbox. The bills of the company may take many months to get straightened out, but do not fear, your accurate record-keeping is your defense. And no company is going to sue you for $5 or $10 despite all those threatening form letters they send out. Do not worry, either, about your file at the local credit bureau. The companies are too busy to bother sending in negative reports about informed consumers who beat them at their own game. Besides, the Fair Credit Reporting Act permits you to add your side of the story in 100 words or less to your credit file any time you want to, should something actually appear in your file. In fact, with good records, you can have any disparaging comments taken out of your file in such a case. (This is discussed in greater detail in Chapter 7.)

An irritated consumer once had a dream: If just 1 percent of the population kept accurate records on these negative-option deals, the companies would soon learn that they could not profitably continue to use that type of sales technique. Furthermore, if 1 million consumers requested that "free sample" of whatever is being sold, kept good records, and sent back all the forthcoming unneeded and unordered products, those companies using the *free-sample* gimmicks would soon go out of business.

By the way, do not forget that postal regulations are very clear in stating that if you receive anything in the mail that you have not ordered, it is yours as a *gift*. Take all the "gifts" you can, keep good records, and when

Another service people sometimes buy is movers. About 20 percent of American families move each year. While most of these moves go reasonably smoothly, problems arise in about 30 percent of moves handled by professionals. (*Kenneth Karp*)

they send those computer-printed form letters, *you* send them a bill for "storage charges" for keeping the "gifts" in your home.

Such individual and collective consumer efforts may well be needed, since the proposed trade regulation rules to tighten up negative-option sales have not yet been implemented by the FTC. Many of the abuses could be eliminated with new regulations that would more carefully control the negative-option and free-sample sales plans.

Mail-Order Sales

Millions of consumers make purchases by mail every year, and a high percentage of them are not satisfied. Mailing a check for something is too often like a lottery: Will you or will you not be a winner and receive the merchandise? National companies with established reputations usually serve mail-order customers well, but the others are something else again.

Most frustrated consumers give up after sending off a letter or two (with no response) and write off their $5 or $10 loss. But this is a $60 billion industry! That is a lot of $5 bills! The responsible consumer should contact the industry's Mail-Order Action Line (Direct Mail Association, Inc., 230 Park Avenue, New

York, N.Y. 10017), the Postal Service, the state Office of Consumer Affairs, the Federal Trade Commission, and if necessary members of Congress.

Federal Trade Commission regulations give consumers some protection. If no date is stated by the seller (such as "4 to 6 weeks"), you have the right to have the merchandise shipped to you within 30 days. If the merchandise does not arrive within the time period, you have the right to cancel your order. If you cancel, the seller must mail your refund to you within 7 business days after hearing from you. If it was a credit sale, the seller has one billing cycle to correct your account.

If there is going to be a delay in mailing the merchandise, the seller must notify you of that delay and give you a free means to reply (such as a postage-paid postcard). If the shipping delay is 30 days or less, you have the right to cancel the order and get your money back, the right to agree to the new shipping date, or the right not to answer. If you don't answer, the seller can assume you agree. If the delay is more than 30 days, you must give your expressed consent to the delay. If you do not, the seller must return your money at the end of the first 30 days of the delay.

It sounds complicated, but the regulations are helpful. Keep in mind, however, that they do *not* apply to services like mail-order photo finishing, magazine subscriptions, serial deliveries (like negative-option book clubs) except for the initial shipment, mail-order seeds and growing plants, COD orders ("collect on delivery"), and credit purchases where the buyer's account is not charged prior to shipment of the merchandise.

Fraudulent Product-Testing and Buying Groups

In spite of heightened consumer awareness, fraudulent product-testing and buying groups are flourishing. World Field Research, a "product-testing" organization, closed up shop after collecting hundreds of thousands of dollars in "enrollment fees." It had tested only a few products. Almost all marketing firms do their own product testing! "Guaranteed refunds" and other advertised lies from such companies continue to bring in new customers to "try out these products and send us your evaluative comments as a typical consumer." Certainly the consumer should beware.

Reputable buying groups, known as *cooperatives,* have existed for decades. It is true that large numbers of organized consumers can get discounts on merchandise, but fast-buck artists have been promoting "buying groups" and absconding with loads of profits. Either they close up shop by declaring bankruptcy or, better yet, stay in business, realizing that a very small proportion of their customers will actually use the services even though they have paid in advance.

Some clues can help show you which buying groups are probably not on the up and up: Those that heavily advertise their new service or use telephone solicitations to entice you to come to their office, or those that set up offices in temporary quarters (such as a motel), or those that charge an enrollment fee of more than $10 or $15, or those that give away a free gift for "just listening to an explanation about our exciting program," or those that want you to sign a contract. Most college communities have one or more buying clubs come through town selling memberships every year. Some of these outfits are nationally based and talk students into signing contracts for $400 or more. This is pure stupidity if you realize that you can get the same products and prices either at discount stores or through a reputable catalog mail-order buying service that charges $10 or less per year to be a member. Claims to the contrary are just untrue.

Fortunately, the Federal Trade Commission is looking into this area and expects to issue regulations to better protect consumers. In the meantime, the claims the promoters make are fantastic! And people sign up. Why?

Employment Agencies

Employment agencies are either privately run or are operated under the direction of the Labor Department. At present, through the government's employment offices, a "job bank'' computerized system is in operation across the country in more than 120 cities. However, most jobs on file are at the lower end of the employment scale. Eventually, the Manpower Administration expects to include professional, technical, and managerial jobs, too. Then the cooperating state employment agencies will be able to have daily lists of thousands of vacancies for job seekers. But until that time comes, private agencies will continue to place many people.

About 14 million applications will be filed this year at the more than 8000 private employment agencies. Together, these private agencies—both good and poor—will probably place about 4 million people. Before using an agency, however, it is wise to spend some time trying to find a job through the help-wanted ads, the local state employment office (which will even give you—free—a series of aptitude tests), and the placement office of the last school you attended.

When fees are charged by private agencies, they range from about 5 to 15 percent of your *annual* salary—higher percentages for higher-paying jobs. When you first apply to a private agency, you must sign a contract listing the conditions under which you must pay the fee. You should read these contracts carefully even though usually you pay no fee unless you accept a job to which they refer you. But occasionally you must pay even if you are sent by one potential employer to another one that the agency never heard of. That contract clause is one to avoid. The trend for the employer to pay the fee is a welcome one. After all, a 10 percent fee on a $14,000 job is $1400, and that is a lot of money.

Choosing an employment agency is also important since you want the best type of job for your talents. Many private agencies specialize in particular types of jobs or in positions in certain salary ranges. So here, too, it pays to shop around. You should interview them to see which one can best serve your needs. It can also pay to have more than one agency working to find you a job, since in any case you will have to pay only one fee.

Be careful about *job-counseling* firms or *job-search* companies. They specialize in writing resumés and sending them out for you. Also, they often give aptitude and ability tests—which could be done free elsewhere, or at least for far less money. The firms do not guarantee results but you still have to pay a fee. The charges run from $50 to more than $1000—quite a price for a little counseling and a search!

Family Portraits

The desire to be able to relive or capture some of life's wonderful experiences is often achieved through the family photograph album. However, some deceptive practices lie in wait for those who fall prey to "family portrait specialists."

Mrs. Mary Harelson of Tampa was extremely pleased with the beautiful pictures of her children that the photographer took. She signed a contract with the Remembrance Studios, agreeing to pay for a series of family portraits to be taken once every 6 months until the children graduated from high school. The cost was only $65 a year, payable at $6 a month. Mrs. Harelson remained pleased—until 2 years later, when the photographer did not contact her for their semiannual appointment. Remembrance Studios had gone out of business and was no longer in town. Nevertheless, a debt collection agency *did* contact her, to demand payment in full on the contract she had signed. The agency took her to court, and eventually she had to pay $200 of the remaining $550 due on the contract to the finance company, even though future pictures were never taken. Instead, *she* had been taken.

Signing a long-term contract for photographic services is always dangerous. Most of the contracts are discounted and sold to finance companies, and frequently the consumer must pay anyhow. Reputable photographic services do not ordinarily use contracts. They send out reminder notices when the time has come for portraits—an honest practice.

Day-Care Centers

The most precious possessions of almost every family are its children. And with the increasing number of working mothers, there has been a corresponding need for more day-care centers. As a result, services of many types, for preschool children especially, are located in almost every community in the nation. Many day-care centers also provide preschool education.

However, all is not well in the day-care industry. Minimum federal standards apply to many day-care centers, but each state and/or community sets up its own licensing requirements. Unfortunately for Louis and Marge Shiller, stringent regulations were not in effect in Chicago a few years ago when all four of their children died in a fire in a day-care center. No fire-alarm system was required, so the center did not have one. Nor were there any regulations concerning the number of exits, and the firefighters could not get to any of the children in the basement room that had only one entrance. Highly flammable curtains and overcrowded conditions gave the children little opportunity to save themselves.

Responsible parents must check local regulations, then visit several centers. They need to check for proper licensing and talk to the people in charge and to the paraprofessional assistants. Find out about any educational program and certainly check on the ratio of the children to the number of people caring for them. And be sure to visit when the children are not napping. Stay long enough to see how the children are actually handled, don't just listen to a description. Take your time comparing day-care centers!

Marriage Counseling

Few states regulate or even license marriage counselors. However, check with your state officials for licensing requirements or recommendations, should you need such services. There are thousands of untrained marriage counselors, including many in the clergy, who try to help people with their problems. Additionally, there are, according to current estimates, probably 50,000 phony marriage counselors swindling the public out of nearly $1 billion a year. The very people who recog-

nize they need help with their marriages and go for it are often the victims of quacks. Check for membership in the American Association of Marriage and Family Counselors (225 Yale Avenue, Claremont, Calif. 91711), as it is the national professional organization that establishes minimum standards for academic and professional preparation; over 5000 people are members.

Funerals

Years ago death was a rather simple affair, a family matter. The deceased was washed, dressed in appropriate clothes, and buried. Times have changed, and so have the events surrounding the death of a member of the family.

Funerals today are for the living. Elaborate and expensive funerals reflect the idea that the dead are honored by lavish burial ceremonies. About 2 million people die each year, and total funeral costs amount to approximately $4 billion. Funeral homes get about half the total, with the remainder going for flowers, cemetery costs, grave liners, and obituary notices. The Federal Trade Commission (FTC) estimates the cost of the average funeral and burial to be $2000. That breaks down to about $800 for the cemetery and grave marker and the remaining $1200 for the funeral itself.

A growing number of people have come to believe that lavish funerals are unnecessary, and that the emphasis should be put on the deceased's life, not death. Among the reasons for this are changes in ideas among Americans, alternative methods being more available, the high costs of traditional funerals, heavy and well-publicized criticism of the funeral industry, and an increasing awareness that the average consumer may be closely associated with several funerals during a lifetime.

Although the courts have ruled that the nation's 22,500 funeral homes may advertise prices (something the National Funeral Directors Association fiercely disagrees with), most have not. The reason: Competition would result in lower prices for almost all funeral homes and put some of them out of business. Three-fourths of all funeral homes do two or fewer funerals per week—hardly a competitive situation. So, instead, the costs remain high and sales techniques make it more likely that relatives will buy a more expensive casket and some services they may not really need.

The psychological pressures on those making funeral arrangements are immense and leave them particularly vulnerable to persuasion. What family wants to be thought of as haggling about the cost of their father's funeral? Abuses have been reported throughout the country.

Frequently the bereaved are shown various caskets, the most expensive one first, working their way down to the cheapest, and then hear disparaging comments about the less expensive ones. The people wind up choosing one of the more expensive caskets. Now the funeral home wanting high profits has the customers right where it wants them because this industry often uses what is known as *casket pricing*. A package of services—virtually all the same—are provided based upon the price of the casket. To illustrate, a $200 casket provides a $1000 funeral (the markup is typically 500 percent to cover all costs), a $300 casket provides a $1500 funeral, and a $500 casket provides a $2500 funeral. There are slight differences in the services, but what can a funeral home do other than remove the deceased from the place of death to the funeral home, embalm the body (which is not required by law anywhere but encouraged under the false premise that "the body will look better"), do cosmetic restoration, arrange for obituary notices and burial permits, use the viewing room and other facilities, and provide transportation to the cemetery? Thus, a $2000 funeral may not differ from an $800 funeral except in the type of casket chosen.

To eliminate some of these practices, several states have passed laws requiring that clients be given a list of the arrangements they have contracted for and the total price before the ceremony. The Federal Trade Commission, to make things even clearer for consumers, has issued a set of proposals which undoubtedly will be appealed by the National Funeral Directors Association (NFDA) to the U.S. Supreme Court. The FTC proposes a list of new requirements: They could not embalm a body without a family's permission; they would generally have to itemize funeral costs instead of presenting a take-it-or-leave-it package that might include undesired services, and they would have to display caskets— typically the largest expense in any funeral— in a way that would not disparage lower-priced coffins. The NFDA has already collected a $250,000 "war chest" to fight the regulations.

You can get a lower-cost funeral by shopping around, but there are more efficient ways. A *memorial society* is a "group of people who have joined together to obtain dignity, simplicity and economy in funeral arrangements by advance planning," as stated in the literature of the Continental Association of Funeral and Memorial Societies (1828 L Street, N.W., Washington, D.C. 20036). These nonprofit societies are founded by church-related, civic, and labor groups and are located in more than 100 cities across the country. More than a million people have paid $10 to $20 to join a memorial society. Each organization operates differently, but most societies have agreements with one or more funeral directors. The society then provides the family with information on what kinds of funerals are available at what cost, and assists in preplanning the funeral. Thus, memorial societies bring the families and funeral directors together with a prearranged understanding of all services and costs. The total expenses for a simple funeral planned with a memorial society could be between $200 and $500. This would, of course, include casket, plot, opening and closing fees, and a small marker.

If cost is the most important concern to a family, the lowest-priced alternative is to donate the body to medical research. This performs a valuable service in addition to saving expenses. Many public-spirited citizens leave their eyes to eye banks, too. Arrangements can be made by contacting your nearby medical school, which will work with the appropriate agencies and supply you with a donor card(s). The only expense the family might have would be for cremation and later disposal of the remains, which would be quite minimal (under $100).

Cremation is growing in popularity, and the costs can be as high or higher than a traditional burial. Or, the cost can be extremely low. Cremation "after viewing" means that the full traditional funeral service is performed and then cremation occurs. What seems ridiculous but often happens is that, although no laws require it, many funeral homes insist that the deceased be cremated *in* a coffin. The result is higher costs (add in the cost of the urn for the ashes, too, not to mention the expense of disposing the ashes unless the family takes them home). And remember, some of those coffins are metal. With metal coffins, you get baked bodies. After "cremation" the charred coffin is discarded and the body cremated properly.

Much less expensive cremation costs occur with the help of a memorial society. Eliminating embalming, viewing, and some other funeral home services and merchandise, often including the casket, can reduce expenses to $250. Combining the standard funeral with cremation might cost $500 if the casket is not required.

POINTS OF VIEW AND PROBLEMS TO THINK ABOUT

This chapter on using services is a long one and for good reasons: More than 40 percent of our spending dollars go for such intangibles, services are difficult to evaluate and compare, traditions and our personal habits dictate many of our spending patterns, and we are experiencing grave social consequences because of some of the problems in the service industries.

This is the first chapter in the unit on effective consumer buying. How do you feel about the marketplace? Are you becoming more aware? Are there some aspects of the marketplace and its regulations that you think need changing? Should you as a consumer consider changing any of your personal spending patterns? Are there some things that you as a responsible consumer should do?

In the future, more and more dollars will be spent on services. Typical consumers have most of the material goods they want, and consequently they now demand more services. That demand, partially a result of changing lifestyles, of course, pushes prices up.

In an age of more services, what can be done to ensure quality repair services? Licensing of repairpersons is one alternative. Licensing of the business firms that perform repair services is another. Or, perhaps competency testing and certification is the way to go. In our gigantic economy, can we depend upon the forces of competition to put shady operators out of business? What can we do? Who can control the quality of doctors? Of dentists? Of lawyers? And how can the nation's legal system be improved?

More than 220 million consumers can make the changes they want. In the marketplace, the informed consumer can cast economic dollar votes or withhold them. The state legislatures and consumer groups can call for reform of health care problems, and perhaps even get health education established as an important priority.

In individual communities, consumers can serve their educational system by participating in it and, if necessary, working to change its direction. Similarly, consumers can cast political votes for the men and women who stand up for what is morally right. Also, individuals can find out how candidates stand on issues of ecology, monopolies, and oligopolies. Not only do consumers need to get out and *vote*, they need to participate responsibly and get out *the* vote! Those who fear their votes will not count need only look at some of the progressive changes in the marketplace during the past decade.

This is your country. It changes slowly, but it does change when the people want it to. This process is perhaps the greatest strength of the system. But changes of any kind will cost. Are you willing to pay more by participating and by spending?

Think about what it might take to change the following two service situations. The first is the "myth of unending consumption," written about by Ivan Illich. This is grounded in the belief that process inevitably produces something of significant value, and therefore production necessarily produces demand. Applied to education, this would mean that instruction produces learning. The existence of schools produces more demand for schooling. We have learned the need for school. "In school," says Illich, "we are taught that valuable learning is the result of attendance; that the value of learning increases with the amount of input; and, finally, that this value can be measured and documented by grades and certificates." What do you think?

A second service problem to consider surrounds a legislative bill in Massachusetts. Henry L. Keller proposed a bill to outlaw the 10-cent pay toilets—"which would make life a little bit happier." Keller was morally indignant about companies that profit by a person's discomfort. Lobbyists for motel and amusement park associations spoke against the bill. One observer commented, "I wouldn't give a dime for the chance of this bill passing."

CHAPTER ACTIVITIES ━━━━━━

Checkup on Consumer Terms and Concepts

Per capita spending	Health-care system
Consumer price index	Social Security benefits
Comparison shopping for services	Workers' Compensation
Professional incompetence	Private health insurance
Peer-review system	Nonprofit health insurance
Minimum fee schedules	Group health insurance

National health insurance	Negative-option clause
Preventive medicine	Nuclear fusion
Quality education	Memorial society
Legal monopolies	

Review of Essentials

1. Describe the relationships between inflation and the purchasing power of the dollar.
2. Describe aspects of the professions that keep them from serving consumers effectively.
3. How can you find a quality professional? List several ways.
4. List the components of the nation's health-care system and comment on the effectiveness of each.
5. Cite examples of the effectiveness and the ineffectiveness of today's private health insurance.
6. Compare and contrast various proposals for national health insurance.
7. How does prepaid health care work?
8. Describe your ideas of an educational system that would provide equal educational opportunity for all.
9. What are some of the problems and proposed solutions to our nation's energy situation?
10. List several guidelines for getting your money's worth when you buy personal services.
11. React and cite examples about this statement, "In our democratic system the majority of the population changes what it wants to change."

Issues for Analysis

1. Health care for middle-income consumers is inadequate. What steps would you recommend be taken to ensure better care? Consider the following factors in your analysis: cost, role of government, profit motive, ethics, morality, and so on.
2. Assume that you have just been elected "dictator for a year" of the health care

industry. With such broad powers and no laws to stop whatever actions you make, draw up a list of policy statements that your subordinates must carry out. Remember, the country will revert to a democracy in 12 months.

3. Assume that you are the attorney general for your state. Write up a list of proposed laws and/or regulations to more effectively control the personal services offered consumers in your state.

5
Buying Food

THE PROBLEMS

The most prevalent disease in the world is malnutrition, and that includes the United States. *Obesity* (overweight), which seriously affects 50 million Americans, is also a major problem. Obesity and *malnutrition* (too little or too much of certain nutrients) mean that we are not a well-nourished people. The nutritional adequacy of most Americans is shameful, and it's getting worse. For most of us, breakfast is a nutritional flop. Even those who eat breakfast cereal with milk have fallen prey to the advertising claims, because you usually don't get much nutrition with that kind of breakfast. Other breakfast foods, such as eggs, toast, muffins, and orange juice, are often nutritionally superior and also cheaper.

For many, the McDonald's Big Mac, french fries, and chocolate shake diet is popular and does provide adequate nourishment. However, this occurs at a cost of nearly 1100 calories. It will take considerable physical activity to burn up that amount of energy.

For all of us, prices of foods are rising rapidly. When we shop for groceries, most of us have a choice of stores where prices vary considerably. It is not uncommon to find one food market with prices that are 10 percent or even 25 percent higher for the same groceries. This is especially true when comparing convenience-type stores. The typical American food shopper could easily save 20 percent on the weekly grocery bill both by becoming more knowledgeable and by comparison shopping. Instead, unaware of the psychology of the supermarket, the shopper pushes the cart along, buying numerous items not normally needed. Curiously, the shopper continues to see products that are virtually the same except for price—and then buys the expensive name-brand product on the mistaken idea that price indicates quality. Then, on the way through the checkout counter, more dollars are often lost by consumers who do not watch what prices the cashier is actually ringing up.

Federal, state, and local governments supposedly protect the consumer in food shopping, and in many ways they actually do. But inadequate laws, nonenforcement, and monopolistic practices permit consumers to be swindled by numerous deceptions, frauds, and misrepresentations. We still eat poisons and other dangerous chemical additives every day—we each consume more than 5 pounds of pesticides, chemicals, and food additives every year. And even though some of these additives have been proven to be linked to cancer, they remain on food-store shelves. Consumers could better protect themselves if they knew more about these matters.

We spend about $200 million a year on bottled water that meets the standards of the Food and Drug Administration. But, surprise! An Environmental Protection Agency study reports that more than 60 percent of bottlers surveyed gave their source as "public supply"—meaning they got their water right out of the tap. Those people who really want bottled water should make sure the label says "Well Water" or "Spring Water," since such claims, by law, must be substantiated.

Fewer than one-half of the people in the nation's households eat nutritionally balanced meals, and these are not necessarily the economically well off. Business executives have been treated for scurvy because, when traveling, they avoided foods other than meat and potatoes. Low-income people have been found to be eating pet food because it is less expensive and more nutritious.

The average consumer needs to learn much more than just "calories" and "taking vitamin pills" to have a healthy diet, to stop wasting money, and to avoid the numerous deceptions, frauds, and dangers in the food marketplace.

UNDERSTANDING NUTRITION

Your body's primary job is to keep your heart pumping. Other necessary tasks include keeping you breathing, maintaining normal body temperature, giving you the strength to get out of bed in the morning and get through a normal day, and seeing to it that you have enough extra power to cope with hard physical work or other stresses. All of these require energy, and you get that from foods that provide energy, which is measured in calories.

Since nearly everything we eat contains some calories, most of us are able to perform our daily chores. Foods give the energy that the body needs throughout the day and even during the night when we are sleeping. Different foods, of course, have various amounts of energy value, or calories. Sweet, greasy, and concentrated foods often have high calorie counts, while watery, bulky, or coarse foods usually have lower ones.

The necessary calories come from three main groups of foods: (1) *carbohydrates* (the starches and sugars found in cereal grains, fruits, vegetables, and sugar added to foods for sweetening); (2) *fats* (found plentifully in butter, margarine, shortening, salad oils, cream, most cheeses, mayonnaise, salad dressing, nuts, and bacon); and (3) *proteins* (found in meat, poultry, fish, milk, cheese, eggs, bread, and cereal). Carbohydrates and proteins have about the same calorie value, while fats have more than twice as much. The number of calories a person needs each day differs with sex, height, weight, age, individual metabolism, and physical activity. Table 5-1 shows recommended calorie allowances for adults by weight. Men need more calories than women, and heavier people need more than lighter ones.

Drinking five milk shakes a day (each with about 500 calories) would give most people all the calories they needed. Eating pies, cakes, and sweet rolls and drinking soda pop could provide a like number of calories. But calories are not the whole story! It is true that you need a certain number of calories each day, and that you need more than other people if you are doing something strenuous. You need fewer calories if you lead a sedentary life. You need still fewer if you want to lose weight. *But* just knowing about calories will not make you healthy. Calories are only one small part of good health. Proper nutrition is something else.

Nutrition is the study of the science of food and its relation to health; in short, it is how your body uses food. The three previously mentioned groups of nutrients (carbohydrates, fats, and proteins) produce energy and are ex-

TABLE 5-1

Calorie Allowances for Adults

Sex	Weight	Calorie Allowances for a 22-year-old Person
Female	88	1550
	99	1700
	110	1800
	121	1950
	128	2000
	132	2050
	143	2200
	154	2300
Male	110	2200
	121	2350
	132	2500
	143	2650
	154	2800
	165	2950
	176	3050
	187	3200

Source: Recommended Dietary Allowances, 7th ed., National Research Council.

cellent sources of calories. But three other groups of nutrients are essential, too—minerals, vitamins, and water. Actually, your body needs more than fifty nutrients. Some are so abundant that we need never worry about them; others are less available and must be sought out. Moreover, we need nutrients not only to supply energy, but to build and maintain body tissues and to regulate body processes.

The Quality of American Diets

It is true that for much of the last 60 years, diets in general have improved, resulting in stronger bodies, physically larger people, and the elimination of many diseases. But in more recent years, this land of abundance, wealth, and education has done little to better the diets of Americans. Studies by the U.S. Department of Agriculture (USDA) show that the American diet has been getting nutritionally

worse. The percentage of people eating *good* diets has dropped to about 50 percent of the population, compared with 60 percent just a decade earlier. This figure is based upon the *minimum* recommended dietary allowances for seven basic nutrients as set forth by the USDA.

Teenagers and Young Adults. Young people have particularly poor eating habits. Dr. Howard Bauman reported that in about 50 percent of families, one or more members skip breakfast regularly. A national USDA study revealed that 20 percent of all people do not eat breakfast. Hurried fathers and mothers are often guilty, but most breakfast-skippers are teenagers and young adults. A 10-year study reported by the University of Iowa concluded that breakfast is the most important meal of the day, especially because "after a 10 to 12 hour period without food a good breakfast provides the necessary energy fuel for the morning's activities." In a separate study, the North Carolina Industry Commission discovered that "75 percent of all industrial accidents in the state occurred to workers who had skipped breakfast."

Dr. Evelyn Spindler of the USDA reported that six out of every ten girls and four out of every ten boys have poor diets. Some are on diets, some are in a hurry, and many just do not care.

Other reasons for the poor diets of young Americans include snacking on poor foods rather than eating full meals, drinking little or no milk, dieting by skipping one or more meals a day, indifference to any kind of meal planning, and lack of nutritional knowledge. A study commissioned by the Harvard School of Public Health reported that teenage girls listed as their favorite snacks, in order, pie, cake, and pastry; candy; fruit; cereals and bread; and ice cream. Boys listed cereals and bread; pie; cake and pastry; soft drinks; milk; and fruit. This trend toward "replacing fruits, vegetables, milk and cereal products with fats and other high-caloric, low-quality foods has compounded the problem." Regardless of which studies are examined, it is apparent that many Americans are not eating good diets.

The Results of Poor Diets. The effects of poor dietary habits vary from a few noticeable effects to severe problems. General problems resulting from malnutrition, cited by Dr. George M. Briggs, chairman of the Nutritional Sciences Department at the University of California in Berkeley, include "poorer health, obesity, mental problems, physical deficiencies and increased susceptibility to diseases." More specifically, says the American Medical Association's Council on Foods and Nutrition, malnutrition results in "growth retardation, weight loss, increased burden of chronic diseases, depression, weakness, retarded convalescence from disease and trauma, and poor performance in pregnancy."

Cancer has been linked to diet also. Dr. Paul A. Marks, director of the Cancer Research Center of Columbia University's College of Physicians and Surgeons, reported that "one-half of the fatal cancers in women and one-third in men may be attributed in part to diet habits." Foods high in fat appear to increase cancer risks, while those high in fiber content appear to reduce them. Fibrous foods include cereals and some vegetables. The National Cancer Institute has accelerated research on the relationship between cancer and nutrition.

Obesity leads to a number of serious health disorders, including hypertension, diabetes, gallbladder, cirrhosis of the liver, osteoarthritis (too much weight on the joints creates excessive pressure), and heart diseases. One in three men in the United States dies of a heart attack or a stroke before age 60. The Senate Select Committee on Nutrition and Human Needs issued a strong policy statement concerning American diets. They recommended, in addition to other things, "a 40 percent reduction in sugar consumption, a 10 percent reduction in fat consumption, and a 50 to 85 percent reduction in salt consumption."

It seems that we Americans are slowly eating ourselves to death. We are making ourselves the victims of overconsumption and malnutrition at the same time. Too many of us are functioning far from our peak physical and mental capacities, and too many of us are also prone to illness. Desirable weights for men and women are shown in Table 5-2.

Nutritional Fallacies

There are many myths about nutrition that people believe. These fallacies need to be better understood if consumers are to get more for their money, stop wasting money, and improve their understanding of nutrition.

Vitamin Pills. Many people think supplemental vitamin pills are needed. In one Food and Drug Administration (FDA) study, three out of four people thought that "extra vitamins provide more pep and energy." Those three out of four people are wrong! Vitamin pills are not needed if you generally eat well-balanced meals and are in good health. Vitamins are essential organic compounds that are found in abundance in everyday foods. Vitamin pills cannot possibly substitute for food nutrients because not even one-half of the known nutrients can be processed into pills. Advertisements suggest that taking one pill a day will solve all nutritional problems.

The Food and Drug Administration is tired of this myth. They conclude that, except for people with special medical problems under the care of a physician, there is no scientific basis for anyone taking vitamin pills on a regular basis. Vitamins will not help grow hair, cure skin problems, ease arthritis pain, prevent ulcers, give one more energy, make one sexier, or cure a cold. A well-balanced diet provides all your body needs. Some doctors prescribe vitamins for individual health problems. In such cases, a low-cost store brand is usually the best buy. Compare the products if you have to purchase vitamins, since FDA regulations concerning labeling *require* strong similarities among products and the ingredients must be listed in the same sequence on the containers.

Health Foods. A heavily promoted cure-all for dietary problems is health foods. Understandably, most foods lose certain amounts of nutrients during processing. But overpriced "health," "organic," or "natural" foods are not the answer. Some people claim that "natural fertilizers" result in better foods. A plant can't tell the difference between organic and inorganic fertilizers. Soil depletion reduces the quantity of the crops grown, not the quality. The reverse is often claimed and is a myth.

"Even if you assume that food additives are bad for you, it doesn't follow that their absence somehow confers safety," reports Dr. Donald Kennedy, head of the FDA. For example, aflatoxin, a mold that grows on corn and peanuts, is as natural as can be and is also one of the worst carcinogens (causes of cancer) that we know about.

Deficiencies are not going to be cured by health foods. In fact, too much reliance on any one type of food will probably result in missing out on some other important nutrients. Furthermore, the "additive-free" (organically grown) foods are frequently not totally free of additives, or even pesticide residues. One final major myth should be exploded: "Organic foods are filled with natural vitamins." Chemically speaking, your body cannot tell the difference between a vitamin taken in by food or one produced in a laboratory. A vitamin is a vitamin.

The phobia against chemicals, the desire to protect our environment, the disclosure of false claims about certain food products, the

TABLE 5-2

Desirable Weights

Weight in Pounds According to Frame (In Indoor Clothing)

Men of Ages 25 and Over Height (with shoes) 1-inch heels		Small Frame	Medium Frame	Large Frame	Women of Ages 25 and Over Height (with shoes) 2-inch heels		Small Frame	Medium Frame	Large Frame
Feet	Inches				Feet	Inches			
5	2	112–120	118–129	126–141	4	10	92– 98	96–107	104–119
5	3	115–123	121–133	129–144	4	11	94–101	98–110	106–122
5	4	118–126	124–136	132–148	5	0	96–104	101–113	109–125
5	5	121–129	127–139	135–152	5	1	99–107	104–116	112–128
5	6	124–133	130–143	138–156	5	2	102–110	107–119	115–131
5	7	128–137	134–147	142–161	5	3	105–113	110–122	118–134
5	8	132–141	138–152	147–166	5	4	108–116	113–126	121–138
5	9	136–145	142–156	151–170	5	5	111–119	116–130	125–142
5	10	140–150	146–160	155–174	5	6	114–123	120–135	129–146
5	11	144–154	150–165	159–179	5	7	118–127	124–139	133–150
6	0	148–158	154–170	164–184	5	8	122–131	128–143	137–154
6	1	152–162	158–175	168–189	5	9	126–135	132–147	141–158
6	2	156–167	162–180	173–194	5	10	130–140	136–151	145–163
6	3	160–171	167–185	178–199	5	11	134–144	140–155	149–168
6	4	164–175	172–190	182–204	6	0	138–148	144–159	153–173

For girls between 18 and 25, subtract 1 pound for each year under 25

Source: Metropolitan Life Insurance Company.

rebellion against convenience foods, and the desire to eat "natural" foods have produced the health-food fad. Nearly $1 billion is spent each year on "health," "organic," or "natural" foods.

There are, of course, some pluses for health foods Even though they can cost 35 to 150 percent more than others, natural foods sometimes look and taste better. This is mainly because they are often grown and sold locally, and therefore are fresher than food that has been shipped hundreds of miles. But this is not necessarily so. For example, many so-called farm-fresh stands are supplied by the same jobbers who supply the supermarkets—which, because of the volume they buy, can pay lower prices, and are supplied with fresher produce. If you want to eat natural foods, go right ahead. But do not believe those wild statements about their curing your health problems. And remember, you cannot *taste* nutrition.

Other Fallacies. Misconceptions about food are numerous. Some of the more common ones are listed below.

- "Toast has fewer calories than bread." This is false, since toasting removes only water, which does not alter the energy value at all.
- "Pizza has little nutrition." Not true. Pizza is often very high in both protein and calcium; the same is also true of peanut butter, which is another favorite.
- "White shelled eggs are better for you than brown-shelled ones." (Or the opposite.) Totally false. They are equal except in price (since many people think brown eggs are less nutritious, there is less demand, so the price is usually much lower for brown eggs). The nutritive value of an egg is determined by the breed of the hen.
- "Adults do not need milk." False. It is very hard to get the needed quantity of calcium from any other milk products. Besides, milk is an excellent source of several other important nutrients.
- "Brown bread is more nutritious than white bread." False again. Besides findings by other researchers, a comprehensive study by Consumers Union found that no one bread was superior to another. The only consistent factor was that prices for brown breads were about 36 percent higher than for white breads.
- "Water is fattening." Many people actually believe this. Water has no caloric value at all; it cannot possibly be fattening.

The Basic Food Groups Provide Good Nutrition

Our food supply, technology, and knowledge of nutrition are enormous. The meals you plan can be tasty and not too expensive, and also provide good nutrition. But consumers are generally not well informed about nutrition. They need to be more aware of the four basic food groups and effective meal planning.

The research division of the U.S. Department of Agriculture has divided the foods we need into four groups: (1) milk and milk products; (2) meats, (3) bread-cereals, and (4) vegetable-fruit products. These four groups of food, essential to maximum health, must also be supplemented with other products, as shown in Figure 5-1.

Nutritious, Healthy, Low-Fat Meals

Fats are necessary but too much can cause problems. For most Americans today, approximately 40 to 45 percent of the daily caloric intake is fat. That is nearly one-half the calories you eat.

The body handles fats in three ways: (1) burning it up to produce energy, (2) storing it in tissues, or (3) silting it in the form of cholesterol along the walls of the arteries (the blood vessels that carry oxygen and food throughout the body). High fat levels are clearly associated with many diseases, most particularly heart problems.

Scientists know that the silting of fats is part of the process of atherosclerosis, in which cholesterol is deposited in the artery walls. A certain amount of cholesterol, however, is needed for good health; in fact the body manufactures some itself.

We are what we eat. *And* we will be the result

Choose from these foods most of the time:	
. . . to get the foods your family needs economically. These are usually among the best buys in the food groups. Use any other foods that you produce at home, get free, or can buy for no more than the foods on this list.	

Milk Group

Nonfat dry milk	Cheese, processed
Fluid milk	Cottage cheese
Evaporated milk	

Meat Group

Try to use in each day's meals—

1 or more helpings from these:

Dry beans	Eggs
Dry peas	Peanut butter

1 small helping* of meat, poultry, or fish, such as:

Hamburger	Bologna
Pork shoulder	Frankfurters
Liver (beef,	Chicken
pork, lamb)	Fish (many kinds)

*To make meat go further, use in dishes with less expensive foods — macaroni, noodles, rice, potatoes.

Bread-Cereals Group

Use "enriched" products when possible.

White enriched bread	Grits
Whole wheat bread	Some ready-to-eat
Crackers	cereals
Flour	Rice
Cornmeal	Macaroni
Farina	Spaghetti
Oatmeal	Noodles

Vegetable-Fruit Group

Try to use some of these at each meal for color, food value, and variety.

For important vitamins:
Cabbage
Carrots
Potatoes
Sauerkraut
Pumpkin, canned
Spinach, canned
Tomatoes, canned
Oranges
Grapefruit
Citrus juices, canned or frozen

For added variety:
Celery
Onions
Turnips
Beets, canned
Green beans, canned
Apples
Bananas
Applesauce, canned
Cling peaches, canned
Prunes, dried
Raisins, dried

Note:
At times, some fresh vegetables and fruits, such as greens, tomatoes, corn, and peaches, may cost less than canned. Sometimes berries and melons may be good buys, too.

Other Foods	Lard	Sugar	Jelly	Coffee	Salt
	Margarine	Corn sirup	Applebutter	Tea	Pepper
	Salad oil			Cocoa	Other seasonings

Source: USDA

FIGURE 5-1   Four groups of foods

of what we eat now. Hence, it is important for better long-term health to cut down on fat intake. Many organizations, including the American Heart Association and the Senate Select Committee on Nutrition and Human Needs, and professionals all across the country agree with that recommendation. Please note the phrase "cut down"—it does not say cut out.

Healthy, nutritious, and low-fat meals can be prepared with little disruption in your present menu planning. Remember, the task is to reduce your fat intake from 40 to 45 percent to 30 to 35 percent. So, a whole lot of changes are not necessary. A couple of examples would include using polyunsaturated oils in cooking and using margarines that are high in polyunsaturates. Preparing foods to remove

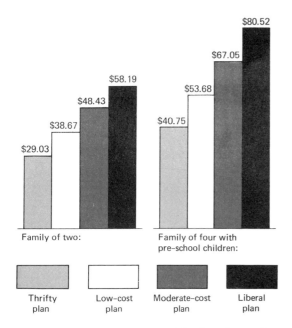

Family of two:

Family of four with pre-school children:

| Thrifty plan | Low-cost plan | Moderate-cost plan | Liberal plan |

FIGURE 5-2 Weekly cost of food at home for young people

extra fats is not that difficult either, and it often results in a tastier meal. For example, if a homemade spaghetti sauce is allowed to cool overnight in the refrigerator, much of the fat will come to the surface and can easily be skimmed off. In any event, isn't spaghetti sauce always better the second day?

Books with low-fat menus can easily be found in bookstores everywhere. Reducing fats in the diet is not a fad; it's a pretty serious thing. With a little help, one can enjoy all the pleasures of fine eating without overdoing the fat business. Even the American Heart Association has a cookbook (3007 I Street, N.W., Washington, D.C. 20037).

SPENDING YOUR FOOD DOLLARS

One of the largest expenditures in most budgets is for food. Let's look at several of the factors that affect food costs.

How Consumers Spend Their Food Dollars

Determining the exact amount people spend for food is difficult because it depends upon

many factors. Do you include money spent on meals eaten out? Do you count money spent on nonfood items at the local supermarket?

Consider the averages first. Eating out in restaurants and fast-food shops now takes one out of every four food dollars. This rapid change in lifestyle (a decade ago only 10 cents of each dollar went for food away from home) is a result of many things. More married women work. More people are single. More people are divorced. More people have more money. And a much wider variety of restaurants is available. Typical consumers spend about 17 percent of their income on food purchases. This translates into about 4 percent for food away from home and 13 percent for food at home.

Weekly costs of *eating at home* are shown in Figure 5-2. Based on extrapolated 1979 prices, the cost of a modest but nutritionally adequate low-cost diet for a young married couple is $38.67 per week; this is projected to be $52.59 by 1982. For a married couple with two pre-school children, the low-cost diet is $53.68 per week; it is expected to be $73.00 by 1982. Costs then rise rapidly with increases in size of family, age of younger family members, and desire to eat "better" meals.

The Supermarket Dollar. Dollars spent in supermarkets do not go entirely for food. In fact, nearly one-fourth (23 cents) of every dollar goes for nonfood items such as toothpaste, cigarettes, headache remedies, and cleaning and household supplies. Spending "food dollars" on these products obviously leads consumers to believe they are spending more on food. This is because most people budget for "food" what they spend at the supermarket. Figure 5-3 shows how the remaining 77 cents is actually spent on food. The four basic food groups are shown, along with two other categories. The same food dollar can also be looked at in terms of the types of items bought according to supermarket departments, as shown in Table 5-3. Such a comparison suggests that buying items from the basic food groups can be difficult, with the hard question being, "Which of all these grocery items will give me maximum nutritional choices so that I can plan meals around the four basic food groups?" We'll examine answers to this question later in this chapter.

Do the Poor Pay More?   This question has been studied frequently over the years. Statistical results are sometimes conflicting, but one needs only to do a week's shopping in a ghetto area to find out personally. The most consistent research finding is that prices charged by chain stores operating in both low-income and suburban areas are virtually the same. But the availability of chain stores in low-income neighborhoods is another matter.

Furthermore, poor consumers spend a higher *proportion* of their income for food, since their take-home pay is smaller. The typical low-income family of four spends 40 percent of their income on food, in contrast to the average of 16 to 17 percent for middle-income families. As the size of the family increases, a higher percentage of spending is for food; it is not uncommon to find large low-income families spending 60 to 65 percent of their income for food.

Common problems facing low-income consumers are limited transportation to chain stores that have lower prices, many "Mom and Pop" stores that offer credit and delivery services but charge much higher prices, and food stores that offer trading stamps and charge slightly higher prices. Studies in Washington, D.C.; Columbus, Ohio; Newark, N.J.; and many other cities show similar findings. Aside from providing poorer consumers with *food stamps* (a federal program which permits them to get more food per dollar), little has been done to increase their buying power. Besides trying to find ways to raise their income, the most promising effort seems to be to encourage more chain stores and large independent stores to enter (or re-enter) low-income areas.

How Important Are Food Stamps?   Food stamps are to low-income people what au-

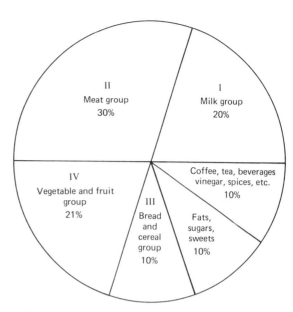

FIGURE 5-3 Dividing the actual supermarket dollar

tomobiles are to suburban middle-income Americans: almost a necessity. Food stamps permit any poor person whosoever—the elderly, the young, the working poor—to increase purchasing power when buying food. At a cost of approximately $6 billion, nearly 20 million people receive food stamp benefits; that's 1 out of every 11 people in the country. In Puerto Rico, more than 60 percent of the population gets food stamps.

TABLE 5-3

Where Does the Budgeted Food Dollar Go?

	Total Food Store Spending	Food Dollars (Percent)
Nonfoods	23.0%	00.0
Meat	23.5	30.5
Produce	9.0	11.6
Dairy	10.0	13.0
Frozen foods	4.0	5.2
Grocery	30.5	39.7

Source: U.S. Department of Agriculture.

It is the only national program providing assistance to all needy families. "My two sons used to go to bed hungry before I got the stamps because I simply didn't have anything to give them to eat," says Carmen Canales, 34, who supports herself and her boys in their four-room wooden shack with $166 monthly in food stamps and an occasional $40 alimony check. "They eat meat now almost every day."

Through a series of complicated formulas, an eligible household can get a certain allotment of food stamps. Those with the lowest incomes, say $100 a month, are permitted to get perhaps $166 in stamps; those with higher incomes would be eligible for fewer stamps. The result is a "food stamp welfare program" for all needy people. Instead of cash, all poor people are eligible for food stamps. Some question whether or not we should have a food stamp program at all. If it were eliminated, what effects would result?

Budgeting and Your Food Spending

One problem facing every consumer is a seemingly continual increase in the price of food. Budgeting for food every week or month can show you where your food dollar is going but, as we have already seen, several factors are involved. Let us look at some of them more closely.

Nonfood Items. When these products are bought at a supermarket, they frequently cost more than they would if they were bought from other retailers. Yet about one out of every four shoppers buys most health and beauty aids at the supermarket, according to Burgoyne, Incorporated, a research marketing firm. Many other nonfood items are also purchased, pushing the total bill still higher: laundry products, brooms and mops, light bulbs, cooking and eating utensils, encyclopedias, tobacco, pet products, reading materials, chewing gum, toys, and even clothing. Yet a "typical" $3 sponge mop would probably cost less than $2 at any nearby discount store. The fact is that the supermarket generally charges significantly higher prices for nonfood items than other retail outlets. But, people like "one-stop" shopping, similar to the old-time general store. It is no wonder that 23 cents of each supermarket dollar goes for nonfood items.

Dining Out. Eating at restaurants is also part of the total food budget. Economically poor families eat out sometimes, but middle-income consumers usually eat out at least

TABLE 5-4

Rising Food Costs*
(Base Year of 1967 = 100)

	1977	1978	1979	1980	1981	1982
Cost of all items	186.1	199.3	214.6	230.5	246.4	261.5
Total cost of food	196.3	215.9	237.5	261.3	287.4	316.1
Food away from home	200.6	220.6	242.7	267.0	293.7	323.1
Total food at home	193.7	213.1	234.4	257.8	283.6	312.0
Cereal and bakery products	189.0	207.9	228.7	251.6	276.7	304.4
Meats, poultry, and fish	179.4	197.3	217.1	238.8	262.7	288.9
Dairy products	176.9	194.6	214.0	235.5	259.0	284.9
Fruits and vegetables	192.5	211.8	232.9	256.2	281.8	310.0

* Extrapolated from 1978 data from U.S. Department of Labor, Bureau of Labor Statistics.

once a day. The trend is toward eating even more meals out in future years. Urban consumers frequently eat their lunches in a restaurant; these are most often working people who prefer not to bring a "brown bag lunch" every day. Some people prefer to call such eating out "entertainment," but basically this money goes for food. And we all know that these costs, too, are rising. Tattered menus are replaced with new ones that usually include new prices as well.

Inflation. While the overall cost of living has been rising in recent years (as discussed in detail in Chapter 4), so has the cost of food. The highest increases in food costs have been for meals away from home, as shown in Table 5-4.

Competition in the Food Industry?
James Hightower, director of the Agribusiness Accountability Project, a Field Foundation–financed research group, developed an interesting menu, "Menu by Corporate America," as shown in Figure 5-4.

The menu suggests the strong presence of large corporations in the food industry. In the past 20 years, more than 150 companies with assets in excess of $7 billion have been bought out by corporate conglomerate giants. Hightower states that, "The manufacture and distribution of the hundreds of items you see on the grocery shelf are controlled by a small number of huge food processors and supermarket chains. These firms have the sheer financial might to overwhelm smaller competitors and the market power to hold up prices and profits like a single monopolist. Unless monopoly power in the food industry is broken, we'll never see the price of food come down."

Oligopolistic and monopolistic practices inhibit competition and also effectively keep new food producers from entering the market. Jennifer Cross, in her book *The Supermarket Trap*, documents the domination of the food industry by large firms, as shown in Table 5-5. Obviously, several food lines are controlled by the four largest firms. The Federal Trade

---

APPETIZER
Sauteed Mushrooms by Clorox wrapped in
Bacon by ITT
SALAD
Tossed Salad of Dow Chemical Lettuce and Gulf & Western Tomatoes
ENTREES
Turkey by Greyhound
Ham by Ling-Temco-Vought
VEGETABLES
Carrots by Tenneco
Artichokes by Purex
Applesauce by American Brands
BEVERAGES
Wine by Southern Pacific
Beer by Phillip Morris
Tea by Unilever
Orange Juice by Coca-Cola
DESSERTS
Chocolate Cream Pie by ITT
Pudding by R. J. Reynolds
Ice Cream by Unilever
Almonds by Tenneco

Source: James Hightower, *Eat your Heart Out — How Food Profiteers Victimize the Consumer*, Vintage Books, New York, 1975.

FIGURE 5-4   Menu by corporate America

TABLE 5-5

Large Firms' Domination of the Food Market

Industry or Product	Percent of Market Shared by Four Largest Firms
Butter	11%
Poultry	12
Meat packing	20
Canned fruit	28
Canned vegetables	36
Coffee	55
Catsup	55
Crackers, cookies	62
Shortening	65
Cake mixes	75
Soft drinks	88
Soup	90
Baby food	95

Source: Jennifer Cross, *The Supermarket Trap,* rev. ed. (Bloomington: Indiana University Press, 1976), p. 186.

"He's okay—it's the first time he's come grocery shopping with me in months.

Courtesy of Edd Uluschak.

Commission calls this a *shared monopoly*. When as few as four companies control 50 percent or more of an industry's sales they can, in effect, act as a monopoly.

That view is shared by others. Senator William Proxmire, head of the Banking and Currency Committee, stated during a period of rising food prices, that food was "one of six concentrated industries whose immense and unjustified price increases are responsible for two-thirds of the current inflation." During the same time, the chief economist at the Department of Agriculture, Don Paarlberg, noted that "four-fifths of the rise in consumer prices" was the result of increasing the middlemen's share of the food dollar. Professor Willard Mueller of the University of Wisconsin, and former head of the Federal Trade Commission's Bureau of Economics, argues that what we have is a shared monopoly. The dominant firms do not bother competing on price because if one lowers prices the others will, too. Thus, "instead of reducing prices, they simply play follow the leader up the price scale. It's similar to what happens in autos and steel. With little fear of being undercut by

competitors, the firms have no incentive to hold down either costs or profits." A Super Market Institute study revealed that 57 percent of the American population "think a few large chains set the prices and everyone else has to follow them."

Not everyone holds the same view, but let's add in a few more facts. The total food dollar, as reported by the USDA, is divided up this way: farmer, 37¢; retailer, 26¢; processor and manufacturer, 20¢; wholesaler, 11¢; and transportation firm, 6¢. Within the numerous food areas, the share of the retail price varies as shown in Table 5-6 for a recent year.

The retail supermarket industry frequently reports that they are not the ones who are "raking in the profits." The supermarket industry shows time after time that their net profit is only 1¢ on each dollar of sales. That sounds low indeed until you think about it a little longer. If this industry is as unprofitable as this figure suggests, why don't they all sell out and buy government savings bonds that earn over 5 percent? Answer—they really make from 12 to 20 percent on their *return on investment* which is typical of most industries in America. Economists agree that "return on invested capital" is probably the fairest way to compare the profitability of companies in different industries.

Thus, it seems that the farmers are not starving, the retailers are doing fine, and the other middlemen are surviving okay, too. So, what is the problem? Prices are rising throughout the food industry, which is dominated by food giants. It has been suggested that breaking up the stranglehold within some food industries will restore competition and result in lower prices. Some evidence to support that position was released by the Congressional Joint Economic Committee, which subpoenaed records from seventeen of the largest national food chains. The study observed that, "Large food chain prices are about 5 percent higher where the largest four firms in a market hold 70 percent of the market than where they hold only 40 percent." Over the 4-year period studied, prices included at least $622 million in what was called "monopoly overcharges."

No less than fourteen cases of antitrust violations affecting food companies are in the courts now, with a far greater number under active investigation by the Justice Depart-

ment. The big one, however, is being pursued by the Federal Trade Commission against the cereal manufacturers. This landmark case, begun in 1972, will reach the U.S. Supreme Court sometime in the 1980s for final adjudication.

The FTC accuses the cereal industry of being a "shared monopoly." It alleges that the four companies, Kellogg, General Mills, General Foods, and Quaker Oats, control over 90 percent of the cereal market, and through various "barriers" managed to overcharge consumers $128 million in one year. It is important to understand that the FTC does not allege that the companies "simply got together every 6 months and fixed prices"; rather, they are saying that because of their concentration and barriers they might just as well have. The barriers, charges the government, include that the "companies tacitly conspired to follow each other's price raises, developed new brands rather than trying to save failing brands with price cuts, and used saturation advertising to maintain their market."

What is especially important about this case is that if the allegations are upheld through the U.S. Supreme Court, it will lay the groundwork for breaking up such concentrations, not only in the food industry but in other industries as well. It is likely that over one-third of the economic activity in the country could be affected, including the auto, steel, oil, aluminum, and tire industries.

The facts seem to be clearly on the side of the FTC and consumers. However, interpretation of the law and of congressional intent is a matter for the courts to decide.

The viewpoint of the successful businessperson is imperative to retaining a perspective about these kinds of important antitrust legal cases. Mr. W. E. LaMothe, president of Kellogg, summarizes the position quite well.

I urge you to think about this: What happens if our industry is splintered apart, broken up because it is found guilty . . . guilty of success, guilty of making whole-

TABLE 5-6

Share of Retail Dollar

	Farmers	Middlemen*
Beef	69%	31%
Eggs	62%	38%
Milk	51%	49%
American cheese	46%	54%
Potatoes	39%	61%
Margarine	32%	68%
Peaches, canned	28%	72%
Bread	17%	83%
Wheat	13%	87%

* Middlemen include processors, wholesalers, retailers, and transportation firms.

Source: U.S. Department of Agriculture.

some products, guilty of providing one of the best nutritional buys in America . . . guilty of succeeding in a system that has up till now <u>rewarded</u> *success, not punished it . . . guilty of working and achieving within a system that has provided the incentive for us to grow and develop and become the greatest country on earth. Success. We're not ashamed of it. We're not embarrassed by it. We don't feel guilty over it. And we don't think it's a crime. And neither should you. Neither should America. Now there is a fiction, a fantasy, a simple-mindedness growing in this land of ours that somehow breaking up the nation's large corporations will result in lower prices. That somehow this would be good for the consumer. That fractionating corporate America, compelling its leading corporations toward a costly, wasteful, time-consuming and contentious breakup is going to benefit consumers. Nothing can be further from the truth.*

Where to Buy Your Groceries

Martha and Felix Johansen of Boston are a typical married couple, and they spend about $50 per week on groceries. They have always shopped at a nearby independent supermarket. Occasionally they shop at small, convenience-type stores when they need just a few items. What they do not realize is that they could save (or not waste) nearly $300 a year by learning a little more about where to shop. Let us look at some of the types of stores available to the Johansens, and to most Americans.

The Markets Where Groceries are Sold. The many thousands of food outlets in this country can be classified into three basic types: (1) *un-affiliated independents,* (2) *affiliated independents,* and (3) *chain stores.* Some characteristics of these types of stores are shown in Table 5-7.

Another type of grocery store not shown in the table is the discount food supermarket.

The trend toward discounting food prices has occurred in both chain stores and affiliated independents. About 15 percent of today's large supermarkets also call themselves discount stores. Prices are commonly lower, and services are kept to a minimum. Such services as games, trading stamps, contests, carry-out service, and neatly stacked merchandise are eliminated or reduced. Success of the discount supermarket depends primarily upon increasing its sales volume and attracting more customers.

Price Variations among Stores. Even between one large supermarket and another in your community, prices can vary by as much as 20 percent. Knowing *which* stores have the best prices and shopping effectively can save you as much as $300 a year. Let's see how you can determine this.

Citing national studies or surveys in large cities is helpful but has little relation to the average consumer's home town. Although the summary observations in Table 5-7 are generally valid, conducting *your own* price study in the shopping area near you is an excellent way to determine differences among stores.

There are three basic approaches: (1) the *brand-name* technique, (2) the *lowest-price* survey, and (3) the *personal-choice* method. The brand-name approach involves making up a list of from fifteen to fifty nationally sold brand-name products and then checking the prices of those products at your local stores. Choose products of all types, including non-food items. The four basic categories used in the consumer price index might be used: (1) cereal and bakery products; (2) meat, poultry, and fish; (3) dairy products; and (4) fruits and vegetables. If you include convenience stores in your study, price variations will probably be quite large.

One *brand-name* study in a Midwest shopping area included forty-two items, checked in eighteen stores. A shopping list was made up, and the store that cost the least charged $27.92 for the items, while the store that cost the most charged $37.36, a range of $9.44. The average cost was $31.92. The price range among the six most comparable supermarkets was still $6.29, with the lowest priced charging $27.92 and the most expensive charging $34.21. Buying brand names cost 23 percent more at the highest-priced supermarket than at the lowest-priced comparable store.

The *lowest-price* survey is more difficult to conduct but does give clear information on which stores are easiest on your pocketbook.

You should use a similar shopping list, but without specific brand names. Instead of "Heinz Catsup, 14 ounces," the shopping list might read, "catsup, 14 ounces." The shopper then searches through the 14-ounce catsup bottles and records the lowest price. A survey in an Eastern community using the lowest-price technique showed prices varying 27 percent among five large supermarkets.

The *personal-choice* survey method is

TABLE 5-7

Places to Buy Groceries

Unaffiliated Independents:	
Mom-and-Pop store	Family owned; small; carries many products that are not brand-name items; low volume sales; high costs; usually carries the smallest size of a product line; mortality rate is high; prices are high; credit often extended; offers delivery service.
Convenience store	Family owned; small; carries about 2000 of the most popular products; many brand-name items; located in busy areas; high volume of sales; high prices; usually clean.
Large independent	Family owned; often the main-street store in smaller communities; carries many brand names; competes with any nearby large supermarket; usually not quite as neat and clean; prices usually slightly higher than chain stores, but certainly less than convenience and Mom-and-Pop stores; maintains full line of products, probably around 9000 (about 6800 are dry grocery foods, 550 frozen foods, 170 produce, and the remainder nonfood items); high volume of sales; normally no delivery service.
Cooperative	Owned and operated by the people who use it; controlled by the members; usually small; carries between 4000 and 8000 products; has name-brand and some private-brand items; not as neat and clean as big supermarkets; emphasis upon lowest prices possible; serves 2000 to 3000 families; redistributes any profits made at the end of each year, depending upon how much each member spent at the store.
Affiliated Independents:	
Small independent	Family owned; affiliated with a franchise name operation or large buying group (national or regional); often is the neighborhood supermarket; carries 3000 to 4000 products, brand-name goods as well as private-label items; lower prices than Mom-and-Pop and convenience stores; usually not as neat and clean as larger supermarkets; serves perhaps 1000 families at most; higher prices than competing larger supermarkets.
Large independent	Family owned, or sometimes owned by a group of local people; carries full line of goods, both brand-name and private-label; neat and clean; prices competitive with any large supermarket; high volume of sales.
Chain Stores:	
Convenience store	Franchise business or owned by the chain; small; neat and clean; carries about 3000 to 4000 popular items; sells brand-name and private-label items; located in busy areas; high volume of sales; higher prices than any large supermarket.
Supermarket	Owned by a corporation; managed locally; carries full line of about 9000 products; sells both private-label and brand-name items; large; neat and clean; high volume of sales; prices competitive with any other large supermarket.

specifically geared to your lifestyle. When you make up the list of items, look in your own kitchen and choose items that *you* normally buy. With any of the methods, the prices recorded should be double-checked for accuracy. Also, if you have the time, you might try checking every few days, weeks, or months for seasonal variations or sales. And if you divide your list into categories, you can see which stores charge higher prices for certain groups of products, like meats or vegetables.

Promotional Costs and Nonprice Competition
With the growing number of large chain stores and affiliated independent supermarkets, large supermarkets account for nearly three-fourths of all food sales. In general, the prices of these supermarkets are similar, and therefore they have turned to *nonprice competition* to attract and keep customers. Advertising, promotional devices, and packaging are the most commonly used methods.

Advertising. Local supermarket advertising, much of it in newspapers, accounts for only 2 to 3 percent of total store sales. Handbills and circulars are used, but since nearly three-fourths of all shoppers read the newspaper ads, this medium seems quite effective. Most such food advertisements give the prices of various products. Few give any nutritional information. *Loss leaders,* items sold at or below actual cost, are prominently advertised to bring people into the store in the hope that they will then purchase more items to make up for the loss on the promoted items. Loss leaders are often a shopper's best buy on that particular day in that particular store.

There is much food advertising on television aimed at brand-name identification. Heavy advertising on television is traditional with food manufacturers, with the oligopolistic industries doing most of it. The cereal industry, for example, spends a substantial proportion of its sales dollar for advertising. Kellogg, with 46 percent of the cereal market, spent $67 million in advertising and special promotions in a recent year, which amounted to approxi-

mately 6 percent of its total sales. Most of its advertising was for Apple Jacks, Special K, Corn Flakes, Rice Krispies, Sugar Frosted Flakes, Raisin Bran, and about twenty other cereal products.

Prices are not advertised, but the virtues of the product are. All the usual appeals—sex, youthfulness, health, peer pressure—are used to influence choices. With the amount of advertising for food products consumers see on television, it is no wonder that, according to a Super Market Institute survey, 72 percent "think prices would go down if food manufacturers would reduce the amount of advertising by 10 percent."

Food advertising regulations from the Federal Trade Commission are likely to be in effect by the early 1980s. The FTC wants to make food advertisements back any nutritional claims with *substantial* evidence. For example, if a product claimed on television that it was "loaded with iron," it would have to contain at least 35 percent of the U.S. Department of Agriculture's Recommended Daily Allowance for iron. If a food was advertised as a source of energy, it would have to say that the energy came from calories and specify how many. The proposed regulations, under consideration since 1974, would apply only to products that make nutritional claims. A company that wants to advertise a product as "fun" or "best tasting" would not be affected.

Promotional Devices. Other nonprice competition devices include trading stamps, coupons, games, sweepstakes, special promotions, and an array of "new" products, all of which are heavily advertised. It has been calculated that manufacturers spend about $90 per year on stamps, games, and coupons to lure *each* family into the store. Such promotional devices are good marketing techniques *when* they work. If sales increase proportionately, costs are covered by the increased profits. However, all shoppers pay for the promotions that do *not* work in higher prices. Jennifer Cross calculated that games cost the retail supermarkets between 0.5 and 3.0 percent of sales, while stamps cost between 1.3 and 3.5 percent (with an average of about 2 percent). (Remember that the supermarket trade publications keep telling us that they earn "only about 1 percent on sales.")

Trading stamps were extremely popular until they reached the saturation point; almost every store gave them away as a promotional device. They lost their effectiveness and, of course, resulted in higher operating costs for most of the stores involved. Price cutting to draw in more customers has been the most common technique in recent years, although trading stamps seem to be making a comeback.

Games and contests which run for a certain number of weeks have been calculated to cost the retail store between 0.4 and 0.7 percent of sales. These include collecting game cards like bingo, probability cards with numbers that one scrapes off, television games (often associated with race horses), and punch cards where "everybody wins" if the card is punched every time one makes a visit to the store. Potential "winners" and the probability of winning are regulated by the FTC, and this has reduced the deceptions associated with such promotions. Even so, these approaches have been losing much of their appeal for customers.

Continuity promotions, where a set of encyclopedias or dishes, for example, are sold for a limited time, still seem to be effective. Also, the in-and-out promotions, those lasting only a week or a month, are useful.

Coupons seem to be a very effective way of reducing the price to get new users for a product. An estimated 60 billion cents-off coupons will be offered to the public this year; about 5 percent will be redeemed. Coupons in either manufacturer's or store advertisements are commonly used. The retailers have considerable handling costs with coupons. Thus, they charge the manufacturer 3 to 5 cents to handle each coupon, which covers their costs quite well. Much evidence is accumulating to indicate that many stores will redeem coupons for

Courtesy of Edd Uluschak.

Games and contests are one form of nonprice competition that supermarkets use to attract customers. (*Guy Debaud*)

cash whether or not the item was purchased. If this is done, coupons lose their effectiveness for the manufacturer. In spite of these problems, stores and manufacturers like coupons because consumer acceptance is very widespread.

New products are often used as promotional devices, too, often in combination with coupons. However, about 90 percent of all new products fail within a year. Yet the manufacturers keep researching and advertising because a successful new product can reap considerable profits. Unfortunately, about 80 percent of all "new" products are just modifications of old products. (Look at the "new" cereals advertised each year, for example.)

Packaging Costs.   The cost of packaging adds greatly to grocery prices. Today's food markets sell groceries, but they also put a premium on shelf space and package design. For example, products displayed at eye level may cost a manufacturer more. For the same reasons, package sizes and colors are often changed because the manufacturer needs to catch the customer's eye, which scans thousands of products during one shopping trip.

The obvious conclusion concerning packaging is that with some products the package costs a lot of money, as shown in Table 5-8. And remember, these percentage figures are based on the retail price. Packaging is a much higher percentage of the manufacturer's costs. Industry-wide, packaging for food in a recent year cost approximately $52 billion: $31 billion for materials, $19 billion for the value added by the manufacturers, $1 billion for machinery, and $1 billion to haul away the trash. Overall, packaging costs about 11 percent of the total consumer dollars spent on food in supermarkets.

A Super Market Institute study revealed that 78 percent of the people "strongly agree" or "agree" that there is too much fancy packaging, such as putting cheese and crackers in one package. Further, 42 percent believe that "money could be saved if manufacturers were permitted to manufacture no more than three standard sizes of products."

A Packaging Conservation Act, sponsored by Senator John A. Durkin, has been introduced in Congress to help resolve some packaging problems from the consumer point of view. It would empower the FTC and the FDA to issue guidelines to eliminate overpackaging, which would reduce solid waste disposal, save natural resources, decrease product costs, and reduce deception. Another problem concerns the U.S. Supreme Court ruling that struck down state laws on package weights all across the country. The Court decided that a package can weigh less when a consumer buys it than when it was manufactured. Natural weight loss for many products is expected, but manufacturers traditionally have added in "a little extra" to compensate. Now, there are fears of widespread deliberate *shortweighting* because of the court decision.

How Cooperatives Reduce Food Costs
There are about 3000 large food cooperatives across the country, and more are being organized each year. This is in addition to thousands of health food clubs and neighborhood food-buying groups. They pose no

TABLE 5-8

Packaging Costs at the Retail Level

Product	Container Cost (Cents)	Percent of Retail Price
1 lb. butter	2.3	3.0
½ lb. American processed cheese	2.1	5.7
14½ oz. can evaporated milk	3.0	20.1
½ gallon ice cream	7.9	9.8
½ gallon fresh milk	3.0	8.3
1 lb. choice beef	1.4	2.0
Broiler (per lb.)	1.5	4.1
1 dozen eggs	3.1	6.0
#303 can tomatoes	4.0	25.0
#303 can corn	4.0	21.0
1 lb. white bread	1.5	7.2
1 lb. breakfast cereals	4.9	11.8

Source: Jennifer Cross, *The Supermarket Trap*, rev. ed. (Bloomington: Indiana University Press, 1976), p. 202.

serious threat to the supermarket industry as yet, even though they are growing in number. But for the nearly 3 million consumers they serve, savings of 5 to 15 percent are quite common.

Buying groups of ten to twenty families can result in lower prices because the groups buy in large quantities and at discounts from local suppliers. These small cooperatives usually specialize in particular types of food, such as canned goods or meats. However, the cash saving is often offset by the time and services each member must *give* to the cooperative. They frequently operate out of a member's home, a church, or a community center. Many small cooperatives fail within a few months or a year for lack of support.

College students are forming cooperatives, too. Students at Boston College organized a food cooperative that has saved them an average of 23 percent on food and as much as 40 percent on health and beauty aids. They have thus saved an overall average of 33 percent, but they, as members, must donate work time and in many cases provide their own "packaging."

Large supermarket cooperatives usually involve 2000 to 3000 families, and the situation becomes more complex. Highly successful co-ops include the Consumer's Cooperative of Berkeley in California and the Greenbelt Consumer's Co-op in Washington, D.C. They need professional management and accounting personnel, and the initial investment is perhaps $250,000. Member owners must pay a fee to join (usually $1) and purchase one share of stock (usually costing $5 a share). This helps raise the capital needed to begin the cooperative. True discount prices are secured and passed on to all customers. Anyone can buy goods at food cooperatives, but often a dual-pricing system is used, one price for members and one for nonmembers. Net earnings at the end of the year are distributed in proportion to each member-family's patronage. To be eligible for the dividends, usually $50 in shares must have been purchased. A law

which would set up a National Consumer Cooperative Bank to assist consumer co-op ventures by lending them money has been enacted by Congress.

Neighborhoods with a relatively homogeneous population that is intent on saving money are most inclined to begin cooperatives. Membership is usually open to anyone, and the organization is democratically controlled. Well-run cooperatives deal directly with manufacturers and wholesalers and pass the savings on to their members. In addition, they often join with other cooperatives to provide health care, prescription drugs, nursery schools, and credit union services. One major effort of large cooperatives is to provide continuous education for their members in all areas of buying. Further information about cooperatives can be obtained from The Cooperative League of the USA (1828 L Street, N.W., Washington, D.C. 20036).

HOW THE GOVERNMENT HELPS FOOD BUYERS

Federal, state, and local governments help consumers in their food buying in many ways. There are laws to help buyers, grading of foods that permits comparisons, and standards of identity that provide consistency among certain foods. Let us look a little further into what governments do.

Laws and Regulations Protecting Consumers
Since 1906, when the first Federal Food and Drug Law was enacted, the federal government has had an important role in helping buyers. Later amendments and new laws have made foods even more wholesome and safe. Almost all the federal laws cited below are amendments to the Federal Food, Drug and Cosmetic Act of 1938.

The Fair Packaging and Labeling Act. This law, the FPLA, was passed in 1966. It brought more honesty to the packaging and labeling of most food and many nonfood products sold in interstate commerce. It requires that the net contents of packages be printed in large enough type to be easily read, that labels give the name and address of the manufacturer, and that the size of the serving be given if the number of servings is stated.

The FPLA and later regulations issued by the government also established some controls to reduce deceptions in "cents-off" sales, prohibited packaging products with grossly excessive amounts of *slack fill* or "air space," and, for many products, required listing of ingredients in order of decreasing weight. The law also encourages manufacturers to voluntarily standardize weights, measures, or quantities for packaging. If necessary, the law permits the government to establish additional regulations to prevent deceptions and to make value comparisons easier.

Consumers now need to compare only five sizes of toothpaste instead of fifty-seven, sixteen sizes of dry cereals instead of thirty-three, and ten sizes of green olives instead of fifty. Also, terms like "jumbo pound" (exactly 16 ounces like all other pounds) have been eliminated.

The Wholesome Meat Act. Passed in 1967, the Wholesome Meat Act requires that all states meet minimum inspection regulations concerning the sanitary conditions of meat processing. Meat sold within states as well as among states is now either federally or state inspected. To ensure that the standards set by the federal government are met, the U.S. Department of Agriculture (USDA) inspects meat in the seventeen states that have chosen not to pass their own legislation.

Wholesome meat and the sanitation of plant facilities were, of course, the main targets of the legislation. However, the law also authorizes the USDA to write specific regulations concerning moving meat from the slaughterhouse to the supermarket counter. The USDA has yet to issue any regulations concerning minimum standards of refrigeration, more honest labeling, or more consistent terms to describe certain grades and cuts of meat.

The Wholesome Poultry Products Act. This act, passed in 1968, was modeled after the Wholesome Meat Act. Now all poultry plants are inspected for sanitary conditions; they must meet federal minimum requirements. Note that although inspection is required, grading is not required under either law; the grading programs are voluntary. Of course, if the meat or poultry has been government-graded, one can be confident that it has been inspected.

The Miller Pesticide Amendment. The Miller Pesticide Amendment of 1954 established specific maximum amounts of pesticide residues that are allowed to remain on agricultural products. The USDA tests pesticides itself or delegates the job to other nationally recognized groups, and finally decides upon a safe level for human consumption. Then, the *legal* residue level is set *100 times lower* to allow an extra margin of safety. This law is one reason why DDT is no longer widely used to spray agricultural products. The USDA continues to test the more than 30,000 pesticides registered with the Environmental Protection Agency.

The Food Additives Amendment. Controversy about the hundreds of food additives being used in processed foods led to the passage of the Food Additives Amendment in 1958. The law requires proof of the safety of any new chemical additive before it can be marketed. The amendment also established a *Generally Recognized As Safe* (GRAS) list of more than 600 substances that have been used for years and are considered safe so long as they are used as they were originally intended and with "good manufacturing practices." The substances on the GRAS list range from salt and sugar to monosodium glutamate (MSG). The Food and Drug Administration is now reexamining all additives on the GRAS list for safety.

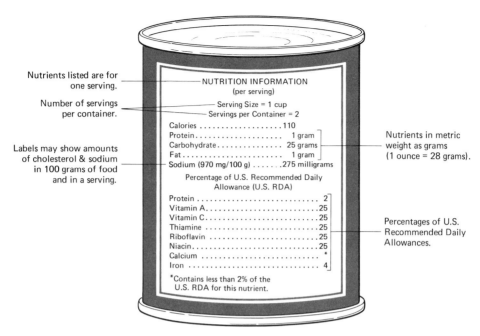

FIGURE 5-5   Sample nutritional label

The Delaney Clause.   This clause of the Food Additives Amendment specifically prohibits the use of any cancer-causing additives in food. When any food being tested with laboratory animals is suspected of being *carcinogenic* (cancer-causing), it is banned. For example, *cyclamates* were banned from all diet drinks and other uses as a sweetener some years ago. A hormone named DES, injected into cattle a few days before slaughtering to help them gain weight, was banned for the same reason. The controversy over *saccharin,* another sweetener, resulted because of the Delaney Clause.

The Color Additives Amendments.   The 1960 Color Additives Amendments required reevaluation of all color additives, including those previously thought to be safe. In addition, the Food and Drug Administration set limits on the amounts of color to be used in foods. Further, no color can be used to conceal any inferiority of a product, as this deceives the public. "Red Number 2" and other

color additives have been banned in recent years because of this law and the Delaney Clause.

Nutritional Labeling Regulations.   Voluntary nutritional labeling regulations established by the Food and Drug Administration went into effect in 1974. The labels are designed to help you identify the nutrient content of the foods you buy. All labels that give nutrition information must follow the same format, which should be helpful in comparing products. Any foods to which a nutrient has been added, or foods which make a nutritional claim, or foods for which a dietetic claim is made, must have a nutritional label. Other nutritional labeling is optional. An illustration of nutritional labeling is shown in Figure 5-5.

The upper portion of the label shows the size of the serving and the number of servings per container. Then, the label shows the number of calories per serving in grams and the amounts of protein, carbohydrate, and fat. As discussed, these are the three major nutrients in all the food we eat. The lower portion of the label shows the percentage of the United States Recommended Daily Allowance (U.S. RDA) for protein and seven vitamins and minerals provided by one serving. Additional information, such as amounts of cholesterol and sodium per 100 grams of food, may be voluntarily shown in the place indicated on the sample label. Other vitamins can be added at the end of the list.

The *U.S. Recommended Daily Allowance* has been developed by the Food and Drug Administration from the Recommended Daily Dietary Allowances set by the National Academy of Sciences' Food and Nutrition Board, which has twenty-four sets of allowances covering different age groups. The FDA simplified the categories and came up with the U.S. RDA. The FDA used the highest recommended allowance in each category for almost every nutrient. Hence, a typical adult male needs only 90 percent of the U.S. RDA for protein; a child of 7 to 10 years old needs only 55 percent of it. The eight nutrients required on the label are considered to be "indicators" of the many nutrients known to be of value.

Unit Pricing. Laws requiring unit pricing of food products are in effect in several states, although the laws apply only to larger stores. In some places, unit pricing is voluntary. The unit price is the price per unit of standard measure, whether that is a pound, ounce, quart, or whatever. The information is frequently shown on unit price labels, which are affixed to the shelves close to the products.

Open Dating. Several major cities and a few states require open dating (which can mean several different things) of many perishable food products. For the residents of those areas, open dating is very helpful. For example, bread sold in one community must be open dated, that is, the *pull date* must be clearly shown. After that pull date, the bread is no longer considered fresh. It is certainly not stale or bad, but it is not as fresh as other bread. Thus, the merchant quite frequently moves the bread after the pull date and places it on sale at a specially reduced price.

Some products have an *expiration date,* meaning the last day on which a product should be used. Others have a *pack date,* indicating what day the item was manufactured. For years, the companies had various secret codes to explain these things to the store personnel so that they could rotate stock when necessary. Consumers were kept in the dark. In New York City, for example, open dating has been quite successful in helping consumers buy fresher perishable products while at the same time saving money for the retailers; 75 percent of shoppers look for open dating. Now the store personnel can understand the codes well enough to rotate stock properly, and losses through waste have been cut substantially. Open dating pays for itself.

Universal Product Code (UPC) and Price Disclosure Laws. The UPC is a national coordinated inventory system being used on about 75 percent of all grocery items. An enlarged symbol is shown in Figure 5-6. The first five numbers designate the manufacturer, and the second five the specific product; the linear bar corresponds to the numbers. It can be smaller than 1.5 square inches and still have space to generate 1 trillion machine-readable numbers. At the checkout counter, an electronic scanner translates the UPC bar information to the store's minicomputer. It flashes back the price to the cash register, which simultaneously prints the type of product and the price on the customer's cash register tape, and records the purchase on a perpetual stock control and reorder system.

All seems fine on the surface, but consumers have raised many arguments to "keep the prices *on* the products," and price disclosure laws have been passed. One of the strongest consumer points is how difficult it is to remember prices of products while walking around the store, thus making it hard to compare, say, frozen and canned peas.

Most stores have relented in view of all the

arguments (and pending legislation in some areas), and now continue to individually price products even when they use electronic scanners to read the UPC codes. Tests reported in supermarket trade publications have shown that it would cost about $155,000 to outfit an average supermarket doing $100,000 a week in business. The system would produce savings of $60,000 per store, and pay for itself in 2½ years. The savings would primarily come from improved inventory control, faster and more accurate checkouts, and reduced labor costs. Consumer groups have calculated that it would only cost $225 a week to continue putting prices on items and keep customers happy. Legislatures of several states have agreed and have passed *price disclosure laws,* which require that most items in grocery stores be individually marked with the price.

Grades for Foods Provide for Comparisons

No U.S. food products are graded on the basis of nutritional value. Rather, they are graded on appearance and flavor. The grades vary from product to product. The U.S. Department of Agriculture establishes the grades for many food products, and their use is voluntary.

Most inspected meats are stamped with a quality grade. The common beef grades include "U.S. Choice," "U.S. Good," and "U.S. Standard." "U.S. Prime" beef, the highest-quality grade, is usually available only in restaurants. They buy up the supply immediately because it has the highest fat content and is the tenderest. The common grades for veal, lamb, and mutton are "U.S. Choice," "U.S. Good," and "U.S. Commercial." Lesser-quality grades are usually taken by food processors who use meats as part of another product, such as in beef and noodle soup. Pork is normally not graded because all cuts are considered tender.

The Wholesome Poultry Act introduced grades for all kinds of poultry, including ducks, geese, and guinea hens. Consumers can usually only buy "USDA Grade A," as the lesser grades are not often sold in super-

FIGURE 5-6   Universal product code

markets. Lesser grades have a poor appearance that does not sell well, and, therefore, such products are used in processed foods.

Both fresh and processed fruits and vegetables (approximately seventy different products) are graded, with different standards for each. The common grades are "U.S. Fancy," "U.S. No. 1," and "U.S. No. 2."

Some cheese products are graded on a voluntary basis. Of the more than 400 types of processed cheeses, cottage cheese may be labeled "Quality Approved," but this pertains to inspection only, not to quality. Only American cheddar is quality graded. The prefix "U.S." must appear on the label if the cheese has been federally graded. Both words and points on a "100 scale" are used for cheddar: "Extra Fancy" (95 and above), "Fancy" (92 to 94), "No. 1" (89 to 91), "No. 2" (86 to 88), "No. 3" (83 to 85), and "Culls" (below 83). Either the word or the number alone can indicate the quality. Another point system is used to voluntarily grade butter. It uses the letters AA, A, or B. However, unless the prefix "U.S." appears on the label, too, the standard is not the federal one.

Eggs are both graded and sized. Grades are AA, A, and B. AA or A eggs have a firm, upstanding yolk and a large amount of firm white—good for poaching or for those who want the yolk to "look good." Grade B eggs have thinner whites and flatter yolks, and are suitable for scrambling and for those who like less yellow and more white. Egg sizes include "jumbo" (one dozen weighing not less than 30 ounces), "extra large" (at least 27 ounces), "large" (at least 24 ounces), "medium" (at least 21 ounces), and "small" or "pullet" (at least 18 ounces). Grade B eggs in the medium or large size are often your best buy.

Standards of Identity Provide Consistency

Today, foods that contain more than one ingredient must either list the ingredients on the label in order of predominance *or* meet a preset specified *standard of identity*. Hundreds of foods, particularly frozen and canned products, must have minimum percentages of content ingredients under regulations issued by the Food and Drug Administration. They are then given a specified "correct name" by which they must be sold. These products do not have to list ingredients on the label because they meet the FDA's preset standards, although a few companies voluntarily list ingredients anyway.

When foods have a standard of identity, consumers can be sure that they are getting a product that meets minimum standards for consistency. The standards are intended to protect consumers from being cheated by inferior products or confused by misleading labels. For example, margarine must contain at least 80 percent fat, which is the same requirement as for butter. Ice cream must have a minimum of 10 percent milk fat and 20 percent milk solids, in contrast to ice milk, which must have a minimum of only 2 percent milk fat and 11 percent milk solids. American cheddar cheese must have at least 50 percent milk fat. Breaded shrimp must have 50 percent shrimp, and *lightly* breaded shrimp must contain at least 65 percent shrimp. The standards are minimums. Manufacturers and processors are, of course, allowed to exceed the minimums to retain the individuality (perhaps the flavor) of their products. About 365 products have standards of identity registered with the FDA; therefore, when you compare two items with the same food names and no list of ingredients, you must assume you are comparing essentially the same product, since both must have met the same standard of identity. Copies of the standards for various foods can be obtained free of charge from the Food and Drug Administration.

HOW TO WASTE MONEY BUYING IN FOOD STORES

Table 5-9 shows many ways in which consumers waste money buying in food stores. If you are willing to pay $5 or more extra each week for your groceries without getting increased value, do as many of these things as possible!

TABLE 5-9

How to Waste Money in the Supermarket

Buy nonfood products at the grocery store	Close to one-fourth of the supermarket dollar is spent on nonfood items. Yet the supermarkets often charge 20 percent more for such products than the discount stores.
Do not recognize the psychology of the store layout	Because of the way certain food products are arranged, consumers tend to spend and buy more than they intended to: "Fresh produce looks very tasty"; "While I'm here I might as well buy that sponge mop I've been needing"; "Since the aisle-end display is so large, the prices must be lower"; "Why not buy a few of these things that I need while I'm waiting in the checkout line."
Buy on impulse	Buying on impulse because you "see it and need it" can raise your grocery bill at least 10 percent; straying from your shopping list is

TABLE 5-9 (Continued)

	almost always impulse buying. Research shows that 40 percent of food purchases are on impulse!
Buy lots of convenience foods	About two-thirds of the products ready to eat or partly prepared will cost you more—these foods often cost from 40 to 80 percent more than cooking from scratch. A turkey that you prepare could cost 36 cents per serving, compared with frozen turkey slices at 79 cents per serving. The "newest" convenience foods being sold are almost always higher in cost.
Buy in extra large quantities	Some boxes are too large for your shelves and are not economy size for you. Or there may be too much in the container for you to use, so you wind up throwing it away or letting it spoil.
Buy a freezer	Economy is not a reason to buy a freezer and load it with food; in fact, it is quite expensive. A Cornell University study estimates "that it costs at least 20 cents a pound to home-freeze and store food in a 15-cubic foot freezer for one year, even if you have an energy-efficient freezer filled to capacity. Higher electric rates, poorly operating freezers and inefficient use of freezer space and materials can drive the *additional* cost to as high as 53 cents a pound."
Buy at trading-stamp stores	Someone must pay for the cost of trading stamps, and that someone is you. The stamps cost the store money, so prices must go up ever so slightly—unless, of course, sales increase from the trading stamp promotion enough to offset the cost *and* the savings are passed on to the consumer in the form of lower prices. If you do not save stamps, yet you shop where stamps are given away, you are probably losing money. If you do save them, you probably lose only a little money, although you must invest the time to lick and stick.
Buy at stores that offer numerous extra services	A supermarket that has carry-out service, a bakery department, a large produce department, and other services has to pay for them. If you do not use them but shop there anyhow, you are paying more than you should.
Always buy name-brand foods	Name-brand foods (Green Giant vegetables, for example) often cost from 10 to 25 percent more than store-brand foods. Often the food processor simply changes labels on the assembly line when filling a large order for a supermarket chain, which then sells the food under the store-brand label; the product is often exactly the same.
Do not bother comparing prices or products	The average consumer can spend an extra 50 percent by buying small packages of cereal rather than one reasonably larger size. And how different can tomato soup be just because one container sells for 15 cents while another sells for 19 cents?
Buy lots of tasty "nonfoods"	Popular products such as Cracker Jacks and other heavily advertised products often provide empty calories for high prices. Prepackaged dry mashed potatoes cost about 50 percent more than fresh potatoes, yet provide only about one-half the vitamin C. TV dinners not only are expensive but provide little nutrition compared with most prepared meals. Lipton's chicken-and-noodle packaged soup actually contains only 2 percent chicken, and more salt than chicken.
Join a food-freezer plan	Almost without exception, people buying food and a freezer under a sales contract are dismally unhappy. Frequent complaints include poor-quality meats, substituted frozen vegetables of less quality, inconsistent delivery of products, and an overall increase in food expenditures. The contract is usually impossible to get out of.
Do not watch the cashier	Those modern cash registers that tell you how much change you get are still being operated by human beings pushing little buttons. It is estimated that cashiers in food stores make an average of one error for every $10 or more in groceries purchased!

HOW TO SAVE MONEY BUYING FOOD

You can begin to save money in the supermarket by not wasting money in the ways listed in Table 5-9. Responsible consumers can continue to save by becoming familiar with and practicing some of the many tips listed in Table 5-10.

DECEPTIONS, FRAUDS, AND OTHER PROBLEMS

Even the informed food buyer has problems in the world of food shopping. There are four areas in which consumers need to become more knowledgeable (and in the process perhaps even help eliminate some undesirable aspects of the marketplace): (1) packaging and labeling, (2) additives, chemicals, and other poisons, (3) some realities in the selling of food, and (4) government problems. Let us look at these more closely.

Packaging and Labeling

Deceptions in packaging and labeling are common. One cause is the government's standards of identity program. Remember, the ingredients of about 365 common foods do not have to be listed on the label. Thus, buy some chicken chow mein and see how much chicken is really there: 4 percent. Chili con carne must contain at least 40 percent meat, while chili con carne with beans must have 25 percent. How many shoppers are going to know the difference, let alone be able to compare values?

Who is likely to know the following kinds of food information? Hamburger or ground beef is not supposed to have more than 30 percent fat. Chicken noodle soup must contain at least

TABLE 5-10

Saving Dollars when Food Shopping

Maintain a file of inexpensive recipes	Recipe books are available by the hundreds, and many are aimed at providing low-cost, nutritionally sound menus. Many inexpensive recipes are also printed in daily newspapers and magazines. Cut them out and keep a file.
Use advertisements to help in planning your shopping	Newspaper advertisements, usually on Thursdays, for all major supermarkets contain the best prices for comparison. Buying the specials that actually are at lower prices can save many dollars. Cutting out and using "cents-off" coupons on items you need can save a dollar or two a week in some communities.
Plan your meals around advertised specials whenever possible	Knowing when certain advertised cuts of meat are being sold at unusually low prices simplifies the most expensive part of most meals. Vegetables and other products on sale can be checked in the advertisements, too. Planning your meals around such good buys can reduce your expenditures considerably.
Make a shopping list	Buying items that are on your shopping list will reduce impulse buying. Sticking to that list will get you in and out of the supermarket at the lowest cost possible and in the shortest time. Remember, the longer you stay in a store, the more you spend.
Shop on weekends	Price surveys consistently show that the best food buys are available on Thursdays, Fridays, and Saturdays. By shopping early in the morning you can avoid the crowds and still take advantage of the lower prices.
Buy at more than one store	Competing stores advertise their best prices on the same days, so take advantage of it. Driving a few blocks or a mile for specially advertised items can often save you many dollars. And keep your eye on the "first-of-the-week" sale items for quick one-stop shopping for these food products. Shopping at "farmer's markets," if available, can save 40 to 50 percent on some foods.

TABLE 5-10   (Continued)

Shop alone	Shopping with a spouse or with children will invariably cost you more. Men are notoriously generous in choosing "this and that" when shopping with their wives; children always want that special item that is strategically placed on shelves at their eye level, not yours.
Shop on a full stomach	A hungry shopper almost always buys more, so buy after you have eaten.
Buy specially priced items	If advertised or unadvertised specials are available—and you know your prices—take advantage of them and stock up if you can use the products. That may mean going off your shopping list, but do so when the savings are evident and the need is there. About ¾ of all shoppers stock up on bargains.
Avoid fads	Heavily advertised items on television and radio usually cost more, particularly when the product is new.
Use unit pricing	Many large supermarkets now have some type of unit pricing (price per ounce, price per pound, etc.) on the shelves along with the food products. You can save 20 to 30 percent by taking an extra few seconds to glance at similar products and see what the unit prices are—and don't assume that the larger package is the better buy. Forty percent of all shoppers use unit pricing.
Trade down	Less expensive cuts of meat, leaner meats, lower grades of eggs, medium-sized fruits and vegetables, and day-old bread are examples of trading down. Try to buy products that fit your needs but are not the most expensive. The largest part of your food dollar goes for meat, so savings are most impressive there.
Buy substitutes	Standard foods are always less expensive than higher-cost versions: regular breads instead of rolls or special breads, ordinary breakfast cereal instead of sugar-added, plain cheeses, standard rice, regular noodles, etc. You can add extra ingredients if you want at a much lower cost. Also, check different forms of food—fresh, canned, dehydrated, frozen—to see which is the best buy.
Buy seasonally	All types of foods vary in price depending upon the time of harvest and the laws of supply and demand. Listening to radio or TV reports and reading newspaper columns can tell you when products are in season and at good prices. Out-of-season products always cost more.
Buy lower-priced brands	You might like chain-store and the less advertised brands, which are similar in quality to well-known brand name products, yet cost less. About three-fourths of all shoppers purchase some store or lower-priced brands.
Buy "no-name" brands	Some canned or packaged foods have simple labels, like "peas," that just list the contents. Stores that offer "no frills" grocery labeling price the item at 10 to 40 percent less than name brands or store brands. There is no advertising, but the food varies in quality.
Buy in quantity	When a staple item is available at a very low price, buy more of it if you can use it up without wasting it or letting it spoil. Similarly, have the produce or meat personnel cut open a package for you and give you only part of it if the quantity is too much.
Consider a buying club	A neighborhood group could form a co-op and save by buying in quantity directly from wholesalers and farmers. A club could check ads for specials and send members to the different stores to buy for the group. Also, consider joining a large food cooperative if one is available.
Read the labels	More than 80 percent of our food products are prepackaged and therefore have labels, so use the information. Only 46 percent of shoppers check the ingredients of products and 33 percent use nutritional labeling. The typical shopper pushes the cart, selects thirty-two items from about fifty locations in the store in about 15 minutes; this averages to making one purchase decision every 28 seconds. And most do not read labels.

TABLE 5-10 (Continued)

	Taking time to do so will save you money, let you buy products you really want instead of what you thought you were buying, and buy more nutritious foods.
Buy products to fit your needs	Purchasing beautiful cuts of meat and fresh produce for a casserole is unnecessary when canned products can save you money. For example, use tomato puree instead of expensive spaghetti sauces, or dry milk with whole milk.
Demand out-of-stock or "oversold" receipts	Often advertised specials are sold out before you get to the store; simply ask the cashier or manager for an "oversold" receipt for such products. Then when they become available you can buy them at the same low prices.
Return poor-quality products	Occasionally when you open a can or a package, you find that the product is obviously of inferior quality. Return it for a cash refund or an exchange. Even if you have cooked the food before you find it is bad, be responsible enough to return it and save the money you would have lost.
Prepare food at home	Starting a meal from scratch may seem like a chore, but with many foods, it is not that difficult. Anybody can mash potatoes. Given the extra time, you can save dollars by preparing more foods at home.
Make shopping a skill, learn, and have fun	Spending $50 in 25 minutes on a shopping trip is commonplace, but if you take a little more time and shop more carefully, you can save $5 on the same groceries. Let's assume it takes you 15 minutes longer—then that $5 is equivalent to $20 per hour savings. Only 18 percent of the people in one study were classified as careful shoppers—reading labels for information on food additives, preservatives, and nutritional value, as well as comparing prices. Learn a little more about how to save at the supermarket. Outwit the heavy advertising, the psychology of the store layout, and the deceptive packaging. Make food shopping a challenge and have fun!

2 percent poultry meat, that is, except for dry chicken noodle soup. In the latter case, if the manufacturer had to list the ingredients in order of weight, the label would read "salt, noodles, other additives, and poultry." Products labeled "beef with gravy" must contain at least 50 percent cooked beef, while "gravy with beef" must have 35 percent. "Meat tacos" must have at least 15 percent meat while "meat taco filling" must have 40 percent (sounds reversed, doesn't it?). And how about the popular frankfurter and similar cooked sausage? It may contain *only* skeletal meat, no more than 30 percent fat, 10 percent *added* water, and 2 percent corn syrup, and no more than 15 percent of it can be from poultry meat (didn't you think those were supposed to be beef frankfurters?).

Proposed regulations, not yet implemented, would require that this kind of information be on *all* labels. Also, another FDA proposal would require listing the *percentages* of ingredients on the label. This is called *ingredient labeling*. It has been required on dog foods for more than a decade, but not on human foods.

Package sizes are often deceptive, too. Sixteen different sizes of cereal may or may not seem like too many, but it is almost impossible to tell the difference between two boxes that look exactly the same in height and width— while one is actually thinner than the other. This is legal. Quart-size soft-drink bottles offer another challenge. To be labeled as a quart, any product must have 32 ounces. But one bottle may be shaped to make it *appear* taller. Many consumers buy a soft drink in the apparent "quart size," only to find that it holds only 28 ounces. Choosing the deceptively shaped bottle at the same price as a competing product in a quart bottle represents a 14.2 percent overcharge! It's no wonder that leading consumer advocate Bess Myerson reports that "even experienced shoppers fail to select the best buys as much as 40 percent of the time. The multiplicity of weights, package shapes and sizes present the consumer with an arduous task of comparison shopping. Standardization of sizes would eliminate this unnecessary problem."

Other common deceptive packaging problems include *short-weighting* and *slack-filling*. For example, short-weighting of meat (giving less weight than the label indicates) occurs in even the largest chain stores. A prepackaged steak might have its weight printed as 14 ounces yet contain only 13½ ounces. Unfortunately, only a few stores have scales in the meat department so that consumers can check the weights. And this is not a small problem. Research studies across the country consistently show that short-weighting of meats (apparently unintentional) occurs between 10 and 20 percent of the time. Two ounces, 1 ounce, or even ¼ ounce may not seem like much loss. But it means millions of dollars in extra profits for the businesses involved. By the way, the meat department is the most profitable in the supermarket.

Slack-filling (leaving empty space in a container) is similar. In other words, how full is the box? Of two boxes of rice, one may be obviously larger, but with slack-filling, the larger box might actually have less in it.

Canned and frozen foods present special labeling problems. The *net weight* (that shown on the label as required by law) is often inflated by the addition of liquids, most commonly water. Cans of fruit are usually filled to the top with water or syrup that raises the net weight. Some canners are voluntarily including the weight of solids on the labels, too. Many experts feel, however, that a better measure to print on such products would be the *drained weight*. The drained weight is that after the liquid is drained, whereas the *solid weight* is that before the liquid is added. The most comparable weight for consumers is the drained weight.

The authority given by the Fair Packaging and Labeling Act (FPLA) simply has not been used to make labels really informative for consumers. Placing the net contents on the front panel in readable-size print, as required by the law, does not solve the problem of the proliferation of package sizes. The buyer is still faced with olive jars, for example, containing 14 ounces, 14¼ ounces, 15¼ ounces, 15¾ ounces, and 16 ounces. Which is the best buy if the olives are priced at 29 cents, 28 cents, 30 cents, 30 cents, and 31 cents, respectively?

Federal grade labels, as presented earlier in this chapter, are almost a joke. Who can remember what the "best" grade for fruits is? Or eggs? Or beef? More than half the time the grades are *not* put on the final food products anyhow, because it is voluntary, so the limited benefits are actually for the processors and buyer-supermarkets. Examine the absurdity of the situation in beef. Less than half of all federally inspected beef is graded. Of this, about 5 percent is graded prime, 78 percent graded choice, 13 percent graded good, and the remaining 4 percent is graded standard and utility. Isn't the choice category just a little on the big side? The range of quality in the 78 percent is wide. Thus, you have to develop expertise in recognizing the degree of marbling in beef in order to pick the kind of meat you want—assuming, of course, that your supermarket grade labels the meats according to the government standards. The trend among the big chains is to have their own grading system or none at all, regardless of whether or not the beef was previously graded by the USDA.

Consumer advocates have for years been promoting a simpler system for grading *all* foods. Just use a scale of "A-B-C-D" or "1-2-3-4," and people (the consumers) would understand that "A" and "1" were the highest. And just as important, consumer groups want the systems to be *mandatory* instead of voluntary. This is a question of freedom of information so that one can choose intelligently.

Solutions to packaging and labeling problems are not easy. The U.S. Department of

Agriculture is responsible only for the labeling of meats and poultry products. The Food and Drug Administration supervises labeling of other food items. And the Federal Trade Commission is responsible for claims made about foods in advertising, not the USDA or the FDA. A complicated situation for sure.

Additives, Chemicals, and Other Poisons

The food supply in the United States is generally considered plentiful, economical, convenient, good-tasting, nutritious, and safe. Some people, however, disagree. Let us take a look into the world of additives, chemicals, and poisons.

Legal Limits of Filth. Our food is not as clean and wholesome as most people believe. After 60 years of secrecy, the FDA was forced by the courts to make public what are known as food *filth allowances.* Technically, the FDA prohibits any food from being sold to humans that contains any filth, or putrid or decomposed substances. In reality this is impossible. So the food industry is given "filth allowances" for various food products.

Some examples of "filth" include legally permitted amounts of insect fragments, rat hairs, bacteria, insect larvae, rodent excreta, worms, decomposed matter, and sticks and stones. The maximum filth allowance for chocolate is "150 insect fragments and four rat hairs per half pound." Canned and frozen blackberries and raspberries are allowed "an average of 10 insects and insect larvae per pound." Peanut butter filth allowances permit an "average of 225 insect fragments or nine rodent hairs per pound."

Hundreds of food products have filth allowances. If some food is found to have an excessive amount of filth, that food is normally seized and destroyed. *Recalls* are another method of removing foods exceeding the legal limits of filth. Recall announcements are made through the news media, alerting the public after such products have been sold. When a food product is recalled, often millions of consumers return products to stores for re-

funds or exchanges, but then again most consumers never hear about such recalls. To find out exactly what the legal limits of filth are, consumers need only write the Food and Drug Administration.

Additives in Our Foods. An *additive* is defined as "a substance or mixture of substances other than a basic foodstuff, which is present in a food as a result of any aspect of production, processing, storage or packaging." This lay definition, from the National Academy of Sciences, is based upon the complex legal definition in the 1958 law. Additives are classified as (1) intentional and (2) incidental. *Intentional additives* are put into foods on purpose. They may be there to preserve quality, add to flavor, or improve the nutritive value. The most common additives are flavorings (about 80 percent of the total); nutritional additives are second. *Incidental additives* are there by accident. The contaminants involved, says the FDA, are usually "hairs, feathers, excreta, urine, or other filth from birds, rodents, or sometimes domestic animals; insects and their fragments, excreta, eggs, and other filth; various molds; decomposition or rot of the food; and dirt, sand, rocks, nonfood plant parts, and other extraneous matter." Legal limits of filth are incidental additives, as are pesticide residues.

There are more than 3000 additives, including those on the GRAS list, in today's foods. Some additives have been used for hundreds of years, such as salt, vinegar, and sugar. Most are flavoring agents, but others include vitamins and minerals. Preservatives are used to extend the usable life of many foods; they help prevent spoilage. Colors are often used not to disguise inferior products but to make foods more acceptable to consumers—such as orange coloring of oranges and yellow coloring for margarine. Additives are also used to provide consistency in many foods, such as mayonnaise and beer. Additives are found in almost all our foods because of the pesticides and chemical fertilizers used to protect crops and give us the larger yields our nation needs.

NEWS ITEM: Mercury pollution in 273 lakes, rivers

Totaling it all up, each consumer eats more than 5 pounds of additives each year.

Ronald M. Deutsch, a specialist in medicine and public health, developed a hypothetical label. See if you can guess what this label means: "acetone, methyl acetate, furan, diacetyl, butanol, methyl-furan, isoprene, methylbutanol, caffeine, essential oils, methanol, acetaldehyde, methyl fermate, ethanol, dimethyl sulfide and prepional-dehyde." It is coffee! Pure, natural coffee with no chemicals added.

Even a list of natural ingredients can be unintelligible to consumers, and thus, labeling is even more important when additives are involved. The FDA allows such terms as "artificial flavor" and "thickening agent" instead of requiring that each ingredient be specified clearly. People with allergies, however, are particularly concerned about this sort of labeling, as they cannot tell what those additives are.

The problems with food additives are multifaceted, and there are many *trade-off* questions involved. For example, should an additive like the sweetener cyclamate be permitted in foods to help those who wish to reduce their weight and those who have diabetes even though research has clearly shown it to be carcinogenic? There are benefits as well as risks involved. Concerns center around questions like: Can the additive cause cancer? How toxic is it? Can it produce mutations affecting the genes, hereditary characteristics, and so on? Does it cause birth defects? Does it affect those with allergies? And what are the effects of combining various additives with others, and with specific foods? Are the nation's consumers being poisoned? Are we a country of 220 million human guinea pigs? Or are additives safely preserving foods and preventing spoilage? The answers are not entirely clear.

Some Realities in the Selling of Food

As already seen, the selling of food is a complex process with many opportunities for consumers to make poor judgments. Some aspects of advertising and packaging and outright frauds further complicate matters.

Nutritional Advertising. Because of the voluntary nutritional guidelines for labeling food products, more dollars now go toward what might be loosely termed "nutritional advertising." However, most of the money spent on food advertising promotes products of little or no nutritional value. Such items include "beer, ale, soft drinks, coffee, candy and peanuts, chewing gum, desserts and pie fillings, spices and seasonings, potato chips, pretzels and snacks." according to James S. Turner in his book *The Chemical Feast*. He further notes that 40 percent of all food advertising in a recent year was spent on such "nonfoods." Instant Breakfast, for example, was widely promoted as providing "all the minerals of two slices of bacon." It does, but bacon is a very poor source of minerals. We eat it mostly because of its flavor.

Perhaps such heavy advertising of similar *nutritional half-truths* (not quite "lies," since the ads just don't give the complete picture) is why children believe what they do. Charles K. Atkins of Michigan State University reported during Federal Trade Commission hearings on his studies with children. One distressing finding was that "many fourth and fifth graders think that a bacon-and-egg breakfast offers the most strength and energy-building qualities." Hopeful signs in the research were that kids enjoyed the more "rational" TV ads and could recall the vitamins and other nutritional ingredients in many products. Atkins urged the FTC to set up guidelines for child-oriented advertising, especially since children over eight are able to learn and understand information about nutrition.

What we have is lots of advertising of foods that are heavily sugar-coated and a general avoidance of nutritional advertising. Partly as a result, Americans consume more than 125 pounds of sugar each year. This, of course, cuts down on the amount of more nutritious foods eaten. According to Dr. Michael Jacobson of the Health Research Group, sugar now "supplies about 19 percent of the average American's caloric intake." This food is unique in that it offers calories but no other nutritional benefit whatsoever. The detrimental effects of too much sugar are well known, especially its role in tooth decay. New re-

search is pointing toward sugar as one of the causes of hypoglycemia, heart disease, and diabetes.

Filling a shopping cart with nutritional gems from the modern grocery store is not the easiest task in the world. Convenience and processed foods make up more than 50 percent of the products and have blurred the four basic food groups. However, you can use the labels to identify products with large amounts of sugar. This will help you shop more effectively.

Pricing and Packaging. Despite the Fair Packaging and Labeling Act, more than one-half of all foods are sold in nonstandard sizes. Often, containers of competing products that actually hold the same amount have different shapes. "It looks bigger, so it must hold more" is a frequent consumer reaction, although the net contents is shown on the front label. But, even with the net contents shown, things can be quite confusing. And 1-ounce, ½-ounce, or even 1¼-ounce differences among products are not only confusing to the consumer, they can be a way to increase profits. (For example, ½ ounce less tomato soup, sold at the same price as a competitor's, times a million cans sold *does* improve a company's profit picture.)

Other promotions include coupons, prizes, toys, free premiums, "cents-off" sales, and multiple pricing (3 for 99¢, for example). These devices may or may not increase sales, but they often confuse consumers. The bill for packaging in a recent year amounted to $50 billion. For that price, one would think we could be getting better packaging and more helpful labeling.

An example of pricing and packaging deception involves the fortified-with-vitamins breakfast cereals. According to Michael G. Jacobson of the Health Research Group, two cereals which are virtually the same except for fortification are Wheaties and Total. The latter is fortified with nine vitamins and one mineral but, in the 12-ounce container, it costs about 18¢ more than Wheaties. This is in spite of the fact that it costs less than a penny to add the vitamins. Some people would call that a huge overcharge.

Favorite Food Frauds. Probably the most popular food frauds are the *food-freezer plans* and the *bait-and-switch* tactics of meat-processing firms. The food-freezer "bargain" occurs when the salesperson persuades the consumer that the company will keep the freezer filled with high-quality foods at guaranteed low prices. Once the contract is signed, the freezer is delivered and the food starts coming. Generally the person has bought a freezer, too! And the quality of the foods often is nowhere near what the salesperson said it was going to be. The long-term contract obligates the customer and the fine print protects the company against irate consumers who soon discover that they have been had. Information about food-freezer plans can be obtained from your local better business bureau, state office of consumer affairs, or the trade association called the Frozen Food Council (Box 5764, Amarillo, Tex. 79107).

The bait-and-switch advertisements for meat promote low-priced beef. The Federal Trade Commission estimates that there are 7500 ethical meat producers in the United States, and another 350 bait-and-switch outlets. Entering customers are shown the advertised meat, which they can see is obviously of low quality, and then are encouraged to buy higher-quality meat. If one does not have the cash, credit sales on an installment basis are encouraged.

The result in such cases is a misrepresented product. The FTC notes: "In one case, an employee of a bait-and-switch operator testified that he had been encouraged to sell the same carcass of beef ten times in one day to ten different buyers. Each of them got meat but not the carcass he selected." This situation can easily occur, since customers are not allowed to watch over the cutting and packaging of meat they select. Baiting customers to bring them into the premises is all too frequent a practice in many businesses. Meat retailers

are the most obvious of such merchants to avoid.

Government Problems

If the food we eat is not as wholesome, nutritious, or safe as most Americans believe, what are the causes? One is that too many companies seem to want to make a little extra profit at the expense of the consumer. But government also deserves its share of the blame. Federal, state, and local governments have a lot of trouble enforcing laws and regulations already on the books and an even harder time passing more effective ones.

Inspection Problems. The Food and Drug Administration spends about $40 million annually trying to enforce legislation concerning food inspection. Those relatively few dollars go to regulate a $250 *billion* industry. Because of its financial limitations, the FDA spot-checks the nation's 60,000 food processing plants on the average of only once every 6 years!

The U.S. Department of Agriculture (USDA) faces similar problems. They have approximately 9000 inspectors across the nation who are supposed to be on hand continually in meat-processing plants checking on wholesomeness. In addition, each plant is visited about twice a month by a USDA supervisor. A General Accounting Office study carefully checked 48 plants to see if they met USDA standards for sanitation and cleanliness. Only *four* plants were acceptable. One big problem is bribery of USDA officials. In the late 1970s, over 100 USDA officials, nationwide, were convicted of bribery and sentenced to jail; the plant managers were mostly just fined.

The wholesome meat and poultry laws have enormous loopholes. The meats are scanned for disease. Chemical residues are not looked for. No check is ever made for salmonella bacteria or any of 100 other possible bacteria. Yet noted consumer columnist Sidney Margolius cites salmonella poisoning as affecting at least 2 million people annually. What is often thought of as a bad stomach is frequently food poisoning. Also, contaminated and diseased meat, infected eyes of animals, and cancerous tumors continually find their way into our food supply. "4-D" animals (dead, dying, diseased, and disabled) are supposed to be destroyed, but they often wind up in other foods. Typical ways of getting rid of such meats are to put them in frankfurters or dog foods. About 10 percent of all meat is diseased before it is slaughtered, and by law any visible defects must be cut off the carcass. The remainder, whether diseased or not, *apparently* can be used just as if it were healthy.

Unlike most meats, fish and seafood products do not have to be federally inspected during any part of the journey from the sea to the supermarket. The Department of Commerce's Marine Fisheries Service provides a voluntary program in the processing plants located in this country, if the plants are willing to pay for the service. About 10 percent of the companies, therefore, are inspected, and most of these are in the tuna fish business. The inspected products carry the seal "U.S. Department of Commerce, Packed Under Federal Inspection." To illustrate the laxity of the U.S. requirements, note this: Canadian carp found unfit for home consumption is being shipped to the United States because Canada has stiffer health regulations than the United States for seafoods as well as fresh-water fish.

Conflicting legislative responsibilities and court decisions further complicate the consumer's world of food. Michigan once had a strong law on packaging and labeling of meats which was more stringent and protective than the federal laws. But the U.S. Supreme Court ruled against it even though the law "had the effect of reducing an ingredient requirement that may result in higher nutritional value for a meat-food product." In Illinois, the Department of Agriculture issued a ruling that prohibits local inspection of food plants if they are licensed by the state and inspected by federal officials. Realizing the problems with federal inspection, many local Illinois inspectors

wanted to check for quality and sanitation themselves. They were stopped. They were not even allowed to check the quality and sanitation of meats sold in restaurants.

Labeling Problems. Enforcing the Fair Packaging and Labeling Act is difficult because little staff time is allocated for that purpose. One study showed that two people on the FDA staff were assigned to enforce that law, five people in the FTC, and three people in the Office of Weights and Measures (in the National Bureau of Standards within the Commerce Department). Labels are tremendously successful in hiding ingredients. Percentages of ingredients need not be shown, and additives generally do not have to be named. And, of course, the hundreds of items with a standard of identity never have to list any ingredients at all.

Standards of identity conceal important information. How many people know that "orange juice" is 100 percent orange juice; "orange juice drink blend" has from 70 to 95 percent real orange juice; "orange juice drink" has from 35 to 70 percent orange juice; "orange drink" has from 10 to 35 percent orange juice; and "orange-flavored drink" contains less than 10 percent real orange juice? Very few. And now that you know, you will probably forget, since the names are so similar. Further, the standards change without most consumers even hearing about them.

Beef standards are an illustration of how consumers can get the short end of the stick without ever knowing it. Since beef graded and classified as "Prime" is in short supply and because more cattle were being grass-fed instead of grain-fed (the latter produces more *marbling,* or flecks and streaks of fat within the tissues), the USDA just decided to change all the standards. Not the familiar labels, just the standards. Grass-fed beef is much leaner than grain-fed and thus could not qualify even for the "Choice" grade. The standards were changed so that about 20 percent of the beef then graded as "Good" would become

"Choice." Consumers and those representing hotels, restaurants, and institutions wanted a new grade to be created called "Lean," which would be between "Good" and "Choice," but they did not prevail. Perhaps now you can stop wondering why "in the good old days" beef seemed to be more tender—it was!

In many food areas, labels with any degree of standardization that is really understandable are almost unheard of. States sometimes further complicate matters. For example, thirty-three states allow the use of words such as "fresh," "ranch," or "country fresh" with eggs. Some states permit such labels only on grade A or grade AA eggs. Others permit them only on products sold by the producer. With meats, the labels often do not show the fat content, nor must the *source* of the meat in meat products be stated, even though you may be eating esophagi, lips, snouts, ears, and skeletal muscle tissue.

Labeling laws also permit the use of confusing chemical names. (Remember our example of a coffee label.) When ingredients *are* listed, few consumers know what the terms mean. And when it comes to additives, few have been tested for safety beyond measuring for outright toxicity. Yet, at the same time, more additives are being approved for the GRAS list, based upon what some critics call faulty research. The procedures used for acceptance are very questionable, since the FDA relies almost entirely upon the manufacturer's research information. Rarely is any independent analysis of the additive requested before it is put on the GRAS list. Besides, the FDA does not have enough staff or money for such studies.

Costs and Benefits of Government Regulation

Addressing the question of costs and benefits is more complicated, as many factors are involved. Let us examine additives as an illustration. Basically, what we have is a benefit-risk equation. Realizing first that there is no such thing as absolute safety, we can begin by looking at benefits. If an additive preserves a certain food longer, more of that food can be produced and shipped to distant places, and with larger quantities the per unit costs drop. Similarly, when a chemical makes a product more nutritious, often at a very low price, the benefits to the consumer are obvious. Moreover, the benefit side of the equation is easy to define and work with.

The risk side is much harder, however. Scientific testing in 1958, for example, regarded fifty parts per million as safe. With improved technology, today we can find chemical residues below two parts per billion, and in some cases, a few parts per trillion. Hence, a chemical like DES, which added weight to cattle, was banned, and this resulted in slightly higher dollar costs for the meat products for consumers. Was the risk worth it?

The dollar costs must be considered, too. The total budget of the Food and Drug Administration costs each of us about $1 a year. After adding in the costs of government protection regarding chemicals and additives, like those of the Environmental Protection Agency and the U.S. Department of Agriculture, for example, the dollar cost still does not exceed $1.50.

Hidden dollar costs exist also in the form of government regulations aimed at preserving the wholesomeness and safety of food as well as its continuous supply. Milk-marketing orders, one of forty-seven controlled marketing programs of the federal government in the food business, inflate the cost of a half gallon of milk an estimated 5 cents. Price supports and import quotas make U.S. cheese prices among the highest in the world.

Another problem is the unknown. Does the use of a certain additive really *cause* more of a specific type of cancer? Or does a chemical *really* cause *mutagenesis* (abnormalities) or *teratogenesis* (birth defects)? In other words, is scientific testing good enough to answer these questions? Another unknown is the alternative cost involved. What is the cost of *not* using a certain chemical in a food product?

Thus, the cost/benefit of a single food additive, one government regulation, or even the whole range of regulatory activities by local, state, and federal governments has no easy answers. The issues are not strictly scientific or mathematical.

Scientists usually come down on the side of "more research." They want more data to "be certain." Advocates, on the other hand, sometimes speak with certainty even in the absence of hard data to back up their statements. As a consequence, the decisions concerning costs and benefits of government regulations are more and more being pushed into the arena of public policy. Issues now often become a question of who shall decide: Business? Government? Consumers?

POINTS OF VIEW AND PROBLEMS TO THINK ABOUT

Consumers can improve their knowledge of nutrition, plan more appetizing and nutritious meals, choose stores that provide food at reasonable prices, and shop more effectively. But only if they want to. Acting responsibly as consumers is the burden that goes along with the rights we enjoy.

Improved inspection and higher standards for the wholesomeness and safety of foods cannot come about without stronger demands from consumers, nor can the additional funds that are needed to study nutrition and additives. Answers to questions must be examined. What shall we do about "meat" products made from soybeans and wheat protein? How should we label imitation "processed meats" made from scraps? Should breakfast cereals have fluoride added to reduce tooth decay?

Some public policy questions need resolution, too. How do we improve the nutrition of lower-income groups? One medical researcher estimates that "pet foods constitute a significant part of the diet of at least 225,000 American households, affecting some one million persons." A more rapid transition to the metric system would make it much easier to compare values—since metric has the com-

mon and easy base of ten—but what will get us there faster? Ingredient labeling, open dating, and competition in the food industry are important issues, too.

Questions such as these must be raised and examined. Without additives, our food supply, in terms of crop production, probably would collapse. And many foods would no longer be available to consumers because they could not be preserved long enough to get them to the markets. But do we need thousands of additives, or should we go the way of Denmark and ban them unless they are absolutely necessary? Some additives are or may be dangerous, and a "temporary" extension to use questionable ones for another 8 or 10 years is certainly suspect.

We need the answers to many questions. But answers cost money. So, which questions are the most important? Finally, where do we get the money so we can search for the answers?

CHAPTER ACTIVITIES

Checkup on Consumer Terms and Concepts

Calories	Fair Packaging and
Nutrition	Labeling Act
Results of poor	Grades for foods
diets	Standards of identity
Basic food groups	Wasting money in
Nutritional fallacies	food buying
Supermarket dollar	Packaging and
Nonfood items	labeling deceptions
Food inflation costs	Legal limits of filth
Shared monopoly	Intentional additives
Profits in foods	Inspection problems
Cooperatives	Costs and benefits
Nonprice	
competition	

Review of Essentials
1. What are some key problems facing American consumers in the food marketplace?
2. Why are calories necessary to sustain life?

3. What is the quality of the American diet and why?

4. Do the poor pay more for food? Why or why not?

5. What factors should be considered in choosing a place to buy your groceries?

6. What is the cost to consumers of promotional devices in the supermarket?

7. What federal laws protect consumers against unsafe foods?

8. Summarize several ways in which consumers can save money when buying food.

9. Name some labeling deceptions and note reasons why these continue.

10. List some suggestions that might help all consumers buying food in today's marketplace.

Issues for Analysis

1. React to this press release: "The American Public Health Association charges that fresh meat bearing the seal 'U.S. Inspected for Wholesomeness' is not necessarily wholesome. The association is threatening to sue the Department of Agriculture if it doesn't require labels warning consumers that inspected meat can cause disease. At the crux of the dispute are microbiological contaminants, primarily salmonella, that are transmitted through meat and that cause food poisoning. The National Academy of Sciences estimates that salmonella alone sickens 2 million Americans a year. Most recover quickly, but infants and the elderly sometimes die."

2. Read this article taken from a newspaper, and answer the following questions. "Four major bread companies, already indicted on price-fixing charges, were sued Wednesday for $12,375,000 on behalf of 20 million residents of the New York metropolitan area. . . . The civil suit charges that the price-fixing conspiracy added five cents a loaf to bread prices in the metropolitan area during the period (five years), in which 750 million loaves of bread were sold at overcharges totaling $3,750,000." Is this a frequent occurrence? In which food industries do you suspect this might occur most often? What can be done to correct these kinds of situations?

3. What powers do you believe that the state, local, and federal governments should have to control the wholesomeness of our foods? Why?

6

Sundry and
Dangerous Products

THE PROBLEMS

Almost every consumer product has built-in hazards. Every year there are more than 20 million accidents related to common household consumer products. The results of these injuries were 30,000 killed, 720,000 seriously injured, and 110,000 disabled. These figures do not include millions of additional injuries associated with tobacco, firearms, aircraft, boats, motor vehicles, environmental poisons, drugs, cosmetics, and food products.

As a consequence, there has been a dramatic increase in product-liability lawsuits against manufacturers and other sellers. *Forbes* magazine reported that in 1960 there were fewer than 50,000 such lawsuits in the courts; in 1963 the number increased to 250,000; in 1970, to 500,000; and in 1980 it is estimated that more than 1½ million product-liability lawsuits will be in the courts each year. The *caveat emptor*, or buyer-beware, concept is being turned around to *caveat venditor*—let the seller beware. More liberal court decisions in recent years no longer require the consumer to ''prove negligence'' on the part of the manufacturer. Also, all products today have an implied warranty to the effect that they will perform as they are supposed to in addition to being safe.

All consumers face hazardous products every day. More than one-half million people were injured seriously enough on ''stairs, ramps, and landings'' last year to require hospital emergency room treatment, according to the U.S. Consumer Product Safety Commission. The rotary lawnmower is another example. It alone was directly related to more than 180,000 accidents in a recent year. And most power mower accidents are severe, resulting in brain damage, amputation, laceration, bone fracture, blindness, or death.

Other accidents and dangers occur frequently. Consider the daily newspaper stories across the country.

- "A Los Angeles man was riding his garden tractor up a 25-degree incline when it tipped over. The blade struck his head, and he died instantly. The tractor's lateral stability was found to be faulty."
- "A 13-year-old Phoenix girl picked up a bottle of soda to open and drink. It exploded. Glass chips resulted in her losing the sight of one eye."
- "Adverse reaction to a deodorant resulted in skin poisoning and 11 days hospitalization for a Lincoln, Nebraska, woman."
- "Little Rock, Arkansas, widow sues cigarette manufacturer because spouse dies of lung cancer."
- "Charleston, South Carolina, woman receives $271,000 judgment because use of a birth control pill caused blood clotting in her legs, resulting in a heart attack and near death."
- "Hopewell, Virginia, man sues former employer because of severe nerve damage resulting from working with a dangerous pesticide."
- "Lawn dart blinds 8-year-old Philadelphia boy while playing with friends."

What are these dangerous, everyday products? What is being done to keep truly dangerous products off the market? How are consumers being protected? And what can responsible consumers do to help themselves and others?

DRUGS

American consumers spent approximately $15 billion last year on prescription drugs not dispensed in hospitals. They spent more than $150 billion on nonprescription over-the-counter (OTC) drugs. These expenditures included billions of dollars for ineffective and dangerous drugs, many of which are also overpriced. The situation is made more difficult because drug-industry advertising and promotion practices actually *encourage* excessive use of drugs.

Prescription Drugs

Getting a "note" from a physician and taking it to a pharmacist is the prescription drug process. Also, it is called the *ethical* drug business. But is it the most efficient and effective process? Let's first consider the matter of prescription drugs.

The Cost of Prescription Drugs. According to the Consumer Price Index, drug prices have not been rising much at all. In fact, the increases have been slower than the overall cost of living. The average cost of a prescription is just over $5. But that is not the whole story.

U.S. citizens are often overcharged for their prescription drugs compared to foreign countries. The Monopoly Subcommittee of the Senate Small Business Committee determined the prices charged by the Eli Lilly company for propoxyphene, or Darvon, for example. For 100 tablets the U.S. druggist pays $7.02, in the United Kingdom it costs $1.92, and in Ireland the cost is $1.66. The Charles Pfizer Company charges $20.48 in the United States for oxytetracycline or Terramycin, but only $4.63 in Brazil and $3.68 in New Zealand. In another study of 12 of the 20 most commonly used drugs, the American prices were highest, sometimes four times higher than in the next most expensive country. Even though lower labor costs are cited as one reason for the lower drug prices, remember that 95 percent of all prescriptions are ready-made compounds.

Not surprisingly the drug manufacturing industry is profitable. In fact, it is the second most profitable industry in the United States. (The soft drink manufacturers come in first.)

On the retail level costs vary widely. Comparison shopping shows that prices for the same prescription can easily vary by 100 to 400 percent even in small communities. One study by the American Medical Association (AMA) revealed price differences as great as 1200 percent for some common prescriptions.

Advertising of prices of drugs is now legal in all states since the U.S. Supreme Court struck down a Virginia law which banned prescription drug advertisements. That ruling also affected the thirty-three other states with similar laws. The landmark case found that such a ban was unconstitutional and violated the First Amendment right of freedom of speech.

The ruling, based largely on the need of individual consumers and society to receive product and price information, said, "Advertising, however tasteless and excessive it sometimes may seem, is nonetheless dissemination of information as to who is producing and selling what product, for what reason, and at what price. So long as we preserve a predominantly free enterprise economy, the allocation of our resources in large measure will be made through numerous private economic decisions. It is a matter of public interest that those decisions, in the aggregate, be intelligent and well informed. To this end, the free flow of economic information is indispensable."

The Federal Trade Commission (FTC) estimated that the savings to consumers from the increased competition through advertising will amount to $134 million a year. The FTC has established guidelines for specific facts to be included in the ads: brand name, generic name, dosage strength, form in which sold, and price of a specific quantity, which must include all costs such as "professional fees" or "handling charges."

In larger communities the best place to buy prescription drugs is probably a discount store. Table 6-1 shows how stores compared in one large study. Don't just go by these generalizations, however. Checking advertised prices in your area or asking the price from pharmacists will probably reveal differences and result in considerable savings.

Interestingly, little antitrust action has been taken against pharmaceutical manufacturers for restraining trade. In one big case in 1973, five major drug companies paid back more than $4 million to consumers across the nation after *18* years of litigation on price fixing. Charles Pfizer, American Cyanamid, Bristol-Myers, Olin, and Upjohn were ordered to make refunds for overcharging by 300 percent for tetracycline. Consumers submitting claims will receive a rebate of 50 percent of the cost of drugs bought between 1954 and 1966. That is, of course, if they kept their receipts that long.

Promotion of Prescription Drugs. Approximately $1 out of every $5 in prescription drug sales goes toward advertising and sales promotion. Sales promotion policies are self-evident. Not only is there a drugstore on almost every corner, but approximately one-sixth of all advertising is for drug-related products. The leading drug companies spend up to 40 percent of their revenues on sales promotion. And this promotional process is very different from others—it is not directed at consumers! About two-thirds of the promotional dollars go toward *detailing* (direct contact between company sales representatives, called detail people, and the physicians and pharmacists), with the remaining one-third going for professional journal advertising and direct mailings.

Studies suggest that doctors get 75 to 80 percent of their drug knowledge from detail people and from ads in professional journals. Most of the doctor's knowledge about drugs, therefore, comes from companies which are promoting their own brand-name products. It costs nearly $8000 per private physician to provide detailing. The average physician writes prescriptions each year averaging $70,000, with about 90 percent being for brand-name drugs. Thus, the manufacturers

TABLE 6-1

Best Place to Buy Prescription Drugs

Discount store—suburb	0%
Discount store—downtown	+5%
Chain store—downtown	+13%
Chain store—suburb	+20%
Discount store—poor area	+34%
Independent—downtown	+37%
Chain store—poor area	+42%
Independent—suburb	+51%
Independent—poor area	+67%

try hard, apparently successfully, to sell the doctors on the virtues of their products.

It has been said that doctors prescribe too many drugs too often, prescribe costly drugs of questionable clinical value, prescribe drugs with serious side effects, and prescribe drugs about which they know very little. Former FDA Commissioner Alexander M. Schmidt said he has "a strong conviction that we have to upgrade postgraduate and continuing education in clinical therapeutics" because he is "appalled" at the ease with which physicians overprescribe or misprescribe drugs for their patients, which can have serious and sometimes fatal consequences.

Brand-name and Generic Drugs. This is an area of controversy for professionals, and of considerable money saving for consumers. There are over 22,000 different prescription drugs, and most are known by their brand names, although about a third of them have generic names. After a new drug patent expires, in 17 years, other manufacturers often produce "me too" drugs that duplicate the chemical ingredients. Prescriptions that specify the generic name instead of a manufacturer's brand name can save the consumer 40 to 60 percent or more. For example, Mylan Laboratories makes the brand-name drug Erythromycin. Other manufacturers use the same ingredients, but because they are not burdened with expensive research, development, and testing, they can sell the product for less. The consumer can buy 100 tablets of the brand-name Erythromycin for $31.74 or a generic product for only $11.40. Aureomycin, an antibiotic, might be prescribed and cost 25 cents per capsule. Should the doctor prescribe it as tetracycline, its generic name, the cost would be 8 cents per capsule. Colace can be bought for $6 for 60 capsules or the generic O.T. capsule at $3.98. Interestingly, both brands are made by Schere Company but bottled by different packagers.

Brand-name manufacturers have long claimed that, if there are two antibiotics containing the same amounts of active ingredients, but formulated into tablets by different manufacturers, one is bound to be better. However, many studies have found just the opposite, showing that there is no significant difference between generic and brand-name drugs.

Antisubstitution Laws. Twenty states have laws that prohibit a pharmacist from substituting a generic drug (which is usually much less expensive) for a brand-name drug. On the other hand, in six states a pharmacist who receives a prescription for a brand-name drug must substitute a generic drug. Other states allow the doctor to make the decision. The Council on Economic Priorities found that 53 percent of the ampicillin prescriptions surveyed were written generically, but 98 percent were sold by brand name. Thus many patients pay extra even though the prescriptions are written for a generic drug. (See Table 6-2.)

In the other states, the pharmacist can substitute a generic drug for a brand-name drug if neither the physician nor the consumer requests otherwise. The American Association of Retired Persons and the National Retired Teachers Association, with more than 10 million members, claim that the generic drugs are just as good as name brands and much cheaper. The Pharmaceutical Manufacturers Association, on the other side, says that there is no way to guarantee that the generic drugs are equivalent to the name brands. The Department of Health, Education and Welfare has announced that they plan to set price ceilings on prescription drugs that are produced by more than one company, and which are paid for by Medicare and Medicaid. This of course has given the generic proponents the start of a victory. The Federal Trade Commission may decide the question by issuing a trade regulation affecting all drugs in interstate commerce (meaning virtually all prescription drugs) after it completes its present study on drug substitution.

Ineffective Drugs. The effectiveness and/or safety of many vaccines are under serious

TABLE 6-2

Sample Prices of Brand Versus Generic Drugs*

Generic Name	Maker and Brand	% of Market	Brand Price	Lowest Generic Price
Penicillin VK	Lilly: V-Cillin-K	54%	$ 8.32	$1.85
Penicillin G	Squibb: Pentids	78	8.36	1.20
Oxytetracycline	Pfizer: Terramycin	99	18.43	1.90
Ampicillin†	Bristol: Polycillin	23	12.81	4.40
Erythromycin	Abbott: Erythrocin	60	13.81	5.70
Chloramphenicol	Parke-Davis: Chloromycetin	90	23.71	8.00‡

* Based on a 1975 study by the Council on Economic Priorities.

† Bristol manufactures 70% of total supply; remainder sold under various names.

‡ No generic; lowest brand price.

question, but they are still being used across the country. A General Accounting Office report notes that the Division of Biologic Standards (DBS) has permitted the marketing of 75 of the 263 biologic products it has licensed, despite claims of ineffectiveness—possibly on the theory that at least they do no harm. The nineteen vaccines licensed for disease prevention are all under question now. Dr. J. A. Morris, a research microbiologist for DBS, raised strong doubts about the safety and effectiveness of vaccines for mumps, measles, influenza, and German measles. (Dr. Morris was fired for "insubordination" after opposing the "swine flu" vaccine program; public interest attorney James Turner is helping Morris get his job back, particularly since all Dr. Morris' warnings were accurate.)

Smallpox vaccinations were stopped in 1972, following the recommendation of the Public Health Service. The last known natural case in the United States was reported in 1949. Yet in 1968, nine deaths were attributed to the vaccine itself. Similar questions about risks outweighing benefits are being asked about the Sabin oral polio vaccine. The Federal Center for Disease Control notes that the oral vaccine has become the leading cause of polio in this country. In 1973, for example, the year after

the last recorded outbreak of the natural disease in this country, 13 of the 14 recorded cases of paralytic polio were linked by federal health authorities to the oral vaccine.

Some critics believe that the popular flu vaccines are virtually worthless. However, Dr. Jonas Salk, who developed the 100 percent safe killed-virus vaccine for polio, believes that the United States' inconsistent approach to influenza vaccines is mostly at fault for not effectively protecting the public. Influenza, or flu, can be controlled, in Salk's opinion, when it becomes a national goal, and he suspects that one flu vaccine can be developed that would provide protection against all variants.

One very effective drug, not vaccine, for A-2 influenza syndromes (Asian, Hong Kong, London, Port Chalmers, and Victoria) has been amantadine. Well known for its effectiveness for shaking palsy or Parkinson's disease, it is not so well known or used against flu. It decreases the penetration of the viruses into body cells. Five separate studies in the 1960s showed its effectiveness, and it won FDA approval. And, as reported by Lawrence Galton, health expert, "the medical profession held back, apparently hesitant to accept the idea that any drug that was safe to use could be effective against viruses, especially tough flu viruses.'' While the United States medical profession either debates or ignores the drug, the Soviet Union recently purchased over 10 million doses from the United States maker. When amantadine has been administered in studies, it sharply reduces both the duration and severity of fever, headache, and respiratory symptoms within the first 48 hours. Dr. Ernest C. Herrmann, associate professor of microbiology at the University of Illinois School of Medicine, said that ''I feel certain that many of the 100,000 or so people who have died in flu epidemics since 1969 could have been saved if they'd been on amantadine.''

In 1962 Congress gave the Food and Drug Administration a mandate to remove ineffective as well as dangerous drugs from the interstate market. In 1967 the National Research Council of the prestigious National Academy of Sciences reported (as requested by the FDA) that 1700 brand-name drugs were ineffective. A more recent study of 16,573 drugs by the National Academy of Sciences showed that 14.7 percent were ineffective, 34.9 percent possibly effective, 7.3 percent probably effective, 19.1 percent effective, and 24.0 percent effective but with qualifications (usually meaning significant side effects). To date, about 6500 of those drugs have been removed from the market, and those were removed voluntarily by the companies, primarily because of low profits.

The FDA is trying harder to remove the more controversial but ineffective drugs from the market, yet they are having little success. Although several drugs were banned during the early 1970s, lobbyists, court action, and congressional pressure have limited any really significant progress to rid the market of these drugs. The FDA recently proposed that manufacturers be required to prove that each ingredient in a combination drug contributes to the product's effectiveness. Much evidence has accumulated to show that combining drugs does not increase effectiveness, and sometimes the drugs actually work against each other. It is reported that more than 100 members of Congress have been enlisted in a lobbying effort to stop the implementation of this FDA proposal.

Dangerous Drugs. Many dangerous drugs have been around for a long time, and most will probably remain. Adverse reactions to some drugs—penicillin, for example—occur simply because it is impossible to make a drug that does not have some side effects. Therefore, one can raise a fundamental question: When is a drug dangerous?

Thalidomide, a tranquilizer and sleep-inducing drug, was responsible for horrible birth deformities of more than 20,000 babies in twenty countries. In West Germany it was marketed from 1957 to 1961. In 1970 a West German court permitted an out-of-court settlement of $27 million to 400 plaintiffs by Chemie-Gruenenthal of Stolberg, a pharmaceutical company. The company admitted no guilt, but began financial assistance to children and parents. In 1975 a similar suit for more than $20 million was settled in England. In other countries, pharmaceutical companies that sold thalidomide are still in court. Fortunately, the drug was not marketed in the United States, although some travelers obtained and used it.

Dr. Frances Kelsey, an FDA official at that time, almost singlehandedly stopped the drug from being sold in the United States. Under great pressure from the American drug industry and many FDA officials, she still refused to license it because of conflicting data concerning birth defects. The shocking scandal of thousands of such defects finally came to the attention of the world. It is unfortunate to note that Dr. Kelsey was later transferred out of her position in the FDA. In 1972 two more doctors who were instrumental in restricting the sale of thalidomide and MER-29, also linked to birth defects, were transferred, too. The FDA director of the Bureau of Drugs told the doctors that the division ''was a major source of complaints from the drug industry.''

Miraculously, thalidomide has recently become the wonder cure for 12 million victims of leprosy throughout the world. The World Health Organization and the Hadassah-Hebrew University Medical Center in Israel joined efforts to treat 4552 patients in sixty-nine countries with thalidomide. In 99 percent of the cases, symptoms of the crippling disease showed improvement in 2 days, and total remission was achieved in 2 weeks.

Imipramine hydrochloride, or Tofranil, is widely used for the treatment of severe mental depression. In 1972 an Australian doctor, William McBride, reported evidence of malformed babies born to mothers who used the drug. The United States manufacturer branded the charges unsubstantiated. The FDA thereupon assigned *one* doctor to examine all available evidence, and later ruled that warnings about "inconclusive side effects" must accompany prescriptions. Court delays and FDA policy reversals have stopped that order.

Chloromycetin was introduced on the American market in 1949 as a broad-spectrum antibiotic. It is still widely sold. Yet as early as 1952 a serious side effect was noted—a correlation between the drug and the incidence of aplastic anemia. Also, persons taking Chloromycetin suffer some damage to the bone marrow. Senate hearings and other exposés have affected sales of the drug, but it continues to be prescribed, although usually now in lower dosages. The National Research Council advised the FDA that "Chloromycetin can no longer be consider the drug of choice for any illness except possibly typhoid fever [680 cases reported in the last big breakout in the U.S. in 1973]."

Although it is not banned yet, the use of estrogen, a drug containing female hormones and used to relieve menopause symptoms (hot flashes, irritability, and depression) has been linked in four separate studies with cancer of the uterine lining (endometrium), vascular disease, and strokes. In 1976 the FDA sent a special Drug Bulletin to some 650,000 doctors, pharmacists, and hospitals across the country indicating that it planned to require a warning on the labels of estrogen drugs sold to more than 6 million users. In the bulletin, the FDA took an unusual stand by naming the manufacturer of the estrogen drug Premarin, Ayerst Laboratories, and describing them as "irresponsible" for sending hundreds of thousands of doctors a letter which did not refer to the studies but instead had the effect of "clouding the issues and recommending 'business as usual.'"

A case that shows one major aspect of the dangerous drug problem in America is the handling of drugs containing female hormones called progestins. In 1973, the FDA removed its approval for their use in treating conditions related to pregnancy, such as threatened miscarriage. They were also prescribed for women with no menstrual flow or with abnormal bleeding from the uterus. Yet, in 1976 doctors wrote more than 500,000 prescriptions for this drug to be taken by pregnant women. Dr. Sidney Wolfe, head of Ralph Nader's Health Research Group, describes the situation as an outrage. "When the FDA removed its approval, it did it in such a quiet, nonscreaming, nonshock way that most doctors—even those who are reasonable and conscientious about their work—were unaware that it was done. Doctors get into prescribing habits—and unless they are jolted out of bad habits, they will stay with them."

A similar dilemma for pregnant women exists with some of the most popular tranquilizers used today. Valium, Librium, and the drug meprobamate (sold under such trademarks as Miltown and Equanil) have been associated with causing birth defects (such as cleft lips) if taken by women during the first three months of pregnancy. Although the findings were not conclusive, the FDA ordered the drug manufacturers to write new label warnings advising *physicians* of the possible hazard.

Another drug highlights the difficulties faced by the Food and Drug Administration. The drug is Syntex Laboratories' Naprosyn (naproxen), designed to help those with rheumatoid arthritis, of which there are more than 100 types. It was approved in March of 1976. Physicians in the United States wrote 3000 prescriptions in March, 63,000 in April, and 98,000 in May before the FDA announced that it might remove the drug from the market. The reason for the action was that the FDA doubted the integrity and reliability of animal testing that supposedly had demonstrated the safety of the drug. The FDA had "reason to believe" that the application for approval "contained an untrue statement of a material fact." When a manufacturer of an approved drug seeks a hearing in such an instance, the drug can stay on the market pending the hearing and further court actions unless the FDA calls it an "imminent" hazard, something the FDA has never done in the areas of drugs. All the "recalls" that do occur are done voluntarily with the assistance of the FDA.

Diet pills (amphetamines, barbiturates, and diuretics) are commonly used for overweight patients and some illnesses. Their danger is primarily associated with misuse or overuse. Stimulants, such as amphetamines, and sedatives, such as barbiturates, are poorly controlled. Although they are habit forming, doctors, drug companies, and the FDA have not made much effort to monitor their use. In 1973 the FDA began a program to educate doctors and consumers away from the almost worthless use of diet pills for reducing. The program has been a total failure. Now an estimated 25 million prescriptions are filled annually, and 2½ million people use "pep pills" or "uppers" (amphetamines) every year. Efforts are underway to ban amphetamines and all such appetite-curbing drugs, known as anorexians, for use in weight control. Barbituates alone, according to a presidential drug advisor, are responsible for as many as 2400 deaths a year.

Birth control pills are used by approximately twelve million women in this country. The oral contraceptives contain female sex hormones, estrogen and/or progestin. The dangers of these drugs in certain uses have been noted above. With so many users of the pill and its attending dangers, the FDA has decided that benefits do in fact outweigh the risks, and sales continue. The pill has been linked with a higher incidence of cancer of the uterus, blood clotting, increased heart attacks, benign liver tumors, breast cancer, and heart defects in the babies of women who take the pill.

After a long battle, the FDA now requires that informational leaflets describing the potential dangers of oral contraceptives accompany each prescription that is given to the *consumer*. Doctors and pharmacists have long had such information available through special leaflets, direct mailings, and the *Physicians Desk Reference,* a volume listing all approved drugs and their uses and available in every professional's office. Now this information is being made available to the public. However, a reading specialist at California State University, Dr. Fred Pyrczak, Jr., reports that the labels are written in a language that is almost incomprehensible to the average person. The FDA is studying his proposal to lower the reading level of all similar warning labels.

Monitoring Perils of Prescription Drugs. In 1977 public and private groups established an independent joint commission to develop a system for identifying and collecting adverse reactions to prescription drugs. Senator Edward M. Kennedy was instrumental in getting the full support of the Pharmaceutical Manufacturers Association in the joint effort. Additionally, the commission reports on trends in drug prescribing and usage in the United States.

Kennedy, during a 2½ year inquiry into prescription-drug problems, was "startled" that the FDA and the industry spend millions of dollars to ensure safe products before they come on the market, but once a drug is on sale a physician may prescribe it "in any dosage, for any purpose—whether or not that purpose has been scientifically evaluated." Thus, he continued, "the actual use of prescription drugs operates outside the regulatory framework, and little is known about how drugs are actually used once marketed." The postmarketing surveillance mechanism is to be set up by 1980, and nothing in the program precludes implementation of any similar program by the Food and Drug Administration itself.

Consumer Responsibilities. It should be clear by now that consumers are all too often in the dark when it comes to knowledge about prescription drugs. Thus, consumers have an important responsibility to learn about drugs. You can begin by asking questions. Since it is your health at stake, you should discuss with your doctor the benefits and risks of medicines prescribed for you. You need to learn what a drug is supposed to do for you, possible side effects you need to watch out for, and what to do if they happen. It is the responsibility of the individual to understand the specific instructions. Brief instructions will be on the label, but if you don't understand completely, ask your doctor to explain it again.

Further, you need to tell both the doctor and the pharmacist about any special drug problems you have had in the past and indicate what other drugs (including over-the-counter drugs) you are using. Common sense and carefully following directions on labels will help a lot, too. Also, consumers should consider costs, quality of services rendered, and the broader social questions as areas of responsibility.

Fundamental Issues of Concern. Do consumers have the right to be fully informed about the possible risks of taking certain drugs? When will ineffective and dangerous drugs be taken off the market? When will strong standards of safety and effectiveness be established before a new drug can be sold?

Child-resistant Packaging

The Poison Prevention Packaging Act of 1970 affects all prescription and over-the-counter drugs. The aim of the legislation is child-resistant packaging, which in turn reduces deaths from accidental poisoning. The most widely used container is the safety top that can be removed only by pushing down on it with the palm of your hand and then turning it. For drugs such as aspirin, the leading poisoner of children age 5 and under, the FDA requires that of a sample group of 200 small children, 85 percent must not be able to open the container in 5 minutes, while at the same time at least 90 percent of the adults must be able to open it. During the first 3 years of safer aspirin packages, annual deaths among children under 5 dropped from 46 to 17, according to the National Center for Health Statistics. Overall poisoning by such substances have declined 47 percent.

Manufacturers, however, are allowed to exempt one size of packaging from the child-resistant requirement. In such cases, the product must be labeled, "This Package for Households without Young Children." For prescription drugs, noncomplying packages are available at the request of the prescribing doctor or the consumer. Unfortunately, in the case of aspirin, many manufacturers have decided to market the 100-tablet size in the unsafe type of container. This is because more than one-third of sales are of the 100-tablet container, and safety packages would probably reduce sales.

Fortunately, most dangerous household substances are also covered by the legislation. Furniture polishes, lighter fluid, turpentine, and the like must be in child-resistant containers. Now fewer newspapers report, "An 8-year-old grabbed a bottle of liniment that he thought was cough syrup and drank it down"; "An 18-month-old boy died after drinking floor cleaner containing pertroleum distillates"; and "A 1-year-old girl spent 9 days in the hospital after swallowing charcoal lighter fluid from a can left in the yard after a family picnic." However, the U.S. Consumer Product Safety Commission reports that thousands of children are still poisoned by household substances every year. Part of the problem is that products look too inviting to little people—should a drain-cleaner container look like a bottle of ginger ale? Irresponsible adults are more often the cause. The best advice con-

THE BETTER HALF By Barnes

1975, The Register and Tribune Syndicate

4-30 Barnes

"I wish you wouldn't buy aspirin tablets in bottles with child-proof caps!"

THE BETTER HALF by Barnes reprinted Courtesy The Register and Tribune Syndicate, Inc.

tinues to be to keep medicines and other dangerous products out of sight and reach of children.

Over-the-Counter Drugs

Self-medication with over-the-counter drugs is an important part of our health-care system. Without nonprescription drugs, consumers would be standing in long lines in front of every doctor's office seeking relief from minor aches and pains. Somewhere between 250,000 and 500,000 over-the-counter drugs can be bought in drugstores, supermarkets, discount stores, airports, vending machines—almost anywhere. Not even the FDA knows how many there are.

The dangers of self-medication include overuse of drugs, reaction to combined drugs, and failure to get professional care when symptoms persist. Another problem is the lack of effectiveness, or efficacy, of many over-the-counter drugs. One FDA study found that approximately three-fourths of all over-the-counter drugs are not as effective as claimed. In addition, the National Academy of Sciences accepts less than 10 percent of the effectiveness claims of these drugs.

A major problem with over-the-counter drugs is in people's expectations: The general public has the very clear idea that over-the-counter drugs can "cure" their problems. The fact is that over-the-counter drugs (and many prescription drugs, too) can *only* relieve symptoms. Advertising in general exaggerates the need for an over-the-counter drug, or creates a problem for you in your mind that does not even exist, or promises more results than you should realistically expect. The Federal Trade Commission tries, but quite unsuccessfully, to regulate such advertising. A shocking finding was recently reported by FTC Commissioner Elizabeth Hanford Dole, who noted that in a survey 43 percent of the population relied upon advertising as the "primary source of information" about over-the-counter drugs, while only 13 percent looked "primarily at labeling."

Aspirin and Other Pain Relievers. The main conclusion of almost all scientific evidence about aspirin and other pain relievers is that two 5-grain aspirin are just as good as anything else in dealing with pain, fever, and inflammation.

Aspirin was prescribed by Hippocrates 2300 years ago; the Greeks extracted it from willow bark. It eased pain, reduced fever, and fought inflammation. Brought to this country in 1899, pure aspirin is defined as acetylsalicylic acid. Aspirin is named in the United States Pharmacopeia (USP), the standard criterion for registering drug formulas. It is in this privately published but government-recognized book that the chemical structures of about 2000 drugs and dosage forms are described. In addition, the book provides detailed descriptions of the physical tests that can be performed to determine the identity, purity, potency, and related characteristics of the drugs listed. Therefore, any products using the name "aspirin" are required by law to meet the same precise standards of strength, quality, and purity. If, for example, any aspirin bottle is labeled "U.S.P. 5 grains," it contains exactly the same acetylsalicylic acid as another bottle with the same U.S.P. designation, regardless of any advertising statements to the contrary.

Approximately 50 billion aspirin and aspirinlike over-the-counter drugs are consumed each year. This is equivalent to 225 5-grain tablets for every person in America. It is truly a wonder drug in that it is a very powerful pain killer.

A recent theory about how and why it works (after more than 170 years, nobody really knows) is that aspirin attacks pain at the precise source, therefore stopping the "ouch" signals from going to the brain. Dr. John R. Vane of the British Royal College of Surgeons suggests that prostaglandins, present in nearly every cell of the body, are the answer. He reports that prostaglandins "are capable of causing pain, fever and inflammation when they are released by tissues in response to stress or other stimulation. When aspirin is taken, the production of prostaglandins stops and the pain, fever and inflammation are allayed."

When properly used, aspirin is safe for almost everyone. Obviously, too much aspirin can kill. Too much aspirin can also cause ringing in the ears, vertigo, or loss of hearing. For people with stomach ulcers, aspirin can cause severe gastrointestinal bleeding. It can also cause allergic reactions, and it speeds up the rate of blood coagulation. It can completely negate drugs used to control gout, or enhance those used for diabetes. Recent evidence from the FDA suggests that pregnant women should not take aspirin during the last 3 months of pregnancy except under a doctor's supervision, since it can prolong labor and lengthen bleeding and clotting times in both mother and baby. Unfortunately, the print advertising and television commericals do not point out the side effects.

Advertising of pain killers, including aspirin, also does not tell the consumer that tablets kept on the shelf for too long may develop a powdery surface, indicating a loss of strength. A strong smell of vinegar similarly indicates a lack of strength—even in a new bottle. Neither does advertising tell the consumer that aspirin has been shown to be as effective a pain killer as propoxyphene hydrochloride (Darvon) or acetaminophen (Tylenol, Datril, and Bayer Acetaminophen).

In spite of advertisements suggesting the contrary, *no* controlled scientific study has shown one aspirin product to be any different from another in relieving pain or reducing fever. Instead, advertisements tell the consumer that Bufferin is twice as fast as aspirin, Anacin contains a special, fortified combination of ingredients, Excedrin has an extra-strength pain reliever, Bayer Aspirin is already the strongest pain reliever you can buy, Vanquish gives you extra strength and gentle buffers, and Cope gives superior relief. Not mentioned is the fact that aspirin is the main pain-killing ingredient in *all* the products.

The cost of advertising, in the multimillion dollar over-the-counter drug business, comes to approximately 20 cents of each sales dollar. Most of the advertising comes from three companies: Sterling Drug (Bayer, Cope, Bayer Children's Aspirin, Midol, and Vanquish), American Home Products (Anacin, Arthritis Pain Formula), and Bristol-Myers (Bufferin, Excedrin, Excedrin PM, Arthritis

Strength Bufferin). The Federal Trade Commission reports that 36 cents of every consumer dollar paid for the ten leading headache medicines goes for advertising. And the FTC has finally begun to clamp down on these over-the-counter drug advertisements that deceive the buyer with unproven and/or misleading claims.

The FTC has asked the companies to stop the alleged misrepresentations. Furthermore, they are asking corrective advertising for 2 years, which would mean that each company would have to spend 25 percent of its advertising expenditures to clear up false impressions left by earlier claims. Some of the ''evidence'' manufacturers have given to the FTC to back up their advertising claims makes interesting reading:

- ''Anacin adds extra strength to every tablet''—''evidence'' is the addition of caffeine, which has no pain-relieving effect whatsoever.
- ''Two Excedrin worked better than twice as many aspirin for pain other than headache,'' says David Janssen—''evidence'' is a very old research study of the discomfort suffered by 22 women who had just had babies.
- ''Anacin contains the pain reliever doctors prescribe most''—''evidence'' is aspirin.

Until the FTC's allegations are taken through the courts, and most likely to the U.S. Supreme Court, there will probably be few changes in the advertisements. More unfortunate for consumers, final action will take years. It took the FTC 13 years to make Geritol stop claiming it cured ''tired blood,'' and 30 years to make Holland Furnace Company stop faking explosions in people's basements.

Way back in 1973 the FTC filed complaints against all the major aspirin manufacturers for false and misleading advertising. This is becoming a long battle, since the FTC wants corrective advertising like that shown below. Although the following will probably never happen, the FTC released suggested corrective statements to be included in future ads:

Bufferin: It has not been established that Bufferin relieves pain faster than aspirin; it has not been established that Bufferin will cause gastric discomfort less frequently than aspirin; and Bufferin will not relieve nervous tension, or irritability, or enable persons to cope with the ordinary stresses of life.

Excedrin: It has not been established that Excedrin is more effective for relief of minor pain than aspirin or any other nonprescription internal analgesics. . . .

Bayer Aspirin: It has not been established that Bayer aspirin is more effective for the relief of minor pain than any aspirin which meets the standards set out in the United States Pharmacopeia.

Cope: It has not been established that Cope is more effective for relief of minor pain than any aspirin; and Cope will not relieve nervous tension, anxiety, irritability, or enable a person to cope with the ordinary stresses of personal life.

Vanquish: It has not been established that Vanquish is more effective for the relief of minor pain than any aspirin or buffered aspirin; it has not been established that Vanquish will cause less gastric discomfort than aspirin, and it has not been established that Vanquish is more effective for the relief of pain than the largest selling ''extra strength'' tablet.

Midol: Midol will not relieve tension, nervousness, stress, fatigue, or cure depression, or improve the user's mood.

Anacin: It has not been established that Anacin is more effective for the relief of pain than aspirin; and Anacin will not relieve nervousness, tension, anxiety, fatigue, or depression, or enable persons to cope with the ordinary stresses of everyday life.

Arthritis Pain Formula: It has not been established that Arthritis Pain Formula will cause gastric discomfort less frequently than aspirin.

Substitutes for aspirin, such as Tylenol, Datril, and Bayer Acetaminophen, are just acetaminophen, an equally old and well-established pain reliever. Sales of the aspirin substitutes in some areas are exceeding the aspirin-based products—at much higher prices, too. But surprise! Aspirin substitutes are *not* as good as aspirin-based products. They lack aspirin's ability to reduce inflammation, which is frequently the cause of pain in the first place, as in rheumatoid arthritis, tooth extraction, a sprained ankle, or a strained back muscle.

Acetaminophen has virtues. It can be used by the small number of people who actually are allergic to aspirin, it does not cause gastric bleeding or retard blood clotting, and it can be prepared in liquid form. Besides its lack of anti-inflammatory capability, it has a serious drawback in the event of an overdose. Both aspirin and acetaminophen are dangerous if a substantial overdose is taken, but acetaminophen can cause fatal liver damage. Efforts by the FDA are under way to require aspirinlike products to carry warnings on the labels about the potential dangers involved.

In any event, regardless of the pain reliever taken, don't take more than 10 to 15 grains (two or three tablets) at a time (to minimize possible stomach irritation, always drink a full glass of water when taking pills), don't take them more often than every 4 hours, don't exceed 12 tablets in 24 hours, and don't take them for longer than 10 days in succession without the supervision of a physician.

In the meantime, the consumer has a choice. He or she can spend perhaps 29 cents for 100 tablets of store-brand aspirin or buy the same quantity of Bayer for $1.24, Bufferin for $1.53, Anacin for $1.57, Tylenol (an aspirin substitute) for $2.29, Arthritis Pain Formula for $2.41, or get a prescription for Darvon at $10.80 for 100 tablets.

Cough and Cold Medicines. After 3½ years of study one of the FDA's advisory panels, the Over-the-Counter Cold, Cough, Allergy, Bronchodilator and Antiasthmatic Drug Products Panel, came up with some interesting findings. Of the 35,000 to 50,000 cough and cold remedies on the market earning more than $900 million, the panel reported that there was not one that would prevent, cure, or even shorten the length of a common cold. The products that have some effectiveness are *only* for the temporary relief of individual symptoms, reported Dr. Francis C. Lowell, chairperson of the panel.

It should be noted that cold weather does not cause colds. Viruses do. Staying inside is more likely to result in breathing air carrying viruses than going outdoors is. Further, there are more than 100 viruses that cause colds, so developing a drug to cure the common cold is most difficult. Antibiotics, for example, have no effect on viruses.

Dr. Lowell also said that neither the drugs nor grandma's prescription of rest in bed, plenty of liquids, and chicken soup will cure the common cold. But, "grandma's advice was as good as any and there is no need for your ultimate welfare to take any medicine at all." Additionally, antihistamines, which have been one of the most widely used anticold drugs, were noted as being one of the ingredients whose effectiveness "has not been established."

Very importantly, the panel recommended that fourteen prescription drugs be reclassified and sold as over-the-counter drugs. The FDA approved ten for immediate change and recommended further study on the remaining four. By 1979 or 1980 a "new generation" of over-the-counter (OTC) drugs for coughs and colds will be on the market. Thus, if you think you need temporary relief it would be wise to check with your physician and get his or her recommendation. Most new OTC products will contain very few ingredients and thus be better aimed at temporarily relieving one or more symptoms.

The panel is one of seventeen "review panels" established to examine many of the over-the-counter drugs. The aim is to establish categories of products and to impose uniform standards of safety, effectiveness, and accurate labeling. The findings on antacids, laxatives, sedatives, sleep aids and stimulants, and numerous other groups of over-the-counter drugs will be publicized, and will provide a basis for FDA action and later FDA/FTC control of product labeling and advertising.

In the meantime, you might want to be aware of the high alcoholic content of some of the more popular medicines. NyQuil, a cough medicine quite heavily promoted on television, is 25 percent alcohol. That means it is a 50-proof product—stronger than all wines and beers. Tonics for older people contain significant amounts of alcohol too. Geritol contains mostly B vitamins and minerals, as does Geriplex, but Geritol contains 12 percent alcohol (24 proof) and Geriplex is 18 percent alcohol (36 proof). National consumer columnist Sidney Margolius notes that "many elderly people think that it's the vitamins that make them feel good right away when they take these tonics. It isn't, our pharmaceutical expert advises. It's the alcohol." Margolius recommends that those who need them buy mail-order vitamin products for perhaps 2 cents per capsule and a little wine costing perhaps 7 cents, instead of paying 25 to 30 cents per ounce for Geritol or Geriplex.

Suntan Lotions. Consumers spend more than $70 million each year trying to get a tan. Suntan products come in creams, lotions, gels, butters, clear liquids, and aerosol forms. The aerosol can is likely to explode when exposed to temperatures over 120 degrees and, of course, should be protected from such high temperatures. Surprisingly, most of these preparations do nothing to protect you against sunburn. An official of the FDA goes even further by stating that "There's nothing that will prevent a sunburn except staying out of the sun."

The American Medical Association, in a study of fifty-six suntan products, found that thirty-two contained *no* ingredients to provide sunscreening. Therein lies the answer. Look at the label. If the product claims to prevent sunburn, it is considered a drug and must list its active ingredients, including chemicals called sunscreens. If the label says it promotes tanning, it is classified as a cosmetic and active ingredients will not be included. By the way, no product can actually tan you; only the sun can do that.

To prevent sunburn, certain protective chemicals must be in the product. Zinc oxide or titanium dioxide reflect the ultraviolet rays; lifeguards use those products to protect their noses and shoulders. Benzophenones absorb the rays before they reach your skin; aminobenzoates, salicylates, and cinnamates screen out the ultraviolet rays and let in only certain others. So, to help prevent a sunburn, buy a product that can do the job.

The best preventive sunburn products do not protect for more than 1 hour. As you probably have heard many times before, the trick is to build up a tan slowly. Tanned skin is its own natural protection. Begin by exposing your skin to the sun for 15 to 20 minutes a day. Then gradually build up the time of exposure. For tanning to occur, your skin must produce melanin pigments, which takes 2 days to get started and 2 weeks to reach a peak. If you burn and peel the melanin is lost and you must begin the process again. The instant-tanning products used at home containing dihydroxyacetone and acetone appear to work pretty well, but many people develop a mottled and spotty appearance when the "tan" stain begins to wear off in a few days, and they do not protect you from sunburn.

Vitamins. Parents are anxious to ensure that their children receive all the vitamins they need. However, most authorities believe that it is wiser to provide youngsters and adults with adequate vitamins from a well-balanced diet than to purchase supplemental vitamins. If you eat anything approaching a balanced diet, you probably do not need to waste money on expensive vitamins. Difficult questions arise in this area because science does not know all that the public would like to know about vitamins. Just how the body uses a vitamin pill is, for example, not completely understood. How much each vitamin helps an individual is another question. One thing is known quite well, however: A vitamin is a vitamin; the body doesn't know if it is natural from foods or from a synthetic capsule. Or even whether it is advertised on television or sold through the mails.

Too many vitamins can be fatal. The parents of Erin Shelton know this all too well. Before a summer outing with the family, Erin ate a whole bottle of Pals because he thought Captain Kangaroo on television had told him that he would become big and strong. Fortunately, Mrs. Shelton noticed that the bottle was empty. She called the Poison Control Center, got him to vomit, and drove him to the hospital. For 2 days Erin remained in intensive care, hovering between life and death. He survived. But there are some children every year, age 5 and under, who do not survive vitamin poisoning.

Vitamins are classified as a food and not a drug. Captain Kangaroo did not tell his television audience to eat a whole bottle of vitamins, but 5-year-olds cannot read labels and do not know that forty pills will start vitamin A poisoning, resulting in vomiting, structural changes in bones, and increased intracranial pressures. Or that taking twenty-five pills can give you iron poisoning, resulting in diarrhea, blood in the stools, vomiting, shock, and coma. The Television Code Review Board of the National Association of Broadcasters has established self-regulatory guidelines to prohibit such ads on children's Saturday morning shows. Other rules, and perhaps some from the Federal Trade Commission, are likely to lead to a reduction of the "looseness" presently associated with television advertising of over-the-counter vitamins. To date the FTC role has been to obtain consent orders from companies on an individual basis to not advertise vitamins for children *after* they have already done so. A recent case was against Hudson Pharmaceutical Corporation, which agreed to stop directing their "Spider Man" vitamins to children. Peggy Charren, president of the Action on Children's Television, a consumer lobby based in Boston, says that the present FTC method "is a ridiculous way to protect children."

Most vitamins, including vitamin C, are water soluble, which means that the body retains what it needs and excretes the rest. Vitamins A and D, however, are stored in the body; thus, one can overdose.

For adults, the big arguments seem to be over vitamins C and E. Nobel Prize winner Dr. Linus Pauling wrote a book entitled *Vitamin C and the Common Cold* several years ago. In it Pauling reported that from his studies of existing literature, vitamin C, or "ascorbic acid, taken in the proper amount, has much value in decreasing the incidence, severity, and integrated morbidity of the common cold and related infections." He suggests as the "proper amount" a minimum daily intake of 200 to 400 mg for "optimal health." This is four to eight times the FDA Recommended Daily Allowance for vitamin C. Interestingly, some of the first researchers to confirm the relieving powers of the vitamin have recently reported that they were wrong. The new study was directed by Dr. John F. Coulehan of the University of Pittsburgh Medical School, and it involved substantially more scientific controls in experimental testing with students at a Navajo boarding school in Arizona. The second study reported no difference among those who took vitamin C and those who did not.

Vitamin E is an antioxidant that inhibits the combination of a substance with oxygen, and thus acts as a preservative. That word "preservative" hit a responsive chord a few years ago, leading people to believe that it was some kind of miracle drug that would keep you young, cure your skin problems, ease your arthritis pain, prevent ulcers, and make you sexually young. An informed American public ought to know better when hearing claims like those, but they didn't. Even though the Food and Drug Administration has yet to see one single controlled study substantiating such claims, the myths go on. With both vitamins C and E, the FDA reports that there is no need for persons in good health and eating a well-balanced diet to use either dietary supplement.

The FDA proposes to limit the amount of food vitamins in such supplementary pills. They want a regulation requiring that there could not be more than 1½ times the average Recommended Daily Allowance of each vitamin. The FDA believes that if the pill is stronger than that, then it should be sold to prevent a deficiency or for some other medicinal purpose and should then be called a prescription drug. Recently, a Vitamin Regulation Law was passed which restricted the Food and Drug Administration's authority to regulate vitamins. Some consumers feel that this law will result in less protection, while others believe that it is good because it stops the FDA from limiting vitamin and mineral potency in dietary supplements. Thus, the controversy continues.

Mouthwashes. For years the advertisements and labels have proclaimed that mouthwashes have therapeutic value. The experts knew that the products had none. The Food and Drug Administration did nothing. In 1970 the Federal Trade Commission charged Listerine and others with misrepresenting mouthwashes as a cure, a preventive, and a treatment for colds and sore throats. The FDA then supported the FTC action and called upon a panel of the National Academy of Sciences to study mouthwashes.

The panel found "no convincing evidence that any medicated mouthwash, used as a part of daily hygiene regimen, has therapeutic advantage over a physiologic saline [salt] solution or even water. Some could kill bacteria in the mouth but in doing so it might upset the natural balances and cause undesirable effects; the desirability of permitting these products to be sold . . . is questionable." The panel advised against the sale or use of mouthwashes without the advice of a physician.

But in 1971 the FDA reversed its stand. It reclassified all mouthwashes and throat lozenges as cosmetics. The reasoning seemed to be that since the claims for these products are no more than can be claimed for water, they cannot be therapeutic and must therefore be cosmetic. The FTC then dropped its action. The advertising continues, and Cepacol ads

can go on saying that it "leaves the mouth feeling fresh and clean and provides soothing temporary relief of dryness and minor irritations." Columnist Arthur E. Rowse noted that "dentists may have a hard time swallowing that, for mouthwashes are not recommended by the American Dental Association (ADA)." Furthermore, the ADA states that "the general use of mouthwashes can be considered to serve no greater purpose than as an aid in the removal of loose food and debris."

A new chapter to the story opened in 1975 and now continues. FTC Administrative Law Judge Alvin Berman found Listerene's ad claims to be false. And since in a consumer perception test 60 percent thought Listerine to be more "effective against colds and sore throats," while Scope, Micrin, and Lavoris, its main competitors, scored in the 7 to 19 percent range, he ordered $10 million in corrective advertising. Berman reported that "The ability of Listerine to kill millions of germs on contact, therefore, is of no medical significance in the prevention, cure, or treatment of colds or sore throats." He further added that colds "are not caused by bacteria. Bacteria in the oral cavity play no role in cold symptoms."

Under the decision by Berman, Listerine must run corrective advertisements for 2 years which include the statement, "Contrary to previous ads, Listerine will not help prevent colds or sore throats or lessen their severity."

Warner-Lambert, of course, appealed the case. The U.S. Supreme Court upheld the government case in 1977. In the mouthwash industry three companies control 79.8 percent of the market, with Warner-Lambert's Listerine having 46.3 percent of the market. Promising nonexistent cures can mean millions of dollars every year. That is a powerful incentive to create "new" advertisements and sell such products in the years to come.

Ask Your Physician for OTC Drugs. With the Food and Drug Administration now in the process of approving many over-the-counter (OTC) drugs which had formerly been available by prescription only, those used to taking certain prescriptions are advised to see their doctor. There very well may be some over-the-counter drugs that you can use rather than certain prescription drugs. In most cases over-the-counter drugs cost much less than prescription drugs, and if your physician is aware of the strength of the OTC drugs, he or she may recommend them instead. Your doctor may want to keep you on a prescription drug and for good reasons. In any event, be sure to follow your physician's instructions carefully and report any adverse effects or lack of responsiveness to the drug (prescription or OTC) to him or her.

Choosing a Pharmacy

Your choice of a pharmacist is likely to be based upon several factors, and one of the most important is convenience. In an emergency, such as quickly getting medicine for a child who is running a high fever, the nearness of the pharmacy is important. When your physician telephones an emergency prescription to a pharmacy, it helps if you have done business there before. The pharmacist will accept the order from the physician in any case, but knowing the prescription case history of members of the family will help the pharmacist spot undesirable combinations of medicines about which you and your doctor may not be aware.

Prices do vary widely, so it is usually quite helpful to shop for the best price for prescriptions that you will be using for a long time. A recent survey by *Money* magazine for three of the most-prescribed drugs in four stores in each of five cities "found as much as a 406% difference in the price for a given drug." Valium (5 mg) ranged from 8.9 cents to 23.2 cents per pill, Darvon Compound—65 from 7.6 cents to 19.8 cents, and tetracycline (250 mg) from 4.9 cents to 24.8 cents.

You may prefer to use just one pharmacy almost all the time, particularly if they keep records of all prescriptions for each member of the family. A good pharmacist is one who is also willing to answer your questions about prescriptions; the pharmacist may give you some information that your doctor did not.

Furthermore, your pharmacist should be willing and able to recommend particular over-the-counter drugs and have *good* reasons for doing so. If your pharmacist doesn't know the answers, then whom can you trust?

Food and Drug Administration Dilemmas

Many critics have written about the weaknesses of the Food and Drug Administration, some of which have been suggested above. It has been pointed out that their budget is too small, their staff spends too much time trying to regulate prescription drugs and neglects the larger over-the-counter drug industry, they give in to industry pressures, and they too often follow the path of least resistance. The major dilemma facing the FDA is how to do the right thing for the public good.

Congressman L. H. Fountain of North Carolina states that "The key to a more effective FDA lies in the appointment of officials who are dedicated to enforcing the laws FDA administers with vigor and objectivity." Former commissioner Alexander M. Schmidt noted that the budget for the FDA's operations amounts to approximately $1 per year per American consumer, and that this is a major drawback.

A frequent criticism is that the FDA takes too long, sometimes 6 or 7 years, to approve a new drug, to take any other major activity, and sometimes to even accomplish a relatively small objective. Once Schmidt assured a Senate subcommittee that a revised label warning for postmenopausal estrogens could be ready "within a week or two." It took 9 months, and he reported that the reason was that the FDA has too few "first-class scientists with good judgment who can write the English language." Action which is too fast has also been alleged. In 1972 Demulen, a low-estrogen birth control pill marketed by G. B. Searle Company, was approved in 10 days! The application was submitted and ordered "expedited" by the Bureau of Drugs head Dr. Henry Simmons. This kind of situation has been highly unusual.

Perhaps a better example of the slowness of

FDA action involves charges against companies who may have submitted altered data to gain approval for new drugs. Several companies are under investigation with regard to particular drugs. Searle and Company's products Flagyl and Aldactone are a case in point. Both drugs were approved and now are in wide use. Flagyl is used to combat trichomonas vaginitis, an annoying condition of the female reproductive tract, and Aldactone is a diuretic used to rid the body of excess fluids. In 1972 Dr. F. Adrian Gross of the FDA's Bureau of Compliance reported that some of the data submitted earlier were "highly questionable." In 1974 Searle submitted an amended report which Gross thought to be still questionable. In at least one instance he stated, "they changed the raw data to bring it into agreement with the summary." In 1975 an on-site investigation and examination of the actual laboratory records revealed startling findings. FDA investigator Alice Ling reported "that three rats observed (according to the earlier report) as being alive and well" actually had died several months earlier. In 1975 the FDA announced that it was contemplating criminal action against Searle; in 1977 the FDA began criminal action. This is one of the first times such action has been taken against a drug manufacturer. The case continues and the drugs are still being marketed, even though both of them are suspected of causing cancer.

COSMETICS AND PERSONAL PRODUCTS

The federal Food, Drug, and Cosmetic Act defines a *cosmetic* "as an article (except soap) intended to be rubbed, poured, sprinkled, sprayed on, introduced to, or otherwise applied to the human body for cleansing, beautifying, promoting attractiveness, or altering the appearance." If the article is to prevent or cure an ailment, or to affect the structure or function of the body, it is classified as a *drug*.

So cosmetics are different from drugs. They do not have to be approved by the FDA before they are sold. They do not even have to register with the FDA. Any premarket testing is voluntary, and laws do not require that cosmetics fulfill their advertising promises.

From all appearances it seems that the cosmetic industry has more than 220 million human guinea pigs to experiment with. A recent FDA study showed that between 2 and 3 percent of all women who use mascara get some type of eye infection. That adds up to hundreds of thousands of women. It is no wonder that the government estimates that approximately 80,000 serious injuries involving cosmetics occur each year. These range from skin eruptions to allergic reactions to itching to burns to serious disfigurement and permanent injury. And the number of complaints is increasing.

The Beauty Industry

Women and men spend $15 billion on beauty products every year, and the industry is growing at a rate of 10 percent annually. To feel better, to look better, to smell better, and to be more appealing are the marketing thrusts of the beauty industry. To cleanse, beautify, scent, and chase the American dream of physical perfection seems to motivate the public to buy more and more products every year. Although there are difficulties, most of the products sold are safe. The notable exceptions demand public attention and action.

A college student from Tuscaloosa, Alabama, was blinded for nearly a year after she accidently scratched her eye with a mascara brush. In Albuquerque, New Mexico, a 2-year old played with an automobile-shaped glass cologne container. He dropped it, spilling the contents, which caught fire from a nearby portable heater. The child suffered burns so severe and deep that both his legs had to be amputated below the knees. Both of these cases are real. Fortunately, they are only a very small minority of experiences with beauty products.

Cosmetics Hazards

With between 200 and 300 chemicals often making up one cosmetic, allergic reactions are frequent. It is estimated that one-half of the population is allergic to some of the chemicals used in cosmetics. Most people who use cosmetics that cause a minor allergic reaction do not even associate the problem with the product. The ingredients in face powders, foundation creams, liquid makeups, shampoos, eye preparations, soaps, deodorants, and many other products all too often cause swelling around the eyes; loss of hair, eyebrows, or lashes; and rashes and skin irritations.

Researchers for the FDA recently reported that most injuries caused by cosmetics were regarded as *minor* and did not require medication or treatment by a doctor. Just over 10 percent of the injuries were considered *moderate*—the reaction would persist and interfere with normal activities. Another 2 percent were *severe*—painful enough to make the patient see a doctor and result in time lost from work or other activities. The highest incidence of adverse reaction involved deodorants and antiperspirants (40.2 injuries per 10,000 products used). In contrast the voluntary reports from industry showed an injury rate of 0.28 per 10,000. Moisturizers and lotions were reported by the FDA to have an injury rate of 18.2 per 10,000 (in contrast to the voluntary figures of 0.07 per 10,000), and hair sprays and lacquers were 14.6 (compared to the industry reports of 0.008).

The allergic reactions to deodorants and antiperspirants are widespread and recently serious concern has arisen because of precancerous lung conditions found in users of aerosol spray products. A Colorado physician, William O. Good, suspects that Freon or other ingredients that are accidentally inhaled lead to this condition. Recently, the FDA banned zirconium from antiperspirant sprays, as it was suspected of causing lung damage in monkeys. Deodorants, hairsprays, and other products often come in aerosol containers.

A further complication exists for consumers buying deodorants. Deodorants are classified as cosmetics and antiperspirants as drugs. Thus a deodorant only covers up odor, while an antiperspirant is intended to stop moisture as well. (Sorry about that, you long-time deodorant users!)

Deodorant soaps are under careful scrutiny now too, since questions are being raised about five germ killers that are widely used. An FDA-appointed panel has described as "not generally regarded as safe for incorporation into toilet bars for personal hygiene use" the chemicals TBS, TCC, TFC, triclosan, and Vancide FP. It appears that these substances are absorbed through the skin in measurable amounts and can "produce damage to internal organs." The review is continuing, since those chemicals are used in many popular soaps, such as Lifebuoy, Phase III, Irish Spring, Palmolive Plus, and Dial. Deodorant soaps must list their active ingredients on the wrapper while other soaps need not, so that products containing such ingredients can be identified. In the meantime, the FDA has requested legal authority from Congress to regulate more than 100 ingredients in cosmetics that are suspected of causing cancer, birth defects, and nervous system disorders.

In cosmetics, forms of methyl mercury are found in creams and lotions—particularly in eye preparations. The problem is that the body stores mercury. Only small amounts of it are used in individual cosmetics, but the build-up question remains a concern.

Another chemical hazard is 2,4TDA. Little is known about this substance, which is used in many permanent and semipermanent hair dyes. But as early as 1966, laboratory animals developed cancerous tumors when they were injected with the chemical. Nothing conclusive has been announced about 2,4TDA since that time. Manufacturers are searching for a substitute chemical; meanwhile, it is reported that the chemical is still used in forty-three brands of hair dye. Twenty million Americans buy hair-dye products each year.

Bacterial infections is another hazard associated with cosmetics. Many cosmetic preparations—creams, for example—provide excellent bases for bacteria growth. Most likely the bacteria are brought to the cosmetic through carelessness of the user, as when the consumer dips a finger into a jar of face cream without first washing. Annually, approximately 150 staphylococcus cases, as well as pseudomonas aeruginosa—which brings loss of sight within 24 hours—and salmonella infections, can be traced to cosmetics.

The cosmetics trade association, the Cosmetic, Toiletry and Fragrance Association (CTFA), recognizes that some methods must be instituted to safeguard consumers, or at least to inform them of possible dangers. After all, 20 percent of all advertising is cosmetic- and drug-industry-related, and that means a lot of money is spent persuading consumers to believe the false assumption that all such products are safe. In 1972 the FDA, with some cooperation from the CTFA, set up a voluntary system under which the cosmetics industry would list ingredients on the containers. This was to be done in a way that would both protect secret formulas and help to trace hazards. More recently, the FDA issued regulations to require ingredient labeling of cosmetics. The labeling, however, an example of which is shown in Figure 6-1, is not only almost impossible to read without a magnifying glass but also unintelligible. On the plus side, the labeling does help the careful shopper avoid certain ingredients. In addition, these efforts have helped to identify some of the more commonly found allergy-causing and primary irritants, and manufacturers have voluntarily stopped using many of those chemicals.

Hypoallergenic cosmetics are now available which when labeled as such actually are "hypoallergenic." Under recent FDA regulations, products that make this claim must undergo dermatological testing first. Thus, the consumer is much less likely to be adversely affected when using a product labeled this way, although it is not a guarantee. There is no known way to produce a cosmetic to which someone somewhere will not have adverse effects. On the other hand, it is interesting to note that only 123 of the estimated 5000 cosmetic manufacturers voluntarily report customer injuries to the government.

Regulations Are Needed in the Cosmetics Industry
In 1977 the cosmetics industry initiated a Cosmetic Review Panel. The Cosmetic,

FIGURE 6-1   Ingredient labeling

Toiletry and Fragrance Association budgeted $800,000 for the first year of operations and expects that it will take several more years to "review and evaluate all scientific data on the safety of cosmetic ingredients world wide." The independent review is expected, in the words of CTFA board chairman William Chaney, to "give the scientific community a source of information to which it can turn for accurate data on health and safety aspects of cosmetic ingredients." Such a study is needed and has been called for many times in the past, once in the form of legislation proposed by Senator Thomas F. Eagleton.

The FDA already has the authority to request safety substantiation data from companies or the Cosmetic Review Panel if they are available. But, therein lies part of the problem. Are the data available? The FDA has long asked for the authority to set safety standards for the cosmetic industry, but it has not been able to get it. In the first place, the needed data have not been available from the manufacturers. Presumably they will be more likely to be available through the Cosmetic Review Panel.

Of tremendous importance, products are regularly brought onto the market without any guarantee of safety. The FDA does not have the authority to require all manufacturers to prove the safety of their products before production and sale. Nor does the FDA have the legal authority to require adverse-reaction reporting from the manufacturers, which is crucial to monitoring the safety of cosmetics already on the market. The FDA does have the power to remove something from the market if they can prove it is an *imminent* hazard, but as noted earlier, this power is difficult to wield and is rarely used. It has been suggested that if the American people want a cosmetic or drug to be removed quickly because of a *potential* rather than a proven hazard, then the legal authority of the FDA will have to be changed.

Senator Eagleton, writing in *Caveat Emptor,* summed up the situation well. "The number of grooming substances we rub, pour, sprinkle, spray and otherwise apply to ourselves under the assumption they are safe is staggering. The majority of these, when used properly in moderation, are safe. Other products are only a waste of our time and money. But still others contain poisonous or dangerous substances. As the law stands now, we have no way of knowing. What we do know is that keeping Americans beautiful can have some ugly consequences."

Acne Victims—Victims of Advertising

Acne can be treated but not cured. This is the conclusion of nine volumes of documents prepared by the *makers* of skin cleansers and released by the Federal Trade Commission. Under its ad substantiation program, the FTC sought backup information from the companies, and that is what they found out from the makers of Clearasil, Noxzema, Propa P.H., Fostex, Listerex, and others.

Many of the more than 150 preparations had the same ingredients, the report noted. The company studies themselves often showed that the products would have no more impact than would the regular use of soap and water. Most products contained ingredients to promote peeling of dead skin (such as sulfur) and to absorb oil (such as resorcinal). Even the American Pharmaceutical Association says that "Most persons will get satisfactory results with the face soap they ordinarily use," and that "It is of prime importance to the patient to realize that acne cannot be cured; in most cases, however, it can be controlled so as to minimize any permanent scarring."

Regular use of soap and water, therefore, will do the job as well as any commercial product, say the manufacturers themselves. Perhaps this substantiation, if you can call it that, will encourage the FTC to take action against some of the advertising claims made by the manufacturers. In the meantime, the confessions of Steve Harvey in a commentary carried by the Los Angeles Times–Washington Post Service might give some insight into the situation:

> One day over lunch when I was 16, I complained about pimples to my grandfather. "Don't worry," he said, "they'll go away." "When?" I pleaded, as if he had some say in my salvation. "When you're 21 or so," he said. "No!" I shouted—and stomped out of the dining room. Unfortunately, he turned out to be right. No amount of medication —or stomping—could change it: I still faced five years of anguish, much of it spent before the mirror.

Toothpaste

Practically everyone uses toothpaste. Technically it is classified as a drug, but this is not evident in the advertising.

The Food and Drug Administration called eight of the ten most popular brands of toothpaste ineffective. The products were tested by the National Academy of Sciences National Research Council. Found to be ineffective were Brisk, Colgate with Gardol, Colgate dental cream with Gardol, Antizyme, Kolynos fluoride, Super Amm-I-Dent, and both Amm-I-Dent toothpaste and powder. Crest was effective against decay, and NDK was possibly effective. The FDA demanded substantiation of all toothpaste claims, but took no action to remove the ineffective products from the marketplace.

To avoid problems, use a good toothbrush with water only. For those who like that tingling feeling, use a mixture of salt and baking soda.

Contact Lens and Glasses

Glasses or contact lenses are worn by approximately 100 million Americans. About 8 million wear contact lenses, while the rest wear regular glasses. Of the approximately 1½ million people fitted last year for contact lenses, about half of them bought the new "soft" lenses. The cost for regular glasses, including the examination, ranges from about $60 to $115, although expensive frames or special lenses can raise the price considerably. The small hard contact lenses generally cost from $150 to $300. The newer soft lenses usually cost between $250 and $450.

Often people buy contact lenses for cosmetic reasons because they want to avoid wearing regular eyeglasses. Indeed, 75 percent of those buying contacts are women. Regardless of the motivation for purchase, it is especially important for contact lens buyers to buy them right and stay away from cut-rate dealers. It is probably smarter to deal with an *ophthalmologist* (a medical doctor specializing in diseases or conditions of the eye) or an *optometrist* (a state-licensed practitioner specializing in vision defects). Their services cost more, but they are highly qualified professionals in eye care. An *optician* prepares lenses based upon a prescription and instructs people in correct wearing habits. Many states require that opticians be licensed according to minimum standards of education and training. Of course, minimum standards for opticians are considerably lower than those for optometrists.

The pros and cons of wearing glasses, hard contact lenses, or soft lenses can be discussed with your eye specialist. For those considering the larger soft lenses, the higher cost means improved safety (as they do not pop out easily) but also considerably more upkeep (they need special equipment) and less durability. Technology in lenses is improving and a new silicone lens (somewhat hard but still soft) is being tested. In any event, contact lenses should not hurt at any time—the lenses can be adjusted until they fit correctly—and the wearer should not be encouraged to overcome pain, unless hard lenses have been prescribed for certain eye conditions, such as severe astigmatism.

Prices in states which do not discourage advertising of prices are consistently much lower than prices in other states. Removing bans on price advertising for eyeglasses and contact lenses is lowering prices. Lower price tags on frames as well as lenses are occurring.

Orthokeratology is a new and controversial procedure for straightening patients' eyes. In orthokeratology, a person wears a succession of graduated contact lenses, each one pressing the cornea a bit more toward its proper curvature. Eyes are rechecked every 6 weeks, and the whole process takes about 2 years. The cost runs from $1200 to $2000. After completing the treatment, the patient receives a set of "blank" lenses, the only function of which is to keep the reshaped cornea from regaining its original distortion. When the blanks are removed, normal vision remains for a while. Proponents claim about 3 percent of the patients are "cured," while critics claim that no scientific research has been conducted to show the value, if any, of this procedure.

Fortunately for the 20,000 children and 100,000 adult wearers of eyeglasses who break their glasses each year, the FDA now requires that all new lenses be impact resistant. They are made of furnace-hardened glass or plastic. Lenses can still break, but perhaps 90 percent of injuries, many leading to blindness, have now been eliminated. On the other hand, another problem for consumers buying glasses is that there are no requirements that frames be flame-resistant. Lighting a cigarette or leaning over a barbecue can cause problems with some frames. The FDA has the authority to issue nonflammability regulations, but it has not done so thus far.

Aerosol Sprays

The banning in 1974 of the propellant vinyl chloride from use in aerosol containers because of its link to cancer of the liver in factory workers did not solve all the problems associated with aerosol sprays. Each year, it is estimated, nearly 5000 people need emergency room treatment for injuries associated with aerosols. The U.S. Consumer Product Safety Commission (CPSC) reports the following kinds of illustrations:

- Wilma discarded an empty can of insect repellant into a wastepaper fire. The can exploded, and a piece of flying metal pierced her jugular vein. Wilma died 15 minutes later.
- Eight-year-old Jimmy used a hammer and nail to puncture an old can of spray paint. The can exploded, hurling pieces of metal into his face and upper chest, cutting him severely.
- Laurie was smoking while she used an aerosol can of hairspray. Her cigarette ignited the spray, and she received severe burns which permanently disfigured her face.

Additionally, the propellants can be toxic if used in poorly ventilated rooms and inhaled in quantity. Some people who "sniff" aerosols (particularly those containing halocarbons or hydrocarbons) to induce a euphoric effect or "high" have suffered dizziness, lack of coordination, nausea, headache, or blurred vision. Some people have died. Aerosol sprays in general are known to cause heart trouble, skin problems, and respiratory problems, and they have been linked with cancer. One recent study showed a higher incidence of lung cancer among beauticians; it was suggested that because the finely divided aerosol droplets remained suspended in the air for quite some time, their exposure was quite high. However, there is no evidence to indicate that aerosol products containing halocarbons and hydrocarbons are health hazards if properly used.

Fluorocarbons, once widely used in many aerosol cans as propellants, have been totally banned from use in aerosols. This occurred through the efforts of the Consumer Product Safety Commission, the Food and Drug Administration, and the Environmental Protection Agency (EPA). Alternative hydrocarbon propellants, such as propane and butane, and carbon dioxide as a propellant may replace the fluorocarbons. So aerosols themselves will remain; it is the propellants that will change for sure.

The problem was that aerosols containing fluorocarbons "present an unreasonable risk of injury to consumers from the destruction of the ozone layer," reports the CPSC. The ozone layer of the stratosphere screens out harmful ultraviolet light—it's about 16 to 19 miles above the earth. The fluorocarbons in sprays, once released, gradually float upward. The ultraviolet rays break the gases into compounds, including chlorine. Chlorine, in turn, interacts with ozone and destroys it. It can take fluorocarbons up to 10 years to reach the stratosphere, but once there, they remain. It takes an estimated 100 years for any ozone destroyed to be replaced. A National Academy of Sciences study reported that "just about all the Freon ever used in aerosol spray cans now resides in the earth's atmosphere." (There appears to be little potential danger from leakage of these gases out of home refrigerators and freezers, however.)

Dangers do result from the breakdown of the ozone layer. They involve possible worldwide weather changes, in part because of a warmer climate; harm to plants and animals because of the effect of excessive ultraviolet rays on DNA, the genetic chemical; and an increase in skin cancers, again because of excessive ultraviolet rays. Fluorocarbons have not been banned in other countries.

The largest increases in skin cancers are likely to be in two forms—basal-cell and squamous-cell carcinomas. These are usually easy to detect and rarely kill, although they sometimes disfigure. The most dangerous form of cancer, which will increase by an estimated 400 cases a year worldwide, is melanoma. Doctors in this country are already seeing an increase of 10 to 15 percent annually in the nation's current 8500 cases a year. About one-third are fatal. Clearly, the breaking up of ozone layer is not the only cause for this increase; increased exposure to the sun

Courtesy of Edd Uluschak.

"His last words were 'I'm dying for a cigarette!' "

among the leisure-seeking is the main cause. Concerned people should examine all moles for signs of the disease, particularly watching for moles with rough, notched edges or red, white, or especially blue speckling.

Labeling of ingredients on cosmetics is required by the FDA. It demands listing by generic names in order of predominance, except for those substances present in amounts of less than 1 percent. This authority was given in 1976 under an FDA ruling. The problem for the consumer is to simply read the labels and see what's there. If the aerosol container says that water bases, hydrocarbons, or carbon dioxide are used, no risk is present. Many other consumers have reacted differently—millions have switched to the "squoosh" of a finger pump or the silence of a roll-on. It is a wise idea economically at least—a 5-ounce pump spray delivers almost twice as much deodorant as a 12-ounce aerosol can, and they cost about the same.

Today's actions, and those in the past, will cost us all in the future, reported Dr. Donald M. Hunten, head of one of FDA's National Academy of Sciences study groups on the ozone problem. He reported some time ago that "even if the use of Freon were terminated by 1978, we would get a reduction in the ozone layer of about 3 percent by 1990. That would be enough to trigger a worldwide increase in skin cancer of about 2 percent in light-skinned people."

Tobacco

Recent studies of *non*smokers show that they are being harmed by the smoke of others in buses, trains, subways, planes, offices, restaurants, and other public places. Labels on cigarettes now display the warning that "The Surgeon General has determined that cigarette smoking is dangerous to your health." Facts back up this statement. Cigarette smoking is the chief cause of lung cancer and has been specifically linked with other cancers, heart disease, chronic bronchitis, and emphysema. Tar is the element in cigarette smoke that causes cancer, reports the National Cancer Institute. According to the American Medical Association, the risk of contracting lung cancer is ten times higher for men smokers than for nonsmokers, and it is sixteen times higher for women. Nicotine is both a poison and a stimulant; it is a prime suspect as a cause of heart attacks. It has been suggested that the label be rewritten so that it might have greater effect: "Warning: Cigarette smoking is a major health hazard and may result in your death!"

Several years ago, all tobacco advertisements were banned from television, *except* for ads for little cigars, which some believe violates the spirit and intent of the law. Congressional action to redefine cigarettes to include little cigars is in the making.

Smoking cigarettes with less tar and nicotine intake has been shown to be less harmful. However, a recent study sponsored and published by *Reader's Digest* reports that some filter cigarettes that are low in nicotine and tar produce more poisonous gases than some nonfilter brands. "Merit King and Fact King put out more nitrogen oxides than such high tar cigarettes as Camel, Winston filter king and Lucky Strike regular." Nitrogen oxides are directly related to chronic bronchitis and emphysema. Other studies have found that those who switch to a brand with less tar and nicotine tend to compensate by taking more and deeper puffs per day to get their "nicotine fix."

It is commonly assumed that cigar smokers do not inhale or, if they do, only very little. Of course, not inhaling cigar or pipe tobacco smoke somewhat reduces the dangers associated with smoking. Or does it? Most cigar and little-cigar packages contain the statement, "These cigars are predominately natural tobacco with nontobacco ingredients added." What are the ingredients?

Adhesives, plasticizers, and asbestos or ceramic reinforcing fibers are frequently classified as hazardous nontobacco ingredients. Asbestos fibers remain in the lungs permanently! Ceramic fibers do much the same. Unfortunately, neither the Food and Drug Administration nor the Federal Trade Commission has tried to study the effect of nontobacco ingredients on the health of smokers. Under the Hazardous Substances Act, both the FDA and the FTC have the authority to monitor the use of additives or chemicals in all cigars. Doesn't the consumer have a right to know what additives are in the tobacco offered for sale?

Further protection for smokers has come from the National Cancer Institute (NCI), which is urging the tobacco industry to produce cigarettes with lower hazards. In effect, the NCI is promoting the development of a "safer cigarette," although they hasten to add that no cigarette is safe. The National Cancer Institute realizes that even though cigarette smoking is on the decline, a lot of people still smoke and should be helped. In spite of the fact that a smaller percentage of adults smoke cigarettes now than in years past (currently about 34 percent of adult Americans smoke, compared with 36 percent in 1970 and 43 percent in 1964), actual cigarette consumption is going up. Senators Edward Kennedy and Gary Hart have proposed a 4-year, $9.3 billion health tax on cigarettes to pay for more research on cancer, heart and lung diseases, and an informational/educational program to tell more people about the hazards of smoking. The tax would increase the average cost of a pack of cigarettes about 30 cents and would be based upon the amount of tar and nicotine in each cigarette.

Nonsmoker protection is coming more into being every day. The about 170 million nonsmokers, including children, are demanding their rights. Minnesota, in 1976, became the first state to pass a law aimed at *effectively* restricting public smoking which would harm nonsmokers. It is controversial but is considered a model law for other states to follow. The law goes an important step further than previous legislation—nearly all public places must have smoke-free areas. Smoking-permitted areas as well as nonsmoking areas may be designated, but if there isn't room for both, smoking is prohibited. Furthermore, the

Courtesy of Edd Uluschak.

"Claims it's air pollution."

size of the nonsmoking section is supposed to be proportional to the number of consumer-clients who want a smoke-free area.

Alcohol

Alcoholic beverages have addicted approximately ten million people to the point where they are classified as alcoholics or people with a serious drinking problem. And millions more Americans consume varying amounts of alcohol every day. Evidence shows that each drink reduces the oxygen supply through the blood to the brain. The result is a deterioration of brain cells, of which each of us has about twelve billion—and these are irreplaceable. Continued drinking affects the health of the individual, productivity, and the stability of the family and the community.

The social cost of alcohol is well into the billions of dollars. More than 25,000 alcohol-related traffic deaths, 15,000 alcohol-related accidents, and 2 million arrests for public drunkenness are recorded each year. An estimated $25 billion is drained from the economy

because of those with serious drinking problems. They lose income because they miss work "every now and then" due to too much alcohol, and lower productivity occurs when workers have been drinking. These factors, in addition to increased occupational injuries, have a depressing effect on the economic health of the nation.

The outlook for the future looks somewhat grim too, particularly since the Research Triangle Institute reported that they found a strong association between parental and adolescent drinking. The findings included that nearly 25 percent of all students in grades seven through twelve were either "heavy drinkers" (5 to 12 drinks on at least one occasion a week) or "moderately heavy drinkers" (2 to 4 drinks on at least one occasion a week). Only 27 percent of the 13,222 junior and senior high school students surveyed indicated that they were nondrinkers. On the college level, a study by *Gallery* magazine reports that alcohol has replaced marijuana as the students' prime means of getting high.

Too much alcohol is obviously not healthy, and research studies dramatize the severity of two recently discovered problems. The British medical journal *Pulse* reported that the children of alcoholic mothers are much more likely to die or suffer permanent and physical disorders than children of nonalcoholic mothers. The researchers concluded that the babies receive the alcohol their mothers drank during pregnancy. Children born to an alcoholic mother never catch up with others even if they are taken away from their mothers and put into foster homes. The U.S. National Institute on Alcohol Abuse and Alcoholism warns that "women who take more than two drinks a day during pregnancy substantially increase the risk of giving birth to mentally retarded and physically deformed babies." In the *New England Journal of Medicine*, researchers reported the first direct evidence that in nonalcoholic males drinking reduces the production of testosterone—the hormone that gives men masculine characteristics. It has long been known that men may be relatively impotent after drinking, while alcoholics are often completely impotent even after they have stopped drinking. In an accompanying editorial commenting upon the research, it was written that "The clinical effects of alcohol ingestion on male sexual function are overt. Corresponding changes in women may have a more subtle function although no results are available yet from studies of women and alcohol."

The consumer's right to know is seriously restricted too. The labeling of beer, wine, and liquor really doesn't tell the consumer much about anything. In the 1960s it was discovered that at least fifty deaths of unusually heavy beer drinkers were directly attributable to beer in which the foaming was enhanced by cobalt salts. Two doctors complained afterward that "Had this metal been known to be present in beer . . . the prompt administration of an antidote might have saved some of our patients." All beer manufacturers immediately stopped using cobalt salts. Today, the FDA has approved fifty-nine additives for use in beer, but present labeling laws do not require that those ingredients be listed.

An exhausting fight is under way to require labeling. Jurisdiction over alcohol is under the Bureau of Alcohol, Tobacco and Firearms (ATF), but the Food and Drug Administration has been leading the fight to require ingredient labeling. The FDA proposed regulations for labeling beer and wine, but a federal district court judge in Owensboro, Kentucky, ruled that the ATF had exclusive jurisdiction over the labeling of alcoholic beverages. An attorney for the liquor industry said that "the cost of listing ingredients would be prohibitive and present regulations are adequate to safeguard the drinking public." With the FDA blocked in its efforts, chief counsel Richard Merril sent a confidential memo to the Justice Department requesting that the Solicitor General appeal the decision. National columnist Jack Anderson reports that the memo charged that the decision "negates Congress' determination that consumers are entitled to know the composition of the products they consume." There the matter now rests.

Metric labeling has come to the liquor industry, and one consumer writer reports that hidden price increases are occurring in some products. Among half-gallon products he noted one marked 1.75 liters. One liter is equal to 1.0567 quarts. Multiplying by 1.75 shows that 1.75 liters is the equivalent of 1.8492 quarts—about 7½ percent less than a half-gallon. Unfortunately, both products were marked with the same price.

WATER WE DRINK AND USE

A quote from J. E. Singley and A. P. Black in the *Journal of the American Water Works Association* puts the finger on the main problem with the water we drink and use. "A visit to a new major water treatment plant is an interesting and exciting experience. One finds accurate and well-designed chemical feeders with automatic controls, completely equipped laboratories, ample facilities for material handling, and instrumentation for communication and control, not only throughout the plant but throughout the entire water system. Approaching the treatment units, however, the calendar rolls back 50 years and one is faced with the melancholy fact that water treatment is still an art and not a science. One sees before him the same old mixing basins, flocculators, and sedimentation basins that have served as treatment units for more than five decades. Nature purifies water by settling and filtration and, after all these years, man still continues to do so too.''

Almost all of the nation's 24,000 community water systems are still geared toward preventing bacterial diseases and stopping unwanted tastes or odors. The recent public concern about water pollution in general has focused upon streams, lakes, rivers, and coastal waters. But, this interest has drawn attention away from an even more serious water pollution problem—safeguarding the water systems used by nearly all Americans.

Several important studies on drinking water were examined in a series of articles published in *Consumer Reports* which point out the major problems and some solutions. Perhaps the largest problem is that most water systems are aimed primarily at preventing bacterial diseases. For the most part they have been successful in that effort. But, and that is a large but, the U.S. Public Health Service (PHS) standards are clearly inadequate in many respects. Most consumers wrongly assume that the PHS standards are being met. One study reported that 85 percent of the water systems "failed to collect and test the prescribed minimum number of water samples." This may be partly because no federal law requires that water systems meet PHS standards. The standards are not so high, either. The PHS permits ten coliforms (bacteria found in feces and in soil) per liter of drinking water. In contrast, Maryland's standard for *sewage* discharged in certain waters is only 1 coliform per liter of water. The World Health Organization standards are twenty times stricter than the PHS standards.

What the water systems do not do is a little

frightening. The federal and state governments do not recommend or require tests for waterborne viruses. Yet evidence accumulates that diseases like infectious hepatitis have been caused by viruses in drinking water. Also, very few systems bother to check for chemicals in the water systems. This includes such hazardous metals as lead, chromium, arsenic, barium, cadmium, selenium, silver, and mercury. The Environmental Protection Agency *recommends* semiannual testing for these metals. One result of testing has been the finding that a higher incidence of certain types of cancer has been found in many communities where these kinds of contaminants are known to be in the water.

In 1959, the U.S. Public Health Service reported that the bladder cancer rate for New Orleans was three times as high as the Atlanta and Birmingham rates. Similarly higher than normal cancer rates have been recently found again for New Orleans, Louisiana; Evansville, Indiana; and Ames, Iowa. Ohio residents whose drinking water comes mainly from Lake Erie and the Ohio River also have higher rates. Numerous other cities are affected in the same way. The Environmental Protection Agency, with some motivation by the nonprofit Environmental Defense Fund, released a report on carcinogens in water supplies. In New Orleans, the EPA found sixty-six possible carcinogens! Further studies revealed that "every water system tested contained measurable amounts of possibly carcinogenic chemicals." Surprisingly, chlorine—the chemical most American water systems use to purify water—was found to combine with some natural substances to form suspected carcinogens. Thus, guidelines for using chlorine are expected to be mandated by the EPA.

Studies through the years have been inconclusive as to the causes of higher cancer rates. However, many of the organic contaminants found in water are known carcinogens. And, as *Consumer Reports* notes, "all of them can be reduced in quantity, and some can perhaps be eliminated altogether, at a very small cost per household, just by routing the water through a bed of activated carbon granules before it is piped throughout the city."

More research is obviously needed. But strong evidence has already shown that use of activated carbon granules instead of or in addition to beds of sand is a much better method of purification. Very simply, the carbon granules efficiently remove organic compounds dissolved in water, which is something that sand cannot do. The use of carbon granules is not a panacea for water problems, but it can go a long way toward making our water safer to drink. The residents of Nitro, West Virginia, and a few other American communities have taken this route. The cost for the residents of Nitro was less than 1 cent per 1000 gallons of water treated. This amounted to an additional 5 cents per month for a family of four. Thus, this community joins the many European countries that have been using this method for years. Concerned consumers need to ask questions about their own local situation.

POISONS AND PESTICIDES

Three areas of poisons and pesticides confronted by consumers are examined below: lead poisoning at home, lead poisoning on the job, and pesticides and insecticides for home and gardens.

Lead Poisoning at Home

Lead poisoning is a serious crippler and killer of children between the ages of 1 and 6. The National Bureau of Standards estimates that 400,000 children may have elevated levels of lead in their blood. The Department of Health, Education and Welfare estimates that 100 children die each year from lead poisoning, with another 30,000 enduring serious symptoms. Dr. Henrietta Sacks, a Chicago pediatrician and national authority on lead poisoning, sees fifty or sixty patients every day in her lead-poison clinic. She estimates that probably 200 children die from lead

poisoning each year and another 6000 are neurologically handicapped or brain damaged.

Lead poisoning seems to be a ghetto problem. It frequently affects children who eat chips of lead-based paint from crumbling walls and window sills. Continued ingestion results in the following types of symptoms: unusual irritability, poor appetite, stomach pains and vomiting, persistent constipation, and sluggishness or drowsiness. Only a doctor can accurately determine if a person has lead poisoning. If it is not caught and treated early, it can lead to irreversible brain damage and even death. One study conducted in Boston by Dr. Herbert Needleman determined that children with elevated lead levels scored lower on intelligence tests than children without those levels of lead in their blood.

Over the last 50 or 60 years lead-based paints have been used in millions of dwellings to paint walls and exteriors. Because of federal laws prohibiting the use of high-lead-content paint for interiors, such paints are now used only for exteriors. However, in older buildings (there are an estimated 500,000 to 600,000 in Chicago alone), children are still exposed to peeling lead-based paint. Classified as a disease among young children, lead poisoning ranks fourth behind chicken pox, measles, and mumps.

Surprisingly, middle- and higher-income families have also been affected by lead poisoning. One study of 500 children conducted by the District of Columbia government and Howard University showed that 42 percent had abnormally high levels of lead in their blood. Less than 1 percent of the homes had paint with lead content greater than 1 percent, but the amount of lead in the dust in the more affluent homes was much higher than that in the homes of inner-city children.

In areas of decaying homes, Dr. Sachs describes the severity of the problem with an account of the death of a 4-year-old boy. He was treated for lead poisoning four times between March and June. Complaints were made to the building inspector, but the landlord did nothing. The family moved to newer and cleaner housing. In February of the following year, the boy died of lead poisoning. Examination revealed that the newer and cleaner home had lead-based paint on the interior walls and window sills.

There are not too many proposals to remedy the situation, and little action is being taken. Paints for interior use now have a maximum lead content of 0.06 percent, according to regulations issued by the Consumer Product Safety Commission. This affects only newly painted homes. During the year 1975, the U.S. Department of Housing and Urban Development (HUD) announced a ban on lead-based paints in all newly acquired housing. The following year, however, it reversed its position—apparently because of pressure from the paint industry and the realization of the high costs involved in removing lead-based paint from existing surfaces. HUD either owns or is in the process of buying 160,000 housing units that will shelter more than 250,000 children. Is it knowingly or unknowingly exposing them to the dangers of lead poisoning?

Only two serious alternatives have been proposed to solve the dilemma: (1) Cover up walls and window sills on which dangerous lead-based paint was used, and (2) scrape off the old paint and apply new, safer paint. At present, a stalemate exists. It costs $3000 to $5000 to remove or cover up the dangerous paint in most of the offending dwellings, and funds have not been forthcoming. What would you recommend?

Lead Poisoning on the Job

Lead poisoning is one of the oldest industrial hazards, first recognized more than 200 years ago. In the 1800s the Germans called it the *huttenkatze*—the cat of the foundries—because it "tortures like a cat tearing at the entrails," said one early writer. Lead from any source is stored in the body, in the bone marrow, and in other organs. After a certain point, probably "above 80 micrograms per 100 cubic centimeters of whole blood, the risk of serious symptoms of lead poisoning increase dra-

matically," says Dr. J. Julian Chisholm of the Johns Hopkins University Medical School and a nationally recognized expert on the subject. It can cause irreversible nerve paralysis, kidney failure, high blood pressure, arthritic-type pains, and brain damage. Also, lead has been associated with birth defects and miscarriage, as well as sterility among both women and men.

The problem of industrial lead exposure is quite large. More than 1 million workers are employed in primary smelters, recycling operations, battery plants, pigment plants, recycling pigment operations, and probably another 100 other occupations involved with lead. Similar problems occur with asbestos.

A 20-year-plus battle against lead poisoning at the Mineral Pigments Corporation factory in Beltsville, Maryland, is typical of the lack of progress in this area. Throughout the years state and federal officials have intermittently tried to clean up the working conditions, to no avail. "It's not a good story," said Morton Corn, Assistant Secretary of Labor for the Occupational Safety and Health Administration (OSHA). He described how deadlines for correcting the situation have been set and repeatedly reset, sometimes with small fines, as "illustrative of the way things worked here" at OSHA.

In 1974 three-fourths of seventy-two Mineral Pigments workers tested by the county health department showed "abnormal" lead levels in their blood. "I'm always tired. I'm run down. I don't have any energy or anything," said Clarence Wolfe, a 43-year-old worker. Robert Steele, a 24-year-old worker in the colormaking department, is typical of many workers. He earns top dollar—over $6 an hour—but wishes the place wasn't so dangerous. "There's been nights I've told my foreman I refuse to work because of the dust. Sometimes you can't see 20 feet in front of you. It gets that bad."

Allen Jaffy, president of Mineral Pigments, says that the company is "continuing to make progress as fast as technology permits. . . . Maybe not as fast as some people from OSHA would like to see it. It's a very slow process.'' Rockwood Industries, which bought Mineral Pigments Corporation in 1973, reports that lead-dust exposure there is "minor" and that the problem pervades the industry. Martin Ross, chairman of the board of Rockwood Industries, says that "There is no pigment plant in the world, as far as I know, which is completely complying with the OSHA dust standard." Obviously, it will be only through the cooperative efforts of government, industry, labor, and consumers that lead poisoning will be bought under control.

Home and Garden Pesticides and Insecticides
Another major area of consumer concern is pesticides and insecticides for home and garden use. DDT, BHC, endrin, heptachlor, leptophos, chlordane, vinyl chloride, aldrin, mercury, and Kepone have been either completely banned or severely limited in use by the Environmental Protection Agency in recent years. However, hundreds of tons of U.S.-prohibited pesticides and insecticides (including DDT, leptophos, aldrin, heptachlor, and chlordane) are shipped abroad for use in other countries.

Persistent pesticides and insecticides leave toxic residues in the environment for many years. In fact, the residues are often found in animals, fish, and plants that are very low on the food chain. Later, however, the persistent residues find their way up through the food chain into everyday products. A *nonpersistent* product is much safer; and many are not toxic to the environment, and they are less toxic to humans and animals. A commercial successor to the DDT types of pesticides may be a product called Emtex. Early research findings show that it is more efficient than DDT but is neither toxic nor persistent.

The dilemma facing the typical consumer is which pesticides to use in the home and garden. Required labeling provides much information that consumers can use. Since all pesticides are potentially harmful to human and animal life, a good rule is to avoid the use of highly toxic pesticides. Examples of toxic and persistent ingredients include chlorinated hydrocarbons (dieldrin, heptachlor, benzene, hexachloride, and lindane) or compounds containing lead or arsenic. If you must use any of these products, be aware of the meaning of the labels. These most dangerous products are marked on the label with the traditional symbol of a "skull and crossbones." Pesticides labeled "warning" are strongly toxic and should be handled with great care. Products labeled "caution" are the least toxic.

A frightening example of an environment disaster from a persistent pesticide is the case of Kepone. Kepone severely disabled more than sixty workers *and* family members who came in direct contact with the "dustlike substance." The product was made over a period of only 16 months in a converted gasoline station in Hopewell, Virginia. The manufacturer was the Life Science Products Company, a subcontractor of Allied Chemical Corporation. When ingested or inhaled in high concentrations, such as by the workers, Kepone attacks the central nervous system. It results in shaking, loss of mental acuity, and sterility. Fortunately, new drug treatments are meeting with success in treating victims. Kepone has been found to cause cancer in laboratory animals.

Being a persistent pesticide, it caused a serious environmental hazard in addition to the numerous personal problems for the workers. The wastes from the plant were pumped into the James River, since the local sewage system became incapable of handling the problem. The James River feeds into Chesapeake Bay. The seafood industry of the entire Chesapeake Bay area has lost hundreds of millions of dollars because of fish contamination. Kepone-contaminated fish have been found in catches as far north as New Jersey and New York. When fish have a tissue concentration above a certain "action level," the EPA or FDA takes action and does not permit that seafood to be sold. Evidence from the EPA and other sources show that Kepone contamination is still spreading and that it is likely to remain a problem in the Chesapeake Bay area for *decades.*

In 1976 President Gerald Ford signed the Toxic Substances Control Act. It banned by 1979 any further use of PCBs (polychlorinated biphenyls), and resulted in the closing of commercial fishing in the Hudson River and Great Lakes for quite some time. PCBs were also found in the milk of mothers sampled in 11 states. PCBs have been used as a chemical in plastics, paints, printing ink, hydraulic fluid, lubricants, electrical capacitors, and transformers. Research showed that PCBs found their way into the food chain, resulting in reproductive failure, gastric disorders, skin lesions, tumors, and human liver cancer (which is always fatal, generally within a year). PCBs and DDT, because they resist decomposition, are believed to be present in the fatty tissue of nearly every person in the United States, Japan, and other industrialized countries. A recent FDA sample of all types of food found PCBs in 3505 of 17,000 samples.

Of great importance, the legislation gave the Environmental Protection Agency the authority to require chemical manufacturers to pretest products that could cause a health or environmental risk. Companies planning on marketing a new chemical or selling an existing one for a new purpose must now notify the EPA 90 days in advance. The EPA can then review the testing done by the company, require more testing, and limit or even prohibit the chemical from being sold. Of course, companies that object to EPA decisions can take the issue to court. President Ford said, "I believe this legislation may be one of the most important pieces of environmental legislation that has been enacted by Congress." Senator Warren Magnuson said that the law would "no longer allow the environment of the public to be used as a testing ground."

Chemical pollution is of serious concern. There are an estimated 60,000 chemicals already in use today and another 1000 new ones marketed each year. The pesticide industry

alone is a $2.6 billion business which produces 1 billion pounds of chemicals for use in the United States and another 600 million pounds for countries abroad. Environmental contaminants such as these are factors in "60 to 90 percent of cancer occurring in the U.S.," according to the National Cancer Institute. There is no doubt that the law will help protect the American public better, but it is not an automatic thing.

Consider, for example, the difficulties the EPA has had in trying to carry out the mandate of the 1972 Federal Environmental Pesticide Control Act. That law requires a review of *all* pesticide products previously registered with federal and state governments, and then a determination of whether or not they should be allowed to stay on the market under new, stricter guidelines. Basically this involves reregistering and reviewing of all such pesticides.

Senator Edward M. Kennedy released a staff report of his Senate Judiciary Subcommittee on Administrative Practice and Procedure that severely criticized the EPA for its failure to "validate testing data" and to meet the deadlines for reviewing the chemicals established by the law. Kennedy said that he "recognized the constraints under which the EPA was operating," since it was unable to obtain the people and resources to carry out the enormous task, but blamed the EPA "because it attempted to conceal its problems from the Congress and the public." EPA administrator Russell E. Train, while agreeing with many of the criticisms, denied any attempt to "shirk its duties or to mislead the public." All agreed that the review process, if it is to be done properly, will take from 10 to 20 years.

Two related issues are under hot debate. First, should the United States bother using pesticides on crops at all anymore? According to Dr. David Pimentel, professor of entomology at Cornell, if we eliminated pesticides altogether, "we wouldn't starve." He reports that while cotton and fruit are heavy users of pesticides, only 6 percent of the total United States crop and pastureland is treated. He estimates that halting the use of pesticides completely would reduce the United States food output by only 9 percent. Many in the chemical and food industries obviously disagree. A second issue is whether or not it is worth risking the health and lives of some U.S. workers, who produce dangerous pesticides, in order to achieve economic and medical objectives which may save those in other countries from death, illness, or malnutrition. For instance, is it worth risking the lives of chemical workers in Bayport, Texas, where the nerve-attacking compound leptophos (which is banned for use in the United States) is manufactured for use in Mexico, Indonesia, and Taiwan to kill insects in crops and help the people of those countries avoid death from starvation and disease? What do you think?

TOY AND PRODUCT SAFETY PROBLEMS

Sales in the toy industry amount to over $5 billion annually. Each year the 900 American manufacturers produce about 150,000 different toys, with 5000 being new ones. Additionally, thousands of others are imported from abroad. These toys are for sale at an estimated 1 million outlets. And it is well known that toys bring safety problems. Some 800,000 people were injured seriously enough last year by incidents associated with toys to require hospital emergency room treatment.

How Toys Injure, Maim, and Kill

Toys injure, maim, and kill children in many ways: by lacerations, contusions and abrasions, bone fractures, bumps and bruises, strains and sprains, cuts, pinches, punctures, electric shocks, burns, lung inhalations, and strangulation. They can also cause deafness, blindness, and other types of injuries.

Injuries from toys often, of course, arise from misuse of the product. However, because of inadequate product design, improper materials, lack of durability, insufficient labeling and instructions, inadequate warnings, and

defects in manufacturing materials or construction, millions of potentially dangerous toys are sold. Some have sharp edges, points, wires, staples, or pins. Others are so flimsy, particularly some plastic and glass toys, that they shatter. Some fragment or even explode. Many have small and easily removable parts that can be eaten, inhaled, or become lodged in a child's windpipe, ears, or nose. Some contain fabrics that are highly flammable. Many electrical toys can shock children or have extremely high temperatures on exposed surfaces. There are toys that pinch; that are unclean and lead to infections; that have contaminants inside that, once released, are harmful; that have almost unextinguishable flames; that contain highly toxic substances; that contain small pellets which are easily swallowed if the seam of a stuffed toy breaks; and that glorify war and torture and affront the morals and ethics of many. Others have noise levels high enough to cause deafness.

Injuries

To determine the nature and scope of injuries from toys and other products, the Consumer Product Safety Commission has a national data collection system known as the National Electronic Injury Surveillance System (NEISS, pronounced "nice"). It collects data from 119 statistically selected hospital emergency rooms across the country. NEISS projections can then help identify those products most often related to injuries. Approximately 38 percent of all injuries are treated in hospital emergency rooms, 41 percent are treated in doctors' offices, 18 percent at home, and 3 percent become inpatient cases.

The estimated number of injuries associated with toys and toy-type products which require emergency room treatment is shown in Table 6-3. The biggest three offenders in terms of numbers are "bicycles," "swings, slides, and playground equipment," and "skates, skateboards, and scooters."

One example of a product on which specific NEISS data are available is the bicycle—one of the most frequent contributors to severe injuries. More than 1000 bicyclists die yearly in bicycle-related accidents. Figures 6-2 and 6-3 show the types of injuries sustained and the body parts injured. Children aged 14 or younger suffer 83 percent of the bicycle injuries.

Protection from Toys and Unsafe Products
Many government groups have been involved in trying to protect people from unsafe products. Yet millions of injuries still occur each year. For more than a decade the Food and Drug Administration had the power to prohibit flammable toys under the Flammable Fabrics Act. Then both the FDA, through the Bureau of Product Safety, and the Department of Health, Education and Welfare were specifically charged with protecting children from unsafe toys. Not much happened. In fact, in 1971 the FDA's Toy Safety Review Committee had a staff of six people. The maximum number of toys they could examine was estimated at 1200, or less than 1 percent of those on the market.

Now, things are improving since the Consumer Product Safety Commission (CPSC)

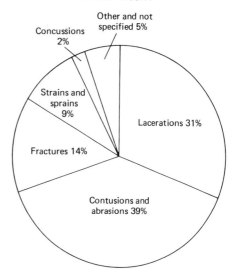

Source: U.S. Consumer Product Safety Commission, Bureau of Epidemiology, February 10, 1978.

FIGURE 6-2   Types of bicycle injuries

was established to centralize federal government efforts to protect against such dangers. In addition to administering other laws related to product safety, the CPSC has certain powers of its own. It can issue mandatory safety

TABLE 6-3

Estimated Injuries Associated with Toy-Type Products Receiving Emergency Room Treatment (Based on NEISS data)

Product Category	Number of Injuries
Bicycles	465,860
Swings, slides, and playground equipment	157,963
Skates, skateboards, and scooters	129,127
Toys (excluding riding or ride-on toys)	84,364
Minibikes and unlicensed motor scooters and go-carts	26,911
Wagons and other ride-on toys	16,434
Tricycles	12,285
Money (paper and coins, including toy money)	10,544

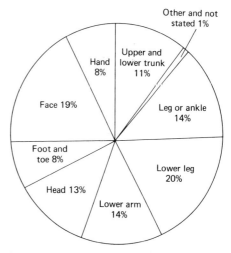

Source: U.S. Consumer Product Safety Commission, Bureau of Epidemiology, February 15, 1977.

FIGURE 6-3   Body part injured by bicycles.

standards; it can issue preliminary injunctions prohibiting distribution of potentially hazardous products; it can ban hazardous products, and require industry to notify the CPSC and the public about any product defect that could pose a substantial risk of injury to consumers; it can require action by industry to correct product defects at no cost to consumers; and it can also engage in educational campaigns to stress safe usage of products by consumers.

Consumer critics of the CPSC suggest that it does too much on the education level and not enough in the protection area. During the first 7 years of its existence, the CPSC issued only a handful of mandatory safety standards, banned 1800 toys, but issued no injunctions. Judy Jackson, a frustrated member of the CPSC Consumer Advisory Board and a professor at Temple University Law School, says that "Rather than trying to regulate the industry, they are trying to say it's all your fault if your child gets hurt and you better watch out. They are saying that business is basically responsible. Oh, maybe there are a few too-rotten apples, but, by and large, they can regulate themselves. I don't agree. The reason the act (empowering banning) was passed was because voluntary regulation failed." Industry critics, on the other hand, think that the CPSC is too strong and unwieldy in its powers. Not many manufacturers like the regulation, for example, that requires electrical toys to have warning labels stating that the products are not recommended for children under a certain age. In the case of toys that contain a heating element, the manufacturer may not indicate that the toy is recommended for children under 8. Few companies, however, have even gone to court to argue against the CPSC.

If you have purchased a product which is a banned hazardous article or substance under the Federal Hazardous Substances Act, one of the laws enforced by the CPSC, you are entitled to redress. In most cases the retailer must prominently display a sign informing people of the fact that particular banned products were sold in that store. The sign must also tell them where in the establishment they can go to ex-amine the list of banned products and the notice of refund or repair procedures. You may then return the article or substance to the retail dealer from whom you purchased it for a refund of the price you paid *and* any reasonable and necessary transportation charges incurred in its return.

Product Safety and Liability

Approximately 1½ million product-related liability lawsuits will be in court this year, and many of these are for consumer products. The others are primarily industrial-product lawsuits for which the consumer ultimately must pay the price because of higher costs of doing business. A Minnesota machinery company with annual sales of $2 million went out of business when its product liability insurance jumped from $2000 in 1970 to $200,000 in 1976. More recently, a propane appliance company's premium increased from $392 for $500,000 in coverage for 1 year to $55,200 for only $300,000 in coverage 2 years later. One packaging-machinery maker saw liability insurance costs rise from $110,000 to $385,000 in only 3 years—this represented almost 4 percent of sales! These examples demonstrate the severity of the problem.

Average settlement costs of product liability suits in Cook County, which includes Chicago, jumped from $93,000 in 1970 to $144,000 in 1975, and are expected to reach $250,000 by 1980. Speaking of the problems of product liability insurance in the future, a spokesperson for the American Insurance Association says "It would probably make medical malpractice look like a common cold."

This has come about for many reasons, but perhaps primarily because of a changing way of life in America and changes in legal thinking. People are now more inclined to sue rather than "just settle" for what the insurance company offers. Also, it has become easier to sue when a product goes wrong and a consumer is hurt. If the product is shown to have a defect in manufacture, design, or labeling, the product can be held liable. Negligence need no longer be shown.

In Westchester County, New York, a 34-year-old woman was awarded $1.2 million because she was injured by a drug. A manufacturer of T-shirts settled for $140,000 a claim involving an 11-year-old boy who received burns on his chest and arms. The T-shirt ignited when the boy came in contact with a power line. The shirt manufacturer had complied with all rules and regulations under the Flammable Fabrics Act, yet the plaintiff contended that the T-shirt was "dangerously flammable," even though the boy had climbed the pole without permission.

Professor Jeffrey O'Connell, long-time advocate of no-fault automobile insurance, proposes some form of "no-fault" insurance to help remedy the problem. The Commerce Department has a study group at work, and the insurance industry is trying to figure out how to avoid a national disaster in product liability lawsuits. National consumer columnist Sylvia Porter suggests that legislation will be needed to help control the number of lawsuits, curb excessive jury awards, and provide insurance for businesses at reasonable costs. Of extreme importance at the same time, however, Porter notes, is to maintain "our rights as consumers to sue for and collect damages, when defects in manufacturers' products cause injury or even death."

NUCLEAR WASTES AND CONSUMERS

The need to expand our nation's energy capacity is quite clear to all. Several alternatives were examined in Chapter 4. However, one source of energy in particular—nuclear power—is quite controversial, as it has a potentially dangerous byproduct.

The dangers of nuclear waste are quite different from those associated with the possibility of a nuclear plant core meltdown or the sabotage of nuclear reactors. Of particular concern are the waste-reprocessing plants planned for future use and what to do with radioactive waste from atomic power plants. Representative John E. Moss reports that by

1983, thirty reactors may have to be shut down because of lack of storage facilities.

The two main sources of radioactive waste in the United States are the 70-plus reactors already generating electricity for commercial consumption, and the federal reactors that produce plutonium for atomic weapons and to fuel submarines, missile cruisers, and some aircraft carriers. Before fast breeder reactors were developed, the United States already had stored in temporary locations throughout the country more than 75 million gallons of high-level radioactive waste and 51 million cubic feet of low-level waste. With the technological situation unresolved, problems abound. No fewer than eighteen leaks at a major storage area at Hanford, Washington, have resulted in the loss of 430,000 gallons of high-level wastes into nearby soil. No deaths or injuries occurred at that plant, but the "hazard will remain for hundreds of thousands of years" reported Dr. Mason Willrich in a special report for the federal Department of Energy. Willrich points out that the potential effects of radiation include "immediate death, life shortened by radiation-induced cancer, radiation-induced genetic change which may affect subsequent generations, or temporary ill health followed by complete recovery."

An example of the latter took place when a chemical explosion occurred at Hanford, contaminating eight workers with radioactivity. No nuclear leak occurred, and the workers were isolated until decontamination. Radioactivity is removed by repeated washings, unless of course it is too serious. The only example in peacetime of a calamity with waste comes from the Soviet Union. Exiled scientist Zhores Medvedev reported that in 1958 hundreds of people were killed and thousands suffered from radiation sickness when buried atomic waste (plutonium) exploded without warning in Troitsk near the town of Blagoveshensk in the Ural mountains. The disaster was caused by an earthquake. Medvedev wrote, "The buried nuclear waste overheated and erupted like a violent volcano. The high winds blew the radioactive debris hundreds of miles, contaminating towns and villages along the way and making hundreds of people so ill with radiation poisoning that many of them died.'' Troitsk is off-limits to Westerners and has never been visited by Americans; however, documents released by the Central Intelligence Agency (CIA) recently confirmed the devastation that occurred. The six atomic factories there make electricity, but their primary purpose is to produce plutonium for nuclear weapons.

That type of calamity is possible here too. It almost happened at Hanford in 1973 but was not reported to the public until 1976. One trench accumulated so much plutonium that a runaway chain reaction almost occurred. According to a *Washington Post* story, ''Alarmed engineers avoided what could have been a serious nuclear accident by pumping into the trench large volumes of cadmium metal, which acts to slow and then halt a nuclear chain reaction.'' The trench was filled between 1955 and 1962 and then sealed off. You don't go about your business and forget about nuclear wastes, however. You must remain watchful—for thousands of years. When this trench was rechecked, the engineers found that it had accumulated much more than the 60 pounds of plutonium they thought it contained. They are still digging up that trench, at a cost of $1 million, and may have to dig up another dozen at Hanford during the early 1980s. Digging up and checking at other repositories is now under way in view of the similarity of problems. Plutonium leaks at the Rocky Flats nuclear weapons plant outside Broomfield, Colorado, have ''left a plutonium blanket on the bottom of the city's 40-acre water supply system.'' Besides solving the leak problem, the governments are trying to decide who should pay for a new $30 million water supply system.

The Department of Energy has announced that it plans to spend $2 billion on six repositories to hold radioactive wastes from nuclear power plants over the next 30 years. Critics claim that $2 billion is low. States high on the list for preliminary field work to determine feasibility include Colorado, Louisiana, Michigan, Tennessee, Utah, Texas, Nevada, Washington, Indiana, Mississippi, New York, Ohio, and South Dakota. Nuclear wastes from the military are expected to be buried in New Mexico and perhaps Kansas.

Simply to close an abandoned and obsolete atomic fuel reprocessing factory near Buffalo, New York, is estimated to cost $540 million. The West Valley plant contains 600,000 gallons of high-level radioactive wastes, including strontium, cesium, barium, cobalt, and plutonium. It has been stored there at a temperature of 195 degrees since 1966. Since liquid waste cannot be transferred, much of the money is needed to build a factory alongside of the original plant which can solidify the liquid radioactive waste. A reprocessing plant at Barnwell, South Carolina, has already cost $250 million without any allowance for converting liquids to cement or glass from solids.

Sweden's Prime Minister Thorbjörn Fälldin announced that if the problem of safe disposal of radioactive waste material for their five nuclear plants could not be solved in 1979, he would shut them down. The United States' solution to nuclear waste, or even the world's, is not clear yet. Perhaps the ultimate solution will be similar to one proposed by the United States at the beginning of the Atomic Age. The so-called Baruch Plan proposed complete international control of nuclear energy from the first stages of mining of uranium to the disposal of the radioactive waste. The United States proposed it at the United Nations in 1946.

POINTS OF VIEW AND PROBLEMS TO THINK ABOUT

The problems facing us in the form of a multitude of products are often overwhelming. Our productive capacities as a nation have given us thousands of products that we cannot effectively compare. Many are also hazardous to our health. In the area of drugs and cosmetics alone, the technology is so sophisticated that only those with advanced college degrees can begin to understand what may be good and what may be bad.

Consumers have to depend upon the regulatory agencies at all governmental levels to provide them with fundamental protection against dangerous products. In fact, consumers must *insist* upon adequate protection. The manufacturers', distributors', and retailers' need for profit must be tempered with greater concern for the safety of consumers, while at the same time consumers must be willing to pay higher prices for increased safety.

Regarding prescription drugs and some over-the-counter drugs, we wonder how many people would continue to take some of them if they knew the serious side effects. Perhaps drug manufacturers, doctors, and pharmacists should have to give *patients* package inserts about drugs before the drug is prescribed. If written in lay language, the consumer-patient could then be aware of the risks involved before deciding to take the drug. Progestins, as noted by Dr. Sidney Wolfe, are still being prescribed to pregnant women. "A question needs asking," says Wolfe. "Would any of those 500,000 pregnant women, informed that these drugs may seriously damage the fetus, and told that they don't even work for preventing miscarriages—their major use—consent to taking them? We believe the answer is no."

On the cancer front, two developments of a positive nature are worth noting. Chlorozotocin is a relatively new cancer treatment drug (of which there are about thirty) currently being tested at Georgetown University's Lombardi Cancer Research Center. Early results suggest that this drug could have much less serious side effects in cancer therapy, as it presumably causes less bone marrow damage while it attacks the cancer. Bone marrow produces the white blood cells necessary to the body's defense against disease. Results are preliminary, but human tests are now under way. In Great Britain, scientists have developed a rather simple chemical test—biphenyl—to determine whether or not a substance is likely to cause cancer. In practical applications with known carcinogens, the biphenyl test has been accurate more than two-thirds of the time. Perhaps one day, as a matter of course, new cosmetics, paints, food flavorings, dyes, and additives will get the biphenyl test first.

Responsible consumers are going to have to put their hand up higher if they want to be recognized. A few examples: In the late 1970s the federal government ordered 427,000 color television sets recalled because of possible radiation from "5 to 25 times the maximum allowable." Despite widespread publicity and two letters from the manufacturer, the record shows that fewer than 40 percent of the purchasers brought their sets in for free repairs. In the first 4 years of the existence of the Consumer Product Safety Commission, it ordered recalls for 33 million individual products—only about 19 percent were ever returned for repairs.

And despite all the talk about protecting our environment, of the consumers who have a free choice between disposable containers and returnable bottles, three-fourths still buy disposables. They prefer convenience to price savings. Oregon and Vermont have had laws restricting throwaway bottles for years, and costs are lower. A twenty-four-state price survey taken by the League of Women Voters in conjunction with the Environmental Protection Agency showed that the returnable bottles were much cheaper than the disposables. A report by the Research Triangle Institute in North Carolina noted "that if current trends continue and a deposit law is not enacted, beer and soft-drink production and distribution in 1982 (the year for which they studied impacts) will require about 0.5 percent of the total energy supply, capital investment of $7.3 billion, and a work force of 369,000 earning $4.1 billion." If a law was in effect nationwide to require returnables, the estimated consumers savings would be "$2.6 billion annually, energy savings equivalent to 70,000 barrels of oil daily, and a net increase of 117,000 jobs." In criticizing the report, Thomas Baker of the

National Soft Drink Association said that "If a deposit system is mandated, the consumer loses freedom of choice. This is still a democracy; why must all citizens have to bear the financial burden for litter cleanup because of the habits of the slobs?"

Responsible consumers must help to ensure that all elements of the marketplace pool their resources and must be willing to pay the price needed for safety in our economy. Such efforts will necessitate (1) increased expenditures to enforce existing laws; (2) legislative action on proposals aimed at more safety in the marketplace; (3) voluntary and sincere actions by businesses to ensure safe products while they seek reasonable profits; and (4) consumers willing to educate themselves concerning the safety, use, and utility of various products.

CHAPTER ACTIVITIES ━━━━━

Checkup on Consumer Terms and Concepts

Hazardous and dangerous products	U.S.P.
	Cosmetics
Prescription drugs	Antiperspirant
Over-the-counter drugs	Nontobacco ingredients
Pharmaceutical trade association	Lead poisoning
Ineffective drugs	Persistent pesticides
Dangerous drugs	"Caution" labels
Generic drugs	Consumer Product Safety Commission
Poison Prevention Package Act	Nuclear wastes
	Product liability

Review of Essentials
1. What is the trend in product liability suits against manufacturers of dangerous products? Why?

2. Discuss the factors involved in the cost of prescription drugs.
3. What are the fundamental issues concerning both ineffective and dangerous drugs?
4. What does scientific evidence conclude about the use of brand-name and generic drugs?
5. Summarize the effectiveness of generic aspirin in contrast to other pain relievers.
6. What must consumers do to be sure of buying a product that really prevents sunburn?
7. What effect do prescription practices and sales promotion policies have on society?
8. Describe the value of toothpastes.
9. What is the possibility of lead poisoning in middle- and higher-income families?
10. What can be done to protect children from dangerous toys?
11. What should be the government's policy toward nuclear wastes? Why?
12. What kinds of things can be done to reduce the number of product liability lawsuits?

Issues for Analysis
1. Should a federal government agency take action to inform consumers about the value of U.S.P. generic aspirin? Why or why not?
2. Assume that you are a happy homeowner with small children. Several small pets in the neighborhood have recently been found dead, including your own dog. The veterinarian told you that your pet died from some type of pesticide poisoning. As a responsible consumer, what courses of action should you take?
3. What should be the role of the federal government in protecting consumers against dangerous products? Include the point of view of business people also.

7

Consumer Credit

THE PROBLEMS

The consumer's dilemma is perhaps more apparent in the area of credit than it is in any other. Credit has become a way of life for most Americans today—it would be difficult for a large majority of adults to conduct their personal and business affairs without it. The consumer, therefore, must understand its advantages, disadvantages, uses, and abuses.

Society is rapidly moving toward a cashless society, with credit and check payments being used so frequently. Now a new problem has been thrust upon us all—a *cashless/checkless* society. Many retail businesses have joined with banks, and all the customer has to do is "sign" when a purchase is made. A charge sale is recorded, and from then on the consumer need not worry about making payments. The bank merely transfers money from the customer's account to that of the store and notifies the customer. What it amounts to is an *electronic funds transfer* (EFT) through the appropriate bookkeeping entry—no cash changes hands, and no checks are written. A primary disadvantage of EFT is that anyone who gains possession of an individual's fund transfer card or code number can empty the account in seconds without detection. And what becomes a real problem to consumers is whether or not they are ready for this sort of impersonal automatic financing of purchases.

Gullible, uninformed, and uneducated appear to describe most of the consumers who buy credit life and/or disability insurance in connection with a loan or credit purchase. *Credit insurance* is short-run term insurance that costs several times as much as most regular term life or disability insurance policies that one might already have. Paying $8.00 for $500 coverage on a loan or purchase for a year may sound good on the surface, but a bargain it is not. What the uninformed consumer is doing is paying excessively for protection he or she may already have or may not even need. Consumers do not need the additional costs or the duplication of coverage. But all too frequently the consumer is given the "hard sell" to buy this "essential" and "inexpensive" coverage. Be alert to this tactic and simply say "no." Retailers or banks can force you to buy this type of coverage as a loan or purchase condition, but at most places it is "suggested" as an option.

Another problem is evident for many uninformed consumers who carelessly make overpayments on their charge accounts. Many retail stores in the country receive overpayments of 50 cents here and $1.00 there and eventually accumulate millions of dollars for their use or investment. Furthermore, many of the stores do not notify consumers immediately or do not notify them at all about the small credit balances. In many cases, if the credit is carried on the account for 3 months, it is "automatically" debited, or cleared right into the general fund of the business. Simply put, through these carelessly made payments, many of the large stores are exploiting thousands of consumers by keeping and using money which is not theirs. Just think about it, an average investment of $1,000,000 for a year of these overpayments, with a modest return of 5%, comes to $50,000! Not a bad return for someone else's money. Would you as a consumer work for nothing? Probably not—but your money will if you are not careful.

Consider the case of Mrs. Thelma Rita, who was in a clothing store buying dresses. Suddenly she realized that she had left all her cash and her checkbook at home. She told the clerk that she would have to come back later for the dresses, only to be told not to worry because she could charge them and pay for them over an extended time. That way, the amount paid each month would be very little. Mrs. Rita agreed to the credit arrangement, since all it required was her signature.

This situation is not unique. Actually, three credit concerns can be seen in this case. (1) The consumer needs to know the specific conditions involved before accepting the credit obligation. (2) The merchant or representative should give the consumer all information about the transactions. (3) Consumers should not let themselves be pressured into accepting credit just to close a sale.

Another problem affects the many consumers who have modest incomes, yet can arrange for almost unlimited credit with merchants.

Since wants can easily exceed ability to pay, they often charge. What they do not always stop to think about is that they must eventually pay the cost of the merchandise *plus* the credit charge. Also, using credit now obligates *future income* for payments.

These and other credit problems obviously present a dilemma to uninformed consumers. Most of these problems are directly related to lack of information and knowledge about credit and/or misinformation from the people extending credit. A more detailed examination of credit—its use, various types, costs, and sources—will help consumers to comparison shop and better prepare them to confront today's credit society.

THE USE OF CREDIT

Basically, *credit* means to trust someone. A questioning comment, however, is "Trust someone for what?" Since time began, some form of credit has been practiced. In early biblical times, when one shepherd lent his staff to another to help rescue a lost sheep from a mountain ledge, a form of credit was being practiced. A trust was demonstrated, since one person lent something of value to another. Part of the trust was the understanding that the item would be returned to its owner, with or without compensation.

Occasionally, when the trust is questionable (in other words, if there is a doubt whether or not the item will be returned, or returned in its original condition), an element of risk develops. The severity of this risk determines the amount of "insurance" that one should take out to *ensure* the return of an item or to *assure* the ability to replace it. Such insurance amounts are generally referred to as charges for credit, credit costs, or interest charges. So the degree of trust is an important factor in credit arrangements.

Why Use Credit?
Most people use credit to get things that are important to them at a particular time and that

they could not otherwise afford. Thousands of people daily create a demand for products and/or services because they want them *now*. Once the demand has been established, the consumer has three options: (1) to resist the demand, (2) to satisfy it and pay cash, or (3) to want to satisfy it but find there is no cash available, and so use credit.

It is, of course, the third option that leads to credit. Generally, to get credit, the consumer can do one of two things: (1) borrow the money from some other source, or (2) sign a *statement of trust* with the seller (a promise to pay) and get the product or service now while making arrangements to pay later.

This desire to "have now and pay later" is the foundation upon which credit is built. The purposes for using credit are almost unlimited today. But most consumers tend to buy on credit for specific types of purchases or services. Generally, credit use is evident to a large degree when buying homes, cars, home furnishings, medical expenses, and education. To a lesser degree, credit is used for travel and vacations, investments, or to start a business.

For some home appliance purchases, the percent of credit use is very high. For example, 44 percent of all refrigerators, washing machines, and television sets are purchased on credit. And, nearly 40 percent of all clothes dryers, dishwashers, ranges, and air conditioners are purchased through credit terms of some kind.

Of course, goods and services do not have to be purchased on credit. Nearly half the consumers, however, cannot afford the cost at one time, yet the need seems to be immediate. Consequently, they arrange to use the merchandise while they pay for it in the future. Immediate use of purchased goods, no matter what they are, seems to be the primary reason for buying on credit.

Why people use credit is as varied as those who use it. Buying major articles, taking advantage of sales, consolidating debts, leveling out monthly payments for necessary goods or services, or using it as an emergency reserve all are viable reasons for using credit. Getting credit and using it properly, regardless of the reason, is the heart of the credit problem.

How Does One Get Credit?

A concern of those who want credit is that they be accepted as trustworthy consumers. A consumer wants a good rating in order to be able to get credit from such places as banks, savings and loan associations, credit unions, consumer finance companies, department stores, and automobile dealers. But if one's *credit trust* has not been established ahead of time, it can be very hard to get when it is needed.

Therefore, to obtain credit one must first establish trust between oneself and a business of some kind. Through the months or years of a person's life various financial activities are performed with businesses. As a result, the consumer seeks credit from *one* business just to help set up some trust and ultimately a credit rating. The consumer's honesty, ability to earn and spend money properly, and willingness to save or gain things of value become evident. Now the consumer can get and use credit on a regular basis.

With the proper credentials of trust and experience, a consumer can openly visit various businesses and get credit. He or she does not have to use this credit without a purpose. But it is available when needed. Also, with this obtained credit goes the right and responsibility to refuse to use it whenever credit is not to a person's advantage.

And finally, credit use is an earned privilege, not an obligation by anyone. Also, it should be used, not abused. Over a period of years of proper credit use, one's *credit rating* (how well you use credit) will be rated tops, and the benefits to be gained by using credit properly are many. Above all, a proper, positive attitude about credit will be the eventual criterion of successful use.

Abuses, Advantages, and Disadvantages of Credit

Mrs. Jalene Harris from Little Rock uses credit a great deal. However, occasionally

Mrs. Harris abuses it rather than uses it. Convenience, ease, speed, and instant money are terms that Mrs. Harris has relied on heavily when making most of her purchases. Although it would be difficult to stop her from using credit, her instant-money rationale has got her into trouble, since she frequently buys unnecessary items on impulse simply because it is so easy. She forgets that her purchases will eventually have to be paid for. Once this resulted in charges of more than $1000 and no immediate way to pay.

The case of Mrs. Harris is not unique; in fact, it is typical of many consumers. A consumer who falls prey to the ease and convenience of credit usually ends up by abusing it and becoming liable for more dollars than he or she can afford. Label these consumers "crediholics."

Credit abuse, of course, is not limited to the individual who cannot resist buying on credit, apparently disregarding ultimate payment. As a result of the widespread use of credit cards, many are stolen or are falsely created and used. A recent study by the U.S. Department of Justice showed that stolen or false credit cards cost private citizens, businesses, and governments $10 billion each year. The widespread, open use of credit cards has almost served as a catalyst for such crimes. Although losses on stolen credit cards are limited by law to $50 per person per card, the ultimate overall loss is staggering.

Credit can be used properly, and most people do so. But those who abuse credit by "not caring," and defaulting on payments for charged merchandise or loans, make it difficult for others who frequently become guilty by association. For example, Joyce Brooks has established a fine credit rating, pays her bills promptly, and generally uses credit very effectively. But sometimes when she uses her Visa card she has to show several pieces of identification and wait for telephone approval of her card before the credit charge is allowed. This is a nuisance for those who use credit properly, and it is thanks to the abusers of credit.

Electronic Funds Transfer (EFT) in banks is another development which stems from widespread use of credit. And it has caused further abuses of credit. Show a credit card, sign a sales slip, and sooner than one realizes money is transferred from one account in the bank to another—untouched by human hands. Although this fund transfer is said to be more convenient, reduce the handling of cash, eliminate the writing of checks, and provide detailed printouts of all transactions, it too can be considered an abuse of credit. All one has to do is present a credit card or some other type of funds transfer card (stolen or falsely acquired), with appropriate false identification, to make purchases readily through the EFT system. Funds are transferred so quickly that it is impossible to check on or stop all fraudulent purchases. Esther Peterson, Special Assistant on Consumer Affairs to the President said in House Subcommittee testimony that if consumers gain benefits from EFT, they must not lose the rights they now have with checks and credit cards. She said that action is needed to give consumers protection against problems that may arise with EFT systems. Errors of transfer that occur (for example, $120 for $12) need to be corrected. There are no provisions currently in effect to do this. With the widespread development and ease of EFT systems, something has to be done to protect consumers. Developed as an effort to benefit consumers, EFT has become a potential problem.

A further problem developed when the Federal Deposit Insurance Corporation and the Federal Reserve Board approved the automatic transfer of funds by a bank from a customer's savings account to a checking account in the case of overdrafts. This approval brings with it a major danger. If someone writes an unauthorized check on your account, causing an overdraft, your savings could be cleaned out before you and/or the bank uncover the error. In effect, what the government agencies have done to protect the interests of banks could cause a further hardship for the consumers. Consequently, consumers need to be continually on guard when using both their savings and checking accounts, particularly when they are in the same bank.

Credit can be used effectively, however, when its purposes and values are clearly understood and a proper attitude is held. To reinforce proper uses, let's look at some advantages and disadvantages of using credit. It has some *advantages,* since it:

- Allows a consumer to shop without having to carry much cash.
- Permits a consumer to act in an emergency when cash may not be immediately available.
- Permits a consumer to use goods and to benefit from services at the same time that he or she is paying for them.
- Permits a consumer to consolidate the costs of goods and services and to budget for them on a monthly basis.
- Enables a consumer to make a purchase when the price is right—on credit—rather than only when cash is available and the price may be higher.

Some *disadvantages* of using credit are:

- Credit tends to encourage consumers to overbuy.
- Credit tends to reduce a consumer's short-term buying power, since the interest costs must be paid as well.
- Excessive use of credit decreases thrift and savings and makes it difficult for consumers to have cash for emergency expenses.
- Excessive credit obligations can result in bankruptcy if the consumer should have a sudden reduction in or loss of income.
- Credit often reduces goal setting by families saving for the future.
- The cost of goods and services is increased by finance charges, further reducing the consumer's cash balance.
- Credit creates a false sense of security because of the possession of the goods.

The abuse of credit has led many people into *bankruptcy,* a legal procedure for wiping out one's debts. Over three-fourths of all bankruptcies have involved persons abusing credit. Furthermore, personal bankruptcies have been steadily increasing in recent years, according to the administrative offices of the U.S. courts. Once a person gets hooked on credit abuse, it is only a matter of time before the threat of bankruptcy can become a reality.

Rights and Responsibilities of Consumers

Consumers also have rights and responsibilities that are unique to the use of credit. Let's take a look at some of these rights and responsibilities.

Consumers have the right to refuse unasked-for credit cards mailed to them. They also have the responsibility to report to the proper authorities those who send these cards.

Consumers have the right to lose only $50 per stolen or lost credit card (they must pay *each* company up to a maximum of $50 for misuse of the credit cards). With this, however, goes the responsibility of notifying the issuer of the lost card. It is a further responsibility of consumers to maintain a record of all held credit cards so that, should a credit card be lost or stolen, the consumer has the number of the credit card and the complete name, address, and telephone number of the credit card issuer. Quick notification limits the liability of consumers.

Consumers have the right and responsibility to shop for credit to obtain the best terms and conditions possible. Also, they have the responsibility to seek information and ask questions appropriate to each potential credit obligation.

Consumers have the right to refuse to use credit if it is not appropriate to their needs and standards of quality. They also have the responsibility to learn enough about credit to judge good and bad credit conditions.

Consumers have the right to pay cash instead of using credit without being intimidated or harassed. Further, they have the responsibility of reporting store personnel who try to push credit unnecessarily.

Consumers have the right to know the credit information maintained about them in a credit bureau file as provided by the Fair Credit Reporting Act. Also, consumers have the responsibility to follow up and try to correct improper or wrong information that is in their files. They have the right to do this without harassment or intimidation or threat by bureau personnel.

Consumers have the right to apply for and obtain credit without discrimination on the grounds of sex, marital status, race, color, religion, national origin, or age under the Equal Credit Opportunity Act. It is a responsibility of consumers to report discriminatory practices to the proper authorities for redress.

Also, consumers have the right and responsibility to use credit properly and not abuse it. With this goes the right to be informed about all aspects of credit use and the responsibility to seek out this information as it is available and needed.

These rights and responsibilities for consumers in regard to credit are not exhaustive. They are, however, primary points to consider toward fair and equitable credit use for the benefit of consumers. If everyone adheres to these suggested rights and responsibilities, the public, business, and government will see a significant reduction in credit abuse.

TYPES OF CONSUMER CREDIT

Consumers should be able to differentiate between installment credit and noninstallment credit, which are the two broad classifications of credit used today. Their characteristics are illustrated below.

Installment Credit

Installment credit involves purchasing goods and services from a merchant or borrowing money from a lender. In addition, it means paying for these goods or services or repaying the money borrowed at a specific date each month (or week) for a set time period. Installment credit usually requires repayment for periods of up to a year or more. However, arrangements can be made for only a few months if desired.

With each potential installment credit purchase, the consumer must choose between two alternatives. He or she may purchase and pay in installments and pay a finance charge, but at the same time enjoy the benefits of the item. Or he or she may save money until it is possible to purchase the item for cash. In the latter situation, the consumer avoids finance charges. In the former, the consumer is saying that it is worth paying extra to be able to use the item now.

Installment Credit in Use Today. In a recent year, installment buying amounted to over $250 billion. Installment loan credit is provided by commercial banks, savings and loan associations, mutual savings banks, credit unions, and consumer finance companies. Other installment credit for merchandise is handled by most auto dealers, department stores, and other small retail stores. The amount of installment credit, the interest charged, and the time allowed for repayment are the main differences among those who provide installment credit. The largest amount of installment credit is held by commercial banks, who hold $97 billion in such debts, compared with the $45 billion held by finance companies. Common reasons for using installment credit include purchasing automobiles, major appliances, and household furnishings and making loans for home improvements or educational expenses.

Collateral Installment Loans. When you borrow money by pledging something of equal or near-equal value in case you default, your loan is called a *collateral loan*. Frequently savings are pledged, although this is only necessary when money is needed quickly and a withdrawal of savings is unwise at the time (perhaps due to the loss of accumulated interest). Most often a car or furniture is used as collateral.

When collateral loans are made, monthly payments are almost always required. A person who borrows $1000 with an annual interest rate of 10 percent is expected to repay the

THE FIRST OF YOUR 48 EASY PAYMENTS IS NOW DUE!

CLICK

Courtesy of Edd Uluschak.

amount plus interest 1 year later. The fact that the consumer has collateral places him or her in a better financial position as far as the lender is concerned. Thus, the borrower can frequently obtain a slightly lower interest rate. If the borrower does not repay the money, the pledged collateral is repossessed, or taken and used for repayment. This type of installment loan is also called a *security loan*.

Financing of many items can be arranged through one of several sources, which are discussed later in this chapter, but two legal devices are commonly used.

The *chattel mortgage* is the means by which most automobiles are financed. Similar to a mortgage on a home, the chattel mortgage always applies to movable goods (such as automobiles and furniture). The title, or ownership, is transferred to the buyer at the time of sale, and the lender holds the mortgage as security.

A *conditional sales contract* is another way to finance a purchase. It has been used much more frequently in recent years. It is similar to a lease on a home. With a conditional sales contract, the title does *not* pass to the buyer until the item is completely paid for. Therefore, there is less safety for the consumer because if he or she misses a payment, the lender can begin the process of repossession.

Noninstallment Credit

The second major type of credit is *noninstallment credit*, which does not involve fixed payments. Instead, the consumer decides whether or not to make more than one payment for a particular purchase. Noninstallment credit includes single-payment loans, charge accounts of various kinds, and service credit. Examples are given below.

Single-payment Loans. Alex Dender borrowed $500 from a bank in order to make repairs on his home. He agreed to repay the total amount in 6 months, along with an annual interest charge of 9 percent. With this single-payment loan, Mr. Dender need not repay anything until the 6 months has elapsed.

Charge Accounts. Mary Furnar bought some linens from a local department store and charged them to her account. Her account is a regular charge account, and her purchases must be paid in full within 30 days from the date of purchase.

There are also other types of charge accounts. For example, one type that varies slightly from Mrs. Furnar's charges a service fee if the account is not paid in full in 30 days, but it allows 30, 60, or 90 days or longer for full payment. The fee is usually a fixed amount—50 cents as a minimum, or 1 to 1½ percent a month or more of the unpaid balance.

A *revolving charge account* is a popular variation of the regular charge account. The revolving account offers the customer two payment choices: pay the entire balance in full in 30 days, or pay a designated amount (depending on the balance) upon receipt of the first statement—which usually provides 30 days to pay—and then pay the rest in later months. There is a finance charge on the remaining unpaid balance each month. This type of account has a number of names, among them an economy account, thrifty account, E-Z charge account, and flexible charge account. Master Charge and Visa are examples of nationwide accounts that follow this procedure.

Service Credit. Service credit is that given when the consumer uses public utilities for a short time before paying for the services rendered. Electric companies, gas companies, water departments, and telephone companies typically extend service credit.

Service credit is a special form of noninstallment credit. A customer must apply for the services needed. Commonly, the consumer is asked to pay a small deposit before the credit is extended, but once the credit is approved, he or she may use the service continuously.

After about 30 days of service, the customer is sent a statement of the amount owed to date, which must be paid in full within a prescribed number of days. If the consumer cannot pay the entire amount at the time, he or she is expected to pay it by the time the next statement is prepared, along with interest charges.

Some utility companies offer a small incentive to pay not only in full but also promptly, as the case of Mrs. Virginia Cummings of Atlanta, Georgia, shows. She was issued a monthly bill for electric services. Gross and net amounts were shown on each statement. Her January statement showed a gross amount of $44.42 and a net of $42.30. If she paid by February 10, the net amount was due. Since Mrs. Cummings never paid her statement until about the twenty-third or so of each month, she ended up paying $2.12 for 2 weeks of additional credit. Over a period of a year (an average of $2.12 for 13 or so days), the equivalent annual interest rate would be 208 to 239 percent! Is this a good use of credit?

Thousands of consumers of electricity and other utilities follow a similar procedure. Although the amount of money involved each month seems small, the annual interest rate equivalent is high.

Utility companies often find it risky to extend credit to new customers. Before they can tell whether the customer will abuse the credit, the service already has been rendered. To help protect themselves against such abuses, most companies require a deposit, temporary or permanent, frequently of anywhere from $20 to $50. That way, if the customer should for some reason not pay the bill, the deposit will absorb at least part, if not all, of the accumulated costs. Sometimes companies require a deposit only until the customer proves reliable—often a period of a year or so. The consumer should then ask for a refund *with* interest!

Overdraft Loans. A special bank arrangement is designed around a system which permits you to carry *overdrafts* (writing checks in excess of your account balance) as you write checks. The bank sets up a credit reserve for you, once your application is approved, ranging from about $500 to $5000 or more, depending on your ability to pay, your needs, and your wants.

Once the amount is set up, you need not use it unless you want to. Essentially, you can write a check for more than you have in your checking account. Enough money to let you cover this check is then transferred automatically into your checking account from your reserve account. The reserve balance is always available when you need it up to the approved amount. And, as you repay, you reestablish your reserve for future use.

Each month you receive a statement showing the amount, if any, which has been transferred to your checking account from your reserve and the amount you have to repay. The cost, included in the statement, is based on the amount of money transferred to your account and not yet repaid. The usual interest charge is 1 percent per month on this balance, although it varies with banks. Often a minimum fee is assessed, and as in the case of service credit the interest rate can become quite high.

A variation of this is the revolving credit checking account, in which a *line of credit* (top dollar limit of credit allowed) is established with the bank. After application, credit investigation, method of payment, and ability to pay have been established, a line of credit is set up for the customer. If, for example, a person can repay $60 a month for 30 months, the bank will allow a line of credit of $1800. A customer is issued special checks which can be used to draw against this agreed-upon amount. He or she is only charged for the amount used but not repaid, and the rate is again about 1 percent a month on the unpaid balance.

Bill Mullins of Memphis, Tennessee, had occasion to use this type of account and found it very convenient. Bill had a line of credit of $1500. He wrote checks for $300 during the first month. His first statement showed he had a balance of $1275. He had used $300 and paid back $75. His charge was $2.25 ($300 − 75 × 0.01 = $2.25). In this case the interest was assessed on the *ending balance*. The charge would have been $3.00 for the first month ($300 × 0.01 = $3.00) had he not repaid the $75. In either case an interest charge for the following months will be assessed if the balance due is not paid in full.

CREDIT CARDS AND CREDIT

Most charge-account customers use a credit card that gives them an option of how to pay for purchases. And there are three types of cards to use: (1) store or company, (2) bank, and (3) business, travel, and entertainment. These are discussed below.

Store or Company Credit Cards
Credit cards issued directly to the customers with no bank or agency used for collection are commonly called store or company credit cards. Typical stores issuing such cards are Sears, J. C. Penney, and Montgomery Ward, all of whom sell nationally. Credit cards of this type are also used by various other local, state, or regionally operating retail stores, and also by oil companies.

Convenience may be one of the main reasons consumers use these cards, but another is that they gain time to make payments. Merchants generally favor the use of credit cards since it encourages people to come back to their store and buy. A card issued directly to the customer means that the user either makes full payment within 30 days of the billing date or pays a portion of the bill each month. A consumer who chooses to pay over a longer time is assessed a finance charge, which generally amounts to 1½ percent per month on the remaining balance. A sample charge account application and agreement which also indicates the minimum payment due when one decides not to pay the bill in full is shown in Figure 7-1.

Bank Credit Cards
Bank charge cards are issued by a bank or group of banks. Examples of bank credit cards are Visa, Midwest Bank Card, and Master Charge. These cards allow consumers to charge merchandise at thousands of stores using only *one* card. Consumers pay for merchandise bought from these many stores with only one check, written to the credit-card company.

With bank credit cards, merchants convert their sales transactions to cash by shifting the collection responsibility of these sales to others. The merchant's cash position is improved, making it easier to reinvest capital in new inventory. Usually a discount rate of from 3 to 5 percent is assessed by the bank for

F. W. Woolworth Co. (Woolworth-Woolco) RETAIL INSTALLMENT CREDIT AGREEMENT

In consideration of the extension of credit to me, I agree to the following regarding all purchases made from time to time by me, my family or others authorized to use my F. W. Woolworth Co. Retail Installment Credit Account.

1. You are to send me a statement each month which will show the previous balance on my account, **FINANCE CHARGE,** current purchases, payments, credits and the minimum monthly payment.

I agree to pay at least the minimum monthly payment shown on my statement upon receipt of each monthly statement. The amount of such minimum payment shall be in accordance with the following schedule:

If the New Balance is:	$.01 to $10.00	$10.01 to $200.00	$200.01 to $300.00	$300.01 to $400.00	$400.01 to $500.00	$500.01 to $600.00	OVER $600.00
Your Scheduled Monthly Payment Will Be:	Balance	$10.00	$15.00	$20.00	$25.00	$30.00	ADD $10.00 FOR EVERY $100.00

REQUESTED PURCHASE LIMIT

I Request An Account Permitting Purchases Up To:	$200.00	$300.00	$400.00	$500.00	$600.00	
Scheduled Monthly Payment Check (√) Desired Amount	$10.00	$15.00	$20.00	$25.00	$30.00	All Amounts Exceeding $600.00 Add $10.00 For Every $100.00

2. I will make the monthly payment as set forth above before the next closing date as shown on my monthly statement. If I fail to make any payment in full when due, you may declare the full remaining unpaid balance immediately due and payable.

3. If I elect to pay the New Balance as shown on your monthly statement before the next closing date, I will not incur any additional **FINANCE CHARGE** on such balance. The next closing date shall be one month from the closing date shown on your statement as indicated in the Schedule of Closing dates below:

SCHEDULED CLOSING DATES

Last Name Starts With	A-B	C-D	E-F-G	H-I-J	K-L	M-N-O	P-Q-R	S	T-Z
Closing Date	2nd	5th	8th	11th	14th	17th	20th	23rd	26th

4. The **FINANCE CHARGE** shall be determined by the periodic rate applied the **AVERAGE DAILY BALANCE** as indicated in the schedule below.

SCHEDULE CODE	F
ON AMOUNT OF AVG. DAILY BALANCE	TOTAL
PERIODIC RATE	1.5%
ANNUAL PERCENTAGE RATE	18%

The **AVERAGE DAILY BALANCE** is determined by dividing the sum of the balances outstanding for each day of the monthly billing period by the number of days in the monthly billing period. The balance outstanding each day of the monthly billing period is determined by adding purchase and debit adjustments and subtracting payments and credits from the previous day's balance.

5. NO **FINANCE CHARGE** WILL BE MADE:
   (a) During a monthly billing period for which there was no previous balance.
   (b) In a monthly billing period during which payments and/or credits equal to or exceed the Previous Balance.

6. The Credit Identification Card issued to me remains the property of the F. W. Woolworth Co. and may be reclaimed at any time.

7. If any payment remains in default more than 10 days after its due date, and if permitted by law, I agree to pay (a) a delinquency and collection charge in an amount equal to 5% of each payment due or $5.00, whichever is less and (b) court costs and other expenses incurred by you in the collection or enforcement of this agreement or such other amounts prescribed by law.

8. The F. W. Woolworth Co. has the right to amend the terms of this agreement as to all purchases. Notice shall be given in accordance with applicable law.

NOTICE TO THE BUYER: DO NOT SIGN THIS AGREEMENT BEFORE YOU READ IT OR IF IT CONTAINS BLANK SPACES. KEEP THIS AGREEMENT TO PROTECT YOUR LEGAL RIGHTS. YOU HAVE THE RIGHT TO PAY IN ADVANCE THE FULL AMOUNT DUE WITHOUT INCURRING ANY ADDITIONAL CHARGE FOR PREPAYMENT.

SEE REVERSE SIDE FOR IMPORTANT INFORMATION REGARDING YOUR RIGHTS TO DISPUTE BILLING ERRORS.

FIGURE 7-1 Charge account application and agreement

this collection service. In effect, the merchant is willing to sell the merchandise for 95 to 97 percent of the selling price in order to get cash sooner. An alternative would be to handle charge accounts and collections individually. A merchant who did this would have to set up a billing and collection process and wait longer for accounts to be paid, and the resulting amount of cash available might be less.

Issuers of credit cards make a great deal of money on outstanding balances. For example, studies show that the average credit card purchase is about $35. To illustrate the impact of use, the average outstanding balance for Master Charge accounts recently was $236. Another major credit-card issuer, Visa, had an average outstanding balance of $208 for the same period. About one-third of all those cus-

tomers pay their bills in installments and thus incur interest costs.

A recent study by the Federal Reserve System revealed that about 13 percent of households with earnings of less than $5000 had bank credit cards, and approximately 44 percent of families with incomes of more than $10,000 had them. Despite these impressive figures, overall bank-card use accounts for only about 3 percent of the total consumer credit and 23 percent of the revolving credit. One reason for this limited use is that major department store chains and oil companies usually do not accept the bank credit cards.

To further expand their use, bank cards have taken on an international flavor. The Visa card has replaced the Bank Americard and a few others, and can be used to charge items all

With a bank credit card or a travel and entertainment card, consumers can charge their purchases at thousands of stores and write only one check to pay for them. (*Guy Debaud*)

over the world. It is especially helpful when cashing checks abroad.

Business, Travel, and Entertainment Credit Cards

Business, travel, and entertainment credit cards are similar to other credit cards. The significant difference lies in the way these cards are issued. For example, Diners Club, Carte Blanche, and American Express investigate a prospective cardholder more carefully; they also charge an annual fee just for issuing the card. These companies are generally more particular about the type of job a person has, annual income, previous credit record, and the amount of use to which the card is put. The annual fee for one of these "prestige" cards is $20 or more.

These special cards are accepted almost everywhere, especially internationally, and consequently the businessperson who must travel or who entertains clients finds them a great advantage. As a result, their cost is often absorbed by the firm as a business expense. Business people also recognize that credit-

card statements provide a good expense record and a reliable control of authorized business expenses.

Credit-Card Protection

Many credit cards are used by individuals today; therefore, certain precautions can be taken to help protect credit-card holders. Four basic steps should be a must as protective measures.

1. Make a record, a copy of both sides, of each credit card used. This will permit quick reference about the name and number of the card in case it is stolen or lost.
2. File records in a safe place; a safe deposit box would be ideal for this. Records of this type are easily lost or misplaced if they are kept in a desk or other such place in the home. Also, fire could destroy these records in a home.
3. Have the telephone numbers and addresses of the credit-card companies along with the account numbers written someplace that is easily and quickly accessible. These data can be used when contacting a credit-card company in case of credit-card loss. This information should be kept in a safe place at work or at home, or again in a safe deposit box.
4. Make a habit of carrying only credit cards that will be used on a regular basis. Avoid carrying those cards that will be used only occasionally; leave these cards at home for safekeeping. Remember, your potential financial loss if eight cards are stolen or lost at one time, even under the protection of the law, could be $400.

All cardholders need to be familiar with the responsibilities, and with the terms and conditions that must be complied with. Each credit-card issuer provides the cardholder with precise information on these rights and responsibilities. It is up to the cardholder to exercise these rights and to fulfill the responsibilities when necessary.

Established legislation, the Truth-in-

Lending law, helps consumers who lose their credit cards by limiting the personal liability of the cardholder. The loss liability limit is $50 *per card*. A person who lost six credit cards, for example, would be held responsible for $300 worth of fraudulent charges but for no more than that. However, if the issuing card company is notified immediately of the loss—before any fraudulent charges are made—the consumer has no liability.

COSTS OF CREDIT

Much discussion by consumers and merchants alike focuses on the costs of credit, especially the "high cost" of credit. The merchant is concerned about the expense of extending credit and other credit considerations. And consumers are concerned about the costs of using it. Above all, consumers need to be aware of what makes up the dollar cost of credit and the specific ways credit costs are assessed.

Credit-Cost Considerations

(1) "Why do consumers pay for credit?" (2) "Aren't credit costs absorbed as part of a firm's operating costs?" (3) "If buying on credit increases sales, why not offer credit at no additional cost?" (4) "If businesses must wait 30 days or more to collect money for charge sales, isn't it fair for them to charge a fee for the deferred payments?"

Answers to these questions or problems generally reflect the bias of the persons responding—consumers, merchants, consumer-sponsored groups, or business-sponsored groups. One needs to examine all sides of a credit-cost situation.

Why Do Consumers Pay for Credit? Costs are incurred when a merchant extends credit. There are record-keeping costs, such as those of statement preparation and mailing. There are additional capital investments in equipment and machines, and subsequent maintenance costs for this equipment. There is the cost of risk, since some consumers never pay for the purchases they make. In some cases, because of wear and tear from use, repossessed goods have little or no resale value. Another cost, incurred to reduce the previous risk, is that of a credit investigation into the character, capital, earning capacity, and collateral of each credit applicant. In view of these expenses, it should be clear that those who use credit must pay for it.

Credit Costs as Part of a Firm's Operation. Most merchants consider credit costs a normal operating expense. But is this practice fair to all customers? When a consumer buys a new stereo system on credit, who bears the cost of credit if it is part of "operating expenses"? And it can also be argued that a cash customer should not have to pay for credit costs incurred by credit users.

If the reason for assessing credit costs is based on increased labor, materials, and equipment related to extending credit, then these costs should be assessed proportionately and directly to those consumers who generate the expenses—the credit customers. In addition, credit charges should be made in direct proportion to the credit costs *per transaction* rather than a flat amount—that is, a percent amount per dollar of transactions.

It is also important to note that on many "big-ticket" items the charge for credit operates as a built-in profit cushion. This is illustrated by the response of a merchant to a consumer who elected to pay cash for a new color television set. "I can't make anything when you pay cash." When questioned about his comment, the merchant admitted he made an extra profit from credit charges. Surprisingly, few credit customers realize that in this manner credit charges contribute to higher list prices for most products and services.

Increasing Sales with Credit Use. Mr. William Aldridge of Plattsburg, New York, was window-shopping and came upon a coat he liked, but for which he could not pay at the moment. The alert salesperson suggested he charge the coat, since it would take only a minute to open an account. Mr. Aldridge opened an account and made his purchase. If the suggestion to open an account and use credit had not been made, the sale could not have been made. Does this support the statement that credit availability increases sales and generates profit that offset expenses related to credit?

Credit Costs by Business for Extending Credit. When a consumer uses a charge account, in essence the merchant's money is being used until payment is made. In the meantime, the merchant must meet operating expenses and replenish inventory in order to stay in business. The merchant has three alternatives: (1) to use cash reserves to cover operating expenses, (2) to seek credit when making purchases from wholesalers, manufacturers, or distributors, or (3) to borrow money from a bank at a fixed rate of interest.

Should the merchant use a cash reserve, it reduces the return on investment. If credit is used, a fee will be charged. If the merchant borrows from a bank, interest must be paid. In each case, the merchant incurs an additional expense that must be passed along to the consumer in the form of a credit charge or an increase in the price. These latter two options similarly result in a lower return on investment.

Dollar Cost of Credit

Each person using credit should know what the actual dollar cost will be for a given transaction or existing balance. Simply stated, the *dollar cost of credit* is the difference between the cash price paid for an item and the credit price (including any finance charges). To illustrate this point:

Given: Purchase amount $200 cash, or $225 credit price to be paid over 12 months.

Credit price	$225	
Less cash price	200	
Difference	$ 25	The dollar cost

This difference of $25 is the dollar cost of credit, the amount the buyer pays for the *use* of credit.

It is, of course, possible to have a cash price and a credit price that are the same, but this would be considered a "penalty for paying cash," since one who pays cash does not gain the "delayed-payment" benefit of one who buys on credit. If you want to look at credit and credit costs philosophically as well as economically, this penalty for paying cash may be interesting to think about.

Assessing Credit Costs

The assessment of credit charges is accepted by most people who use credit. Few people, however, understand the different ways in which these costs are assessed. The more frequently used methods are discussed below.

Simple Interest Method. Interest which is determined by a simple calculation—*amount borrowed or owed* (principal P) $\times$ *interest rate* (rate R) $\times$ *the time* (T) *used (in years)*—$I = PRT$—is referred to as simple interest. No monthly repayments are included. You are charged an amount of interest for using a specific amount of money for a certain length of time. For example, Stanley Polen of Kalamazoo, Michigan, borrowed $300 from a bank at a rate of 8 percent for 1 year. His interest could be determined as follows:

$$P \times R \times T = I$$
$$\frac{300}{1} \times \frac{8}{100} \times \frac{1}{1} = \$24.00$$

He is not required, under this method, to repay monthly. At the end of 1 year he will repay the loan of $300 plus the interest of $24. Had he borrowed the money for only 6 months, the interest would be half as much as for a year under the same circumstances, or $12.

In reality, it is important to note that most banks or other lending institutions require a *monthly* payback of the borrowed amount. If this is true, the computed interest method is not simple, since it involves installment payments. Interest calculated under these circumstances is handled differently and is discussed later in this chapter.

Interest Add-on Method. Under this method the interest calculation is identical to that in the simple-interest method. However, the method of repayment is different. To illustrate, suppose that Stanley borrowed $300 from a bank with an interest rate of 8 percent for 1 year. Only this time he agrees to repay the loan in twelve installments. His obligation then would appear as follows:

$$\frac{300}{1} \times \frac{8}{100} \times \frac{1}{1} = \frac{24}{1} = \$24.00 \text{ (interest charge)}$$

Therefore

$300 + 24 = 324/12 = \$27.00$ monthly payment

Consequently, Stanley would repay the loan at $27 per month for 12 months. The inequity of this method as illustrated is that Stanley is being charged $24 for using $300 for a year. But in reality he is using less than $300 each succeeding month (first month, $300; second month, $300 − 27, or $273; third month $273 − 27, or $246; etc.).

Discounting. Discounting means deducting interest charges before any payments are made. It therefore always carries a higher annual percentage rate than any other method because from the beginning the customer has less than he or she actually borrowed. Consider a loan of $100 with an interest charge of $8, or 8 percent. If it is discounted, the customer leaves the lending agency with $92, or $8 less than the amount financed, while the loan amount is $100. Therefore, the customer's available monthly cash balance would be $92, assuming there is no monthly repayment. The interest would still be $8, but when the $8 is divided by $92, it results in a higher true annual percentage rate (8.675 percent in this case).

Simply put, when discounting is used, most frequently by commercial banks, the true annual percentage rate is going to be greater than when other methods are used. This is because the net amount of money available to use has been reduced by the discounted amount. If you want to borrow $500 and it is discounted

by the bank, you will have to borrow more than $500 to realize the net cash amount of $500 after deducting the interest paid in advance.

Unpaid Balance Method. Another way of assessing credit costs is to base them on an unpaid balance. In these instances, it is difficult to know in advance exactly what the cost of credit will be. One would need to know precisely how the payments would be made, how much each would be, and what each monthly unpaid balance would be. But since it is often necessary to estimate the needed information, the amount calculated is also an estimate. To determine the interest amount and rate under the unpaid balance method, follow the plan suggested in Table 7-1.

Note that the total dollar cost of credit is determined by adding up all the figures in the "credit charge" column. In this case, $17.84 is the dollar cost of credit on $275 for the time shown. This seems to be an annual rate of approximately 6.5 percent ($17.84 ÷ 275 =

TABLE 7-1

Approximating the Dollar Cost of Credit on an Open-end Type Credit Account

Beginning Balance	Credit Charge	Payment	New Balance
$ 275.00	$ 2.75	$ 25.00	$252.75
252.75	2.53	25.00	230.28
230.28	2.30	25.00	207.58
207.58	2.08	25.00	184.66
184.66	1.85	25.00	161.51
161.51	1.62	25.00	138.13
138.13	1.38	25.00	114.51
114.51	1.15	25.00	90.66
90.66	.91	25.00	66.57
66.57	.67	25.00	42.24
42.24	.42	25.00	17.66
17.66	.18	17.84	00.00
$1781.55	$17.84	$292.84	

$1781.55/12 = $148.46 average balance

TABLE 7–2

Monthly Payment (Principal and Interest) and the Dollar Cost of Credit to Amortize a Debt of $1000

Annual Percentage Rate	Monthly Dollar Payment on Principal and Interest on Loan for:				
	12 months	24 months	36 months	48 months	60 months
8	86.99	45.23	31.34	24.42	20.28
10	87.92	46.15	32.27	25.37	21.25
12	88.85	47.07	33.21	26.34	22.25
14	89.79	48.02	34.18	27.33	23.27
16	90.74	48.97	35.16	28.35	24.32
18	91.68	49.93	36.16	29.38	25.40
20	92.64	50.90	37.17	30.44	26.50
22	93.60	51.88	38.20	31.51	27.62
24	94.56	52.88	39.24	32.61	28.77
26	92.53	53.87	40.29	33.72	29.94
28	96.51	54.89	41.36	34.85	31.14
30	97.49	55.91	42.45	36.01	32.35
32	98.47	56.95	43.55	37.18	33.59
34	99.47	57.99	44.67	38.37	34.85
36	100.46	59.05	45.80	39.58	36.13

Annual Percentage Rate	Approximate Dollar Cost for Interest on Loan of $1000 for a Certain Number of Months				
	12 months	24 months	36 months	48 months	60 months
8	43.90	85.50	128.10	172.16	216.80
10	55.00	107.50	161.60	217.76	275.00
12	66.20	129.80	195.70	264.32	335.00
14	77.40	152.30	230.40	311.84	396.20
16	88.80	175.10	265.70	360.80	459.20
18	100.20	198.20	301.50	410.24	524.00
20	111.60	221.50	337.90	461.12	590.00
22	123.20	245.12	375.20	512.48	657.20
24	134.70	268.90	412.40	565.28	726.20
26	146.36	292.88	450.44	618.56	796.40
28	158.12	317.36	488.96	672.80	868.40
30	169.88	341.84	528.20	728.48	941.00
32	181.64	366.80	567.80	784.64	1015.40
34	193.64	391.76	608.12	841.76	1091.00
36	205.52	417.20	648.80	899.84	1167.80

Source: Some data from Household Finance Corporation, Chicago, Ill.

6.487 percent), with a rate of 1 percent a month assessed on the unpaid balance. But the amount of money available per month *on the average* was only $148.46. Therefore, comparing the cost of $17.84 for using $148.46, the rate amounts to 12 percent (17.84 ÷ 148.46 = 12.016 percent), or 1 percent a month.

Also, as shown in the table, the monthly payments were equal. In some instances a variable monthly payment is allowed. In such cases, the interest would be determined on a month-to-month basis. All payments, however, would have to be made before the total interest charge and the overall annual interest rate could be determined. Although this method of calculation is cumbersome, it is precise. Most retail stores or lending institutions have charts that provide this information rather quickly.

Why Shop for Credit Terms?

The total difference in dollar costs from one lender to another over the period of the loan can be staggering, as shown in Table 7-2. A 10 percent loan compared with a 14 percent loan does not sound like much, because what are percentage points anyhow? And the difference in payments over 36 months—$32.27 and $34.18—does not sound like much either. But, in this example of a $1000, 36-month loan for a used automobile, the total dollar cost of credit at 10 percent is $161.60 as compared to the 14 percent figure of $230.40. Shopping for credit in this instance saves $68.80. For a $3000 loan, the amount saved would be triple—$206.40—or enough to buy a new set of good tires.

The cost of credit over time is dramatic also. An 18 percent loan of $1000 repaid in monthly installments in 1 year results in interest charges of $100.20. When the loan is stretched over 2 years, the cost rises to $198.20, and to $301.50 over 3 years. If this were a $3000 loan, just the cost of credit of a 3-year loan ($904.50) rather than a 2-year loan ($594.60) amounts to an extra $309.90!

PERCENTAGE COST OF CREDIT

Any reference to credit costs that uses dollars and cents only is misleading. The percent cost is a fairer, more meaningful way to express the actual credit costs. Let us consider this concept in a little more depth by examining open-end credit costs and those involving special formulas.

Open-End Cost Rates of Credit

Open-end credit does not specify an exact beginning or a specific periodic payment. The balance can be variable, and the monthly payments increase or decrease accordingly. The open-end terms of Woolworth shown in Figure 7-1, page 200 illustrate how the amount of the monthly payment fluctuates with the balance.

Open-end-credit-account charges are almost always stated in percentage terms; they are generally 1½ percent per month on the unpaid balance. Because of different purchase and billing dates and the "unpaid balance" figure used, the true annual percentage rate for open-end-credit accounts cannot be determined exactly until an account has run its payment cycle.

Businesses use different "unpaid-balance" figures when assessing credit charges. The balances typically used are the previous month's balance, the average daily balance, and the ending balance. Let's take a look at how these are used.

Previous-Balance Method. An unpaid balance exists when a person does not pay in full upon receiving a monthly statement. A "previous-balance" amount is considered to be the highest first unpaid balance in an account. To illustrate, let's examine the data in Table 7-3, which provides some sample amounts.

Following the previous-balance method, $300 is the amount used. The $100 payment has no effect. Interest charges of 1.5 percent a month on the unpaid balance would be $4.50

TABLE 7-3

Purchasing Data to Illustrate Previous,
Average, and Final Unpaid Balance

Purchase	Pay-ments	Balance
April 1 beginning balance		$300
April 22 payment	$100	$200

(0.015 × $300). Certainly the method favors the business in its calculation, since the customer made a partial payment and reduced the balance to only $200. The customer pays interest on the total previous balance as though he or she really had the use of the funds for the total time, which was not the case.

Average-Balance Method.   When the average-balance amount is used to calculate interest, the customer is treated quite fairly. Just as the name "average balance" implies, an average of the balance in an account is used in calculating the interest.

Using the same data from Table 7-3 and the average-balance amount, the interest is $4.05. The calculating takes longer and is a little more difficult, but computers usually do the math anyway. To illustrate:

$300 balance for 21 days (April 1–21)
$$= \$6300$$
$200 balance for $\dfrac{9 \text{ days (April 22–30)}}{}$
$$= 1800$$
Total   30 days
$$\overline{\$8100}$$

Average balance = 8100/30 = $270
Interest = $270 × 0.015 = $4.05

A person is in a more favorable financial position using this method, since it results in less interest being paid. More businesses are using this method, since so many consumers have complained about the costly previous-balance method, used so much in the past.

Ending-Balance Method.   Under this method the interest is calculated on the last balance on the statement if it is not paid in full. Again using the data shown in Table 7-3, the interest would be only $3.00. The ending balance is $200, and the calculated interest is $200 × 0.015, or $3.00. In this instance the customer would be in a yet more favored position, since he or she pays the smallest amount of interest. Some businesses still use this method of determining the unpaid balance.

As you can see, it is important for consumers to know which unpaid balance method is used and how the interest is calculated. Table 7-4 summarizes the "real" true annual percentage rate based on the interest charges and the specific unpaid balance used.

As can be seen, the "real" annual rates reveal that the *ending-balance* method has the lowest rate (18 percent) and the *previous-balance* method the highest (27 percent). This difference of 9 percent should be enough to encourage consumers to compare the methods, the actual interest charges, and the "real" true annual percentage rates before using open-end charge accounts. As shown, this is especially important when an unpaid balance is being carried forward to a new billing period.

Cost Rates Using Special Formulas
Interest charges are expressed in various ways. Some are expressed in dollars and cents, others in dollar amounts and time. One may know the dollar interest charges, but yet may not know the percentage rate. Two special formulas used to determine interest rates more precisely, when predetermined payments and times are used, include the simple annual percent method and the true annual percentage rate formula.

Simple Annual Percent Rate.   When Mrs. Allen Ashburn of Ogden, Utah, bought merchandise on credit and was charged $9 in finance fees, she wondered whether or not the charges were too high. Although she only owed $76, she had a full year to pay and made only one payment. Was the $9 charge fair?

TABLE 7-4

"Real" True Annual Percentage Rate for Specific Balance Illustrated

"Unpaid Balance" Used	Monthly Rate	Monthly Charge	Opening Balance	Payments	"Real" True Annual Rate
Ending balance	0.015	3.00	300	100	18.0
Average balance	0.015	4.05	300	100	24.3
Previous balance	0.015	4.50	300	100	27.0

A more exact measure to use would be a *simple annual percent rate* to determine the cost of credit. A basic, simple interest formula to determine the annual rate cost of credit applied in the above illustration is the following:

$$R = \frac{C}{PT} \times 100$$

where R = Rate (percentage)
  C = Credit charges (in dollars and cents)
  T = Time allowed (in *years*)
  P = Purchase amount financed or loaned

Using the above formula and substituting Mrs. Ashburn's data, the percent cost of credit is calculated as follows:

$$R = \frac{9}{76(1)} \times 100 = \frac{9}{76} \times \frac{100}{1} = \frac{900}{76} = 11.842\%$$

To cite another example for comparison, Mr. Ricky King of Athens, Georgia, owed $3.00 in interest charges for $35 worth of merchandise, to be paid in full within 6 months. Is his percentage cost of credit more or less than Mrs. Ashburn's? On the surface, all one can do is offer an educated guess, but by using the above formula a more precise figure can be found.

$$R = \frac{3}{35(0.5)} \times 100 = \frac{3}{17.5} \times \frac{100}{1}$$
$$= \frac{300}{17.5} = 17.142\%$$

Mr. King's annual percent cost of credit is 17.142 percent and Mrs. Ashburn's is 11.842 percent. Since all percentages are related to an identical base, these two figures can easily be compared. An important point to keep in mind in these cases and other similar ones that use the simple interest formula is that the person assessed makes only *one* payment at the end of the prescribed time. *No* periodic payments are made. The simple annual interest rate formula should not be used when installment payments are made.

True Annual Percentage Rate. Loans with monthly payback arrangements can be changed to an accurate percent cost by means of a special formula called the "true" *annual percent rate* formula (APR). It is so called because it takes into consideration all factors that could have any bearing on the true annual-percent cost of credit.

But why bother with a special formula when a merchant or banker can tell you this rate? One reason is that when a merchant or banker quotes you a rate, it does not always allow for periodic repayment of the amount owed. Such quotations are commonly referred to as the *stated rate* ("the rate is 8 percent"). The "true" annual percentage rate is very different. Also, many banks or merchants provide the true annual percentage rate *after* the purchase or loan has been agreed upon and the necessary papers are being signed. But by using the special formula, this distinction, its importance, and its value as a comparison factor can be shown.

The formula for determining the true annual percent of credit costs is as follows:

$$APR = \frac{2YF}{D(T + 1)}$$

where 2 = a constant.

> Y = the number of payments made per *year*. Usually this figure is 12 (for 12 monthly payments), but it can be some other figure, such as 4 for quarterly payments or 52 for weekly payments.
>
> F = the total *finance* charges. This figure includes the regular credit charge, or interest, plus other *required* charges stemming from a credit investigation or credit life insurance. It is the dollar cost of credit.
>
> D = the *debt*, or amount to be paid. This is the difference between the total amount of purchase and a down payment; it is the total amount borrowed in the case of a loan from a finance institution.
>
> T = the *total* number of payments to be made. This figure is the same as Y when the payments are to be made within a year. When the period exceeds a year, the total payments will be some multiple of the number of payments per year—i.e., for a 2-year credit arrangement with monthly payments, $T = 24$.
>
> 1 – a constant.

Mr. Harry Lylewell of Columbia, Missouri, visited two stores when he was shopping for a new stove. At Store A the cost of the stove was $235 plus $29 credit charges, the total to be paid in 12 monthly payments. At Store B the cost was $247.50 plus $35 credit charges, the total to be paid in 16 monthly payments. Mr. Lylewell did not know which terms to select, but he did know how to apply the APR formula:

Store A	*Store B*
$Y = 12$	$Y = 12$
$F = \$29.00$	$F = \$35.00$
$T = 12$	$T = 16$
$D = \$235.00$	$D = \$247.50$

$$APR = \frac{2 \times 12 \times 29}{235(12 + 1)} \qquad APR = \frac{2 \times 12 \times 35}{247.50(16 + 1)}$$

$$= \frac{696}{3055} \qquad\qquad = \frac{840}{4207.5}$$

$$= 22.78\% \qquad\qquad = 19.96\%$$

Store B obviously charges a lower rate.

This formula can also be applied when periodic payments are made in different ways. For example:

Given	Store A	Store B
Amount owed	$550	$550
Payments	Monthly	Weekly
Credit terms	3 years	3 years
Finance charges	$150	$150

Store A

$$APR = \frac{2 \times 12 \times 150}{550(36 + 1)} = \frac{3600}{20,350} = 17.69\%$$

Store B

$$APR = \frac{2 \times 52 \times 150}{550(156 + 1)} = \frac{15,600}{86,350} = 18.07\%$$

Although only the total number of payments differs, there is a difference of 0.38 percent in the true annual percent of credit. This difference is not great, but you are practicing sound money management—and the amounts do add up—if you make it a practice to choose the source of credit that charges the least.

CONSUMER CREDIT LEGISLATION

Many pieces of legislation are introduced in Congress each year; a smaller number of the bills introduced get to the various committees; a still smaller number come out of committee for congressional discussion and debate; and finally a few are passed and become law. Five major laws that have been enacted during recent years to benefit consumers using credit are the Truth-in-Lending law (Consumer

Credit Protection Act), the Fair Credit Reporting Act, the Fair Credit Reporting Act, the Fair Credit Billing Act, the Equal Credit Opportunity Act, and the Fair Debt Collection Practices Act. Let's examine each of these laws as to their characteristics and merits.

Truth-in-Lending Law (Consumer Credit Protection Act)

The Truth-in-Lending law is a popular title for the Consumer Credit Protection Act. Primarily the act protects the consumer by requiring a statement of the costs of credit—dollar finance charges *and* true annual percent rate charges. It also states the conditions of wage *garnishments* (withholding salary to satisfy the claim of creditors) and advertising guidelines. Of particular concern to the consumer are the provisions giving credit or finance charges in dollar amounts and the true annual percentage rates.

Merchants, bankers, and lending agencies for many years opposed this legislation, which took effect in 1969. Much of the opposition was motivated by the fact that many merchants and lending agencies did not want to give out specific, comparable credit-cost information, since few consumers realized how much and what rates they were really paying. Now that the law has been in effect for a number of years, most businesses have complied with little difficulty.

Disclosure Statement. A major outcome of the Truth-in-Lending law is the consumer's *disclosure statement* for credit transactions. In Figure 7-2 you can see a typical disclosure statement, which is part of the retail installment contract of a bank. This also gives a summary of the credit costs and terms.

Items 4 and 6 on the form are particularly important, since the figures called for are requirements of the disclosure statement. Item 4 is the *dollar finance charge*, which is usually taken from a book or schedule of charges based on the amount financed and repayment

time. Item 6 shows the calculated true *annual percentage rate*. This percentage is calculated (using the APR formula discussed previously) on the basis of financing $5000 at a cost of $900.76. If a lender *requires* credit life insurance, the cost must be included in the amount to be financed; if credit life insurance is optional but the consumer wants it, it is not considered part of the cost of credit.

Several copies of the agreement are prepared; they are signed by all parties to the transaction. Each receives a copy, including the disclosure section, and is equally informed as to what took place.

The critical things to be aware of when negotiating a separate disclosure statement, or a section on an installment contract, are the total dollar finance charge, the annual percentage rate, your understanding of every figure shown, and the voiding of all items not executed in the agreement—which you can easily do by drawing a line through the space provided for figures. Leave no space blank. If you have any problems or doubts, do not sign! Get outside help and clarify the situation.

Stated versus Annual Percentage Rate. An important fact brought out by the Truth-in-Lending law is that the *stated rates* sometimes quoted by lending agencies and the *annual percentage rates* are rarely the same.

A lending agency, for example, may lend money at a *stated rate* of 8 percent (of $8 per $100 per year) but require the borrower to repay the loan in installments. As a result, the borrower does not have the use of *all* the money borrowed for the *full* period of the loan. With a $100 loan at 8 percent for 1 year, repaid at $9 a month, for example, the borrower has use of the full amount for the first month, $91 for the second month, $82 for the third, $73 for the fourth, and so on. Actually, on the average, the borrower has the use of only about one-half the money lent. Therefore, instead of 8 percent, the true annual percentage rate is closer to 16 percent. Generally speaking, when installments are made, the true annual

NOTE
FIRST NATIONAL EXCHANGE BANK OF MONTGOMERY COUNTY
INSTALMENT LOAN AND DISCLOSURE

Blacksburg , Virginia   January 25   , 19 79

Lois Testerman
NAME OR NAMES
                Route #2, Blacksburg, Virginia 24060   } "Borrower"
ADDRESS

FOR VALUE RECEIVED, Borrower (jointly and severally if more than one, hereinafter called "Borrower") hereby promises to pay the Total of Payments set forth below to the order of First National Exchange Bank of Montgomery County ("Bank") at any of its offices in the State of Virginia, in 36 monthly instalments, beginning Feb. 25, 1979 each of said instalments being for $ 163.91 , except the last for $ 163.90 . All subsequent instalments shall be paid on the same day of each succeeding month until paid in full. If the last payment is more than twice a regular payment, it is a Balloon Payment. Bank is not obligated to refinance a Balloon Payment if not paid when due.

Personal Insurance is not required and is not provided unless Borrower signs below and the insurance is issued by the insurer. Only the persons signing below will be covered.

☐ Credit Life for term of
loan.   Premium $ _____

_____   _____
SIGNED   DATE

_____   _____
SIGNED   DATE

☐ Accident and Health
for term of loan.   Premium $ _____
☐ Accident Death and
Dismemberment for
_____ months   Premium $ _____

_____   _____
SIGNED   DATE

1. Net Loan Proceeds.................		$5,000
2. Charges Related to Loan		
Personal Insurance........	$_____	
Property Insurance........	$_____	
Filing Costs	$_____	
Other................	$_____	$_____
3. Amount Financed (1 + 2)...........		$5,000
4. FINANCE CHARGE		
Interest	$ 900.76	
Service Charge	$_____	$_____
5. Total of Payments (3 + 4)...........		$5,900.76
6. ANNUAL PERCENTAGE RATE.....		11.07 %

LATE CHARGES AND ACCELERATION: In event of nonpayment of any instalment when due continuing for 10 days or more, a late charge of up to 5% of the amount of each late payment may be imposed. Further, in such event the Bank, at its option, may declare the entire indebtedness due and payable, but the balance owing shall be computed as if the Borrower had made a voluntary prepayment and obtained an interest rebate as set forth below, and thereafter such accelerated balance shall bear interest at the Annual Percentage Rate shown above.

PREPAYMENT: Except as stated below, in event of prepayment, Borrower will receive a rebate of the amount of the unearned interest portion of the Finance Charge, computed under the Rule of 78's. Notwithstanding the preceding sentence, if the Bank has not earned a minimum of $25.00 in Finance Charge at the time of prepayment, then the Bank shall withhold from the rebate otherwise payable an amount equal to the extent such minimum was not earned. Further, in the event of prepayment from proceeds of credit life insurance, there will be no rebate to Borrower.

SECURITY: Borrower, any guarantor, surety, indorser or other party hereto (hereinafter collectively referred to as "Party") agree that Bank shall have the right to offset the amount owed by a Party hereunder to the holder hereof against any account, checking, savings or otherwise, which a Party may have with the holder. Further, this loan ☒ is ☐ is not secured. If secured, Bank has been granted a security interest in the property described below ("Collateral"), together with all accessions thereof and proceeds thereof. To create the security interest, if any, Borrower ☐ has executed or caused to be executed a security agreement granting Bank a security interest in the Collateral and/or ☒ hereby grants a security interest in, and has caused, and/or hereafter will cause, the Collateral (including any certificates evidencing ownership) to be deposited with, assigned and pledged to Bank. The Collateral is described as follows (if any): 1978 Thunderbird automobile; identification number 1978-4127878
_____
_____

PROPERTY INSURANCE: ☐ is ☒ is not required. If required, Borrower may choose the person through whom any property insurance in connection with this loan is obtained. Such insurance ☐ is ☒ is not obtainable through the Bank. If obtained through the Bank, the cost will be $_____ for the following coverage and term: _____

DEFAULT: Upon default as set forth on the reverse side hereof, Bank may, at its option, without notice or demand, declare all obligations evidenced hereby immediately due and payable, together with an attorney's fee of 20% of the amount then owing and unpaid by Borrower, if services of an attorney are employed to effect collection, and other expenses of collection and enforcement.
    REFERENCE IS MADE SPECIFICALLY TO THE PROVISIONS APPEARING ON THE REVERSE SIDE HEREOF, ALL OF WHICH ARE EXPRESSLY MADE PARTS, TERMS AND CONDITIONS HEREOF.
    Borrower hereby acknowledges that he has received a completely filled-in copy of this Note prior to consummation of this loan.
    WITNESS the following signatures and seals as of the date first above written.

923-83-76

_____ (SEAL)

_____ (SEAL)

FIGURE 7-2 Disclosure statement

percentage rate is about double any stated rate. A more precise comparison can be made using the APR formula discussed earlier.

Other Major Provisions. Another provision of the Truth-in-Lending law has provided some financial protection for many consumers. Under it, if a credit card is lost or stolen, a person's financial liability for charges made is limited to $50 per card. If a person loses four credit cards, the liability is $50 per card, for a maximum of $200. This liability applies even when the card issuing company has been notified, if there has already been fraudulent usage. However, a reasonably responsible person would notify the issuing company as soon as possible after missing the card. If the lost credit card is located early enough, there may not be a financial loss at all. Also, as soon as you notify the company of the loss of the card, you are not liable for further fraudulent usage.

According to the Federal Reserve System, one of the monitoring agencies for this law, four conditions must be met before you can be held liable for any unauthorized use: (1) you requested or used the lost or stolen credit card; (2) a means of identification of the card user (photograph or signature panel) is provided by the card issuer; (3) you have been notified of your $50 liability potential; and (4) the card issuer has given you a form on which to notify them of the loss or theft of your card. The law also prohibits the issuance of credit cards unless you specifically request it.

Advertising of credit terms is also regulated by the law. Essentially the law states that if a business is going to advertise anything about credit, it must include *all* the important terms. Number, amount, and period of payments to be made are examples of terms to be included. "Only $5 down" in an advertisement would be too limited, to be in compliance; the ad must also state that you will pay $20 a month for the next 2 years and give the true annual percentage rate. The intent of the regulation is to provide you with full and accurate information.

Cancellation procedures are another provision of the law provided to protect consumers. If you enter into a credit transaction in which your home is used as security—major repairs or remodeling involving a "second mortage" is typical—you have 3 business days to think about it and cancel if you wish. You also must be given written notice of your right to cancel. If you decide to cancel, you must also notify the creditor in writing to rescind the contract.

Fair Credit Reporting Act

The federal Fair Credit Reporting Act is designed to protect consumers from the potential ill effects of credit reports. If you are denied credit, insurance, or a job on the basis of information provided by a credit-reporting agency, the act requires that the denying party give the name and address of the agency that submitted the negative report. The discredited person may then ask for and get at no charge the information the credit-reporting agency has on file. You can't really "look at" the file but are told the substance of particulars involved. If there are errors in the file, the agency must either verify or delete them. If information cannot be verified, the credit agency must send a retraction to all those who recently received the false information. If it is verified, the discredited person has the right to know who verified it and what was said. Then the consumer can check the original source if there is still a question. Also, it is important to know that you may take another person with you when you visit the reporting agency.

A disputed item in a file can be labeled as disputed and the discredited person can provide another version of the facts. The person can write up his or her side (maximum of 100 words) and have it placed permanently in the credit file. In such cases the total file must then be sent to all those who recently may have received the information. Because of the far-reaching effects a credit report can have, checking your credentials perhaps every other year could well be justified. In such cases—when you are acting on your own without having been denied credit or employment—a small fee, probably $3 to $5, is charged to check on and discuss your file.

Other rights include obtaining free of charge, within 30 days, information to which you are entitled when you have been denied credit; being told who has received a credit report on you within the previous 6 months, or 2 years if the report involved an employment denial; having incorrect or inaccurate information removed from your file once it has been proven to be so; having agencies who have been provided with incorrect data to be told of this; and suing a credit-reporting agency for damages if it knowingly and willfully violated the law.

These, then, are the major rights that consumers have under the act. Most important, it gives consumers the opportunity to react when inaccurate or misleading information is kept on file and reported by the numerous consumer reporting agencies.

Fair Credit Billing Act

Today, more consumers than ever are using revolving charge accounts and other kinds of consumer credit. And, of course, mistakes are occasionally made on the billing statements. Consumers too often find that trying to get the mistakes corrected can be difficult and frustrating. Most of the mistakes are simply clerical or mechanical errors which frequently are blamed "on the computer." The Fair Credit Billing Act, passed by Congress in 1975, helps consumers fight billing errors.

The act applies only to open-end credit plans. *Open-end* credit includes all types of consumer credit involving the use of a credit card and other types of revolving credit, including regular store charge accounts and special overdraft checking plans. The act does not apply to installment loans or purchases where a repayment schedule has been set (*closed-end credit*).

The act allows persons who use covered consumer credit to get help with billing errors on monthly statements, such as charges made by a person not allowed to use your account; wrong description, amount, or date on charge items; property or service charges which you did not accept or which were not delivered as agreed; payments or goods you have returned which have not been properly credited to your account; accounting or other arithmetic errors on charges, payments, or finance charges; a billing statement not delivered to your current address if an appropriate notification is given (10 days) of any address change. These errors are specifically covered under a standard dispute procedure of the act. And it outlines the step-by-step process to follow if these types of billing errors occur and you want to get more information or get the error corrected.

In addition, the act:

- Permits retailers to give a discount, not in excess of 5 percent, on cash purchases; retailers who give discounts must post a sign explaining the discount.
- Requires that any written complaint to a store or credit-card company must be acknowledged within 30 days, and that the dispute should be resolved within 90 days after receiving notice; during this period, the consumer does not have to pay the amount in question or any finance charges on the amount.
- Entitles the consumer not to have to pay for a defective product if he or she first tries to resolve the problem with the merchant.
- Allows you the right of redress against the credit-card company *as well as* against the seller if you purchase unsatisfactory goods or services on a credit card of any kind.
- States that if the consumer returns any item charged on a credit card, the store must notify the credit-card company of the return; the credit-card company must then credit the customer's account.
- Requires that a bill be sent to the consumer 14 days in advance of the deadline for payment.
- Prohibits a bank, where a consumer has both a credit card and an account, from collecting credit-card payments from the account to pay the overdue debt.

The above provisions of the act provide needed protections for those consumers who use credit properly. Often in the past there have been careless or wanton errors, and sometimes a reckless disregard for accuracy by businesses; and there has been little assistance or methods established to correct these problems. This act has and hopefully will continue to reduce or eliminate billing errors and abuses.

Equal Credit Opportunity Act

Credit use in this country has been revolutionized with the passage of the Equal Credit Opportunity Act by Congress in 1975. Essentially, the act opens the credit doors to *every* person who has the ability and willingness to repay. Furthermore, the act applies to all who regularly extend credit—banks, finance companies, department stores, and credit-card issuers.

The basic protective provisions of the act provide equal credit opportunity for all applying for credit and require that a creditor:

- Must not discourage you from applying for credit, on the basis of sex, marital status, race, color, religion, national origin, or age, or refuse to grant you a *separate* account if you are a worthy applicant.
- Must not ask your marital status if you apply for an unsecured separate account, except in a community property state or when other state laws govern.
- May ask and consider to what extent your income is affected by obligations to pay alimony, child support, or maintenance, or must tell you that you do *not* have to disclose this income if you will not be relying on that income to obtain credit. If you choose, however, to rely on such income, the creditor may request information as to its source.
- Must not prohibit you from opening an account in your maiden name.

And in evaluating applications for credit, a creditor:

- Must request and use information about your spouse *only* when your spouse will be using or will be liable for the account, or when you are relying on your spouse's income or property.
- Must consider alimony, child support, or maintenance payments as income to the degree that such payments are likely to be made.
- Must not discount your or your spouse's income because of sex, marital status, race, color, religion, national origin, or age, or discount income from part-time employment that is shown to be reliable.
- Must not use sex, marital status, race, color, religion, national origin, or age as factors in any method of evaluating creditworthiness.
- May not ask about birth control practices or child-bearing plans or assume that because of a woman's age, she may drop out of the labor force to have a baby, causing an interruption of income.
- Must not use unfavorable information about an account you shared with a spouse or former spouse, if you can show that the unfavorable history does not accurately reflect *your* willingness or ability to repay.
- Must consider, on your request, the credit history of any account held in your spouse's or former spouse's name which you can show is an accurate reflection of your credit experience.
- Must provide, if you request, the reasons for any denial of credit.

As can be seen, most of the provisions of the act close the door to refusing credit on the basis of personal characteristics of a person or couple. With the establishment of the act, refusals of credit must be more completely explained and documented. And if a creditor is to be in compliance, that creditor can refuse credit to someone only on the basis of the likelihood of an inability or unwillingness to repay if and when credit is established.

Er . . . just dropped by to wish you a good day, sir.

Courtesy of Edd Uluschak.

The Fair Debt Collection Practices Act

The Fair Debt Collection Practices Act, which took effect in March 1978, was passed to protect consumers from such abuses as unsavory language, threats of violence, harassing phone calls, and publication of shame lists that name debtors who are in default. Additionally, the legislation bans all forms of misleading or false representation. Anyone from a collector's office will not be permitted to pretend he or she is a lawyer, police officer, or government official in the process of debt collecting. Furthermore, the collector is not allowed to make false statements to the effect that if the debt is not paid, the debtor will be arrested, hauled into court, lose property, or have wages withheld.

Stores, hospitals, and other establishments that handle their own collections are not covered under the act. Banks, credit unions, and other businesses whose principal purpose is not the collection of debts are also not covered by the provisions of this act. The new law is aimed directly at the specialists in debt collecting.

There has been and will continue to be incentive for debt collection. There are over 5000 debt-collection agencies throughout the country, and they "go after" the over $5 billion in unpaid debts. Collectors usually retrieve about a third of the money sought and receive fees of as much as 50 percent of the amount eventually collected. The act will in no way prevent or disavow legitimate debt collection so long as it falls within its provisions.

To comply with the act, when trying to collect a past due debt, the collection agency, after making the first contact with the consumer, has 5 working days to send a written notice that spells out the amount of the debt and the name of the creditor. The notice must also carry a statement that the collector will assume the debt to be valid unless the debtor contests it in writing within 30 days of receiving the notice. If the debt is disputed, the collector must go back to the creditor for a certification that the amount is owed and mail that to the consumer.

In summary, the debt-collection law, enforced by the Federal Trade Commission, strongly limits the tactics a collector may employ in trying to collect a debt. For example, collectors cannot (1) call you at unusual or inconvenient times, (2) call you at work if your employer objects, (3) reveal your debt to a third party other than your spouse or legal adviser except with court permission, (4) communicate with you after receiving your written refusal to pay, except to inform you of possible further action of the creditor, and (5) use harassing or intimidating language or falsely threaten arrest.

Although the new act is designed primarily to protect persons from debt-collection abuses, it does not allow "deadbeats" to escape payment of legitimate debts. And an added built-in safeguard for any violations of the law is that individuals who sue debt collectors may be awarded damages of up to $1000. In class action suits by groups of persons, the court may award up to $500,000 in damages.

CREDIT CLAUSES TO AVOID

All credit purchases involve a legal contract which is either implied or express. The most frequently used credit contract takes the form of a written sales contract in which the terms, conditions, and special clauses are spelled out as shown in Figure 7-2 (page 211). These clauses can be for the benefit or detriment of the purchaser depending on how they are used. To be sure of getting the full benefits of any sales contract, the consumer should understand the details of these special clauses before entering into the contract. And a buyer should especially check these several clauses before signing the contract because some should be avoided if possible. If the creditor agrees, these clauses in the contract can be scratched out and initialed by both parties to void them.

Acceleration Clause

The acceleration clause holds that if you miss a single payment, the entire balance of the loan is due. All later payments are essentially accelerated into one; thus, the acceleration clause. If this is applied, the loan is due and payable at the demand of the lender. So if you miss one installment payment, the lender can ask for full payment immediately, and begin the process of repossessing the charged merchandise if you do not pay.

Add-On Clause

This clause is used to cover *additional* installment purchases. Essentially, the seller retains title to *each* purchased article until the *last* purchased item is fully paid for. Joyce Abrams of Las Vegas, Nevada, purchased several hundred dollars worth of household furnishings over the past few years from one department store. Not long ago, she lost everything because she failed to make a $25 payment on a recently purchased $125 item. This is one clause consumers can definitely do without.

Balloon Clause

Under this clause the last payment on a loan is abnormally large compared with the other scheduled payments. For example, you might have installment payments of $75 per month for 35 months but the thirty-sixth payment might be for $980. Seasonal workers can use the balloon clause to their advantage by having lower payments during the off-season of their employment; when they have more income available, they may be able to make a larger payment more easily. But for most people the balloon clause is one to be avoided. A very important point, ethically and morally, to emphasize is that one should be told that the balloon clause is being used *before* signing a contract. Some individual states have outlawed this clause because of its abuse and because its use exploits ignorant or otherwise uninformed consumers.

Rule of 78s (Sum of the Digits)

A large prepayment penalty is charged the person who pays a debt early under this clause. Its name is derived from the sum of the digits of the months of the year—12 + 11 + 10 . . . + 2 + 1 = 78. The term "rule of 78s" is, however, a little misleading, since it applies only to those installments covering a year. A more appropriate term would be *sum of the digits for payback period.*

On a 6-month installment loan the figure would be 21 (6 + 5 + 4, etc.); for 18 months it would be 171 (18 + 17 + 16, etc.); or for 2 years it would be 300 following this system. Although the "rule of 78s" is the suggested term, it is the "sum of the digits" that is being used to determine the interest to be charged, or rebate to be made.

An example of its application will show its bias toward the creditor. Sally Wilson of Columbus, Ohio, borrowed $1500 to buy a used car and agreed to make payments for 18 months with an interest charge of $180. She contracted to make monthly installments to repay the loan. After paying on the debt for 3 months, she decided to pay off the loan with her fourth payment. Using the *sum-of-the-digits* method her interest charges would be 66/171 (18 + 17 + 16 + 15) × 180 = $69.47. Accordingly, she will have to pay 39 percent of the total interest charge for using the money only 22 percent of the time.

A special formula can also be used to determine the interest to be charged for early payment by Sally Wilson. The formula is

$$PI = OI - OI \left[\frac{0.5PR(PR + 1)}{0.5TP(TP + 1)} \right]$$

where

PI = interest with prepayment
OI = original interest charge
PR = number of payments remaining
TP = total number of payments

Using Sally Wilson's data, the calculation would be

$$PI = \$180 - \$180 \left[\frac{0.5(14)(14 + 1)}{0.5(18)(18 + 1)} \right]$$

$$= \$180 - \$180 \left[\frac{105}{171} \right]$$

$$= \$180 - \$110.53 = \$69.47$$

A more equitable way to calculate Ms. Wilson's interest, but still not entirely fair, would be 4/18 (4 months out of 18) × 180 = $40. Under this method, however, she is being charged interest on the use of $1500, although she has already repaid part of the money borrowed. Regardless of which of these methods is used, Ms. Wilson is penalized by repaying the loan *early*. This is hardly an incentive for anyone to prepay a loan!

Confession of Judgment

This clause means you waive your right to a legal defense if the contract is contested in court. You sign away your right to defend yourself if you miss a payment on a loan. The court will always find you guilty, since the clause lets the lender's lawyer plead you guilty. Therefore the court must award damages to the plaintiff-lender.

Wage Assignment

This clause permits the lender to notify your employer that you are behind in your installment debt. The employer must then legally withhold part of your wages and send this directly to the creditor. In effect, it says that since you are not competent to pay your creditor, your employer will have to do it for you. Consumers often unknowingly agree to and sign wage assignment clauses when the

MASTER CHARGE ACCOUNT NUMBER

PERSONAL (1)

PRINT FULL NAME	DATE OF BIRTH	AGE	FIRST NAME OF SPOUSE	HOME TELEPHONE
William Paul Zinter	3-30-34	45	Margaret	332-4562

HOME ADDRESS	CITY	STATE	ZIP CODE	HOW LONG
1205 45th Street	Chicago	Ill.	60103	3 YEARS 6 MONTHS
PREVIOUS ADDRESS (IF WITHIN 3 YEARS) —	CITY —	STATE —		HOW LONG — YEARS — MONTHS

NUMBER OF DEPENDENTS INCLUDING SPOUSE: 4 — SOCIAL SECURITY NUMBER: 123-46-1945 — DRIVER'S LICENSE NUMBER: E 227 24 21376

EDUCATION: ☐ HIGH SCHOOL ☒ COLLEGE ☐ COLLEGE DEGREE(S) — COLLEGE MAJOR: Business Administration

EMPLOYMENT AND INCOME (2)

FIRM OR EMPLOYER'S NAME: ABC Construction Co. — POSITION: Asst. Mgr. — HOW LONG EMPLOYED: 11 YEARS 2 MONTHS

BUSINESS ADDRESS, CITY, STATE: 95th and Jeffrey Blvd — TELEPHONE: 336-4683 — TYPE OF BUSINESS: Construction — MONTHLY SALARY: $ 1050.00

PREVIOUS EMPLOYER: Sears Roebuck and Co. — ADDRESS — CITY: Gary — STATE: Indiana — HOW LONG EMPLOYED: 5 YEARS 0 MONTHS

SPOUSE'S EMPLOYER: None — POSITION: — — HOW LONG EMPLOYED: — YEARS — MONTHS

BUSINESS ADDRESS: — CITY: — STATE: — TELEPHONE: — TYPE OF BUSINESS: — MONTHLY SALARY: $ —

SOURCES OF OTHER INCOME: None — MONTHLY AMOUNT: $ —

BANK ACCOUNT (3)

BANK AND BRANCH: 1st National — ☒ CHECKING A/C NO. 193-45 ☐ SAVINGS A/C NO. ☐ LOAN

BANK AND BRANCH: Merchants Savings — ☒ SAVINGS A/C NO. — ☐ CHECKING A/C NO. ☐ LOAN

HOUSING (3) & (4)

☒ OWN ☐ RENT — MONTHLY RENT OR MORTGAGE: $ 205.00 — PURCHASE PRICE: $ 46,500 — ORIGINAL MORTGAGE: $ 16,000.00 — PRESENT BALANCE: $ 10,300.00

MORTGAGE HOLDER: Northern Savings and Loan Assn — ADDRESS: North State St. — CITY: Chicago — STATE: Ill.

CAR (3) & (4)

MAKE AND YEAR: Dodge 1970 — FINANCED BY (NAME AND ADDRESS—EVEN IF FULLY PAID): 1st Natl Bank — PRESENT BALANCE: $ —0— — MONTHLY PAYMENTS: $ —0—

CREDIT REFERENCES (1)

PLEASE LIST DEBTS OUTSTANDING (EXCLUDE ANY LISTED ABOVE)

NAME AND ADDRESS	BALANCE	PAYMENTS
1. Sears Roebuck and Co.—Chicago	$ 242.00	$ 12.00
2. Allied Furniture Co.—Chicago	$ 460.00	$ 40.00
3. Marshall Field & Co. Chicago	$ 80.00	$ None Specified
4.	$	$

CREDIT CARDS (INCLUDE OIL COMPANY) (1)

NAME	NO.	NAME	NO.	NAME	NO.	NAME	NO.
		Amer. Express	143 3030517400	Sears Roebuck	1604336808	Gulf Oil Co	683501064

MASTER CHARGE CARDS DO YOU HAVE A MASTER CHARGE CARD WITH ANOTHER BANK? ☐ YES ☒ NO BANK

I have read and agree to all the terms and conditions of the agreement set forth on the reverse side hereof wherein applicant is called Holder. I certify that the above information is true and complete, and I further authorize your bank to obtain any information that you require concerning the statements in this application. I agree that this application shall remain the property of the bank whether the credit is granted or not.

SIGNATURE William P. Zinter DATE

ISSUE ADDITIONAL MASTER CHARGE CARDS TO: ☐ SPOUSE ☐ OTHER

FOR BANK USE ______ BY ______ LINE OF CREDIT ______

FIGURE 7-3 Illustrative credit card application form

contract is originally signed. Usually the wage assignment ranges from 10 to 20 percent of your total earnings.

CREDIT RATINGS

All businesses that lend money or grant credit of any kind to customers are very much concerned about repayment. Firms try to see in advance if you are a good risk and if you have certain personal and financial characteristics that will ensure that the payments be made. This section discusses various criteria and ratings that are used to determine if a person is a good credit risk. Some suggested guidelines on how to establish and maintain good credit ratings are also given.

Criteria for Granting Credit

There are several criteria that credit-granting institutions study before they decide whether to extend credit. These include:

1. *Character*—the general behavior, attitude and personality of the person, past and present.
2. *Capacity*—the person's earning power—type of job, salary, other income.
3. *Capital*—the net worth of the individual, his or her accumulation of things of value.
4. *Collateral*—any items of value the person can use as security.

A typical credit application blank is shown in Figure 7-3. As you can see, specific sections are numbered. These numbered sections are for the information requested of each applicant; they indicate to which of the credit criteria it might apply. Those items marked 1 measure some degree of a person's *character*; those marked 2 show aspects of *capacity;* those marked 3 cite *capital* information; and those marked 4 label *collateral* data.

In addition, a fifth "C"—*conditions*—must be considered. These conditions are not under the control of the applicant, but the company extending credit must be alert to them—they are conditions that exist in the economy. For example, under tight money conditions, only limited amounts of money may be available to lend. A person may have difficulty obtaining a $3000 personal loan, for example, because the lender does not have much money to lend and would prefer a security loan such as on an automobile. Under such conditions, the cost of credit also rises. Of course, the opposite is true in times of "loose" money, or readily available credit.

Each business must decide for itself how to evaluate an applicant for credit. For example, if a customer has very good earning power, *capacity,* that may be all that matters. On the other hand, if the capacity to pay is in question, other factors, such as *collateral* or *capital,* may be given more consideration. And all other criteria notwithstanding, if *conditions* are bad and money for lending is not readily available, only those with the very highest credit credentials are given credit. But qualified customers can almost always get credit.

Point System for Credit Ratings

In an effort to be objective in rating the creditworthiness of customers, various point systems have been developed. Under a point system, points are alloted for various criteria that tend to be good credit-risk indicators. One list of factors and applicable point value ranges that has been used is the following:

Occupation	0–7 points
Job tenure	1–5 points
Residence	0–5 points
Time at present address	1–3 points
Bank accounts	2–6 points
Income	0–5 points
Credit references	−2 to +2 points

The assigning of points to an applicant and the interpretation of the point system is left to the individual creditor. Using the above list, each firm establishes an upper point for automatic approval of credit and a base (perhaps 12 points or less) for automatic denial.

Many personal factors are considered when deciding on a person's credit rating. And many laws and regulations have been enacted that either help or hinder establishing credit ratings and credit granting by firms. Consequently, many credit-granting institutions are seeking more objective bases for establishing credit ratings. Therefore, any objective point system appears to be more favorable than the subjective analysis used so frequently in the past.

Establishing and Maintaining Credit Ratings

Common sense, good buying and work habits, and a reasonable ability to handle family or personal finances are essential to help establish and keep a good credit rating. Unfortunately, not all credit ratings are good. Some people are reckless and careless with the use of credit; before too long what was once a good rating becomes quite questionable.

Many factors contribute to the establishment of a credit rating. In addition to those outlined earlier, having a job, working steadily, being of legal age, or having savings or checking accounts are just a few things considered. Bill Manners of Norman, Oklahoma, recently graduated from college with a degree in marketing. He was a B+ student, well liked, and a very amiable and energetic person. Yet, Bill did not have a credit rating at all because he always prided himself on being able to pay cash for everything. What Bill forgot was that to establish a credit rating he would have to use credit of some kind. In other words, Bill would have to be trusted by someone in regard to financial transactions in the marketplace. Bill would have to buy something on credit, or borrow money, and then pay for the items or repay the loan. His pattern of repayment would be noted, and he would be rated. Essentially, he would be given a credit rating based on his credit use.

Bill's situation illustrates one way people misinterpret credit ratings. Paying cash *is not* a way to establish credit. Using credit is the only way one can establish a credit rating. A good credit rating can be established in two phases (1) apply for credit to show you can be trusted; and (2) practice good credit use by making payments regularly and promptly. Reports of your credit payments habits sent to other businesses and agencies will contribute to your credit rating. A credit rating is not too hard to establish, but maintaining a good credit rating is another matter.

How well you use credit of various kinds will determine how your credit rating is maintained. When you use credit, you need to do so properly. When payments are due, you must make them. If you find that you cannot afford to make payments, you should not buy on credit. You must understand what credit is, what it can do, what it can't do, what its obligations are, and above all what your responsibilities are when you use it. One thing is for sure—if you abuse credit, it will hurt your rating. If you use credit properly, it will help your rating.

A final point to remember about maintaining credit ratings. If a credit report is sent to some business about you and you find it is not correct, follow it up. Under the Fair Credit Reporting Act, discussed earlier, you have the right to know about any items in your report that are unfavorable to you and can therefore limit or alter credit approval for you. You must know about these credit reports, be familiar with their contents, and know what to do if inaccurate reports are circulated. It is another of your responsibilities as a consumer credit user.

SOURCES FOR CREDIT USE

Commercial banks, credit unions, consumer finance companies, and "loan sharks" are examples of agencies that lend money directly to the consumer. Insurance companies, sales finance companies, and pawnbrokers also lend money, but usually under special conditions. Other sources from which approved forms of consumer credit are available include department stores, specialty shops, and discount stores.

Lending Institutions

Lending institutions have different operating practices and policies. Some practices are imposed by federal, state, or local laws, but nevertheless there is competition in the money-lending marketplace. Listed below are several types of institutions and certain operating characteristics of each.

Credit Unions. Reliable and good personal service; payroll deduction usually available; membership (through place of employment, church, community residency, or fraternity for a cost of less than a dollar) in credit union required of all who borrow; usually quick, easy service; have upper limit on amount borrowed; usually fixed interest rate, 3/4 to 1 percent a month (APR 12 percent) on the unpaid balance (varies in some cases, depending on amount borrowed or security provided); commonly installment loans only.

Commercial Banks. Very reliable, and usually have available funds; stated rates from 6 to 10 percent annually (APR 12 to 20 percent) depending on conditions and location; expect high personal qualifications of customers who borrow; generally no limit on the amount borrowed, or a very high limit; serve primarily low-risk customers for lending; minimum service fee for early repayment required; will usually discount amount of loan; single-payment loans usually available as well as installment loans.

Consumer Finance Companies. Controlled primarily by special state laws; have maximum loan limits; will assume poorer-risk customers; usually charge high rate of interest—stated rate ranges from 8 to 24 per-

Imagine—not buying something just because you can't afford it.

Courtesy of Edd Uluschak.

cent per year (APR 16 to 48 percent); greater pressure to collect from customers; personal, household, or auto loans are common; high degree of advertising and promotion; frequently a penalty or service fee assessed for early payoff of loan.

Sales Finance Companies. Usually lending is arranged through consumer-goods store or dealer; consumer cannot borrow directly; assume medium- to high-risk customers; generally screening of customers is handled by seller of product; primarily finance automobiles [for example, General Motors Acceptance Corporation (GMAC), Ford Motor Credit Company, and Chrysler Financial Corporation]; rates are higher than commercial banks, but lower than consumer finance companies; amount loaned backed by purchased consumer goods (for example, new car as collateral for loan).

Insurance Companies. Borrower must hold a *permanent type* of life insurance policy with the company from which he is borrowing; amount borrowed is based on cash value of existing permanent insurance policy; usually a low interest charge—5 to 6 percent annual APR; no specific payback arrangement required; charge interest only for period money used; no service or early prepayment fees; often charge lowest available interest rate; loan limit based on cash value of insurance policy.

Pawnbrokers. Loan amount based on exchanged item; borrowing is on something of value owned by customer and surrendered to pawnbroker; charge interest for services even though items of value are collateral for money loaned; customer can repay money and get property back; usually no specified date for redeeming pawn ticket (paying back money); generally high-risk customers served; must have something of value in exchange for money lent, and loan amount borrowed is generally much lower than value of item given as collateral; usually charge very high interest rates (APR 24 to 48 percent).

Loan Sharks. Operate outside the law; "last-chance" risk customers; exorbitant rates of interest—100 to 200 percent per week, month, or year are not uncommon; threats of harm are common to urge collection from customers; easy lending practices; personal qualifications or characteristics seemingly unimportant for borrowing.

Other Consumer Credit Sources

In addition to the money lenders of various kinds, there are numerous other sources of consumer credit. Department stores, specialty shops, discount stores, gasoline stations, restaurants, motels, and various recreational resorts are just a few places where consumers can use credit for products or services.

Business firms honor various forms and types of credit. Bank credit cards (Master Charge, Visa), store credit cards (Sears, Wards, Penney's), travel and entertainment cards (American Express, Carte Blanche), oil company cards (Gulf, American, Exxon) are used by many consumers. The acceptance of the particular card will depend on the policy of the business. Yet if desired, many businesses still offer regular charge accounts where no "plastic identification" is needed—just sign your name on the sales slip.

Consumer credit in all forms is a multibillion-dollar business. Almost all firms extend credit to and encourage credit use from its customers. And about half of all consumers use credit in some form. But, however it is extended or encouraged, the users of consumer credit must use it intelligently and responsibly.

HOW DO YOU KNOW IF YOU ARE OVEREXTENDED?

Proper credit use carries with it a major responsibility for consumers. Credit is now relatively easy to get, and it can provide one with most material goods or services. Consequently, there will be a few people who use credit with reckless abandon, disregard their responsibilities, and wind up overextending themselves financially. In effect, by using credit too often, some consumers have so obligated themselves with credit and don't know it until it is too late.

Consumers need some guidelines or signals to help them realize if they are becoming or already are overly indebted. Indebtedness measures, credit limits, debt pooling, add-on loans (flipping), repossession, garnishments, and bankruptcies can be used as clues that excessive credit use has been the practice. Let's learn how these signals can be used to help avoid this credit abuse.

Overindebtedness Measure

Determining at frequent times that you may be an overextended credit user is essential. There are different ways to estimate a person's overindebtedness, but one that has been frequently recommended and used has been developed by Dr. Gwen Bymers of Cornell University. Three financial areas of concern are measured to determine the degree of indebtedness.

1. The amount of cash you have to meet emergencies—for this you add all money in savings accounts, government savings bonds, checking accounts or other liquid assets. If this amount is greater than $1000, give yourself an A; if less than $1000, give yourself an F.
2. The length of time necessary to pay your present installment debt—for this measure, add all your outstanding installment debts and divide the total by the total debt payments made per month. The result will be the number of months you need to pay your debts. If this amounts to 12 months or less, give yourself an A; if greater than 12, give yourself an F.
3. The amount of monthly income that is being spent for installment debt payments—for this figure, divide your estimated monthly installments for debt payments (from step 2) by your monthly take-home pay. Your result will be the percentage of take-home pay that is allocated to debt payments. If the percentage is less than 20 percent, give yourself an A; if greater than 20 percent, you get an F.

If you have given yourself three F's, you are extremely overextended in debt; if two F's, you are somewhat in debt—you need to be careful here; one F may be all right, but don't stop watching. All A's would indicate that debt management is being handled with little difficulty. As a user of consumer credit, it is your responsibility to strive for all A's.

Credit Limits

Frequently, issuers of credit—retail stores or credit-card issuers—may limit the amount of credit that can be extended. If not, you may ask any extender of credit to do so. This credit limit helps to discipline you, the credit consumer, on using credit.

For example, George Lindsey of Portland, Oregon, had a Master Charge credit limit of $500. But he sought to raise his limit because he constantly had $500 outstanding. Master Charge was willing to raise this limit to $800. The important signal here for George is that he is gradually becoming overextended by seeking to raise his limit. George should consider reducing his indebtedness by cutting back on his credit purchases rather than raising the limit. You as a user of credit must be aware of your credit-buying habits and if you are continually at your credit limit, stop, reflect, and perhaps reduce your spending and your credit debts outstanding. It's your responsibility.

Debt Pooling

When you borrow money or refinance existing loans to consolidate your debts in order to make one monthly payment, you are debt pooling. This is also known as *debt consolidation*. This signal becomes evident to the person who is overextended on credit.

Ellen Stoucher of Macomb, Illinois, had monthly debt payments totaling $372 with a monthly take-home pay of $600. It was extremely hard for Ellen to make payments and still provide other necessities, such as food and medical help for her family. Ellen decided to pool all her debts; she borrowed $4800 from a consumer finance company. Now she makes monthly payments of only $180 per month. But she is paying more interest and for many more months. Debt pooling or consolidation is the number one reason why people borrow from consumer finance companies.

When you find yourself wanting to pool your debts to "get out from under the financial pressure," stop and think. You may have too much debt and must consolidate. But if you do, it is your responsibility to resist future buying on credit and reduce your indebtedness in a consistent manner in the months ahead.

Add-On Loans (Flipping)

An indication of too much debt related somewhat to debt pooling is called add-on or "flipping." To illustrate, Jim Edwards of Terre Haute, Indiana, borrowed $300 from a bank to be repaid in monthly installments. When the debt balance was at $152, Jim refinanced the loan and added on another $300. Now he owed $152 + $300 or $452 plus interest. He has "flipped" his original loan over to a new loan and will continue to pay, and pay, and pay. In the future he may decide to add on again. And he may never repay the ultimate loan completely.

When you find yourself wanting to add-on or "flip" on an existing loan, stop and think—you are probably overextended. Be alert to the signal and act accordingly. Resist temptation, reduce spending, and at least analyze the situation carefully and perhaps repay the first loan before contracting for another.

Repossession

This indebtedness signal is hard for anyone to overlook. Ginger Jordan of Washington, D.C., purchased a 25-inch console color television recently and agreed to make installment payments. Shortly, other credit payments took most of her take-home pay; so she skipped her television payments for 3 months. Subsequently, her creditor proceeded legally and repossessed her television. It did not take Ginger long to realize she was too much in debt, since she had lost her television and still had some of the debt to repay, in addition to court costs that were assessed.

Of course, had Ginger checked her total indebtedness carefully before she purchased the television set, she probably would have realized she could not afford it. As she gradually reduced her indebtedness, she could have taken on additional debts without the subsequent embarrassment of repossession. Moreover, it is the responsibility of each credit-using consumer to determine the extent of debt and to resist buying when the debt is high.

Garnishment

A legal directive of the court given to one's employer to take/withhold part of the salary or wages and pay it to a creditor is called garnishment. It is a legal right sanctioned and determined by the courts.

Garnishments are not automatic; they are usually a result of action by a creditor against someone who has failed to pay a debt. But when garnishments happen, this indicates that there has been overindebtedness and/or careless handling of debts.

The federal Truth-in-Lending law puts limitations on the use of garnishments. It limits the amount of a person's disposable income for any week that can be garnished. More specifically, up to 25 percent of a worker's disposable income for the week, or the amount by which disposable income per week exceeds 30 times the federal minimum hourly wage prescribed under the Wage and Hour Act when payable, can be garnished. Furthermore, employees whose wages are garnished cannot be discharged for this reason alone. Also, when a state law regarding garnishment is more strict, it will prevail. Therefore, persons who are concerned about garnishments should seek legal advice and check the state statutes.

Garnishments, therefore, are another signal of being overextended. They are, however, extremely serious, since once a garnishment has been authorized, little can be done except to live with it. The only other option is to repay the debt in full immediately. Credit users need to recognize other, less serious measures of debt overextension and avoid being caught up in a garnishment.

REMEDIES FOR POOR CREDIT USE

Those who use credit should make every effort to use it properly. However, if persons are caught up in abusing credit, they need to do something to forestall the drastic measures described earlier. Here are some suggestions to help persons who are addicted to poor credit use or who just don't understand all the ramifications of using credit properly:

- Admit that you are using credit improperly when it seems apparent. If you can't help yourself, get help from someone who can.
- Contact the firms extending credit to you and try to arrange for reduced or delayed payments. This will give you some time and reduce the pressure until you can get back on your feet financially.
- Learn more about credit—what it is, what it can do or cannot do, its advantages and disadvantages—through self-education or educational programs at schools or community organizations.
- Contact your local banks, credit unions, community action workers, or county extension agents, as they may offer debt counseling on a formal or informal basis. But you must seek out their help, since they normally do not solicit.
- Seek help from reliable registered and licensed *nonprofit* consumer credit-counseling offices. Trained professional credit counselors can help you get back on a proper credit-use path. This service is usually for little or no fee. (Write to the National Foundation for Consumer Credit, 1819 H Street, N.W., Washington, D.C. 20006, for the address of the Consumer Credit Counseling Service nearest you.)
- Contact legal aid societies to get help on the legal problems related to overextension of credit. This help is also at no cost to the user.
- Check the nearest Family Service Agency. These agencies, located throughout the nation, offer financial counseling or can refer you to an agency that does.
- For the aged in particular, many towns and cities offer assistance through the "Council on Aging" or a similar agency. Competent, knowledgeable persons offer credit-counseling services on a volunteer basis. "No strings, no gimmicks, no cost, just help" is the rule.

Of these suggestions, the first is perhaps the most important. If one doesn't recognize that a credit-use problem exists, there is no motivation for finding remedies.

A final note: Stay clear of the so-called *debt consolidators* who wrongly pass themselves off as credit counselors. These companies will pool your debts for you—provide you with smaller payments and extend your payments—but frequently do so at a very high interest rate in addition to charging you a service fee. The fee often comes out of the first 2 or 3 months of payments—*all* the money one pays in. Such practices, including the service fee which one cannot afford to pay, in fact, often place one further in debt as a result.

POINTS OF VIEW AND PROBLEMS TO THINK ABOUT

Credit will continue to play an important and significant role in the American economy. Continued growth in the total use of consumer credit is an indication that credit is an important contributor to economic growth. Easy access to consumer credit can present problems; although it allows consumers to improve their level of living, credit use still obligates future income. It is safe to conclude that credit has a considerable impact on both the economy and the buying habits of individual consumers.

Credit use, however, does not have to result in credit *abuse*. If consumers abuse their credit, stronger efforts must be made to introduce them to more efficient credit-management practices. More credit-counseling programs must be made available and publicized. Special omnibus offices might also be made available to those who have difficulty coping with credit transactions, contracts, and finance charges.

With so much emphasis on credit, what about cash customers? Cash is a negotiable financial commodity, and persons who use cash frequently should not be penalized. The prices charged by businesses that extend credit do reflect the operating credit costs, which includes the costs of offering credit.

Should cash customers pay for this service that they do not use?

Education is an important element of credit counseling. Judges frequently order automobile drivers with serious traffic violations to attend driver-education classes. Perhaps credit-use "violators" should be required to attend classes on the proper use of credit—especially those consumers who are heavily in debt or are in bankruptcy proceedings.

Overextending oneself with credit is a major problem in our society. Getting credit is too easy for many people because of the overly generous actions of many businesses and credit-card issuers. Should the responsibility of this overextension of credit be solely on the shoulders of the consumers? What is the role and responsibility of business in restricting credit for those who already have credit over-extension signals? Should the government pass laws to treat the abuser of credit as a "crediholic" as we do with severe traffic violators?

Credit legislation needs to be continually reviewed and strengthened. To what extent should a person's credit file be open to issuers of credit? This becomes an invasion-of-privacy versus freedom-of-information argument. What information should be kept on each credit user? Are the Fair Credit Reporting Act, the Fair Credit Billing Act, the Truth-in-Lending law, the Equal Credit Opportunity Act, and the Fair Debt Collection Practices Act sufficiently effective? And when will legislation be passed to protect consumers in electronic funds transfer situations?

The reporting of credit costs, as part of the Truth-in-Lending law, has been very helpful, but consumers do not widely use these costs for comparison-shopping purposes. Are they ignorant of the availability of this information? Or lazy? Or apathetic? Perhaps there should be more checks and balances, particularly on the amount of credit charges as well as the interest rates charged. Should state and local laws be studied and revised to make credit costs more equitable for all consumers?

Does the explosion of credit suggest that we

are headed for a "cashless society" (exclusive use of credit when purchasing goods)? Or, in effect, are we venturing upon a "checkless society" as well? Present technology, including computers and other electronic devices for processing credit data or transferring funds, would indicate that this is a likely direction. If that is the wave of the future, are enough safeguards built into the system to protect consumers? In the final analysis, the consumers, business people, and government officials will determine how well both cash and credit transactions will exist in our society. But the consumer voice must be heard, or all the needed checks and balances may not be put into place.

CHAPTER ACTIVITIES

Checkup on Consumer Terms and Concepts

"Crediholic"
Consumer credit
Installment credit
Single-payment loan
Revolving charge
  account
Service credit
Overdraft loans
Bank credit cards
Travel/recreation
  credit cards
Dollar cost of credit
Interest add-on
  method
Discounting
Shopping for credit
Open-end credit

Simple annual
  percentage rate
True annual
  percentage rate
Truth-in-Lending
Disclosure statement
Stated rate of interest
Equal Credit
  Opportunity Act
Balloon clause
Rule of 78s
Condition
Consumer finance
  company
Sales finance
  company
Garnishment

Review of Essentials

1. How can a person abuse credit?
2. What are some advantages of credit?
3. What are some disadvantages of credit?
4. What are some rights and responsibilities of consumers in using credit?
5. Explain why credit costs charged by businesses to consumers are necessary.

6. Distinguish between the simple interest method and the interest add-on method.
7. Cite the advantages of using the ending-balance method when calculating interest on open-end credit accounts for consumers.
8. What is meant by the dollar cost of credit? How is it determined?
9. Explain why the true annual percentage rate for installment loans is usually about double the stated rate.
10. What should be the main things looked for when examining a completed credit disclosure statement?
11. At what population segment is the Equal Credit Opportunity Act primarily directed and why?
12. Why has the "balloon clause" been shown to be one to probably avoid in credit?
13. Identify ways consumers can maintain a good credit rating.
14. What ways or sources can persons use to remedy problems resulting from improper credit use?

Issues for Analysis

1. Should merchants and lenders of money be obligated to do a more thorough check on their credit applicants to help keep the "crediholics" from getting deeper and deeper into debt? Why or why not?
2. Should a credit user ever be allowed to be completely absolved of indebtedness because of insolvency (as is now permitted under the Federal Bankruptcy Act), or should there be only a temporary moratorium on payments until the debtor is again solvent? Why?
3. Is it fair if a store or service agency charges 1½ percent a month finance charge on the opening balance rather than on the unpaid balance? Why or why not?
4. Is it necessary for consumers to know how to calculate the true annual percentage rate for installment loans or purchases? Why or why not?

8

Purchasing Clothing

THE PROBLEMS

New fashions in clothing seem to be foisted upon the consumer by the designer and manufacturer. Especially until a few years ago, consumers bought certain clothing articles mainly because they were in fashion or because nothing else was available. Some important questions: "How often are opinions about clothing design sought from consumers? How willing are consumers to offer opinions on clothing design? And how many consumers really care?"

Regardless of consumer concerns, merchants must stock and merchandise clothing that sells. There is certainly no criticism here. But often the merchant relies too heavily upon the advice of the manufacturer. The merchant then stocks and sells *only* the big-selling designs. People who want high-style trousers or dresses, for example, may be in good shape right now. But those who want more conservative designs may have to do considerably more shopping to find what they want; not-so-fashionable clothing is often hard to find. This is true in both men's and women's clothing. Whatever is "in" is what the consumer is expected to buy.

Also, consumers are frequently forced into lengthy shopping tours because sizes are not consistent among manufacturers. Mrs. Billie McIntyre of Charleston has worn size 12 dresses for years. Recently, while shopping in New Orleans, she saw a dress she liked. She tried on the only size they had left in stock—a size 12—but found it too small. The next dress she tried was too large, even though it too was a 12. Consequently, she bought nothing.

And what about the man who keeps himself trim and does not "naturally" bulge at the middle? He will find it difficult to get a suit from the clothing racks. For example, if he wears a 44-long suit, the trousers will have a 38- or 39-inch waist. The man who has a 32- to 34-inch waist must have the trousers tailored to fit. The problem is one of the manufacturer keeping in touch with the public to be reasonably sure that a 38-inch waist is "average" for one who wears a 44-long suit. Most manufacturers do try to meet the average-size demands of their customers, but the problem still exists. One answer might be that the "average sizes," for both men and women, have changed, or that there are several "averages" and that therefore more careful measurement research may be necessary.

Judging quality, or how well clothes are made, is difficult for many consumers—another problem. Most people rely almost exclusively on the word of the salesperson. But can their word be relied upon? Frequently, salespersons working on commission want only to "sell, sell, sell" and are not concerned with service and a thorough product knowledge. Many clothing sales people are not well trained to sell clothing, and furthermore are not trained to recognize quality.

Freedom to choose is one of the basic rights of consumers. Problems develop, however, when outside forces, such as advertising, make direct or indirect efforts to influence this choice. It is correct to inform the consumer about clothing facts, such as material, care, size, and price. However, when the practice goes beyond informing to heavily influencing, it becomes a consumer problem. How to cope with it remains unanswered.

REASONS FOR CLOTHING CHOICES

"I like it." "Everyone's wearing them." "It's the 'in' look." "I want to be different." These statements are typical of the reasons given by hundreds of thousands of consumers daily—reasons that vary with age, sex, and economic and social status, as well as group and peer influences, the youth culture, women's and men's liberation, and socio-psychological bases. Styles, fashions, and fads reveal further insights into the clothing choices of consumers in the American marketplace. Let us look at some of these influences.

Youth Culture

A father was overheard telling his two sons that he would give each of them $20 if they would get a different style of haircut. His motive was to see how loyal they were to the peer pressure, or youth culture. Both sons refused his offer for the same reason—their friends would think they looked "creepy and odd." Other boys, of course, might have felt differently—or their peer groups might have.

This reaction to haircuts can also be related to the clothing choices of many young people today. A young person's reasons for choosing a particular style or color are varied, ranging from what is functional and comfortable to what the peer group is wearing—which may or may not be the same thing. Essentially, there are both social and psychological reasons for deciding what to wear. It is a means of self-expression ("the clothing I wear is me"). It presents a self-concept or image of prime importance for many young people; clothing is their means of striving for it. Recognition becomes a byproduct of clothing choices for any one person. What dad or mom thinks is practical and proper may be fine, or it may be ultraconservative and out of the question.

This is not to say, however, that all young people are guided strictly by peer pressure. These people spend a significant amount of money on clothing, and their choices are usually made independent of their parents. Regardless of who or what influences their thinking—the designers or certain youth groups (like entertainment)—young people are going to be greatly influenced by what is in fashion and what best gives them the identification they are looking for. Consequently, their choices of clothing are limited, yet, in another sense, independently made.

Women's Continued Liberation

In the seventies, when fashion designers decided to drop the mini and emphasize the midi length instead, they started a snowball rolling that has not stopped yet. For women did not accept the midi. Instead, they turned increasingly to pantsuits and other clothing designs. They made up their *own* minds. The influence of designers is still apparent, but it is not quite as strong. Designers now look more to what women want.

Surely, the decade of the seventies can well be described as the "womens rights" years. Recently established and proposed federal legislation and constitutional changes have opened up more choices and freedoms for women. Increased employment opportunities, more equitable salaries, and other equally important benefits are being demanded. Also, along with this goes a movement to equalize opportunities for all people. In the long run it will be up to each individual to decide how she is going to implement these newly won rights, and even whether she wants to exercise her rights to the fullest.

Women have continued to seek their own means of self-expression and individuality. Being liberated from the so-called traditional "women's clothing" has allowed most women to speak out in their own way and say indirectly "I am not inferior," "I am at least equal," "I am myself," and "I want to be able to express myself as an individual, not just as one of a larger group."

Many women and women's groups have been using their consumer rights by rejecting the styles (which sometimes denote a subservient role) being thrust upon them. Others are using their right to choose. Some are rebelling against being regarded as "sex symbols," an image that fashions tend to promote. Others are using their choice to find physical and psychological comfort, self-expression, or emotional release.

Yes, a continual change in women's ideas on clothing design is evident. More alternatives for selection are available. And women in general are increasingly able to cast their economic votes for *their* clothing choices, basing these choices largely upon socio-psychological or their own personal reasons, not on some designers' and manufacturers' ideas.

Although most women want to choose their clothing for personal reasons now, there still remains that interest and desire to maintain femininity. Initially, demand tends to move to the extremes in most areas of consumer buying; clothing is no exception. Many women have been buying more feminine-looking clothing as well as reflecting their individuality with nonconforming clothing styles. For a while, however, as the "liberated" women started to break loose from the mold to seek a new self-image through pants and pantsuits, many other clothing alternatives were not as

available as before. But, once the freedom to express in different clothing styles was established and accepted, a return to some of the basics became evident.

If some women choose to buy clothing that makes them less sexy, this is their right. If others want to choose clothing so sexy that it borders on unacceptability, that, too, is their right. If they want to dress to reflect their self-concept or self-image or to please their friends, a boyfriend, or a husband, that is also their right. The alternatives are numerous.

Men's Renewed Role

Historically men have been rather conservative in their dress, although it is true that there have also been many "peacock" eras. From the early seventies to the present there has been evidence that men are moving from a conservative to a "peacock" era again. Years ago a man could wear a suit for several years and not feel old-fashioned. Not today! Men have become more style-conscious.

A reversal seems to be developing between the demand and buying habits for clothing among men and women. Conformity was in vogue for many years in the clothing men purchased. Now men are superconscious of fashion and style. In the past most women were the only ones possessed by this "fashion conformity."

Perhaps the greatest impetus to creating this "new" men's image in clothing has been the influence of young adults. Their choices of clothing have had an impact on many older men as well, who enjoy the new clothing designs. Ultimately the "new" clothes-conscious male introduced flare trousers into the business world, whereas before such trousers were worn only by navy personnel.

The choices in men's clothing have also expanded greatly in recent years. Gone are the days of selecting clothing merely for protection and decency—although such reasons are still good, of course. Styles, individuality, employment, social pressures, self-expression, status, and a desire for conformity or nonconformity have taken over now and give the male shopper a new framework for his choices. Clothing of a certain type may also give a psychological lift to one who is under tremendous pressures. Furthermore, new style variations let men use clothing as an expression of their personalities, moods, or self-concept.

Styles, Fashions, and Fads

There are important distinctions among such terms as "styles," "fashions," "fads," "tastes," and "rages," which are frequently used when one speaks of clothing. To illustrate, *style* is the characteristic or distinctive way a garment looks; it is the sum of the features that make that garment different from other garments. Women's pants styles, for example, might include tapered legs, bell-bottom legs, straight legs, shorts, culottes, or gauchos. So that you can better see the relationship of these terms in regard to clothing choices, a brief examination of how they differ will help. Figure 8-1 illustrates the distinctions.

As can be noted, all terms are based upon consumers' behavior in the marketplace. It is their economic voting that determines whether or not an item of clothing will be accepted. To gain this recognition, an item must be accepted for a period of time and by many people.

Characteristically human beings are a peculiar lot. Logically one might think that people in our society would look at quality as being of strong importance when buying clothing. This is not always the case. The average consumer looks for fashion, price, and quality, in that order of importance, when it comes to shopping for clothing. In fact, one could say that fashion "wears out most clothing." Literally, of course, this is not true, but it is true indirectly as consumers buy new clothing because of fashion change. The older clothing, no longer considered fashionable, is disregarded or given to someone else who is not quite so fashion-minded.

Of course, fashion can be created honestly or falsely. If an item of clothing is designed

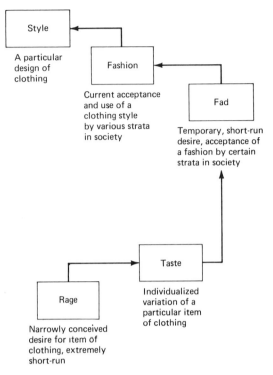

FIGURE 8-1 Distinguishing market characteristics in clothing

and follows the normal progress of acceptance by persons in the marketplace, it can be considered an honest style. If, on the other hand, it is designed and then all but pushed into the minds and hands of consumers through high-powered advertising, extreme sales pressure (optimal power of suggestion), or limited or no competition, it can be said to be falsely created.

Consumer voting dictates the life or death of styles. The acceptance or rejection of clothing (economic voting) as it is designed and manufactured becomes an economic game of chance for both manufacturers and consumers. When choosing clothing, consumers are influenced by peer or social pressures, economic necessity, self-expression, emulation, *conspicuous consumption* (keeping up with the Joneses), advertising, common decency, or protection. These influences and many others eventually create styles. Moreover, if a newly

Courtesy of Edd Uluschak.

"You're in luck, sir—cuffs are back this year."

established clothing item really catches on, more will be bought, and this may firmly entrench it as a style in the marketplace.

As styles, fashions, or fads exist in the marketplace, they are, in and of themselves, a tremendous influence on why consumers choose certain types of clothing. That is, most consumers buy clothing because it is in fashion, or it is the latest fad. One problem continues, however: consumers often disregard *purpose, function, price, quality,* and *need* when their purchases are guided exclusively by fads and fashions.

Unfortunately, many men and women continue to accept unequivocally the designers' and manufacturers' styles of clothing. Essentially, many consumers become addicted to designer creations solely. "You design it, manufacture it, advertise it, and sell it, and I will surely buy it with no questions asked, and no matter how I look" is perhaps a harsh way of describing this addiction, but one that is too often true. For example, on many people,

slacks, shorts, hot pants, etc., did not create the image the designer had originally intended; they did not suit everyone. Then again, the fallacy of trying to be a nonconformist through buying the recently created styles in reality makes one a conformist to the styles created by designers. Invariably, nonconformity soon brings about conformity in another way.

CLOTHING NEEDS AND WANTS

One cannot completely disregard external influences when rationalizing clothing choices. Clothing needs for one person may be wants for another, and vice versa. But a person's lifestyle, position, economic status, and attitude will be among the deciding factors in classifying items of clothing as *needs* or *wants*.

Clothing Needs
Clothing needs can be described as the things one "must have" to exist according to the dictates of society or one's particular lifestyle.

Such needs would, of course, be individualized. No general blanket list of clothing could be established for all. Needs in clothing have two general classifications, *primary* [to include protection (both physical and psychological), decency, and esthetics], and *secondary* (to include employment, social, and status).

Primary Needs. Three primary needs for clothing are for physical protection from the weather, for psychological protection from mental stress and fatigue, and—in our society—for decency and esthetics. These three needs are accepted by most consumers in the United States, although of course there are some who will challenge them—especially decency—unless the law or society steps in.

Only the most meager wardrobe would be needed to satisfy one's most basic clothing needs—a dress (or pants and blouse), perhaps stockings, and shoes for women and girls; and a shirt and trousers (or coveralls), and socks and shoes for men and boys. But this would hardly fill the needs of most people. Ms. Janie Braunig of Houston "needs" twelve dresses of various kinds, ten pairs of shoes, many skirts and blouses, several pairs of pants, and other items of wearing apparel to satisfy her needs. In contrast, Ms. Olivia Williams of Detroit needs only two dresses, three pairs of shoes, two or three styles of pants, a few blouses, and a few other garments. Neither woman is gainfully employed—both are housewives with small children—yet their needs are vastly different. Consumers must decide for themselves what their needs are and what they can do without.

In addition to needs for physical protection and decency, there also are psychological needs. A "good feeling," "a brief respite from the drudgery of work," "looking nice," and "general relaxation" all could be classified as *psychological advantages* that one gets from wearing clothing. In essence, specific items of clothing worn can provide protection from the mental stress in work, school, or play.

If buying a new dress or suit makes a person feel more mentally alert and more able to cope with the problems of the day or evening, then why not? If wearing a new suit of clothes makes some persons more confident, and provides them with a way of reflecting self-expression or a better understanding of themselves, then so be it. No one practice or behavior of consumers in the use of clothing is considered standard. Each need is different, and each satisfaction of any psychological need will be different. The choices are numerous, and the freedom to choose a particular kind or quantity of clothing is available to all.

Of course, not all persons have uniformly shaped bodies. Consequently, custom, time, and designers have dictated that clothing can be used as the equalizer to make persons look similar and to give them a nice appearance. People recognize the need to alter or hide obvious physical imperfections with clothing. As a result, it makes them feel good, and above all it gives them a new appearance. Under such circumstances an esthetic need has been satisfied. This need for satisfaction goes on all the time; however, the specific esthetic needs and how they will be met is going to be different among consumers.

Secondary needs. Certain clothing needs depend upon a particular event or phase of a person's life. Needs of this type are referred to as *secondary* needs. Examples of secondary needs include lifestyle, social status, place of employment, and type of employment.

These secondary needs are going to vary among consumers. As each person or family adopts a particular lifestyle or other status, their needs will change. For example, Janey Groves worked hard to achieve a high skill in playing the violin in the school orchestra. She was successful and was chosen to play with the orchestra beginning in the fall semester. Her needs also changed, since she now had to buy some evening gowns to wear when she played. Because she took on another activity, she developed a secondary need for a certain type of clothing.

Persons employed in certain places and certain jobs have a need for special types of clothing. Suits, ties, white or colored shirts, and polished shoes may be the type of clothing required by some employers. Others may only require shoes, a pair of pants, and any kind of shirt. Still others may insist that all women employees wear dresses rather than pantsuits at work. And too, clothing needs of this type may not be in accord with a person's own lifestyle, but because of the employer's request or the nature of the work, the person will have to make some adjustment.

Social status is important to many people. Thus, it also influences their clothing needs. If a person's social position demands looking nice all the time, and that certain types of clothing be worn for specific occasions, then these needs must be satisfied if the social position is to be maintained. Whether the secondary-clothing need is chosen or mandated by a special situation, it must be satisfied according to the dictates of society. That does not mean, however, that ski clothes for a skiing vacation are necessarily a secondary need; circumstances of this nature become wants of individuals, and these will be discussed later.

The need for clothing does not, of course, guarantee that it will be bought. A low-income family, for example, may feel that each of their boys needs two shirts for school, but they may be able to afford only one. Therefore, the one shirt must be washed frequently to keep it clean, and, if possible, rips and tears must be immediately mended. Those with more money, on the other hand, can afford a half-dozen or a dozen shirts per child.

Clothing Wants

When one talks of clothing wants, this usually means certain items that one does not basically need, or more items than one has to have to fill these needs. Inwardly one feels a want to satisfy one's desires.

Often in order to keep up with fads and fashions, people begin to buy new items of clothing even though their wardrobe is full of clothing in good condition. Pressure may be felt from neighbors, peers, coworkers, or social groups; and persons try to satisfy these *clothing wants* to meet the pressure or to be in high fashion. Clothing wants are frequently justified on the basis of their function, comfort, or convenience.

Clothing function. A person buying special clothing to go skiing (as referred to earlier) considers the functional use of clothing. Unless a person is required to ski for a job, the desire for specialized clothing is a *want*, not a *need*. Many a young man or woman has gone skiing without special kinds of clothing, and has done well. (This assumes, of course, that the person has clothes that can be worn for skiing.) In some cases, however, part of an outfit could be a need for safety or health reasons. An example would be the specially designed boots for skiing. It would be very difficult, if not impossible, to ski without them. Other activities which involve the use of functional clothing include swimming, skin diving, mountain climbing, cycling, trap shooting, jogging, and skating.

Comfort. Recently certain undergarments that women had worn for years (such as girdles) began to be given up because they were considered restrictive and uncomfortable. When these items were first designed, it was primarily for appearance. But attitudes and ideas change, new products help to displace the old (a special panty hose to displace the panty girdle), and thus the comfort of particular items of clothing takes precedence, and manufacturers tend to adapt accordingly.

In men's and women's clothing the leisure suit and pantsuit were designed primarily for comfort. Neither outfit was considered a need. It was a want that provided comfort and relaxation, yet had a somewhat dressy appearance. In some places of employment the standards for dress were relaxed to let employees wear leisure suits or pantsuits. In both cases the emphasis was on comfort. In other places leisure suits and pantsuits were not allowed. Consequently, persons wore these styles at functions and activities other than work, mainly because they were comfortable.

Convenience. A very frequently used reason for buying clothing and for wanting certain items is convenience. Consider, for example, the car coat. For a person who gets in and out of a car frequently on cold days, a car coat is much more convenient than a long coat. A women's shoulder bag may not be essential; a small clutch bag might serve the same purpose. But a shoulder bag often has more room and of course can free the hands for other uses.

One does not apologize to anyone for a want for specific clothing items. What is important is that the want should have some substance to it and the purchase should be made in an informed manner. The want should have a personal value and purpose; it should not be haphazardly satisfied without justification.

WHAT TO LOOK FOR WHEN BUYING CLOTHING

The average consumer knows little about what to look for when buying clothing, yet much of this ignorance is not the consumer's fault. Often it is the fault of the economic system. Information about quality, fabric, care, and many other items is frequently misleading, obscure, or missing. Let us discuss a few of these important points.

Quality

Consumers are continually trying to learn more about the quality of clothes—how well made they are and the kind of fabric used. Unfortunately, this information is not readily available to consumers, especially in a form they can understand. Often information is too technical, and it therefore takes an expert in clothing construction to judge quality.

Currently it is hard to understand quality terminology because it is in large part subjective. Until definite and clearly defined standards are established, one must learn about and use whatever quality measures are available when shopping for clothing.

Clear, concise, standardized consumer information about the quality of clothing is practically nonexistent. Workmanship and durability are just two terms typically used to measure standards of clothing quality. But what do they mean?

Workmanship. The quality of construction that goes into an article is referred to as *workmanship*. Examples of workmanship that can be identified by careful inspection include neat, straight, even stitching with thread of the proper weight and color; seams that are flat and, where necessary, have finished edges; hems that are of proper width with invisible stitching; smooth, correctly aligned lining and interfacing; hooks, snaps, or buttons firmly attached and correctly placed on the garment.

Durability. How long a particular fabric is expected to last is generally called *durability*. Fabric with high durability should be used for clothing that is worn frequently; fabric with low or moderate durability is sufficient for clothing worn only once or a few times. How well a garment wears and how much abuse it can take are further indications of its durability. A term often used interchangeably with durability is *wearability*. Both terms are used synonymously in analyzing material quality. Ultimately the consumer must learn about the fabrics used in clothing construction to be any kind of judge of durability or wearability. Consumers must read labels to learn about the types of fabric used in the making of clothes. Table 8-1 identifies characteristics and suggested uses of certain fabrics.

Fibers and Fabrics Used

Different fibers and fabrics used in clothing manufacture are often labeled and described in technical language. Nevertheless, some knowledge about the four natural types of fibers and several synthetic fibers is essential

TABLE 8-1

Characteristics of Natural and Synthetic Fibers

Fiber	Common or Brand Names	Characteristics	Uses in Clothing
Natural Fiber			
Cotton	Pima, Egyptian, Sea Island	Natural resistance to abrasion; versatile, durable, strong, absorbent, wrinkles badly unless treated	All types of lightweight apparel
Linen	Crash, damask, huckaback	Natural resistance to moths; durable, strong, absorbent, quick drying; wrinkles badly unless treated	Women's and children's dresses, blouses, and skirts; summer suitings, handkerchiefs
Silk	Cultivated, raw, spun, Tussah, or Wild	Natural resistance to wrinkling, flame; resilient, shape-retaining, strong, absorbent, heat-sensitive	Women's blouses, skirts, and suits; casual, cocktail, and evening dresses; accessories; lingerie; men's robes, shirts, ties, and summer suits
Wool	Virgin or new, reprocessed, reused; alpaca, camel's hair, cashmere, llama, mohair, guanaco, vicuna	Natural resistance to abrasion, wrinkling, sunlight, flame; resilient, versatile, durable, absorbent	Men's, women's, and children's apparel: skirts, sweaters, dresses, suits, coats, and socks
Man-made Fiber Acetate	Acele, Celacloud, Celanese, Celara Estron	Able to take beautiful color; shrink-resistant; economical; able to retain crispness; has a pleasing drapability; luxurious feel and appearance	Dresses, foundation garments, lingerie, blouses
Acrylic	Acrilan, Creslan, Nomelle, Orlon, Zefran	Soft, warm, and lightweight; shape-retentive, resilient, quick drying; light, fluffy construction	Sweaters, skirts, dresses, suits, socks, sports and work clothes
Modacrylic	Dynel, Verel	Soft, resilient, flame-resistant; quick drying; noted for warm, luxurious handling	Deep-pile coats, trims, linings, fleece fabrics
Polyester	Avlin, Dacron, Encron, Fortrel, Kodel, Quintess, Trevira, Vycron	Strong resistance to stretching and shrinking; easy to dye, resistant to most chemicals; crisp and resilient, wrinkle-resistant, abrasion-resistant, able to retain heat-set pleats and creases, quick drying	Men's, women's, and children's apparel; durable (permanent press) garments
Rayon	Avisco, Avron, Avicron, Enka, Fortisan, Cupioni	Highly absorbent, durable, soft and comfortable; versatile, economical, easy to dye, good drapability, wrinkles easily	Dresses, suits, blouses, coats, lingerie, pants, ties, lining fabrics

TABLE 8-1 (Continued)

Nylon	Ayrlyn, Caprolan, Enka, Nytelle, Blue C, Qiana	Exceptionally strong, elastic, abrasion-resistant; able to be dyed in a wide range of colors; smooth, resilient, low in moisture absorbency; lustrous, easy to wash	Hosiery, dresses, lingerie, underwear, suits, stretch fabrics
Olefin	Amco, Amerfil, Beamette, Diamond Herculon, Vectra, Polycrest, Olane	Very lightweight; able to give good bulk and cover; abrasion-resistant, quick drying, highly stain-resistant, very sensitive to heat	Knitwear, sportswear, pile fabrics
Spandex	Duraspan, Elura, Glospan, Interspan, Lycra, Numa, Vyrene	Lightweight, resistant to body oils, strong, durable, abrasion-resistant; supple, great elasticity and recovery power	Girdles, bras, bathing suits, support and surgical hose, ski pants
Triacetate	Arnel	Shrink-resistant, wrinkle-resistant, fade-resistant, easily washed; good pleat retention, maintain crisp finish	Sportswear, garments where pleat retention is important

Sources: Adapted from *Shoppers Handbook,* Cornell Extension Bulletin 1093, January 1969, and *Guide to Man-Made Fibers,* Man-Made Fiber Producers Assn., Inc., New York, N.Y., 1970.

for all consumers. Table 8-1 also identifies the fiber types and their common or brand names. Although it is not necessary to become an expert on fibers and fabrics, some knowledge of them will help the consumer to judge durability, make appropriate selections, and avoid careless choices. One serious problem occurs for some consumers who are allergic to certain fabrics and who do not read the label carefully. If one has an allergy to wool, for example, a label should show any wool content of the fabric being purchased.

Special fabric treatment is also important to consumers who buy clothing. Certain treatments will let consumers get nicer-looking clothes, get more use from clothes, and ensure easier maintenance of clothes. Table 8-2 identifies several fabric finishes that give improved appearance and/or resistance to soiling.

Proper Fit and Size

"The sleeve is too tight, and the jacket cuts my arm." These are the words of a model who is trying to help a manufacturer develop the best possible fit for her particular size. Frequently these models are referred to as "duplicate models," in that they duplicate the physical proportions of an average person of each clothes size. A size 12 duplicate model, for example, gives the manufacturer an idea in advance of how the size 12 consumer will probably react to the fit of a garment. These efforts to arrive at a proper dress size help manufacturers to maintain reasonable control over garment sizes. There is certainly room for more precise techniques, however. For example, when June Simpson purchased a size 8 dress for her daughter, it did not fit like the size 8 she had bought 3 weeks earlier, and she had to return it. Mrs. Simpson was annoyed and inconvenienced when she found that the two dresses were not reliably sized.

The consumer has the right to expect reasonable standards in the sizing of garments, and the National Bureau of Standards is researching the problem. As a result of their efforts, specifications for girls' and women's clothing are being reviewed, and new voluntary standards will be very helpful.

The first few standards will establish a nationally recognized sizing system for girls, based on body measurements. The classifications included are "slims," "regulars," and "chubbies." Each classification will be defined by more than thirty body measurements. But until sizing techniques become more sophisticated, the consumer must continue to be patient and careful, and prepared to try on almost all types of clothing before buying.

Color

The color chosen for an article of clothing depends largely on the tastes of the person. Color can, when properly used, give a priceless look to an inexpensive garment. Also, careful color choices can let you combine various articles of clothing and thus have a wider selection of outfits.

Although typically a noncost item, color is one of the first things people notice about clothes. Some colors seem to "make you sparkle," while others do the opposite. Generally, when you choose colors for your wardrobe, consider very carefully your natural coloring (skin tone, hair, and eyes) and your physical proportions. Skin tones of white people may vary from fair with a tinge of blue to pink, with redheads having an orangish tone. And those who display more olive coloring have yellow skin tones. Black people also show a similar range of tones in their skins, including some with a more yellowish or orangish tone. There is a range of flesh tones about which people probably need to learn more. Once aware of skin coloring, you can begin to do some more intelligent choice making about clothing colors and overall clothing selection.

To use color effectively, one must understand some basic color characteristics. The name of a color, its *hue*, may be warm or cool. Warm hues include reds, oranges, and yel-

TABLE 8-2

Fabric Finishes

Finish	Description
Colorfast	Fabric treatment that ensures sufficient color retention so that no marked change in shade takes place during the normal life of the garment.
Drip-dry	Treatment that enables the article to be washed and worn with little or no ironing because of its wrinkle-resistant properties.
Flame-retardant	Fabric treated so that it will not ignite into a torch; flame will be reduced, causing smoldering, charring, or melting of fabric.
Permanent-press	Fabric finish that permits clothing to keep its shape throughout its life, such as sharp creases, smooth surface texture and appearance, and seams that are free from bulges.
Shrinkage-control	A manufacturing process or chemical finish that removes the tendency of a fiber to shrink when washed.
Soil-release	Fabric treatment which allows soil to be released from the fabric more easily during washing.
Spot-repellent	Fabric treatment that makes sure that spills will not sink in and can be easily wiped or sponged off to prevent permanent soiling or damage.
Wash-and-wear	Fabric treated so that garments usually washed will have few wrinkles and article can be worn with little iron touchup.
Water-repellent	Finishes that resist the absorption and penetration of water, but are not fully waterproof. Nylon and polyester, for example, have repellent qualities in their structure.
Wrinkle-resistant	Fabrics treated chemically to maintain a smooth appearance. Usually wrinkles will hang out overnight.

lows, while cool hues consist of blues, greens, and purples. *Value,* the lightness or darkness of a color, may add to or subtract from your size, depending on the colors worn. For example, soft shades of cool, light colors can make one appear slender, while warm, bright colors give a heavier appearance to the wearer. The brightness or dullness of a color is called its *intensity.* High-intensity (bright) or low-intensity (dull) colors also have an effect on whether persons appear bigger or smaller than they really are.

Combining colors is very important in dress and the selection of clothing. The colors chosen for various articles of clothing can have very effective results for the wearer. For example, you will look taller if you wear a green matching sweater with a green skirt or pants because the eye moves from bottom to top without hesitation. On the other hand, if a contrasting-colored sweater (red) is worn, the eye stops at the line of contrast (red and green), and the wearer looks shorter. Furthermore, the shopper should coordinate wardrobe items by having several combinations that look well together. Choose a sweater that looks good with several different pairs of pants or skirts. Your clothing choices should emphasize groupings of color and/or style that blend harmoniously. Selected shades of brown, for example, along with various shades of red or yellow will give you many combinations of clothing to wear. If you add several choices of neutral colors, clothing combinations become virtually unlimited.

Design
Technically, a *design* in clothes is a specific or individual interpretation of a style. It is the use of different colors, fabrics, and trimmings that differentiate one design from another. Much of design is for show. There are times, however, when it has a purpose. For example, the design of certain women's dresses gives the wearer freer movement. Some designs of men's suits (leisure suit) or women's dresses permit greater air flow around the body. Some designs can be ego-building by making individuals appear taller or shorter, slimmer or huskier.

Four components that contribute to effective design in clothing are (1) *balance,* which is produced by proper relation of weight or forces to a central point (the head balanced equally over the shoulders); (2) *emphasis,* which helps to focus on the most important area of clothing design (a V neck on a dress, or stripes or lines which accentuate a narrow waist); (3) *rhythm,* which brings about a continuous, flowing movement in clothing through the use of straight or curved lines, or shapes of various kinds; and (4) *proportion,* which has to do with sizes and ratios of shapes and areas to one another (width of shoulders in a woman's dress or man's suit or width of cuffs are considerations for proportion).

Figure 8-2 illustrates how different people can see design in different ways. Note the appearances and descriptive terms suggested by the various types and shapes of lines—and also the way these lines can reflect an appearance other than the real, underlying one. Design in clothing is obviously as important as quality, proper fit, color, or cost.

Labeling
General information about the type of fabric has been on clothing labels for several years now—labels bearing such statements as "100% virgin wool," "65% Dacron, 35% cotton," or "75% wool, 25% cotton."

The Federal Trade Commission (FTC) has continually been the watchdog to enforce federal statutes relating to these specific fabric qualifications, household textile articles, and wool and fur products. Certain federal labeling laws require that all wearing apparel, floor coverings, draperies, bedding, and other textile goods used in the household be informative and truthful in the labeling, and should be advertised accordingly. The Textile Fiber Products Identification Act requires that labels on all clothing and piece goods specify the amount of such fibers and their name. The Fur Products Labeling Act was designed to make it unlawful to misbrand, falsely advertise, and

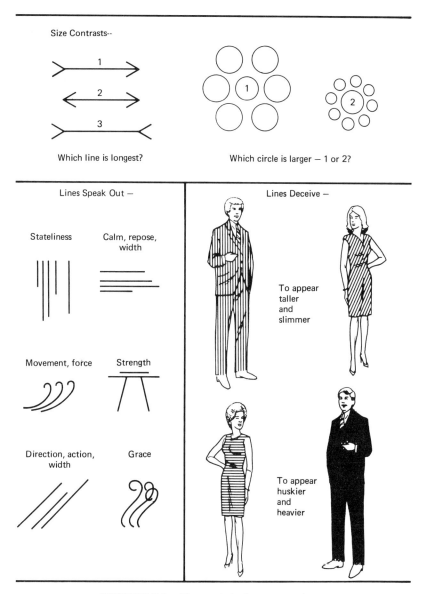

FIGURE 8-2 Size and design perception

falsely invoice fur products. The Wool Products Labeling Act requires that manufactured wool products be uniformly labeled to indicate all fibers contained therein and to specify percentages of wool. A recent legislative enactment is directed toward care labels which tell you how to clean and take care of your garments.

The Trade Regulation Rule of the Textile Fiber Products Identification Act requires that "permanent care labels" be attached to most clothing sold. This rule is enforced by the Federal Trade Commission. Most wearing apparel falls within the scope of this regulation. Permanent care labels must disclose fully, clearly, and thoroughly *regular* care and

That's our new graduate's model—no pockets, just flaps.

Courtesy of Edd Uluschak.

maintenance required by the mere use of the product. Spot-care information is not required.

Care labeling is extremely helpful to consumers. Now that these labels are required to be a permanent part of all apparel, if they are somewhat consistent in their language, consumers will know how to wash and dry most clothing and will not have to guess and hope as they did in the past. Illustrative of the recommended "care label" terminology as advocated by the FTC include "dry clean only," "leather cleaner only," "machine wash and dry," "tumble dry," "machine wash in sudsy water at medium temperature," "machine wash warm, gentle cycle," "do not use chlorine bleach," "hand wash cold," "do not twist or wring," "do not dry clean."

Figure 8-3 shows a label from one clothing manufacturer that complies with the new regulation. With such precise and readable wording, more responsibility is shifted to the consumer. The consumer can no longer blame the manufacturer for washing something that should have been dry cleaned. The consumer is responsible.

SHELL
CALIBRE CLOTH ®
WOVEN EXCLUSIVELY FOR
LONDON FOG®
by **REEVES**

65% DACRON POLYESTER FIBER
35% COMBED COTTON
MACHINE WASHABLE
DO NOT SPIN DRY OR WRING-
RINSE THREE TIMES REMOVE
ALL SOAPS-HANG TO DRIP DRY
—OR—
COMPLETE WASH CYCLE
PLACE IN MACHINE DRYER

TOUCH UP IRONING HELPS
RETAIN RAIN REPELLENCY

THIS COAT MADE FOR

M

FIGURE 8-3 Illustration of a permanent care label

CHOOSING CLOTHING

Whether the motivation to buy clothing is based upon a need, a want, fashion, style, color, or what have you, careful selections should be made. All too often certain clothing purchases turn out to be based on unsound reasoning. This is because of poor selection.

Let us consider some of the major points to be taken into account when you buy clothes— *how, when* and *where* one buys, and the *cost*.

How to Buy Clothing

Shopping for clothing does not have to be the disorganized chore some people make it to be if certain steps are followed. These steps are listed in the three sections of Figure 8-4: *Things to Do before Leaving Home, Things to Do while Comparison Shopping,* and *Things to Do while at the Store.*

At first, this process will take time, but as you become familiar with it, you will *save* time as well as money, even though, obviously, different people shop for different clothes and the time, effort, and procedure they use will also differ slightly.

When to Buy Clothing

To many, the obvious time to buy is when clothing is needed. Others buy when it is convenient. And most of us buy when money is available. Let's look at some aspects of the calendar-year cycle, the fashion cycle, and sales that can help us decide when to buy clothing.

Calendar-Year Cycle. A timetable can be set up for when to buy clothing to get the best values. A suggested clothing calendar is shown in Figure 8-5. This is a guide to selected items that are typically bought by most consumers. However, there will certainly be times other than those shown when clothing can be a good buy. For example, men's and boy's clothing are considered good buys in March, but a sale for the same items could also take place after the Thanksgiving holiday. All one has to do is read the newspaper and the best times to buy clothing will emerge.

Fashion Cycle. Most consumers are becoming more aware of the best times to buy clothing in the calendar year. However, few consumers know about a time to buy cloth-

FIGURE 8-4 Pointers on how to buy clothing

Section I. Things to Do before Leaving Home

- Check clothing inventory
- Plan overall wardrobe
- Identify needs and wants
- Know sizes, jot them down
- Find a tape measure to take with you
- Learn about items to be purchased
- Check for sales advertisements
- Check informational advertising
- Determine purpose of clothing to be purchased
- Estimate amount to be spent for each item

Section II. Things to Do while Comparison Shopping

- Visit several stores
- Compare prices of all items
- Identify and compare quality factors
- Talk with knowledgeable store personnel
- Be sure there is more than one item from which to choose (do not buy if only one item is available)
- Carry copies of advertising with you
- Isolate several alternatives from which to choose among clothing and stores

Section III. Things to Do while at the Store

- Try on all clothing that you are considering buying
- Evaluate quality factors
- Compare prices and quality for similar clothing items within each store
- Consider your complete satisfaction with the garment you select in terms of your purposes
- Check on necessary garment care
- Inquire about returning clothing if you are not satisfied

ing as part of a fashion cycle. Characteristically the fashion cycle has five phases:

Phase	Characteristic
Introduction	High fashion, very costly, keen individuality, "couture clothing," specialty-shop offerings.
Rise	High-quality products are offered by most specialty shops; department store sales are increasing. Consumers should buy near the end of this phase when copied-down reproductions appear.
Culmination	Mass market, department store selling largely, also discount stores and factory outlets; little individuality.
Decline	Yard and neighborhood sales; getting rid of clothing; need and value gone.
Obsolescence	Goodwill Industries, and Salvation Army selling; virtually no market left; salvage only.

It is extremely important that the consumer know at what point in this fashion cycle to buy clothing. For example, wise consumers would buy clothing before the culmination phase to gain any quality or individuality in the style before other phases develop. Also, consumers should not buy a coat or other item for more than one season's wear in the culmination stage or later. If they buy at the wrong time, consumers will be faced with the "also ran" markets where there is lower quality, little or no individuality, and run-of-the-mill design and fabrics.

Sales Cycles.   Sales are an extremely important part of the decision of when to buy. Clothing sales normally include the same garments that were sold at regular prices only a few days or weeks earlier. Some sales also include specially purchased goods of lower-quality merchandise. Knowledgeable shoppers learn to recognize such false values. Of-

ten, sales may be only for those items that the public does not want, so the merchant reduces the price to get rid of them, even though the merchandise may be just as good as that sold for a higher price. To take advantage of such sales, however, a person may have to modify desires. Perhaps the idea of design or color, or fashion goals, may have to be changed.

If done wisely, buying clothing on sale can save you a great deal. Consequently, it is important to have a general idea of when good buys are available and to be aware of special sales. Merchants usually do not send you a personal invitation to a clothing sale. This is where sales informational advertising helps. Read the newspapers, listen to the radio, watch television, and pay attention to handbills distributed to your home.

Buy with caution, however, when you buy clothes on sale. A wise consumer will evaluate carefully the need, purpose, and price of the sale item before choosing. Do not get caught in the "sale syndrome" by buying solely because an item is on sale. People who do this end up going through a process of deciding "how to wear," "whether to wear," "if to wear," or "can I wear." Buying clothing only because it is on sale can be wasteful and costly in the long run.

For the truly fashion-minded person, when to buy can be a special problem. These people prefer to buy the most up-to-date fashions, so they sacrifice a good sales price later on—but this is their choice. You, too, will have to make such decisions.

Avoiding Common Mistakes in Buying
The tips listed below give many ways to avoid making mistakes when shopping for clothing:

1. Do not buy an item if it is the only one available (unless it's perfect).
2. When making a decision, do not be hasty. Take your time.
3. Know exact sizes. Do not guess. Try things on. This is especially true when you are buying shoes.
4. Do not select an article of clothing

FIGURE 8-5 Suggested Clothing Shopping Calendar

Stores follow a fairly standard schedule for their promotions. Some of these are sales; others are new displays of merchandise on which prices may or may not be a bargain. Here is a month-by-month rundown.

January	February	March	April
Storewide clearance, resort wear, infants' wear, coats and furs, dresses, hosiery, handbags, shoes, lingerie, housecoats, men's and boys' clothing.	Washington's Birthday sales, coats, furs, dresses, active sportswear, millinery	Men's and boys' clothing, hosiery, infants' wear, boys' and girls' shoes.	Easter merchandise, after-Easter clearance, fur storage campaigns, men's and boys' clothing, dresses, lingerie, housecoats, infants' wear.
May	**June**	**July**	**August**
Lingerie, handbags, sportswear	Sportswear, camp clothes, dresses, lingerie, housecoats, boys' clothing, fabrics.	July 4th clearances (throughout the month), hosiery, handbags, shoes, children's wear, dresses, active sportswear, millinery, lingerie, housecoats, men's furnishings.	Summer clothing clearances, fur sales, back-to-school specials, fall fashions, coats, men's coats.
September	**October**	**November**	**December**
Back-to-school specials, fabrics, children's clothing	Columbus Day specials, fur fashions, lingerie, housecoats, back-to-school	Veteran's Day specials, Thanksgiving weekend sales, pre-Christmas specials, fabrics, dresses, children's clothing.	Children's wear, men's and boys' wear, winter clothing specials (late in the month). After Christmas sales.

Source: *The Smart Bargain Shopper in the Market,* Cooperative Extension Programs, The University of Wisconsin, Madison, Wisconsin.

merely because it has a higher price. Check for durability and workmanship.

5. Determine the true purpose of clothing before buying. Do you need it? What for? Do you *want* it? Why? And will it go with the rest of your wardrobe?

6. Compare similar clothing characteristics, particularly quality, when you are shopping for the best prices.

7. Consider *all* cost aspects. For example, add mailing and handling costs or shipping charges to the regular price. Also, consider cost of dry cleaning versus washing.

8. Avoid letting emotion and clothing design be the primary reason for your purchases.

9. Select a fabric that looks nice and will hold up under normal wear and repeated cleaning.

10. Do not buy clothing *merely* because an item is on sale. Think about need and purpose for items before purchasing.

HOW MUCH TO SPEND ON CLOTHING

How much money a consumer should spend on clothing depends to a large extent on that consumer's lifestyle and also on the availability of funds. Enough money for one lifestyle could be too much or too little for another. Let us see what a few others spend and then see what you can do.

What Others Spend

The average family spends about 9 to 11 percent of its annual income for clothing. This amounts to about $350 for each man, woman, and child in the country per year and ranks fifth in total family expenditures after shelter, food, health and recreation, and transportation. These figures can be useful, as a rough index, in determining one's own clothing spending. It is an imperfect index, however, since so few people are completely "average." Another factor that partly indicates how much one spends on clothing is the level of education of the head of the household. The more education a consumer has, the more that consumer generally seems to spend on clothing.

Recent data released from the Department of Labor revealed that women and men spend significantly different amounts of the family-clothing dollar. Typically women spend about 60 percent, with men spending the remainder. Infant wear and hosiery, outerwear garments, dresses, and footwear dominate clothing purchases by women. Outerwear garments, suits, trousers, and sport coats and accessories form the spending pattern for most men's clothing purchases. This dominance of clothes spending by women is based largely upon the keen fashion and clothes interest displayed by most women.

Although there are no hard-and-fast rules upon which a family can rely to tell them how much they should spend on clothes, a number of spending patterns are evident:

1. The amount spent for clothing increases as the young family gets older.
2. Peak clothing expenditures come when children are in their mid-teens.
3. Annual personal clothing expenditures seem to taper off when people reach about age twenty-five.
4. As the family's level of living rises, the percentage of money spent on clothing for

husbands and sons declines, and that spent on wives and daughters rises.
5. As the level of living rises, the cost of clothing services goes up for everybody, especially for women and girls.

Analyze Your Clothing Inventory

Periodically everyone should take stock of his or her wardrobe. This taking of inventory is most helpful and consists basically of a few simple steps:

1. Take inventory of your present wardrobe. List every item of clothing you own. Examine each item carefully to see how much life it has left.
2. Determine your current clothing needs and wants. Note all the items you should buy to give yourself a well-balanced wardrobe.
3. Consider exceptional clothing needs (for example, for funerals, weddings, or other special occasions) as you inspect your wardrobe.
4. Sort and examine your clothing by season and by activities (school, social events, church, home chores, or work).
5. Look for all-purpose types of clothing in your wardrobe—those with versatility (for example, a dress that works for several purposes by just changing accessories, or a topcoat to be used in both rain and cold weather as it has a zipout lining).
6. Establish priorities of purchases among the needs and wants.

Too often consumers act impulsively and buy clothing they do not need. They jump at sales, they buy simply to keep pace with fashion, or they try to "keep up" with a friend or neighbor.

A balanced wardrobe is the result of careful planning. In making a plan, coordinate colors and styles, strive for versatility, and correlate your fall-winter and spring-summer clothes. And in the cooler climates, remember the in-between days of spring and fall. Your task will be made easier if you use an inventory form like that shown in Figure 8-6. Children

PRESENT WARDROBE INVENTORY

Fall-Winter (Season)	Suits or Dresses	Separates — pants, skirts, sweaters, shirts blouses, jackets	Coats — jackets, topcoats, over-coats, raincoats	Accessories — shoes, gloves, scarves, ties, jewelry, belts, purses
Casual clothes and sportswear for relaxing or working at home, dates, spectator and active sports, school		8 Jeans 5 shirts 2 sweaters 2 skirts	1 Raincoat	3 pr shoes 1 pr gloves 2 scarves 3 belts 1 handbag Asstd Jewelry
Tailored clothes for school, work, dates, shopping, travel	5 dresses 2 suits	2 pantsuits	1 overcoat	
Semi-dress clothes for dates, parties, entertaining, dinner out	2 dresses			
Evening-dress clothes for parties, dances, formal occasions	1 dress		1 coat	1 handbag

In addition to the articles listed above, also include:		
Undergarments	Sleepwear	Miscellaneous clothes for special activities such as tennis, bowling, swimming
6 pr panties 4 half slips	3 shortie nightgown 2 long nightgowns	3 swimsuits 2 shorts

FIGURE 8-6   Format for wardrobe inventory

and young adults in the family can use the same form.

Each person must decide personally, of course, how various clothing items should be ranked in the priority listing. However, children need guidance from their parents. Young adults should make as many decisions for themselves as they can and then live with them.

Spending for Clothing
Intelligent spending for clothing results when the consumer puts all these "how to's" to work and gets a good buy for the money. It is here that the wise consumer uses all his or her knowledge and background about clothing. Let us look at some of the points that wise consumers should consider.

Values and Resources. Good materials pay off. Put your money in materials that will be easy to care for and that will be serviceable. Insist on good workmanship and durable materials. Look for labels that guarantee against fading, shrinking, wrinkling, spotting, and sagging. If a garment must be dry cleaned,

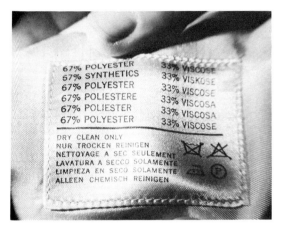

Clothing labels will tell you what a garment is made of and how much care it will need. If you check the labels, you will be able to choose clothes that will be easy to care for and suitable for the purpose you have in mind. (*Guy Debaud*)

consider that expense as well as the purchase price.

Purpose. If you will use an item of clothing infrequently, or even only once, consider buying something really inexpensive. Or, if possible, buy something that can be altered later and then worn for another purpose. Occasionally women are asked to buy a formal gown for a wedding, which they will use only once. Rather than buy a really cheap gown (frequently there is little choice on the type), pay a reasonable amount, then shorten or otherwise alter the gown and wear it as a dinner dress. Also, if durability is essential, but not the general outward appearance, you can usually save money. This is because it costs more to make material look nice.

Out-of-Season Spending. When one can save from 20 to 50 percent by taking advantage of out-of-season spending, many of us just should not overlook it. Often, if you can wait a few weeks before buying a particular item, you can buy at end-of-season sales, which have drastically reduced prices.

Special "after" sales—after Christmas, Thanksgiving, or Easter—or holiday, back-to-school, or general clearance sales are also typical. Many reductions are available on those crowded shopping days. The wise shopper should still compare prices among stores before buying. And one word of caution—do not buy clothing merely because it is on sale. There are high-priced bargains and low-priced booby traps. Telltale signs of a cheap garment are poor fabric, harsh colors, and gimmicky style. Follow your wardrobe planning needs even when taking advantage of sales.

Buying Standard Items. Clothing bought in large quantities can save you money, too. This practice can be followed, for example, with shirts or socks for men and hosiery for women. Buy one color or shade of socks, and then when one wears out, another can take its place without your having to replace a complete pair. Shirts and underwear in lots of three, six, or twelve, prepackaged in a variety of colors in one size, can often be purchased at lower prices. Ask about volume buying of these standard items the next time you shop.

Buying "Seconds" or "Irregulars." Clothing marked "seconds" or "irregular" sells at lower prices. It usually has some minor flaw that could not pass the manufacturer's inspection tests but often is not even noticeable to the average consumer, and if it is noticeable, it can usually be quickly repaired if one is skillful. These flaws may consist of slight deviations from a straight seam, off-center buttonholes, or minor mismatching of material designs. Generally these items can be a good way to save money, but be sure that if clothing is a "second" or "irregular," it is so marked.

Home Production. Making clothing at home is one of the least expensive ways of filling most of the family's needs. Of course, one needs to know how to sew to have this process pay off! Sewing has become increasingly popular and is being done by millions of women, as well as by many men. In fact, if you *really* want to save money, you would be wise to take a few sewing or tailoring courses first. Savings would be tremendous over just a year—often 30 to 60 percent.

Consider carefully, however, the *opportunity costs* (the cost of what you give up to enable you to do something else) before you sew your own clothes. *Time* spent on anything is a valuable commodity; therefore, you should realize that if you spend time on sewing, you must give up the opportunity to spend time on other equally important projects or activities. Weigh the cost differences and then decide—in the long run it may be less costly to buy rather than sew your own.

Just about every type of material made is available to those who want to sew. Be careful when you buy materials, however, since frequently labels on bolts of material come loose and get lost. Hurried clerks may also replace a found label on the wrong bolt of fabric.

Clothing Care

Garment life can be greatly increased through proper maintenance and cleaning; therefore, clothes should be treated with care to achieve a longer-life goal. As a matter of fact, day-to-day clothing care is essential in order to get the most use from your clothes. Ripped or popped seams quickly stitched, buttons resewn, zippers replaced, skirts and trousers lengthened, and simple tears repaired are just a few things that you can do to extend the life of a garment.

Wise consumers of clothing should make the following points standard practice in care of clothing:

1. Hang up clothing after taking it off to allow wrinkles to disappear; hanging will also let moisture buildup dry and the clothes air.
2. Hang clothes loosely in a closet, and store them in uncrowded space in drawers. Avoid crowded conditions for all clothing when possible.
3. Use padded, contoured, or shaped hangers for hanging clothes to prevent unnecessary stretching.
4. Rotate clothes when you plan what to wear—give clothes a rest.
5. Change to different types of clothing when the activity dictates (for example, wear work clothes for yard work).
6. Mend clothes promptly when they need it.
7. Store out-of-season clothes properly to protect them from dust, moisture, and moths.
8. Stuff shoes with paper or shoe trees if wet, to absorb moisture and retain shape.
9. Check for spots and stains and remove them with stain or spot removers if possible.
10. Brush clothes frequently to remove surface dirt before it embeds.
11. Press or iron clothing when required.
12. Use proper temperature setting to wash and dry washable clothing; improper heat can literally destroy some fabrics.

Unfortunately, maintaining clothing can be costly in some cases. For example, if you are bothered by the high cost of dry cleaning, try buying mostly wash-and-wear clothes. However, be warned that some so-called wash-and-wear clothing may need a quick touch-up with an iron. Sometimes, of course, the purpose of the clothes or the need for a particular type of appearance will rule out wash-and-wear, but since these garments are continually being improved, there may come a time when dry-cleaning establishments will become obsolete.

Care of clothing, like care of many other consumer goods, is based on a positive—"I believe"—attitude of the consumer. A need for clothing care must be felt by consumers first. Perhaps if the clothing-care skeptics would treat clothing purchases as an investment rather than as a short-run expense initially, they would care for them better.

LEGISLATION AFFECTING CLOTHING

In most manufacturing industries, sooner or later problems develop and remedies and improvements are sought and developed. The clothing industry is no exception. Several federal regulations directly related to the manufacture and merchandising of clothing have been enacted to solve problems of the industry and/or protect both consumers and the industry.

The Wheeler-Lea Act of 1938

This legislation is directed against false, deceptive, or misleading advertising; claims made on the label by the manufacturer must be adhered to. Moreover, an unwillingness to state pertinent facts about the product is classified as false advertising. If the advertising is written so that the consumer is led to believe that a fabric will act in a certain manner when it actually does not, this is considered deceptive.

The Wool Products Labeling Act of 1939

Requiring that products containing any amount of virgin wool, reprocessed wool, or reused wool be labeled to show the fiber content percentages is essentially the thrust of this act. Consequently, textile mills must keep records identifying the yarn and fibers that went into each piece of cloth. Lot number labels on most wool clothing items relate to a manufacturer's production ticket so that it can be traced back through other manufacturing processing records to the original raw stock if necessary.

The Fur Products Labeling Act of 1951

Preventing deceptive labeling of lower-grade furs is the emphasis of this act. For example, Hudson seal, mink-dyed muskrat, mountain sable, and others were the deceptive titles for such lesser grades of fur as opossum, muskrat, and rabbit. The fur act requires that every article display a label which includes (1) whether the fur is artificially colored, natural, or dyed; (2) a product-identifying mark to enable tracing it back to its source; (3) accurate identification of the animal from which the hide was taken; and (4) the country from which the animal came. As a result of this legislation, both consumers and retailers are protected from deceptive practices.

The Flammable Fabrics Act of 1953

The manufacture or sale of wearing apparel made from fibers or fabrics that were flammable was prohibited by this act and a 1967 amendment. A 1972 ruling enforced a flammability standard for children's sleepwear. This ruling required that a designated number of specimens of each item of sleepwear be tested. If the standards were not met, the garments could not be sold. As a direct result of this act, the clothing industry was forced to produce flame-retardant sleepwear. Because of the added cost of testing and the subsequent price increases, some smaller clothing manufacturers were forced out of business. Not all legislation intended to help, protect, and improve ends happily for all parties involved. Another unfortunate problem resulted when TRIS, a flame-retardant chemical added to sleepwear, turned out to be a carcinogen. Under provisions of the federal government's Consumer Product Safety Commission, it was banned, and now other chemicals are used.

The Textile Fiber Products Identification Act of 1958

Essentially a "truth-in-fabrics" law, this act covers the labeling of all apparel textiles not covered by the previously enacted wool act. Accordingly, all products must be labeled with the fiber content by percentage. Also, the listing must be by the highest to lowest weight of each fiber in the fabric.

Trade Regulation Rule—1972

This special regulation under the Textile Fiber Products Identification Act requires that all textile apparel products and piece goods have a permanent, legible, easily read and understood care label attached to the product for its useful life. Although initially costly to the clothing manufacturers, this regulation was a significant step toward better informing consumers on clothing care. It has reduced some of the care confusion that has existed for years and consumer advocates hope that this is the first of many steps for more informative labeling in clothing.

POINTS OF VIEW AND PROBLEMS TO THINK ABOUT

Problems in the selection and purchase of clothing will continue to exist. Consumers must, together, try to eliminate at least some of these problems. They must voice their opinions on such topics as clothing design, standardization of sizes, and quality measures.

Designers and manufacturers can be expected to continue their efforts to control. Consumers should realize, however, that when designers set the fashion, they do so with the approval of consumers. A consumer who does not like a particular fashion should not buy it. If possible, he or she should choose an alternative, or else the consumer should cast a negative economic vote by not buying at all. Contrary to what some think, many designers and manufacturers are becoming more and more attentive to the voice of the consumer.

Consumers should also enlist the help of local merchants to protest the manufacture and sale of poor-quality clothing. Local merchants should recognize that consumers will not shop at a store that carries shoddy merchandise. If this kind of message is repeated often enough, even the most reticent merchant will pass the complaints along to the manufacturer.

Legislation relating to the safety, quality, labeling, grading for durability, or maintenance of clothing is helpful. One should question why manufacturers seem unwilling to accept more responsibility for their products. On the other hand, one can also question why the government finds it necessary to legislate in order to provide higher standards, such as flame-retardant fabric for children's sleepwear.

Voluntarily personnel of a large department-store chain refused to sell any apparel treated with the flame-retarding chemical TRIS. The basis for their decision pointed out a new problem in clothing merchandising. As noted, this chemical was found to be a possible cancer-causing agent, according to laboratory tests. The Consumer Product Safety Commission eventually ordered the end of the sale of clothing treated with TRIS. During that 3-year investigation, clothing manufacturers, retailers, and consumers were faced with a dilemma. If manufacturers complied with the flame-retardant regulations in clothing, they would be selling possible cancer-causing materials to retailers and in turn to consumers. What would you have done?

To make reliable comparisons, consumers need more specific information about clothing quality. Manufacturers can help by collectively establishing criteria for judging quality; they can print more data pertaining to durability and workmanship and make it available to all consumers. Such information should not have to come by accident, after years of experience, or through the help of a salesperson. A few manufacturers are now making written statements to the effect that "if this garment wears out within 1 year from date of purchase, it will be replaced free of charge." Such statements should be applauded, but they are only a beginning.

CHAPTER ACTIVITIES

Checkup on Consumer Terms and Concepts

Peer pressure
Styles
Fashions
Fads
Esthetic needs
Secondary clothing
  needs
Durability
Synthetic fabrics
Natural fabrics
Duplicate models

Permanent-care
  labeling
Fashion cycle
Clothing inventory
Standard clothing
  items
"Seconds"
Home production of
  clothing
Wash-and-wear
  clothing

Review of Essentials

1. What are several reasons for buying clothes of a particular type or design?

2. Why do many young people not want to buy clothes chosen by their parents?

3. What has been the primary impetus for the changes in men's clothing?

4. How do the terms style, fashion, and fad differ as applied to clothing design and use?

5. What are the primary and secondary needs for buying clothing? Give an illustration of each.

6. Needs for buying clothing are numerous, but what identifies a psychological need for clothing?

7. What are the basic differences between needs and wants in clothing?

8. Three steps are involved in how to buy clothing: name them.

9. What is a "shopping-for-clothing calendar," and of what value is it?

10. How does a designer try to get an "average consumer's" opinion on proper fit and size on new clothing?

11. As new clothing standards are developed, what appear to be the three classifications of sizes to be included in girls' clothing?

12. Identify ways in which color coordination can be helpful in clothing selection.

Issues for Analysis

1. In the past, clothing designers and manufacturers largely directed what fashions would be worn by consumers during a coming season. Should such practices be permitted to continue? Why or why not?

2. Should import duties (taxes) be lowered or eliminated to enable foreign clothing to compete with American manufacturers and merchants? What could be gained? What lost?

3. Needs for clothing are varied. Justify a person buying clothing to satisfy esthetic, psychological, or employment needs. Also, illustrate situations where such needs can be used effectively.

4. Quality of clothing is difficult to determine. Should more precise and tangible information about quality be made available to consumers before they buy? Who should provide the information? How should it be disseminated?

9

Buying Household Furnishings and Appliances

THE PROBLEMS

"Going out of Business! Sale!" is a sign one frequently sees in merchants' windows. And many of these merchants are dealers in home appliances and furnishings. However, when any business displays such a sign too long or too often in its window, the ethics of that business must be seriously questioned. The practice of continually "going out of business" is an effort to get consumers to buy products on the pretense that they are greatly reduced in price.

Another unethical practice is that of *almost* telling the truth in sales signs. Recently a sign was displayed in a large furniture store in Oakland with the words GOING OUT   BUSINESS in capital letters. Closer inspection, however, revealed the word "for" in much smaller letters printed between the words OUT and BUSINESS. The sign really read GOING OUT for BUSINESS. Is this clever advertising? Or is it an attempt to mislead?

Warranties and guarantees that accompany most household appliances and furnishings are not consistently reliable. In spite of recent laws, some are still written in such technical and uncommunicative language that it is nearly impossible to figure out what they actually cover.

"Truth in quality" of products sold is perhaps the major problem facing purchasers of household furnishings and appliances. It is nearly impossible for the average consumer to cast an accurate economic vote when buying because of the lack of comparable shopping information on many household furnishings and appliances. What criteria can the consumer use to judge the quality of chairs, tables, washers, dryers, and glassware? Statements of product quality made by sellers are often merely "sales puffery." Reliable product-quality data seem to be unavailable except for those found in reputable consumer publications like *Consumer Reports* and *Consumers' Research Magazine*. Unless efforts are made to improve the identification of quality in products, consumers will remain on the edge of ignorance.

Furniture that breaks under ordinary use is of poor quality, and this points up another problem. Too many consumers are injured, some quite seriously, when furniture does not hold up under normal use. Appliances that are manufactured in an unsafe, faulty manner or are improperly installed or do not work properly cause both fires and electrocutions. Furthermore, the design of many pieces of furniture and appliances often leads to unexpected injuries and deaths. Range dials and burners within easy reach of small children, ovens with nonprotective catches, easily breakable glass, appliances that topple over, and beds that break through the "slats" injure consumers every day. What priority, one wonders, does safety have?

Recent product safety data shows that every year approximately 20 million Americans suffer product-related injuries in or around the home; about 110,000 are disabled; over 30,000 are killed; and at least $5.5 billion of unnecessary and wasteful spending occurs because of these product-related injuries. New products are being manufactured daily, and consumers continue to buy some which are poorly designed or defective, so that injuries occur regularly. What is done? When one remembers the great numbers of injuries and deaths due to problems with household furnishings and appliances, effective product selection by consumers becomes even more important.

Another problem that we are faced with is the energy consumption of appliances. Many salespersons do not know how much energy various appliances use. Also, the comparative cost of operation of appliances seems to be difficult for both salespersons and consumers to understand.

Delivery of large, heavy appliances is a welcome service for most consumers. When the retail store delivers, few problems result with damaged merchandise. However, if an independent carrier delivers an appliance that is damaged, there are problems about how to determine and handle damaged merchandise. Most drivers do not let you inspect the merchandise before they leave. "Too busy," "a long way to travel," "just can't wait," "got to meet a deadline" are typical excuses drivers offer for not waiting until goods are uncrated and inspected.

"A rose by any other name will smell as sweet." This line from Shakespeare has been often quoted and applied in many situations. But a term used by any other person does not mean the same in certain areas of the appliance industry. For example, "heat resistant glass" means one thing to the manufacturer, often something different to the salesperson, and still something else to the consumer.

Consumers mistakenly use price as a sign of quality in buying many household furnishings and appliances. They assume that because it costs more, it will necessarily last longer. This assumption is not right. Consumers don't even know the average expected life, under normal use, of the appliances and furnishings they buy. Surely, therefore, an overriding difficulty in buying household furnishings and appliances is that of product information.

BUYING MAJOR APPLIANCES

A difficult task for many consumers is choosing major appliances. Some of the problems facing buyers are the overwhelming number of appliances from which to choose, the helpless feeling of not knowing what to look for in quality, and just plain ignorance about appliances in general. Let's try to address and solve some of these problems.

Types and Purposes

There are several types of major appliances. Each type has many manufacturers, and each manufacturer typically sells several models. Therefore, it is no easy task to buy the appliance you want and to be able to come away with a feeling of complete satisfaction.

Some typical types or classifications of major appliances are: *refrigerators*—single door and double door; *freezers*—upright and chest; *combination refrigerator-freezer*—upright or doors side by side; *ranges*—gas or electric, free standing or built in, *ovens*—gas, electric, or microwave; *dishwashers*—free-standing, portable, or built in; *trash compactors*—free-standing or built in; *washers*—front or top loading; *dryers*—

gas or electric; *air conditioners*—installed or portable, electric or gas; *humidifiers*—self-contained portable or attached; *dehumidifiers*—self-contained, portable, or attached; *vacuum cleaners*—canister or upright, disposable or nondisposable bags. Then there is also that broad classification of home-entertainment appliances, including *television*—black and white or color; *stereo systems*—phonographs or tape, stereo, 4-channel, or cassette.

Let us consider what one can or should expect in the matter of performance. When Ed Netsen of Birmingham bought an air conditioner, he continually complained to his wife about its poor performance in keeping their apartment cool. He was running it at maximum capacity, but the apartment was always warm. Furthermore, his electric bill was extremely high for the period. It took an alert air-conditioner salesperson to point out that Mr. Netsen had an air conditioner rated to cool only one large room, and he was trying to cool four. Since Mr. Netsen had made his choice mostly on price, he had originally bought a very inexpensive model. After he bought a larger, high-efficiency (to conserve energy) unit, his wife stopped teasing him about neglecting to consider the important aspects of cooling efficiency and capacity.

Determining Quality of Appliances

One of the headaches of buying appliances is not knowing a "good" appliance from a "poor" one. Certain quality characteristics of an appliance seem too technical for the average consumer to fully understand. For example, what does the term BTU mean? What is the difference between watts and amps? Fortunately, however, consumers will find that some of these things are not that hard to learn about and understand. Then they can use that understanding about specific products *before* buying.

To help determine quality and learn about appliances, consumers need to (1) study appliance-rating tests such as those reported in *Consumer Reports* and *Consumers' Research*

Major appliances can be so complicated that judging their quality seems impossible, but when you consider the price of these appliances, it is well worth spending time investigating quality. (*Guy Debaud*)

Magazine; (2) study appliance information provided by the American Gas Association, Underwriters' Laboratories, the Association of Home Appliance Manufacturers, and others; (3) read materials available from manufacturers and dealers on particular appliances under consideration; (4) ask someone who owns one to get reactions on the strengths and weaknesses of the appliance; and (5) visit and talk with several dealers and salespersons who can often provide valuable factual information (aside from "sales puffery") about an appliance. Salespersons cannot give you all the information you want, but much of what you get from good salespersons may be helpful.

Lazy and uninformed consumers are frequently unwilling to spend time gathering information in the ways suggested above. But when a person spends from $75 to over $1000 for a major appliance, the time invested is often well worth it. A person who spends half an hour gathering information and comparing prices and then buys a stereo system for $200 instead of $225 has in effect earned $25 for the half-hour's work. And just as important is being satisfied with what you buy. If you are unhappy with a major appliance purchase and you could have avoided the problem by shopping more carefully, you will be reminded about that unhappiness every time you use it.

Energy Operation and Cost

For many years it was common for people to try to get all types of time-saving and labor-saving appliances for the home. For many families it was achieving a long-sought goal when they bought a new "frost-free" refrigerator or microwave oven. They often thought that the overall cost of operation of these major appliances was justified by the savings over the life span of the appliance. Unfortunately, all these new products in the aggregate consume a lot of energy compared with the products used 10 or 20 years ago.

Ever since the oil blockade by the Arab oil-producing nations in 1973, there has been a rising concern over the overall use of energy in this country. It is clear that we do have an energy crisis of serious proportions. The blockade, in addition to some colder-than-usual winters, alerted the citizens of this country to the fact that our present energy sources were inadequate. The choices for the United States were having to depend on oil from other countries (on their terms), finding other, more viable sources of energy, and/or reducing consumption of energy. Being dependent on foreign oil is risky and costly; finding other sources—nuclear energy, solar energy, or renewed use of coal energy—is expensive, has other high social costs, and will take time. A reasonable and partial stop-gap solution is the conservation of energy whenever and wherever possible by all consumers (business, government, and the public alike).

With all the concern for energy saving, many manufacturers have tried to produce and sell lower-energy-consumption appliances. Typically the efforts meant redesigning appliances, like the "high-efficiency"

air-conditioning unit for lower energy consumption. Other efforts have included promoting the substitution of newer lower-energy-consumption products, like the microwave oven, for older high-energy-consumption products, like electric ranges. Table 9-1 compares the various amounts of energy consumed by household appliances.

In addition to conserving energy, buying one household appliance rather than another can also mean lower operational costs. Utility companies have had to increase costs for the production of gas and electricity, for various reasons, and these extra costs are being passed on to the consumer in the form of higher utility rates. Consequently, the consumer can ill afford to waste energy. The less energy used (kilowatt hours or cubic feet of gas), the lower the cost.

Using the data in Table 9-1, for example, and given an electric rate of a certain amount per kilowatt-hour (1000 watts used per hour), it is fairly easy to calculate how much it would cost to operate a particular appliance. To determine the operating cost of any appliance, multiply the number of kilowatt-hours (kWh) by the kilowatt-hour rate charged by the utility company serving your area. For example, if the kilowatt-hour rate is 3 cents in your area, the cost of operating a range with an oven (according to chart) would be $35.25 per year. In comparison, operating a microwave oven would cost only $5.70 per year.

Also, to estimate the operating cost per year of any appliance you already own, look at the label for the *wattage* (the number of watts consumed by the appliance) and multiply this wattage by the estimated number of hours used per year; multiply the local kilowatt-hour rate by the result; and then divide by 1000. The operating cost for several of your household appliances may be so high that it may be wiser and less expensive in the long run to go out and purchase a substitute product with a lower energy use.

Energy labels have been prepared as the government has sought more energy conservation from all consumers. This label, its use and

TABLE 9-1

Electrical Major Appliance Operating Costs

Appliance	Average Wattage	Average Hours Used per Year	Approx. kWh Used per Year	Cost per Year at 3¢ per kWh
Air cleaner	50	4,320	216	$ 6.48
Air conditioner (room)	860	1,000	860	25.80
Broiler	1,436	70	100	3.00
Clothes dryer	4,856	204	993	29.79
Dehumidifier	257	1,467	377	11.31
Dishwasher	1,201	302	363	10.89
Fan (attic)	370	786	291	8.73
Fan (window)	200	850	170	5.10
Floor polisher	305	49	15	.45
Freezer (15 cu. ft.)	341	3,504	1,195	35.85
Freezer (frostless 15 cu. ft.)	440	4,002	1,761	52.83
Humidifier	177	290	163	4.89
Microwave oven	1,450	131	190	5.70
Range with oven	12,200	96	1,175	35.25
Range with self-cleaning oven	12,200	99	1,205	36.15
Radio	71	1,211	86	2.58
Radio/record player	109	1,000	109	3.27
Refrigerator (12 cu. ft.)	241	3,021	728	21.84
Refrigerator (frostless 12 cu. ft.)	321	3,791	1,217	36.51
Refrigerator/freezer (14 cu. ft.)	326	3,488	1,137	34.11
Refrigerator/freezer (frostless 14 cu. ft.)	615	2,974	1,829	54.87
Roaster	1,333	154	205	6.15
Sandwich grill	1,161	28	33	.99
Sewing machine	75	147	11	.33
Television (b & w, tube)	160	2,188	350	10.50
Television (b & w, solid state)	55	2,182	120	3.60
Television (color, tube)	300	2,200	660	19.80
Television (color, solid state)	200	2,200	440	13.20
Trash compactor	400	125	50	1.50
Vacuum cleaner	630	73	46	1.38
Washing machine (automatic)	512	201	103	3.09
Washing machine (nonautomatic)	286	266	76	2.28
Waste disposer	445	67	30	.90
Water heater	2,475	1,705	4,219	126.57
Water heater (quick recovery)	4,474	1,075	4,811	144.33

Source: Adapted from Edison Electric Institute, EEI-Pub #75-61, New York, N.Y. and *Changing Times,* February 1975.

Before Buying

Check Energy Cost

How much will your yearly energy cost be with this model? How does it compare with other models? Check the figures and spend less on energy.

Help the nation conserve energy.

Compare Energy Costs

Estimated Yearly Energy Cost of this Model

$84

Compare Energy Costs

This model has 23 cubic feet of inside space. All brands and models with 21.5 to 24.5 cubic feet have about the same space inside.

These brands and models have different yearly energy costs:

| Model with lowest energy cost $63 | | Model with highest energy cost $122 |

$84
This Model

Name of Corporation

Refrigerator/Freezer
Model: AH503
Capacity: 23 cubic feet

More Cost Information

The $84 estimate for this model is based on the 1977 national average electric rate of 3.8¢ per kilowatt hour.

Check this table to estimate your yearly cost.

Cost per kilowatt hour

2¢	4¢	6¢	8¢	10¢
$44	$88	$132	$176	$220

Warning

Removal of this label before consumer purchase is a violation of federal law. (42 U.S.C. 6302)

Source of Cost Information

Estimates are based on U.S. Government standard tests. Your cost will depend on your utility rate and how you use the product.

FIGURE 9-1 Example of energy label for household appliances

content to be monitored by federal agencies, is or soon will be on all household appliances sold. Figure 9-1 is a sample label developed by the federal government that could fulfill its energy consumption goals. Furthermore, these energy labels will give consumers energy cost comparison information about an appliance they wish to buy *before they buy.* More specifically, energy consumption and the approximate energy usage costs for each appliance labeled will be emphasized on each label.

Once one knows the approximate operating cost of these household appliances, costs can be cut very easily. Cutting the use of high-energy-using appliances will reduce your utility bills automatically. This is becoming more important every day now, as rates for most forms of energy are clearly on the increase with no slowdown in sight.

Expected Life of Appliances

The life span of an appliance is primarily related to its quality and use. Of course, high-quality appliances normally last longer than inferior products. The average estimated life of several major appliances is shown in Table 9-2. These are averages only, depending in part on care and use. And of course, repairs may be necessary during the life span of the appliance.

A serious problem facing buyers of household appliances is *built-in obsolescence.* Basically, this means that the manufacturer, through deliberate underengineering, plans in advance just when a given appliance will wear out or become obsolete. Of course, these statements, or suspicions, are all but impossible to prove. But when appliances break down or seem to wear out too quickly, one questions the engineering and technology of the manufacturer.

Similarly, it appears more than likely that the high repair costs for many appliances arise from the manufacturer's basic design of the product. Often it is cheaper to buy a new appliance than to pay the repair bills. Consumers often get the impression that many

TABLE 9-2

Estimated Life of Major Appliances

Appliance	Average Estimated Life*
Dishwasher	11 years
Electric clothes dryer	14 years
Electric range	12 years
Electric refrigerator	16 years
Freezer	20 years
Gas clothes dryer	13 years
Gas or electric water heater	10 years
Gas range	13 years
Sewing machine	24 years
Stereo set	12 years
Tank vacuum cleaner	15 years
Television set, B & W	11 years
Television set, color	12 years
Washing machine	11 years
Upright vacuum cleaner	18 years

* Does not take into account replacement of parts.

Source: Department of Agriculture.

dealers and manufacturers do not even want to repair an appliance; it seems that the manufacturers would rather sell new ones. This is part of planned obsolescence and characteristic of our wasteful "throwaway" attitudes in society. Careful checking on reliable product-testing information can help consumers choose appliances that are less likely to need repairs. Also, prospective buyers should keep in mind that the appliances with the most complex dials and gadgets inevitably are more expensive to repair.

BUYING SMALL APPLIANCES

Hundreds of different kinds of small appliances ranging from those used for food preparation to those used for personal grooming are in constant demand by consumers. Almost all small appliances sold bring convenience to consumers, who are willing to pay whatever is necessary to get it. Therefore it is important to have general information about these appliances, as well as information regarding the quality of a specific model. Further, the energy consumption of these appliances must be given consideration when buying. And tips to help make careful selection of small appliances are essential to ensure efficient consumer buying.

Types and Purposes

There are many different types of small appliances. Small appliances manufactured for a particular purpose are not very different one from another. Frequently the purpose and function are quite similar; however, specific manufacturer designs and general overall appearance usually influence people heavily when they buy these appliances.

Two-tone or multicolored appliances could help some people decide which brand to buy; lightweight plastic casings as opposed to metal might influence others; or general esthetic design by some manufacturer could influence still others. No one characteristic is likely to be the only reason to buy one particular appliance when the general purpose and function are the same. Therefore, consumers must study and learn about basic functional and operational characteristics of these small appliances before looking at those characteristics that are purely esthetic in nature.

The small appliances available are numerous and varied. Some are classified as being used for *food preparation*—blenders, hot plates, broilers, rotisseries, frying pans, coffeemakers, or toasters. Another classification is for *general convenience or comfort*—electric heaters, fans, can openers, electric knives, knife sharpeners. And yet another classification is for *personal grooming*—hair dryers, combs, brushes, shoeshine machines. These classifications are not exhaustive, but they do serve to distinquish one type from another.

Frequently, consumers do not know how to go about shopping for small appliances intelligently. Many times they are received as gifts, or the cost is not felt to be high enough to spend time on comparison shopping. Consequently, consumers shopping for small appliances end up doing a rather mediocre job. To help reduce the mediocrity, Table 9-3 identifies some points to consider when shopping for certain small appliances—before shopping, what to look for when shopping, and questions to ask.

Determining Quality of Small Appliances

A most difficult task for consumers is trying to determine the quality of small appliances. Quality becomes quite elusive, since little specific information is available in a store when one is shopping for these appliances. And a main reason why consumers do not investigate, study, and compare among the small appliances is because quality information is not known, is scarce, or is hidden. Consequently, consumers have to dig and seek out sources to determine the quality.

To check on the performance quality of small appliances, consumers need to get help just as they do when comparing quality for major appliances. These include (1) reading and studying the tests and ratings of *Consumer Reports, Consumers' Research Magazine,* or other similar sources; (2) studying information provided by small appliance industry associations; (3) reading and comparing material available through the manufacturer and dealer; (4) getting information and opinions from someone who owns and uses a particular appliance or brand; and (5) visiting and talking with dealer or manufacturer personnel to get more specific quality information, aside from the normal sales puffery.

Another reason why many consumers do not take the time to check for quality is because small appliances cost so little compared with major appliances or furniture. Also, many consumers generally do not expect small appliances to last very long, so they treat the purchase as a short-run, expendable item. If an appliance doesn't work properly or doesn't last very long, some people merely throw it away and buy a new one. Behavior of this kind is both wasteful and uneconomical. Many

small appliances are quite costly now compared with a few years ago. Also, many small appliances can be expected to last a number of years with proper care and usage. Toasters, for example, can be expected to last 15 years.

Regardless of how affluent he or she is, a consumer has the responsibility to check as many product characteristics as possible *before* buying. The time spent investigating quality is often worthwhile and can save time and aggravation (returning for repair or replacement) as well as money.

Energy Operation and Cost

What with today's vital concern about energy use, consumers must also be concerned about the energy consumption of each appliance they buy. Although various appliances are similar in their purpose or function, the cost of operation may be markedly different.

Arnold and Janie Hearsch were looking at coffeemakers one day. They were not necessarily sold on any one brand, but they did want a capacity of 10 cups. Looking at the labels and other information on these appliances, they noticed a difference in energy consumption. For example, one used 675 watts per use, another 900, and yet another 1100 watts. A pot of coffee could be brewed in 13, 9, and 8 minutes, respectively. The Hearsches sought to find out how much it would cost to operate each of the appliances. Table 9-1 (page 255) illustrates average energy consumption and typical kilowatt-hour (kWh) costs to enable consumers to determine operational costs for various appliances. Once the Hearsches found out the cost of electricity locally, they could calculate their cost quite easily.

Using the three coffeemakers they compared and the displayed wattage information the Hearsches calculated use costs. They found out that the kilowatt-hour cost was 5 cents locally, and they estimated they would use the coffeemakers 13, 9, and 8 hours per month, respectively. First, they determined the number of kilowatt-hours to make coffee per month—watts × hours ÷ 1000 = kWh. Next they multiplied the rate ($0.05) times the

TABLE 9-3

Points to Consider when Buying Selected Small Appliances

Things to Do before Shopping	What to Look for when Shopping	Questions to Ask when Shopping
Can openers—Decide if it is necessary. Choose extra features such as magnetic lid lifter, table rest, knife sharpener attachment. Set an approximate price range. Consider number of watts needed to operate. Is there an electrical outlet handy for use? What size cans do I use?	Comparison-shop for different brands and prices. Check additional features, directions for use, and electrical information. Read cleaning instructions.	Does it open cans of all sizes? If not, what sizes? Is there a fast and slow control button? If not, what is the approximate speed per can? How are the blades sharpened? Does it require a special type of storage? Is it easy to dismantle? What are the provisions of the warranty? Is it easy to clean? How does one go about cleaning the can opener?
Irons—Check consumer publications on ratings. Decide on size, weight, and type—steam, dry, or combination. Decide on the type and number of vents wanted. Choose extra features such as heel rest, self-cleaning, water-level gauge, and instant spray.	Shop and look at different styles and costs. See if the settings are appropriate and conveniently located; check the weight, size, length of cord, electrical information; check warranty also. Check to see if the iron rests carefully while on its heel. Try the grip to make sure it is comfortable while using.	Can I use any type and temperature of water? Is the interior designed to resist rusting? Is it designed to give a quick, smooth finish to any type of fabric? Is a fabric guide included? How long is it warranted? Is it necessary to empty water after each use?
Coffeemakers—Check consumer publications for quality ratings. Is it really necessary? What type and size do I need? Consider the time it takes to brew. Decide on extra features wanted. Check out the price of accommodations such as filters. Set a price range.	Comparison-shop for different types and prices. Notice extra features such as strength selector, serving signal light, twist-lock safety top; compare prices of filters; check warranty. Check ease of making coffee. Inspect safety features against burns and shocks.	How long does it take the coffee to brew? Do I have to make the maximum amount each time? How long does the coffee stay fresh and warm after brewing? Is it easy to clean? What are the best filters to use? Is there a filter inside designed to trap stray grounds and strain out sediments? How many watts does it use? How long is the coffeemaker warranted?
Electric Blankets—Is it necessary? Decide on size needed, number of settings, type of fabric. Is there an electrical outlet conveniently located? Is it safe? Choose extra features such as lighted-dial and two-way temperature control. Set a price limit.	Compare types and prices. Check the length of the cord, number of temperature settings, safety precautions, type of fabric, electrical information, Underwriters' Laboratories seal. Look for dual temperature controls. Read cleaning instructions.	Do I have to worry about overheating? How is the blanket to be cleaned? Does this fabric shrink or stretch after cleaning? Is it an energy saver? What are the provisions of the warranty? Is it safety proof? Does it have an automatic cutoff if there is a short circuit or damage to the wiring?

TABLE 9-3 (Continued)

Things to Do before Shopping	What to Look for when Shopping	Questions to Ask when Shopping
Frying Pans—Is it necessary? Determine what cooking surface you want (stainless steel, nonstick coating, or aluminum). Consider the size, weight, and place of storage. Decide extra features wanted, such as signal light, plug-in cord, temperature control, warming tray, and lid prop. Set a price range. Consider what foods you want to cook in the pan. Are appropriate electrical outlets available where the pan will be used?	Comparison-shop for types and costs. Check dimensions, weight, and ease of handling. Look at cooking surface, temperature settings, and length of cord. Consider cleaning procedures. Check warranty. Check Underwriters' Laboratories seal.	Does the heating element distribute a reasonably uniform temperature across the entire pan? What other performances does this pan provide? Do the handles get hot when in use? Will this pan retain its cooking surface? For how long? How much electricity does it use? Are the handles removable? Are there any special cleaning procedures? Where is the safest place to use it? What are the provisions of the warranty?
Hair dryers—Decide what type of hair dryer you want—salon, bonnet, or blow dryer. Is it easy to carry when traveling? Choose extra features such as mist feature, brush, comb/detangler, and blow dry pistol. Consider low-energy-consumption dryer. Consider length and type of hair. Set a price range.	Look for different brands, types, and costs. Compare extra features included. See if bonnet is adjustable; if vents are directed away from neck and face. Notice length of cord, folding size. Read electrical information. Check for Underwriters' Laboratories seal. Check warranty. Check on energy consumption. Look for temperature controls (flexible heating degrees). Check on fan speeds.	Do I have to worry about overheating? Approximately how long will it take to dry my hair? What is the noise level during operation? Does it interfere with radio or television? Are air vents designed to distribute equal air flow? How much current does it draw? What is the wattage? Is it easy to adjust for height? What are the provisions of the warranty?
Electric combs/brushes—Consider length and type of hair. Determine watts needed. Select accessories such as brush, drying comb, style comb, and separate attachments. Decide on size and weight. Set a price range.	Look for accessories and features desired. Compare prices and makes. Check wattage, length of cord, Underwriters' Laboratories seal. Notice location of control lever. Is it easy to carry when traveling? Check warranty.	Do I have to worry about the heat damaging my hair? Is there an automatic cutoff when it gets too hot? If so, how long does it take to cool? How long will the comb or brushes last? Is it easy to dismantle? What are the provisions of the warranty? Should the combs or brushes be cleaned? If so, how?

TABLE 9-3 (Continued)

Things to Do before Shopping	What to Look for when Shopping	Questions to Ask when Shopping
Electric knives— Determine purpose for using the knife. Consult consumer publications on quality ratings. What size and type of blade is needed? Consider type of handle. Set price range. Decide upon energy usage.	Comparison-shop for different brands, models, and prices. Judge the comfort of the knife. Check the length and width of the blade, safety lock, speed control, and Underwriters' Laboratories seal. Notice the number of speed settings. Check for energy consumption.	How often does the blade need sharpening? How is the blade sharpened? What is the best type of handle to buy? Is there a manual on how to use it and special safety tips? How easy is the blade disassembled from the handle section? How much electricity does the knife use?
Slow cookers—Check several published sources that have done quality ratings. What specific electrical hook-up is necessary? Check electrical outlet, countertop space; select extra features desired. Consider size of cooker, and removable pot.	Compare models, brands, and prices. Check size, weight, services provided, operation cost, and cooking time for different foods. Check Underwriters' Laboratories seal. Determine if interior of pot is removable for cleaning.	Do I need a special electrical hook-up? Can I place the oven anyplace in my kitchen? How long does it take to cook various foods? What are the cleaning procedures? Are special products needed? If so, the cost? Is it safe? Is there a bacteria-control lever? Can I store food in the refrigerator in this cooker? Does a cookbook come with the purchase? What are the provisions of the warranty?
Toasters—Decide whether to get a toaster oven or a toaster. Check consumer publications. Determine size of toaster. Is it appropriate where used? Choose extra features such as adjustment button and automatic ejector. Is there a convenient electrical outlet? Set a price range.	Comparison-shop for styles and models. Check the size, length of cord, other services provided. Compare additional features and prices. Look for darkness control. Lift to check on weight and ease of moving.	Does the toaster toast other types of bread besides white or brown (muffins, cakes, waffles, etc.)? How can the texture be controlled? How long does it take to toast different types? How is it cleaned? Is it safe? What is the wattage? What is the estimated life under normal use? How long is it warranted? What are the provisions of the warranty?
Blenders—Decide on size of container, speed controls, cycle speeds; check for convenient electric outlet; determine whether you want a plastic or glass container; choose extra features such as pouring lip, nonskid feet, automatic shut-off, visible measurements. Set a price limit.	Shop and look at different styles, models, and prices; check information on blending time for certain foods, electrical information, warranty, and dealer's guarantee. Check on weight for portability. Look for available attachments for later use.	What services does this blender provide (whip, chop, puree, etc.)? What is the noise level during operation? Does it interfere with the radio or TV? What are the cleaning procedures? Are the blades stainless steel? If not, what are they made of? What are the provisions of the warranty? Is a blender cookbook included? Is the blender easily disassembled and cleaned?

TABLE 9-3 (Continued)

Things to Do before Shopping	What to Look for when Shopping	Questions to Ask when Shopping
Broilers—Decide whether you need a broiler. Check several published sources that have tested and rated broilers; measure the space for the broiler; choose a safe place; select the type of body wanted—polished steel or woodgrained. Determine electric circuitry available. Decide what extra features you want, such as extra shelves, signal light, and toast attachment. Decide on price range.	Comparison-shop for styles, brands, and costs. Check size and additional features; compare services provided and cooking time for various foods. Check for energy consumption. Read electrical information and warranty. Lift broiler for weight and ease of movement.	Can I place the broiler anyplace in my kitchen? Is there any maintenance that needs to be provided? What are the temperature settings? Do I have to be concerned about burning? How long will this product last? Does it provide other services such as baking and roasting? What is the cost of operation? Is a food preparation manual included? What are safe cleaning procedures to follow?
Food mixers—Check several published sources that have tested and rated mixers; select type of mixer—portable or tabletop; check to see if there is a conveniently located electrical outlet; determine size, how many speed controls, and other features needed. Set a price range. If hand model, check for weight and ease of handling when using.	Compare different styles, models, and cost. Check length of cord, speed controls, and dimensions (for storage purposes). Check size, weight, ease of using, and electrical information. Determine number and capacity of bowls. Compare extra features offered such as extra bowls, positive ejector, nonsplash beaters, and two-position turntable. Weigh the advantages and disadvantages—conveniences and inconveniences of the two types. Check to see if the mixer has a good balance and is easy to grip (if portable).	Do I have to worry about the motor overheating? Are there certain foods that cannot be mixed in this mixer? Are the beaters easy to clean? What are the manufacturer's warranty and dealer's guarantee? Are the beaters nonsplash? What is the noise level during operation? Does it interfere with the radio and/or television set? Is there a special cooking manual available for using the mixer?

kilowatt-hours to find the cost. The energy consumption cost figures for the three coffeemakers are summarized on the next page.

In studying the calculations and estimates used by the Hearsches, coffeemaker B is the best buy according to cost of energy use. All other factors were equal as far as the Hearsches

were concerned, so they bought coffeemaker B. Many consumers, however, might consider other characteristics more strongly. They may decide that although one appliance uses less energy and is cheaper to operate than another, it is not their choice. Style, design, material used, or color may be much more important than energy use to some consumers. But as

Energy Consumption Cost for Three Coffeemakers

Coffeemaker	Wattage	Estimated Hours Used per Month*	kWh (W × H ÷ 1000)	Usage Cost ($0.05 × kWh)
A	675	13	8.775	$0.439
B	900	9	8.100	0.405
C	1100	8	8.800	0.440

* It is assumed that less time is used with the higher wattage.

energy becomes more scarce, the amount of energy used by each appliance will have to be given higher priority. If not, consumers may have the appliance, but not the energy. Or the operational costs of high-energy-consumption appliances may be prohibitive.

TIPS ON BUYING MAJOR AND SMALL APPLIANCES

Many factors should be considered when buying appliances. Of course it is impossible to look at all things. However, there are some

TABLE 9-4

Electrical Small Appliance Operating Costs

Appliance	Average Wattage	Average Hours Used per Year	Approx. kWh Used per Year	Cost per Year at 3¢ per kWh
Blanket	177	831	147	$4.41
Blender	386	39	15	0.45
Carving knife	92	87	8	0.24
Clock	2	8760	17	0.51
Coffeemaker	894	119	106	3.18
Deep fryer	1448	57	83	2.49
Egg cooker	516	27	14	0.42
Fan (circulating)	88	489	43	1.29
Frying pan	1196	156	186	5.58
Hair dryer	381	37	14	0.42
Heat lamp (infrared)	250	52	13	0.39
Heater (portable)	1322	133	176	5.28
Heating pad	65	154	10	0.30
Hot plate	1257	72	90	2.70
Iron (hand)	1008	143	144	4.32
Mixer	127	102	13	0.39
Shaver	14	129	1.8	0.05
Sunlamp	279	57	16	0.48
Toaster	1146	34	38	1.17
Toothbrush	7	71	0.5	0.02
Vibrator	40	50	2	0.06
Waffle iron	1116	20	22	0.66

Source: Adapted from Edison Electric Institute, EEI-Pub #75–61, New York, N.Y. and *Changing Times,* February 1975.

I still say we should have bought furniture instead of a color TV.

Courtesy of Edd Uluschak.

tips, several of which are listed below, to help consumers with their buying.

1. *Read* literature on appliances *before* beginning to shop.
2. *Check all* aspects of warranties and guarantees offered.
3. *Look* for any and all forms of energy-use information for the appliance.
4. *Identify* the source for repair service on the appliance before buying.
5. *Note* the built-in safety innovations on appliances.
6. *Check* on the electric circuitry of the appliances for safety and check on needed voltage, to ensure maximum operational efficiency.
7. *Determine* if an owner's manual is available for a particular appliance and examine it.
8. *Inquire* about the availability of a low-energy-consumption appliance.
9. *Compare* the initial price *and* the operational costs of different products when you are shopping for electric or gas appliances.
10. *Check* for industry, government, or private agency approvals, such as Underwriters' Laboratories, American Gas Association, Association of Home Appliance Manufacturers, or the General Services Administration (approval of government product purchases) of the federal government.
11. *Check* for private consumer publication ratings, such as those from *Consumer Reports* and *Consumers' Research Magazine.*
12. *Survey* home energy capacity and local ordinances to ensure that you can use the appliance (for example, some ordinances forbid the use of trash compactors).
13. *Comparison-shop* for *all* appliances on price, quality, utility, operating costs, and service.

FURNITURE

Probably the most important component of the household is furniture. Families may do without certain appliances, curtains, fancy glassware, or complex home-entertainment systems, but most homes have some basic pieces of furniture, no matter how inexpensive or crudely constructed they are. Wood and upholstered furniture are two of the most common and traditional types. Plastic, metal, and wicker or cane are others that are used less frequently.

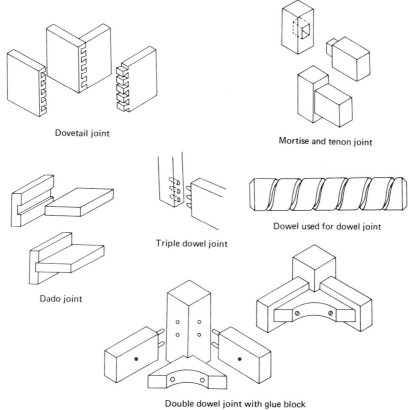

Dovetail joint

Mortise and tenon joint

Triple dowel joint

Dowel used for dowel joint

Dado joint

Double dowel joint with glue block

FIGURE 9-2   Quality wood joints

Upholstered Furniture

Many problems in buying result from consumers not knowing what they want. They just choose "a style." But other factors, such as quality, durability, material, color, size, and price, must also be considered.

Types of Furniture and Fabric.   Types of upholstered furniture are based largely upon the style or design, and they are called by a designer's name or a period in history. Examples would be Chippendale and Early American. When one plans furnishings for a temporary apartment, for example, style or type may or may not be important. However, when one wants to furnish a more permanent home, it may be wise to consider particular styles before the other factors are considered.

In addition to the types and styles of furni-ture, one must also consider the type and color of fabric. Although fabric is generally looked upon as an appearance factor, it is most assuredly important in terms of wear and comfort.

Quality.   In upholstered furniture, quality is of primary importance. But determining quality is more easily said than done, since such furniture necessarily includes wood and metal, too. When an informed consumer looks at the overall construction of a piece of upholstered furniture, both inside and out, many questions on quality can be answered. Type of wood used (hardwood or softwood, especially), foam padding, springs, and types of joints used in construction of the basic framework are essential points. All the wood joints in Figure 9-2 would meet quality construction standards. A lesser-quality joint often uses *butt-joint* construction only. Butt joints are put together with glue and/or screws.

The upholstery fabric affects furniture durability, too. Specifically, one should compare upholstery fabric using the following guides:

1. Mohair and frieze fabrics wear longer than flat woven material; they also collect dust faster.
2. Although nylon and olefin fabrics are highly resistant to stains, many other fabrics now have stain-repellent finishes such as Scotchgard and Zepel to achieve the resistant quality sought.
3. Choose heavy fabrics rather than light fabrics for longer service.
4. A nylon blend is generally better than 100 percent nylon fabric. A nylon-mohair blend, for example, has greater durability.
5. Select material with contrasting colors (patterned) and textures, since it tends to hide soil better than single colors and smooth fabrics.
6. Choose tightly woven material because it will wear better than looser fabrics.
7. Avoid a plastic that is not fabric backed, since it wears poorly.
8. Check to see if the furniture guarantee also includes the fabric, and find out if it involves replacement, refund, or just repair.

Utility. The use of the particular furniture and its fabric should be given ample consideration. Is it going in a room where it will be used heavily? Or is it to go in a bedroom as an extra piece of furniture, primarily for appearance? Are children or adults going to use the furniture? The answers to these and similar questions must be considered. Utility must be recognized as part of the purpose or function of the furniture being purchased.

Price. Furniture prices are usually uppermost in the mind of the shopper. But the initial price of upholstered furniture should *not* be the only or even the primary consideration. It is only one of several factors.

Admittedly, there are times when one only has a certain amount to spend. For example, after Carol and John Isenbach were married, they discussed their finances and their needs for furniture. They decided to allow $600 for a set of upholstered living-room furniture. This restriction actually encouraged the Isenbachs to consider other factors carefully in order to get the best buy for their money. The quality and overall appearance of their furniture may not approach that of a $900 set, but the satisfaction of money well spent is equally important.

A fair or good price for any piece of upholstered furniture is difficult to determine. But an effective comparison-shopping plan (including quality, type, utility, and price) is without a doubt the best method of getting a good buy. Table 9-5 shows some general points to consider, including things to do before shopping, what to look for when shopping, and questions to ask when shopping.

Wood Furniture

In selecting wood furniture, quality, style, finish, and price are all factors that must be carefully considered. Essentially these factors are similar to those considered in the purchase of upholstered furniture.

Purpose. In most cases the kind of furniture selected indicates its purpose. A chair is for sitting, a table for eating, a chest for storing items. Consumers should decide in advance actually where, how, and how heavily wood furniture is to be used in their home. Style of wood furniture is another point to consider. An advance decision to choose Early American, Danish Modern, French Provincial, or Mediterranean, for example, will reduce time and effort in the final selection. Figure 9-3 shows some styles of wood furniture.

Quality. An essential concern of all consumers choosing wood furniture is quality. Overall construction, design, kind of wood used, type of wood joints (shown earlier in Figure 9-2), and finish are all quality characteristics. The

TABLE 9-5

Points to Consider when Buying Upholstered Furniture

Things to Do before Shopping	What to Look For when Shopping	Questions to Ask when Shopping
Chairs, couches, sofas, etc.—Decide on the style and design of furniture. Be aware of present color scheme of rooms where furniture will go. Decide upon approximate price. Have a general idea about fabric to be used for covering. Know the room where furniture will be placed. Select a reliable furniture dealer. Read published materials on various types of furniture.	Compare styles, models, and prices from one store to another. Choose a particular style of furniture. Check basic frame, type of wood, joints for strength (look for double dowelling and also for glue blocks for reinforcement of joints); rigidity of the overall frame; look for convoluted springs, coil springs, and high-carbon spring wire; for crossed steel-wire supports in the underconstruction; to see if springs are held in place with steel wires; for booster springs and a spring edge on the furniture. Read the label to verify materials used for filling. Look at types of filling for cushions and padding (polyurethane or latex foam rubber). Select a durable fabric. Check for stain-resistant materials. See if there are zippers on cushions. Check on quality of welting. Sit on furniture to see how it feels. Bounce on furniture to check springs. Push back to see how far you sink. Look for quality of detail in construction.	What warranty or guarantee is there on the furniture? Can I remove the upholstery covering and replace it with another? Are there any delivery charges? Are all joints in the frame reinforced? Are there wooden corner blocks on joint-stress points? Is the wood solid or veneer? If it is plastic, how good a quality is it? Is there firmness on the front edge of the furniture for added support? Is the webbing on the underside of the furniture closely interfaced? Are the seat and back springs firmly tied? Does price necessarily mean quality in what I buy? How long will the fabric last before it shows wear? Can I give my fabric a protective finish by spraying it with some solution? Will the fabric lose its shape when it is washed or dry cleaned?

finish, although primarily associated with appearance, is important to both quality and durability, as some finishes last much longer than others.

Quality is difficult to determine in wood furniture, but generally it is held that solid hardwood used in construction is better quality than most veneers. Also, *lumber core* (softwood between two thin pieces of hardwood veneer) is considered a much better quality than *regular veneer* (several thin layers—three to five—of various wood products sandwiched between two thin layers of hardwood veneer). Plastic-coated surfaces provide more permanent protection from most liquids or heat. And plastic as used is more durable in some types of furniture when rough use is anticipated. Consequently, purpose and use must be considered carefully when selecting quality furniture. Table 9-6 suggests many other points to consider when buying wood furniture.

Middle Georgian Chippendale

Early American

Italian Provincial

Shaker

French Provincial
City Style

Pennsylvania Dutch

Mediterranean

FIGURE 9-3   Styles of wood furniture

Unfinished Furniture.   This furniture offers an excellent opportunity for the shopper to save money. But one must be handy with a paint brush or other finishing supplies and have or quickly develop the ability and the know-how to finish furniture. If the consumer can get style, quality construction, and the right type of wood in unfinished furniture, the finished product can be more valuable than a comparable product bought fully finished. The option of buying finished or unfinished furniture is fast becoming attractive to many consumers, especially when savings as high as 80 percent can be realized.

TABLE 9-6

Points to Consider when Buying Wood Furniture

Things to Do before Shopping	What to Look For when Shopping	Questions to Ask when Shopping
Chairs, tables, desks, dressers, bed frames, etc.—Decide upon style and design of furniture wanted. Select a compatible grouping of furniture. Decide upon approximate price you can pay. Read published materials on various types of furniture.	Comparison-shop from one store to another. Consider design first. Check type of wood (lumber core vs. solid wood vs. veneer); glue joints in all types of furniture you select; all sides of furniture including the bottom for excessive glue on glue joints; for quality jointing of legs, corners, and drawers; for dovetail joints on all drawers; for dustproofing panels and gliders for drawers in all bureaus, dressers, and chests. Select hardwood whenever possible. Consider plastic tops for added durability for tables and desks in particular. Compare the grain pattern in wood. Finish should be clear, have visual depth, and be smooth to the touch. Slip out a drawer to see if it slides freely. Touch between drawers to check for dust paneling. Pull on drawer handles to see if they are attached firmly. Swing out doors to see if they hang properly. Check on dealer or manufacturer warranties.	Is the surface stain- and burn-resistant? Is the delivery free? What guarantees do you offer for furniture? How will humidity affect the joints of the furniture? Will the color darken or fade over a period of years? Will sunlight affect the surface? Can I replace drawer pulls and knobs? What type of glue joints are used in the construction? Is veneer wood of lesser quality than solid wood for construction? Will the furniture warp in any way? Do I have to have a plastic surface to get stain-resistant quality? If the furniture is metal supported, what is the thickness of the metal (for strength)?

Refinished Furniture. This alternative is another way to reduce the cost of buying wood furniture. Generally, when furniture is professionally refinished and sold, it is because the businessperson knew there was quality in the original construction. Many times people are attracted to a very old chair or table, not because of its finish, but because of its style and apparent high-quality construction. Often, however, the finish may be burned, stained, chipped, or otherwise deteriorated. In such cases one practical answer is to have the piece refinished. By buying old furniture and having it refinished or refinishing it yourself, you can gradually save money while also becoming the owner of high-quality furniture.

Price. Quality and price of wood furniture do not necessarily go hand in hand. A price of $500 for a dining-room table does not necessarily mean that it is better than one that costs $350. One still must look at the construction and finish of the furniture. The reputation of both the manufacturer and the dealer will often give a clue to whether or not the price is reasonable, but that is absolutely no guarantee either.

To say a piece of furniture is "quality" to justify a high price does not in and of itself make it quality. Unfortunately, the average consumer buying furniture is not well equipped to judge quality. Consequently he or she does a mediocre job. A recommended way to reduce this type of mediocrity is to be better informed through reading literature about the furniture you intend to buy and to plan purchases well in advance so that you can be better informed.

Tips on Buying Furniture

Identified below are twenty-five tips which can be used by consumers when shopping for and buying furniture. The list is by no means exhaustive, but it serves as a summary of facts, ideas, dos and don'ts, and things to check so that consumers can be better informed when shopping for furniture.

1. Determine the price that is right for your budget.
2. Compare the quality of merchandise available at that price.
3. Do comparison shopping.
4. Study advertisements, hang tags, permanent labels, and furniture literature.
5. Check for an informative label telling you something about the hidden features, such as type, quality, springs, padding, webbing, and wood.
6. Examine the covering to see if it is durable, closely woven, easily cleaned, and pleasing to the eyes.
7. The difference between poor-quality and high-quality upholstery can often be seen in the raised seams. These are called *welts*. In good welted upholstery, two pieces of fabric are joined to a third piece that is wrapped around a cord.
8. On carefully constructed upholstered furniture, stripes and patterns should be carefully matched at the seams.
9. In some pieces, fabric is stretched across

unpadded areas. If you poke on such a span and the fabric does not resist your finger, it lacks backing. This is a sign of poor construction.

10. You should not feel the frame when you squeeze an upholstery arm. Feeling the frame beneath the upholstery can indicate inadequate padding and slipshod construction.
11. Look for firmly woven, closely interlaced webbing securely attached to the frame.
12. Check to see if each spring is tied several times with strong twine which is securely fastened to the frame; springs of tempered steel placed closely together and firmly anchored to webbing are essential in quality construction.
13. Muslin covering to permanently hold stuffing is usually used in good-quality furniture.
14. Construction components that are important to consider include:
    a. If the piece isn't solid wood, the maker must specify "veneered construction"; *veneer* refers to a material consisting of several thin wood layers permanently bonded to each other with an adhesive. The core or center layer of the veneer is thicker than the others.
    b. *Solid* means that all exposed furniture surfaces are made of solid wood (named on the tag) without a veneer.
    c. *Genuine* used with the name of a particular wood, walnut, for example, means that all exposed parts are made of walnut veneer over hardwood plywood. To be sure you are getting the real thing, thump the panel. Genuine wood sounds dead. A panel on a frame echoes.
    d. The term *combination* applies if more than one type of wood is used in exposed parts of the furniture.
    e. *All-wood* construction means exposed parts are made of wood for the full thickness of the panels.
16. Wood finishes on all-wood pieces should

have an even color and gloss even on "distressed" surfaces.

17. Fillers and stains are often used to conceal ill-fitting cabinetry; look closely at the surfaces.

18. Feel for carelessly cut veneer on wood furniture. It may be frayed along the edges; if so, poor craftsmanship is evident.

19. Look for dovetail joints. These joints must be precisely mated, and should fit together perfectly. Dovetail joints are an excellent sign of quality construction.

20. Inspect cabinet backs. The front is what you see, but the back may be more revealing. Staples, although used, should never replace screws or bolts where good support is needed in cabinet construction.

21. Drawers when pulled out should glide smoothly without binding and have stops to prevent them from accidentally coming out completely. Take out the drawers and check out their overall construction.

22. Check on the pulls, handles, hinges, and knobs. These should be well made, solid, easy to grasp, firmly attached, and carefully aligned.

23. Tables should feel smooth on the undersides. Simply running your fingers along the bottom edges of a table can reveal any roughness.

24. Excessive table wobble can be identified by rocking the top; too much wobble indicates poor-quality construction.

25. Sturdiness of chairs should be tested by leaning back in a chair, putting your weight on its back legs, then twisting slightly; wobbling or creaking indicates trouble.

GETTING SATISFACTION FOR YOUR MONEY

American consumers will spend billions of dollars on retail household goods this year. Nearly every home has a refrigerator, over one-half have a clothes dryer, three out of four families have a washing machine, one-third have a freezer, and almost one-fourth have a dishwasher. Consumers are buying more appliances every year. And there are clear indications that many consumers are not getting their money's worth. To improve the situation, consumers must first recognize their responsibilities in buying; and second, be aware of action programs for their benefit.

Responsibilities of Consumers in Buying

Consumers spend over $200 billion annually for durable goods, including furniture, appliances, and other household furnishings. Consumers sometimes have been characterized as spending with reckless abandon, mostly because they often act emotionally and lack specific buying information. It is imperative that consumers *study, learn,* and *know* more about the products they are buying.

How does the average consumer go about preparing to buy these household goods? If classes in consumer information are not available or convenient, other excellent sources are as close as your nearby newsstand or library. Among published materials, *Consumer Reports, Consumers' Research Magazine, Changing Times, Better Homes and Gardens,* and *The American Home* are but a few of the magazines that can help. They contain pertinent and up-to-date information. Also, to help inform consumers the federal government makes a wide variety of publications available in the area of household furnishings—often free. These publications are offered by mail through the Federal Consumer Information Center in Pueblo, Colorado 81009. (Write for a free catalog.)

In addition, the consumer should ask questions of persons who might know about household furnishings. You should write letters to manufacturers asking for information about products. A very simple letter is fine. You should also complain when you are dissatisfied with a product. Yes, complain! By doing so you are (1) trying to gain satisfaction for an unsatisfactory product or service, (2) letting the seller know that the product is not operating as advertised, and (3) able to get results and additional information that will help you another time.

Most complaints do not go unheeded. Businesses, volunteer consumer groups, and government agencies are increasingly wanting to listen and resolve problems. Keep in mind that a dissatisfied consumer can complain to the highest source if need be. One can write to the president of a company. Names and addresses of most corporate officials can be found in *Moody's Investors Guide* or *Standard and Poor's Register,* available in most public and school libraries. And, of course, the dissatisfied consumer can seek help from outside volunteer and government sources.

Action Programs for Consumers' Benefit

Businesses and independent consumer action groups are serving our needs as they see them. And consumers should be the first to praise those organizations that come up with positive programs. Consumer action groups or specifically identified industry-supported agencies are becoming more and more important to consumers. They serve as vital links between the dissatisfied consumer and the manufacturer in helping to resolve a problem or dispute over merchandise sold.

CAPs as Aids. Voluntary action programs to help consumers are commonly referred to as Consumer Action Panels (CAPs). The Major Appliance Consumer Action Panel (MACAP) and the Furniture Industry Consumer Action Panel (FICAP) are groups which are very active in helping consumers with specific problems. Such CAPs mediate otherwise difficult disputes between consumers and sellers. MACAP, for example, the oldest of the CAPs, is a group of consumer experts representing the public at the upper management level of the major appliance industry. When still dissatisfied with dealers and manufacturers, many distraught consumers have turned to MACAP. Of the over 2000 complaints received each year, MACAP has been able to resolve about 74 percent in favor of the consumer. Only about 3 percent of the complaints have been considered unreasonable. The other 23 percent are problems that are still pending—awaiting information from the manufacturer or the consumer.

Most complaints come to MACAP as a last resort. Yet MACAP's chairperson readily admits that in most cases, a written notification to the manufacturer is enough to satisfy all parties concerned. Of course, there are times when the consumer is unreasonable, as in the case of a woman who demanded her money back for a range she "had used for 8 years."

The Furniture Industry Consumer Action Panel (FICAP) and the AUTOCAPs (for consumers with problems concerning automobiles) are fairly new groups compared with MACAP. These two panels operate in the same general fashion as MACAP. CAPs consist of members from industry and the public to help solve these consumer complaints.

Like MACAP, these other CAPs usually do little until just about all other avenues for solving these problems have been exhausted. If complaints to a dealer or manufacturer have been unanswered, or the remedy is unsatisfactory, consumers should write the appropriate CAP. The CAP will then work within the industry toward a solution that will satisfy all concerned. Sometimes a manufacturer is unwilling to do anything or to do more than has been done already, but in the great majority of cases the decision of the CAP has been followed by the manufacturer. All information given to the CAP must be factually correct and documentable to ensure fairness when the CAP serves as the mediating body between the manufacturer and the consumer. Specific addresses for these CAPs are noted in the Appendix.

WARRANTIES AND GUARANTEES

"You get what you pay for!" This statement of despair is frequently made by consumers when they are disenchanted or dissatisfied with an appliance purchase. And it is even more irritating when an expensive appliance does not hold up as well as an inexpensive one. The consumer's only hope seems to be the warranty, if not the local reputable dealer. On

Think I found the problem—the warranty's expired.

Courtesy of Edd Uluschak.

the surface, warranties seem to be a panacea for all the ills an appliance might ever develop, but this is not quite the case.

Types and Purposes

Implied and express warranties and guarantees are the two types most frequently used. An *implied* warranty is a promise of quality that a buyer has a legal right to expect. *Implied warranty of merchantability* is a term often used interchangeably with implied warranty. For example, a clothes dryer has an implied warranty that it will dry clothes—its intended purpose.

An *express* warranty is an oral or written promise of a specific degree of quality and/or performance. The express warranty usually covers features other than those covered in an implied warranty, such as replacement of parts that wear out before a specified time, and who shall bear the costs. Usually a warranty covers only parts replacement, and a guarantee covers both parts and labor. In practice, however, both terms are used interchangeably.

Problems of Warranties and Guarantees

Upon purchase of an appliance, the consumer usually receives instructions for its proper care and/or operation. This information is most helpful. Purchasers should read these materials carefully. The buyer also receives a guarantee or warranty which appears to be a manufacturer's promise of performance, durability, mechanical precision, and long life. The fact is that warranties have traditionally been designed to protect the manufacturer. The warranty protects the manufacturer against what was not done, rather than protecting the purchaser against poor product performance or liability damage. The warranty essentially limits the manufacturer's liability if something goes wrong with the product.

The warranty itself has not been the whole problem. In the past most people have been confused by the "mesmerizing jargon" of a warranty. Consequently, the consumer's interpretation of the carefully deciphered words is drastically different from that of the manufacturer. Misunderstandings, misinterpretations, and confusion often result. The buyer paid for most of or all the needed repairs, and was not paid for losses incurred if he or she was hurt by a dangerous or malfunctioning product. Fortunately, these problems will be reduced somewhat in the years ahead as a result of new warranty legislation, discussed below.

A related warranty problem is the "mailback" warranty card given to many purchasers. If one forgets to mail it, loses it, or

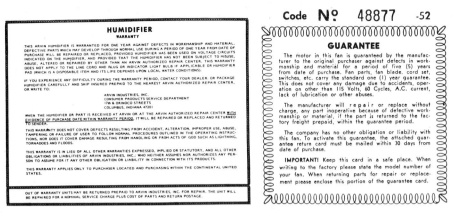

FIGURE 9-4 Older warranties of manufacturers

does not want to be bothered, the warranty may be affected. One question to be raised is, should the purchaser be forced into these clerical duties in order to have the product covered by a warranty? An alternative would be to have the merchant send the warranty to the manufacturer with the needed name, address, date, and place of purchase.

Most mail-back warranty cards also ask for personal information: Where did you buy the appliance? How old are you? What sex? What brought you to the store? Is this a case of the manufacturer invading the privacy of the consumer? To make the warranty effective, just record your name and address, the date, and the place of purchase, and skip the rest of the personal questions. The manufacturer's marketing research department should get this information some other way. On the plus side for returning these warranty cards, the manufacturer may need to get in touch with all the buyers of a specified year or model or an appliance later found to be malfunctioning or dangerous. The warranty cards on file (actually put on computer tape) are the quickest and best source for names and addresses in the event of a product recall.

Assuming that a warranty or guarantee is understood and that the card is mailed in, the consumer still has other problems: inability or refusal to get proper service, delays in service, delays while someone decides where blame

should be placed (manufacturer, dealer, service agency, or customer), and excessive labor charges (especially where travel charges are added to a high hourly rate). Responsible consumers should continue to actively pursue their rights in spite of such obstacles when necessary.

Warranty Readability and Understanding
Some manufacturers' appliance warranties that were used in the past and how they differed are shown in Figure 9-4. Careful reading shows the differences in the degree of confidence or lack of confidence that the manufacturers have in their own products. Figure 9-5, on the other hand, shows a newer revised warranty that complies with the new legislation, which in part requires easier-to-understand language.

Warranties that are printed for the buyer vary in readability. One easily gets the impression that some warranties are not meant to be understood, although now the consumer is beginning to find that they are written more and more in simple language.

You should ask yourself questions about the warranty for any product you are considering buying: Is the warranty readable? Can you understand what is to be done? What is covered? What is not covered? How long does the warranty run? What do *you* have to do? Who is offering the warranty, and who is responsible for carrying out the services? What will the manufacturer do as the warrantor? You should be able to find the answers clearly stated. If you cannot, be careful, and get the answers before you buy. Then be sure and get these points clarified and put in writing *and* signed by the dealer.

Magnuson-Moss Warranty Act

Legislation for federal regulation of warranties covering consumer goods became effective in 1975. The legislation gave the Federal Trade Commission the power to require clearly understandable and accurate language in warranties. It also authorized the FTC and the Justice Department to seek injunctions and bring lawsuits against companies that violate the FTC regulations or fail to carry out the terms of their own warranties.

Senator Warren Magnuson and Representative Frank Moss, authors of the warranty act, have continually urged manufacturers to write warranties that people can read and understand. This strong bill puts an end to most of the misleading practices of putting promises in large print and then hastily retracting them with confusing small print. Warranties on consumer products costing more than $10 must be available for consumers to look at *before* they buy. Also, the provisions of the act let consumers force companies to keep their warranty promises. The Warranty Act provides that all warranties must be easy to read and understand; they must be written in ordinary language; fine print isn't allowed; and every term and condition of the warranty must be spelled out in writing.

There are two basic types of written warranties covered under the Warranty Act: full and limited. A *full warranty* means that a defective product will be fixed (or replaced) free, including removal and reinstallation if necessary; it will be fixed within a reasonable time after the complaint; and the warranty is good for anyone who owns the product during the warranty period.

Limited warranty, as provided in the act, gives the buyer anything less than what a full

Norelco®

LIMITED WARRANTY

North American Philips Corporation warrants each new Norelco Nail Dazzler™ Model HB 9400 (except batteries and accessories) against defects in material or workmanship for a period of one (1) year from the date of original purchase for use, and agrees to repair, or, at our option, replace any defective unit without charge for either parts or labor.

IMPORTANT: This warranty does not cover damage resulting from accident, misuse, or abuse, lack of reasonable care, the affixing of any attachment not provided with the product, loss of parts or inserting any but the specified batteries.* THIS WARRANTY IS VOID WHEN SERVICE OR REPAIRS ARE PERFORMED BY A NON-AUTHORIZED NORELCO SERVICE CENTER.

NO RESPONSIBILITY IS ASSUMED FOR ANY SPECIAL, INCIDENTAL OR CONSEQUENTIAL DAMAGES.

You may obtain warranty service at any of the Norelco Service Centers listed on this card. Simply take or ship the unit prepaid to the nearest Norelco Service Center. Damage occurring during transit is not covered by this warranty.

Enclose $1.50 to defray cost of return shipping and insurance.

NOTE: No other warranty, written or verbal, is authorized by North American Philips Corporation.

This warranty gives you specific legal rights, and you may also have other rights which vary from state to state. Some states do not allow the exclusion or limitation of incidental or consequential damages or limitations on how long an implied warranty lasts, so the above exclusion and limitations may not apply to you.

*Read enclosed instructions carefully.

HB 9400 © Copyright North American Philips Corp. 1977   Printed in Japan

FIGURE 9-5   Current manufacturer's warranty

warranty gives. Limited means be careful—something's missing. For example, a limited warranty may cover only parts, not labor; allow only a pro rata refund or credit; require the return of any product to the store for service; cover only the first purchaser; or make a charge for handling.

Also, for a full warranty, your rights don't run out at the end of the warranty for problems complained about during the warranty period. The company must still take care of those problems, no matter how long it takes. Listed below are some suggested steps to follow in case trouble develops with warranties.

1. Read the warranty carefully when a problem comes up. A warranty is a contract that spells out the buyer's rights.
2. Make sure you contact the right person in the company. If the manufacturer gives a warranty, don't stop with the seller; write the manufacturer at the address given on the warranty.
3. Contact a local consumer-protection office or complaint center; they may be able to help and explain more about buyers' rights.
4. In some cases there will be an organization that hears and decides disagreements informally, if both sides are willing. A company or a local consumer-protection office can tell you who to contact.
5. If the amount of money involved is small, go to a small claims court. Their costs are low, procedures are simple, and a lawyer is usually not needed.
6. If the product was manufactured after July 4, 1975, you can sue the company under the Warranty Act. If the suit is decided in favor of the buyer, he or she can get money damages or any other type of relief the court decides to give. This includes the cost of bringing the lawsuit and the buyer's attorney fees. If the product was manufactured before July 4, 1975, you can still sue the company under state law. Contact a lawyer or consumer protection office for further information.
7. Report violations of the law to the Federal Trade Commission. The FTC cannot help directly with a warranty problem, but it needs to know if companies are obeying the warranty rules. Write the FTC if a company does not make warranty information available.

REPAIR AND DELIVERY SERVICES

Two service areas that need special mention are repair and delivery. Whether or not a particular business provides these services is important to the consumer. And if it does, questions need to be asked. What kind of services are provided? Is the repair service on the premises? Does the product have to be shipped to the manufacturer? Can the customer carry the merchandise and save delivery charges?

Repair Services

Mass production, spot inspection, lack of pride in workmanship, and rising consumer expectations have all contributed to what some believe to be lower quality in the end product. Whether today's products are of higher or lower quality than 10 years ago is debatable. However, one can be certain that there is a need for repairs on most household furnishings and appliances used in the home.

General Repair Need. Quality workmanship in many manufactured products seems to be gone. In some cases, getting the product home and working can be considered an achievement in itself. In other cases, the product never needs repair for several years. In essence, the degree of manufacturing quality varies considerably. If your new refrigerator is manufactured on a Monday, for example, it is less likely to be up to the manufacturer's high standard. (Some suggest that high absenteeism and the "Monday morning blues" are a factor.) It is impossible to predict with accuracy how long a particular product will work or how long it will last without something going wrong. Most necessary repairs should occur and be fixed during the warranty period.

Consumers must face the facts—appliances and other operating home furnishings are going to need repairs occasionally, and they are going to wear out from use eventually. "Planned obsolescence" may be part of the problem, but with the manufacturing procedures, large-scale production, and complexities of products today, it is impossible to produce products that will perform 100 percent of the time.

Repairs often can be done by the consumer—a loose belt or screw can be tightened, a fuse can be replaced, or a wire that has worked loose can be connected. In such cases it is most important to locate and read the owner's manual which came with the product when it was new. Specific suggestions and safeguards are often given in such manuals. When a problem is serious, it is necessary to call a qualified repairperson. Of great importance is to make sure the repairperson is qualified, certified, and licensed for the product being repaired. A manufacturer's certified repairperson is important, but others can also become licensed or certified equally as well. In other words, shop around, compare, and be selective in choosing who shall do the needed repair. One should definitely know or find out about the reputation of any service people before asking for their help.

Repair Service Contracts. Selling service contracts is a way to get consumers to pay for repairs in advance. Most service contracts are issued by appliance dealers. They are sold and paid for at the time a purchase is made, and they cover repairs on the product beyond those covered by the warranty. It is a type of "insurance." Usually the contracts last for a specified period, often 1 or 2 years.

It is somewhat ironic when a consumer asks, "If the product is supposed to be quality and should last, why do I have to buy a service contract to guarantee repair of this quality product?" This valid question deserves an answer. You probably don't need a service contract if the product has any kind of decent warranty. Not only are they highly overpriced, but independent research shows that consumers don't get their money's worth because the products hold up pretty well and don't need all the repairs that consumers were led to believe would be needed.

Mr. and Mrs. J. C. Gibson of Manhattan, Kansas, decided not to buy the service contract for a new gas furnace. The contract would have cost them $80 for the first year and $100 for the second year. But 11 months after purchase, while the 12-month warranty was still in effect, repairs amounting to $177 became necessary. They did, however, purchase a service contract for a new color TV set at a cost of $81.50 per year. No repairs of any kind have been made on the TV in 3 years.

Service contracts are a risk—if you buy a contract, you are saying, in effect, "I believe something will go wrong, and I will prepay the cost with a service contract." If you do not buy a contract, you are saying, "I hope nothing goes wrong, but if it does I feel I can pay for the repairs myself."

Service contracts are not inherently bad. If consumers are careful about buying them and have weighed the pros and cons, they can be advantageous. But studying the contract to learn its basic provisions and what it covers is often more difficult than one might imagine. In any event, a consumer must fully understand what he or she is paying for, what are the risks, who is to do the repairs, and other aspects of the contract before buying it.

Repairs by service contracts and other repairs are very profitable. One large appliance dealer grosses over $1 million a day on repair service. It is important for the consumer to weigh the advantages and disadvantages carefully on repair services of all kinds. Figure 9-6 summarizes some questions that should be asked in regard to service-contract purchasing.

Consumer Repair Tips. Many home appliance repairs are not necessary if the consumer will stop and think. Some helpful tips to consumers include:

- Check to see if the electric cord is plugged in.
- Check to see if the outlet is working properly.
- Check the power source (a fuse may be blown).
- Check the owner's manual (Always keep it handy and available for all appliances.)
- On *refrigerators or freezers,* check to see if the temperature control is set properly.
- On an *electric range,* check for small fuses within the range itself; make sure all elements fit securely.
- On a *gas range,* check to see if the pilot

FIGURE 9-6 Know a good service contract when you see it

- Does the contract guarantee speedy repair service? Some don't. Is there an extra charge for holiday service and weekend or after-hours calls?
- Under what conditions can you cancel and get a refund? You may want to if an appliance is stolen or you move out of the service area. Ask about transferability, too. A contract may go with an appliance when it is sold or given away. In other cases, coverage stops.
- If you are buying a contract to cover a new appliance, what will the contract do for you that the warranty won't? If a two-year policy is basically an extension of a one-year warranty, think about waiting 11 months to see whether problems develop. Then buy a one-year contract (usually at no extra cost) if you've been having trouble.
- Does the contract limit the number of free calls? When work done by one free call isn't satisfactory, don't let a return call be counted against your free limit.
- Does the contract cover the whole appliance or just part? With a TV, it may cover only the picture tube; for a microwave oven, only the magnetron. For ranges, refrigerators and washers, contracts are unlikely to exclude any part except inexpensive "trim," such as a light bulb.
- Are there hidden costs or exclusions? Parts but not labor? Some contracts provide free repairs, but customers have to pay extra for the repairer's travel time and for any work that can't be done in the home.

Source: *Changing Times,* August 1976, p. 31.

light is on if the burners do not light. (Do not light a match!)
- On *automatic washers,* if they should stop, in addition to checking the power, check to see if the load is too heavy or out of balance; poor drainage from washer may indicate that too much soap is being used.
- On *dishwashers,* make sure the door is closed. Improper cleaning could be due to the water not being hot enough, or to too little or too much soap being used.
- On a *garbage disposer,* if it is jammed or inoperable, press reset button first, defuse, then probe with nonconducting instrument (wood). Overheating may mean too much garbage or too tightly packed.
- On *clothes dryers,* check controls for setting, push start button again firmly, make sure door is closed, check lint trap if clothes are not drying, or if drying takes too long. Check for overloading if drying is ineffective.

Of course, these hints are not complete. When an appliance does not work, these basic quick checks might correct the problem. If not, check the owner's manual and/or call a repairperson.

Delivery Services

Most persons will need some type of delivery service when buying large household furnishings and appliances. Consequently, the delivery service available will be a factor in deciding where to buy. Several problems and options need to be understood concerning delivery services.

Delivery Availability. Is the delivery service going to be provided by the store? Is delivery going to be provided through a local independent carrier? Is delivery to be provided by a statewide or a nationwide carrier? The answer to these questions should be given to a consumer who purchases a major household furnishing.

Locally provided delivery service appears to be most favored by many consumers. Usually the driver is employed by the firm from where the purchase was made and is more likely to be cooperative and helpful. Nonlocal carriers don't seem to be quite as accountable. They are usually in a hurry, or do not wait for inspection of goods before leaving.

Delivery Time and Damage. All too often people have waited in vain for a delivery truck to bring a new appliance; they just did not show up when they said they would. Sally Hill of Burlington, Vermont, took off work one afternoon because it was understood that she had to be at home to receive her newly purchased clothes dryer. She gave up $20 in pay to slowly find out that the delivery was not made. The company called about 6:00 p.m. and said they were running late; they would deliver the next day. Ms. Hill had to repeat the same procedure the next day. It cost her $40 in lost wages to get the dryer delivered. To make matters worse, the driver and helper stayed long enough to only uncrate and install the dryer; nobody showed her how to run it. Ms. Hill's situation has been repeated hundreds of thousands of times in the country over the years.

Delivery service is provided, but too often in a rather mediocre fashion. Consumers need to inspect delivered merchandise, if at all possible, before the carrier leaves. This is to help determine if it is damaged, and if so, where, when, and by whom it was damaged. Usually damage is caused by the shipper before transportation or by the carrier enroute to the purchaser. The cause of the damage and who is at fault need to be determined *at* delivery time so that the proper claim can be made. Unnecessary delays on damage claims are a nuisance, result in dissatisfaction, and sometimes cause financial hardship for consumers. If there is no damage—no problem. If there is, a report and damage claim can be filed immediately for repair, allowance, or replacement.

Delivery Costs. An increasingly common practice in regard to delivery of merchandise is followed by a furniture store in Jackson, Mississippi. It advertises a lower price if the consumer handles delivery. Figure 9-7 illustrates this way of giving the consumer certain alternatives, such as delivery service on certain products. As noted, there is a 13.4 percent reduction in price if the direct cost of delivery is shifted to the consumer.

FIGURE 9-7 Advertisement showing alternatives for consumer toward cost reduction. Courtesy Buzzy Tatum's Furnitureland, Jackson, MS

Consumers are given the option of accepting or not accepting the available delivery service at a particular price. They are made aware of the cost difference in these options. Furthermore, a customer who chooses to pay a higher price should be able to get "topnotch" delivery service for the additional price, especially since, as shown in the figure, it amounts to $60. Delivery service may be one of a consumer's main reasons for purchasing merchandise at a particular store. In any event, it should be made clear whether the delivery service is "free" or at extra cost. However it is provided, the service should be performed properly and completely.

WHERE TO BUY VARIOUS PRODUCTS

A major function of the American market system is to provide the right goods, at the right time, in the right place, and at the right price. Only through a good working relationship between businesses, governments, and consumers can this be done. Consumers, through their

TABLE 9-7

Characteristics of Types of Businesses that Sell Household Furnishings and Appliances

Type of Business	Characteristics
Demonstration stores	Highly specialized; usually handle single manufacturer's goods only; highly trained and specialized personnel; limited product selection, but high standard of selling and customer service.
Specialty stores	Volume selling of specific types of household furnishings and appliances; special repair services on premises; more styles and sizes from which to choose; in some cases limited brands to compare; can offer lower prices as a result of high-volume selling.
Wholesale stores	Lower prices, sometimes must belong to special group in order to buy; few or no services; no returns; no charging; cash only; no delivery; usually only manufacturer's warranty; products not always available.
Department stores	Variety of products from which to choose; no high volume on one line of products; all shopping in one place; price range competitive; usually many services provided at customer cost; can be overcrowded, but often open during evening hours; hard to get to and present parking problems unless located in shopping center; generally operate at higher profit margin than specialty stores; frequently do not handle repairs on premises; subcontracts for certain repair services for customer, or ships to manufacturer; often sells by mail and telephone.
Discount stores	Largely self-service; large assortment of merchandise, but not many quality choices; high volume and turnover of stock; emphasis on frequent sales; usually located in low-rent areas for location with easy access; maximum shopping hours and days; eliminate or reduce services to pass on savings.
Variety stores	Varied price ranges along with merchandise; narrow selection of products available; usually no charge accounts or delivery service; occasional free delivery on expensive items.
Catalog showrooms	Deal in high-volume selling; reduced overhead, open displays to see catalog items; prices usually as low as wholesale prices; code for customer pricing is standard practice; few frills and services offered; usually honor most major bank credit cards; little opportunity to get help from sales specialists in store; most products sold from catalog after seeing display item; handle most name brand items with wide variety of products; low markup on products.
Manufacturer's outlets	A variety of products from one manufacturer; don't have products supplied by other manufacturers; most products less expensive than wholesale and retail prices; usually operate with low overhead to keep prices low; open displays for self-service; individual help available, but generally few salespersons are employed; mostly cash basis, but many honor major bank credit cards; most services have additional charge (alteration extra in clothing).
Furniture showroom outlets	Extremely low overhead; high-volume selling; few services offered; self-service delivery is standard practice; "cost plus 15 percent" is generally accepted markup; usually operated by furniture manufacturers; often seconds are available at considerable markdown; cash (check) is expected for purchases; no provisions made for installment purchases; salespersons are specialists in furniture and can provide excellent help; not usually available in the country, must seek them out.

comparison shopping, decision making, and economic voting, are letting the businessperson know what goods to produce. Knowing what to buy, being knowledgeable about certain characteristics of products, and being willing to comparison-shop are essential to getting a high degree of satisfaction when buying household furnishings and appliances.

In addition, consumers must learn where to buy these products. The nine general types of stores handling household furnishings and appliances are demonstration, specialty, wholesale, department, discount, and variety stores, catalog showrooms, manufacturer's outlets, and furniture showroom outlets.

Certain characteristics are both unique with and common to each type of business. Table 9-7 identifies several characteristics of each. Consumers must take care when buying from certain types of retailers or wholesalers. For example, some stores call themselves "discounters" when in reality some of their "discount prices," although below the price on the price tag, are higher than prices at other retail stores. This is sometimes true of the *catalog showroom* dealer. A catalog distributed by a catalog showroom discounter may list a Zenith 23-inch console color television set to retail at $599.95. Their pricing code would be T103496-99000. Dividing the last 5 digits by 2, the selling price to the consumer would be $495.00. Sounds great—over $100 discount being given. However, by comparision shopping the identical television set could be found at a local Zenith dealer for $479.00, including delivery and other services. So what appears to be a great money saver may be in reality a sales gimmick to dupe the uninformed.

Other fast-growing businesses are the *manufacturer's outlets* and *furniture showroom* outlets. They too suggest to the consumer "low, low prices," "eliminate the middleman and save," or "low display costs mean low consumer prices." Although these advertised cost reductions to consumers may be true, occasionally they are selling gimmicks at best, and they need to be studied carefully. But generally these outlets have a pricing structure of "costs plus 15 percent" plus shipping. If this pricing is followed, the outlets may be worth investigating and considered along with other sources for comparison purposes.

Below are listed eight tips that you can use when deciding on places to shop for household furnishings and appliances:

1. *Decide* exactly what you want to purchase before you go out shopping—if possible, identify model, brand, features you want, amount you can afford to spend, and expected quality.
2. *Determine* how much time you can devote to decision making and comparison shopping.
3. *Use* advertisements, catalogs, and the telephone to gather information before you visit stores.
4. *Combine* shopping for several items whenever possible.
5. *Begin* at a specialty shop that handles a variety of the item being sought to let you comparison-shop.
6. *Shop* at several stores even though you are considering a particular brand and model. Stores that carry the same brand and model will still have price and service differences worth noting.
7. *Compare* stores for delivery and repair service, installation (and costs), warranties, credit arrangements available, and merchandise return policies.
8. *Be alert* for exceedingly low priced items being advertised; it may be a "bait and switch" tactic.

POINTS OF VIEW AND PROBLEMS TO THINK ABOUT

Trade associations and individual manufacturers have shown some improvement in recent years in identifying specific quality characteristics of furnishings and appliances. However, more needs to be done to inform consumers of these characteristics through labels, tags, or literature. Why can't they put consistent and comparable fabric quality ratings for durability on furniture, for example?

Many complaints are handled to the satisfaction of the consumer. But in too many cases, complaints would never have been made had the manufacturer set higher production standards in the first place. A case in point is the use of plastic in home construction and furnishings. A recent experiment showed that selected plastic furniture was literally destroyed by fire in only 7 minutes. The potential flammability of these products has been largely ignored by those who manufacture and those who regulate. Until standards of flammability are established, consumers are advised to be wary about buying "fire-resistant" plastic furniture.

Although new laws appear to have closed the door on many problems related to warranties, these laws must still be implemented and enforced. The FTC, industry, consumer groups, and consumers must be careful about adherence to these regulations. Hopefully, the warranties offered will be understandable by all and open to only one interpretation. Warranties and guarantees can protect both the manufacturer and consumer.

President Carter and other state and local officials keep urging consumers to "jump on the energy conservation bandwagon." Great! But they must also urge the appliance manufacturers to more readily display energy consumption labels and tags on household appliances of all types with *comparative* information. These data would then inform consumers more easily, rather than having consumers use pencil and pad to make all their calculations.

Consumers themselves are still one of their own greatest problems. Mr. and Ms. Consumer too often accept poor merchandise; they frequently do not comparison-shop; and they remain rather quiet, almost passive. Yet, they need *not* "demand," "resort to violence," "defame," or "practice civil disobedience" to make themselves heard! Several channels are open to help people voice their complaints and compliments, and both are important. Whether these channels lead to private agencies, consumer agencies, industry-supported agencies, government agencies, or the dealer or manufacturer directly should make little difference to the responsible consumer. One must take the first step, then pursue any others, as necessary, if they—retailers, wholesalers, dealers, distributors, and manufacturers—are going to help improve the marketplace.

CHAPTER ACTIVITIES

Checkup on Consumer Terms and Concepts

Appliance quality	MACAP
Appliance life	Warranties
Consumer Reports	Guarantees
Consumers' Research	Express warranty
Magazine	Implied warranty
Comparison shopping	Warranty readability
Furniture style	Warranty Act
Quality furniture	Discount stores
Furniture utility	Specialized dealers
Refinished furniture	Wholesale dealers
Unfinished furniture	

Review of Essentials

1. What are some problems the consumer finds in buying household furnishings and appliances?

2. Name five points that consumers should consider when shopping for upholstered furniture.

3. What are three quality points to look for when buying wood furniture?

4. What purpose does comparison shopping serve in buying furniture and appliances?

5. Major appliances come in several categories and styles. Name several of each.

6. Explain how consumers can better determine quality and can gain information when buying appliances.

7. Explain the difference between implied and express warranties.

8. Identify the major provisions of the Magnuson-Moss Warranty Act.

9. What have several companies done to

help the consumer with warranties and product problems?

10. Explain how one can determine the amount of energy used for major or small appliances.

11. What are some reading materials that the consumer can use to get more information before shopping for household furnishings and appliances?

12. What sources can consumers use to find the names of corporate officials?

13. What is meant by CAPs, and how do they help consumers?

14. What are some basic differences in shopping for appliances at large department stores and at discount stores?

15. Name some characteristics of stores that sell household furnishings and appliances that will help consumers in their shopping.

Issues for Analysis

1. Do professional associations such as the National Association of Manufacturers or the American Home Appliance Manufacturers really work to help the consumer, or is their action merely a token effort to keep the consumer from making too many complaints to federal agencies and legislative bodies?

2. Many stores throughout the country selling household furnishings and appliances call themselves discount stores. Are they really? Are their prices lower than those of a regular department store or specialty store? Should the consumer be given more information about whether or not a store is truly a discount store?

3. What is the consumer's responsibility when it comes to comparison shopping for household furnishings and appliances? Should consumers accept mediocrity as a standard on much of the merchandise they buy?

4. What is the responsibility of the manufacturer, dealer, wholesaler, distributor, and retailer when it comes to providing quality products and services?

10
Automobiles

THE PROBLEMS

More Americans complain about their automobiles than they do about any other consumer product or service. Since cars contain about 15,000 parts and there are more than 140 million of them on the streets and highways, it seems logical that this would be a product to complain about. Not surprisingly, design is a major area of complaint. Federal officials report that "design flaws were responsible for about two-thirds of the 52 million cars and trucks recalled during the past 10 years to correct safety defects."

When choosing a new or used automobile, consumers find that they must buy a vehicle that is a heavy contributor to air pollution. In addition, American cars have long been criticized by many European manufacturers for having poor brakes, poor suspension, and poor steering. Federal regulations require that bumpers be able to withstand a collision of 10 miles per hour. But at 12 miles per hour—a slow speed—the grillwork, nearby sheet metal, and fenders are damaged at a cost of hundreds of dollars!

There are other problems too. The selection is wide. There are about 300 American and 200 foreign models available. Many are virtual look-alikes (Mercury Monarch and Ford Granada; Plymouth Volaré and Dodge Aspen; Ford Pinto and Mercury Cougar). All the possible makes, models, and options can become somewhat confusing. When one decides to spend no more than a certain amount, such as $4800, for a new car, the task is very difficult. A medium-priced Ford with a list price of $4300 might be appealing, but any optional equipment might run the cost to $5500. On the other hand, a higher-priced Ford for $5600 might include many of the "options" as original equipment. Which of the two models should be chosen? Should you compare a Ford to a Plymouth? A Chevrolet? A Pontiac? Then, how do you go about comparing the different warranties? And how do you know when a dealer has offered you the best possible price? What about that salesperson? Are the statements the salesperson made really trustworthy?

A popular practice of some automobile dealers is "low balling." The husband and wife have finally talked the salesperson into selling an almost-new Chevrolet for only $3400—a really low price. The salesperson writes up the contract, congratulates the family on their new car, and goes away to find the manager who must okay all sales. The children play in their new automobile while the husband and wife smile about the good buy they made. Then the salesperson returns with the manager one step behind, shouting at the salesperson and threatening to fire him or her. The salesperson explains that the manager will not okay the contract because the price was incorrectly quoted. The salesperson apologizes profusely. Less than one hour later, the family drives home in the very automobile they wanted, but it cost them $3850. To the family, it was still a "fair price for such a fine car," and besides, they did help get the salesperson out of trouble. To the dealer, it meant an extra profit of $200 above the market value, which was really $3650.

Financing automobiles is a major problem area. Unknowingly, millions of consumers are financing their automobiles at interest rates that are simply too high. Why waste money when you don't have to? They are often uninformed about how easy and valuable it is to shop for better credit terms. Shopping for a better source of credit (which can often be done on the telephone) can easily save $200 to $400. Automobile dealers who advertise "bank rates" have not been to the bank lately. Those dealers are advertising *stated* bank rates, which differ considerably from the effective true annual percentage rates.

Another area of concern is a special financing technique that keeps the monthly installment smaller—the "balloon payment." A new Buick at $5450 can be priced the same at two different dealers, but the financing plans may differ radically. The first dealer says that a 3-year contract requires a monthly payment of $166, while the second says that for the same $450 down payment and length of contract, the monthly payments will be only $151. What the consumer may not fully realize is that the first dealer offers thirty-six equal installments, while the second has thirty-five payments of $151 and a thirty-sixth "balloon" payment of $846.

Repossession of cars happens often with sales finance companies. Big profits do go to those who finance cars as well as to the sellers. Selling a car which cost a dealer $1100 for $1400 yields a profit. A larger profit may be made by selling the promissory note to a sales finance company that later repossesses the car when payments are missed. Owners of cars that break down can raise all the fuss they want to with the auto dealer, but they had better not miss those installment payments. Usually, the consumer has little recourse. Upon repossession, the sales finance company sells the car for whatever it can get and bills the consumer for the difference. Often a court judgment is entered against the consumer demanding that he or she pay the amount then due. If the consumer owed $600 on a car worth only $475, and it is sold for only $200 after repossession (sometimes at an "auction" to the dealer's brother-in-law), the consumer still owes the $400 difference plus repossession charges of another $100 or so. Sometimes this unfortunate situation can be avoided, but to do so consumers must become knowledgeable.

Equally staggering amounts of money are spent on insurance premiums. A 17-year-old boy must pay as much as 3⅓ times what his father pays for the same coverage. Some consumers find that because of accidents and/or traffic citations, they are classified as "high risks" and cannot buy insurance in the voluntary market at all. In all states, however, such persons can be classified as "assigned risks"; they are then assigned to a selected company, which must write them coverage. Of course, premiums are much higher, but they do have coverage.

What can a good driver do when a company for some unknown reason simply decides not to renew the insurance and sends a cancellation notice? If your car is totally wrecked in an accident and the company offers you a check for $2600 when you know the car is worth $3000, what can you do? And what can we all do about the one-fifth of the nation's drivers going around without insurance?

Automobile products and related services

are another large area of consumer concern. Fraudulent repair services, deceptive transmission "specialists," emergency-towing frauds, gas station gyps, and ordinary incompetence take billions of dollars from millions of consumers every year. One enterprising gas station hired a man to drive on a certain section of the highway and yell to motorists driving along beside him, "Hey! Your back tire is wobbling!" Of course, most drivers pulled over at the nearest service station, which just happened to be the station under discussion. The "repairs" usually resulted in a bill of $80 or more.

Tires and gasoline are other products that are almost impossible to buy with confidence. Amazingly, a 7.75-14, or 7.50-14, or 195-R 14, or ER 78-14 or P195/75R14 tire will all fit the same car, since they are basically the same size. Several cord materials are available in each of those sizes, but how do you compare the twenty or more types and sizes of tires that can fit your automobile? Or the 1800 different brand names? Similarly, consumers cannot compare gasolines effectively because accurate octane ratings are not posted on all gasoline pumps. And since lubricants do differ, what type and weight of oil is best for your car?

Yes, consumers have problems in the automotive world. In most cases, there is ignorance and in others a lack of information. Sometimes, misinformation, deception, or fraud exists. An examination of the topic of automobiles reveals several areas of consumer interest: the cost of operating and choosing an automobile, financing an automobile, maintaining it, automobile insurance, and some social concerns about automobiles in general.

THE HIGH COST OF OPERATING AN AUTOMOBILE

The average of 10,000 to 15,000 miles driven every year costs each driver many dollars. And only the individual driver can calculate the precise costs for a particular vehicle. However, there are some estimated costs for driving a car. Data from the U.S. Department of Transportation's Federal Highway Administration (FHA) suggest that it costs 20.5 cents per mile to drive a standard size car, 16.8 cents for a compact, and 14.5 cents for a subcompact.

Although this information is useful, it just isn't realistic. The FHA assumes that the car will be driven for 10 years; the figures do not include a personal property tax; and no account is taken of finance charges. The Hertz Corporation puts out cost data for automobiles too, and their figures are much higher, as shown in Table 10-1.

Hertz's method assigns a higher proportion of costs to the first years of ownership because of the higher depreciation during those early years. When a new car leaves the showroom

TABLE 10-1

Hertz Estimates of the Cost per Mile of Automobile Ownership*

Years of Use	Subcompact	Intermediate	Standard
1	27.6 cents	34.3 cents	38.7 cents
2	25.7 cents	33.6 cents	37.6 cents
3	24.6 cents	32.3 cents	36.2 cents
4	22.5 cents	29.6 cents	33.4 cents
5	19.7 cents	26.5 cents	30.2 cents
10	15.8 cents	20.5 cents	22.2 cents

* Extrapolated to 1979 based upon earlier data.

Cost of Owning and Operating an Automobile
1979*

SUBURBAN–BASED OPERATION TOTAL COSTS: CENTS PER MILE							
SIZE	ORIGINAL VEHICLE COST DEPRECIATED	MAINTENANCE, ACCESSORIES, PARTS, & TIRES	GAS & OIL (EXCLUDING TAXES)	GARAGE, PARKING, & TOLLS	INSURANCE	STATE & FEDERAL TAXES	TOTAL COST
STANDARD** WITH STANDARD EQUIP- MENT, WEIGH MORE THAN 4000 LB EMPTY.	5.6	4.8	3.8	2.5	2.0	1.8	20.5
COMPACT WEIGH MORE THAN 2700 LB BUT LESS THAN 3600 LB EMPTY.	4.4	3.9	2.9	2.4	1.8	1.4	16.8
SUB COMPACT WEIGH LESS THAN 2700 LB EMPTY.	3.7	3.6	2.1	2.4	1.7	1.0	14.5

Source: U.S. Deptartment of Transportation, Federal Highway Administration, Office of Highway Statistics Division.

*Extrapolated data from earlier FHA estimates.

**Not shown in this study are the intermediate-size cars that weigh 3600 to 4000 lb empty.

FIGURE 10-1   Cost of owning and operating an automobile

floor, it *depreciates* (or loses) 30 to 33 percent of its value simply because it is now a used car. Using a $5000 car as an example, the depreciation for the first year is approximately $1650. Maintenance for the same year will probably be about $100. Depreciation during the second year (estimated to be 25.5 percent) amounts to another $1275, while maintenance costs rise to over $100. Often the best time to trade in the automobile is during the fourth year, since from that point on maintenance costs usually exceed depreciation. Thus the more realistic data from Hertz suggests that it costs 38.7 cents per mile to drive a standard-

What ever gave you the idea that it was hard on gas.

Courtesy of Edd Uluschak.

size car for the first year, 34.3 cents for an intermediate, and 27.6 cents for a subcompact.

All these estimates assume reasonable increases in the cost of gasoline and the taxes on it. Should, for example, a special tax of 30 cents per gallon be added to help reduce consumption and encourage people to conserve, the cost per mile for driving would necessarily be increased. Using the 30-cent figure and assuming driving 10,000 miles per year at 20 miles per gallon, the driver would have to pay an extra $150 in taxes. This amounts to an additional 1.5 cents per mile.

If you are anywhere near typical, transportation costs will rank only behind shelter and food costs as your biggest yearly outlay. Amounts of $1500 to $3000 a year are common. Transportation costs can be lower, however. The age of the car, type of vehicle, running condition of the car, miles per gallon it gets, distances driven, taxes, driving habits, insurance, and other factors all affect the final cost. Can you beat the average costs? Yes, in many cases, if you learn how and are willing to make some of the necessary trade-offs. For example, deciding to drive a subcompact instead of a standard-size car can reduce costs during the first year of ownership from 38.7 cents per mile to 27.6 cents—that's more than $1000 per year!

TO LEASE OR BUY OR NOT BUY AT ALL

When faced with the need for a new automobile, you might look into the possibility of a long-term lease. Sears, Roebuck & Company is so confident that in the future people will be leasing rather than buying new automobiles that they plan to offer leasing arrangements through their catalog. Sears figures that it won't be too many years before three-fourths of all new automobile buyers will become lessees instead.

Closed-end lease contracts are commonly for 12 to 36 months. With a closed-end lease, you pay a set amount per month for the term of the lease, and that's it. You turn the car in at the end of the term. *Open-ended* leases are

actually conditional sales contracts. With an open-ended lease, which costs less per month, at the end of the lease period the customer is legally obligated to pay the company the difference between what the car will sell for and the amount that has been set aside for depreciation as part of the monthly payments (monthly depreciation reserve). Suppose a car cost $8000 to start with. Lease payments are $145 a month, $100 of which goes into the depreciation reserve. Over 3 years, the reserve amounts to $3600, leaving a balance of $4400. You can either buy the car yourself for the balance owed ($4400), have the leasing company sell it for you, or sell it yourself. Leasing companies try to estimate depreciation as accurately as they can, but lots of factors are involved. If the car has depreciated more than expected and is worth only $3800, you have to come up with the extra $600. Of course, if it depreciates less than expected, you get that amount back.

The average costs of operating a well-maintained leased automobile are very similar to those of owning one—but the consumer should remember that the leasing agency has to make a profit too. If you do decide to lease an automobile, comparison shopping is strongly recommended. Rates vary by as much as 12 to 15 percent, and leasing contracts are not standardized.

Most of the advantages of leasing are noneconomic. (1) Once the contract is signed, the consumer has a more definite estimate of the cost of driving. (2) With a good contractual lease covering an extension of the warranted parts, which costs more, the consumer does not need to worry about major repair costs. (3) The lease may call for a monthly cost of $155 for a small Chevrolet, of which $20 is for maintenance, an arrangement that means that the driver's only other expenses will be for gasoline and oil. (4) The driver usually does not have to bother with insurance, as the leasing company generally provides it. One economic advantage is that the consumer has less capital invested in the car; he or she has to put up the first and last months' payments and then just make the monthly installments.

There are also disadvantages to leasing. The major one is economic, because a careful shopper with a good credit rating can get the same low price when buying a new automobile and the same low interest rates as the big companies. Additionally, more competitive insurance rates could probably be obtained through comparison shopping. If the consumer wants to get out of a leasing contract before it expires, there is an extra charge. Another disadvantage is that at the end of the lease you have nothing. You may have the option to buy the car after the expiration of the contract, but in that case it would probably have been cheaper to have bought it in the first place.

A growing number of people have decided to avoid the entire problem of deciding whether to buy or to lease. They are doing neither! They walk, use public transportation, ride bicycles, get occasional lifts from friends and acquaintances who have cars, and sometimes rent cars on a short-term basis. Depending upon your values, where you work and live, and the availability of other forms of transportation, you could save many hundreds of dollars each year by choosing not to have an automobile. And there are all kinds of noneconomic health and psychic benefits too. Shouldn't you think about the possibilities?

BUYING A NEW AUTOMOBILE

A consumer considering buying a new automobile must answer many questions: Do I just want a new car or do I really need a new one? How much can I afford to pay? Should I trade in my old car, or should I try to sell it? What make of car should I buy? Which model? Which optional equipment or accessories should I get? When should I buy? Where? What about service? What about warranties? Answers to these and many similar questions must be found by the wise automobile consumer.

Needs and Wants

An investment of $4000 to $9000 for a new car should hardly be taken lightly. Except for buying a home, the purchase of a new automobile is probably the largest financial decision a consumer will ever make. The individual or family must decide whether a new car is a true necessity or something that is merely "wanted."

A teenage daughter or son may exert heavy pressure in the decision-making process. The teenager may want a sportier model than a four-door sedan, for instance. Or perhaps the old automobile will become the teenager's after—and if—the new car is purchased. The teenager may clearly see the need for the family to buy that new car, even though a parent might feel no real need exists.

Another family might feel that a new car is a necessity, particularly if both parents work and one uses a car to commute long distances. In such cases, a highly dependable new automobile may be needed. Retired family members may or may not need a new car. Perhaps they will not drive the car often, but they feel that they need a really dependable one. Maybe they need a new car, since a retired couple may have more time to travel and may want the security of a new car. Or, for once they might simply like to have a new car. The young married couple, as well as young singles, have similar considerations.

For all of us, the automobile is a type of status symbol. In some cases it is a reverse status symbol—a wealthy person may drive a lousy-looking car. We may not consciously buy with status in mind, but when others see us stepping in and out of *our* car there is a tendency to label us and our position in life according to the make, model, and year of that car. The automobile is a reflection of how we would like others to see us or as we see ourselves. Cars symbolize our self-reliance and our yearning for private adventure. For many, a car is a love object. Moreover, automobiles are a form of *conspicuous consumption*—they demonstrate to others that "I am somebody" and "I can afford" this car.

Obsolescence

Being obsolete implies being "of little or no value." And obsolescence is a very important part of the automobile world. *Planned obsoles-*

cence involves changing a product, usually just superficially, in order to increase sales. The annual model changes from one year to the next are rarely the result of engineering breakthroughs. Instead, the changes are usually slight and made so that you might be encouraged to look at your "2-year-old car and think that it's out of style." *Built-in obsolescence* is different. It involves deliberate under-engineering so that the product wears out and needs replacement. With the average American car lasting only 5 or 6 years, one wonders about built-in obsolescence. Consider only two examples. Cars are simply not designed to withstand crashes at even 12 miles per hour. At that speed, repairs to an average car can cost nearly $1000. Also, rustproofing technology is far ahead of the limited amount of rustproofing done to American cars. The question is, why?

This question, among others concerning obsolescence, is being raised by the Federal Trade Commission (FTC). Owen Johnson, Director of the FTC's Bureau of Competition, has recently begun a new probe into the automobile industry. The aim is to determine if antitrust violations exist. This investigation differs from that being conducted by the Justice Department, which may eventually break up the "big three" auto makers into several competitive companies. Johnson's thrust in part is to determine whether frequent styling changes and the necessary retooling make the business too expensive for any other companies to enter the market; in other words, does planned obsolescence keep out competition?

The buyer concerned about obsolescence and engineering technology should know that Detroit makes more major changes in style every 2 years. Thus, the second year of a particular model—normally the even-numbered years—usually has more of the kinks out of it and is a better vehicle.

Automobile Selling Is Different!

American automobile sales are clearly one of the last bastions of *caveat emptor*—let the buyer beware. The puffery in advertising is unbelievable.

"Selling below dealer cost—come see our invoices" is one common line. The truth is that the manufacturer gives the dealer rebates for every car sold *after* it has been sold. Thus, the "invoice" does not show the true full cost of the vehicle to the dealer. Fake scientists quoting unrealistic mileage figures (that are approved by the government) and slinky starlets draped over the hood of the latest models are but some of the techniques designed to appeal to the buyer. And then we have the new car awards. So many new car awards are being given out by *Motor Trend, Road & Track Magazine,* and others that one wonders when the industry will start giving out its own awards. Perhaps they will be called "The Best of the Rest." Seriously, as *Automotive News* questions, how can so many groups come up with standards that would be meaningful to consumers? "After all," the editorial asked, "what qualities make a car stand out above all others? Engineering? Mechanical innovation? Reliability? Economy?"

Once in the showroom, the consumer is fair game for some of the most polished techniques ever thought of in the field of sales. And occasionally ethics are put aside. Recently the Federal Bureau of Investigation (FBI) seized bugging equipment that was used to eavesdrop on the conversations of prospective customers in Tampa. Roger Whitley Chevrolet and Hawke Chrysler-Plymouth dealers were charged with violation of federal laws. It seems that when customers, often a wife and husband, are left alone in a salesperson's office, they assume privacy and talk more freely about the "highest amount they will pay" and similar matters. An intercom system permits listening in on conversations. Assistant U.S. Attorney John Lund said that "We have information that the use of these devices in auto dealerships is fairly widespread, and our investigation is continuing."

When shopping for almost any other product or service in America, the buyer is given a price. Only when buying automobiles are we forced to go back to the centuries-old buying practices of Arab and Mexican markets. As Ralph Ginsberg says, "The list price affixed to the car window (mandated by law) is a fiction. To pay that price would be sufficient evidence to have the buyer declared incompetent and remanded to the funny farm." Comparing prices on many models, considering gobs of accessories, and bargaining with different dealers makes car buying in America truly a unique experience.

Budgeting for a New Automobile

A major purchase such as an automobile must be considered in terms of the entire budget. Any car can easily cost 10 to 13 percent of a family's budget, and a new car is likely to cost a little more. The only way to determine whether or not you can afford a new car is to sit down with a pencil and paper and figure it out. Briefly, you need to review your total financial status and then place a hypothetical figure into the budget for the *real* cost of the car. If you finance your new car, you must determine a total monthly cost figure. This is *not* just the amount of the monthly payment on a loan. You need to add in amounts for insurance, registration fees, license plates, personal property taxes (if applicable in your state), gasoline and oil, maintenance, and miscellaneous. The miscellaneous figure should be enough to cover all the washing, waxing, and polishing that people usually do to new cars. Also, just because an automobile is new does not mean that it will need little maintenance. The U.S. Department of Transportation estimates the annual repair and maintenance costs for a car valued at $4379 to be $81.84 for the first year, $115.37 for the second, $242.65 for the third, and $296.09 for the fourth. Some of the newer models have to be serviced quite often at first.

Thus, you need to examine your financial status and see if you have the necessary down payment, then determine how much it will cost you each month to operate the vehicle above and beyond the monthly installment payment figure. If you made a down payment

of $800 (including $300 in sales taxes, registration, dealer fees, etc.) on a car that cost $4500 with a 3-year loan on the balance of $4000, your monthly payment would be $161.60 at 10 percent interest. Add perhaps $55 for gasoline and oil, $20 for maintenance, $20 for parking and tolls, $10 for personal property taxes, $30 for auto insurance, and $10 for miscellaneous. This adds up to "out-of-pocket" costs per month of $306.60. Actually, the *real* cost should include depreciation (likely to be 33 percent for the first year), so we should include another $125 per month, for a total cost of $431.60 per month for that first year of owning the new $4500 automobile with an $800 down payment. Using this example, you should be able to calculate the cost of an automobile you may be thinking about buying. However, since insurance costs vary so widely, it might be wise to call a couple of companies to get an estimate on what the coverage on a new car will cost. More than one potential buyer has decided against a new car because the budget couldn't handle the combined price of the car and the insurance.

The important step is putting the final hypothetical monthly *real* cost figure into your budget and seeing what happens. If you are in a strong financial position, you may want to recalculate and plan on buying a more expensive model to better suit your tastes. Or, on the other hand, you may decide to wait and save up a larger down payment. Or you may decide to buy a less costly car. Or to keep driving the car you now have. Or to use public transportation. Or to ride a bicycle. Or to walk.

Selection of a New Automobile

Ordinarily, one does not buy a new car merely by going to the nearest automobile dealer and saying, "I'll take that one." Such a hurried, slipshod method of shopping is hardly the behavior of a rational, intelligent, informed consumer. Several points must be considered very carefully. Once the decision to buy is thought out, the next move is to follow a step-by-step, carefully established plan for

"That reminds me—we received a recall letter a little while back—something about a minor defect in the steering wheel and door-latch."

Courtesy of Edd Uluschak.

buying the new car. Then you'll get satisfaction as well as your money's worth. These processes are described below.

Choose the Make and Model. This choice should be made *before* you actually visit the showrooms. Many of us can give a quick answer when someone asks, "What make of new car would you like to buy?" A Ford! A Chrysler! A Buick! Others might say that they are not sure and would need more information.

Several magazines publish information about new cars, including *Motor Trend, Road & Track, Car & Driver, Popular Mechanics,* and *Popular Science.* Consumer rating publications, such as *Consumer Reports* and *Consumers' Research Magazine,* rate new cars and survey the complaints of thousands of customers. Much pertinent information can be found in these publications. Check some well-known "bad news" about your new car before you buy it, as well as the good features.

Beware of Deceptive EPA Mileage Data. Each new automobile must display either on

the price sticker attached to the window or adjacent to it the gasoline mileage estimates as calculated by the Environmental Protection Agency (EPA). Actually, the EPA figures are an offshoot of the agency's testing of new cars for their antipollution performance. The vehicles are tested in simulated situations in a laboratory using a chassis dynamometer. A precise series of starts, stops, and accelerations result in gas-mileage estimates in three types of driving: city, highway, and combined city-highway. Although the tests do measure all models consistently, they are quite unrealistic when compared with actual road tests. Gulf Oil Company ran a series of experiments to compare the EPA estimates with Gulf's "actual road tests." The results were, on the average, a flat 20 percent lower! So, despite the EPA figures—and the accompanying warning that "the actual fuel economy will depend on factors such as individual driving habits and the maintenance condition of the vehicle"—one would be safe in lopping 20 percent off all the mileage claims just for starters.

Helpful information on the sticker includes a comparison of mileage estimates for other models in the same-size class. This is figured on interior volume of the cars, so comparisons do not always include the ones you might expect. In that event, every new-car dealer can give you a free copy of the *EPA/FEA Gas Mileage Guide*. Of considerable value in the guide is the estimated cost of fuel for 15,000 miles. Be aware, however, that the more economical the car, the less meaningful are the gains in mileage. For example, a car that gets 15 miles per gallon (mpg) of gasoline for 15,000 miles will cost $162 more for fuel than a car that gets 20 mpg. But for a car that gets 25 mpg compared with one that gets 30 mpg, the extra cost is only $65. This is in spite of the difference in both cases of 5 mpg. Keep in mind too that certain optional equipment directly affects fuel consumption. Air conditioning will reduce mileage by about 10 percent, and the Federal Energy Administration (FEA) reports that an automatic transmission may reduce mileage 10 to 15 percent in some models.

More realistic and accurate gasoline mileage information can be obtained through the consumer product testing magazines, such as *Consumer Reports*. They use a variety of actual driving tests and "evaluate the overall fuel economy for each car tested during the time we own it (usually six months or more and 3,000 to 10,000 miles)." In one series of tests, the EPA had figures of 22.8 to 24.9 mpg for four subcompacts; all quite similar. *Consumer Reports* discovered "a significant difference in gas mileage between the two Japanese cars and the Vega and Pinto. The Toyota and Datsun were 4 to 7 mpg better in traffic, 5 to 8 mpg better at constant speed, and 5 to 7 mpg better on our one-day trip. Thus, our figures show that there should be an important difference regardless of the type of driving you do." With such dramatic differences in mileage, one might do well to check the consumer publications for this kind of information.

Choose the Accessories and Optional Equipment. These decisions can also be made before you actually go shopping. The same consumer publications cited above give information about the numerous accessories you may

want. Early decisions on such equipment can save you hundreds of dollars when you are faced with a persuasive salespersons. Remember that the training and psychology of the salesperson is to sell you all the options you "need." This equipment can quickly raise the price of your car an extra $1000. Average costs for some accessories—and costs vary according to make and model (the bigger the car the less the charges for optional equipment)—might be as follows: automatic transmission, $300; air conditioning, $475; power brakes, $60; power steering, $150; rear-window defogger, $80; and vinyl roof, $140. The list is almost endless: sun roof, racing stripes, white wall tires, digital clocks, special instrument panels, quadraphonic radios, tape decks, speed regulation devices, adjustable steering columns, etc. Some manufacturers have a lot of this equipment as "standard," while for others a lot of these things are "options." A recent trend is to make almost all these things "options" to help keep the sticker price as low as possible—it looks better in the advertising.

Be sure you get what you pay for, too. Some dealers are putting in foreign radios at the dealership instead of the name-brand factory-installed product. The catch is that the consumer is charged the same price even though the foreign radios cost less. One dealer, who asked not to be identified because of his "delicate relationship with GM," said, "Foreign radios are a better product and they're cheaper. Frankly, I think Delco is substantially overpriced."

Shopping for Your New Automobile

Once you have a firm idea of the make, model, and optional equipment you want, you can begin your comparison shopping with vigor. But when?

When to Buy. This sounds like a peculiar question when you have already decided to buy. However, some months are better than others for getting a good deal. Late summer discounts of $600 to $800 on intermediate-size makes are common because when the new models arrive the old ones will depreciate by

20 to 30 percent overnight. Keep in mind, too, that more than 40 percent of all new-car sales are made with discounts of $600 or more off the "sticker price." If you plan to keep the car for several years, buying just before or after the new models come out will save you many dollars. But if you plan to trade in every 2 or 3 years, your end-of-the-year savings will be offset by heavy depreciation during the first years of ownership.

Other good times to buy are in December and February. At Christmas, few customers are shopping for new automobiles, so the dealers are more willing to "deal." In February, or perhaps early March, when the weather in many parts of the country is bad and customers are disinclined to go shopping, dealers give customers the red-carpet treatment simply because they may be the only prospective buyers that day. A general rule, therefore, is that dealers are more willing to bargain during slack periods.

Buying during a dealer's "big sale" or "special sales promotion" is often good too, especially during the last couple of days of the sale. Competition among salespersons to "win their contest" is keen. Look around the office area for the names of the salespersons, their quotas, and their sales to date. Choose a salesperson close to the leader; if that salesperson wants to win badly enough, he or she might be willing to "reach into his or her own pocket" to make up part of the difference between your offer and what the sales manager will accept.

The Early Phase of Shopping. After the above-mentioned preliminary actions, there are several steps that are quite important in getting the best new automobile for you.

1. Decide whether or not to trade in your old car (if you have one). You may want to sell it outright by advertising in the newspaper. You can easily find the wholesale and retail values of your car by looking it up in *Red Book, Official Used Car Market Values.* It adds or subtracts for various options on your car, its mileage, and its general condition. You can order a copy from the publisher[1] for $5.00 or look at one at your local bank or credit union. A new issue comes out every 45 days. Also, the *Annual Buying Guide of Consumer Reports*[2] lists average retail used-car prices for 1-year old models. If your old automobile is in excellent condition, you may be able to sell it for more than the listed retail value. Regardless of its age, it will pay to clean it up. You will probably get a better resale price. Some minor repairs may also be necessary, but it is usually not wise to have any major work done.

2. Use a worksheet to help you decide which new car to get. As shown in Figure 10-2, list all the important factors that will affect your decision. This simple problem-solving device will make it much easier to compare different makes or models, dealers' prices, and value judgments.

3. Line up your tentative financing for the new automobile (if you are not going to pay cash). For your peace of mind, and to get the best possible credit terms, it is smarter to shop for credit before you actually shop for your automobile. When you have found suitable credit terms, fill out the necessary forms so you can speed up the process when you actually need the money.

4. Visit the various showrooms in which you are interested. It may pay to go to a dealer about whom you have heard favorable comments from friends. Visit some of the heavy advertisers in your immediate area also. The purpose of your trips to these dealers is not to buy a car, it is to get firsthand information to supplement the published data you have already read. Fortunately, some comparative information is available at the dealers. All new-car

[1] National Market Reports, Inc., 900 South Wabash Avenue, Chicago, Ill. 60605

[2] Consumers Union, Mount Vernon, N.Y. 10550

FIGURE 10-2 Comparison Shopping Worksheet

Dealer's name			
Model and make of car			
Base price			
Extra equipment			
Radio			
Automatic transmission			
Power steering			
Air conditioning			
Other extra			
Other extra			
Dealer preparation			
License fees			
Transportation charges			
Taxes			
Other			
Other			
Warranty			
Dealer service quality			
Total price			
Subtract trade-in			
You must pay			

dealers must now, by law, provide written performance data for consumers, including stopping distance, acceleration, passing ability, tire reserve loads, and mileage ratings. Your worksheet will be most helpful here if you are comparing different makes. Keep in mind that it is smart to shop by yourself because your spouse and you (if both of you are informed) can cover twice as much ground and you can explain to those high-pressure salespeople that you "cannot make any final decisions without the better half."

5. Poor warranty service is one of the biggest complaints about automobiles, so check this item carefully. Most manufacturers offer a limited warranty for 12 months or 12,000 miles, whichever comes first. Chrysler and AMC will lend you a car if the repairs take more than 1 day. Warranties are designed to limit the liability of the manufacturer, not just to satisfy customers. Thus, most manufacturers offer a "limited" warranty. AMC provides a "full" warranty, which covers almost everything for the specific number of miles. Of great importance with full warranties is that by law the repairs must be satisfactorily made within a *reasonable amount of time*. Those broad words have not yet been clearly defined by the Federal Trade Commission, but it is obvious that a full warranty is much more valuable than a limited one—especially if you buy a "lemon."

So, examine those warranties. Pick up copies of the warranties that the new cars will have. It is helpful if you briefly discuss the warranty with each dealer, get an explanation of what it covers, get an impression of that dealer's ability to service the vehicle, and then later take the time at home to read the warranty. Some are difficult to read, and specific differences may be important to your decision. Make notations about the warranties on your worksheet.

The Final Phase of Shopping. To put that new car in front of your home, you need to be concerned with getting the best price, making your final decision, and finalizing the financial details.

1. Getting the best price—the lowest possible price—is not as difficult as one might imagine. Fewer than 10 percent of all new-car buyers pay the manufacturer's suggested price on the window sticker. The FTC proposed, with no success, that the "deceptive sticker price" be cleared up so that it would have to be within 3 percent of a level "at which substantial sales have been made."

Several available books will tell you the exact price that a dealer must pay for the various models and the optional equipment.[3] Knowing what the dealer paid the manufacturer for the new car will go a long way toward helping you bargain for the best price.

If you cannot discover the exact price the dealer paid, simply estimate it, using the figures in Table 10-2. For example, if you want a compact model with a base sticker price of $3855 plus air conditioning at $471, rear-window defogger at $43, special instrument package at $45, dual exterior mirrors at $27, and AM-FM stereo radio at $110, the total comes to $4551. Since the car is a compact, multiply the total by the cost factor of 0.86, as shown in the table. This results in a *base figure* of $3913.86, which is likely to be within $50 of what the dealer had to pay for the car. A dealer must earn between $125 and $300 per car to cover the cost of doing business and to make a profit.

A sticky area is what to add to your base figure. Of course you have to add in

[3] *Auto Dealer Costs,* Box 708, Dept. 94, Liberty, N.Y. 12754; *Car Fax,* Fax Publications, Inc., 220 Madison Avenue, N.Y. 10016; *Price Buying Directory,* Consumer's Digest, 6316 North Lincoln Avenue, Chicago, Ill. 60645; *Better Homes and Gardens Car Prices,* Box 374, Des Moines, Iowa 50336; and the April issue of *Consumer Reports,* Consumers Union, Mount Vernon, N.Y. 10550.

TABLE 10-2

The Dealer's Cost for New Automobiles (within $50)

Total of the Sticker Price of the Basic Auto without Options and the List Price of Each Option You Want	Dealer Discount	Cost Factor
Subcompact	13%	0.87
Compact	14%	0.86
Intermediate	18%	0.82
Standard	20%	0.80
Luxury	22%	0.78
Specialty	15%	0.85

transportation costs, sales taxes, and license plate fees. But what about "dealer preparation" charges? On most American models this is already figured into the posted sticker price, but on foreign makes it usually is not. Consumers should beware of any additional stickers on the window showing such charges, as they are likely to represent an extra cushion for profit for dealers and include things you may not want. Dealers deserve some money for preparing the automobile for sale, but how much? A charge of more than $100 is suspect, and anything above that should be considered as part of the dealer's profit.

Following this example through, we then have a base figure of $3913.86, $70 for transportation, $30 in license fees, and $205.14 in sales taxes, for a total of $4219. Your target bargaining price should be between $4344 (allowing for a profit of $125) and $4519 (allowing a profit of $300).

If you are going to trade in an old car, you must be careful because here is where some dealers will get you unless you are careful. For example, let us say that the dealer offers you $850 for your old car and you know that it is only worth $550. Certainly something is fishy—and it is the high new-car price to which you may not have been paying close attention. This is called *high balling.* When people trade in an older car, dealers have a tendency to want to discuss the value of the trade-in rather than the price of the new car. If you seem to be getting a high trade-in on your old car, it makes you feel better—that is, until and unless you realize you are paying too much for the new car. Get the price of the new automobile settled first, and then talk about the value of the trade-in. If the dealer offers you within $150 of what you think your car might bring, it might be better to let the dealer take it rather than go through all the hassle and expense of selling it yourself.

When the consumer knows the dealer's cost and adds in a profit, the consumer is in control of the situation. You must now as a wise consumer offer a low but realistically fair price. After the salesperson stops laughing, convince him or her that you are serious and stand your ground. If the salesperson wants to make the sale or dicker some more, fine, but get the best offer in writing. Also, have the itemized counteroffer signed by an officer of the company. This will prevent *low balling,* where the irate sales manager chews out the salesperson for offering such a "good deal" and cancels it, and then the price rises—after you've had your heart set on buying that car. Do not sign anything yourself! Get another firm price on the car you want from another dealer or two and you will be getting much closer to your final decision. Also, be prepared for a telephone call from any of the dealers you visited, because they usually will give you another lower counteroffer after you have left the premises. Their business is selling cars, even if the profit margin is sometimes small.

There are some national buying clubs which, for a $10 to $15 membership fee, will send you the names of new-car dealers in your area who will sell you the exact automobile you want for $125 over dealer cost.[4] Sometimes such a service is available through your local credit union too. Many people use such services just to get the computer printout on the dealer's costs for the model and options they want. They then take it to their local dealer to be in a stronger bargaining position. After all this shopping for price, do *not* accept the final low price offered to you because there is *more* than price to consider in buying a new automobile.

2. Choose your dealer with service in mind. The warranty on your new automobile is only as good as the dealer. For most warranty work on new cars, "authorized" servicing and repair work must be done or the warranty becomes void. Your neighborhood garage may qualify as authorized service and repair, but you may decide to have much of the servicing done by the dealer from whom you buy the new car. When checking for service, you might go to the waiting-room area and ask a few customers to comment on the quality of work done on their cars. So, carefully consider this factor on your worksheet and note your comments under "dealer service quality." If you find that one dealer in particular does a poor servicing job, avoid that dealer, even if the quoted price is $100 to $150 less than the competitors. You want a dealer who willingly handles complaints, does repairs that are not necessarily covered under warranty for free, charges fair prices, does quality work, and does business reasonably close to where you live.

3. Accept only the car you want with the options you want. If the exact car you want is unavailable, let your "new-car fever" subside and order what you want—it will only be 6 to 8 weeks. That's not much time compared with how long you will be keeping it.

4. Make your final decision within comfort-

---

[4] For example, Car/Puter International, 1603 Bushwick Avenue, Brooklyn N.Y. 11207.

able surroundings, preferably at home. Take out your worksheet and look it over carefully while narrowing your choice. Look over every item. Reexamine those categories that you feel are really important and weigh them accordingly. Perhaps sleep on it, then make your decision. Feel relieved? You should, because you have carefully decided how to make the second largest expenditure in your life. You are about to make a *good buy*—one at a fair price that satisfies your needs and wants.

5. Before you go back to your chosen dealer, stop by your lending agency and complete the loan forms. More than likely the final figure you will pay the dealer will be very close to the estimate you and your lending agency previously arrived at. Pick up the check to take to the dealer. And be certain to road-test your new automobile (as if it were a used one), since a typical new car has more than 30 defects. Have the dealer make needed repairs and adjustments before you hand over the check, or get a promise in writing that all problems found within the first 2000 miles of driving will be fixed by the dealer.

BUYING A USED AUTOMOBILE

People buy used automobiles rather than new ones for a variety of reasons. The biggest reason, of course, is money. After reviewing their budget, many consumers find that they cannot afford a new automobile. Or they just do not want to pay for all that depreciation. Or if the car is mainly to drive around town, perhaps just to work or for shopping, it might be more economical to buy a used automobile. Some people never buy a new car, figuring that after a year or two the original owner will have taken care of all the little, nagging problems, in addition to having "paid" for the early heavy depreciation. The depreciation versus maintenance relationship shows, however, that buying a used car may mean buying someone else's problems. On the average, the maintenance costs of a car become rather high during the fourth year. The big expenses usually occur between 50,000 and 60,000 miles; after that repair costs are rather constant. Therefore, when shopping for a used car, be very careful that you are buying a car that is mechanically and structurally sound and safe, is not overpriced, and will not cost too much to repair and maintain.

What Type of Car?
The make, model, and year you finally decide on depends mainly on how much money you intend to spend. Besides price, you probably will want to consider such factors as gas mileage, appearance, power, and special equipment. Most of your decisions in buying a used car should be the same as those described in the previous section on buying a new automobile. However, several aspects of buying a used car are different and should be examined.

Once you have decided how much to spend (remember in your estimating that maintenance and repair costs will be somewhat higher, so raise that figure), you can concentrate on which make, model, and year to buy. Several well-known guides are available, and any lending agency is likely to have one or more of them: *N.A.D.A.* (*National Automobile Dealers Association*) *Official Used Car Guide, Kelley Blue Book Market Report, Red Book Official Used Car Valuation,* and *Black Book Official Used Car Market Guide.* These books on selling prices for used cars are an invaluable source of help in finding out how far your money will go. Visit any bank or credit union and look up the information you need. Also, the *Annual Buying Guide* issue of *Consumer Reports* lists suggested retail prices that you might expect to pay for cars that are 1 year old. The magazine offers descriptive comments about desirable and undesirable features on the numerous makes and models in addition to the frequency-of-repair record for each automobile.

From one of the official guides to car prices, $4000 for a used automobile will probably buy you a 2-year-old, 6-cylinder, 2-door Ford

Er . . . appears to have been a spelling error.

Courtesy of Edd Uluschak.

Maverick; a 3-year-old, 6-cylinder, 2-door Chevrolet Nova; a 3-year-old, 8-cylinder, 2-door Ford Torino; a 3-year-old, 6-cylinder, 2-door Plymouth Duster Satellite; a 3-year-old, 4-cylinder, 2-door Ford Mustang; a 4-year-old, 8-cylinder, 2-door Oldsmobile Cutlass; a 6-year-old, 8-cylinder, 2-door Cadillac Fleetwood El Dorado; or a lot of other cars. When you consider licensing, gasoline, and repairs on a 6-year-old Cadillac as compared with a three-year-old Mustang, you are likely to discover that the Cadillac would be too expensive to maintain. Therefore, when deciding on what type of car you hope to buy you will have to be somewhat flexible on both the make and year. If you simply must have a certain make of car, you can still be flexible about the year and the different models of that same car.

It is important that you narrow your selection down to a few specific models. Otherwise, you could wind up being very unhappy. Persuasive salespersons have been known to talk customers into buying the kind of car that the salesperson wants them to buy—the one the salesperson wants to get rid of.

Where to Buy

Once you have chosen two or three models that fit your budget and needs, you are ready to begin shopping. You are more likely to get a better automobile from a friend, relative, or neighbor or from a new-car dealer than from a dealer specializing in used cars or from answering private newspaper advertisements. New-car dealers usually resell their better used cars to the public and wholesale the poorer ones to the used-car dealers, either directly or through auctions. Also, new-car dealers have more complete service facilities to back up the short-term warranty they commonly offer with used automobiles. Used-car dealers often do not have service facilities. And compared with new-car dealers, they do not stay in business as long. It's important to have someone reliable there at the dealership to back up the warranty and perhaps provide other service.

Choosing a Used Car

After you have located several used cars that fit the basic description of what you want, it is time to undertake the serious process of choosing the best one. Be curious, cautious, suspicious, and observant, since the previous owner must have had some good reason for getting rid of it. You would do well to avoid used cars that have had their appearance cleaned up with body and engine paint. A slightly dirty car could be a more honest purchase. Perhaps you will immediately eliminate two or three because the seller seemed a little "unfriendly" or "not trustworthy" during your first visit, or because the seller will not provide the commonly accepted warranty of "30 days/100 percent parts and labor" *and* "90 days/50 percent parts and labor." Make sure you understand the warranty clearly because you may need to use it later.

Some states have legislation pending for a "report-card" warranty for used cars. "A" would mean that the vehicle is unconditionally warrantied for 30 days or 1000 miles, and the power train (engine, transmission, and rear axle) warrantied for an additional 60 days or 2000 miles. "B" would carry the 30-day unconditional warranty with no power train coverage. "C" would have a 30-day or 1000-mile power train warranty only. "D" would have no warranty and be sold "As Is." A Federal Trade Commission proposal will require that the 13 million annual used-car customers who buy from dealers be told about dealer repairs or defects already discovered, and if the car came from a rental firm or fleet owner. Each major system, from brakes to transmission, would be checked either "OK" or "not OK."

To avoid buying someone else's problems, you should use common sense in addition to making several tests upon the vehicle. Never buy in a hurry, at night, in the rain, or under any condition that hides aspects of the car or keeps you from examining everything about the car, inside and out. If you do not know enough about automobiles to feel reasonably confident, get a knowledgeable mechanic to check your final selection. Pay $20 or so; it will be well worth it in the long run. Consumer's Union provides a descriptive checklist on what to look for when buying a used automobile,[5] and the important factors are summarized below.

On-the-Lot Tests. Look for/at (1) freedom from signs of wear and tear, such as on seat cushions, brake pedals, arm rests, and carpet-

[5] *How to Buy a Used Car*, Consumers Union, 256 Washington Street, Mount Vernon, N.Y. 10550 (28 pages).

ing; (2) tire wear, particularly uneven wear (the front tire might have been exchanged with the spare in the trunk to mask a front-end problem, so check it too); (3) freedom from bad rust spots and flaking paint; (4) body and frame damage, such as ripples in the fenders, dents or paint that doesn't match, repainting, or excessive rust; (5) the fit of windows and doors; (6) front-wheel bearings and suspension joints, such as looseness when each front wheel is shaken in and out at the top of the tire; (7) freedom from internal leaks of brake fluid, such as having the brake pedal sink slowly under steady heavy pressure for one minute or so; (8) lights, switches, controls, and safety devices (including seat belts); (9) shock absorbers, such as continued bouncing when you push down hard on one corner of the vehicle.

Driving Tests. Look for/at (10) front wheels and back wheels in line (have someone else drive it and you follow); (11) engine's pickup action; (12) transmission performance (smooth shifts and absence of noise); (13) performance of the brakes (pulling to one side, noises, etc.); (14) steering performance (ease, lack of more than 1 inch of free play); (15) piston rings (blue or white smoky exhaust after slowing down from 45 mph to 20 mph and then accelerating); (16) road testing over a rough road (for steering and noises); and (17) freedom from overheating.

Shop Tests. Look for/at (18) the engine's compression pressure; (19) the brakes and the wheel bearings; and (20) several important things with the car raised on a lift (such as oil leaks, worn mufflers, and signs of repairs). Use of the Consumers Union checklist will help you to conduct on-the-lot and driving tests consistently and effectively on several used automobiles.

You can narrow your choice to perhaps two cars by combining a comparison-shopping worksheet (such as shown earlier in Figure 10-2) and a checklist. Simply change the headings on the worksheet to compare specific vehicles. Should the testing indicate that something is wrong with a particular car, note it on the worksheet and estimate the cost of repairing it, because you may decide to buy a car that has a defect or two. Used cars *are* used, and some wear is to be expected. If an automobile is in basically good condition, one or two repairs might put it into excellent condition.

Accurate mileage is better assured now because of the federal law (part of the Motor Vehicle Information and Cost Savings Act) which requires that a signed mileage disclosure statement indicating the truthfulness of the odometer be given to the buyer. If you have the slightest doubt, however, it is simple to telephone the prior owner to be sure. Consumers who are wronged can sue the seller for civil damages in the amount of $1500 or three times the amount of actual damages, whichever is greater, in addition to court costs and reasonable attorney's fees. You must be able to prove intent to mislead and defraud as well as who committed the violation. It is not as hard as you might think.

It is also possible that the vehicle may be one of the 15 million that have some unrepaired safety defects. By calling the National Highway Traffic Safety Administration's toll-free hotline (800-424-9393) and giving them the make, model, year, and vehicle identification number (VIN), you can get a report on that car. Defect recalls can then still be repaired by an authorized dealer for free.

The final choice of your used car depends on many things, but perhaps most important is the shop test. For the final one or two choices, take the checklist and car(s) to your local mechanic and give him or her a fee of about $20 per inspection. Or you can take the vehicle to a reliable automobile diagnostic center, where for a flat fee of $20 to $25 they will thoroughly examine the car and give you a written report of their findings. Either way, the car you buy will be one about which you have learned much, and it will probably perform as you expect.

MAINTAINING YOUR AUTOMOBILE

The total cost per mile of operating a vehicle can be broken down into *fixed expenses* (such as insurance, taxes, license, registration, and depreciation) and *variable expenses* (such as gasoline, oil, tires, and maintenance). The totals, of course, are different in various parts of the country.

To save money, a consumer can buy an automobile with smaller fixed costs (such as a compact model). But once you have bought any automobile, you have to operate it. The wise consumer, therefore, tries to maintain the automobile properly, but at reasonable cost. Let us examine some of the factors in maintaining an automobile.

Warranty Coverage

For most new automobiles the warranty lasts for 12 months or 12,000 miles. Some manufacturers have more liberal benefits, and the informed consumer carefully reads the warranty and uses the warranty service when it is needed. For used cars, the warranty period is usually much shorter, and the responsibilities of the consumer become greater. Should the consumer suspect something is beginning to "go" when the car is still under warranty, this must be brought to the attention of the dealer. Get the dealer to examine the situation carefully and certify in writing that it is okay or that the dealer investigated for that particular problem and found nothing. Should the car break down because of that problem just after the warranty period expires, the consumer would have no recourse without something from the dealer in writing.

Secret extended warranties are special programs made available by all manufacturers but not known to all customers. After the warranty has expired, many repairs are selectively paid for by the manufacturer, based upon the factory's experience with the failure of a component. You usually don't find out about it unless you have a good relationship with the local new-car dealership. It is a "word-of-mouth extended warranty." If you have not been having your new vehicle regularly serviced at the dealership, you will probably not find out which items may be eligible for extended replacement or any other extra benefits authorized by the factory. Ford fixed more than 12 million vehicles for rust damage under such a plan. Chevrolet replaced front fenders on millions of Vegas because of rust also. And almost all manufacturers have had extended secret warranty coverage on premature engine failures because of design problems in valves, rings, pistons, etc.

The Ford rust program was brought out into the open by Ralph Nader's Center for Automotive Safety, which reported in a statement that: "Ford never announced the program to the general public. It has not notified the owners of the cars of the program's existence. Instead it was made available to favored customers only at the discretion of Ford regional factory representatives." This type of secret program is designed to pacify the customers who complain loudly, but unfairly discriminates against those customers who do not. The Federal Trade Commission is considering making regulations in this area, but in the meantime it pays to get to know your dealer and find out what characteristics about your car have already been or might be covered under such an extended warranty program. You have to ask—the dealer is under no legal obligation to tell you anything.

Automobile Complaints and Repairability
The federal Office for Consumer Affairs and most state offices for consumer protection report that automobiles bring more complaints than any other product. Problems range from rattles in new cars to poor warranty service, and from high labor costs to outright fraud in repairs. Many of the complaints stem from the design and manufacturing quality control of cars in the first place. But, then again there is the age-old problem of consumer ignorance.

The problems of automobile safety and repairability are basically controlled by the Detroit manufacturers. Safety has improved in recent years, and not just because drivers are not going as fast as before. Many agree that it is because of the numerous safety regulations required to be built into automobiles. In the last 10 years the number of deaths per mile has dropped, and they could be lower with additional safety regulations, says the Department of Transportation's Brock Adams. Former National Highway Traffic Safety Administration head Douglas Toms believes that today's 45,000 deaths could be cut to 20,000 for an additional cost of $150 per car. He labels industry figures running as high as $1000 for the same safety devices as being "vastly overstated and exaggerated."

Repair bills for accidents are soaring. In a study done for the American Mutual Insurance Alliance, the cost for labor and parts were calculated for a front-end collision. Parts included were a fender, headlight, bumper, grille, hood, radiator, windshield, fan, and water pump. For a Chevrolet Impala the 1970 cost was $825.73; in 1976 it was $1576.53—an increase of 91 percent. For a Ford Mustang, it was $847.60 in 1970 and $1576.12 in 1976—an increase of 98 percent. It is estimated that over the following 6 years—through 1982—similar price increases will occur. These increases are far greater than the general rate of inflation and seem to be primarily the result of two factors: the more rapid increase in prices for parts themselves, and the tendency of mechanics to replace parts instead of repairing them.

General repairability of automobiles is often a result of poor design. To simply replace the spark plugs in some models requires the physical abilities of a contortionist. And if the plugs are hard to replace, the repairperson must charge the consumer more. Another example of poor design: it costs $15.80 to replace a $4.00 headlight on most Toyota models—to get to the bulb, the entire grill has to come off. At present, automobile insurance and government officials are developing and refining "damageability and repairability" indexes of different makes and models of automobiles. These rating systems will be most helpful to consumers and insurance people, as those cars more susceptible to losses should have larger premiums. Allstate was the first company to develop and use such an indexing system.

Where to Go for Service
Before we describe the various places to get auto service, let us examine a characteristic common to all. An automobile mechanic who performs work on your vehicle automatically has a *mechanic's lien* on your property. This is a legal right to keep and perhaps sell your car if the bill is not paid. Note that this right is not absolute. The U.S. Supreme Court and most recently a federal district court have ruled that such acts are unconstitutional unless there is a court trial or hearing. So, any mechanic can hold your car until the bill is paid, but the mechanic must go to court to establish the legality of the bill and get the court's permission to sell the car. The consumer/owner would therefore have a hearing.

There are distinct differences among the six basic types of places to take your vehicle for maintenance and repairs.

New-Car Dealership. The highest prices are paid here mainly because mechanics are factory trained to handle your car's particular make and model, and they are the highest-paid mechanics in the industry. Replacement parts are factory authorized, and all warranty work on new cars is done. Most dealers are large enough to have many specialists on hand to work on air conditioning, tune-ups, brakes, transmission, and wheel alignments. You don't necessarily get a better job, but you normally will.

Independent Garage. The owner is usually the chief mechanic and on the average employs three others. The charges are generally lower than at a new-car dealership. Since the garage doesn't advertise, the business needs good word-of-mouth comments from satisfied customers—like you. They often lack the sophisticated diagnostic equipment of large operations, and they sometimes have difficulty in keeping experienced mechanics, since they

cannot pay the highest wages. Listen for recommendations of others and you will probably find an independent garage that pleases you at the right price.

Service Station. Since they have such convenient hours, service stations do about one-third of all maintenance work on cars. However, recognize that mechanical work is a sideline of the service station. Most of the work done is minor, and no one is trained in your particular make and model. Also, they have very little specialty equipment available. Very importantly, you cannot judge the quality of the work until they have already done some work on your car. If it is a station where the people know you, or if it is a neighborhood operation, they will try harder to satisfy you since they must depend upon repeat business. If it is a service station on a well-traveled tourist route, any suggestions for immediate repairs should be suspect. In fact, much of the gouging of the public that gives the industry a bad name occurs in such stations.

Franchise Specialty Shop. These people have specialized and usually do just a single job—mufflers, tires, brakes, or transmissions. Because the employees are well trained in the one area and because of bulk buying, costs are normally lower. But this is true only if you are certain you need their service. Such specialists develop "tunnel vision" and often can only see the *one* problem that they are trained to solve. Don't let the brand name outside fool you, because it is not guarantee of quality—anyone with enough money can buy a franchise. Additionally, little or no policing or even training is available from most automobile franchisers.

Mass Merchandiser. Big stores like Wards, Sears, or Woolco that are located in a suburb mass-merchandise auto repairs too. They specialize in the most common kinds of repairs and are not equipped for large jobs. They can offer low-cost parts because of their large buying power, and the parts are generally of the same quality as those available at new-car dealerships. Service and prices for minor repairs and periodic maintenance are probably good.

Diagnostic Center. These are automobile laboratories where for a $20 to $25 fee all the latest diagnostic equipment is applied to your car and you are given an itemized list of what is wrong and what is likely to go wrong. If you have a true diagnostic center available, great, but the concept has been corrupted. Many "diagnostic centers" are set up next door to a repair service which does the work prescribed. Some are so blatant they do the work themselves. Tony Swan, national consumer columnist on automobile affairs, recommends asking two questions. First, "Do you perform repairs?" If the response is yes, they are not a true diagnostic service. The second question is, "Do you have a dynamometer?" If the answer is no, then they are not good enough to diagnose all the things that need to be examined. A dynamometer is an expensive piece of equipment designed to simulate all kinds of actual road conditions, like accelerating, braking, turning, hill climbing, etc.

You have to make the choices according to your needs. However, a few suggestions might be helpful. Generally speaking, the closer you can get to the mechanic who will be working on your car, the better off you will be. And, of course there is no substitute for knowing whom you are dealing with. In a totally new area, ask for recommendations and look for a shop where some of the mechanics have passed one or more of the eight voluntary tests of the National Institute for Automotive Service Excellence (NIASE).

Repair Frauds

Today's safer but increasingly more fragile cars often need repair. During any year one out of every four drivers will be involved in an accident requiring repairs. Also, periodic maintenance is always needed in addition to those occasional emergency repairs when something goes wrong. Therefore, the owners are quite frequently susceptible both to mechanics who are too often incompetent as well as the gyp artists.

Each year, consumers are charged $10 to $12 billion for auto repairs that were not done, were not needed, or were overcharged for. The tricks are innumerable. For example, a Santa Clara, California, Aamco transmission specialist showed a car owner "metal filings" in the transmission pan to convince him of the need for repairs. Actually, the "filings" were harmless grease-sweep, a kind of sawdust used to clean floors, that the "specialist" had put there in the first place. The particular company made more than $1 million before being shut down by the district attorney.

Another nationally known franchise transmission business in New York was cited for "repairing" nonexistent items and unnecessarily replacing parts. One customer was charged $160 for a 22-cent repair. The same firm in Texas was charged with "changing a few bolts" for which the customer paid $350. Car owners don't have to know how to repair a transmission, just take care of it. Simply checking the transmission fluid once a month is easy preventive maintenance. An additional pint or two every 20,000 or 25,000 miles can prevent serious trouble.

Outlets of large companies are also sometimes guilty of similar fraudulent practices. The Montgomery Ward auto-repair shop in Canoga Park, California, charged consumers for brake jobs that were not done, failed to rebuild or replace parts and perform the work necessary in a complete brake job, and made false and misleading statements. Ward agreed to pay $15,000 in costs and obey all state auto repair laws in the future. John Raymond, a reporter for television station KHQU-TV in Houston, tested local repair services in the area. The Sears, Roebuck & Company outlet billed him for $122.33, including charges for a front-end alignment and new shock absorbers. Raymond had put new shock absorbers on just 1 week earlier and had applied ultraviolet spray to the front-end sections of the car. Inspection revealed that no alignment work had

"Of course, it's only a very small leak, but since we'll have the radiator off, it would pay you to have us check the pump and the fan while we're at it, and if we're going to take *them* off we might as well take the front off to check over the timing chain, and there's not much point in having the front off unless you take the head off to check over the valves, too, and . . ."

Reprinted with permission from CHANGING TIMES Magazine, © Kiplinger Washington Editors, Inc.

been done. The county judge found Sears guilty of deceptive business practices and fined the firm $500.

One Maryland independent businessman, Riley T. Ferebee, in a rare criminal action, was sent to jail for 1 year and had his business closed by the Prince Georges County Department of Licenses and Permits. He was convicted on two separate occasions of fraud, which in most places simply results in a civil case and a fine. Numerous customers testified that he "had improperly repaired their cars, raised prices on repairs without informing them, and refused to honor warranties." One man testified "that a new battery was taken from his car while it was at Ferebee's business, and replaced with an older one." He said he "discovered the switch when one of Ferebee's repairmen used my battery to 'jump start' my own car after it wouldn't start."

Newspaper reporters, as well as television investigative reporters, in major cities occasionally do something to make an automobile run poorly and then take it to several mechanics to be repaired. One Dallas newspaper had the distributor rotor ground down so that it was defective and made the car "cough" when the accelerator was pressed. The plastic and brass part cost 99 cents to replace; however, getting it repaired in the marketplace resulted in some surprising findings.

Twelve different repair shops in the Dallas area tried to fix the coughing, backfiring automobile. The standard charge for diagnosing and repairing a defective rotor should range from $9.50 to $11.50, according to the commonly used rate book, *Chilton's Labor Guide and Parts Manual*. The bills ranged from $1 to $54.60. Two of the repair shops wanted the car to be left for additional work, estimated to cost up to $130. One mechanic correctly diagnosed the problem and replaced the part for $1. And, in spite of the fact that the car was otherwise in tiptop mechanical condition, six repairpersons found other things that needed fixing or replacement.

The rate-book gimmick is also popular. The need for a job-estimate book for the cost of labor and parts is very real, but there are some problems associated with it. The average dealer-employed mechanic earns $7.50 an hour, while the shop owner charges about $16.00 per hour for work done. Therefore, the skilled mechanic can increase earnings by completing a repair job in less time than the book estimates, while the customer is charged for the full time. This technique is used at all types of places. Most mechanics get an equal split of the hourly service charge customers pay after the mechanics have been credited with 40 hours in 1 week. One convenient way to beat the time estimates in the book is to fail to perform follow-through tests: not checking or adjusting everything. Or the mechanic can replace parts rather than repair them, since it is quicker. Of course, for consumers these actions raise prices.

The highway gasoline station cheats take millions of dollars with ingenious gimmicks. A dishonest mechanic can quickly pull a coil, loosen a cable, cause a spark in the distributor, puncture a radiator hose, cut a fan belt, or squirt oil on a fuel pump or shock absorber to simulate a leak, reports Jack Anderson. This nationally known columnist claims he has evidence that "some of the nation's biggest service station chains use these modern highwaymen to push tires, batteries and accessories upon unwary motorists."

An accomplished dishonest mechanic can puncture a tire by thrusting a sharpened screwdriver between the treads while checking the air pressure, even while the consumer is watching. Once the car is up on the rack, the customer really begins to pay. The gyp artists prefer to deal with men because they are less likely to ask questions while the work is going on (something about "knowing it all already"), and also they are less likely to complain when they realize they were taken. The big oil companies claim to know nothing about such large-scale operations, but certainly many stations are selling more than their share of tires, batteries, and accessories.

A footnote to this story is the recent action by the House Small Business Committee recommending that the oil companies be prevented from owning retail outlets, and placing strong restrictions on their power over independent stations that sell their brands of gasoline. This would directly involve about 15,000 of the nation's 190,000 service stations. Representative John D. Dingell observed that the "effect of oil companies' control was to stifle competition. Independent businessmen who depend on contracts with large refiners are being squeezed by pressures to sell gasoline at unprofitable prices and to sell products other than gasoline—such as tires and batteries—forced on them by the oil companies."

The really desperate dealers might purposely foul up a car and then repair it, but most dishonest automobile repairpersons do not have to go that far. It is too easy to use more foolproof ways. By raising your car improperly on the rack, any mechanic can show you a loose wheel. Sixty-five dollars later for ball joints (which were not replaced because they were just fine), the car is raised on the rack again—this time properly—and the wheel is solid.

A resealing job on your transmission will cost you $55 when all you might really get is a $10 rear seal replacement. Carburetors, which cost $45 to $90, almost never need replacing; a $9 needle valve and seat is usually all it takes (but try and find a mechanic that will do the job that way for you instead of replacing it). The list of repair deceptions is almost endless.

What ought to be done and what you can do are two good questions. Voluntary certification of mechanics is more widely needed in order to identify the qualified people. Look for the orange, blue, and white seal on a plaque or on shoulder patches of persons working in auto shops. These are for mechanics who have passed one or more of the voluntary certification tests given by the National Institute for Automotive Service Excellence. Many states have moved in the direction of required licensing of mechanics. Some states also license the automobile repair shop itself and suspend the license when a mechanic working there is found guilty of fraudulent practices. Another step is to establish more independent automotive diagnostic centers throughout the country. Alabama, Arizona, Tennessee, Puerto Rico, and Washington, D.C. have begun state-run programs, which give free inspection for safety hazards, with funding under the federal Motor Vehicle Information and Cost Savings Act. In addition, independent clinics can completely check out a car for a flat fee of $20 to $30. Some clinics exist now, but most are suspect, as they are connected with repair shops. Such shops must remain independent or the repairs become more important then the diagnostic work. Unfortunately, some of the good, honest ones are going out of business because of a lack of customers.

Individually, there are three "dos" for consumers. *First, shop around for a good mechanic.* Listen to comments from friends and neighbors and you can get a good lead on a knowledgeable one. This mechanic may seem to cost you more, but it will be worth it. *Second, always ask the mechanic for a specific estimate in writing before he or she begins the job, but leave a little leeway for some unforeseen additional costs.* This will give the mechanic the freedom to properly diagnose the repairs, to give you an accurate picture of the costs, and to avoid an overcharge of $10 to $20 for hurry-up jobs that occur when someone says, "How much will it cost?" or "How soon can I get my car back?" Third, *make it a point to get your old parts and examine them.* If new parts go in, then old parts must come out. If you don't understand what was wrong with a particular old part, ask the mechanic to point out the problem on the part itself.

Also, there are some "do nots" in automobile servicing:

- Do not have repairs done in transient areas where you will not see the mechanic again. If you can, have the car towed home; you will probably save money. If repairs are a must, watch the mechanic "like a hawk."
- Do not leave your car where a lot of "kids" work. They need cars to practice on.
- Do not pick a mechanic because he or she can give you quick service. A mechanic who does not have many customers will have to heavily charge those he or she has.

Automobile Maintenance

Fraud and misrepresentation in automobile maintenance occur because the work usually involves the same business firms. The general guidelines noted above are useful in maintaining your automobile, although there is one additional suggestion: practice preventive maintenance.

All new cars have an owner's manual that recommends that certain services be performed after so many miles. Consumers must follow these recommendations for the sake of their own lives and the life of their automobiles. Take the manufacturer's advice, but also consider the type of driver you are and the driving you do. If it is heavy (short trips, cold weather, lots of dust), you should service more frequently. Also, for $5 to $10 the consumer can buy a do-it-yourself shop manual that is detailed and gives enough information for an ordinary consumer to do a lot of basic car servicing. A well-serviced automobile will need fewer repairs than a poorly serviced one.

Most consumers spend about $15 per month for automobile maintenance, as estimated by a U.S. Bureau of Public Roads survey. If consumers would spend a little more, perhaps another $6 or $7, repair work for mechanical failures would be greatly reduced.

Consumers can save money if they have a little mechanical ability and the time to do some of the maintenance. Buying batteries, air filters, oil filters, tune-up kits, and other items from parts stores and installing them yourself can save 50 percent or more of the cost. Wasting money occurs all too often. Field tests by the American Automobile Association "uncovered the fact that over 30 percent of all vehicles waste 21–35 percent of their fuel" because the cars need tune-ups. At that rate it costs more than $80 in wasted gasoline to drive 5000 miles. A tune-up costs much less. An informed consumer and a competent mechanic can provide the best maintenance for an automobile.

AUTOMOBILE INSURANCE

Every 10 minutes there are about 500 automobile accidents, 88 persons are injured, and 1 person is killed. The 18,000,000-plus accidents each year account for more than 4,500,000 injuries and approximately 45,000 deaths. Such staggering economic losses encouraged all states to enact *financial responsibility* laws. These laws are designed to protect the public from those drivers who cannot afford to pay for the damages or injuries they cause. When an accident occurs that involves bodily injury or substantial property damage, all parties must file a report with the proper state agency. It is then that one must provide proof of ability to pay damages up to the minimum amount set by the state. Proof usually takes the form of a bodily-injury and property-damage liability insurance policy, but it can be in the form of putting up cash or other assets. If proof cannot be supplied, the driver's license is supposed to be taken away until financial responsibility is proven.

Financial responsibility laws are one reason for consumers to have insurance protection. Also, sensible persons simply will not drive on today's highways without protecting themselves. The moral argument and the possibility of killing or maiming others is also a reason to buy insurance. An Oregon woman, Lou Guthrie, recently was ordered by the courts to pay $325,000 for injuries to a child caused by her automobile. Since Ms. Guthrie was uninsured, she will be sending a large part of her paycheck to that child's family for the rest of her life. Drivers can avoid such problems

by understanding the types of insurance protection available and buying sufficient coverage.

Types of Insurance Protection

Liability insurance protects the driver in cases where he or she injures or kills someone or damages another's property. The driver is legally liable for the damages, but the insurance protects him or her up to the amount of coverage. There are two types of liability coverage: bodily injury and property damage.

Bodily Injury Liability. This coverage applies when your car injures or kills pedestrians or persons riding in other cars; in some states it covers guests in your car. Liability limits are expressed as a series of numbers separated by diagonal lines. For example, 20/40 indicates that the policy will pay a maximum of $20,000 for bodily injury to one person or $40,000 for all persons in the same accident. Therefore, if three persons were injured in an accident and each successfully sued for $25,000 in bodily-injury damages, the driver with the above coverage would be liable for $75,000. The insurance company would pay the maximum amount of $40,000, and the driver would be responsible for the remaining $35,000.

Bodily-injury policies are often written for the following amounts: 10/20, 20/40, 50/100, and 100/300. The driver in the example above would have been adequately insured with the 50/100 coverage. Bodily-injury coverage is always sold in conjunction with property-damage liability insurance.

Property-Damage Liability. This coverage applies when your vehicle damages the property of others. Usually in an accident the damaged property is an automobile. This insurance also covers damage to telephone poles, lampposts, buildings, and so on. The limit of property-damage liability per accident is expressed as the last figure in a series of numbers separated by diagonal lines, such as 25/50/10. The first two figures refer to the limits of bodily-injury coverage, and the third figure to the amount for property damage. The entire series of numbers is interpreted as: the insurance company will pay a maximum of $25,000 for bodily injury to each person in an accident but will pay only a maximum of $50,000 to all persons involved, and they will pay up to $10,000 for damage to property.

Both bodily-injury and property-damage liability insurance are in effect when the car is driven by the insured. Members of the insured's immediate family and others who drive the car with permission are usually also protected. One should check the policy to see who is insured and who is not.

The costs of liability insurance vary according to many factors, but more complete coverage normally does not cost too much more. A car owner who lived in an area where 20/40/10 cost $163 a year should be able to buy 25/50/20 for $178 a year, and 50/100/25 for $189 a year, or 100/300/50 coverage for $201 a year. This difference in cost between the 20/40/10 and the 100/300/50 coverages is only about $30 or $35.

Some companies combine both types of liability coverage into a single liability coverage, such as $100,000 for any and all types of bodily-injury and property-damage claims. Since the single limit coverage will cover more claims, premium costs are more than for comparable split limits. Collision and comprehensive physical damage coverages insure the driver's *own* vehicle and not others.

Collision. This coverage applies to damage to one's own car as a result of colliding with another vehicle or object, or of turning over. Damages are paid regardless of who is at fault. If you have an accident where the other driver was clearly at fault, your insurance company will usually pay for the claim under your collision coverage and then collect from the other company later. This coverage is designed to restore the insured's automobile to its previous condition. One major problem with this is the high cost of repairing automobiles. If a $5000 auto is ¼ damaged, it is considered by the insurance companies to be "totaled," since it will cost at least $5000 in new parts

With collision insurance, your insurance company pays for damages to your own car, regardless of whose fault the accident was. If another driver was at fault, your insurance company will later collect from the other driver's insurance company. (*Bruce Gilden*)

and labor to fix it up. The insured in such a case will get a check for $5000 and will hopefully find a similar car to replace the other one. Institutions financing automobiles always require their credit customers to buy collision insurance. Should the car be in an accident while $2500 is still owed on the loan, the car would be repaired and the lending agency would still be protected.

Most collision insurance is sold on a $50, $100, or $250 deductible basis. In the event of an accident, the consumer pays the first part of the loss. This is a form of *coinsurance*. Both the owner and the insuring company are "coinsurers" because the owner pays the first $50 or $100, and the company pays the remaining amount ($350 or $300 in the case of a $400 accident).

Comprehensive Physical Damage. This coverage provides for protection against many things that may happen to a car. It protects against losses from theft, glass breakage, falling objects, fire, earthquake, windstorm, hail, water, flood, vandalism or malicious mischief, riot or civil commotion, or collision with a bird or animal. The premiums are relatively inexpensive, $20 to $50 annually. If a deductible clause of $50 is used, the costs are usually halved.

Three additional types of automobile insurance are commonly available and are worth consideration: medical payments, towing and labor costs, and uninsured motorists.

Medical Payments.   This coverage applies to medical expenses resulting from accidental injury to anyone in the *policyholder's* car. Such things as ambulance, hospital, medical, and surgical expenses are covered up to the limits of the policy. It also applies to members of the family whether they are in the policyholder's car, in someone else's car, or struck down while walking. Medical-payments coverage of $2000 usually costs about $12 per year.

Towing and Labor Costs.   This coverage applies to towing and labor when the policyholder's car is disabled. The labor is that involved at the scene, not that after the car has been towed to the garage. The annual premium is about $3.

Uninsured Motorists.   This coverage applies only to bodily injury caused by an uninsured motorist or a hit-and-run driver. It covers all members of the policyholder's family, whether in their car, in someone else's automobile, or walking. It does *not* cover property-damage losses. The coverage is usually $5000 at a cost of about $3.

How Much Insurance Is Needed?
Regardless of the age of the automobile, the owner should have bodily-injury and property-damage liability insurance because of the financial responsibility laws. Required minimum limits of 10/20/5 are in effect in many states, but for any serious accident this coverage would be grossly inadequate. Heavy property damage and payment for injuries are better

covered by policy limits of 25/50/20 or higher. Moreover, one can increase liability coverage to 100/300/50 for less than a 20 percent increase in the premium for minimum coverage.

If the automobile is fairly new or is being financed, the owner probably should protect the investment with collision insurance. If it is an older car (usually 4 years or more), the owner may want to assume the risk personally because of the relatively high cost of collision coverage. But, with rising inflation one should carefully check the retail value of an older car to see how much it is really worth—it might be much more than you think—before dropping collision coverage. Comprehensive insurance is also a good buy for newer cars, as it protects against unforeseen loss. For older cars, the cost of comprehensive coverage is not usually prohibitive, but many companies do not write that coverage for automobiles older than 8 years. In some instances, however, nondeductible coverage on an old second car may cost as little as $10 per year. In a high-risk neighborhood this coverage may be desirable.

The low cost of medical-payment coverage makes it a good buy, but only if it does not duplicate personal medical and hospitalization insurance. Towing and labor cost coverage is also inexpensive. Since today's fragile automobiles must be towed away from almost any type of accident, towing and labor insurance is valuable unless this is already paid for by membership in an automobile club. Although the probability of being in an accident with an uninsured motorist is relatively small (four out of five drivers are insured), the cost of this limited coverage is negligible, and it could be a wise purchase.

How Much Does Automobile Insurance Cost?
Automobile insurance rates are determined by such factors as the type of driver operating the vehicle, marital status, age, driving record, previous accident claims, recent traffic violations, place of residence, and the use made of the car. For collision and comprehensive coverage, the value of the car is especially important, since the amount of loss is directly

TABLE 10-4

Youthful Operator Rates (Suburban Area)

Type of Coverage	Limits	Cost
Bodily-injury liability	20/40	$ 491
Property-damage liability	10	147
Collision	100 deductible	699
Comprehensive physical damage	50 deductible	128
Medical	500	26
Uninsured motorist	10/20	4
Total		$1495

related to the cost of the car. Using the above information, drivers are classified into different groups according to types of coverage desired, and premiums are then determined.

Let us take an example of a young male driver from a suburb of Houston. He is a 19-year-old junior-college student who uses his new Mustang for 8 miles travel to and from his part-time work in the city, has had one accident within the past 3 years, and received a speeding ticket about 2 years ago. His recent coverage and premiums are shown in Table 10-4.

TABLE 10-5

Adult Operator Rates (Suburban Area)

Type of Coverage	Limits	Cost
Bodily-injury liability	20/40	$201
Property-damage liability	10	59
Collision	100 deductible	290
Comprehensive physical damage	50 deductible	49
Medical	500	10
Uninsured motorist	10/20	4
Total		$613

On the other hand, an adult operator has a new Chevy Impala which he drives to and from work, over 10 miles each way, and has no accidents on his record. His coverage is the *same* and the premiums are shown in Table 10-5.

There is no doubt that young drivers pay more for insurance than older people, as the figures show. Because younger drivers are involved in more accidents, they must pay a "surcharge" for insurance, above the base rate that adult drivers pay. Also, youths with poor driving records may be limited in the amount of coverage they can purchase. A 17-year-old boy with his first car pays more than three times as much as his parents for the same coverage. Girls also pay more for insurance than do adults, but their premiums are not as high as boys' because they have fewer accidents, probably because they drive less often and not as much during late hours.

According to the National Safety Council, drivers aged 20 and under are approximately 10 percent of all licensed drivers, but they are involved in more than 17 percent of all accidents. Drivers aged 25 and under make up approximately 20 percent of the licensed drivers, yet they are involved in more than 36 percent of the accidents. Therefore, the rates for young drivers must be higher to pay for their accidents. In high-density areas insurance on a new car for a youthful driver could cost as much as $3000 per year; in rural areas costs drop substantially.

Factors that Reduce Premiums

The junior-college student with the bad driving record in the earlier example might have done a few things to reduce his premiums. For example, he could have reduced the limits of his coverage on certain types of insurance. This option is always available, but it could be dangerous. Let us review four ways of reducing insurance costs.

1. Buy deductible collision coverage. If $50 deductible coverage costs $699, then $100 deductible coverage will cost about $580, and $250 deductible will cost about $475.

2. Buy deductible comprehensive insurance. If full coverage costs $160, the $50 deductible coverage will cost about $128, and $100 deductible will cost about $90.

3. Before buying a particular model of car, consider other models that will cost less to insure. High-performance vehicles and insurance company data on how frequently specific cars are stolen or damaged and how expensive they are to repair all figure into the final cost of the insurance premium. A different model car might cut the cost of insurance for the same coverage in half, especially for youthful drivers.

4. Keep the title of the vehicle in the name of a parent who then allows the youthful driver to borrow it whenever wanted. A 20-year-old male will have to pay 100 percent more than what his father pays for auto insurance if the car is in his name; if in the parent's name, the increase will amount to about 60 percent.

These are *direct* methods of reducing the cost of premiums. Other ways to reduce automobile insurance premiums include *special discounts* if the driver qualifies for the following:

1. *Driver Training Discount.* The driver usually saves approximately 10 percent if he or she has completed a certified course. Statistics show that graduates of these courses have fewer accidents. A similar discount is sometimes available for adults who complete a refresher "safe-driving" or "defensive-driving" course every 3 years.

2. *Good Student Discount.* In most states a good student can get a discount of from 10 to 25 percent. Students usually must rank in the top 20 percent of their class or have a B average.

3. *Small Car Discount.* If the driver's car is a small foreign model or a Detroit subcompact vehicle, he or she can often qualify for a 10 percent reduction in the premium. Sporty models are not eligible for the discount.

4. *Nondrinker Discount.* If the driver totally abstains from drinking alcoholic beverages, companies may allow a 10 percent discount. Some companies even allow slight reductions for those who drink moderately.

5. *Multiple-car Discount.* If there are two or three cars in the family and all are insured with the same company, a discount of 5 to 10 percent is usually available.

6. *Limited-use Discount.* This applies to those students who are away from home, probably in college, and do not use a car very often. (The school usually must be more than 100 miles from home.) Youthful drivers who use a car for only a small percentage of the time find that premiums are reduced from 10 to 20 percent.

7. *Special-policy Discount.* Special policies differ from the usual family multiple-car policies. The special policy limits liability coverage, often to a maximum of $100,000. If this and other special-policy limitations are acceptable, a savings of 10 percent or more may be available.

8. *Good-driver Discount.* A driver who has maintained a good driving history in terms of accidents, tickets, and claims may be eligible for a reduction in premiums. Normally, this discount applies only to adult drivers, but some companies make this discount available to youthful drivers also, with a savings of about 10 percent.

Usually, few of these discounts are disclosed unless the consumer asks about them. A salesperson may question you to see if you qualify, or then again may not. To get the best price for auto insurance—ask.

If you could qualify for all these discounts, would you have to pay any automobile insurance at all? Of course. Even if you qualify for more than one discount, companies have a maximum total discount they can give any particular driver or family. These discounts are based upon statistical averages and the patterns of driving established by certain groups of drivers, and are given by insurance companies in varying degrees across the country. A driver who believes that he or she can qualify for some of these discounts should search out the companies and policies which best suit his or her needs.

Some people have such poor driving records and/or simply live in such a high-accident-rate area that they must pay an extremely high price for auto insurance. These drivers are normally refused insurance in the voluntary market. Since all drivers should have access to insurance, all states have an *assigned-risk* classification. Each company writing insurance in the state must participate in an assigned-risk pool, and they must accept a certain number of assigned risks according to how much insurance they sell. The more insurance a company writes, the more assigned risks it must accept. People who are classified as assigned risks pay considerably more in premiums, but at least they can buy insurance coverage *if* they can afford the premiums. Most people in assigned-risk pools have *no* history of accidents or traffic violations; they are often young and/or live in high-risk neighborhoods. In New York State, the pool known as the New York Automobile Insurance Plan is the second biggest insurer in the state (behind Allstate). Rates are often prohibitive, usually triple traditional rates, so that many finally decide to drive without

insurance. Nationwide, only 80 percent of drivers have automobile insurance.

Shopping for Automobile Insurance

Two major factors are involved in shopping for automobile insurance: (1) determining the coverage and (2) selecting the insurance company.

A driver considering insurance needs should first examine how much he or she values protection. A wealthy businessperson with many assets to protect may want millions of dollars of liability coverage. A young couple with children may feel empathy toward the possibility of injuring another family's children and want $300,000 worth of bodily-injury liability insurance. Another person may feel that when the time comes for an accident he or she is really going to have one (perhaps smashing a big $60,000 tractor-trailer), and may want maximum property-damage protection. A driver who has a fairly new car, paid in full, may want to be protected against loss by securing collision and comprehensive insurance; if the car is worth less than $600, collision insurance is surely not necessary. The way to determine one's automobile insurance needs is to simply write them down on a form such as the one shown in Figure 10-3.

The automobile owner should also talk to various sales agents on the telephone, which

FIGURE 10-3 Insurance Needs and Rate Comparison Worksheet

Types of Coverage	Needed Policy Limits	Cost from:	Cost from:	Cost from:	Cost from:
Bodily-injury liability					
Property-damage liability					
Collision (amount deductible)					
Comprehensive					
Medical					
Towing and labor					
Uninsured motorist					
Other					
Discount (what type)					
Discount (what type)					
Total Cost					
Merit surcharge					

will eliminate much of the pressure to "sign on the dotted line." The shopper can discover the recommendations of the salespersons *and* the reasons behind them. In addition, the consumer can get a "feel" for the kind of service that the companies would be offering if and when a claim needs to be settled. Policies from different companies vary and must be compared. Some combinations may not be available, special factors may become important, and the rates may vary widely for the same coverage. Most states permit price fixing of rates as approved by a regulatory agency. With the insurance industry exempt from federal antitrust laws under the McCarran-Ferguson Act of 1945, price fixing is the norm. State Farm Insurance Company frequently testifies in favor of ending traditional state regulation of premium rates. Jean Hiestand, vice president of State Farm, recently testified before a Senate committee that the industry "historically has been dominated by price cartels." She argued in favor of free enterprise and price competition among insurers.

In other states rate competition is available and prices do differ. In Illinois, for example, a study by the state insurance department revealed price differences as great as 200 percent for the same coverage.

Some shocking findings about consumer buying habits were reported in a study by Kemper Insurance Company. They found "that 72.9% of those surveyed only considered one insurance company before making a purchase." This certainly shows an apparent lack of interest in comparison shopping for auto insurance. It is also a surprising finding in view of the savings that can be obtained by comparison shopping.

An example of a special factor that might be important when comparing policies is a *merit surcharge,* or, as it is more commonly known, the *safe-driver discount.* This should be listed on your worksheet because you may or may not want it. The safe-driver discount frequently permits the insurer to add a surcharge to the base premium if the car owner later becomes a not-so-safe driver. The initially low rates may go up drastically, as they are based

upon a point system. Traffic violations count as one, two, or three points, and the rates may go up accordingly: one point equals a 30 percent surcharge, two points equals a 70 percent surcharge, three points equals a 120 percent surcharge, and four points (usually reckless or drunken driving) equals a 260 percent surcharge. Having automobile accidents or even making minor claims can result in additional points. With comparable policies and premiums, the shopper should probably avoid this type of safe-driver discount. At the very least, compare the details of how the surcharge systems vary.

The selection of an insurance company, as already noted, is important for many reasons. Quality of service could be imperative. A study of thousands of complaints received by the Pennsylvania Insurance Department revealed that 50 percent involved dissatisfaction with claims, 28 percent involved cancellation/nonrenewal of insurance, and 12 percent had problems with the premiums. Only 1 percent had problems with the policy or agent, and the remaining 9 percent had a variety of other complaints. Many state insurance departments have similar studies available free for the asking. The findings can often be surprising. In one state, some of the largest companies (such as Allstate and Aetna) did not rate well on service. In a recent study by *Consumer Reports* magazine, thousands of consumers responded to the question "Which companies handle claims best?" Companies rated "much better than average" (less than 3.8 percent of consumers saying they were dissatisfied) included Amica, Erie Insurance Exchange, New Jersey Manufacturers, and United Services. Companies rated "worse than average" (14.1 percent of consumers reporting that they were dissatisfied) included Allstate, Liberty Mutual Fire, and Liberty Mutual.

Another factor to consider in shopping for an insurance company is whether it is financially solvent. Between 15 and 30 insurance companies go bankrupt every year. Ask for financial details on the solvency of the company; if in doubt, go with one of the larger ones. Keep in mind also, that it is usually wise to deal through an agent and not directly with the insurance company. If group auto insurance is not prohibited by law in your state, the rates are likely to be so much lower that you might want to give up the personal service of an insurance agent. If you have an agent, he or she can help protect your interests. Should the company want to cancel your policy, the agent can warn you and you can cancel first, thus leaving you with an unblemished record.

Canceled policies and those not renewed by insurance companies do cause problems for the consumer. Most other companies will not write a new policy for a customer who has been canceled elsewhere. Thus, such customers wind up being "assigned risks." If your policy is ever canceled, try to find out why. Some states have laws requiring insurance companies to disclose the reason and additionally forbid the dumping of a policyholder because of race, religion, age, or occupation. The only recourses available are to: (1) complain to the state insurance department, which might produce an explanation; (2) try to get insurance from another company; (3) get assigned-risk coverage; (4) sue the company for dropping the policy without legal cause; or (5) lobby to help get a law passed in your state which would force companies to disclose the valid reasons for dropping policies.

Realize too that an *agent* or sales representative for one company, such as Allstate or State Farm, can only sell you one of their policies. A *broker* can sell any one of several companies' policies. Thus, the broker is in a better position to compare the coverages and rates of several companies. Still, it is best to comparison-shop among companies using both agents and brokers.

NO-FAULT AUTOMOBILE INSURANCE AND ALTERNATIVES

Here are some startling facts about the automobile insurance industry:

- The nation's automobile drivers paid more than $24 billion in premiums last year, but only 14 percent of the money came back to pay the out-of-pocket expenses of accident victims. The traditional automobile insurance premium dollar is broken down this way: 56 cents goes to the insurance companies and agents for overhead costs; 8 cents pays for costs the auto victim has *already* received from another source, such as health insurance; 22 cents goes for pain and suffering and lawyer's fees (more than a third of the amount); and the remaining 14 cents pays for the actual net economic loss of the victims.

- Premiums for youthful drivers can go as high as $3000 per year, and high-risk adult drivers in major metropolitan areas are often required to pay more than $4000 for automobile insurance each year if they want the coverage.

- In 1978, more than 250,000 lawsuits were filed as a result of 2.6 million accidents injuring 4.4 million people; by 1982, more than 300,000 lawsuits are expected. The court system is overloaded with automobile lawsuits. One study noted that 13 percent of federal judges' time was spent on automobile cases instead of perhaps more important civil cases. Court delays of more than 2 years are common; it takes nearly 5 years in Chicago and Detroit to get an accident case to court.

- A study in Massachusetts showed that 35 percent of automobile accident victims were unable to prove which driver was at fault and consequently never got a cent! Nationally, studies suggest that one in four accident victims cannot prove who was at fault and do not collect.

Overhauling the automobile insurance industry to rid it of some of the above problems is under way—and "no-fault" insurance plans of one type or another are a reality in 24 states (although only 16 are considered "true" no-fault plans). No-fault insurance differs from the traditional "fault system" of automobile insurance that we have had for years.

Under the *fault system* of the common law of torts, the principle is that the driver that was negligent pays for the losses incurred. Since it is often very difficult to put the "blame" on just one driver, most of the premium dollar is spent for investigation costs, general overhead expenses of the companies, and legal fees. One insurance company "fights" another (and sometimes itself, as when a State Farm driver hits another State Farm driver), and legal battles are frequent. In the meantime, the victims end up having to pay their own medical bills, getting their own cars repaired, and trying to make up for lost wages.

The *no-fault* principle eliminates the need to prove fault. In addition, losses for some immediate expenses are paid for by one's *own* insurance company. Thus, the need for traditional liability insurance is reduced. In effect, liability insurance would be put on the same basis as homeowner's fire insurance or private medical insurance. Under good no-fault plans, bills for the medical care of those injured and some of the wages lost because of an inability to work are paid for immediately. Traditional liability insurance is still needed, but rates are much lower since almost all accidents can be paid for under the no-fault coverage.

No-fault plans vary widely from state to state, primarily because of opposition by the American Trial Lawyers Association (ATLA). More than a quarter of the income of most members of the ATLA comes from automobile accident cases, and they have vigorously fought no-fault insurance in every state. Where the plans have become law, they are often watered-down versions of a more effective no-fault approach. The ATLA also has been successful in preventing the federal government from passing legislation to establish minimum standards for no-fault insurance.

Most no-fault plans include variations of the following: Everyone must pay premiums; compensation is paid for medical expenses to each injured person, up to certain maximums, or in the case of death for funeral expenses; insurance companies must provide compensation quickly; lost income, up to a certain amount, must be reimbursed; amounts can be paid to persons hired for essential services, such as child care; the right to sue is limited to those who suffer expenses above a certain amount, or "threshold"; victims who are disfigured or permanently disabled are still free to sue, as are the survivors of those who die; there are safeguards against cancellation or nonrenewal by insurance companies; the expenses to be paid will be only those not paid for by another type of insurance; accidents caused by felons will result in their being liable; drunks and drugged drivers have to reimburse an insurance company for damages; motorists found guilty of driving violations will have to pay surcharges; pedestrians are covered for hit-and-run accidents; and large vehicles such as trucks would have to pay more of their share for economic losses.

No-fault auto insurance is not a panacea. It does not and cannot solve all the problems of automobile insurance. What a good no-fault law does do, however is (1) get adequate and quick compensation for injuries or fatalities, and (2) effectively eliminate most liability claims (lawsuits). Limiting the liability claims keeps many unnecessary cases out of the legal system, and this reduces costs of liability coverage. A study by Paul Gillespie, a proponent of no-fault plans, reports that in several states "95% of negligence claims were wiped out by no-fault." In Michigan, which has a very comprehensive no-fault plan, the delay in settling claims used to be 16 months; it is now less than 30 days.

Lowering the cost of insurance is only one purpose of no-fault insurance. In Massachusetts, during the first 4 years of their no-fault plan, rates for the minimum amount of automobile insurance coverage dropped 37.5 percent. Keep in mind that this reduction refers to about a quarter of the total auto insurance bill. In years when insurance rates have been climbing because of the skyrocketing costs of parts and repairs, and for other reasons, the increases in rates in states with no-fault laws have consistently been smaller (about 3 to 5 percent lower) than in the traditional fault states. A special report conducted for the Senate Commerce Committee by independent actuarial consultant Philip O. Presley concluded that "the use of no-fault auto insurance systems in Michigan and Colorado hasn't caused accident claims and costs to skyrocket and probably won't in the future."

Rates for no-fault coverage vary widely, as does coverage for other types of automobile insurance. William J. Sheppard, the insurance commissioner for the state of Pennsylvania, found variations of "up to $169 annually for compulsory auto coverages" in that state. In no-fault states, consumers must buy "wage loss" and "substitute-service" coverage. *Wage loss* provides part of the income you might lose because of an accident. *Substitute-service* coverage pays for services you cannot perform while recuperating from an accident, such as child-care expenses.

AUTO SAFETY AND SOCIAL IMPACT

Auto safety, meaning all aspects of the automobile's impact upon society, has a most dramatic effect upon our economy and lifestyles. We use personal vehicles as a primary source of transportation throughout America mainly because of the various subsidies given to automobiles over the years. Yet, the economic costs of accidents and pollution are tremendously high. To promote mass transportation rather than the automobile would cost billions and billions of dollars and mean severe lifestyle changes for many of us. In the meantime, we've got millions of automobiles and some definite safety problems.

Improved auto safety requires the efforts and cooperation of many. Business, with its voluntary safety improvements in vehicle design, is the very first component. Some new ideas came with no pressure from outside. These included four-wheel brakes, shatterproof windshields, compressible steering columns, and dual-system hydraulic brakes that prevent total brake failure. More safety also requires the continued efforts of government. On the federal level, more than one hundred safety improvements in design have been

mandated since the passage of the 1966 Motor Vehicle Highway Traffic Safety Act. Stronger bumpers, safety belts, padded dashboards, safety glass, and many other changes have made driving safer. Also, government guidelines on exhaust emissions have lessened pollution from automobiles—even though automobiles are still the number one contributor to air pollution. On both the federal and state levels, we have seen many improvements in general highway safety, such as breakaway signs and lampposts, empty drums placed in front of highway abutments, raised bumps to mark the center line, and grooved highways to reduce "hydroplaning."

People themselves are the final important ingredient in improving auto safety and reducing the tremendous economic waste caused by automobile driving. In some communities more people are using public transportation, and this certainly helps. More common sense by drivers would be an even bigger help. More than 80 percent of today's American drivers simply do not use their lap and shoulder safety belts. Many western European and other countries have mandatory belt-use laws, and if all of us "buckled up," the National Motor Vehicle Safety Advisory Council estimates that the traffic death toll could be cut by a half to three-fourths. The National Safety Council estimates more conservatively that 12,000 lives would be saved annually. The Research Triangle Institute reports that seat belts could be the most effective lifesaver on the highway if everyone used them. Mandatory usage, they report, would save 89,000 lives over the next decade.

Passive restraint systems like air bags could also save thousands of lives annually. Even if they were mandated in all cars, it would still take several years before most people were protected because older cars have to wear out first. With the present negative attitude toward seat belts, one wonders how concerned the average American really is. Driving under the influence of alcohol figures in nearly half of all fatal accidents. It's a well-known fact, yet people still take to the road when they know they should not. Makes you wonder, doesn't it?

Automobile pollution, injuries from accidents, lives lost, economic waste, and personal tragedies will not be stopped tomorrow or even 10 years from tomorrow. But progress can be made if industry, government, and consumers work individually and collectively toward making driving safer and reducing some of the negative social impacts associated with automobiles.

POINTS OF VIEW AND PROBLEMS TO THINK ABOUT

Consumers in America live in a world full of automobiles. And these automobiles have left their imprint upon society. We have traffic deaths, serious injuries, economic losses, superhighways cutting across the country, miles of secondary roads winding almost everywhere, congested traffic in both large cities and small towns, and an increasingly polluted environment. The great mobility of the population and the economic growth of this great country owe much to the progress and development of gasoline-powered vehicles. But we are beyond the point of permitting continued destruction of our environment by such cancerous vehicles.

Something dramatic must be done—*today*, not 5 or 10 years from now. We need a pollution-free vehicle, be it electric, steam, methane, turbine, hydrogen, diesel, multifuel (such as the Stirling engine), atomic, or solar powered. Industry and government must cooperate even more closely on this important national priority. Despite all the efforts toward improved "emission controls," autos are far and away the most important cause of air pollution.

Perhaps as much as two-thirds of the costs of death, injury, and destruction caused by automobile accidents could be eliminated by development of vehicles which can withstand crashes at speeds of up to 50 miles per hour, and which can also protect the occupants. The technology exists to protect at 30 miles per hour, but it is not being mass produced.

We also need a realization that big cars may be more dangerous than small cars—not the opposite as is commonly believed. Professor Po Lung Yu in a major research study conducted in Texas reports that "Even though you have less protection in a small car, the highest number of accidents involving big cars makes them more dangerous overall." He found that the largest cars made up only 33 percent of the registered vehicles but accounted for 60 percent of the accidents in the study. These autos "produced 53 percent of the serious or fatal injuries, and were involved in a staggering 73 percent of the accidents involving drunken drivers." Professor Yu theorizes that the smaller cars are a more difficult target, as they are more maneuverable and can thus avoid accidents more easily.

Another major contributor to the economic and personal losses caused by auto accidents is our present highway system. It is woefully inadequate both in terms of its ability to handle the vast number of cars and in terms of design safety. Many innovations in building safer highways already exist, but they need to be used on *all* highways. Traffic congestion could be greatly alleviated with the development of efficient mass-transit systems, both for commuters and for long-haul passengers. Strong incentives—probably financial—need to be offered to encourage use of mass-transit systems too. These efforts could also save energy.

Speed kills too, and often people drive faster than the posted limit. To dramatize the problem, Stephen Long and five friends drove the 50 miles of Interstate 94 between Ann Arbor and Detroit at 55 miles per hour, the legal limit. They drove the entire distance two and three cars abreast and when they got to Detroit, approximately 600 cars were backed up behind them! It makes one wonder about the typical American driver, doesn't it?

There are immediate needs for stronger automobile safety requirements, including federal tire standards and grading. All fifty states, instead of the present forty, should operate car-safety inspections at least to check on brakes, steering, and tires. One survey by the National Highway Traffic Safety Administration reported that 6 percent of all auto accidents were *caused* by mechanical failures; in another 11 percent, such failures were probably involved. Diagnostic clinics, which would be independent of any repair services, need to be established in more communities. Strict licensing of the businesses that repair automobiles and the mechanics who work in them (in addition to gasoline-station mechanics) would help ensure honesty and quality workmanship. The National Institute for Automotive Service Excellence already has a voluntary testing program for auto mechanics. Hopefully, thousands more mechanics will soon be wearing the shoulder patches showing that they have passed some or all of the certification tests.

And consumers need to be made *more* aware of the places for redress concerning automobiles. Autocaps (Automotive Consumer Action Panels) exist in almost every state and can resolve most such complaints. Problems concerning insurance may be resolved through consumers contacting ICAP (the Insurance Consumer Action Panel). See Appendix.

Finally, minimum standards for no-fault auto insurance are definitely needed. The inequities in rates, the crime of nonpayment to accident victims, and the clogged court system could be greatly relieved. Only enlightened leadership, encouraged by consumers who vocally express their feelings on such critical issues, will successfully meet the needs of an informed and improved American society.

CHAPTER ACTIVITIES

Checkup on Consumer Terms and Concepts

Depreciation	On-the-lot tests
Optional equipment	Variable expenses
Low balling	Real costs

Repairability	Collision
Mechanic's lien	Comprehensive
Chilton's Labor	physical damage
Guide and Parts	Medical payments
Manual	Uninsured motorists
Financial	Coinsurance
responsibility laws	Merit surcharge
Assigned risks	No-fault automobile
Bodily-injury liability	insurance
insurance	

Review of Essentials

1. The realistic estimated cost for driving is approximately how much per mile?
2. How much do new cars depreciate during the first year of ownership?
3. What is "high balling"?
4. When is the best time to trade in a car?
5. What should a young adult examine to determine needs or wants in buying an automobile?
6. Name several magazines that contain descriptive information about new cars.
7. How much do you deduct from the sticker price of a new compact-model automobile to find out how much the dealer paid?
8. What does a 20/40 bodily-injury liability policy mean?
9. Comprehensive physical-damage coverage provides for protection from what types of occurrences?
10. What factors determine automobile insurance rates?
11. What four direct methods to reduce insurance costs are available to all consumers?
12. What courses of action are available to consumers who have had their automobile insurance canceled?
13. Out of every dollar collected by automobile insurance companies in premiums, what proportion pays for the actual net economic loss of the victim?
14. Where can you complain about automobiles and auto insurance when you cannot get satisfaction on the local level?

Issues for Analysis

1. Discuss what can be done about the extensive model changes every year that result in first-year depreciation amounting to 30 percent or more.

2. What would be the effect of having new-car warranties written more clearly and covering "all" types of needed repairs for a certain length of time?

3. Should individual states or the federal government establish mandatory no-fault insurance for automobiles? Defend your position.

11

Housing

THE PROBLEMS

The need for suitable housing is a problem that all consumers face, particularly since about 40 percent of all Americans live in substandard housing, according to the Department of Housing and Urban Development. John Barton, for example, could not find a decent apartment close to the college he was attending, and all because of his pet cat. He finally accepted a less-than-adequate upstairs apartment in a private home because the owners liked animals. Similarly, Susie Wong and Carrie Chan were refused by many apartment managers in their community because they were told they would probably have lots of parties and be too noisy, "like those other college kids." Of course, it did not help that they were both Chinese-Americans.

Apart from the quality of the housing, 80 percent of Americans cannot afford to buy a median-priced new home. The prices are so high that they cannot afford the monthly payments. The Charles Boardlins were shocked to find that to rent a simple one-bedroom apartment in Atlanta, they had to pay more than $300 per month. Being newlyweds, they could not afford the necessary $11,000 down payment for a home valued at $55,000.

About 9 years ago, the Ed Nickson family purchased a modest home in Kansas City. Since the selling price then was $32,000, Ed did not have the large down payment needed for a conventional mortgage, so he used all his savings—$4050—and bought the home on contract. His monthly payments were $195. The total payments made over 8 years came to $20,117, which reduced his loan by only $2153. He calculated that his home would be paid for in another 35½ years, if he lived that long! Some neighbors, the Richard Jacksons, were also buying their home on contract, and they were evicted after paying installments for more than 12 years. Their furniture and clothing were piled in the front yard on a cold January morning. They were given nothing, even though they had paid in more than $24,000 during those years. A *contract purchase* usually means that the buyer acquires no equity in the property or title to it while paying off the purchase price, no matter how many payments are made. If one payment is missed, in such a legally enforceable contract, the entire balance is due, and if it is not paid, the "owners" may be evicted.

Homeowners in many states lose their property through deceptive but legal tax sales. This occurs simply because they do not realize their property is in danger. Often they do not understand the law or cannot read English. Apartment dwellers sometimes lose their rent deposits, which they give to landlords in good faith to cover possible damages that they might cause. Many landlords just keep the money. And when the deposit (or part of it) is returned when the tenant moves, the tenant often does not receive interest on the money.

More unfortunate are the blatantly illegal situations where realty firms practice a "double X" discrimination code. Such a code identifies homes in black or integrated neighborhoods. Homes for sale without the "double X" are in white neighborhoods, and prospective black buyers are steered away from them. A recent study by the Department of Housing and Urban Development found that "blacks trying to rent houses or apartments encounter discrimination by rental agents three out of four times they look." Similarly disgraceful are landlords who collect rent from ghetto apartments but never make any attempt to correct building code violations. Not surprisingly, such landlords exist in rural as well as in urban America.

Nondiscrimination laws exist, but a recent study by the U.S. Comptroller of Currency showed that "blacks seeking homes were found to have been refused about twice as often as whites, even when applicants of both races earned $20,000-a-year or more." This happens even though various regulations and laws make it illegal to discriminate against minorities and women. "Redlining," the refusal to make loans to people living in designated neighborhoods (usually those with a large number of minority residents), is illegal too. But it still occurs in spite of requirements that savings and loan associations maintain detailed mortgage records to help bank examiners detect redlining.

Many housing problems result in part be-

cause of personal greed or biases. Other problems occur because of inadequate federal, state, and local laws. Enforcement of present laws, at times, also seems scant at best. But a large part of the problem is the uninformed consumer. The consumer must become better informed.

HOW MUCH HOUSING SPACE IS NEEDED

Regardless of the type of housing you choose—apartment, townhouse, single-family dwelling, or whatever—the actual amount of space you need and get is determined by your values and goals, housing costs, and your stage in the life cycle.

Values and Goals

A long-standing traditional value among Americans is home ownership. One study was recently conducted by the National Association of Homebuilders. When they asked new homeowners why they bought their homes, approximately 40 percent reported that they simply "desired to become a homeowner." Another study conducted by Investors Mortgage Insurance Company surveyed unmarried women. It revealed that three out of five single women would prefer to live in a single-family home. They wanted the tranquility of the single-family dwelling instead of the publicized "swinging" high-rise apartment dwellings.

These findings say something about the values of Americans. They want space, privacy, and not very much noise in their neighborhood. As a matter of fact, the two most frequently heard complaints about a family's present housing are "too much noise" and "insufficient storage space." Each situation is different, but there are six basic goals that determine how much housing space is needed.

One goal is the *use* of housing space and its function. There needs to be space for all activities. There should be a satisfactory interrelationship of public, private, and work space. Public areas are usually for some leisure activities, active games, entertaining, dining, and so on. Private areas are for sleep, privacy in general, dressing, bathing, and grooming. Work areas are for food preparation and serving, clothing care, and storage. Also, the traffic patterns among these areas should be conveniently laid out. For example, having to walk through two bedrooms to get to the only bathroom may *not* be convenient.

Ease of care is also important. If one dislikes housework in general, it may be wise to get a relatively small home. Larger units have more places to dust and much more floor space to vacuum and/or scrub. If one spends a great deal of time away from home in work and/or pleasure activities, there may be little need to have a large house or apartment.

Economy is a goal, too. One should not, of course, buy such expensive housing that it ruins the family's whole money-management program. But economy also means choosing housing where one's human and material resources are used efficiently. Examples of inefficient uses are a third-floor walk-up apartment for a large family that has to carry many bags of groceries upstairs each week, or a spacious kitchen for a single person who usually eats out.

Safety is high on the list when most people consider housing space. For a person concerned about the possibility of a fire, a small apartment with only one exit might be too "nerve racking." Similarly, others might think that too large a home might seem too inviting to a burglar.

Beauty and attractiveness is more crucial than most people think. One should choose housing that is pleasing to look at and that lifts the spirits. Who wants to come home from a hard day at work, open the front door, and frown? Who wants to spend the weekend at home when it is just not a very attractive place?

Individuality in your housing space is a reflection of your personality, and will develop naturally from your own interests and preferences. Families that value privacy might not be wise to choose a home with few rooms and lots of open space. A person who likes to entertain is likely to choose a home with a large kitchen and recreation area. Moreover,

people choose housing according to their own values, goals, and aspirations.

Housing Costs

If you earn $15,000, it is very doubtful if you can afford to buy a home priced at $45,000. It is more likely that you might be able to buy or rent housing space valued at $30,000. In all likelihood, of course, the housing space will be much smaller in the lower-priced home. Thus, housing costs definitely relate to how much space you can have.

The median amount of living space in new homes is about 1700 square feet. This home typically has three bedrooms and two baths. With inflation and other costs, that *same* type of home sold for $20,000 in 1963, $23,000 in 1967, and $42,000 in 1976, and is projected to cost $63,000 in 1980 and $78,000 in 1983. These figures not only show the increase in prices of new homes but emphasize the fact that the typical homeowner is going to have to pay a relatively stiff price for new housing space. Keep in mind, however, that the median price is somewhat misleading because it only shows the increase in sales price. It does not show the size of the home, the amenities, and most important, the lack of demand for and sale of inexpensive homes.

The cost of housing varies according to many factors, and ample space can be obtained for less than the median amounts. However, one major reality of the seventies has been the high cost of housing and the utilities; in other words, the high *total* cost of shelter. One result has been an attempt to decrease the number of square feet of living area in many new homes to keep costs down. There has been some effort to reduce the square footage of land for each home. Some builders have tried to cut back on the amenities (such as appliances and fireplaces); most have not, however, because consumers continue to prefer them. The renting or buying of housing space depends upon factors such as these, since they affect the price so greatly.

Housing costs must be considered in their entirety when comparing alternatives. The important amount spent for utilities (heat,

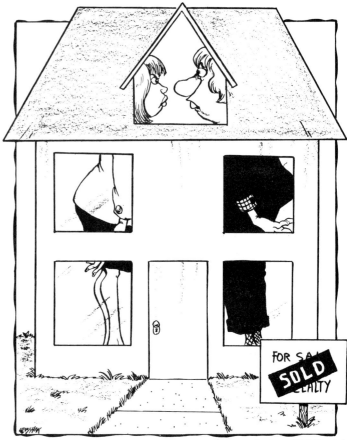

Well it looked a lot bigger in the picture.

Courtesy of Edd Uluschak.

electricity, water, and sewage) must be known in advance or one can find oneself spending too much for housing.

Life-Cycle Stage

The particular stage of the life cycle one is in is another factor in choosing housing-space needs. A single person may demand only very limited space, perhaps 600 square feet, but he or she may also want a private entrance. A young couple may need 800 square feet to be content. A couple with one child may demand more in actual space, perhaps 1000 square feet, and may also want housing from which they can readily move when they need a larger home. A family with teenage children may need still more space, perhaps 1800 square

feet, for private bedrooms, entertainment, hobbies, and perhaps a garage for two cars. For a couple whose children have grown and moved away, housing-space needs contract, and they may require considerably less, perhaps 1000 square feet.

FACTORS AFFECTING WHERE TO LIVE

Many factors affect the decisions people make when they choose where they will live in the United States. Of course, the opportunity for employment is perhaps the most important reason. However, people's values, goals, and desired lifestyle play a strong part in their decisions about where to live. Some like hot weather, some like cold. Others prefer mountains or easy-to-reach places to hunt and fish. Many love the life of the big city, and an increasing number prefer suburbia.

There are several specific factors that people consider when deciding where to live:

- *Proximity to employment*. How close do you want to live to your work? Do you want to be only 10 minutes away? Or do you really want to "get away from it all" and commute for 45 minutes or an hour?
- *Cost of housing*. Is the price of housing in accordance with your budget? Will you be living in the least or most expensive residence in the area?
- *Type, use, and cost of energy*. What kind of energy is used for heating and cooling in that area? Is solar heat both available and practical? Do you have a choice about what kind of energy you can have? Is the housing designed in such a way and well insulated enough to keep energy use down to a minimum? How much does energy from the utility companies cost? What are the cost projections for energy in your area in the future?
- *Neighborhood and location of the home*. Do you want to live in an average-income neighborhood where the homes are generally similar? Do you want to live in an older and established area in contrast to a newer subdivision? Do you want a corner location, or is the middle of the block all right?
- *Attractiveness and safety*. Is the neighborhood clean and attractive? Is the area well lighted? Is it relatively safe from crime? How dangerous would it be should there be a fire in your home or at a neighbor's? If there are children, are environmental hazards such as a creek or pond too close?
- *People in the neighborhood*. Are a fair number of the neighbors in about your age group? Do they have similar social, ethnic, religious, educational, and economic backgrounds? Do the neighbors have similar occupations and status? How many children are there, and in what age groups?

How friendly and sociable are the people? And, very importantly, do you want such things in common with the people in your neighborhood or not?

- *Nearness of schools and colleges*. How close do you want to be to a local college? (You may want to be a part-time student.) Is there an elementary, middle, junior, or high school nearby for children?
- *Convenience*. How close is it to a small neighborhood shopping area and to a larger shopping area? Is the church of your choice within a reasonable distance? How far away are gasoline stations? Is a public transportation system, such as bus or train, nearby? Are playgrounds or parks close? How convenient are the recreational facilities that you might use frequently?
- *Noise and odor pollution*. How much noise is there? Census Bureau data show that fully one-half of American households feel their neighborhoods are "too noisy." How dense is the population of the area? Is there much automobile traffic? What about airport noise? Do many of the neighbors have noisy air conditioners? How about barking dogs? Are there any industrial or environmental situations nearby that occasionally cause odor problems?
- *Mobility possibilities*. Could you quickly *sublet* your apartment (rent it to someone else with your landlord's permission) or sell your home should you want to move? Would others consider this a desirable residence and neighborhood?

Each of these factors is a personal consideration, and the consumer should study certain information before making any decision.

DECIDING TO BUY OR RENT

Fred and Mary Wodell, married a year and a half, will both graduate from college this year and are faced with a difficult decision. Should they buy or rent housing after they move to Newark, New Jersey, and begin working? Fred has a job in counseling with a social service agency, and Mary has a position with an accounting firm. They have limited savings at this time, but they could get some extra money from Mary's mother if needed. They do not plan on having a family right away and may decide never to have children. Of course, they could change their minds on this, too.

Nobody can decide for the Wodells as to buying or renting. Nor can anyone tell you what to do. Each situation is different and includes considerations in two broad areas. First is the long list of values that a family holds and the personal preferences of each member. The second is financial considerations.

Values and Preferences

Questions need to be raised in order to assess your values and preferences more accurately. The answers will affect your decision to buy or to rent. Is the idea of "putting down roots" in a community by buying a home important to you? Do you share that American dream held by so many to "own your own home?" Is the "higher status" of being a homeowner something to consider? Are you willing to incur a large debt in the form of a home mortgage? Do you dislike being responsible for maintenance, small repairs, and perhaps lawn care? Would plumbers, painters, fuel bills, and tax bills simply be too much of a bother? Do you have the time available for such activities?

The mobility possibilities must be considered too. How secure are you in your job? How likely is it that you might be moved or would want to move from one community to another? How likely is it that the size of your family will increase and that you will need more space? What about your social life? Renters can remain rather anonymous, but homeowners are often forced into social situations. Also of tremendous importance are the attitudes and preferences of other members of the family. A most difficult task is trying to weigh these various subjective factors which will enter into the decision.

Cost Considerations

Many costs must be examined when weighing the alternatives. Not only must you determine how much you can afford to spend on shelter, but you must also figure out if you might be better off renting at a low price and investing the difference. Very simply, the cost considerations can be put into the form of an equation when deciding to rent or buy: Net ownership costs = Rent + Savings. Manipulating figures here and there and making different kinds of assumptions can tip the scales either way. Generally speaking, however, if you are going to live in one place for less than 3 years, it is better to rent. Let's examine some of the reasons why.

Moving-in Costs. The moving-in expenses are certainly less for those renting than for those buying. Purchasing a $50,000 home may require a $10,000 or $12,000 down payment, as compared with "one month's rent in advance plus a damage deposit" for renting. Renting a furnished apartment can also eliminate the need to buy furniture. Even when they rent an unfurnished home, renters usually spend less than homeowners on new purchases. People often feel better about spending money on furnishing and decorating an owned residence rather than a rental unit. New homeowners spend about $2900 on furniture and equipment (shrubbery and lawn and power tools, for example) during the first year of ownership. Pride of ownership provides an added incentive to make such purchases.

Budgeted Expenses per Month for Housing. You must be careful when comparing housing alternatives. A $50,000 home purchase, for example, with a $5000 down payment and a loan at 8½ percent interest might require a monthly payment of $346. Comparable rented quarters could cost $425 per month. Buying sounds like the less expensive choice, but upon closer inspection it is not.

The other costs of shelter push up the total monthly cost to $633, as shown in Table 11-1. The $25 in lost interest must be considered as a cost, since the $5000 down payment could easily yield that much in monthly interest if it were put into a savings account. Even if the apartment expense did not include utilities (heat, electricity, water, and sewage), the additional $91 or so would leave it costing less than owning.

Rent payments are slightly less inflationary than home-ownership costs. Landlords do not pass on all the increased costs to tenants when the rental market is poor and when many vacancies exist. When vacancies in a community run above 5 percent, consumers can pick and choose somewhat, and the competition helps keep the rise in rental costs behind that of housing construction and financing costs. When there are few vacancies available, increases in costs are passed on quickly and rents rise accordingly.

How Much You Can Afford to Pay.   The often quoted statement that a person can afford to pay 2½ times annual income for a house is simply not true. Most people cannot afford this much and in fact do not spend that amount. A better generalization is that consumers probably can comfortably spend from 20 to 25 percent of their *take-home pay* on

TABLE 11-1

Comparing the Costs of Renting and Buying Housing Worth $50,000

Expense Items	Monthly	Annually
Mortgage charges (principal and interest)	346	4152
Real estate property taxes	80	960
Homeowner's insurance	7	84
Maintenance, repairs, and improvements	80	960
Heating fuel and electricity	85	1020
Water and sewage	6	72
Refuse collection	4	48
Loss of interest on down payment of $5000	25	300
Total monthly housing costs	633	7596
Comparable apartment rental	425	5100

housing-related expenses. This includes (for those buying a home) repayment of principal borrowed, interest, taxes, insurance, maintenance, repairs, home improvements, heat, electricity, water, sewage, refuse collection, and special assessments. For nonhomeowners, the figure would include the amount paid for rent in addition to some of the above items.

Some people may indeed decide to spend more and, in fact, do. Such a decision depends upon your values and your budget. To determine how much you can afford to spend on housing, examine the worksheet in Table 11-2. The final dollar amount in the budget is the amount you have available for housing-related expenses.

See Table 11-1 for examples of the kinds of expenses that are related to shelter. The amounts vary according to the type of property, its value, tax rates, utility costs, and other items. In general, you can figure $3 to $6 a month per $1000 of house price for expenses other than the amount needed to pay for mortgage principal and interest. Remember, this is an approximation, and you should check the details carefully before making an actual decision. Figure perhaps $3 for a small community and up to $6 for a large city or metropolitan suburb.

Cash Resources.   Part of the cost consideration question is, "Do you have the down-payment money and are you willing to part with it?" Renters may or may not have enough savings for a down payment. Or, they may rent because they do not wish to obligate themselves to a large mortgage debt on a home. A related factor is, "Do you have enough cash resources to weather a temporary reversal in finances should that occur?" Those with little cash reserves or who fear loss of income because of potential unemployment or poor health may want to rent rather than buy a home.

Future Buying Intentions and Tax Laws. Homeowners usually find that because of the tax laws they must buy another house after they sell their first one. The profits made on

TABLE 11-2

Worksheet for Determining Amount Available for Housing

1. Add Up Your Monthly Living Expenses Other Than for Housing
   Food $\$$ _____
   Automobile upkeep, insurance   _____
   Clothing   _____
   Medical and dental bills, insurance   _____
   Commuting to work   _____
   Entertainment and recreation   _____
   Education, school, and college expenses   _____
   Church, other contributions   _____
   Hobbies, books, magazines, records   _____
   Personal gifts, Christmas expenses   _____
   Special luxuries, pleasures (sports, pets, eating out, etc.)   _____
   Personal (barber, beauty shop, bathroom supplies)   _____
   Vacations   _____
   Life, disability, or other insurance   _____
   Savings, investments, pensions, etc.   _____
   Installment payments (washer, auto, other)   _____
   Miscellaneous   _____
   Other   _____
         Total living expenses other than for housing $\$$ _____

2. Determine Monthly Income Available for Housing
   Total gross monthly income (omit spouse's income unless
       he/she will continue to work) $\$$ _____
   Minus all deductions for income taxes (federal, state,
       and local, Social Security, etc.)   _____
   Net take-home pay $\$$ _____
   Subtract total monthly nonhousing expenses from above   _____
         Total monthly money available for housing $\$$ _____

Source: Adapted from Arthur M. Watkins, *How Much House Can You Afford?*, New York Life Insurance Company.

selling a house are subject to federal long-term capital gains taxes unless the person buys another, more expensive home within 1½ or 2 years. The statement that "renters should stay renters and homeowners should stay homeowners" is not true, but the tax laws imply that it is. Since people who own their homes move every 7 years on the average, it is possible that in less than 30 years one could have owned four or five houses. If a more expensive house was purchased each time (to avoid the capital gains taxes) and then the family decided to rent after all those years, the capital gains tax for that 1 year might be $10,000 or more.

Investment Aspect. When comparing the housing alternatives of renting versus buying,

one often considers the investment potential. Would you be better off financially in the long run through home ownership or by renting, thereby saving the down-payment money and investing it along with a specific amount each month? Numerous cost considerations, assumptions, and mathematical calculations are needed to determine the answer.

Recent data from the Bureau of Labor Statistics indicate that over many years the homeowner has about a 2 percent edge over the renter. This is after considering the capital gains situation, the extra income tax deductions allowed the homeowner, and many other factors. However, do not let this general finding keep you from carefully examining your own situation. Your preferences, cost considerations, and assumptions may very well tell you the better alternative, whichever it might be.

Government Assistance. When comparing renting and buying, consider the availability of special government assistance programs. For potential homeowners a variety of assistance plans are available, particularly for those with lower-than-average incomes. These programs include the Department of Housing and Urban Development's Federal Housing Administration insured mortgage loans, guaranteed Veterans Administration mortgage loans, Farm Credit System, and Farmers Home Administration. Check your telephone book for aid.

For renters, most government assistance comes through Section 514 of the Housing and Rural Development Act, financed by the Farmers Home Administration. Under this program consumers go to their local Public Housing Authority to determine eligibility; if they qualify, they get help in obtaining suitable housing. Eligible consumers can sign a lease with a participating landlord and pay only 15 to 25 percent of the family income for rent.

Rent subsidies are given to those applicants with annual incomes, adjusted for family size, of no more than 80 percent of their area's median income. To date, the elderly have received most of the assistance. However, more than 30 million families would qualify for this program if it were fully funded.

CHOOSING AN APARTMENT

Since more than 40 percent of the people aged 20 through 24 move each year, renting an apartment allows them to change residences easily without the bother of selling or buying. Let's first examine the various types of apartments that are available.

Types of Apartments

There are six basic types of apartments for rent.

Small Multiunit Structures (Three to Five Floors). Usually found in neighborhoods with mixed types of housing. Lighting and ventilation are not good in older structures except in corner apartments. Sometimes there is no elevator. Heating is often not controllable in each apartment.

Large Multiunit Structures (over Five Floors). These vary in size and in number of tenants. Lighting, ventilation, and heat are usually good. The apartment can be on two floors instead of one. The apartments can range from *efficiency* (just one room) to whole-floor residences. Sometimes they are rather noisy.

Garages, Lower Level of Houses, and Garden Apartments. There are few other apartment dwellers. Privacy varies with choice of apartment. Ventilation and heat vary with age and construction of structure. The noise level is lower.

Townhouses and Row Houses. Size of the total unit varies from three in a row to ten or more. The floor plan is somewhat limited because windows are only in the front and the back. Often two stories are available for each apartment. There is a variety of styles of outside siding. There are separate entrances and usually a small, fenced backyard.

Duplex (Two-Family Dwelling). This is usually one structure with apartment units side by side. Sometimes the duplex has a unit on top and another on the bottom, which permits a more varied floor plan. A duplex is most often located with single-family dwellings. An attached garage is common, and there is ample yard space. Ventilation and light are excellent. Sometimes there is a basement.

Quadraplex (Four-plex) to Six-plex. This is located with other apartments. Ventilation and light are good except in center apartments in a six-plex. There is a limited, common yard area. There is a variety of floor plans, which sometimes include a basement and a second floor.

Once you have decided on a particular type of apartment to rent, and this would probably include visiting the different types to be sure, there are several other factors to consider before you make a final decision. You should consider location, rent, apartment layout, interior items, safety features, leases, landlord-tenant relationships, tenant unions, and general rights and responsibilities.

Location

Where do you want to live? Downtown near all the conveniences and cultural activities? But what about all the noise? The air pollution? The limited access to play areas for children? Suburban apartments can be just as noisy and bustling if the complex is too large, and then you still have commuting costs. If you like to party and socialize or if you like solitude, it would be wise to ask the manager about your potential neighbors. Perhaps look around and meet some of the present tenants. Also, drive or walk around the neighborhood. Where are the grocery stores? Is public transportation nearby? How about playgrounds and parks? Also, does the neighborhood look like one you would want to come home to? Is it well lighted at night and does it appear safe?

Rent

The amount of rent you pay is usually related to the neighborhood as well as the age of the building. Similar housing in a more expensive neighborhood could cost $50 to $60 more per month. Older apartments are generally lower in price but cost more to heat.

Perhaps by now you have determined how much you can afford for rent. Unfortunately, many consumers are too optimistic on estimating that amount. Thus they overextend themselves with high payments. It is smart to be conservative, since paying too much for shelter may mean not buying any new clothes for 6 months, not buying that car you had in mind, or not taking a vacation.

Keeping in mind that maximum rental figure, be sure to ask about special fees for particular services. Are utilities included in the rent? Also, realize that an all-electric apartment will cost about 25 percent more than one heated with fuel oil or gas in spite of all the advertising to the contrary. Is there a special charge for parking? For hooking up the cable television antenna? For extra storage space?

The rental fee may or may not include certain services, and these need to be checked. How about window washing, mowing grass, and shoveling snow? Is the advertised security guard really there? Is the main door to your building actually secure? Are laundry facilities available in the proper quantity, and do they work? Is there a swimming pool? Game or recreational area? Tennis courts? Whether or not you get or even want these services, it is still important to find out if they are available and at what cost.

Location of Apartment

The location of the apartment within the building can be very important. The first floor may be convenient, but there may be many people using the hallway. The top floor may be quieter but require long waits for the elevator. Apartments in the center part of the floors may be less expensive to heat, but you will have less outside light, and having neighbors on each side may mean more noise. Also, what about refuse disposal? How accessible are the facilities?

Layout

It is wise to look at several different apartments if only because the floor plans vary so much. Walking into one may give you a view of the entire apartment, including the kitchen and bedrooms. Another may have a private foyer with a closet. Once in the apartment, check to see if the rooms are big enough. Take along a tape measure and be sure that a particular wall is wide enough for your couch or king-size bed. Can you sit in the living room without having to look directly into the kitchen all the time? Are the bedrooms constantly in view? Is the bathroom near the living room?

Interior Items

The interior of the apartment is where you are going to live, and it is well worth your time to check it out carefully. If the appliances and equipment do not work now, the manager probably will not fix them later. Check and see if the heat is controllable in each room. Does the system seem to be in good working order and providing adequate heat? Does the air conditioning work well? Does the air conditioner make so much noise that you can hardly hear someone talk?

Are the windows easily opened and closed? Can they be securely locked? How is the ventilation? Are screens provided? Is it too drafty around the windows? Does the garbage disposer work? How about door locks, drains, dishwasher, toilets? Do all the burners on the range work? Are the walls, ceilings, and floors clean? Any signs of roaches, mice, or rats?

Check for the two things people complain about the most—noise and storage space. Are the walls solid, or do they seem hollow? Can you hear the next-door neighbors? Besides important storage and counter space in the kitchen is there adequate closet space for the rest of the apartment? How about extra space not located in the apartment itself?

Safety Features

Nearly twice as many fatal or disabling accidents occur at home as occur on the job. Many of these accidents could be avoided by using good common sense, but some are definitely related to features in the home.

When checking the apartment, think about some of these safety features. The kitchen sink, stove, and all work surfaces should be well lighted. Gas ovens should have pilot lights and have an automatic cutoff in case of flame failure. In the bathroom, the tub should have a nonslip surface. Tub and shower enclosures should have sturdy grab bars, and the doors should be made of safety glass.

Stairways should be well lighted with switches at both top and bottom. Steps should be secure and have a nonslip surface, and the railings should not be wobbly. For fire safety, check that each room has enough wall outlets so that you will not overload them. If there is evidence of do-it-yourself wiring, have the local building department check the adequacy of the system. Also, see if each room has at least one door to the outside or a window low enough and large enough to be used as an emergency exit. Check if the apartment has smoke and/or fire detectors located near the bedrooms.

Leases

A *lease* is a legal agreement specifying the financial terms and general conditions of renting property. Leases for apartments are most often for 1 or 2 years. Many landlords use what they call a "standard lease." Each city and state has its own laws on rental matters, and these may affect the terminology of leases. However, if it is a commonly used lease form, it is designed to protect the landlord. The renter usually has no real protection in a typical lease.

Some examples are in order. Suppose you sign a lease and the landlord verbally promises to make certain repairs after you move in. The repairs are not done, but you cannot break the lease, especially if it is the popular standard lease form 955 (used in Los Angeles). Suppose the heat goes off and the landlord does not come to repair it in spite of cold weather. The standard lease form 42, used in Philadelphia, excuses the landlord, as in most other cities, unless he or she is "grossly negligent." If the toilet does not function properly, can you withhold a portion of the rent until it is repaired? No. Suppose you are told that utilities are included in the rent, you sign the lease, the heating bill comes, and the landlord apologizes, but you must pay it. If it is in the lease you signed, in all likelihood you are legally responsible.

If several people are interested in renting a highly desirable apartment, there is not much you can do about the terms of a lease. But some apartment houses are not that full, and you might get the landlord to agree to add in or cross out some of the items in the lease before you sign and move in. Be certain that both of you initial the changes on all signed forms, however. Such changes in leases are not too common, since prospective tenants rarely demand them.

Landlord-Tenant Relationships and Tenant Unions

Better leases, ones that protect tenants as well as landlords, are being used more commonly now but not everywhere. Changes in leases to the renter's benefit, safer housing, improved maintenance, and legally equal power for tenants in negotiating contracts with landlords have come about mainly through the formation of tenant unions in addition to legislation.

A *tenant union* is a confederation of individuals for the common purpose of protecting and expanding their rights as tenants. Tenant unions have had considerable success, even to the point of withholding rents—with the permission of the courts—until some condition was met. Some groups have been successful in repair-and-deduct actions, rent withholding, rent strikes, and legal suits for specific action. Tenant unions have found that simply requesting a housing code inspector to visit the premises can get landlords to act. (Most housing code inspectors by law have to follow up on every complaint and file a written report.) Laws in several states and many cities in recent years have tried to improve the rights of tenants.

Better landlord-tenant leases now include fairer provisions concerning application fees, security deposits, lease rules and changes, landlord obligations and tenant remedies, and tenant obligations and landlord remedies. Should your state or city not require more equity in the leases, listed below are some clauses to cross out and some others to write in if the landlord is willing. Cross out statements which permit the landlord to evict you if he or she is "dissatisfied" with your behavior, to enter your apartment without your permis-

sion unless it is a real emergency, to make you pay for repairs and maintenance, to make you put up more than 2 months rent as a security deposit, to make you immediately liable for the entire rent if you pay the rent one day late (*acceleration clause*), to prohibit you from subletting the apartment, to make you waive your legal rights, or to make you pay the landlord's attorney's fees.

Add in clauses that require the landlord to give you an itemized list of damages to the apartment before you move in, giving 5 days after moving in to add things to the list that you have discovered. Also, interest earned on the damage deposit should be given to the tenant. Add in a requirement that the landlord submit an itemized list of damages to you within 72 hours of your vacating the apartment. Also add in a statement giving you the right to cancel in the event your employer transfers you to another location before the end of the lease.

Perhaps you could visit a local tenant's organization, a community landlord-tenant relations committee office, a state consumer protection agency, a local legal aid office, or a local housing code office for further information and ideas. In any event, it is important that you read any lease carefully before signing it. Perhaps while visiting an apartment you could ask for a copy of the standard lease (it is probably only standard to *that* manager), so that you can look at it at your leisure.

Rights and Responsibilities

The rights and responsibilities of both landlords and tenants must be more clearly understood to be of benefit to all concerned. New Jersey became the first state to pass a truth-in-renting law which is aimed at making tenants know and understand their rights and responsibilities. Landlords must give out to all tenants state-prepared leaflets which explain a variety of topics covered by the law. With both landlords and tenants more informed, much of the friction between them is eliminated.

Some of the responsibilities of landlords and

tenants are implied in the lists above. However, a brief notation of some tenant responsibilities may serve a useful reminder: Keep the dwelling clean and safe; place all waste in the proper receptacles provided; keep all plumbing clean; use all appliances and facilities in a reasonable manner; abide by all reasonable rental rules; do not deliberately or negligently harm property or permit others to do so; and do not disturb the neighbors or allow your visitors to do so.

When choosing an apartment it should be quite clear by now how important the written lease is. Careful inspection and comparison of leases can avoid much dissatisfaction with what otherwise might be a wonderful apartment.

TYPES OF HOUSING AVAILABLE

We know that most people live in single-family detached homes or rental apartments, but actually there are many other types of housing available. Since many families spend 25 to 30 percent of net income on housing-related costs, each should carefully consider all available types of housing to decide what is best for them. Owned apartments, houses, and mobile homes are alternatives.

Owned Apartments

Almost every type of apartment that can be rented can also be owned. The two ways to buy an apartment are through a condominium or cooperative.

Condominium. Each owner in the multiunit structure holds a specific legal title to a unit and a proportionate interest in the common areas and facilities. Condominiums are governed by an elected board of directors or council of co-owners. Most condominiums are townhouse, multiplex, or highrise buildings. Some are old apartment buildings cleaned up and sold as condominiums. A recent survey in Washington, D.C., found that the three most frequently cited reasons for buying condominiums were (1) tax benefits and rising

value of the property, (2) reduced obligation for maintenance, and (3) desirable locations.

Each owner has basically the same rights as any homeowner and can sell whenever he or she desires. The deed specifies many responsibilities of condominium ownership. These are the rules and regulations that are binding upon the owners, such as that each will pay a certain fee per month for maintenance of grounds and that no exterior changes will be permitted without the consent of the council of co-owners. Approximately one-fourth of new homes built this year will be condominiums. Housing economists predict that by 1995 probably 50 percent of the United States population will live in some form of condominium housing.

Cooperative. Each apartment dweller in the multiunit structure owns shares in the cooperative, which is organized like a corporation and operated by an elected board of directors. The owners do not hold title to their specific apartments, but instead hold many shares for a large apartment or few for a smaller one. This gives the residents an absolute right to occupy their specific units for as long as they own stock.

Costs of upkeep are divided among shareholders, and rules are specified and can be voted upon (as in a condominium). Depending upon the charter of the cooperative, sometimes applicants who want to live there can be "blackballed" and not allowed in. Both cooperatives and condominiums arc growing in number and availability, since the costs of such housing are somewhat lower than single-family detached homes.

Cautions Concerning Owned Apartments. The old days of building condominiums just to "make a buck" hopefully seem to be gone. This improvement resulted in part because more states have passed strong condominium laws (Virginia, Georgia, and Florida, for example) and because of federal regulations (specifically Section 234, the Condominium Program of the 1974 National Housing Act).

When a federal agency such as "Fannie Mae" (Federal National Mortgage Association) or the VA (Veterans Administration) approves a condominium project for financing, you can be sure that their lawyers and appraisers have gone over the details carefully. Of course, not all projects are reviewed by such agencies. Even then, one still needs to be quite careful about the details of condominium ownership; fewer safeguards exist for cooperatives.

Things to be wary about include low-quality construction and soundproofing; project management continuing to own some amenities (such as swimming pools, tennis courts, and parking lots) and then leasing them back at high prices; and "sweetheart contracts" (which permit the manager's brother-in-law to do all the maintenance at inflated prices). The prospective buyer should be aware of the fair market value of the property, be sure that the operating budget is sound, be sure that there are sufficient funds being accumulated to pay for needed and expensive improvements in later years (such as heating systems, hallways, parking lots, and swimming pools), and watch out for underestimated condominium fees which later must be raised significantly (purposely set low to seem inviting). One must also make sure there is a "cooling off period" for changing one's mind after signing a contract. Make note of the following: sufficient parking for the owners (anything less than 1 ½ spaces per unit is probably not enough), too many units being permitted to be rental units (the more individual owners there are, the more likely it is that the project will be successful, and when the developer is allowed to rent out more than 20 percent of the units, this attribute is reduced), and unnecessary control by the developer for an extended period of time. Finally, any language in the documents that restricts owners' resale rights and documents written in such legalese that you cannot understand them are things to watch out for.

With such an imposing list of warnings about owned apartments, one naturally wonders how wise such a purchase would be. The answer is an individual one, of course, but such ownership requires responsibilities. With such a large expenditure you should know what you are getting. When buying any home, numerous checks and precautions must be made, whether it is an owned apartment, a house, or a mobile home.

Houses

When considering which style of house to live in, most people already have certain preferences. They may have "always wanted to live in a house like that." Or perhaps they just like "that particular style." Certainly one should be happy with one's choice, but to make the wisest decision, many factors must be considered. Here is a capsule summary of different styles of houses.[1]

Ranch. This is generally easier to construct. Stair climbing is eliminated. Maintenance is easier. There is more opportunity to create a relationship between indoors and outdoors. It is easier to control sound and little inside space is wasted. It usually requires more land. Bedrooms are not as private as some people prefer. Horizontal walking distances may be greater. A ranch requires more foundation, roofing, and insulation. The cost per square foot is usually higher.

Two-story. The two-story house permits more interior space on less land and often has an impressive exterior appearance. Bedrooms usually can be larger and more private. The upstairs need not be meticulously groomed when casual company drops in. Maintenance of the second-floor interior is more difficult. It involves more stair climbing and there is wasted space in the stairway area. There should be at least one extra bathroom. Cost per square foot is usually lower than ranch.

Split-level. The split-level (where floor levels are about a half story above or below the adja-

---

[1] Text adapted from "Housing Pros and Cons," *Chicago Daily News*, October 1, 1971, p. 45.

cent ones) can be built on rolling terrain, and it blends better with two-story houses than ranches. It has more livable space for the money than a ranch, but requires more land than a two-story. It lends itself to attractive exterior design. There is some wasted space in stairway areas. There is less stair climbing when going from one level to another, but overall stair climbing may be as much as in a two-story. Room controls are needed to provide even temperatures at various levels.

Cape Cod (One-and-a half-story). The Cape Cod (with sloping roof and protruding windows) can be built on a small lot. The second floor need not be finished at the time of the original construction. It permits the master bedroom to be on the first floor, the children's bedrooms upstairs. It provides extra storage space under eaves. A second bathroom is a must on the upper floor. It has knee walls and sloping ceilings upstairs.

For all types of houses, prefabricated construction is available from various builders. Construction of components, such as walls, trusses, or doors, before delivery to the building site reduces costs considerably. Depending upon how readily the local building-code requirements are met by the manufacturer, prefabricated houses can be erected in weeks rather than months. With some prefabricated houses, the buyer can do most of the construction and finishing work, thus reducing costs still further.

Mobile Homes

The mobile home of today (preferably called a "manufactured" home by the industry) is truly a complete home built for year-round living. It is constructed entirely in a factory and transported to the site by special equipment. Usually the homes are moved only once because they are designed, engineered, and constructed for use as a permanent residence.

Today, more than 12 million people live in more than 5 million mobile-home units. The numbers are rising rapidly each year, and now about one-third of all new homes are mobile homes. The key attraction is price. Almost all new homes in the under $25,000 bracket are mobile homes. The cost per square foot is less than one-half the cost of a conventional house, and you get furnishings and appliances with the mobile home. With the rising costs of other forms of housing, one can readily see why mobile-homes sales are booming.

Types and sizes. "Single-wides" are the most common type of mobile home. They are 12 feet wide by 65 feet long, providing 12 by 62 feet of living space, or 744 square feet. Other single-wides run up to 14 by 70 feet. "Expandables" have an "addition" telescoped inside the home during transportation. At the site the sections are placed in position and add 60 to 100 square feet to the room in which they are located. "Double-wides" are two single units built and towed separately to the site. Then they are joined together to make one large living unit.

Things to Look For and Look Out For. As with any important purchase, careful shopping is imperative. Particularly consider quality and the different floor plans. Be sure to compare different brands *and* different dealers. Also, never buy a mobile home or sign a contract until you know *exactly* where you will locate the home. Often, the best parks are full and you will be in a dilemma if you have already signed. If the homesite is in the country, get advance written approval from local authorities, including the health officer, before committing yourself to the purchase.

Construction standards related to safety for mobile homes were established nationally in 1976 by the Secretary of Housing and Urban Development. These newer units are to be more fire- and wind-resistant even though the standards contain about 90 percent of existing voluntary codes, which were already enforced by forty-six states and met by 98 percent of mobile homes built during the previous 4 years. The HUD seal appears near the main entrance of mobile homes constructed since that date. Older units are likely to have a similar seal (near the doorway) from ANSI (American National Standards Institute) or the NFPA (National Fire Protection Association). The HUD seal is helpful, as it establishes minimum standards. However, like almost any seal, it represents a minimum. Mobile homes are certified within the manufacturer's place of business, and the actual inspections are done on a spot-check basis only. Fortunately, many manufacturers exceed the minimum standards. Therefore, it pays to inquire and find out which standards are exceeded and why when considering a mobile-home purchase. Warranties for mobile homes vary widely, and the Federal Trade Commission is expected to establish minimum standards for such warranties.

Serious problems occur in many mobile-home parks, and these need mentioning. Entrance fees are sometimes so high that when park space is tight the owners may charge a fee of $300 to $1500 just to let you in. Other parks are "closed" unless you buy the home *from* the mobile-home park owner. Most parks do not have leases, and the owner can raise the rent sharply almost at will. In the states which do not have strong laws protecting mobile-home residents (particularly good laws are in California, Florida, Colorado, Wisconsin, and New Jersey), eviction after 15 to 30 days notice can occur at the park owner's whim. Some state laws now guarantee mobile-home owners the right to sell their unit without the approval of the park owner and permit mobile-home owners to put up a "for sale" sign. Another sometimes illegal practice is charging an "exit" fee or "commission" when a unit is sold, whether or not the owner helped in the sale; this can amount to 10 percent of the price. Tenant organizations for mobile-home owners have had some success in recent years in getting improvements in products and services from the park owner as well as changes in the arbitrary manner in which rules were made.

Fortunately, not all mobile-home park owners provide such problems for consumers.

However, the situations are not being cured overnight, mainly because of a supply and demand problem. Local zoning officials and laws generally prohibit more mobile homes in their areas; thus, there is a shortage of mobile-home park space, and the present park owners have a monopoly. Most communities do not allow mobile homes on private land unless it is in a remote area. Breaking down the resistance against in-town and close-in mobile-home parks in the years to come will require working closely with real estate interests, zoning officials, and the general public (especially those who own detached single-family dwellings), and changing the tax laws. Although mobile homes are normally used as permanent dwellings, in most states they are still licensed as cars and taxed as personal property.

SPECIAL FACTORS TO CONSIDER IN PURCHASING

If you have decided to buy an apartment, a house, or a mobile home, there are several special factors that you should understand.

Why Housing Costs Are Rising

The rising cost of construction of new single-family detached dwellings is due in part to inflation, increased space needs of consumers, and additional amenities, but that is not the whole story. The average selling price of a new home in 1979, estimated to be about $58,000, is expected to be $78,000 in 1983. Such dramatic increases are often blamed on the high wages of skilled labor, but this is simply not true.

On-site labor costs have actually decreased as a percentage of the total price of a new home. This is mainly because of the increase in factory-constructed housing modules. The two factors that have pushed up the real cost of housing are land and financing. Land now amounts to about 20 percent of the cost of a home, and financing is about 10 percent.

The "No Frills" House and the "Expandable" House

Increasingly higher costs for single-family detached houses in particular have brought new pressures to the market. With a smaller number of people able to buy new homes, builders are offering the "no frills" house. This means a smaller house without the fireplace, and linoleum instead of carpets. Of course, the total cost of the house is lower than the cost of a house with the usual amenities. Many first-time buyers, however, have become accustomed to such niceties. As a result, there has been general consumer resistance to buying such homes.

Instead of the "no frills" house, people seem to want good old high quality at prices they can afford. Thus, there is quite an emphasis on "expandable" homes. Here, the builder of a new home usually finishes out two larger-than-usual bedrooms, plus the usual package of den, dining room, kitchen, and bath. But the upstairs is not finished. It is likely to contain the rough work for a bathroom and two bedrooms. The homeowner puts in labor and buys materials for such expansion when he or she can afford it. On a $45,000 home, for example, the sales price can be dropped $5000 for an "expandable" home. For $1500 in materials and a fair amount of the homeowner's time, the consumer can first afford the home, and second save some money by doing some of the work personally.

Real Equity Buildup Is Slow

The John Steins of Boston complained to an official at their savings and loan association recently that they had been bilked out of $4200. They explained that when they bought their home 5 years ago, they made a down payment of $5000 and obtained a 25-year mortgage for $35,000 at 8 percent interest. Since they had made payments for one-fifth of the mortgage term, they expected that they would have reduced the loan by 20 percent, or $7000, leaving them with a balance of $28,000. They intended to sell the home, take the proceeds of $7000 plus other profits, and buy a bigger house. The lending institution told them that the original debt had only been reduced by $2800, and the balance was $32,200.

Equity, the value of the property beyond what is owed on it, and the Steins' misunderstanding of it, caused their dilemma. One's equity in a home builds up very slowly during the early years of a mortgage. The Steins' $270.20 monthly payment on their conventional mortgage loan included payments toward both the principal and the interest. The *principal* is the debt upon which interest is paid. The first monthly payment was divided this way: $233.33 in interest and $36.87 toward the principal. This is calculated in a similar manner for almost all mortgages. (See Figure 11-1.) In the first month the debt was $35,000, and the interest rate was 8 percent. The interest cost for the first month was one-twelfth (12 months or payments in each year) of 8 percent

FIGURE 11-1   Monthly loan reduction

Monthly Payment	$270.20
Principal Amount of Debt	$35,000
Rate of Interest	8% annually

First Month

$35,000 \times 8\% \times 1/12 = $233.33 interest
$270.20 - $233.33 = $36.87 principal
$35,000 - $36.87 = $34,963.13 balance

Second Month

$34,963.13 \times 8\% \times 1/12 = $233.09 interest
$270.20 - $233.09 = $37.11 principal
$34,963.13 - $37.11 = $34,926.02 balance

Third Month

$34,926.02 \times 8\% \times 1/12 = $232.84 interest
$270.20 - $232.84 = $37.36 principal
$34,926.02 - $37.36 = $34,888.66 balance

of $35,000, or $233.33. The remaining $36.87 went toward reducing the principal owed. So, for the second month the mortgage balance was $34,963.13. The second monthly payment of $270.20 was divided as follows: one-twelfth of 8 percent of $34,963.13, or $233.09, for interest charges, and $37.11 toward the principal.

As illustrated in Figure 11-1, each month a slightly larger amount goes toward retiring the amount of the principal and a smaller amount is paid in interest. Understanding this, the Steins decided to stay in their home for a few more years so they could build up more equity. After 5 years with an 8 percent mortgage with a term of 25 years, one still owes 92 percent of the original balance; at the end of 10 years, 81 percent; after 15 years, 64 percent; and after 20 years, 38 percent. Therefore, homeowners realize little equity buildup during the early years and may think that it is impractical to sell their home for at least 6 or 7 years. But that is not the complete picture. "Real" equity includes *all the value* beyond what is owed on it. This, therefore, includes any *appreciation* (increase in value) of the property. In the Steins' case, for example, they purchased a home 5 years ago valued at $40,000 with a $5000 down payment and a $35,000 mortgage. Because of inflation, landscaping the Steins had done, some interior decorating, and the fact that their neighborhood has become more "desirable" in recent years due to its exclusiveness, the fair market value of their home is now $57,000. Thus, the real equity they have is $24,800 ($57,000 minus the present debt of $32,200). Keep in mind, however, that that equity becomes truly real *only* when the property is sold.

Amortization of Mortgage Loans

Each monthly mortgage payment is divided into so many dollars for repayment of the principal and so many dollars for the interest. The figures (proportions) change each month even though the total payment remains the same. This is discussed above and shown in Figure 11-1. This payment plan is known as *amortization*. The debt is repaid in monthly installments, gradually reducing the mortgage balance upon which the interest rate is calculated; and the interest is paid each month on the amount of money you still have the use of.

An amortization schedule similar to the one in Table 11-3 is available to each buyer taking out a mortgage loan. The interest rate, amount of principal, and term of the loan determine the actual amortization schedule. Payments for property taxes and insurance are *also* often made directly to the lending agency. Since these figures are fairly constant and can easily be estimated, lump sums of $9 per month for insurance and $80 per month for taxes may be added for purposes of illustration. Different estimates, of course, are necessary in various localities.

A controversy rages in some states because the lending agency may not apply monies paid in for taxes and insurance toward the principal and thus reduce the total interest charges. In effect, what happens is that the consumer prepays the taxes and insurance by giving the money in monthly payments to the lending agency, which then pays the amounts due once a year. More enlightened lenders recognize that, ethically, they should pay interest on funds which they hold and then later pay out for taxes and insurance.

The actual rate of interest paid on a mortgage depends greatly upon the supply and demand for housing funds. The rate has varied considerably in recent years, from a low of 7 percent to a high of 11½ percent. Comparatively high rates, of course, are expensive to consumers. A change of only ½ of 1 percent (from 7 to 7½ percent, for example) for a $35,000 loan over 30 years costs the buyer an extra $11.90 a month. A 1 percent increase in the rate of interest on the same mortgage loan costs an extra $23.80 per month.

The cost of increased interest rates based upon each $1000 borrowed is shown in Table 11-4. For example, a $40,000 thirty-year mortgage at 8 percent will cost $293.60 per month (40 times $7.34). The same loan at 9 percent will cost $322.00 (40 times $8.05). Thus, a person with a steady income, saving for the down payment, may find that interest rates have climbed to such a point that

monthly payments cannot be met even though the savings are enough to make the down payment. Viewed another way, a buyer with the above 8 percent mortgage would pay $79,260 for repayment of principal and interest

TABLE 11-3

30-Year Amortization Schedule for Principal and Interest ($35,000; 8% Rate)

Years	Payment Number	Amount of Payment	Interest	Principal	Balance of Loan
	1	$256.82	$233.33	$ 23.48	$34,976.52
	2	256.82	233.18	23.64	34,952.87
	3	256.82	233.02	23.80	34,929.08
	4	256.82	232.86	23.96	34,905.12
	5	256.82	232.70	24.12	34,881.00
	6	256.82	232.54	24.28	34,856.72
	7	256.82	232.38	24.44	34,832.29
	8	256.82	232.22	24.60	34,807.68
	9	256.82	232.05	24.77	34,782.92
	10	256.82	231.89	24.93	34,757.99
	11	256.82	231.72	25.10	34,732.89
1	12	256.82	231.55	25.27	34,707.62
2	24	256.82	229.46	27.36	34,390.98
3	36	256.82	227.18	29.63	34,048.05
4	48	256.82	224.73	32.09	33,676.66
5	60	256.82	222.06	34.79	33,274.45
6	72	256.82	219.18	37.64	32,838.85
7	84	256.82	216.05	40.77	32,367.16
8	96	256.82	212.67	44.15	31,856.19
9	108	256.82	209.00	47.81	31,302.88
10	120	256.82	205.04	51.78	30,703.65
11	132	256.82	200.74	56.08	30,054.67
12	144	256.82	196.08	60.73	29,351.84
13	156	256.82	191.04	65.77	28,590.66
14	168	256.82	185.58	71.23	27,776.32
15	180	256.82	179.67	77.15	26,873.55
20	240	256.82	141.88	114.94	21,167.29
25	300	256.82	85.58	171.24	12,665.84
	355	256.82	10.04	246.78	1,258.80
	356	256.82	8.39	248.43	1,010.37
	357	256.82	6.74	250.08	760.29
	358	256.82	5.07	251.75	508.54
	359	256.82	3.30	253.43	255.12
30	360	256.82	1.70	255.12	0

TABLE 11-4

Monthly Payments for a Debt of $1000 in a Stated Number of Years

Interest Rate (Percent)	Payment Period (Years)		
	20	25	30
7½	$8.06	$7.39	$7.00
7¾	8.21	7.56	7.17
8	8.37	7.72	7.34
8¼	8.53	7.89	7.52
8½	8.68	8.06	7.69
8¾	8.84	8.23	7.87
9	9.00	8.40	8.05
9¼	9.16	8.57	8.23
9½	9.33	8.74	8.41
9¾	9.49	8.92	8.60
10	9.66	9.09	8.78

over the life of the loan. This compares to $86,940 with a 9 percent mortgage. The extra $7680 represents the higher cost of credit.

Property Taxes and Benefits

The real property of homeowners, such as permanent buildings and land, is taxed. Specific exemptions are allowed for churches, government-owned buildings, and a few others, but the homeowner pays taxes regularly. The property taxes in some localities are collected indirectly through the lending institution, which then makes the tax payments for the consumer. In such cases, the monthly payment includes monies for repayment of principal and interest, and an additional estimated amount for real estate taxes. In other localities the government simply sends you a bill each year.

An $800 tax bill is not excessively large for a rather new home valued at $45,000. Rural areas usually have lower taxes, while larger cities sometimes have higher ones.

The benefits received from taxes are many. Local schools depend heavily upon property taxes. If you had children of school age, the benefits would be especially obvious if you were suddenly confronted with the alternative of sending your children to a private school with a tuition of $1200 or more per year. Similarly, fire and police protection are provided for with revenues from property taxes. A new city hall building, improved streets and roads, a wider bridge, funds to support the local community college, public parks in the town, even Christmas decorations over Main Street are paid for with property taxes. One needs only to reflect upon the local city and county government services to see where property taxes are going. The rising demands of consumers for increased government services have been from all the people, and, as a result, local taxes often increase 5 to 10 percent each year. Renters also pay property taxes, but indirectly, since they are considered part of the monthly rent.

The Income Tax Advantages

There are federal income tax provisions that give homeowners an advantage over renters. The two basic ways in which homeowners save money on their tax returns are that interest charges and real estate property taxes are both deductible.

People pay income tax to the federal government based upon *taxable* income (after subtracting exemptions and deductions), not on *gross* income (the grand total). The law allows homeowners to deduct property taxes and interest charges, thus lowering their income tax liability.

Consider the situation of two couples. The Smiths have an income of $19,000 and rent an apartment for $300 per month ($3600 per year). The Martins have the same income, but they bought a home with a mortgage loan of $40,000. Their payments are also $300 per month (for principal and interest). During the year, the Martins paid $2940 for interest and an additional $1800 for real estate property taxes. Since these amounts are deductible they reduced their tax liability by roughly $2400. In other words, it cost the Smiths about $2400 in extra taxes just to live in an apartment. This clearly shows that there is a distinct tax advantage for homeowners.

The tax savings for a single person are shown in Table 11-5. The direct tax savings during the first year for the single homeowner earning $25,000 amount to $2072, which is a considerable sum of money. In future years, the income tax bracket, amount of real estate taxes due, and amount due for interest will vary. Thus the amount of tax savings for the homeowner will also vary. In the analysis, however, do not overlook the lost opportunity cost of perhaps $600 (in interest if the money was put into a savings account instead) on the down payment that was made in the first place.

Nearly 20 percent of home buyers are single, and discrimination against singles in general and single women in particular is steadily declining. In 1974, 1 out of every 35 home-loan applicants was a single woman. The Investors Mortgage Insurance Company of Boston estimates that in the 1980s 10 percent of those applying for home loans will be single women. The Equal Credit Opportunity Act, effective in 1975, helps ensure those rights for women in all credit transactions.

Money Management and Maintenance

Homeowners must of course maintain their residences and occasionally make repairs. The renter's maintenance problems are taken care of by the landlord, since maintenance is part of the rent. Owners of apartments pay a fixed monthly maintenance fee for such expenses (which rises over time). But owners of single-family detached dwellings must budget for those expenses themselves and hope that they can pay for them when they occur.

Simple maintenance costs for homeowners average at least $25 per month. A figure of $40 might be more realistic when one considers the increased costs of hiring skilled workers to make repairs. The money management solution is to set aside a certain amount each month for such expenses.

Hidden maintenance costs can drive up the price of a home considerably unless they are anticipated in advance. Check the home for additional maintenance costs, such as air conditioning, cleaning a septic tank or chimney, special sewer assessments, too much moisture in the basement, ants or termites, cleaning

TABLE 11-5

The Tax Advantage of Ownership for a Single Person

Using a $25,000 annual income for a single taxpayer, given below is a theoretical tax return, showing the financial advantage of ownership. This assumes the purchase of a $50,000 home with an earlier $10,000 down payment.

Regular Income Deductions		Extra Ownership Deductions
Annual Salary:	$25,000	(1st year of 80%, $40,000, 30-year mortgage)
Itemized Deductions:		Mortgage payment (based on 8% interest rate):
Medical	$ 800	$293 per month, or $3505 per year
Income and sales taxes	1,700	Tax-deductible interest on that mortgage (first year
Contributions	350	is 90% interest): $3150
Interest on loans, installment		Tax-deductible real estate tax (based on average of
credit, etc.	200	$4 per $100 valuation): $2000 per year
Miscellaneous deductions	450	Total deduction for ownership costs: $5150
TOTAL	$ 3,500	Taxable income ($20,500) less deductible owner-
Personal Exemptions:	1,000	ship costs ($5150): $15,350
Taxable income (without owner-		*Tax to be Paid:* $3443
ship deductions)	$20,500	*Tax Savings* ($5515 minus $3443): $2072
Tax to be Paid:	$ 5,515	

Rest assured we do a first rate job.

Courtesy of Edd Uluschak.

the furnace, and the upkeep of a swimming pool.

Utility costs are not only rising but difficult to estimate when considering housing alternatives. Keep in mind that the main part of the utility bill involves the cost of heating and cooling the home. This amounts to about four-fifths of the total. Hot water alone may account for 25 percent of that figure. The remaining one-fifth goes for lighting and appliances.

Thus, it pays to carefully estimate the utility costs. Check with the seller. Ask owners of similar dwellings in the neighborhood. Inspect the insulation to be sure that it meets or exceeds the Federal Housing Administration's (FHA) minimum standards. Get a satisfactory explanation from the seller and/or do a visual check of the insulation. The insulating materials for ceilings should have an "R-19" or "R-22" number, indicating increased resistance to heat flow. Some "super-insulated" homes have been reported to be producing savings of from 25 to 60 percent. Also examine windows and doors for proper weather stripping and caulking. Effective money management requires knowledge and control of various maintenance expenses.

FINANCING THE PURCHASE OF A HOME

Financing the largest purchase of your lifetime—a home—is perhaps the most important aspect of the decision to buy. Financing arrangements can save owners thousands of dollars and make ownership a pleasure. Or the terms can be costly, place a tremendous burden on the family budget, and lead to great dissatisfaction.

Just because lawyers are involved does *not* mean that the financial aspects are necessarily confusing. On the contrary, the major concepts of financing a home are few. The different kinds of mortgages, special financing plans that may benefit you, and your own financial ability to purchase a home must be examined.

Kinds of Mortgage Loans

A *mortgage* is a lien or claim against real property by the lender when the buyer provides such property as security for money borrowed. A *mortgage note* is the written agreement to repay a loan which is secured by a mortgage, and it specifies the terms of repayment. In some places the common term "mortgage" refers to a deed of trust and a note. People in general use the terms "mortgage'' or ''mortgage loan'' to refer to both the mortgage and the promissory note. Mortgage financing is available from many sources, although savings and loan associations provide more than one-half of all family housing loans.

Savings and loan associations, mutual savings banks, commercial banks, government agencies, and the other sources of funds for housing are just that—sources. The mortgage itself is a type of loan agreement, and the sources of housing loans provide different types of mortgage loans. The four most common types of loans are conventional, FHA-insured, VA-guaranteed, and builder-assisted (GNMA).

Conventional Loan. Approximately three-fourths of all loans for family housing are provided through conventional financing. A conventional mortgage loan is one in which the creditor and the borrower have a direct legal agreement, pledging the real property as security for the loan, and the creditor has a first lien on the property. (A *lien* is a claim by one person on the property of another as security for money owed.) The lending institution lends its own money. Conventional loans are subject to the laws of each state.

Commonly loans can take up to 30 years to repay. Conventional loans are usually for not more than 75 to 80 percent of the value of the home. The borrower must pay the difference in cash as a down payment. In some instances, lenders will make conventional loans for 90 to 95 percent of the value of the property. In such cases the lenders always require that the buyer take out private *mortgage insurance.* The charge is usually ½ of 1 percent of the mortgage loan amount. If the consumer defaults on the loan, the mortgage insurance company will pay the *lender* for any loss. The additional cost for this is included in the repayment schedule. For example, on a mortgage debt of $33,800, the private mortgage insurance premium is $7.02 per month.

To protect the lending agency, mortgage insurance is required of all small down-payment purchasers. A $35,000 conventional mortgage loan on a house appraised at $50,000 (the value of the house for resale) is a safe loan. This is because if the borrower cannot make the payments and the lending institution *forecloses* (takes legal action to regain title to the property), the home will almost certainly sell again for at least $35,000. But a home appraised for $45,000 with a $43,000 mortgage loan might be mistreated by the owner, so that a later repossession and resale might bring only $40,000. The lending institution would lose money unless it protected itself by requiring the consumer to buy mortgage insurance. Mortgage insurance usually arranged by the lender through a private insurance company simply guarantees repayment of a certain amount of the mortgage in case of default to the holder—the lending institution. A controversy exists, since buyers are normally required to continue paying the mortgage insurance fee until the loan-to-*original*-sales-price ratio is less than 80 or 75 percent. This occurs, regardless of an increased appraised value, 5 or 10 years later.

FHA-Insured Loan. The Federal Housing Administration (FHA) of the federal Department of Housing and Urban Development (HUD) tries to encourage the purchase of housing by insuring qualified loans. The FHA does not make loans itself; the consumer secures the loan from a lender qualified to make this type of loan (savings and loan association, mutual savings bank, commercial bank, etc.). The prospective buyer must meet FHA qualifications concerning income, creditworthiness, and so on. New properties must be approved by the FHA in that the builder warrants that the home conforms *substantially* to the plans and specifications on which the FHA based its appraisal. No new or older house can be advertised as having ''FHA Approval'' to imply that the house is superior. Such ''approval'' does not occur, and this would constitute false advertising.

The government, through the FHA, encourages those without large savings to purchase homes. The maximum mortgage amount for a single-family detached home is $60,000. A minimum cash investment is required as follows: 3 percent on the first $25,000 of appraised value and 5 percent of the amount above $25,000. Terms can be for as long as 30 years.

The FHA acts as an insurer of the mortgage in case of default by the consumer. The mortgage insurance premium is ½ of 1 percent of the amount of the mortgage loan. Because private mortgage insurance companies insure conventional mortgages, the FHA does not insure as many mortgages as they have in past years. A major problem is that unlike conventional mortgage loans, which can be taken out in a matter of 2 or 3 weeks, FHA loans often take 6 to 8 weeks from the date of application.

VA-Guaranteed Loan. The Veterans Administration (VA) will guarantee against default on the mortgage loans of qualified veterans. The guarantee on a veteran's house is for $25,000 or 60 percent, whichever is less, with terms as long as 30 years. For example, if Jose Gonzales of San Antonio buys a small house for $38,000, 60 percent is $22,800. If the VA approves, that is the amount it will guarantee. If he buys a $60,000 home—and the VA approves—it will guarantee $25,000. In the event of default and subsequent loss of value in the property, the VA will repay the lender up to the amount specified. In effect, the VA guarantee is much like FHA's insurance.

The purpose of the VA's home-loan guarantee program is essentially to permit eligible veterans to buy housing when they don't have the down-payment money that is required for a conventional loan. Eligible veterans must make their own arrangements for loans through the usual lending sources. The lender will notify the VA, which will determine the eligibility of the veteran. Almost all veterans qualify, since they served in the armed forces; however, they must also meet income and expense requirements in addition to showing creditworthiness.

If the lender approves, no down payment is required. Of course, with the VA guarantee, there is no need for mortgage insurance, so it is not required either. Commonly an eligible veteran can secure a VA-guaranteed loan for a down payment as small as $100 to $200. The buyer of a new home is protected somewhat because the home must substantially meet VA standards of construction. Further, the veteran is not allowed to pay more than the VA-appraised value of any new or older home because the VA will not guarantee a loan for more than their appraisal. And the veteran is prohibited from borrowing extra down-payment money when the home has a VA guarantee.

In a very small number of cases a direct loan from the VA is made available. This occurs only in rural areas and small towns where private financing is hard to get. The maximum direct loan is $33,000. Interested veterans should contact the VA for details.

Builder-Assisted (GNMA) Loan. The Government National Mortgage Association (GNMA) is a quasi-governmental organization designed to promote more housing in America. It is also known as the Brooke-Cranston program, since those two senators were instrumental in passing the legislation. What happens is that GNMA agrees in advance to buy mortgages from lenders for less than the going rate for conventional mortgages. For example, the lender issues the mortgage to a new home buyer or apartment builder at perhaps 7½ percent instead of the then prevailing interest rate of 8½ percent for conventional mortgage loans. The lender can do this, since GNMA guarantees to *buy* that mortgage from the lender at the specified lower rate. These loans are called "builder assisted" because the lenders involved normally cooperate with specific builders, often large developers, when making such loans.

When mortgage credit is tight (difficult to

obtain) and expensive, the prospective home buyer is likely to see advertisements by builders for loans at below-market interest rates. The builder, in cooperation with a lender which already has an agreement with GNMA, helps the buyer to get a mortgage loan. The government, therefore, is subsidizing the difference between the two rates of interest. The individual home buyers with builder-assisted loans realize considerable savings because they pay a lower interest rate.

New Kinds of Mortgages

New approaches to home financing for consumers are becoming available throughout the country. The main objectives are to permit people who have previously been "priced out of the market" to be able to buy. These mortgages are also to help meet the demands of the lending industry.

A conventional mortgage is contrasted with three new types of mortgages in Table 11-6. As shown, a conventional mortgage at 9 percent on $40,000 means 360 monthly payments of $321.85, with a resulting balance of zero after the 30 years. The *variable-rate mortgage* is quite different. When a home buyer takes out a variable-rate mortgage loan, the interest rate is frozen for a certain period of time (in this example 5 years). Then it is allowed to go up or down according to the general cost of mortgage credit. The frequency and size of interest-rate changes are subject to limits, such as a maximum rise of ½ of a percentage point in any one 6-month time period with a maximum limit of 2½ percent. The rate changes are tied to an index approved by the Federal Home Loan Board.

Variable-rate mortgages benefit consumers who are trying to get a loan in times of rising interest rates, since lenders may otherwise be reluctant to commit funds. After signing such a contract, the consumer would also benefit if interest rates then declined (as shown in the

TABLE 11-6

Conventional and "New" Kinds of Mortgages (Example: A 30-year Mortgage Loan of $40,000 at 9 Percent)

	Conventional Mortgage	Variable-Rate Mortgage (Rising)*	Variable-Rate Mortgage (Declining)†	Partial-Payment Mortgage	Graduated Payment Mortgage
First 5 years	$ 321.85	$ 321.85	$ 321.85	$ 311.75	$ 305.00
Second 5 years	321.85	335.08	308.82	311.75	310.00
Third 5 years	321.85	346.90	297.65	311.75	315.00
Fourth 5 years	321.85	356.85	288.73	311.75	320.00
Fifth 5 years	321.85	364.29	282.43	311.75	325.00
Last 5 years	321.85	368.48	279.08	311.75	330.00
Payments over 30 Years					
On principal	$ 40,000	$ 40,000	$ 40,000	$ 21,511	$ 21,335
On interest	75,866	85,607	66,714	90,719	92,965
Total payments	115,866	125,607	106,714	112,230	114,300
Amount owned after 30 years	0	0	0	18,489	18,665

* Assumes rate goes up ½ of 1 percent every 5 years.

† Assumes rate goes down ½ of 1 percent every 5 years.

third column of Table 11-6, where the variable rate is assumed to decline every 5 years). Since this type of plan takes more of the risk out of financing home mortgages, lenders are offering inducements to those who will choose this type of mortgage over the conventional style. Some lenders offer a beginning rate of ¼ or ½ percent below the prevailing rate, while others permit prepayment of the loan with no penalties (when a home is later sold, for example). Consumers lose in times of rising interest rates, since they will have to pay more per month. Also, the precise amount for principal and interest in one's budget would change when the rate varied, and this could present some difficulty. Another problem is that consumers will probably have to meet tougher standards to qualify for a variable-rate loan, since they will have to prove they can meet the possible higher monthly payments in the future. Thus, the elderly, women, and members of minority groups might find it harder to get such a loan.

Table 11-7 shows the change in monthly payments on a 30-year $30,000 mortgage loan with the interest rate varying ½ percent each year. This is a more typical time span for variable-rate mortgages. In a period of rising interest rates, the monthly payment rises to $283 from $231 over 5 years. If rates declined steadily, the amount due monthly would drop over 5 years from $231 to $183. It is likely that options such as a variable-rate mortgage loan will be available when you want to buy a home.

Table 11-6 also shows the *partial-payment mortgage,* where the monthly installments are less, but at the end of the mortgage term the balance is not paid off. The *graduated-payment mortgage* installments are relatively low during the early years, but they rise every 5 years. Both plans assume that the family will have an increasing income to be able to meet the ending large *balloon* payment. In most cases the buyers will move to another home and sell the one with the new kind of mortgage. Should they remain, of course, the owner can take out a new loan to pay the balloon payment.

Other new kinds of mortgage plans include a *renegotiation clause,* which requires the borrower and the lender to renegotiate the interest rate at specified times, perhaps every 4 or 5 years. The cost of money might remain the same, or it might go up or down, thereby raising or lowering the monthly payment. The *participating mortgage clause,* which initially permits lower monthly payments, gives the lender a "piece of the action," or part of the profits if and when the owner sells. Perhaps the most radical plan is the *split mortgage,* which amortizes the home itself over 50 years (since it will probably last that long), amortizes improvements such as the heating system and appliances over 15 years, and does not amortize the land at all (since it will be there forever). All the newer methods of financing have laudable purposes, but in most plans the buildup of equity is extremely small

TABLE 11-7

Rising and Declining Variable-Rate Mortgage Monthly Payments (30-year Term with $30,000 Mortgage)

Rising Rates

Date	Rate	Payment
January 1979	8.5%	$231
January 1980	9.0	241
January 1981	9.5	252
January 1982	10.0	262
January 1983	10.5	272
January 1984	11.0	283

Declining Rates

Date	Rate	Payment
January 1979	8.5%	$231
January 1980	8.0	220
January 1981	7.5	210
January 1982	7.0	201
January 1983	6.5	191
January 1984	6.0	183

(even less than conventional mortgage plans), and this may be undesirable. Nevertheless, potential buyers who cannot quite afford the type of home and mortgage they would like should carefully consider all mortgage plans.

What Can You Afford to Buy?

Today the Department of Housing and Urban Development estimates that fewer than one in five families can afford to buy a new home with either a conventional or a government-insured mortgage loan. Even with the subsidized-interest programs, such as FHA sections 235 and 502, only about one in four families becomes eligible. The rising costs of homes have seriously dampened the desires of those wishing to buy.

Down Payments. For young couples just starting out, the first hurdle is the down payment. There is no substitute for at least $3000 unless they can qualify for a government-assisted program. More than that may well be needed; how much depends upon their housing goals and what financing method(s) they choose.

Let us assume that a young couple wants to buy a single-family dwelling or an owned apartment that costs $40,000. They expect that it will meet their space and location needs for perhaps 5 years, and they do not qualify for a subsidized-interest mortgage. How much of a down payment do they need?

The required FHA down payment on a $40,000 home would be $1500 (3 percent on the first $25,000, and 5 percent on the remaining $15,000). A 95 percent conventional financing loan would require $2000. If only 80 percent conventional financing were available, the down payment would be about $8000 (20 percent of the $40,000). Unfortunately, the down payment is not the only figure involved. There are many closing costs which must be paid at the time of purchase, and these would probably come to at least another $900. Therefore, the money needed to buy and move in for that $40,000 home would probably be $3000 to $9000 under existing lending terms.

Income Qualifications. The second problem is, can the family afford the monthly payments for all shelter costs. Three rules of thumb are often used by lending agencies. Rule one is that you should not buy a home that costs more than 2½ times your yearly gross income. Rule two is that your monthly mortgage-loan payment for principal, interest, taxes, and insurance should not be more than 25 percent of your monthly net income. Rule three is that all your debts, including repayment of principal, interest, taxes, and insurance on the mortgage loan, should not exceed ⅓ of your monthly gross income. But with today's high home prices and high interest rates, these rules of thumb are *not* practical and are of dubious value.

Assuming that the family has the down-payment funds, the first job is to determine the amount available for total shelter costs (including the mortgage loan). An approach to determining this figure was shown earlier in this chapter in Table 11-2 on page 328. Next, one must determine the amount needed for repayment of the principal and interest. Table 11-4 on page 340, which shows interest rates, may provide this figure. Finally, the family needs to estimate the other expense items included in the total cost of shelter. These would include such items as heat, electricity, water, sewage, refuse collection, special assessments, insurance, maintenance, repairs, and home improvements. Adding up these amounts gives the family a more realistic assessment of their ability to afford a home.

An income of about $1500 per month is probably the minimum needed to qualify for a mortgage of slightly more than $35,000. However, the loan amount considered acceptable depends upon much more than just the size of one's income. Important factors include the type and stability of income, the family's current indebtedness, the size of the family, previously demonstrated ability to live within one's income, past credit history, and cash reserves available. Excessive financial obligations or meager savings could postpone the application for a mortgage loan for 6 months, a

"Here's one in the price range you mentioned."

Courtesy of Edd Uluschak.

year, or longer. To avoid possible embarrassment and to learn more about home financing, many wise consumers complete an unofficial application form and then consult an appropriate lending agency about the possibility of a mortgage in the future.

THE PROCESS AND COSTS OF BUYING HOUSING

Buying housing is like making any other major purchase, except that buying a house is probably the largest financial decision of a lifetime. Hurrying the process can easily result in buying the wrong kind of home, having the wrong type of mortgage, and perhaps being stuck with a home that one cannot readily resell.

Finding the Right Home

Shopping for styles by actually looking at different homes will help you discover your own values and tastes in housing. Spending 6 months "just looking, thank you" on Sunday afternoons, visiting different housing developments and/or privately advertised homes, can give you a wealth of information. Model-house and owned-apartment sales people almost always have brochures that they are happy to give you. When you feel you are getting close to making your decision, it may be wise to go to a reputable real estate broker. If you choose an owned apartment or a house in a development, you may not want to use a broker. But if you need to do some real shopping and need more assurances about making the best buy, a broker's knowledge of the area can be invaluable.

Many real estate brokers sell in an area that has *multiple listings*. This means that all real estate in a given area is listed with and available through any broker who, in the event of a sale, splits the usual 6 percent commission equally with the broker who originally listed the home. If property is not multiple listed, the buyer has to visit several brokers and ask to see the properties each one has for sale. Needless to say, in communities that do not have multiple listing, it is more difficult to shop around. A U.S. district court recently ruled that brokers involved in multiple-listing service must be careful to not "conspire" because they would possibly be in violation of the Sherman Antitrust Act.

In any event, if you use a broker, keep in mind that the broker represents both the seller and the buyer. Multiple-listed sales bring a lower commission, so his or her bias toward the seller may be somewhat less when showing you those properties rather than those originally listed with him or her.

Inspecting a Home

Older homes as well as newer ones might at first appear to be a bargain but in fact turn out to be a headache. A thorough inspection may reveal hidden defects and specific remodeling needs.

If you have doubts about the soundness of the home you have chosen, get an expert appraisal of the property to both establish its value and point out any deficiencies. In many communities there are reputable inspection firms that will examine the home and give you a detailed written report. The $50 to $100 fee may be well spent. Some unfortunate buyers must face the expense of replacing basic equipment, such as the wiring, plumbing, or heating unit, during the first year of ownership. If you have doubts, the owner may permit you to have it checked by an expert. You probably will have to pay for this inspection but sometimes the seller will.

Should you want to call in experts, first check their reputations because there are some unscrupulous operators in the business. They often justify their fee by exaggerating flaws which they themselves (or their relatives) may want to repair at inflated costs. If it appears that repairs and improvements are needed, be sure to get estimates in advance of the cost of the work and find out who will pay for it—you or the seller.

Especially check the following items as possible problem areas: termite infestation, wood rot, sagging structure, inadequate wiring, heating and cooling units, insulation, plumbing, hot-water heater, roof and gutters, wet basement, street and driveway paving, sewer lines, and sidewalks. Furthermore, the day before you take title to a home (closing day), make a thorough inspection trip. Check all equipment, windows, and doors. This is your last chance to request any changes.

When Is the Right Time to Buy?

"There is no better time to buy than now" is probably an accurate generalization. Prices for homes keep rising every year, and money seems quite expensive too. Even in a period of declining interest rates it may be wiser to buy now rather than wait. Table 11-8 gives some figures on the possible financial disadvantages of waiting instead of buying in an inflationary period. Keep in mind that housing prices commonly rise even in times of recession.

To illustrate, using data from the table, let's say that you buy the $45,000 house now with a

TABLE 11-8

Buy Now or Wait? (Assuming a 10 Percent Increase in the Price of the Home in 1 Year)
If You Buy Your Home Now

Purchase price	$45,000
Down payment at 10 percent	4,500
Amount of mortgage loan	40,500
Term of mortgage	30 years
Monthly payment at:	
7 percent	269.73
8 percent	297.27
9 percent	326.03
10 percent	355.59

If You Wait One Year to Buy

Purchase price	$49,500
Down payment at 10 percent	4,950
Amount of mortgage loan	44,550
Term of mortgage	30 years
Monthly payment at:	
7 percent	296.70
8 percent	327.00
9 percent	358.63
10 percent	391.15

9 percent mortgage loan instead of waiting 1 year and buying the same house with an 8 percent mortgage. Do you save by waiting? The answer is no. If you buy now, your down payment is $4500 compared with $4950, which means a saving of $450. The monthly payment at 9 percent now is $326.03 as against $327.00 next year at the lower rate of 8 percent, which would result in an extra expenditure of $11.64 per year, or $349.20 over the life of the loan. The total net savings by buying now amounts to $799.20 ($450.00 plus $349.20) over the life of the mortgage. If you were wrong about guessing future interest rates and they remained at 9 percent, you would have to pay an extra $32.60 per month for a payment of $358.63, or $11,735.00 over the life of the loan (plus the extra $450 down payment).

Selecting a Mortgage Plan and Lender

Careful consideration of the mortgage plans noted earlier will narrow your choices. If you are not a qualified veteran, for example, you cannot get a VA-guaranteed loan. If you think you might qualify for a subsidized mortgage loan, check with your area FHA office. A visit to your local savings and loan association or mutual savings bank can give you preliminary information about the types of mortgages available to you, if you are willing to discuss your finances and housing goals rather thoroughly.

Shopping for better mortgage terms in a nearby community may save you ¼ or ½ percent on a loan. However, many lending agencies are hesitant to make loans for property that is too far away from their offices. Big city institutions, for example, rarely make loans for housing that is 30 or 40 miles away. On the other hand, a trip to a nearby community to check on rates might save you thousands of dollars over the life of the mortgage loan, in addition to requiring lower monthly payments.

When you select your lender and the mortgage plan, there are two other important factors to consider: How discount points work, and whether or not it is wise to take out a really big mortgage loan.

How Discount Points Work. A special mortgage charge is often made when financing is arranged with FHA or VA and many conventional loans. The fee is called *discount points* or just *points*. A point is 1 percent of the amount of the mortgage loan. For example, if a loan is for $35,000, one point is $350. Lenders charge points to raise the *yield* (or return) on the loan, which is, of course, an investment to them. Lenders charge points when money is *tight* (difficult to obtain), when interest rates are high, and/or when there is a legal limit to the interest rate that can be charged on a mortgage loan.

Usury laws in some states prohibit lending funds for home mortgage loans above certain rates. But if the money markets demand a higher rate than is legally allowed, traditional home-financing institutions will not make loans. This is simply because they can, at that time, better invest their money elsewhere. A similar situation exists with FHA and VA loans, since their mortgage rates cannot by law exceed a specific percent, such as 8¼. To equalize the yield, lenders charge points to make up the difference. Buyers are not allowed to pay points on FHA or VA loans (sellers can pay, however). On a conventional mortgage, points may be paid by either buyer or seller or split between them. Points vary according to market conditions; there may be as few as one or as many as eight or nine.

For the buyer, points mean more money. If a mortgage loan is signed for $40,000 with a discount of four points ($1600), the borrower might receive a discounted loan of only $38,400, yet would owe the full $40,000. (Now you can see how the term "discounted" came into existence.) More commonly, what happens is that someone pays the $1600 for points and the full amount of the loan is made.

Since the FHA and VA prohibit the buyer from paying the points, the price of the house is often raised to cover the cost of the points. Of course, the amount of the mortgage is similarly raised. This in turn leads to another problem—for any FHA or VA loan, the house must be appraised by FHA or VA representatives, and the loan cannot exceed the appraised value. Therefore, some sellers actually wind up having to pay the discount to the lender. But in most instances the buyer is paying the points, which are hidden in the increased sales price.

Should You Take a Big Mortgage and Save? Another important factor concerns the size of the mortgage. It is true that you can save many thousands of dollars in interest by taking out a smaller mortgage (making a larger down payment) or by shortening the term of the mortgage loan. However, you can also realize considerable savings with a *larger* mortgage. The only assumption is that the family can afford the higher mortgage payments.

Let us say that a family has an extra $5000 and is arranging a $35,000 mortgage loan on a home with an 8½ percent rate of interest and a term of 25 years. Monthly payments would be $282.20, which would total $84,660 over the life of the loan. If instead they paid the extra $5000 down, their mortgage loan would be for $30,000. Payments would be $241.80, or $72,540 over the 25 years. The savings would be $12,120, a net return of $7120 on their $5000.

It sounds good, but it is not! Those earnings could easily be tripled if the $5000 were put to work elsewhere. One conservative alternative would be to put it into a 5 percent savings account. Compounded annually, it would grow to $16,950 over those same 25 years. If it was put into a savings account at a 6 percent rate, it would amount to $21,450. Meanwhile, all those higher interest payments would be tax deductible, providing further savings. And, finally, in these ever-continuing inflationary times, you are paying back the larger loan in future years with dollars that are easier to earn because they are worth less.

Making an Offer to Buy—The Purchase Contract

This is one of the most important steps of the entire buying process, since the signed "purchase contract" or "agreement to purchase" sets forth the rights and obligations of both buyer and seller. It is a legal document binding you and the seller for a limited amount of time (usually 30 days) to the agreed price and stating exactly what is included in the price. The buyer should be careful to include all wanted and needed qualifications and contingencies. A reputable broker or lawyer can help.

Many things are important besides the actual price for the home and the "earnest money," the amount, probably several hundred dollars, given to the seller or agent to show that the buyer is serious about buying the home. Needed provisions include a cancellation clause should you be unable to obtain financing at the terms and interest rate specified in the contract; provision that the earnest money be applied against the down payment; a clause that provides for refund of the earnest money and prohibits any charges against the buyer if the sale does not go through; papers from the seller proving that he or she has clear legal title and that no liens against the property exist; provision for prorating the payment of taxes; identification of all movable items (screens, drapes, appliances, etc.) that are part of the sale; a list of repairs to be made or work to be completed before you take possession; which party pays for points; who pays for home appraisal and/or inspection visits by experts; and the specific day and place to close the sale. Setting the closing date for the sixteenth of the month, for example, instead of the fourteenth might mean that the new owner will not have to make a mortgage loan payment for 45 days instead of 15. Once the prospective buyer and seller sign the purchase contract, it becomes legally enforceable. The consummation of the contract occurs at the time of closing the sale.

The Closing Process and Costs

The closing process for buying a house is very complex. Chief Justice Warren Burger was quoted as saying, "It's much easier to transfer ownership of an ocean liner than it is for a home." Several people need to be present, and there are many forms to sign. But for the informed consumer, even the closing of a first house can be fairly simple.

When the purchase contract has been signed, the *closing day* is final. This is the day when all the formalities of a real estate sale are concluded. All parties come to a specified place, usually the lending agency, the necessary legal documents are signed, and various payments are made. The closing merely confirms the original agreement reached in the purchase contract.

The numerous expenses which buyer and seller normally incur to complete the transfer of property are called *closing costs*. These costs are in addition to the price of the property and are paid only once, on the closing day. They might include charges for a credit report, loan application, or origination fee (sometimes called "points"); property appraisal; *title search* (to pay a lawyer to search the records of previous ownership); *title insurance* (to protect the lender if there is an old claim against the property); attorney's fees; *survey* (to determine the precise location); *closing fee* (a charge for handling the settlement transaction); recording fee (charged by the local authorities); state and local transfer taxes; *mortgage insurance premiums* (to guarantee the lender against loss if you fail to make payments); and escrow fees for taxes and insurance (this includes prepayment of premiums for fire and homeowner's insurance and taxes paid in advance for which the seller must be reimbursed).

Such fees may total $400 or $800, or possibly even $1000 or more. It depends upon the state, the type of mortgage, the amount of the loan, the legal costs, and a variety of other factors. Although having a lawyer present to represent you during the closing process is not required, and will cost you about 1 percent of the sale price of the house, such protection for such a large purchase is highly recommended, unless you are truly knowledgeable in closing procedures and legal documents.

The potential confusion and overwhelmingness of closing day have fortunately been reduced by the Real Estate Settlement Procedures Act. On or before the closing day, the lender must give the borrower a consumer settlement information booklet which explains the closing process and your rights as a borrower. At the time of the loan application, the lender is encouraged but not required to make a good faith estimate of the closing costs which the buyer may end up paying. Informed consumers will insist upon early disclosure of the costs. The law does permit the borrower to inspect the statement of settlement charges the day before settlement, but if some charges are unavailable at that time, you are out of luck. Knowing the costs earlier will mean fewer surprises on closing day. The buyer will not only know more about what questions to ask, but also probably bring enough money for the closing.

Charges for title search and title insurance are a bit controversial. On one side the people want the present procedures continued to certify clear title to property and then insure against any later claims. Opponents want to transfer land by registration, more popularly known as the Torrens system. A recent HUD-VA report revealed that title-related charges were 1.21 percent of the sales price of an average home. This amounts to $60.50 on a $50,000 home. In larger communities a cost of $180 for the same-price home is common. A Ralph Nader organization, the Housing Research Group, is suing the Department of Housing and Urban Development for delaying a congressionally mandated study to find ways to revamp the title search system, which they allege costs home buyers $500 million a year more than they should be paying. The results of the study, when available, and the ensuing debate may result in more than the present few states registering property by certificate with local government authorities. In the meantime, should you buy title insurance, keep in mind that it protects only the lender up to the amount owed; you have to buy additional protection for yourself if you want it.

Several suggestions are in order to help reduce the settlement costs, and most of these things should occur before signing the purchase contract. Negotiate with the seller to share some of the settlement cost items. If a survey is required, commit the seller to give you the old survey and an affidavit that no changes have occurred; some lenders will accept this procedure. Shop for title insurance, since the rates vary widely (unless your state has fixed the rates), and check with the seller's original title insurance company, since they might give you a lower rate which is called a "reissue rate." If you want a lawyer, choose your own, but make sure the lawyer you choose is thoroughly acquainted with real estate procedures. Ask if he or she is to receive a rebate or commission from the title company or broker, and if so, ask that it be refunded to you. Keep in mind that a lawyer can only give you advice in a house purchase; a lawyer is *not* legally liable for errors in judgment unless he or she is grossly negligent. It also pays to shop for mortgage-loan rates, a surveyor, or any other necessary supplier of settlement services.

The new owner usually takes possession of the house as soon as desired after the closing, which should specify the date of possession. The house is now the new owner's. The seller has the money, and the lending agency will shortly send the new owner an installment book for those monthly payments.

INSURANCE FOR YOUR HOME

Since the owner and the lender both have a considerable investment in the property, homeowner's insurance is necessary to provide against loss. The basic concept of sharing the risk works well, since insurance companies, for example, can accurately predict how many houses will be lost because of fire each year. There are many things that can happen to one's real and personal property, and there are various types of policies to provide coverage against the general perils of property and personal liability.

Most companies sell several types of policies, including one for tenants. Each pol-

icy, or form as it is called, provides coverage for a number of perils, with the higher form numbers giving greater protection (they range from one through six). The most common forms are one, two, and five. HO-1, called *Basic* coverage, covers damages from a limited list as shown in Figure 11-2. HO-2, or the *Broad* form, protects against more risks and is the most popular. HO-5, the *Comprehensive* form, gives the greatest protection. Figure 11-2 shows the differences. Protection under HO-1 and HO-2 is on a named-risk basis, and anything not listed is excluded; under HO-5 the opposite is true—all risks are covered except those noted.

Changes in policies in recent years have been led by the Insurance Services Office, an industry organization that serves most insurance companies with loss data and other ratings information. Policies are easier to understand, and the print is bigger. Perhaps, as a survey by Sentry Insurance Company showed, more than one out of ten people will *try* to read the policies now.

To varying degrees every homeowner's policy (except tenant's policies) provides protection in six categories:

1. *Damage against the house.* If the house is destroyed, the policyholder will receive full "replacement value" only if the face amount of the policy equals 80 percent or more of the house's current replacement value. Should the house be underinsured when a loss occurs, depreciation will be taken into consideration and the homeowner will receive significantly less than the replacement value.

    For example, in the event of a $10,000 fire on a $55,000 home that was insured for only $30,000, one could only collect $6818. In effect the principle of coinsurance will prevail. Essentially, the insured and insurer "coinsure" for the loss because the insured did not purchase a policy which equals 80 percent or more of the house's replacement value. When a loss is experienced, this formula applies:

PERILS AGAINST WHICH PROPERTIES ARE INSURED
HOMEOWNERS POLICY

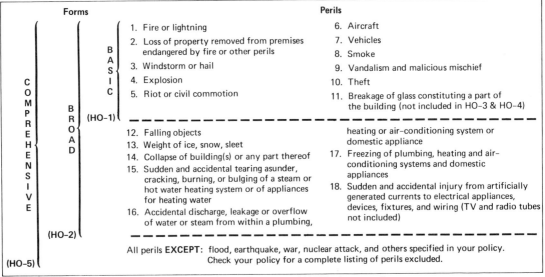

Source: Insurance Information Institute, "A Family Guide to Property and Liability Insurance."

FIGURE 11-2   Perils against which properties are insured

Amount of insurance carried

Amount of insurance required

× amount of loss = amount collectible

Putting in the above figures results in

$$\frac{\$30,000}{\$44,000} \times \$10,000 = \$6,818$$

Thus, it is obvious that it is important to review one's policy occasionally and update it if necessary. Most companies have an automatic inflation clause to raise your coverage and premiums accordingly.

2. *Damage against other structures on your property.* Coverage is usually restricted to 10 percent of the face value of your policy to protect a garage or workshed. If these items are worth much more, you can buy additional coverage.

3. *Damage to or loss of personal property.* Newer policies provide protection for the full value of the property. Personal property includes household contents and other personal belongings used, owned, or worn by members of the family. This coverage also extends to the policyholder while away from home on trips or vacation. Very importantly, it covers a college student who lives away at school under the parent's policy, providing the student has been at the temporary residence (at school) at any time within the last 45 days. Credit-card, forgery, and counterfeit-money protection is provided to a limit of $500. Certain items, such as jewelry, money, stamp and coin collections, and securities, have limits on coverage. For example, there is a $100 limit on money and $500 on jewelry. To get additional coverage, a "floater," or scheduled personal property endorsement, on these possessions may be necessary. For those who want high protection on the dwelling and need very little protection on their personal property, a *Special* form, HO-3, is available.

4. *Necessary living expenses.* When a fire occurs, it is often necessary to move into

temporary living quarters, and the policies pay for these expenses. A maximum amount of 20 percent of the face value of the policy normally will be paid.

5. *Personal liability.* This coverage protects against legal claims arising from bodily injury to others or damage to their property. It does not matter who is at fault—you, your child, your dog, or a visitor slipping on your sidewalk. Minimum coverage is normally $25,000, but for a few dollars more one can increase the liability coverage by three or four times.

6. *Medical expenses.* This coverage provides payments to those persons who are accidentally injured, at or away from your home, if the injury was caused by you, members of your family, or your animals. The payments are limited to $500 per person and do not cover members of your own family.

Renters are protected in categories three through six above with the *Tenant's* form, HO-4. It insures household contents and personal belongings against all the perils included in the broad form, HO-2. Premiums are quite a bit lower than for homeowners, since there is no exterior structure to insure. The cost might be as low as $30 a year for $5000 in coverage.

Mobile home protection is also available, and the policy provides basically the same coverage as the broad form, HO-2. Premiums are sharply higher, since mobile homes are more susceptible to fire and wind damage.

Condominium unit owners have a special *Condominium Unit-Owners* form, HO-6. The coverage is basically the same as in the broad form, HO-2. Exterior insurance coverage, of course, is paid for by the condominium association under a master policy.

Special situations have caused the government to step in and provide coverage in two very important circumstances. Damage from flood is excluded in all homeowner's policies; however, if you live in an area highly susceptible to flooding, you can buy low-cost flood insurance on your home through the federal government. Check with your local insurance salesperson for further information. Fire insurance is available through the federal government for those who live in deteriorating areas or areas with high crime rates. Under the Fair Access to Insurance Requirements (FAIR), limited maximum coverage is available at reasonable rates.

To help keep costs for insurance down, shop around. If rates are not fixed by state regulatory agencies, they may range to twice the amount that the least expensive company will charge. And that is for the same coverage! Also, having a deductible clause of perhaps $50 on your policy, can lower the premium substantially. If the company goes bankrupt, policyholders in four states should be concerned: In Alabama, Arizona, Arkansas, and Oklahoma, claims will only be paid to the extent of the bankrupt firm's assets. The other states have established pools of funds from which the insurance commissioner can make full payment of claims.

POINTS OF VIEW AND PROBLEMS TO THINK ABOUT

The quantity and quality of housing in America is not good. With approximately 40 percent of American consumers living in substandard housing and with more than half the housing in most large cities 40 or more years old, problems abound. Yet slum housing in large cities cannot be eliminated without massive local, state, and federal efforts. Incentives to destroy, renovate, and/or rebuild must be combined with standardization of building codes within states, and with planned zoning changes which do not violate U.S. Supreme Court guidelines against discrimination.

The national housing goals, which have been set realistically low, are not effectively met. Yet planning for totally new communities and large use of modular factory-built housing can be as successful in this country as it has been in many Western European countries.

Also since development in many present communities has been blocked because of inadequate sewage facilities, pollution controls and adequate facilities need to be established and funded to meet the needs of the people.

The possibility of owning adequate housing is, of course, limited in part by the relatively small number of houses being built. However, high interest rates also keep 80 percent of today's families from being able to buy new housing. Low-income families cannot afford housing either. Under most subsidy programs, help is legally available to those families whose incomes do not exceed 80 percent of the median income of the area. This amounts to 30 million households in the United States containing 75 million people—roughly one-third of the total population.

Raising interest rates (by tightening the supply of funds) to help fight inflation is one thing, but severely limiting the accessibility of housing is another. It results in a depression in the housing construction industry. Taking mortgage interest rates out of the battle against inflation and reducing the cost of home financing will take considerable effort on the part of federal and state governments, and then we will be on the road to meeting the national housing goals established by law more than 30 years ago.

One idea of former Senator Edward Brooke is a Young Families Housing Act. It would permit the young family to accumulate enough cash for a down payment by establishing a savings account called an "individual housing account." A family could deposit up to $2500 a year to a maximum of $10,000. This money would be tax deductible (the motivation), and would have to be applied as a down payment on a home (the desired result). Another idea is that the taxpayer could simply tell the Treasury how much extra to withhold from a paycheck for a "housing account."

Subsidizing interest rates for all homeowners, particularly the forgotten middle-income consumers, could reduce the monthly cost of a $40,000 mortgage by 40 percent or more, thus creating tremendous demand for new construction. Repeal of the Davis-Beacon Act, which forces the payment of "prevailing" high wages to those working on federally financed construction, could also reduce the labor costs of new housing.

The rights of homeowners—which are the rights of all Americans—need many changes to reduce the inequities. All newly constructed housing should have a clear warranty concerning quality. In Great Britain, a person who buys a house automatically acquires a 10-year guarantee: all ordinary defects are corrected for 2 years, and structural defects for 10 years. And 95 percent of new housing built in that country is covered by the guarantee. The best we have is a voluntary HOW (Home Owners Warranty) program, and the FHA and VA do not even insist on correcting defects in homes even after their inspectors find the homes have problems. Why is it that we cannot do as much?

To alleviate many slum-housing problems, an implied warranty should not only exist but be enforced, specifying that rented housing is in fact habitable and meets all building code requirements, such as heating, lighting, availability of water, freedom from rodents, and safety. Publicly controlled housing, often guilty of the same violations, should give tenants hearings before evicting them or levying assessments for damage to the premises. Elimination of many legal "hidden-trust agreements" (where the names of the true owners of slum housing are protected) might also embarrass some owners into making needed changes. Criminal, not civil, charges should be filed against flagrant violators. Remedies should be sought to eliminate out-of-state land frauds, to stop inequitable tax sales of property without full legal notification and due process before the exchange of title, to make low-cost federal flood insurance more widely available, to prevent unfair contract sales of homes, to eliminate exorbitantly overpriced title insurance, and to reduce the one-sidedness of many clauses in mortgage-loan contracts.

America's housing problems are serious. It

is the social and ethical responsibility of government, labor, business, and the consumer to try to solve them.

CHAPTER ACTIVITIES ▬▬▬▬▬

Checkup on Consumer Terms and Concepts

"Double X" discrimination code	Lease
	Tenant union
Modular housing	Equity
Private area	Purchase contract
Split-level house	Mortgage
Multiunit apartment	Mortgage insurance
Quadraplex or six-plex apartments	Second mortgage
	Contract buying
Condominium	Closing costs
Cooperative	Fire and extended
Amortization	coverage
Multiple listing	Broad form
Discount points	Floater

Review of Essentials

1. What are some of the problems consumers face in the area of housing?
2. What are some of the reasons why we have failed to reach our national housing goals?
3. Name the basic goals related to the amount of housing space needed.
4. Name several types of rental apartments.
5. Differentiate between the two types of owned apartments, condominiums and cooperatives.
6. Compare the down payments necessary with conventional, FHA, VA, and builder-assisted home financing.
7. Differentiate among the kinds of mortgage insurance available.
8. Explain the effect the rate of interest has on both the monthly payments and the total mortgage payable.
9. What are some dangers in the newer kinds of mortgages?
10. What factors should be considered when one is trying to find a house and choose a mortgage lender?
11. Explain the effect discount points have on closing costs.
12. Why might it be advisable to take a big mortgage rather than a small one?
13. What kinds of things should perhaps be written on the "purchase contract" to more fully protect the potential buyer?
14. What kinds of closing costs must normally be paid, and how much do they usually total?
15. Comment upon the problems that affect the quantity and quality of housing.

Issues for Analysis

1. Should the building codes in your community inhibit the growth of modular homes? Why or why not?
2. Should tenant unions be established in your community? Defend your position.
3. Should the "ideal" of home ownership have any effect on the available land in the United States? Discuss.
4. Could the presence of more homes and apartments affect water and air pollution in your community? Explain why or why not.

12

Money Management

THE PROBLEMS

Would you believe that a person with an annual income of $34,000 could not make ends meet? Jack Richmond of Boise, Montana, had such an income. Yet he recently filed for bankruptcy. He had been earning a good salary for several years, but his problem was that he could not stop spending. Furthermore, his wife was equally careless. They never made plans for spending, for savings, or for future goals. Simply put, they had no plans at all. Since their debts amounted to over $41,000 and their assets amounted to only $9500, Jack and his wife filed for bankruptcy.

Is the case of Jack Richmond typical? Perhaps, perhaps not. Yet 183,000 personal bankruptcies were filed in 1971 and nearly 200,000 in 1977, and 230,000 are projected for 1982. The number of bankruptcies filed increased by 90,500— or 54 percent—between 1965 and 1975, while the population of the country increased by only 11 percent for the same period.

The great number of bankruptcies is attributed largely to the careless use of credit. But the real problem lies with the credit users themselves. Many consumers simply have not been able to handle their finances effectively. When they run out of money, they use charge accounts. They "forget" that they must pay these charges. Before long they have far exceeded their ability to repay and find themselves filing for bankruptcy—and bankruptcy is, in effect, the ultimate reward for poor money management.

Too many marriages end in divorce, suicide, or desertion—and the number one reason for this is poor money management! It is a case of not enough money and too many demands. More specifically, there is a lack of discipline or know-how when it comes to handling family finances.

When Jane and Paul Holly were married, they were riding on a cloud. Both were working and making good salaries. They had a nicely furnished apartment with an inexpensive rent. Everything seemed fine. But they had not set goals or made any plans for handling the family finances.

Is the case of the Hollys serious? Yes, according to a study involving 400 marriages. Couples took an average of 7 years to end disagreements on management of income. About 15 percent still considered it their main problem after 20 years of marriage. Fortunately, many young people recognize the problem early and either solve it or get help. Others are not so lucky. They end up with broken marriages. Floyd and Edie Fulton of Dallas were recently given a divorce. In retrospect, both agreed that no divorce would have been necessary if money-management help had been available. Of over 1100 divorces recently granted in Dallas, for example, a study showed that 75 percent of the couples pointed to some financial or money-management problem as the basis for the divorce.

MONEY MANAGEMENT—PURPOSES AND DEFINITION

Money management means using a systematic method of planning for spending, based on the expected income of the individual or family unit, and founded on a favorable attitude toward the use of effective buying knowledge and practice.

There are three key points in this definition. First, there is the *use of a systematic method*. This is necessary for effective organization. Second, there is *a plan for spending*. Essentially this is to let one know where the money is to go and/or has gone. And third, there should be *a favorable attitude* toward both the first two points. This is really the firm foundation of the whole plan.

Realistically, the purpose of money management is to help an individual or a family to achieve predetermined goals. Further, the purpose is not to guarantee more income, but to ensure a better use of what income there is. Money management can be considered a method of disciplining oneself to plan spending. It permits people to appreciate the value of the money earned and to plan for and be accountable for money spent. It also lets people realize both short- and long-range goals. Money management is a very personal

process. It should not be patterned after what some other person or agency has decided.

Money management is the broad picture, and a *financial plan* (an estimate of income and expenditures for a period) is one of its important elements. Furthermore, *record-keeping* (keeping a record of actual income and expenditures) is an essential step in developing and operating a financial plan. Figure 12-1 graphically illustrates this relationship.

MAJOR FACTORS INCLUDED IN THE MONEY MANAGEMENT PROCESS

Many factors are involved in a comprehensive understanding of money management and its operation. Some of these factors are the value of the dollar, family income, use of credit, level of education, buying habits, and the needs and wants of individuals and families. All of these are discussed below.

The Dollar Value

Inasmuch as one of the major purposes of money management is to get the most for

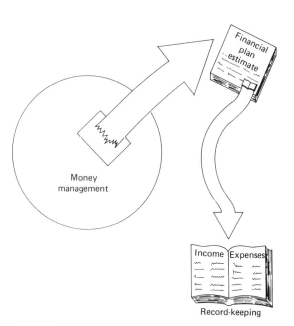

FIGURE 12-1 Relationship of money management, financial planning, and records

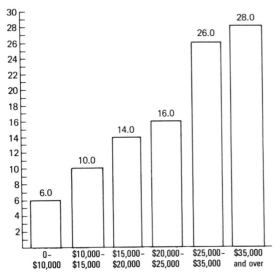

Source: The Conference Board

FIGURE 12-2 Annual income of families by income group, 1985 estimate

one's money, one must be aware of the influences on the value of the dollar.

Inflation. Inflation is an economic term that means that prices are rising rapidly—*more rapidly* than the real value of the commodities or services. From the consumer's viewpoint, this means getting less for one's money. In the language of the shopper, "It costs too much money to buy, and I get less and less for more and more."

Deflation. Deflation can be considered the opposite of inflation. A sudden decrease in prices would be a short but apt definition. Commodities cost less. Prices are reduced. In essence, the dollar increases in value.

Of course, inflation or deflation have other results in the economy, too, such as increased or decreased productivity, employment, and demand and supply, to mention but a few. It is sufficient to say that the value of the dollar, as it is affected by both inflation and deflation, is an important consideration for the consumer.

Since planning is a major part of money management, the consumer must realize first

that no plan is foolproof. During inflationary times, the plans of today may not work as well in a month or a year because of the diminished value of the dollar. Furthermore, since a deflationary period could bring about more unemployment, the consumer may be laid off and faced with loss of income. These are factors that must be considered.

Consumer Income

A person or family with an annual income of $15,000 to $20,000 will consider plans for spending in a very different way than one with an income of $10,000 to $15,000. The range in family income can be seen in Figure 12-2 as estimated by the Conference Board. Family income classifications range from under $10,000 to more than $35,000. The median income in 1977 was $14,720. The median figure is projected to be $17,500 by 1982 and $26,000 by 1985.

Earnings must surely be counted when considering appropriate money management. Also, answers to pertinent questions are needed: "Are my earnings fairly stable and predictable for the selected period of time?" "Should the wages of the earner be the only income consideration?" "Do I have income other than regular salary that I can rely on?" Answers to these and other questions are needed if one is to move toward a greater understanding of money management.

Although each family unit must of course consider its own financial situation, one can hardly ignore the impact of aggregate (total) consumer income. For example, in a recent year the aggregate personal income for Americans was $1464 billion. This amount represents the total amount of money that consumers had available to spend. To be sure, some of this money went for taxes. However, even after taxes, net personal income was $1246 billion.

That is a lot of money for over 220 million people. And rather than having one person or agency allocate these dollars, the hundreds of thousands of employers throughout the country allocate them to their employees. Each employee, in turn, is supposed to give a fair day's work for a fair day's pay.

People who draw Social Security or get other pension or retirement checks on a monthly basis have what is called a *fixed income*. Many people on fixed incomes cannot foresee any appreciable increase in the amount of their earnings, although Social Security recipients do get cost-of-living increases. Prices may go up, rents may go up, costs of services may go up, but income remains pretty much the same. Effective money management is much more difficult for the fixed-income person, yet it is a necessity if one is to survive economically.

Credit Buying

Credit buying is an important factor in money management. Credit use is convenient, and it is easily available to most consumers. But again, it can be used excessively.

Mrs. Carla Kirkland of New Orleans was window-shopping one day when she saw a dress she liked. She had no cash or checkbook with her, but she did have her Master Charge card. And so Mrs. Kirkland bought the dress and charged it. It is a common story.

Using credit in this way is most assuredly not bad—unless it reaches the point where the consumer disregards the proper use of credit and creates future financial problems. Then it becomes a case of "not being able to resist."

When using credit, one must be aware of a major point—its cost. The use of credit cards does not necessarily mean that there will be additional costs, but there often are. If credit is used wisely, the costs can, for all practical purposes, be avoided. Credit use, therefore, must be controlled to eliminate or reduce the cost.

Education and Income

Two areas closely associated with an understanding of money management hinge directly upon education: amount of income, and the use of that income.

The amount of income that a person is likely

TABLE 12-1

Lifetime and Mean Income of Persons Aged Twenty-five and over by Years of School Completed

Years School Completed	Lifetime Income (Dollars)	Annual Mean Income (Dollars)
Elementary		
8 years	369,000	10,300
High school		
1–3 years	401,000	11,700
4 years	510,000	13,900
College		
1–3 years	599,000	15,300
4 years	815,000	21,600

Source: Statistical Abstract of the United States, 1977, extrapolated to 1979.

to earn usually increases in relation to the number of years of schooling. Table 12-1 shows the expected lifetime earnings of persons with varying amounts of education.

As can be noted, the more education a person has, the more income he or she can hope

TABLE 12-2

Expected Monthly Earnings of Individuals Graduating from College with Bachelor's Degree, By Occupational Fields

Occupational Field	Average Monthly Salary (Dollars)
Engineering	$1453
Chemistry	$1296
Accounting	$1248
Mathematics, statistics	$1223
Others	$1207
Sales, marketing	$1141
Economics, finance	$1103
Business administration	$1038
Liberal arts	$1012

Source: Extrapolated to 1979 from Frank S. Endicott, *The Endicott Report 1977* (Evanston, Ill.: Northwestern University, Placement Center).

to earn. This education/earnings relationship has a bearing on establishing a money-management plan. For example, a person with 2 years of college may consider going back to school for a bachelor's degree.

A different view of the importance of education as it relates to earnings is presented in Table 12-2. This table shows expected earnings according to occupational field.

Both the number of years of formal education and the field studied affect one's earnings. Also, as income rises, its distribution will vary somewhat, as shown in Table 12-3. A family with an income of $12,537 per year, for example, will spend an average of $3752 (30 percent) for food, $2447 (20 percent) for shelter, and $1117 (9 percent) for medical costs. In comparison, a family with an income of approximately $20,254 will spend $4810 (24 percent) for food, $4790 (24 percent) for shelter, and $1116 (6 percent) for medical care. In summary, typical budget figures of three income levels differ noticeably in both dollar and proportional amounts.

Consumer Buying Habits

Several factors influence the buying habits of all consumers. Let us examine some of them.

External Influences. Advertising (newspaper, magazine, television, or radio), family pressures, societal demands, religious ties, ethnic background, type of neighborhood, and occupation are all examples of external influences that affect buying habits. To be influenced by and through external forces is natural, but when one fails to recognize these influences for what they are, it becomes difficult to counteract them, when necessary, with common sense and planning.

You should make a reasonable effort to resist undue influence, whatever the source. To buy simply because an item is advertised as being "better than any other brand" seems almost robotlike. "Everyone is wearing it," may be one teenager's remark to his parents, or "I want a pair of shoes just like Harry's," may be another's comment. Each shows the domination of some external influence for buying.

TABLE 12-3

Average Living Cost Estimates for a Family of Four in Urban United States (1979)

	Lower Budget $	Lower Budget %	Moderate Budget $	Moderate Budget %	Higher Budget $	Higher Budget %
Food	3,752	29.9	4,810	23.7	6,059	20.4
Housing	2,447	19.5	4,790	23.6	7,276	24.5
Transportation	954	7.6	1,745	8.6	2,287	7.7
Clothing and personal care	1,330	10.6	1,867	9.2	2,703	9.1
Medical care	1,117	8.9	1,116	5.5	1,188	4.0
Other family consumption*	590	4.7	1,096	5.4	1,787	6.0
Total cost of family consumption	10,190	81.2	15,424	76.0	21,300	71.7
Personal taxes	1,782	14.2	3,917	19.3	6,831	23.0
Other Costs†	565	4.5	913	4.5	1,544	5.2
Total budget	12,537	100.0‡	20,254	100.0	23,759	100.0

* Includes reading materials, recreation, education, tobacco, alcoholic beverages, and such miscellaneous things as bank service charges, legal fees, and children's allowances.
† Includes allowances for gifts and contributions, life insurance, occupational expenses, and Social Security, disability, and unemployment taxes.
‡ Percentages may not add to 100 due to rounding.
Source: Bureau of Labor Statistics, U.S. Department of Labor, 1976; extrapolated to 1979.

Courtesy of Edd Uluschak.

"Of course we had to give something up to be able to afford it—namely, gasoline."

It is important that you be able to recognize external influences for what they are when you plan and spend. Go along with them when you can and want to, but do not let them dominate you.

Self-indulgence. "I could use," "I would like to have," "I want," "I need." Each of these statements typifies the self-indulgent consumer. What may start out as a "could use" soon becomes a "want" and finally winds up as a "need." It is amazing how many consumers can mentally move a product from a "would like" to a "need" in a matter of minutes.

Self-indulgent consumers need to reexamine very carefully their values and goals in life before they decide to shift these "would likes" to "needs." Of course, some people just allow themselves to be self-indulgent, but a firm basis for effective money management is to describe one's goals realistically. Such goals reflect concerns of other family members, too.

Consumers tend to spend most of their earn-ings, and they do not save much. But if consumers learn to plan, to do without, to live within their income, and to save regularly, they will not be faced with so many financial frustrations. Occasionally they will even be able to indulge themselves.

Unlimited Wants versus Limited Income. Economics revolves around one central problem—deciding how to satisfy society's unlimited wants with its limited resources. Consumers have the same fundamental problem—deciding how to satisfy unlimited wants with limited income. Effective money management can help. The limited income will still be there. So will unlimited wants. Yet these unlimited wants can be listed in order of importance and given a priority. Soon one can see the list of priorities change and many of what were once thought of as absolute wants will change to "would like to have, but really can do without," or simply "luxuries." One caution—no matter who puts together this list of priorities, there will probably be some disagreement. Occasional reexamination of priorities will help to clarify established family or individual goals.

Choice Making and Opportunity Costs. An important concept is that of *opportunity costs*, sometimes called *alternative costs*. Opportunity cost means what a productive factor could return if it were used in some other activity; the amount needed to attract a productive factor away from some alternative use. In consumer terms, this means that if resources (primarily labor or capital) are used to satisfy one human want (clothing, food, housing), they cannot be used to satisfy another want (transportation, medical costs, recreation).

Fundamentally, opportunity costs, as related to choice making, become a series of decisions that must be made constantly. A college student, for example, realizes that if she has only $30 and she spends it on repairing her television set, she will have to forego the new skirt on sale at a local store. Similarly, the student who decides to play poker for money before school, and loses, learns about opportunity costs rather suddenly. He finds that the cost of his lunch was given over to the alternative cost of playing cards for money. Each time a decision is made, other alternatives have been put aside, at least temporarily.

Comparison-Shopping Skills. Often family money-management plans fail because of careless shopping. A desire to have a product is frustrating if, when the time comes to buy it, the consumer is overwhelmed with the dilemmas of which price, what quality, and which brand to choose, and makes a poor choice.

This is when money management and comparison-shopping skills go hand in hand. Money management can be considered as a major plan, developed according to predetermined goals. Comparison-shopping skills can be a primary force in the successful use of the major plan.

Ms. Judy Moore, a junior college sophomore from Senatobia, Mississippi, wanted to take her vacation in England during the summer following her sophomore year. To do this, she made some very thoughtful money-management plans during the year before her trip. The trip was estimated at $935, using special excursion rates. Ms. Moore's resources were very limited, but through carefully planned comparison shopping for books, supplies, clothing, and other essentials, and by the sacrifice of several costly recreational outings, she was able to achieve her goal. In the same way, through thoughtful planning, practicing comparison-shopping skills, and making a few sacrifices, other consumers can reach the goals they set for themselves in their money-management plans.

College-Student and Young-Adult Spending. College-student spending is somewhat different from that of other people of the same age who are not in college. Spending for tuition, books, and other school supplies reflects students' special needs. Table 12-4 shows some typical amounts spent. As noted, the bulk of the expenditures (almost 60 percent) goes for the essentials of room and board, tuition,

TABLE 12-4

Typical Monthly College Student Spending*

Expenditure Category	Amount	Percentage
Room and board	$119	23
Tuition	134	26
Books and supplies	46	9
Transportation	26	5
Recreation	31	6
Snacks, food, etc.	26	5
Gifts	16	3
Personal care	21	4
Laundry and cleaning	21	4
Medical care (other than college provided)	21	4
Other miscellaneous	57	11
Total	$518	100

* Based on funds provided from parents, savings, earnings, scholarships, or other.

books, and supplies. Excluding these items, the strictly college-student expenses come to about 40 percent of the total expenditures. Seemingly, little is left for truly discretionary spending.

Family and Individual Needs and Wants in the Life Cycle

Obviously the needs and wants of consumers will vary according to their particular stage in the life cycle. Let us look at some of these stages.

The Cycle Begins. When Bill and Ellen Creiger were first married, they both worked. Sensibly, however, Ellen Creiger's salary was not used to cover regular household expenses. Most of her weekly take-home pay was put into a savings account. The Creigers planned to have a family, and when their first child was born Ellen planned to leave her job, at least temporarily.

In the meantime, Bill and Ellen made plans to buy household furnishings they wanted before they began their family. They planned on a piano for Ellen and some hunting and fishing equipment for Bill. They knew that if they did not get these items now, they might not be able to get them for a long time. After children were born, most of their income would go only for "must have" items.

Through a carefully thought-out money management plan, the Creigers worked toward their goals. Fortunately, they discussed their ideas together often and knew pretty much what they wanted as first-priority goals: children, furnishings, a few luxuries, a home of their own, and a sound insurance program. With their money management plan in full operation during the first 3 years of their marriage, it was easy to predict that the Creigers would realize their goals. They did have some unexpected expenses, and after 3½ years, Ellen Creiger was expecting her first child.

Young Children's Needs and Wants. The world is full of surprises, as the Creigers discovered. Ellen Creiger gave birth to twins,

Scott and Dana. But did the Creigers have to make any major financial adjustments? Not necessarily. They had been planning for more than one child over the next few years. The only difference was that the few years telescoped into a few minutes. Bill and Ellen made a few adjustments in their plans, then continued on their way toward enjoying life and achieving their other goals.

Immediately, of course, they had to plan for two of many items instead of one—or enough for two instead of one. But this doubling-up routine did not fluster the Creigers. By now, they were well used to money management. The Creigers were also lucky enough to have very devoted grandparents for their children, who gave the twins many toys. But if such grandparents had not been available, the Creigers would have provided these items themselves by sacrificing other items or rearranging their priorities.

Teenagers' Needs and Wants. When Scott and Dana Creiger were in the tenth grade in high school, they were aged 15. What changes had come to the Creiger family when their children had reached this age? To be sure, basic food and clothing costs had risen, but so had income—Bill got a recent promotion, and Ellen returned to work. Any additional expenses to speak of? Not many, but Scott and Dana had thrust themselves into hyperactive roles in school activities, and some of these cost money. Scott tried out for football and made the team, which meant that additional medical-insurance coverage was necessary. Dana wanted to take voice lessons so she could try out for some roles in a production her music/drama club was to be presenting later in the year. And, of course, the twins needed increased allowances for recreation and personal expenses, even though they also earned money on their own.

These are normal types of costs for a family with two teenage children. And Bill and Ellen had not forgotten that within a few years Scott and Dana would probably be going to college. Their written management plans had become worn and had been adjusted many times. But they been enjoying life while achieving their goals and objectives.

College Students' Needs and Wants. Needless to say, the expenses of sending two children to college are high. There are tuition, books, lodging, and food to pay for. Then there is laundry and dry cleaning, and money for travel and personal expenses. Fortunately, the Creigers planned ahead and purchased mostly machine-washable clothes for the children, thus reducing dry-cleaning expenses. A small saving was realized when Bill and Ellen were able to lower their own at-home food budget. After all, two children eating at college were not eating at home. Furthermore, a college regulation prohibited cars on campus, and so automobile operational costs and insurance premiums were reduced markedly, since Scott and Dana were not home 9 months of the year. And too, Scott and Dana were able to get part-time jobs to help with the expenses.

The college expenses strained the Creiger finances, but with Scott and Dana almost finished—Scott in engineering and Dana in medicine—Bill and Ellen can look over their plan once again and set some new goals.

Later Family Needs and Wants. And so it goes. The children were born, grew up, finished high school, went on to college, graduated, and are now about to begin the same life cycle on their own. And what of Bill and Ellen? Well, back to the money-management plan. Currently heading their list is an often planned, but never realized, trip to Europe.

Both Bill and Ellen are relatively young—fifty-two and forty-nine, respectively. So now they can plan for other things in life. The financial focus is no longer on the children—it is more on Bill and Ellen. Perhaps before long it will even include plans for assuming the roles of devoted grandparents.

The life cycle of the Creigers is not meant to be typical of all families throughout the United States. It does, however, demonstrate suc-

cessful money-management planning throughout the life cycle. Using it, they were able to realize their goals and objectives. They were not just lucky—they planned.

Surely different people have different needs and wants throughout the various stages of their lives. We each have our own values and lifestyles, and these may change as the years go by. One's own money-management program is, therefore, both short-and long-term so that it can reflect these values.

PERSONAL/FAMILY FINANCIAL PLANS

"The whole is equal to the sum of its parts" is a familiar statement in mathematics. The same statement is true of the relationship between a financial plan and money management. One of the most important factors leading to successful money management is the financial plan, which contributes significantly to the whole money-management process.

Goals and Purposes of the Financial Plan

A financial plan is meaningless unless it relates to a "picture" clearly painted by its creator—the individual or the family. The goal of a financial plan is to meet the primary needs and wants of its makers in accordance with their expected income. Such income is distributed among the various expenditure classifications and projected for later spending. Characteristically, spending is controlled and records are kept. Finally, comparisons are made to see how well the plan was followed.

The purposes of such a plan are to set direction, establish pace, and set a limit or boundary. Limits are usually set in terms of dollars of income and spending needs. The direction is set on the basis of personal needs, wants, tastes, and—occasionally—external influences. The pace is the speed at which the individual or family wants to approach the limits based on the direction.

Why Use a Financial Plan?

Regardless of the size of their income, many families have the problem of not being able to make ends meet. Financial planning does not increase the income. However, it is used to systematically determine the most effective way to spend the income that the family expects to earn. It is for that reason we can make the statement that the ability to accomplish financial objectives is not equal to the size of the family's income. A carefully made financial plan can use income to improve the family's level of living in many ways. Let's consider some of the ways in which financial planning can help families and individuals.

An obvious reason for financial planning is to allow the family to improve their material level of living, to buy more and better goods and services. In turn it often improves the social status of the family in their neighborhood and among colleagues and peers. This is usually a result of the family's reaching the goals set for themselves. To some families this status seeking is a goal in itself. Along with improving one's image in the eyes of others, these material goods provide many hidden psychological satisfactions for the family members. This is a factor that cannot be overlooked in making the financial plan.

As mentioned earlier in this chapter, money problems have been a primary reason for many divorces and suicides in the past. This shows how important financial planning can be in helping to smooth relationships within the family. Using a predetermined financial plan, the family members can see the improvements and changes that are being made in the management of the household. Relieving pressures, providing a sense of sharing and togetherness, and maintaining fairness and equality among the family members in dealing with financial matters help to improve family relations. One study of young families revealed that in 67 percent of these families, women controlled the day-to-day finances; in 31 percent, men handled the family funds; and *only* 2 percent of the households shared the responsibility.

Setting Goals in Financial Planning

We have mentioned indirectly the importance of setting goals in financial planning. Many families set goals, but do not plan financially to accomplish them. Both long-term and short-term goals can be achieved more satisfactorily if they are included in a financial plan. Setting goals is very important for a family, as it forces its members to examine and clarify their values. They must decide what is important to them, what they will give up to attain this, and what values will take top priority in their lives. The priorities for the family will often depend on the stage in the family life cycle. The same basic goal, for example to purchase a second car, might have low priority for a young couple, have first priority for a family with children in high school, and not even be considered by a retired couple. Whatever the situation, setting goals and working toward them leads to better organization of family activities. In particular, it requires the family to devise ways to use available economic and noneconomic resources in order to best attain the desired goals.

Throughout this process of clarifying values, setting goals, and incorporating these goals into the financial plan, it is very important that the family be realistic in what it hopes to accomplish. Unrealistic goals will only disappoint the family and frustrate its efforts.

Another purpose of financial planning is to help the family avoid financial difficulties. With a financial plan, the family can allocate its income and see exactly where the money needs to be spent. Through the use of stated goals, the family can look at its objectives and decide which ones might be postponed for a while in order to avoid overindebtedness. For families who are already having financial difficulty, a plan can help them see where they are overextended in their credit use; it can also help them identify ways to cut down on spending to reduce debts.

DEVELOPING A FINANCIAL PLAN

In setting up the actual, or "master," financial plan, the first thing to do is assess family resources. Second, consider other resources available to the family (including present financial position, income, and nonmonetary re-

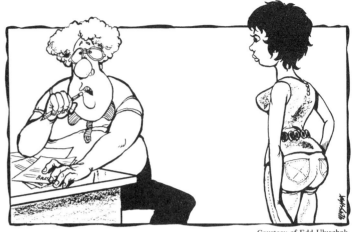

Well, our financial worries are over—we're out of money.

Courtesy of Edd Uluschak.

sources). Third, the expenses for the period of time being planned for must be projected. After a careful look at these factors, the family can begin to write out its financial plans on paper and soon arrive at a well-organized plan.

Determining Family Resources

The resources that a family has for use in planning for improving its level of living may be of a wide variety. However, the first resource most of us think of is money. And so estimates of present financial condition, future income, and other resources must be made.

Present Financial Position. For a family to assess its financial status in terms of money, the net worth must be determined. *Net worth* means what's left when the family's *liabilities* (what is owed) are subtracted from its *assets* (what is owned). It is a balance, just as in a checkbook, and can be figured easily by using a balance sheet or financial statement such as the one in Figure 12-3. The assets—the current values of car, house, antiques, etc., plus cash, savings, and other monetary items on hand—are listed separately and totaled. The list also helps you identify your total liabilities (installment debts, mortgages, etc.). When the two totals are subtracted, the remaining figure is the *net worth*. What does this mean to a

family? It tells them what they are "worth" at present, and what they would have if all debts were paid. This gives them a place to start in making a financial plan, and lets them compare their progress from one period to another.

Income. Another major resource to determine is the actual income the family is likely to receive during the period. This income may be in the form of wages and salaries, or it may be from Social Security benefits, pensions, welfare payments, and/or the value of food stamps. Other possible sources of income might be investment dividends, interest from savings, tax refunds, gifts, and bonuses. In financial planning, it is important to distinguish between gross income and disposable income. *Gross income* is the money you get from all sources of income. *Disposable income*, also called *net income*, is the amount left after federal and state income taxes, Social Security tax payments, retirement fund contributions, insurance, credit union, and other such deductions have been taken out of the salary or other source of income. This is the amount that the family actually has to spend.

In estimating the family's income for a particular period, it is generally a good idea to list the sources and estimated amounts of income

FIGURE 12-3   Balance Sheet or Financial Statement

	Beginning of the Period	End of the Period
Assets		
Money in savings accounts	$_____	$_____
Cash on hand and checking account balance	$_____	$_____
Cash value of:		
Home and other real estate	$_____	$_____
Automobile and other vehicles	$_____	$_____
Household equipment and furnishings	$_____	$_____
Insurance (cash value of policy)	$_____	$_____
Bonds, stocks, and other investments	$_____	$_____
Annuity or retirement plan (cash value)	$_____	$_____
Money owed you	$_____	$_____
Other_____	$_____	$_____
_____	$_____	$_____
_____	$_____	$_____
Total Assets	$_____	$_____
Liabilities		
Mortgage	$_____	$_____
Debts owed (installment and single-payment loans)	$_____	$_____
_____	$_____	$_____
_____	$_____	$_____
_____	$_____	$_____
Total Liabilities	$_____	$_____
Net Worth		
Total owned minus total owed	$_____	$_____

on a chart such as the one shown in Figure 12-4. This will let you clearly visualize the income you have to work with and where it is coming from.

Other Resources.   Other nonmonetary family resources are often taken for granted or not used to their full advantage. The production that goes on within the household is an invaluable resource and greatly determines how effectively the monetary resources are used. The special talents, skills, and knowledge of family members can be used to make household production more efficient, as well as to provide entertainment, pride, and psychological satisfaction to the family at minimum cost. An example of this would be the ability to raise a garden and preserve your own fruits and vegetables. Another is the talent of a family member in arts and crafts, which

provides recreation and also allows the making or renovating of items for the home. Other "bargain" resources are offered to the family by the community. Free libraries, parks, and museums offer education and entertainment, and community recreation programs and organizations offer opportunity for leisure activity and for self-improvement. These noneconomic resources must not be overlooked in the financial plan, even though a monetary value is not assigned. The ultimate difference will show up in your savings and enjoyment.

Projecting Expenses

Perhaps the hardest part of making a financial plan is to determine as accurately as possible approximately how much the family will spend during a month and then during a year. To begin, expenses can be *fixed* or *variable*. *Fixed*

FIGURE 12-4   Determining Disposable Income

	Previous Year's Income (to Help as a Guide)	Income Expected Current Year
1. Determining Gross Income	$_____	$_____
Salary, wage, or commission	$_____	$_____
Other salary, wage, or commission	$_____	$_____
Interest	$_____	$_____
Tax refunds	$_____	$_____
Gifts	$_____	$_____
Pensions	$_____	$_____
Social Security	$_____	$_____
Annuity	$_____	$_____
Bonuses	$_____	$_____
Rents	$_____	$_____
Dividends	$_____	$_____
Special fees	$_____	$_____
Welfare payments	$_____	$_____
Food stamps	$_____	$_____
Other income_____	$_____	$_____
_____	$_____	$_____
_____	$_____	$_____
2. Total Gross Income	$_____	$_____

3. Deductions from Income (Record these deductions on a monthly basis)

Federal income taxes deducted	$_____
State income taxes deducted	$_____
Social Security taxes	$_____
Health insurance	$_____
Life insurance	$_____
Accident insurance	$_____
Disability insurance	$_____
Retirement fund contributions	$_____
Union dues	$_____
Company savings plans	$_____
Credit union savings	$_____
Other deductions_____	$_____
_____	$_____
4. Total Deductions (monthly)	$_____

5. Total Deductions on an Annual Basis (multiply the total of deductions in 4 by 12)
$_____

6. Total Annual Disposable Income (Subtract total of these deductions in 5 from Total Gross Income in 2)
$_____

7. Total Monthly Disposable Income (Divide annual total in 6 by 12)
$_____

expenses are those of fixed amounts, occurring on a regular basis. Examples of these are rent and auto-loan payments. *Variable expenses* are those whose amounts vary and can be controlled. Food and clothing are good examples of variable expenses. But before any of these expenses can be estimated, the family must list the goals they hope to accomplish in their spending.

Goals. In listing financial goals, the family can divide their goals into long-term, intermediate, and short term. *Long-term goals* are those things which the family hopes to accomplish some time after the next 5 years. These goals might include paying off the mortgage on the house, accumulating savings to provide education for children, or saving to sustain the couple or individual during retirement years. The goals to be accomplished within the next 1 to 5 years are *intermediate goals*. Buying a new automobile or major appliance or saving enough money to make a down payment on a house might be intermediate goals. *Short-term goals* are those immediate wants and needs of the family for the current year. Examples are reducing present debts, going on a vacation, buying special recreational equipment such as a boat or bicycle, or merely meeting the fixed expenses each month.

After the goals have been listed in the proper categories, the amount needed for each can be estimated. These must be divided into yearly and/or monthly savings amounts in order to be of value in projecting planned expenses. The list of goals serves a specific purpose here and can referred to time and again as the financial plan is implemented.

Determining Spending Patterns. The list of goals explained above gives the family some idea of the spending and saving they hope will take place in the future. But, how can the family estimate the other day-to-day or month-to-month expenses that must be covered? One good way to do this is to refer to previous records. Old bills, receipts, check stubs, etc., allow the family to see what it has spent for various purposes in the past. Correcting these figures for the rising cost of living gives a general estimate of future costs.

Many families fail to keep these records, so they have no way, other than guessing, to estimate their expenditures. These families would be wise to have each family member keep an accurate record of all money spent for a period of time, such as 2 weeks or a month or 2 months. This will probably show a more typical spending pattern. This record keeping,

When you make up a financial plan, you need to find out how much you usually spend. One of the best places to get this information is from old bills, receipts, and check stubs. (*Kenneth Karp*)

combined with referral to past records, can give an excellent picture of the family's spending patterns.

Making a Written Long-Term Financial Plan

Now that net worth, income, and expenses have been determined and projected, the individual or family must sit down and write out their specific financial plans. How much time this master plan will cover is totally up to the persons involved. A young family with children might want to lay out plans that will cover from the present until the children have completed their formal education. Another family might want their plan to take them to retirement. A widowed or divorced woman with two small children may want to plan only to resolve some short-term debts. It is important for all concerned to consider their own needs and stage in the life cycle before they decide on the length of the plan they are making.

Savings. The most important item in attaining financial goals is savings. Far too many families plan to save only whatever is left over *after* expenses are covered, rather than having a plan *for* savings. In the end, there is usually nothing left to save. Thus, they either go into debt to try and accomplish their financial goals or do not accomplish them at all. A set amount of planned savings should be determined and subtracted from disposable income before any of the income is allocated for expenses. A form like the one shown in Figure 12-5 might be valuable in determing a personal plan for savings.

In this case, the Andersons, a family of five, has as its goals for the year to purchase a new refrigerator for approximately $600 and also to have $1000 for a vacation the next summer. These are totaled and listed as specific wants. They have $500 on hand that was left over from the amount they had saved for last year's vacation. This is subtracted from the total goal to arrive at the actual savings amount that they must include in their budget. They would also like to give each of their three children a $25 savings bond on their birthdays. Purchased at $18.75 each, this amounts to $56.25. Since they do not have any funds to carry over for this purchase, they must budget for the entire $56.25. Other savings the Andersons might plan, such as a college education fund for the children, would be entered in the other column in the same fashion. When the monthly budget is planned, these amounts are added and divided by 12 (for 12 months), and this figure included with the other expenditures budgeted for. Thus the family has a much greater chance of actually reaching these goals than they would have had without planning.

When many families are asked what they are saving for, the answer is often "a rainy day." This certainly has merit, but if the family is trying to achieve certain goals, this type of savings might better be called a special emergency fund. An emergency fund must be budgeted for separately from the savings that are earmarked for "other" goals. Again, the amount depends on the individual family's situation. One suggestion is that an amount equal to 2 months of the "breadwinner's" take-home pay should be kept on reserve for an emergency fund. In the case of the Andersons, this is approximately $2000. The amount would certainly vary according to family size, stage in the family life cycle, and the amount and types of insurance and other benefits held by the family. This type of savings should be listed on the savings plan too. Unless the emergency fund is used up completely, there will usually be an amount carried over from the previous year that will merely have to be added to in order to maintain the fund.

Expenses. We have already distinguished between fixed and variable expenses. In making out the written long-term plan, the family must estimate the approximate yearly total of these. The expenses that are easier to view at the yearly level are those large *irregular* or *revolving expenses.* Examples of these are insurance payments, tuition, and taxes, all of which come due at a certain time of the year rather

FIGURE 12-5   Sample Savings Plan

	Specific Wants	Emergencies	Security	Other (Specify)	Total
Goals for Year End	$1600	$2000	$56.25		$3656.25
Less: Now on Hand	$ 500	$1400	$ .00		$1900.00
Budget for Year	$1100	$ 600	$56.25		$1756.25

than being monthly expenses. However, it is important to plan and save for these on a monthly basis, or the funds will not be available when needed. Figure 12-6 will help families plan for meeting these expenses. These planned savings will be included in the family's monthly budget along with the regular fixed and variable expenses.

Using the Plan. When a financial picture for a year has been developed, the next logical step is to break the plan down into monthly, or perhaps even weekly, budgeting periods. Then the plan becomes usable.

When you start using your plan, you will no doubt see that you have to make some adjustments to realistically meet the goals you have set. In some cases the goals must simply be postponed in order to meet other expenses adequately. Remember that even though your plan is written, it still must be flexible. Make necessary adjustments to achieve short- and long-term goals.

IMPLEMENTING THE FINANCIAL PLAN THROUGH BUDGETING

Now that written guidelines have been set up for long-term financial planning, the family must turn to the task of implementing their plans on a regular basis. Keeping a close enough check on finances to achieve long-term objectives can only be done effectively by budgeting of each month's expenditures. Reviewing each budgeting period in terms of how it fits in with the total master plan assures the family that their planning, spending, and saving are going in the right direction.

It has become apparent in our discussion that budgeting is not financial planning in itself. This is a misconception that many people have, and therefore their financial plans are not as future-oriented as they should be. It is important to remember that budgeting is a vital short-term tool to be used in implementing total financial plans. We should also remember that the planning of a budget should

Year 19___ Month Date	Amount Needed to Cover Large Expenses	Deposit in Reserve Savings Fund	Paid from Reserve Savings Fund	Reserve Savings Fund Balance
(Describe Expense Item:)				$ 600
January *Auto insurance*	$ 250	125	250	475
February		125		600
March		125		725
April *Federal income tax*	400	125	400	450
May		125		575
June		125		700
July *Auto insurance*	250	125	250	575
August		125		700
September *Tuition*	600	125	600	225
October		125		350
November		125		475
December		125		600*
Total	1,500	1,500	1,500	

Total Large Irregular Expenses: $ _1,500_ Divided by 12 = $ _125_ which is the amount to be deposited in Reserve Fund each month.

*Should equal balance at beginning.

FIGURE 12-6   Reserve fund worksheet

be a joint family effort, as it affects each member of the family. For that reason, it is a good idea for each member of the household to be given a personal allowance so that he or she is totally responsible for maintaining at least one small part of the budget. Before just sitting down and selecting a rigid form that will be used for the budget, there are many factors the family must consider. A budget will not work unless it has been planned to fit around the family's basic lifestyle, values, and objectives. The budget must be "personalized" for that particular family. How do you go about doing this?

The Budgeting Process

In setting up the personalized family budget, there are seven basic steps that can be identified: (1) Determine what goals you want to achieve in the budgeting period. (2) Estimate the disposable income that will be available for the family's use during the budgeting period. (3) Categorize the types of expenses the family will normally encounter during the budgeting period. (4) Estimate the approximate amounts the family will spend in each of these categories. (5) Devise a worksheet for the budget that suits the family's individual needs. (6) Accurately record the actual expenditures on the worksheet. (7) Evaluate and modify the budget periodically as needed.

These steps seem clear-cut, but there are certain reminders and aids that can help. We need to consider each step in greater detail.

Goals. Earlier in our discussion we said that goals can be classified as long-term, intermediate, or short-term. Long-term and intermediate goals appear in the family budget under savings, since achievement of these goals is likely to occur through savings. Short-term goals might also be covered in the savings category of the budget, or they might be listed in a specific category of the budget, or they might be listed in a specific category if they are to be a current expenditure during a particular budgeting period. If the family has listed several short-term goals, it will need to determine when each of these is to be accomplished so it will know exactly what current goals are to be included in each month's budget. It is only logical that these financial goals be looked at first in the budgeting process, as their accomplishment is a major purpose of financial planning. Setting priorities for spending is essential to the entire organization of the budget, or the budget will not fit into the total financial plan.

Income. One important purpose in setting up a budget is to help the family live within a certain income. Before considering expenses, the family must take time to estimate very carefully the amount of income available for its use. Estimating disposable income was discussed in detail earlier. For the monthly budget, a similar estimate of income should be made for each month. This is a definite pre-requisite to making out the actual expense budget.

Expenses. Steps 3, 4, and 5 of the budgeting process deal with expenses. A logical step in estimating expenses is to list the major categories under which the family's expenses fall. The two basic subdivisions in the budget would be *fixed expenses* and *variable expenses*. *Fixed expenses* will be either *regular*, such as rent and installment payments, or *irregular*, such as insurance, tuition, and taxes. List these expenses first, since that income is *already committed*. Be sure to include in the budget *each* month the amount that you will need to save to meet those large, irregular fixed expenses when they come due.

Variable expenses are also of two types. *Regular variable expenses* include food, transportation, etc. These occur regularly, but they are variable because the amount you spend on them can be controlled to a certain extent. The other type of variable expenses is *occasional variable expenses*. These expenses include clothing, entertainment, furnishings, medical costs, and other expenses that do not occur on a regular basis. These might also include funds planned for vacations, Christmas gifts, and large purchases of clothing for back-to-school needs. The amounts spent in many of these categories can be drastically cut or eliminated entirely, depending on the family's situation.

Categorizing expenses may be easy, but the difficult part of budgeting comes when you try to estimate how much you will want to spend in each category. The fixed expenses are set, so that part is already done. But how will you estimate the amount your family spends or should spend on food? on entertainment? We have already noted that the best way to do this is to refer to previous records, check stubs, and bills, and to keep an accurate record of all money spent for a certain period of time. This should provide a fairly good estimate of what you are likely to spend during this budgeting period. One point to remember is that what you have spent for certain items in the past is *not* necessarily a good indication of what you

Courtesy of Edd Uluschak.

At least we've got something money can't buy—poverty.

should be spending; it is only a guideline for setting up the initial budget.

Record-Keeping and the Financial Plan

Before one can compare actual income and expenses with the estimates, these amounts must be recorded. Recording estimates has been discussed. Recording actual income and expenses is the primary task in this phase.

The Mechanics of Record-Keeping. Recording actual income and expenses can be done by one of two methods: the cash method or the accrual method. With the *cash method,* you record every transaction only when there is an actual payment or receipt of cash. With the *accrual method*, you record these transactions when they actually occur, even though payment may be made much later.

Bill Johnson from Beloit, Wisconsin, liked the accrual method because he felt he always knew his overall financial position. When he bought a suit, for example, he charged it, but he recorded it as an expense for clothing for this month. He knew also, of course, that he would eventually have to pay for it.

Ms. Zelpha Berglund from Tucson, Arizona, prefers the cash method. She feels that the only way to keep accurate track of cash is to record when it actually comes in and goes out. Of course, it is important that she remember what the cash was paid for and record this as soon as possible. Recording problems can occur with partial payments. Ms. Berglund, for example, regularly charges clothing, services, and gasoline to her charge accounts. Last month she charged $250 for such items. This month she will make several payments, amounting to $75, to be applied against what she owed. When she makes her payment, she must know what portion of her $75 is for clothing, gas, and so forth, then record the amount for each type of expenditure. A little more effort is involved for Ms. Berglund, but if it works, then this is the method she should use.

In addition to selecting the method of recording, one must also decide on the amount of detail to be recorded. "Should I record every item regardless of amount?" "Should I record whether the purchase was for children's clothing or for father or mother?" "Should I record expenditures separately (such as gas $17.00, electric $32.00, water $8.50) or as a group (such as utilities $57.50)?" Each financial planner will have to answer these questions personally. So long as the

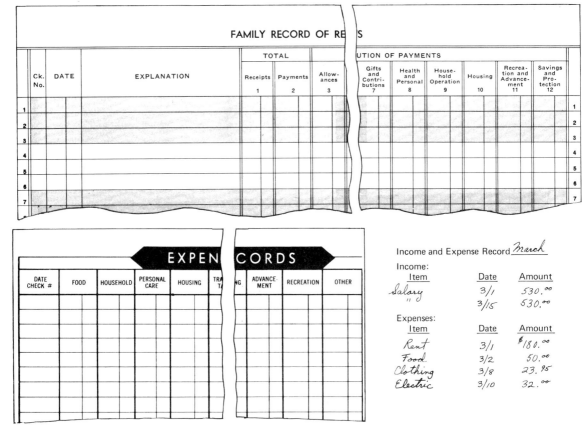

FIGURE 12-7   Illustrative record-keeping forms

method used or details kept and recorded help to achieve the goals, the system is all right.

Suggested Formats to be Used in Record-Keeping. As we said, the style of record-keeping is of little importance so long as it serves its purpose. Figure 12-7 shows a few suggested formats that one could follow.

The Budget Worksheet. A specific form that can be used successfully is the budget worksheet, an example of which is shown in Figure 12-8. The important thing to remember in setting up a budget worksheet is that it should suit the needs of that particular family. The number and types of categories will vary with the family's lifestyle and desire for detail. And the format of the worksheet that is most con-

venient for record-keeping will also vary with personal preference and need. It is highly unlikely that any two families will set up exactly the same worksheet. For those who need suggestions, textbooks and other publications give many variations of forms for budgeting purposes. Separate budgeting forms, often called family financial records, are available at stationery, office supply, and department stores. Setting up the worksheet that best suits your own income, spending patterns, and time schedule is the key to easy budgeting.

Evaluating the Budget

A family using the form shown in Figure 12-8 could easily record and compare income with the planned budget, and accurately record the actual amounts spent in each category. The

FIGURE 12-8   Monthly budget worksheet

	Month_____ 19_____		
Disposable Income	$_____		
Fixed Expenses	**Planned**	**Actual**	**(+) or (−)**
Taxes	$_____	$_____	$_____
Real estate	$_____	$_____	$_____
Personal property	$_____	$_____	$_____
Federal income tax	$_____	$_____	$_____
State income tax	$_____	$_____	$_____
Mortgage or rent	$_____	$_____	$_____
Fixed utility payments			
Water	$_____	$_____	$_____
TV cable	$_____	$_____	$_____
Other	$_____	$_____	$_____
Insurance			
Life	$_____	$_____	$_____
Medical	$_____	$_____	$_____
Auto	$_____	$_____	$_____
Other property	$_____	$_____	$_____
Installment payments			
_____	$_____	$_____	$_____
_____	$_____	$_____	$_____
_____	$_____	$_____	$_____
Notes payable	$_____	$_____	$_____
Licenses, fees, and dues	$_____	$_____	$_____
Tuition	$_____	$_____	$_____
Planned savings	$_____	$_____	$_____
Emergency fund	$_____	$_____	$_____
Fixed Expense Total	$_____	$_____	$_____
Variable Expenses			
Food			
Meals at home	$_____	$_____	$_____
Meals out	$_____	$_____	$_____
Entertaining	$_____	$_____	$_____
Alcohol and tobacco	$_____	$_____	$_____
Housing			
Furnishings & equipment	$_____	$_____	$_____
Housekeeping supplies	$_____	$_____	$_____
Maintainence & repairs	$_____	$_____	$_____
Variable utility expense			
Electric	$_____	$_____	$_____
Telephone	$_____	$_____	$_____
Fuel	$_____	$_____	$_____
Other	$_____	$_____	$_____
Clothing			
Purchase	$_____	$_____	$_____
Dry cleaning & Laundry	$_____	$_____	$_____
Alterations	$_____	$_____	$_____
Transportation			
Gasoline and oil	$_____	$_____	$_____
Repairs	$_____	$_____	$_____
Tires	$_____	$_____	$_____
Public transportation	$_____	$_____	$_____
Medical care			
Doctor bills	$_____	$_____	$_____
Medicines	$_____	$_____	$_____

FIGURE 12-8   (Continued)

Dental care	$_____	$_____	$_____
Personal care			
Cosmetics	$_____	$_____	$_____
Barber and hairdresser	$_____	$_____	$_____
Other	$_____	$_____	$_____
Recreation			
Vacation and trips	$_____	$_____	$_____
Recreational equipment	$_____	$_____	$_____
Entertainment	$_____	$_____	$_____
Education			
School Supplies	$_____	$_____	$_____
Books & reading materials	$_____	$_____	$_____
Gifts and contributions	$_____	$_____	$_____
Personal allowances	$_____	$_____	$_____
Variable Expense Total	$_____	$_____	$_____
Fixed Expense Total	$_____	$_____	$_____
Total	$_____	$_____	$_____

final step is to evaluate the budget. The last column on the budget worksheet is to record the difference between planned spending and actual spending. This will show where the family has underestimated as well as overestimated either certain items or the whole budget.

EVALUATION OF THE TOTAL FINANCIAL PLAN

We have explained above some of the considerations in evaluating the budget. A similar evaluation of the total financial plan should be made each year. Begin this annual evaluation with the same point you started planning—*net worth*. This new net worth figure can be compared with last year's to give a general idea of how successful the financial plan has been in increasing the monetary resources of the family while achieving the goals. Notice where changes in assets and liabilities have occurred. Are your savings larger this year? Have debts been increased? Questions such as these will let you see in what direction your financial planning is going.

Next, look at the overall plan in terms of each monthly budgeting period during that year. Figure 12-9 provides a form to transfer the planned and actual spending for each month onto a year-long chart (3 months per sheet). The individual or family should enter subtotals for each major expenditure category into the appropriate space on the yearly budget worksheet. At the end of the year, this record should be looked at in terms of the individual's or family's goals. With this total picture you can best see where the individual's or family's needs and goals are not being met and note adjustments that should be made in the future.

During this process of planning and spending, if the family's goals have been met, well and good. If not, a reassessment of the plan needs to be made. Maybe the goals were unrealistic to begin with. It is also possible that some values or aspects of the individual's or family's lifestyle have changed during the course of the year, making certain goals no longer important. New goals may need to be listed in order for the overall plan to remain adequate.

Throughout our discussion of financial planning, we have emphasized that things must be planned to suit the *particular individual or family*. By the same token, the ways in which the individual or family chooses to adjust their plans will also be very individualis-

FIGURE 12-9 Budget worksheet for Year 19_____

Item	Month_____			Month_____			Month_____		
	Planned	Actual	Total to Date	Planned	Actual	Total to Date	Planned	Actual	Total to Date
Fixed Expenses:									
Taxes									
Mortgage or rent									
Fixed utility payments									
Insurance									
Installment payments									
Variable Expenses:									
Food									
Housing									
Clothing									
Transportation									
Medical care									

tic. Cutting back on spending, shifting goals, using more human resources, and other measures will depend upon the lifestyle of the individual or family and the efforts made. Thus, financial planning requires you to have a better knowledge of yourself and the family. It demands awareness and analysis.

HANDLING FINANCIAL PROBLEMS

Although financial planning should be looked at as a preventive measure, many people begin to consider budgeting or any form of planning only after they are already in serious financial trouble. Financial planning can be part of the remedy, but before any permanent solution can be found, the specific problem(s) and cause(s) must be identified.

The Need for a Positive Attitude

A positive attitude is a must when it comes to practicing money management. Yet there are thousands of people who do not consider the consequences when they try to manage their finances. Poor credit ratings, continual indebtedness, misuse of income, little or no goal achievement, divorce, and personal bankruptcy are frequent results of a poor attitude toward money management. Positive attitudes toward money management result in effective use of income, realization of goals, and personal satisfaction.

Financial Problems and Their Causes

Financial problems are of a wide variety but center on or result in either the loss of income or the overextension of income. Many financial problems come from mismanagement of money and credit, but there are other outside causes as well. Let's examine these problems and causes in greater detail.

Loss of Income. Loss of income is a financial problem that sometimes happens to individuals or families through no fault of their own. Unemployment, resulting from illness, disability, change in economic conditions, seasonal work, or other reasons, just happens. Since this problem is often out of the individual's or family's control, the major implication here is that an emergency fund can help alleviate this type of problem if it should occur.

Overextension of Income. This widespread problem can have a variety of causes. Individuals or families who do not have a planned, balanced budget can easily spend more money than they are making. Individuals or families who do budget may encounter medical emergencies or other unexpected expenses that require them to spend more than they planned. In such cases, the emergency fund is eventually used up and the savings account is also dipped into. When an individual or family uses planned savings for current expenses, their goals are not met and they are depleting their savings.

Beyond unexpected expenses, a major cause of overextension of income is the misuse of credit. This can happen in a number of ways. One common pitfall is the accumulation of an overload of installment debt. Another problem is the overuse of credit cards. Both of these actions can lead to dangerous indebtedness. The credit rating is downgraded, and then one may face the problem of not being able to obtain credit at all. This, of course, greatly limits one's spending power.

Other mismanagement problems plague the overextended individual or family, too. *Impulse buying* (spur of the moment buying) is one practice that, if it is done too often, can create financial difficulty for the individual or family. Planning the budget around the individual's or family's goals and working toward

these can help reduce this problem. Additionally, when large irregular expenses such as taxes, insurance, and tuition are not budgeted for, the individual or family may have to use up their savings or go into debt to pay for them. Previously a plan was suggested to create a reserve fund in anticipation of these expenses. This can be a problem-solving device too.

Poor Decision Making. Many students will be breaking out into the real world where they get money instead of grades for their performance. Most wouldn't be too dissatisfied with perhaps $13,200 a year, meaning a monthly salary of $1100. For purposes of illustration, let's see how things can get really messed up.

TABLE 12-5

Illustrative Monthly Budget (Single Person)

Income:	
Salary ($13,200 annually)	$1100
Expenses:	
Income tax (federal)	220
Income tax (state, 5%)	55
Social Security tax (6.13%)	68
Automobile installment payment (36 months)	188
Rent	225
Food	140
Medical insurance premiums	60
Gasoline, oil, and maintenance	75
Automobile insurance premiums	———
Life insurance	———
Household furniture and furnishings	———
Clothing	———
Recreation equipment	———
Personal entertainment	———
Vices	———
Reading material and education	———
Savings for . . .	———
Emergency fund savings	———
Investments	———
Gifts and contributions	———
Trips to relatives	———
Vacations and long weekends	———

How can one flirt with financial disaster? How might a person get locked into a lifestyle he or she really doesn't want? All it takes is to go out and buy a nice new car on the installment plan soon after graduation.

Let's see what happens. Table 12-5 shows what a typical budget might look like after buying a nice new car. Putting in those known figures like taxes and making a few assumptions about some other expenses quickly tells you the bad news. The items listed amount to $1031! Buying a car on credit will seriously affect your lifestyle. You won't be able to do some of the other things you'd like to do. You have *only* $69 left to cover the remaining expense items. Buying a new car upon graduation may end up being a poor decision.

Other Symptons of Poor Money Management

Listed below are several financial involvements that are symptoms of poor money management:

1. You have lost track of what your debts add up to, and the balances owed don't seem to decrease much.
2. Your checking account has an overdraft loan feature and you use it too frequently.
3. Both husband and wife write checks and have not developed a system to show the correct current balance.
4. You can't figure out where your money goes, and there is not much to show for all your outlay.
5. You have no reserve cash to meet emergencies.
6. You find it harder and harder to save; you show more withdrawals than deposits in your savings account.
7. You depend heavily on extra income—bonuses, overtime, moonlighting—to get you over rough spots.
8. You take out a new loan to pay off old ones in order to extend the payment time.
9. You find yourself dipping into funds accumulated for one item, such as insurance premiums, to pay for other bills.
10. You use credit to purchase things like clothing which you previously bought with cash.
11. Some of your creditors have started sending you reminders about overdue payments.
12. You pay only the minimum amount due each month on your revolving charge accounts.
13. You tend to be late in paying bills or you shuffle them around, paying some creditors this month and others the next.
14. Bills once paid promptly are now placed on the bottom of the pile, and you wait longer and longer to pay them.

How to Get Out of Debt

When the family finds itself leaning toward overextension, careful budgeting may be the only answer. Analysis of the budget will show where expenses for specific items might be reduced and where variable spending might be curbed. If, after budgeting, the family realizes that they are in serious financial trouble, then other measures must be taken.

Reducing Overindebtedness. The first logical step in seeking help with overindebtedness is to call the creditors. Many creditors will make arrangements to *prorate payments* so that the debtor can pay what he or she can afford to each creditor and not fall behind in paying any particular debt. In effect, the creditor(s) agrees to accept less than the proper amount and "stretch out" the payments by lowering the amount of each payment. Another approach is to ask each creditor to let you skip one payment, if that will help the situation, and finally make that payment at the end.

In any event, let your creditors know about your overindebtedness. You are likely to find that they are reasonable people and will help you help yourself to resolve your debts. After all, they have just as much to gain as you do.

Financial Counseling. If the family needs in-depth financial counseling to help them change planning and spending patterns, many services are available. The traditional source of financial counseling has been the family minister. This may be helpful, but such persons are rarely trained in financial counseling. The Family Service Association and the Consumer Credit Counseling Services (CCCS) are two agencies that have offices across the country staffed by people trained in financial counseling. They are nonprofit organizations. Counselors can help people determine why their finances are in poor shape and help them get out of trouble. In about 40 percent of the CCCS cases, the counseling service intercedes with creditors to cut down monthly payments to manageable levels. There are also many private debt counseling agencies to help persons get out of debt, but beware of "hidden charges" if you go to a profit-making organization. Finally, there are legal aid societies and other social service agencies to help families with financial difficulties. The important thing is to realize when you need help *and* to ask for it before matters become even worse.

Bankruptcy. If all the options mentioned above fail, then bankruptcy may be the only course left to take. There are two types of voluntary bankruptcy that a family may file as outlined in the Federal Bankruptcy Act. The first is straight bankruptcy in which certain assets of the individual or family are sold in order to pay off creditors. You are allowed to keep such necessities as the house, automobile, clothing, and other household goods. To file bankruptcy under Chapter XI, a fee of $50 to $100 is charged. This results in a "clean slate" for the debtor and the opportunity for a fresh start. Once this type of bankruptcy has been declared, it cannot be declared again for 6 years. This means that the individual or family will have to manage finances carefully during this period, and are *not* necessarily seen as a "bad risk" by creditors and have a chance to rebuild their financial status. All records of this type of bankruptcy are removed from the credit file after 14 years.

The second type of bankruptcy is referred to as Chapter XIII of the Federal Bankruptcy Act and is known as The Wage Earner Plan. This plan is available to any person whose income is from wages, salary, or commissions. To file this type of bankruptcy, the debtor petitions the court for an extension of time in which to pay debts. The debtor must submit a plan for paying these debts. At least one half of the debtor's creditors must agree to this plan. The court then appoints a supervisor to counsel the debtor and help with the arrangements for paying the debts, such as determining the percentage of income that will be used for living expenses and the amount that will be deducted from wages to pay the debts. The debtor has 3 years in which to pay off debts. Through this procedure the individual or family is not subjected to the social stigma of going through a straight bankruptcy, as they still can pay old debts. A great advantage of bankruptcy proceedings is that once the petition is filed, creditors are prohibited from harassing the consumer/debtor and trying to collect the entire debt. Thus, the individual or family is protected under the bankruptcy laws.

It is up to the individual or family, with the advice of an expert, to decide which type of bankruptcy, if either, would be better for their situation. Legal advice from a private lawyer or a legal aid society can help with this decision and with the procedures that follow. *Remember, this is the last resort.* Hopefully, careful financial planning has kept the individual or family from coming to this point, and instead, given guidance to successfully achieve financial objectives.

POINTS OF VIEW AND PROBLEMS TO THINK ABOUT

Bankruptcy, financial problems, ruined marriages, misuse of earnings, and other money-management problems will continue to exist in the years to come. But individual consumers need not accept these problems as personally inevitable. Surely the financial and money-management problems facing consumers are both solvable and preventable.

With 10 million people earning less than $5000 a year, and with about 200,000 personal bankruptcies filed each year, it is no wonder that some consumers have formed a negative attitude about handling financial problems.

Fortunately, some laws are designed to help those who have money-management problems. This is especially true of Chapter XIII of the Federal Bankruptcy Act. This act allows the district courts to keep creditors from harassing the indebted consumer. When you file a "Chapter XIII," the pressure from creditors stops. Future interest on bills and loans, except for secured loans, ceases. Landlords cannot evict you for back rent; creditors may not contact you, and if they do, they are in contempt of court. Your fixed indebtedness is established, and you pay it off over a definite period of time, usually 3 years. A court-appointed trustee receives your money and gives to your creditors. Essentially, Chapter XIII is a legally established process that allows consumers to repay debts under controlled conditions without pressure from creditors. Even creditors favor the Chapter XIII plan, since they receive 100 cents on the dollar, which they would not under straight bankruptcy.

Concerted efforts must be made to help all persons with their money-management affairs. These efforts must come largely in the form of education. Individuals and families must be given the skills and knowledge they need to be financially solvent.

An income of $5000 or less for any family is definitely low. An income of $7500 or more would help such consumers. Little can be gained, however, unless consumers have a positive attitude about using money wisely, regardless of the amount of income available. Efforts to provide more income for the poor, the culturally deprived, the aged, the sick, the crippled, and those low in ability will be in vain if money management and consumer education programs are not established first. Government, businesses, private agencies, educational institutions, and individual citizens must work together to provide a learning environment that will help people help themselves solve family financial problems.

CHAPTER ACTIVITIES

Checkup on Consumer Terms and Concepts

Money management	Long-term goals
Dollar value	Net worth
Inflation	Intermediate goals
Fixed income	Financial goals
External influences	Revolving expenses
Self-indulgence	Fixed expenditure
Opportunity costs	Budgeting process
Comparison shopping	Budget worksheet
Financial plan	Accrual method
Disposable income	Financial counselors
Variable expenses	Positive attitude
Present financial condition	Bankruptcy

Review of Essentials

1. Name three major problems which have occurred because of poor money management.
2. What are the key points to consider in the definition of money management?
3. State the relationship between money management, financial plans, and record keeping.
4. What effect does the dollar value have on the financial plan of any consumer?
5. Name some reasons why fixed-income persons are handicapped in their spending during inflationary times.
6. What are some external influences that could have an effect on the buying habits of consumers?
7. Explain the relationship between choice making and opportunity costs as applied to money management.
8. What effect do comparison-shopping skills have on the success of money management?
9. What are some guidelines for the development of a financial plan?
10. Describe the several steps used in developing a financial plan.
11. What specific types of income should a

person or family use in developing a financial plan?

12. Explain the difference between fixed and variable expenditures and give examples of each.

13. Of what value is the comparison between the estimated and the actual amounts in a financial plan?

14. What are the two methods used for handling income and expenses in the record-keeping process? Explain the differences.

15. Of what value is a budget worksheet to one who is using a financial plan?

16. Identify several symptoms of poor money management.

Issues for Analysis

1. What can be done to reduce the number of personal bankruptcies, divorces, and suicides that are often caused by poor money management practices?

2. What can community service agencies do to help people who are having money-management problems, even though they appear to have adequate incomes?

3. Should poor money managers be allowed to free themselves from overindebtedness through straight bankruptcy? Why or why not? How about allowing relief from over-indebtedness through Chapter XIII of the Bankruptcy Act only? Why or why not?

13

Consumer Savings

THE PROBLEMS

Developing the discipline of saving is very difficult for some people. One main problem is that these people do not have a goal. And until one develops a goal, one is likely to continue to spend all one's income. The goal for saving can be almost anything—from buying a new dress to making a down payment on an automobile. To get started, you need to save only a small amount each week or month. This is true of people from all income levels, because both poor people and people with substantial incomes often do not save.

The next question is: Where can a person save to make sure that the money will be safe, readily available, and earning a reasonable rate of return (interest)? There are many differences among financial institutions. Also, knowledge of the frequency of paying interest on savings, liquidity, risk, how interest is calculated, and the concept of compounding are valuable pieces of information. Not knowing them costs consumers many dollars.

Those who put money in a savings institution need more complete information. For example, some banks advertise that they are paying "5 percent annual interest, payable quarterly" on savings. Is this really 5 percent annually, or is it less than 5 percent? Or more? The answer depends largely on how the interest is calculated, what amount of savings is used for the calculation, and the amount of time involved. Information of this type is seldom given to the savings consumer, although many say that it should be.

Some consumers have been exploited over the years *because* they are practicing thrift. Savings clubs have been encouraged by banks and other financial institutions. Christmas Club accounts are the most popular. Many financial institutions have, under pressure, started to pay interest on these short-run accounts. However, many still do not pay any interest at all. In these cases, banks and other financial institutions continue to use the saver's money. This is hardly an equitable business arrangement and does not encourage knowledgeable consumers to save.

Less than 45 percent of small savers understand what is meant by "compounding of interest." Over 50 percent do not know the different ways interest is calculated at commercial banks and at other thrift institutions, and nearly 45 percent are not aware of the exact interest rate paid on their savings accounts, as shown in a recent research study. The real problem is not having, not seeking, or not caring about information in regard to savings accounts. Is this ignorance or consumer apathy?

Regulations and other laws regarding financial institutions can have a negative effect, although the intent is positive. Federal regulations, for example, limit the maximum interest rate that commercial banks and savings and loan associations can pay on savings accounts. Because of these limitations, savers have been discouraged from saving on a short-term basis because the rates are too low.

Furthermore, there is overt discrimination by thrift institutions on the way and how much persons may save. Banks pay consumers interest rates of only 5¼ percent a year on their savings—well below the inflation rate. On the other hand, banks pay corporations and wealthy persons rates as high as 9 percent per year for their deposits. Collectively, the corporate deposits and the small-saver deposits earn the *same* return for the bank, but individually the small saver is paid nowhere near as much interest.

In another instance, banks are allowed by law to pay a higher rate of interest on $100,000 certificates of deposit—made by corporations and the extremely wealthy. But the small saver cannot afford the minimum deposit of $100,000. In the words of the chairman of the board of the nation's second largest bank, "This is a real ripoff."

When consumer interest groups and other agencies strive for congressional financial reform, the voice of the banking industry—the American Bankers Association (ABA)—always screams loud and clear against reform. Any long-term action to benefit the small saver is going to have to come from the consumer and more importantly from enlightened bankers who are interested in equity, competi-

tion, and fair play for the consumers' savings dollars.

THE PURPOSE AND IMPORTANCE OF SAVINGS

Savings take many forms. They range from a few pennies in a child's piggybank to millions of dollars in banks or other financial institutions. *Savings* can be defined as including all basically risk-free ways that consumers can use to better their financial positions. Investing in stocks and bonds, although considered a form of savings by many consumers and economists, is not covered under this definition. Saving is a way of putting your money to work, with virtually no risk, to enable you to better your financial position.

The Value of Savings to Consumers

"A penny saved is a penny earned." This statement implies that there is value in saving. And it is true that consumers who save regularly will be able to enjoy the benefits of their savings in the future. These benefits can come in the form of material things, such as a new car or a new boat, or in less material forms, such as recreational activities or vacations. Some people, of course, just enjoy watching their money grow. Another important value is having money available when and if an emergency arises. Easy access to cash from savings on short notice, known as *liquidity*, is extremely important. Also, these savings can earn interest until such a need or purpose arises.

A very important value of savings for the consumer is enjoyed by many, because it is savings dollars that provide millions of dollars to lend. Money borrowed is someone else's money saved. Banks, savings and loan associations, and credit unions depend on savers to provide the funds to make loans to others. Thus money saved by many is valuable to other individuals and businesses, and consequently to the American economy. As more money is saved, the likelihood of more loans increases, and with more loans the probability of economic growth also increases.

The Whys of Savings

Why save? The answers are many and vary with the individual. People save for a better home, to educate their children and themselves, for the future, and for retirement. Many save for security. Others save for a new television set, for a vacation, or because it is "the thing to do." Regardless of why people save, the important point is that they do save, and save with a purpose. Most people also save because they want to earn interest on their money. Interest is the money earned by saving at commercial banks. However, for those who save at savings and loan associations, these earnings might be more accurately called dividends. Interest and dividends are the same in regard to savings, and the terms are used interchangeably in this chapter.

There are persons who want to save but for some reason are unable to. Yet, if some of these consumers would take "inventory," they might be pleasantly surprised to see their gradual accumulation of earnings from some *indirect* sources. For example, a monthly mortgage payment on a house shows a saving every month as one's equity increases. Many people also have a gradual buildup of cash value in a permanent life insurance policy, and this, too, is an example of saving.

Another indirect saving occurs when one has reduced any outstanding credit balances during the past year, and with them the credit charges. Here, of course, the consumer is involved in a forced-savings plan, since he or she has to make those payments. Buying needed goods on sale, or using a "no-service-charge" checking account are other forms of indirect savings.

How Much Is Saved by Consumers

The confidence people have in the economy has a significant effect on savings. Consumers tend to save anywhere from 5 to 8 percent of

A special vacation is one of the reasons why people save. (*Bruce Gilden*)

their disposable (after taxes) personal income. But after wage and price controls were instituted in 1971, most savers had less confidence in the economy, so they began to save more.

Of course, the amount of money saved also fluctuates with the income people earn. Although the proportion of earnings saved was as high as 25 percent in 1945, the actual dollars amounted to only $37.3 billion. Although the dollar amount has increased greatly, the percentage of income has remained relatively stable in recent years at just over 7 percent.

Who Does the Saving and Where

Millions of consumers save. The amounts vary primarily according to income. Low-income consumers have more difficulty saving, since their money must go for necessities. The lower middle-income consumers, those families earning between $8000 and $12,000, are the most consistent savers. They more often see the need for saving in order to reach their goals. Families earning $12,000 to $18,000 are also regular savers, and they save a significant percentage of their income. Those with incomes over $18,000 also save, but usually not consistently. Nor do they save a proportionately larger share of their incomes. The spending habits and values of upper-income consumers result in some families saving and others not. On the other hand, persons with high incomes lean more toward investments than toward pure savings.

The question now is, where are these people doing their saving? Where people save and the total amounts saved are shown in Table 13-1. Of the savings institutions noted, commercial banks are the leaders in amounts saved. They hold about one-half of such funds. Nevertheless, these banks do not pay the highest interest rates. Maximum interest rates payable are set by law, and banks are therefore limited in what they can pay. For example, in 1978 banks were allowed to pay 5¼ percent on regular accounts, 5½ percent on 90-day minimum savings, 6 percent on 1-year maturities, and 6½ percent on 2½-year maturities. Savings and loan associations were permitted to pay ¼ of 1 percent *more* on each type of savings. Credit unions can pay up to 7 percent legally on regular savings accounts if they want and have enough earnings to make such payments. Even though banks do not pay the highest interest rates on savings, people frequently save at a bank because that is where they have their checking accounts and it is convenient.

Savings Flow

Typically, savings follow a steady flow pattern to and from individuals, businesses, and savings institutions. Figure 13-1 illustrates what happens to such money in a commercial bank.

TABLE 13-1

Places and Amounts of Personal Savings (Primary Sources) (in billions of dollars)

Commercial banks	$560
Savings and loan associations	343
Mutual savings banks	132
Credit unions	64

Source: Statistical Abstract of the United States, 1976, U.S. Dept. of Commerce, Bureau of the Census; extrapolated to 1979.

Contrary to what some people think, money saved does not remain in the bank. As shown in the figure, money saved is generally lent to another individual, a business, or a government. A person who borrows money may then buy goods at a store. The store merchant, in turn, may pay some expenses, pay salaries, buy more merchandise to sell, or deposit money in another savings account. Subsequently, the merchant's bank will lend that deposited money to another of its customers—perhaps a manufacturing concern, as shown in the illustration. The manufacturing firm may also save part of its income in various ways, perhaps for later investment in new equipment. Employees will receive salaries. Part of their salaries will be used to meet their living expenses, and part may go into savings.

There are many other savings flow patterns that are more complex because there are many variations of savings, investments, businesses, or governments. However, one basic premise remains constant: Most of the money saved by individuals or business firms earns interest and also "works" for the savings institution by allowing it to make further investment or loans to others.

FACTORS TO CONSIDER IN SAVING

One cannot save effectively without first taking into account several factors. Among these factors are risk, convenience, liquidity, earnings on savings, and overall planning. Let us discuss there factors further.

Risk

Risk in savings is the degree of possibility that a person will lose some or all of the deposited savings. Most people who save in commercial banks, savings and loan associations, mutual savings banks, and credit unions have little or no risk. There have been occasions, however, where schemes to defraud depositors have been perpetrated.

The City Savings and Loan Association scandal in Chicago some years ago is one

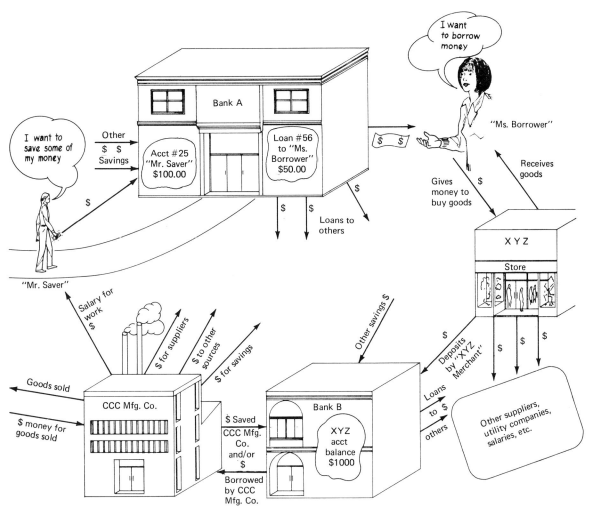

FIGURE 13-1   Flow of savings

example in which honest depositors lost millions of dollars. The association president, Oren Mensik, defrauded the organization of nearly $30 million through the use of just about every fraud imaginable. That particular savings and loan association was *not* insured against loss, since it was a *state*-chartered association and the federal law requiring insurance did not apply. Recent reports, however, after over 10 years of hard work and service, show that some depositors have gotten back 98 percent of their money and others over 45 percent. Still other depositors have not been

located at all. But during all this, Mr. Mensik escaped from prison and has fled the country.

Fortunately, the case of City Savings and Loan Association and others like it are the rare exceptions. They do show, unfortunately, that such things *can* happen. At the very least, your savings institution should be insured. Check carefully if you save at a state- rather than a federally chartered institution.

To help reduce risk, most savings institutions buy enough insurance to give their depositors up to $40,000 of protection per savings account. There is no direct cost to the depositor. The insurer (the organization that provides the loss protection) is usually directed by the government. The Federal Deposit Insurance Corporation (FDIC) covers savings in all nationally chartered commercial banks and most state banks. The Federal Savings and Loan Insurance Corporation (FSLIC) covers savings for savings and loan associations. The National Credit Union Administration (NCUA), an agency of the federal government, handles the protection for money in all federal- and most state-chartered credit unions. Those state-chartered institutions not required by individual state laws to provide deposit insurance *may* buy it through a private insurance company if they wish. Protection is provided to the depositors based on assessments of the amount of deposits the financial institution holds. For example, a state-chartered credit union is charged ½ of 1 percent per month on the amount of money held for its members. Other financial institutions that have this protection are assessed in a similar manner.

The protection provided is up to $40,000 for each separate account. For example, if a person has $39,500 on deposit, the account will be fully covered. On the other hand, if a person has $42,000 on deposit, only $40,000 is protected; $2000 could be lost if the savings institution was suddenly penniless. However, there are ways to protect such savers. Accounts can be written and deposits made in the names of different family members. Bill and Charlotte Owens of Cincinnati, Ohio, have separate accounts, each of which is insured for $40,000. They also have a joint account, insured for $40,000. Therefore, the Owenses have $120,000 of protection on their combined savings. If they have children, separate and combined accounts can be established, with each protected for up to $40,000.

A financial institution's overall reputation and integrity is also a risk factor. If an institution has many years of service and no appreciable losses, no embezzlements by employees, continued payment of competitive interest or dividends, and honest employees who give good service, this also helps to assure the saver of the safety of the institution.

Convenience

Not being able to get to a savings institution may be an excuse some people use for not saving. However, saving by mail could be a convenience for those who do not have transportation. Having access to a local savings branch office could be convenient for others. The branch office which is most convenient may not pay the highest rate of return compared with another type of savings institution, but it may mean saving *or* not saving. Yet some saving, even with a lower interest rate, is better than none. Commercial banks can make savings easy by merely transferring money from your checking account to a savings account as you request. All you have to do is to be aware of the amounts transferred until the bank notifies you formally.

Liquidity

Of great concern to many savers is how *liquid*—how quickly available—their saved money is. Getting the money when it is needed or having to wait a few days can sometimes make quite a difference. With most banks, savings and loan associations, and credit unions, there is no problem. However, most passbook savings rules do state that the institution can legally wait 30 or 60 days to give you your money—although this rarely occurs. Small institutions without large amounts of ready cash may need to do this—as, for example, a very small credit union. But all such institutions have the capacity (assuming they have more assets than liabilities) to either convert some of their assets to cash or borrow from other lending institutions in order to meet unexpected demands for withdrawals.

Earnings on Savings

Naturally, people who save want to get some earnings on their savings. Also, they usually want to know what rate of earnings they can expect, how these earnings are computed, and how often they are paid.

Rates. The amount of interest or dividends paid on each savings account each year is usually stated in terms of an annual rate. These rates vary from one institution to another and from one type of account to another. The typical range would be from about 5 percent on a regular passbook account to 7¾ percent on some long-term accounts such as certificates of deposit.

As one begins to look at places to save money, the rate of return on savings should be considered. All other things being equal, the consumer should choose the institution that will pay the highest interest. Realize, however, that the advertised rate does not tell the whole story. One must also know how the earnings are computed and the frequency of those earnings, and understand the concept of compound interest.

How Earnings Are Computed. It would be nearly impossible to understand all the ways financial institutions use to compute earnings. A report of the American Bankers Association (ABA) revealed that over fifty methods were used! More important, the saver should know *how* his or her particular earnings are calculated. Once this is known, the saver can go to other institutions, get similar data, and then compare.

Four common methods of computing interest are fifo, lifo, average balance, and day of deposit to day of withdrawal. Figure 13-2 shows the four methods and illustrates how the earned interest will vary based upon the method used for calculating the interest. *Lifo* (last-in, first-out) means that when withdrawals are made, it is assumed that the deposits made most recently have been withdrawn. The earliest deposits therefore remain intact and earn interest from their date of deposit. For example, consider a consumer who made deposits of $100 each on January 1, March 1, and June 1, and of $300 on September 1. A withdrawal of $200 was made on December 1. After the December withdrawal, all deposits continued to earn interest from their date of deposit except the one in Sep-

tember. Because the consumer withdrew $200 on December 1, only $100 of the $300 September 1 deposit continued to earn interest for that period. About 5 percent of the commercial banks use this method.

The opposite of lifo is fifo. *Fifo* (first-in, first-out) means that withdrawals are assumed to come from the earliest deposits in an account. Under this method, and using the example cited above, the deposits of $100 each made in January and March will earn no more interest after the December withdrawal of $200, assuming that interest is paid annually. Although an institution that follows this method is using the saver's two $100 deposits for 11 and 9 months, respectively, no interest is paid on them. Institutions using the lifo method therefore pay a better return than those using fifo. Approximately 16 percent of commercial banks use the fifo method, according to the ABA. Any method of calculating interest is, of course, based on the type and amount of activity (deposits and withdrawals) in the saver's account.

The *low-balance method* is popular. It is used by nearly 30 percent of the banks. Here, the lowest balance of an account during the interest-payment period is used to calculate earnings. This is certainly the most unfavorable method for the saver, as any withdrawal will, of course, bring about a lower balance. To understand the real disadvantage, let's look at an example. Suppose you have a balance of $800 in your savings account and you need to withdraw $500. After you withdraw, the balance is only $300. Then, 2 weeks later you put $800 into your savings account, and the balance becomes $1100. You would earn interest only on the $300 "low balance" for the period.

Another method of computing interest used by a few (less than 1 percent) institutions is the *average-balance* method. Here, the average balance is determined for each account and the interest is calculated on this average. For example, the average can be determined by taking the opening and the ending balances for 1 year and dividing by 2. Another, more tedi-

These four banks all pay the same interest rate—yet interest payments range from $44.93 to $75.30.

There are many ways of computing interest, as the text of our report indicates. Here are four passbooks showing the identical deposits and withdrawals (made on the same days), with explanations of how the interest has been computed under four common methods. All four assume a 6 percent interest rate and quarterly crediting and compounding.

	DATE	WITHDRAWAL	DEPOSIT	INTEREST	BALANCE	TELLER
1	JAN–1		**1,000.00		**1,000.00	
2	JAN 10		**2,000.00		**3,000.00	
3	FEB–6		**1,000.00		**4,000.00	
4	MAR–3	*1,000.00			**3,000.00	
5	MAR 20	**500.00			**2,500.00	
6	MAR 30	**500.00			**2,000.00	
7	APR–1			*14.79	**2,014.79	
8	JUL–1			*30.14	**2,044.93	

LOW BALANCE

Under this method, interest is paid only on the smallest amount of money that was in the account during the interest period. Despite a balance that reached $4000 during the first quarter, this account earned interest only on $1000—the lowest balance during that period. (There are no withdrawals during the second quarter, so the low-balance formula is not important there.) This method, which tends to discourage deposits, is the most punitive to savers. Yet 30 per cent of commercial banks still use it, according to a study last year by the American Bankers Association.

Interest: $44.93

	DATE	WITHDRAWAL	DEPOSIT	INTEREST	BALANCE	TELLER
2	JAN–1		**1,000.00		**1,000.00	
3	JAN 10		**2,000.00		**3,000.00	
4	FEB–6		**1,000.00		**4,000.00	
6	MAR–5	*1,000.00			**3,000.00	
7	MAR 20	**500.00			**2,500.00	
8	MAR 30	**500.00			**2,000.00	
9	APR–1			*22.19	**2,022.19	
10	JUL–1			*30.25	**2,052.44	

FIRST-IN, FIRST-OUT (FIFO)

With this method, withdrawals are deducted first from the starting balance of the interest period and then, if the balance isn't sufficient, from later deposits. This erodes the base on which your interest is figured and means you automatically lose interest on withdrawals from the start of the interest period rather than from the dates on which the withdrawals were actually made. Another variation of this method is to apply the first withdrawal to the first deposit, rather than to the beginning balance; this would earn $53.93. About 16 per cent of commercial banks use the FIFO methods, according to the ABA.

Interest: $52.44

	DATE	WITHDRAWAL	DEPOSIT	INTEREST	BALANCE	TELLER
2	JAN–1		**1,000.00		**1,000.00	
3	JAN 10		**2,000.00		**3,000.00	
4	FEB–6		**1,000.00		**4,000.00	
6	MAR–5	*1,000.00			**3,000.00	
7	MAR 20	**500.00			**2,500.00	
8	MAR 30	**500.00			**2,000.00	
10	APR–1			*28.10	**2,028.10	
11	JUL–1			*30.34	**2,058.44	

LAST-IN, FIRST-OUT (LIFO)

Under this plan, withdrawals are deducted from the most recent deposits in the quarter and then from the next most recent ones. This method, which does not penalize savers as much as the two FIFO methods, is used by about 5 per cent of commercial banks. **Interest: $58.44**

	DATE	WITHDRAWAL	DEPOSIT	INTEREST	BALANCE	TELLER
2	JAN–1		**1,000.00		**1,000.00	
3	JAN 10		**2,000.00		**3,000.00	
4	FEB–6		**1,000.00		**4,000.00	
6	MAR–5	*1,000.00			**3,000.00	
7	MAR 20	**500.00			**2,500.00	
8	MAR 30	**500.00			**2,000.00	
10	APR–1			*44.71	**2,044.71	
11	JUL–1			*30.59	**2,075.30	

DAY-OF-DEPOSIT TO DAY-OF-WITHDRAWAL

Under this arrangement, the bank pays you interest for the actual number of days the money remains in the account. This method, which is sometimes called daily interest, instant interest, or day-in day-out, is the fairest to consumers. It is used by almost 50 per cent of commercial banks and 60 per cent of insured S&Ls (there are no industry figures for savings banks). It yields the greatest return.

Interest: $75.30

Source: *Consumer Reports.* Consumers Union, Mt. Vernon, NY.

FIGURE 13-2   Ways of computing interest

ous way is to add the *ending daily dollar balance* and then divide the total by the number of days. Yet another variation would be to use the balance at the end of each month and then divide the total by the number of months.

A method that is gaining more widespread use—almost 50 percent of commercial banks and 60 percent of savings and loan associations use it—is that of calculating interest from the *day of deposit to the day of withdrawal*. Thus, interest is computed on a daily basis. Each deposit receives interest for the total number of days it actually remains in the institution. When a withdrawal is made, the interest is calculated for the number of days the money remained on deposit. This method is the most costly for the institutions, but it is certainly best for the saver. The last example in Figure 13-2 illustrates the calculation of interest under this method. It provides the highest interest of any of the methods used. If interest rates are the same, then the institution using the daily interest calculation method may be the one to choose.

Compounding Interest. All savers need to understand the concept of *compounding interest.* Compounding interest simply means calculating interest upon interest. For example, if interest is paid on $500 at 5 percent annually, and is payable quarterly, the interest earnings on this $500 would be $6.25 for the first quarter (0.05 × $500 × ¼ = $6.25). The total value of the savings would then be $506.25, assuming the earned interest was left in savings. For the second quarter, the interest would be paid on the $500 *plus* the $6.25, or $506.25. The amount of interest for the second quarter would be $6.33. As a result of compounding (calculating interest upon interest), the saver earned an additional 8 cents. This looks small, but it is better than a 5 percent account that does not compound interest. Moreover, the true annual interest rate will be greater; how much depends on the frequency of compounding. Table 13-2 shows this increase based on semiannual, quarterly, and daily compounding. When one is talking about $500 or $5000 in

TABLE 13-2

True Annual Rate when Compounded

Stated Annual Rate	Paid Semiannually	Paid Quarterly	Paid Daily
4.5	4.551	4.577	4.603
4.75	4.806	4.835	4.864
5.0	5.063	5.095	5.127
5.25	5.319	5.354	5.390
5.5	5.576	5.615	5.653
5.75	5.833	5.875	5.918
6.0	6.090	6.136	6.183
6.25	6.348	6.398	6.448
6.5	6.606	6.660	6.715
6.75	6.864	6.923	6.982
7.0	7.123	7.186	7.250
7.25	7.381	7.450	7.518
7.5	7.641	7.714	7.787
8.0	8.160	8.243	8.328

savings, the "small differences" in compounding interest become very important.

Table 13-3 illustrates the importance of increasing the frequency of paying and subsequently compounding interest based on dollar earnings. As can be seen, daily payment and compounding bring the largest earnings.

PLANNING FOR SAVINGS

To meet a specific savings goal, careful planning is necessary. Besides comparing places in

TABLE 13-3

The Relationship of Frequency of Paying Interest and Compounding ($1000 Deposited, 5% Rate)*

Frequency	Value
Annual payment	$1050.00
Semiannual payment	1050.62
Quarterly payment	1050.90
Daily payment	1051.13

* In all cases the annual value would be $1050 without compounding.

which to save, one should consider goals, consistency and frequency of savings, specific amounts to save, and long-range planning and savings.

Goals

To help one save, one should establish some type of goal. The goal can be either short- or long-term. Perhaps it is to save enough money for a new television set. Maybe it is to save enough to pay for 1 year's tuition in college. Table 13-4 provides a suggested guide for monthly savings. Once a goal of saving a certain amount of money is set, the table indicates how much should be saved *per month* at various rates of interest. The table shows quarterly interest payments and compounding. Regardless of what the goal is, it will give a purpose and make the saving worthwhile.

Consistency and Frequency

Steady saving (consistency) and frequent saving will help you achieve your goal. Once your goal is set, you can decide how much to save each week or month and be consistent about it. The consistency is important. Why not "pay" yourself regularly by saving? It is the consistency that seems to get the job done. Perhaps it is partly in knowing that each week or each month you can *see* the amount of savings grow. A sporadic saving pattern does not help one reach one's goals very rapidly. Remember, a small amount saved regularly is usually better. Trying to save too large an amount and finding it is a burden often ends up meaning no saving at all.

Amounts to Save

Your goals for saving, your timetable, your budgeted expenses, and your earnings must all be examined before you can decide on an amount to save. Most important, the amount saved should be realistic and not so high that you cannot enjoy life. If you earn $325 per week, it would be unrealistic to try to save $100 of it. But saving $25 might be feasible. It would depend upon your savings goals, values, and money-management plans.

Long-range Planning and Savings

Once you decide to save on a regular basis, you also need to think about some long-range planning. All savers need short-run goals, but early consideration must be given to long-range needs in order to achieve them later.

Let's look at some long-range goals or objectives that the regular saver could consider. A long-range saving plan might include:

- *First,* have protection against loss of earning power, particularly for the primary wage earner. This can be provided by disability insurance or investments, but having 2 months income put away in savings usually provides adequate protection.
- *Second,* have an emergency fund for immediate need. (Costs of doctor or hospital care, money to take a quick trip home, etc.) Various amounts are recommended (2 to 4 months take-home pay), but it will vary with each individual depending on what may constitute a need for ready cash.
- *Third,* save in order to buy a home at some time. A down payment may be the only goal, but even down payments can be very high.
- *Fourth,* if children are going to be raised, some money is likely to be needed for college or other education beyond high school. Again, the amount you will need will depend upon whether or not you want to get your children started and/or provide the entire education costs.
- *Fifth,* plan for retirement when saving. Although a young person or couple may consider this too far away, it is part of the long-range plan and should be studied. Even persons receiving Social Security benefits as retirement income must begin saving some amount early in order to have any extra retirement income later. Other ways of providing money for retirement—individual savings is but one—must be investigated and planned as well. Young persons may give retirement income only cursory attention. As one grows older, however, retirement income ranks higher on

TABLE 13-4

A Guide for Monthly Savings*

Find Your Savings Goal In This Column	4½%	5%	5½%	6%	6½%
$1000 in 5 Years	$ 14.85	$ 14.66	$ 14.47	$ 14.28	$ 14.09
10 Years	6.60	6.43	6.25	6.09	5.92
15 Years	3.90	3.74	3.58	3.44	3.29
20 Years	2.58	2.43	2.30	2.17	2.04
$2000 in 5 Years	29.69	29.31	28.93	28.55	28.18
10 Years	13.20	12.85	12.50	12.17	11.84
15 Years	7.79	7.47	7.16	6.87	6.58
20 Years	5.15	4.86	4.59	4.33	4.08
$3000 in 5 Years	44.54	43.96	43.39	42.82	42.26
10 Years	19.79	19.27	18.75	18.25	17.76
15 Years	11.68	11.20	10.74	10.30	9.86
20 Years	7.72	7.29	6.88	6.49	6.11
$4000 in 5 Years	59.38	58.61	57.85	57.10	56.35
10 Years	26.39	25.69	25.00	24.33	23.67
15 Years	15.57	14.93	14.32	13.73	13.15
20 Years	10.29	9.72	9.17	8.65	8.15
$5000 in 5 Years	74.22	73.26	72.31	71.37	70.44
10 Years	32.98	32.11	31.25	30.41	29.59
15 Years	19.46	18.67	17.90	17.16	16.44
20 Years	12.86	12.15	11.46	10.81	10.19
$6000 in 5 Years	89.07	87.91	86.77	85.64	84.52
10 Years	39.58	38.53	37.50	36.49	35.51
15 Years	23.35	22.40	21.48	20.59	19.72
20 Years	15.44	14.58	13.76	12.97	12.22
$7000 in 5 Years	103.91	102.56	101.23	99.91	98.61
10 Years	46.17	44.95	43.75	42.58	41.43
15 Years	27.24	26.13	25.06	24.02	23.01
20 Years	18.01	17.01	16.05	15.13	14.26
$8000 in 5 Years	118.76	117.22	115.69	114.19	112.69
10 Years	52.77	51.37	50.00	48.66	47.34
15 Years	31.13	29.86	28.63	27.45	26.30
20 Years	20.58	19.43	18.34	17.29	16.30
$9000 in 5 Years	133.60	131.87	130.15	128.46	126.78
10 Years	59.36	57.79	56.25	54.74	53.26
15 Years	35.02	33.59	32.21	30.88	29.58
20 Years	23.15	21.86	20.63	19.46	18.33
$10,000 in 5 Years	148.44	146.52	144.61	142.73	140.87
10 Years	65.96	64.21	62.50	60.82	59.18
15 Years	38.91	37.33	35.79	34.31	32.87
20 Years	25.72	24.29	22.92	21.62	20.37

* Compounded quarterly.

the priority list. Eventually, retirement income will be an integral part of one's savings plan.

Unfortunately, many savers never develop any kind of plan, let alone a long-range one. Long-range planning forces a person to establish long-range goals. Planning for savings must be both short-run and long-run in its development. Only the priorities will change as one gets older and achieves and/or changes the short-run goals.

WAYS TO SAVE

Financial institutions today are competing for savings. Through advertising and giving away gifts they are almost begging you to save with them. Among the factors that attract new savers are the various types of accounts available.

Regular Savings Accounts

A regular savings account is frequently called a *passbook* account. A person can put money into or take it out of such a savings account whenever he or she wants. In either case—deposit or withdrawal—a record is kept in a passbook, or there is some other type of record. The earnings (interest) paid by the financial institution are paid on money that has been in the account for a certain length of time and that was deposited by a specified date.

Certificates of Deposit

Certificates of deposit (C/Ds) are accounts in which you must leave your money for a certain length of time and in doing so you receive a substantially higher interest rate. Included in the C/D classification would be 1-year, 3-year, 4-year, and 6-year maturity savings certificates. This means that the depositor must leave the money in the bank for the time specified before he or she will receive the interest rate set for that holding. If the money is needed before the maturity date, by federal law some interest is lost as a penalty. Unfortunately, minimum amounts for deposit are a restriction on most C/Ds—usually $500, $1000 or

$10,000. A person who saves through a C/D should fully understand its time limitations— but if the funds can be tied up longer, the interest rate is higher than it is with a regular savings account. To illustrate: 1-year C/Ds may pay 6 percent annually; 3-year C/Ds pay 6¼ to 6½ percent annually; and 6-year C/Ds pay 8 percent annually. What you lose in giving up your money for a longer time, you gain by a higher return on your savings.

Special Savings Accounts

To encourage longer-term savings and fewer withdrawals, most savings institutions offer various types of special accounts. Typical names include "Golden Passbook," "Special Account," and "Golden Dividend Account." Generally these accounts pay more interest than regular accounts, usually ¼ of 1 percent higher, but *only* if the institution is notified of a withdrawal 90 days in advance. Should the depositor need to withdraw money without the 90 day notice, he or she can, but as a penalty any interest due is paid at the lower passbook rate instead of the higher special savings account rate.

Another recently established way of earning interest on monies placed on deposit at savings institutions is through the *Negotiable Orders of Withdrawal* (NOW) accounts. This type of account offers the consumer a "middle line" between savings and checking accounts. Essentially, the NOW accounts provide consumers with an attractive alternative to regular savings and checking accounts.

A NOW account pays interest, just like a savings account, but an individual can also write checks against it. The accounts are available to individuals only and not to businesses or associations.

These accounts are offered by mutual savings banks and savings and loan associations. A uniform interest rate on NOW accounts has been established by a panel of government agencies. Generally, the rate is less than that of regular savings accounts.

This type of account, where available, has improved competition among financial institutions. Some banks, for example, are offering interest-bearing checking accounts. With careful planning and usage on the part of the astute consumer, once-dormant checking-account funds may earn interest.

Government Savings Bonds

Series E government savings bonds are the most popular type of government bonds. Series E bonds can be bought in denominations of $25, $50, $75, $100, $200, $500, $1000, and $10,000. They are purchased at 75 percent of their face value. The purchaser receives the full face value at maturity, which is about 5 years after bonds are issued. For example, one can purchase a bond for $18.75 and receive $25 at maturity. The difference between what you pay and what you get back is your interest. You do not have to pay income tax on Series E interest *until* the bonds are cashed in. Also, if you want to, you can cash in Series E bonds any time after 2 months from issue date and get back your cost plus all accumulated interest to that date. The interest return on your investment in Series E Bonds is nearly 6 percent annually if they are held until maturity. Also, there is a guaranteed 10-year extension privilege for continued earnings if the bondholder chooses.

Series H bonds are different from Series E. They are designed to provide a steady income for savers. Holders receive a Treasury check every 6 months for the interest earned during that time period. Income received during the year is reported for tax purposes. These bonds can be bought only in denominations of $500, $1000, $5000, and $10,000. Series H bonds must be held for at least 6 months before they can be cashed in. The normal maturity date is 10 years from date of purchase. The overall yield on Series H bonds amounts to about 6½ percent annually. With both types of bonds, the *yield* (amount earned) is less if they are cashed in before the maturity date.

Forced Savings

Another type of savings is referred to as forced. It is not a type of account, but a pro-

cedure. Basically it amounts to making oneself deposit a certain amount of money regularly into some type of savings account. An example would be payroll deductions for deposits to your credit-union account or to purchase U.S. savings bonds from your bank. Another method is to authorize a bank to transfer money automatically from one's checking account to a savings account every payday.

Other Ways to Save

Many persons have not been able to discipline themselves into saving through the more formalized ways described above. However, some consumers have other ways to save.

- *Emptying excess change into a jar.* As money accumulates, wrap the nickels, dimes, quarters, etc., and periodically deposit the wrapped coins into a formal savings account.
- *Saving a particular coin.* Some people save Kennedy half dollars or Bicentennial quarters, for example. You can do this individually or as a family. The savings could be used for vacation money or some other special item or event.
- *Unexpected money.* Examples include inheritances, bonuses, and money available after making the final installment payment on a debt. Earmark these funds for saving, since they weren't available for spending earlier. In regard to the installment-payment money, make the payments to *yourself* now in the form of savings deposits.
- *Money won at games*, such as cards, bingo, golf, or a lottery. This requires a great deal of discipline, but saving such winnings can be done. It is surprising how much one can save in a year by saving small winnings.
- *Reimbursement for travel expenses.* This is one primarily for salespersons who are reimbursed for job travel expenses by their employer. That check at the end of each month, or a portion (such as 50 percent), could mount up rather quickly.

Remember that nest-egg we saved up? Well, it's now a goose-egg.

Courtesy of Edd Uluschak.

- *Eliminate habits.* Examples include coffee and roll, smoking, and alcoholic beverages. Many of us are victims of habit, and we pay accordingly. Two packs of cigarettes a day will cost over $500 a year. Stop or cut down smoking, and instead of buying a pack, put the money in a safe place. When a large amount accumulates, deposit it in a savings account. Eliminate the roll or doughnut with your coffee break and save the 20 to 30 cents a day, which could amount to $75 per year.
- *Do it yourself.* Examples: repairs, car washing, and one's own hair. Instead of calling a carpenter or plumber, study the problem yourself. It is more than likely that you can fix it. The library is full of books on repairs and "do-it-yourself" ideas. All you have to do is read and get at it. Put the money you would have spent into your savings account. Also, for the one (either male or female) who runs to the hairdresser every week—skip a time now and then or go every other week. The savings can really add up in a year's time.
- *Moratorium on entertainment.* Decide to eliminate entertainment expenses for a month, for example. When you do this, the money you save can be earning interest for you in a savings account. Entertainment is

often considered a semiluxury expense item. It can be reduced or eliminated occasionally without any ill effects.
- *Walk and be healthy.* If you now take a bus, cab, or train for short distances (less than a mile or two), consider walking instead. Then, save the money you would have spent on transportation. Also, the walking will be good for you, and in the long run you may reduce your visits to the doctor—this could be another saving.
- *Take your own lunch.* Spending $1 to $2 a day or more for lunch can add up—more than $350 per year. That might be enough to pay for a needed vacation, for example. Although it may be somewhat embarrassing for some to carry a lunch, once it becomes a habit, it is amazing how nice it is (no crowded restaurants, no harassment by waiters and waitresses, reduced food consumption, etc.).

These and other special ways to force yourself to save are possible and are used by many people. But unless you take the initiative, develop a positive attitude, and discipline yourself to save, no matter what gimmicks or games you use, saving will always be secondary or nonexistent. You must decide.

COMPARISON SHOPPING FOR SAVINGS OUTLETS

Once you have a plan for saving (both short- and long-range), you need to decide where to save. A person who has carefully considered the numerous factors of saving must follow through with one additional step—comparison shopping for the best place to save. Various places must be investigated, and one must take the time to read any literature on them. Any places that deserve serious consideration should be visited. Then, with the basic knowledge and information in hand, the informed consumer can make an intelligent decision.

Things to Look For When Shopping

Each individual who compares the important characteristics in selecting a savings institution needs to establish his or her own evaluative criteria. What is important for one may not be for another. For example, Al and Shirlee Grayling of suburban Knoxville feel that service is more important than getting the highest interest possible. Marilyn McElaine of Memphis wants the institution that is most convenient for her. Earl Halbert of St. Louis always wants the highest interest rate.

When you are comparing financial institutions for savings, consider each of the following criteria:

1. Annual rate of interest paid on savings
2. Type of plan used for computing interest (lifo, fifo, low balance, day of deposit to day of withdrawal)
3. Frequency of paying interest (daily, quarterly, semiannually)
4. The "true annual rate"
5. All money deposited federally insured up to at least $40,000 for each account
6. Overall size of the institution (number of depositors, amount of financial holdings)
7. Location of institution (easy to get to and from)
8. Number of years in business
9. Availability of money deposited for emergency withdrawals
10. Minimum length of time money must remain on deposit before interest can be earned
11. "Grace days" offered ("deposited by the tenth, earn from the first")
12. Penalty for early withdrawal of savings
13. Convenience for making deposits and withdrawals (drive-up service, branch offices, mail, etc.)
14. Personal services (help when needed on transactions, financial counseling)
15. No history of problems with safety, security, or misappropriation of funds.

Places to Save

Trying to determine the best place for your savings is not as hard as it might seem. Looking at what is most important to you will lead to your proper choice.

Primary Sources. There is some competition among the several types of institutions where one can save money. There is also competition among the institutions, although it is limited within each classification (commercial banks, for example, compete primarily through services provided to customers). Consequently, to attract dollars, they must be able to offer something in return.

Since the institutions are competing for the saver's dollars, it stands to reason that the saver should make an effort to get the best offer. Figure 13-3 identifies the primary financial institutions and some specific characteristics of each. These include savings and loan associations, commercial banks, credit unions, mutual savings banks, and government savings bonds.

Indirect Sources. Occasionally there are persons who cannot save at one of these types of financial institutions. They cannot afford to save anything from their take-home pay. Or they have simply decided not to save. These people need to know that not all saving is direct saving.

Jack Yung of San Francisco uses two indirect or secondary types of savings all the time.

FIGURE 13-3 Comparative Factors in Places to Save

Place to Save	Types of Savings Available	Ease of Saving	Annual Interest Rates Paid (Percent)	Frequency of Paying Interest	Liquidity	Insurance Coverage
Savings and loan associations	Regular; certificates of deposit	Good	5.25–7.76	Quarterly or daily most common	Good— usually on notice	$40,000 per account (FSLIC)
Commercial banks	Regular; certificates of deposit	Good	5.0–7.5	Quarterly most common; some daily	Good— usually on notice	$40,000 (FDIC)
Credit unions	Regular	Very good (close by)	5.0–7.0	Semiannual; some quarterly	Good— usually on notice	$40,000 (NCUA)
Mutual savings banks (legal in seventeen states)	Regular; certificates of deposit	Good	5.0–7.75	Quarterly; some daily	Good	$40,000 (FDIC or other insurance)
Government savings bonds	Series E (5-year maturity)	Very good if purchased by payroll deduction	6.0 (average)	Semiannual	Adequate	100%
Government savings bonds	Series H (10-year maturity)	Very good if purchased by payroll deduction	6.0 (average) (5, 1st year; 5.8, next 4 years; 6.5, next 5 years)	Semiannual	Adequate	100%
Government bonds	Treasury notes and bills	Good	Range 6–8½	Quarterly or semiannual	Adequate	100%

As a result of his job as a teacher, he pays regularly, once a month, into a pension plan for his retirement. This is a form of savings to him. And he may be able to realize more than he has contributed, since he can take his contribution to his pension and the interest it has earned with him if he leaves his job; this is known as a *vested* retirement program. Also, Jack has a permanent type of life insurance called *straight life*. He makes quarterly payments on it, and part of each payment goes toward building cash value in his policy. The remainder gives him life insurance protection. This is another form of savings to him. If an emergency develops, he can borrow against the built-up cash value of his policy. Jack Yung is not alone. Millions of people make similar types of payments but do not consider them savings.

Social Security is another type of indirect savings, and it includes about 90 percent of all workers; part of it is a pension plan administered by the government. The amounts of money an individual pays into the Social Security fund should be looked upon as indirect savings. True, the funds paid in cannot be withdrawn whenever a person wants. But in the long run one may be able to get back more than the amount paid in. This assumes, of course, that one lives long enough to collect a retirement pension and has paid into the fund for the required number of years. Or, surviving spouses and children can collect survivor's benefits for a number of years. The primary disadvantage of Social Security as a secondary source of savings is that the money cannot be used until death, disability, or retirement has occurred.

Effective buying practices are also a form of secondary savings. Taking advantage of a sale and saving 30 percent, for example, is a form of indirect saving. Buying goods at wholesale or *truly* discount prices saves money. Whether you save directly at a financial institution or save very indirectly by taking advantage of a clothing sale, the important fact remains that you are saving in some way with a purpose.

TRUTH-IN-SAVINGS AS AN AID TO CONSUMERS

More and more savers are becoming interested in the finer points of computing interest on their savings. No longer are they willing to accept at face value the statement that $9.63, for example, has been credited to their account as interest for the first quarter. Many want to know exactly how the interest was computed. In other words, they are seeking a "truth-in-savings" disclosure.

What Is Truth-in-Savings?
Basically, truth-in-savings is letting the saver know exactly how an account is going to be considered in the computing of interest, the rate of interest, the frequency of compounding, and whether crediting of interest payments (depositing interest earned to savings account directly) is practiced—in other words, knowing the full facts.

Surveys on savings accounts have shown that a difference of from 60 to 150 percent in earnings can result merely from the way the interest is computed over a 6-month period, using the same interest rate. Factors that tend

to bring about this spread of interest payment include the method used (low balance; first-in, first-out; last-in, first-out; average balance; or day of deposit to day of withdrawal); frequency of compounding (daily, quarterly, semiannually, or annually); automatic crediting to the savings account; a *grace period* (deposits received by the tenth of the month will earn from the first); and penalties (such as a charge for more than two withdrawals during the interest period).

It is hard for the average saver to determine exactly how each of these factors will come into play on a particular savings account. Therefore, savers should be told the full facts on how interest is to be computed. Most differences in interest payments are a direct result of the deposit/withdrawal activity. Generally there is little difference in the interest paid if no withdrawals are made during the interest period. How deposits and withdrawals will alter account balances and amount of interest simply be changing the factors when interest is computed was shown in Figure 13-2 (page 392). Note that the rate of interest is held at a constant 6 percent in each case. Information, not misinformation, presented clearly shows the differences that develop with various methods of calculating interest.

The Importance of Truth-in-Savings to Consumers
The more information you have about your savings institution, the better you will be able to evaluate it. And you are entitled to know more than you are usually told. "Truth-in-savings" is important to all savers. At the urging of Professor Richard Morse of Kansas State University, legislation has been introduced to enact a Truth-in Savings Act, but with little success to date. The most recent effort has been by Congressman Robert F. Drinan of Massachusetts. He offered a bill to establish a Consumer Savings Disclosure Act that would provide for uniform and full disclosure of methods of computation and payment of earnings on certain savings deposits. Essentially, the act, if it becomes law, will give con-

sumers clear and thorough information about their savings accounts.

POINTS OF VIEW AND PROBLEMS TO THINK ABOUT

Persons who save need to have the discipline to save regularly. All too often consumers who try to save do so *only* if there is some money left at the end of the pay period. No money, no savings. A plan must be made to save a specific amount regularly. Why not "pay yourself" first? If you also receive some extra income or spend less than the usual amount, some of those funds could be saved, too.

The informed saver should seek out the best places to save. Getting the highest earnings on one's savings, and with the best protection, should be a major goal of each saver. Other factors, such as convenience, may be considered minor, depending upon one's needs.

Savings institutions are normally completely risk-free because of federal insurance. But some institutions are still *not* insured. They are state chartered and exist where state laws do not *require* them to purchase insurance. Critics think these institutions should not be allowed to operate, since consumers customarily think that all savings places are insured and safe. We agree.

Savers are still being discriminated against by savings institutions that deny high-earning deposits to the small saver. Because of prohibitive minimums ($10,000 or $100,000) on deposits, the small saver is unable to earn the higher rates (up to 9 percent in some cases). The federal government's policies often dictate what the minimum amount will be. Yet, at the same time, the thrift institutions invest the pooled sums of the small savers' money (10,000 savers at $100 each = $1,000,000) to earn higher rates for themselves. They are unwilling to pass along anywhere near this amount to the small saver. Historically, thrift institutions and banks have been guilty of paying only modest interest rates.

Perhaps one of the "lowest blows" has been dealt by the American Security and Trust Company in Washington, D.C. It has started to assess a service charge of $1 a month on savings accounts with balances below $500. This is an annual cost of approximately 2 percent with a balance of $499. If the interest earned is, say 5.25 percent paid annually, the net gain would be $14.20 ($26.20 − $12.00) instead of $26.20. One might not complain about earning $14 a year, but what about a person who has only $50 in an account? The cost would be $12 per year, or 24 percent (12 ÷ 50). The earnings would be $2.63, and a net *loss* of $9.37 (service charge $12.00 − earnings $2.63) would result. This is hardly an incentive to save for the small saver. Could it be that the big thrift institutions are trying to eliminate the small savers completely from their books? Have these executives forgotten that if 100,000 savers have $50 account balances, this amounts to $5,000,000, and this aggregate amount invested at 5 percent paid annually earns $250,000? These sort of penalties are simply not needed and should not exist in a competitive business world.

Negotiable Orders of Withdrawal, also known as NOW accounts, are being offered at several financial institutions. This is equivalent to a checking account offered by commercial banks. The difference is that the money left in the account earns interest. NOWs look and act like checks, but legally they are different. The NOW accounts have brought about more competition among financial institutions for consumers' checking-account dollars. Persons can deposit money in NOW accounts and gain an extra benefit—interest. Many savings and loan associations and mutual savings banks provide NOW accounts.

Another incentive being used today by some thrift institutions is to offer to pay interest on savings accounts in advance—"interest-to-go." Essentially, here is how this works. You agree to deposit and leave on deposit, for example, $5000 for 3 years. The savings institution will pay you $896.85 when you make the deposit, which amounts to about a 6 percent annual rate. Now you may reinvest the $896.85 if you want or spend it. What this amounts to is that you are receiving about $900 in return for someone's right to use your $5000 for 3 years. This is another reason for savers to look around and compare. There are new devices, incentives, and gimmicks being developed every day to get you to deposit your money in one place instead of another.

Consumers must make continued efforts to get truthful savings-account information from savings institutions. Institution personnel should first be given the opportunity to provide information about earnings and how they are calculated. If they fail to help, then state or federal laws requiring them to do so may be the only solution. Consumers are entitled to this information.

CHAPTER ACTIVITIES ▬▬▬▬▬

Checkup on Consumer Terms and Concepts

Savings	Compounding
Savings flow	interest
Risk	Regular savings
FDIC	accounts
FSLIC	C/Ds
Liquidity	Special savings
Lifo	accounts
Fifo	NOW accounts
Low-balance	Series H bonds
method	Forced savings
Average-balance	Indirect sources
method	Truth-in-savings

Review of Essentials

1. Other than not having enough money, what seems to be the main reason why some people do not save?
2. What is the primary reason for saying that savings in most commercial banks and savings and loan associations are risk-free?

3. Why can the savings of some consumers be considered a help to those persons who do not or cannot save?
4. How can various savings institutions afford to pay interest on savings?
5. In which types of institutions do people generally save their money and in what proportions?
6. Explain why the money consumers place in savings accounts does not remain in the institution until it is withdrawn.
7. Institutions offer different types of savings plans, so why would a saver wish to choose a special type of savings account instead of a regular account?
8. Explain why a 3-year certificate of deposit would be able to earn more interest than a 1-year C/D.
9. What are the names of the organizations that protect savings in commercial banks, savings and loan associations, and credit unions?
10. What items are considered essential in a long-range plan for savings and why?
11. Why would a savings institution that computes and pays interest on its savings accounts from the date of deposit to the date of withdrawal be more attractive than others?
12. How does the frequency of paying interest on savings accounts affect the earnings of a saver when compounding is used?
13. In what way can the concept of comparison shopping be used to the advantage of the saver?
14. What are three ways in which a person can save indirectly when he or she is unable or does not wish to save in a direct manner?
15. Name three things that truth-in-savings is trying to remedy in regard to savings accounts.

Issues for Analysis

1. Since a few savings institutions have had problems with fraud, should there be new

regulations to offset such activities in the future? Why or why not?

2. Concerning the possibility of a truth-in-savings law, what could be some of the problems if such a law were passed?

3. Should all types and forms of savings, including those with higher returns, be accessible to *all* individuals regardless of income and initial amounts saved? Why or why not?

14

Investments

THE PROBLEMS

Thousands of people lose millions of dollars each year through careless investments. Ironically, most of those people supposedly understand investments.

George Putnam of Oklahoma City recently read a book entitled *How I Made a Million Dollars through Stock Investments*. On the basis of this book, he invested over $5000 in various securities. In less than 2 years Mr. Putnam's investment had dwindled to a value of $300; most of his investments turned out to be totally worthless. Considering the limited information that he used, it was no wonder.

Unfortunately, thousands of people daily use Mr. Putnam's investment approach. The "get-rich-quick" method always finds believers. People are often very susceptible to suggestions about how to invest their money. Such suggestions usually involve rash promises to double their money in 3 to 6 months. These promises or guides are offered through books that successful investors have written, through newspaper articles, through newspaper and magazine advertisements, or as a tip from a well-meaning friend.

A recent widow whose husband has left her thousands of dollars is particularly vulnerable. Getting a large amount of money at one time is not easy, especially if one is still emotionally upset. All too frequently a ready and amiable salesperson will quickly offer investment services. Yet persons with large sums of money need not fall prey to unscrupulous investment counselors. There are legitimate places to turn to for help, such as commercial banks, registered independent stock and bond brokers, and *bona fide* investment firms.

But even the knowledgeable investor can have careless moments and rely upon a tip about a certain stock to buy. Relying on these tips can lead to financial ruin for even the experienced investor unless he or she carefully checks into their authenticity.

Problems occur for many investors because they cannot or will not devote the time necessary to thoroughly investigate the variety of investment alternatives. The millions of people who invest billions of dollars annually cannot all become experts on investments. Therefore, they shift much of this responsibility to the experts. Care and judgment must, of course, be used in selecting a licensed expert who will help you, not fleece you!

Perhaps the most serious problem in investments is that the investor lacks basic knowledge. Many people feel they will never have enough money to make any investments, and these feelings may be true, even though one out of four adults owns some shares of stock. But far more important, when some of these same people come into unexpected money, they do not have the common sense to seek professional help.

Not too long ago, only people with incomes over $25,000 usually did any investing. Now, however, many persons with less income are investing on a smaller scale through carefully chosen investment plans.

Unfortunately, the small investor is unable to readily attract the attention of investment experts. Too often these experts tend to give their time to the big investors so as to earn higher commissions. Most trust departments of commercial banks provide no help to the investor with less than $10,000. Economic discrimination in its most blatant form seems to be practiced by many banks and other experts in investment firms when it comes to helping the small investor.

Also, the small investor is sometimes kept out of the market by the relatively high commission rates charged by brokers. These rates are based on a percent of the purchase price of the stock and the number of shares purchased. And the rates may be higher for the smaller purchase. For example, at one broker, the small investor may invest $200 and the fee may be 6 percent (or a minimum of $20). Another may invest $2000 and the fee may be about 2½ percent. The larger investor is paying more dollars than the small investor, but percentagewise considerably less. These kinds of factors tend to keep the small investor out of the investment market.

WHY PEOPLE INVEST

For our purposes, investing is limited to buying stocks (both common and preferred), bonds (corporate, municipal, and government), mutual funds, and real estate. Typi-

cally, investments carry a greater risk than savings.

The three primary objectives for investing are *safety of principal* (the amount invested), *income* (the amount of interest or dividends returned on the investment), and *growth* (increasing the value of the amount invested). People and businesses invest their money mainly to earn more money. It is that simple.

The motivation for wanting to improve their financial position, however, varies among the 30 million investors. In a recent survey of individual investors who were asked why they invested in stock, the most frequent response given was for retirement. Following this came family security, education of children, building an estate, additional income, and long-term growth.

Regardless of one's reasons, it must be fully understood that with each investment comes a degree of risk. In certain types of investment, such as government securities, the risk is very small. For other types of investments, such as some common stocks, the risk is much higher.

The person who chooses to invest in securities rather than save in a savings account is simply saying that he or she is willing to assume some risk. For the willingness to take this risk, one also assumes the potential of earning more income from investments than one could from interest on a savings account. For example, Mary Jo Morton of Santa Barbara, California, chose to invest in the common stock of an electronics firm. She realized that she could lose her whole investment if the company went out of business. But Mary Jo studied the company's operation and financial history very carefully and felt she was making a sound investment; thus, she assumed the risk.

Jesse Parker of Los Angeles took a more conservative approach. He was going to put his money in a savings account, which is literally risk-free, when he saw an opportunity to earn more income through investing in long-term corporate bonds that paid a higher rate of return. The bond is only backed by the finan-

"You'll find a copy of 'How to Get Rich in Today's Economy' in the fiction department."

cial integrity of the company, but Mr. Parker was willing to assume this difference in risk to gain the additional earnings.

Another reason for selecting a particular type of investment is based on the economic behavior of the marketplace. An inflationary economy with rising prices is an example of turmoil. Under such conditions some persons invest in common stock because its value usually (but not always) increases and decreases with prices in general. For example, if a person owns 100 shares of XYZ Company, presently valued at $1500, and the prices on most consumable items increase about 2.1 percent in 3 months, that person might expect the value of the common stock to increase in the same way. There is no guarantee that its value will rise as prices do, but historically it generally has. Investments in preferred stock or government and corporate bonds do not lend themselves to quite the same type of price fluctuation. This is mainly because common stock is traded in a much larger volume than other investments.

Some investors choose a preferred stock with its fixed rate of dividends; the return is usually not guaranteed, but it is paid before common stock dividends. Thousands invest in short- and long-term government bonds be-

cause of their safety. Finally, the novice investor often chooses a mutual fund, leaving the selection of the particular stocks and bonds up to the experts who manage the fund. These and other types of investments will be discussed in more detail later in the chapter.

Although people choose their types of investments for individual reasons, each choice should be rational and justified. This justification should come in the form of careful planning and an understanding of investments and the risks involved, the economic situation of the economy, the costs of the investment, and the expected return of the funds invested.

IMPORTANCE OF INVESTMENTS

The investments made by the various sectors of the economy keep the wheels turning in the American marketplace. Benefits accrue to all: consumers, businesses, governments, and the total economy.

To Consumers

Investments are important to individuals in many ways. Persons who invest money in businesses or governments do so for the primary purpose of gaining a return. But personal satisfaction can also be gained by contributing to a company's or a government's operation through investing.

Buying twenty shares of Telex Company stock at $2.50 per share may seem to be a rather small investment. But to the small investor it represents a piece of ownership in one company in the American economy. Although these twenty shares may represent only $1/1000$ of 1 percent of the total shares outstanding, this is unimportant. There are many more stockholders with many more shares in the company, but those twenty shares still represent ownership. Interest and enthusiasm are often high with small investors. And the investment gives a personal opportunity to see how business operates. Furthermore, one can better understand the relationship of the Telex Company and the free enterprise system when one becomes a shareholder-owner of part of a business.

The aggregate investments of the millions of people in the economy constitute a faith in the business and governments in which they invest. In addition, these investments earn millions of dollars in dividends and interest for the investors. These dollars can be used to buy consumer goods or services, or they can be reinvested.

To Businesses and Governments

Most businesses and governments could not exist without investments. A typical large business corporation depends almost completely upon money invested by others in order to operate effectively and grow. Investments, whether in stocks or bonds, help the business immeasurably. It is through them that the business has funds with which to operate. These funds are then put to work to earn a profit for the firm. As profits increase, the business can turn part of them back to the investors in the form of dividends or interest.

Governments, of course, also need funds to operate. Taxes are usually their major source of income. But a cash-flow problem often occurs, since tax monies do not come in as regularly as a paycheck. So borrowing by selling bonds becomes necessary. Often, schools and other expensive municipal facilities cannot be built out of current revenues. So governments, at all levels, like businesses, must borrow.

Figure 14-1 shows how important invest-

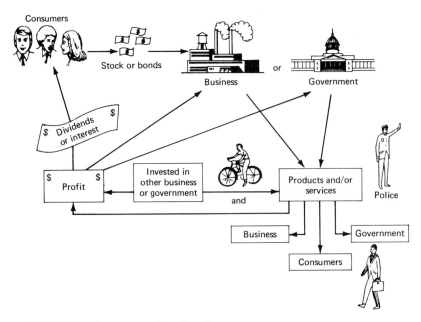

FIGURE 14-1   Investment benefits all segments

ment is for all. Similarities can be noticed among the three segments of the economy—individuals, businesses, and government. Each invests in various ways to help the others. And each benefits from these investments, which help its own cause through earnings, profits, or both. Additionally, all segments benefit from the products or services manufactured or performed by the others.

Products are manufactured for consumer, producer, or government use. At the same time, services are performed by government bodies for the benefit of consumers and businesses. Without investments many businesses and governments would have to operate on a far smaller scale. Consumers, too, would suffer. Fewer products would be produced and fewer services could be performed.

To the Economy

Individuals, businesses, and governments together make up the economy. The investments and spending of each segment ultimately benefit all, as shown in Figure 14-1. The individual has a chance to work and earn a living; businesses can manufacture, sell products and services, and hopefully make a profit; and governments can perform needed services for all.

Investments help all to help themselves and at the same time to help the economy grow. An improved economy in turn benefits all through stability, security, and freedom.

TYPES OF INVESTMENTS

There are types of investments for almost every kind of personal desire. Degree of risk, amount of money needed, rate of return on investment, and length of time before benefits can be gained are but a few investment variables. People can choose a high risk and possible high return on their investment dollars, or they can choose a long-term low-risk investment with a moderate return. The choice is up to them. But they must first know the

All investments involve some degree of risk, but some, such as short-term investments in gold and silver, involve more risk than others. (*Kenneth Karp*)

basic differences among the available investments.

Stocks

Probably the most common type of investment is stock in a corporation. Persons who want to invest in corporations can do so by buying shares of stock. Each share represents a certain proportion of ownership. For example, if a person buys 100 shares of one stock, and the corporation has a total of 2000 shares of stock to sell, the 100-share investment represents one-twentieth, or a 5 percent ownership. Shares of stock vary in price, depending on the issuing corporation and the existing market conditions. If a particular type of stock is in high demand (many people want to buy it) and the number of shares is in short supply (too few are available), then the price usually rises to that offered by the highest bidder. The profitability or potential for profits greatly affects the price.

Two important stock prices or values to note are par value and market value. *Par value* is the issue price of each share according to the corporate charter; it has little meaning once the stock has been issued. *Market value* is the price at which the stock is currently being sold. It is the market value that fluctuates with the earnings of the company and the economy. Once the stock is issued, the market value is the primary figure of concern.

Common Stock. One of the major types of stock is a corporation's common stock. This stock provides a percentage of ownership, and holders of common stock also enjoy certain other rights and privileges. These may include *voting rights,* which entitle a stockholder to vote at annual corporation meetings, usually to elect the board of directors; *stock splits,* which give the stockholder double or triple the number of shares owned, although at a reduced value per share (for example, if the market value of a share is $30, and there is a two-for-one stock split, the value of each new share is $15 and the investor now has twice as many shares but the same ownership; reverse stock splits are possible, too); and *stock rights,* which give the stockholder the right to buy new corporate issues of common stock, in proportion to his or her current holdings, before anyone else can buy them on the open market. In addition, and most importantly, common stockholders share in *dividends* (a financial return) as declared by the board of directors. Dividends are declared on a per-share basis, and are usually paid quarterly. For example, a company with a market value of $30 a share may make a first-quarter payment to shareholders of 40 cents for each share.

Many investors buy common stocks because they tend to keep abreast of rising prices. But there is no perfect direct relationship between prices in general and the value of a particular common stock. Just because overall prices increase 4 percent in 6 months does not guarantee that the value of a share of common stock will do the same. However, the value of most common stocks does keep up with or slightly ahead of prices in general and the cost of living.

Preferred Stock. Many corporations offer another type of stock in addition to common, and this is called preferred stock. It gives the stockholder special privileges and a completely different kind of ownership. For some people, preferred stocks are the best investment. Some investors like to have a fixed rate of return, and this is a characteristic of preferred stocks.

The rate of return to be paid to the preferred stockholder is stated on the face of the *stock certificate* (a document showing evidence of ownership). Each time the board of directors declares a dividend for preferred stockholders, the amount paid is usually the precise rate printed on the certificate. For example, stockholders who hold preferred stock with an original par value of $200 and a 6 percent rate of return would be paid a $12 dividend. As with common stock, there is, of course, no guarantee that a dividend will be declared. A company may suffer financial reverses, or may decide to reinvest all profits in the corporation.

Some preferred stocks, called *cumulative,* offer a kind of guarantee that a dividend may be paid eventually. If a dividend is not declared, the holders of cumulative preferred stock receive these past-due dividends later, when money is available for payment. And, in all cases, preferred stockholders must be paid *before* common stockholders.

Another feature of many preferred stocks is that they are *participating.* In high-profit years the corporation may decide to declare extra-large dividends. Normally, such dividends go to the common stockholders, since they have the greatest risk of ownership. But a participating preferred stockholder could receive additional dividends, should the board of directors declare them. Should the corporation go bankrupt, preferred stockholders also have a higher priority, insofar as the distribution of remaining assets is concerned, than do common stockholders.

Bonds

A *bond* is a promissory note (an "IOU") of a corporation, municipality, or government, and is usually issued for multiples of $1000. It is a written contract-certificate of debt in which the issuer promises to pay back to the bondholder the amount borrowed in addition to a specified amount of interest for a particular period. A bond represents debt; its holder is a creditor of the corporation or government. Bonds become due and payable after perhaps 5, 10, 20, or even 50 years.

Corporate Bonds. One who wishes to lend money to a corporation buys corporate bonds. A major reason for buying corporate bonds over government bonds is that they normally pay a higher rate of return. They are bought through investment firms or banks, normally in minimum amounts of $1000. Selling bonds is one of four basic ways a corporation has to raise funds. The other three ways are by making good profits, by borrowing from a bank or other financial institution, or by selling stock.

A corporation that issues bonds realizes that the debt will cost interest. However, it can take the money raised by selling bonds and use it for capital improvements. In the long run, hopefully, these improvements will help to increase profits, and the corporation will be able to repay the borrowed money when it becomes due. A corporation that issues 20-year bonds at 6 percent annual interest in the amount of $2 million will have to pay $120,000 in interest payments during the first year and hundreds of thousands of dollars more over the 20-year period. But the $2 million will start working for the corporation immediately. And through careful use of the money, the corporation hopes to get a return greater than the 6 percent it is paying out in interest over the 20 years.

Through issuing bonds, the corporation can partially realize its goals, and the bondholder also benefits. The interest paid is fixed, so the bondholder knows the exact amount that will be coming in each year. And, although the interest paid is stated annually, it is usually paid on a semiannual basis.

Payments are usually made by one of two methods. Bondholders *of record* are automati-

cally mailed their interest checks. *Coupon* bondholders present their tear-off coupons and receive interest as they turn them in. In either case, a large commercial bank is normally designated as the trustee who pays the interest. One advantage of buying bonds is that, should the company become bankrupt, the bondholders will be the first to be paid off, in part or in full.

Municipal Bonds. A type of indebtedness unique to villages, towns, cities, and states, but similar to corporate bonds, is the municipal bond. Its distinction lies in the fact that it is issued by a municipality, not a corporation. Basically the purpose of municipal bonds is the same as that of corporate bonds—to raise money. One basic difference is that corporate bonds are used essentially to earn profits, and municipal bonds are used essentially to finance municipal building costs and improvements.

An advantage of buying municipal bonds is that the interest earned is not taxable on one's federal income tax. Also, most states do not tax interest on municipal bonds issued in their own states. Although the interest paid on these bonds is generally lower than that on corporate bonds, people in tax brackets of 32 percent or higher, for example, gain more by buying them. To illustrate, a person with a taxable income of $40,000 may be able to realize an after-tax return of 7.35 percent on municipal bonds instead of the stated rate of 4 percent. The return is higher because the income is tax exempt. If the same person were to buy corporate bonds paying 8 percent interest, some of the interest would go for taxes, reducing the real return to perhaps 5½ percent.

Government Bonds. The federal government has historically borrowed money to operate the economy. One way of borrowing money is by issuing government bonds. Government bonds are usually distinguished from government savings bonds in that they are issued for definite, short or long periods. These securities are backed by the credit of the U.S. Treasury and are classified as follows: (1) *Treasury bills* have the shortest maturities, from 3 to 6 months. They are also considered safest because of their short life span. (2) *Treasury notes* usually mature in from 1 to 7 years and pay a fixed rate of interest semiannually. (3) *Treasury bonds* generally have a minimum maturity of 7 years and are considered to be a long-term investment; interest is paid semiannually. These bonds can be purchased through banks or brokers, usually in minimum denominations of $1000 or $10,000.

Bond Ratings.   Typically, the soundness of the U.S. Treasury makes all U.S. government bonds considered the highest quality, whereas the quality of corporate and municipal bonds varies considerably. To help determine quality, the investor must rely on ratings from specialists in the bond field. Most banks and brokers can provide these ratings, and other good guides include *Moody's Investors Service* and *Standard & Poor's Corporation.* From the highest to the lowest quality, the ratings are:

- Moody's—Aaa, Aa, A, Baa, Ba, B, Caa, Ca, C
- Standard & Poor's—AAA, AA, A, BBB, BB, B, CCC, CC, C

Bonds that fall into one of the first four ratings are considered top investment quality. Bonds rated lower should probably be avoided.

Mutual Funds

Investment of the members, by the members, and for the members is a general description of the basic operation of a mutual fund. It is actually a type of holding company, and shares are "sold" to investing consumers in much the same way as a share of stock in a corporation is sold. Instead of buying stock in one company, however, an investor buys a share of a mutual fund corporation.

Operational Principles.   Mutual fund administrators specialize in investing funds from thousands of people. Rather than trying to

choose from a variety of investments by oneself, a single investor need only turn to a mutual fund and let an expert do the work. However, mutual funds differ in purpose, and this can be determined by examining the objectives of the fund as recorded in its *prospectus.* This is a document providing many details about a company, required by the Securities and Exchange Commission. Some mutual funds specialize in growth stocks, some in income bonds, and still others have a diversified approach. Getting the prospectus, therefore, is an important step in getting information.

With a mutual fund, any operational costs are deducted from earnings. Through this form of investing, the investor can put money into a fund by buying shares and then let someone else worry about how it will be invested for growth, income, or both. The investor, of course, must have confidence in the mutual fund itself and its investment specialists.

Figure 14-2 illustrates the basic principles of how mutual funds work. The fund begins with an investor, continues through the several financial steps, and returns to the investor—hopefully with dividends and/or growth. The investor in the fund has nothing to do with the actual investing. This task is left to the investment management specialists, whose job is to invest all money received from the thousands of investors.

Types of Funds.   There are two important types of mutual funds: *load* and *no-load.* These two terms mean charging or not charging a commission. A *load fund* charges the investor anywhere from 8 to 9 percent of the invested amount as a commission for the salesperson. If, over a period of a year, you invest $500 in a fund with a load charge of 9 percent, you will end up with only $455 actually invested in fund shares. In fact, the true percentage charge is higher, since it should be calculated on the $455; the real rate is 9.9 percent.

New regulations prohibit charging the entire commission to the customer's account during

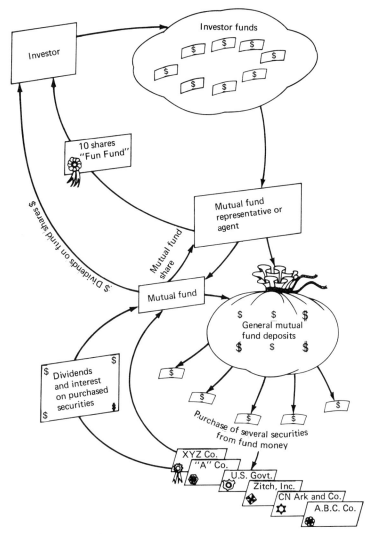

FIGURE 14-2   Mutual funds and how they work

the first year. For example, a 9 percent commission on a $1000 investment would be $90 total. Since only 50 percent of the commission ($45) can be assessed during the first year, the consumer has $955 in shares earning dividends from the beginning.

No-load (no commission is paid) funds are normally purchased from the fund company itself by contacting them directly. The middleman (broker) is eliminated from the buying process. No-load funds are growing in number, since no commission is paid and the overall performance of both types is about the same. Naturally, you should seek out a no-load fund if you want to avoid paying additional charges. If a fund is particularly attractive to you regardless of the load charges, you will have to weigh the advantages and disadvantages and make a decision.

A mutual fund investor needs to be aware of two other types of funds—*closed-end* and *open-end* funds. *Closed-end* funds issue a fixed number of shares to be traded on an exchange or over the counter like common stock. New issues are not made as a result of investor demand or market activity. Essentially, the *net asset value* NAV (market value of assets minus liabilities, divided by shares outstanding) does not change because of a change in the number of shares issued. However, the market value of shares can increase or decrease, depending on the profitability of the fund.

Open-end fund companies continually sell or buy shares to meet the public demand. There is no limit on the total number of fund shares that can be sold. A new net asset value per share is computed at the end of each day based on the number of shares outstanding—including new issues. For example, if today net assets were $8,500,000 and the total shares issued were 800,000, the net asset value would be $10.63 (8,500,000 ÷ 800,000). If, however, tomorrow an additional 10,000 shares were issued, the net asset value would change to $10.49 (8,500,000 ÷ 810,000). The open-end funds are more popular because the issuing of new shares makes more shares available and allows more people to invest in the fund.

Methods of Purchase. Three primary ways to purchase mutual fund shares include the regular account plan, accumulation plan, and contractual plan.

A lump-sum purchase is called the *regular account plan.* A specific amount of money is invested at one time. A load charge (a commission charged by the seller of mutual fund shares) of up to about 9 percent may be assessed against the total purchase amount. For example, if you invest $20,000 at a 9 percent load charge, $1800 goes to the seller of the shares as commission. The rest, $18,200 worth of shares, will go to the purchaser. In some instances, the load charge is reduced, that is, the larger the purchase amount, the less the load charge. Also, some funds do not have a load charge at all.

After you make your purchase, you will get a certificate of ownership with the noted number of shares. Subsequent dividend checks will be sent to you in the mail. This is usually done quarterly. In some instances, however, dividends may be paid on a monthly basis. Another alternative that you can arrange for under this regular account plan is to reinvest your dividends to purchase additional fund shares. Also, if the fund gains in value and this is redistributed to the shareholders, you may again reinvest the payment and gain additional shares. This, however, is optional.

Sometimes called a voluntary plan, an *accumulation plan* starts with an application stating the amount of the initial purchase, usually from $100 to $500, depending on the particular fund. Also, the investor must state the amount to be invested periodically in the future and when the payments will be made. Generally speaking, this will vary with the fund, but there is a minimum of $25 to $50 required for each periodic payment. The purchaser has the option, however, of changing that amount so long as the amount paid does not fall below the minimum. With each purchase a confirmation is sent to the investor. The specific fund certificates are usually not sent to the purchaser unless specifically requested. Under many funds, stock certificates are held in the name of the broker. This practice enables the holder of the stock to easily transfer the stock or shares at the request of the investor.

As in the case of the regular account, both load and no-load funds can be bought this way. In the case of a load fund, as was true of the regular, a specified rate will be given to the investor. Under the accumulation plan, the load charge is deducted from each payment that is made. For example, if the load charge is 8 percent and the investor is investing $100 a month, $8 of that monthly investment will go toward the load charge, and $92 a month will actually be invested in the fund.

If you use the accumulation plan, you can treat it like the sort of open account that would normally be used by anybody investing in stock on a periodic basis. You can invest money (staying above a minimum amount) according to a predetermined plan. Yet whenever you want you can stop your contributions to the fund, and everything that you have in the fund will remain unless you specifically ask to have it sold or transferred. The accumulation plan gives the investor a great deal of flexibility.

Generally speaking, the *contractual plan* operates like the accumulation plan except that there is an agreed-upon (contractual) amount that will be eventually paid into the fund. Under the accumulation plan no such maximum exists. The contractual plan is similar to paying an installment debt, although this is an investment rather than a debt.

Let's look at an example. Under the contractual plan, suppose you agree to invest $10,000 over a 10-year period with a load charge of 9 percent. Also, you agree to pay $1000 a year. Normally that 9 percent or $900 (9 percent × $10,000) would be paid before anything else is invested. If you invested about $90 a month in order to have a total amount of $1000 invested in a year, your first ten monthly payments would be used for the load charge, and it wouldn't be until the eleventh month that you could realize shares in the fund as a result of your purchases.

The usual interpretation of the contractual plan is as described above. However, there is a modification of this that many investors do not know about. No more than 50 percent of the first twelve monthly payments can be deducted for sales commission (load charge). So if you were paying in $1000 a year, no more than $500 of that amount could be deducted for commission the first year. In the illustration cited, although the total load charge would be $900, only $500 could be deducted the first year, and the remaining load charge would be paid over the next few years of the contract.

One disadvantage of the contractual plan is that if you decide to discontinue the plan in the early years of your contributions, very little of the money you paid would be actually working for you because at least half of the load charge is deducted first.

Regardless of which plan is used in the fund,

once the shares have been purchased and/or dividends are paid and/or subsequently reinvested, the ownership is treated the same way. Dividends are paid per share in all plans. Withdrawal from the fund or falling back from paying is quite similar. Should the investor want to sell shares, it would make no difference how they were purchased so long as they were owned by the investor; he or she has the right to sell at any time.

Real Estate

Not too many years ago only wealthy people were able to invest in real estate. This was mostly because of the large initial investment required. Real estate investment is no longer as restrictive because of *real estate investment trust* (REIT) organizations throughout the country.

This type of trust is based on a premise similar to that of mutual funds. It lets the middle-income consumer invest money in relatively small amounts. The people operating the trust accumulate funds from numerous investors, small and large, and invest these funds in real property. The trust sells shares to the investing public, commonly in amounts of $5000, although an increasing number of funds are permitting share purchases of $1000 amounts. The funds are then professionally invested in one or more real estate projects.

Although real estate trusts date back as far as 1850, they did not gain prominence until recently when the Internal Revenue Service gave them a limited tax-exempt status. They are not taxed on any money paid back to the shareholders as investment returns. By law the real estate trusts must pay out 90 percent of their ordinary income to shareholders to qualify for tax-exempt status. It is because of this status that the real estate trusts have grown so in recent years.

THE PROCESS OF INVESTING IN STOCKS AND BONDS

If you want to invest, you should get a sound basic knowledge of the field of investments.

Then you should study the information about the investments that interest you the most. The more knowledge you acquire, the less complicated the process will seem, and the probability of achieving your goals will be higher.

Obtaining Information

Some investors do a great deal of studying before they buy or sell securities. Others find a reliable broker and rely on that person's advice while perhaps understanding less about the situation. In either case, there is plenty of information available that is useful for the investor.

Published Sources. For the investor who wants to gather investment information and stay abreast of what is happening in the business world, several publications are available. Valuable weekly publications include:

Business Week
P. O. Box 430
Hightstown, N.J. 08520

Forbes
60 Fifth Avenue
New York, N.Y. 10011

Financial World
590 Exchange Street
Marion, Ohio 43302

Fortune
541 North Fairbanks Court
Chicago, Ill. 60611

The Exchange
11 Wall Street
New York, N.Y. 10005

Barron's
200 Burnett Road
Chicopee, Mass. 01021

Other periodic publications that are extremely helpful to the investor are:

The Commercial and Financial Chronicle
National News Service, Inc.
110 Wall Street
New York, N.Y. 10006

Moody's Handbook of Common Stock
Moody's Investors Service
99 Church Street
New York, N.Y. 10007

Federal Reserve Bulletin
Division of Administrative Services
Board of Governors of the Federal Reserve System
Washington, D.C. 20551

Survey of Current Business
Supt. of Documents
U.S. Government Printing Office
Washington, D.C. 20402

Three excellent sources which can supply more detailed investment information in addition to providing special publications are:

Standard and Poor's Corporation
345 Hudson Street
New York, N.Y. 10014

Value Line Investment Survey
Five East 44th Street
New York, N.Y. 10017

Moody's Investors Service
99 Church Street
New York, N.Y. 10007

In addition, one excellent daily publication is:

The Wall Street Journal
30 Broad Street
New York, N.Y. 10004

Another source would be the financial section of most large city newspapers.

Many problems of beginning investors come from a communications gap. They just do not understand the language of investing. Most investment firms, trust departments of commercial banks, the New York and American Stock Exchanges and others, and many brokers have basic glossaries on terms unique to the investment world, in addition to other useful general publications. Usually these "language-of-investing" publications are free.

Corporation Reports. All public corporations publish annual reports that are available to the

BERRY'S WORLD

Ye Olde Bookshop

HOW TO MAKE MONEY IN THE STOCK MARKET

Now ½ PRICE.

© 1970 by NEA, Inc.,

Reprinted by permission of Newspaper Enterprise Association.

potential investor too. Of course, the scope of the reports varies from company to company, but under regulations of the Securities and Exchange Commission, these reports must provide much valuable information. Financial statements commonly show assets, liabilities, sales, earnings, dividends paid, corporate research activities, new developments and particular plans for expansion, pertinent information about the people who run the business (particularly its officers, board of directors, and key workers), and future outlook for both the company and the industry.

Periodic short-term reports that include quarterly listings of earnings and dividends paid to stockholders are also available from corporations. Although some reports are restricted to employees and stockholders, any good broker can get copies of most reports of this type if you are interested.

Be certain to check information sources carefully. Choose reliable ones (keeping in mind that corporate reports usually do their best to show how good the company is). Also, compare one source with another, and double-check any conflicting information.

Moody's Industrials, Standard & Poor's, and *Value Line* are excellent reference books found in most libraries that provide detailed analysis of companies and industries. Of course, deal only with licensed investment specialists.

Making Decisions on Investments

More people than ever before are investing in stocks and other types of securities. The New York Stock Exchange reported recently that the number of stockholders has more than tripled in the last 10 years and now stands at over 30 million. Wise investing, however, requires knowledge, planning, and, of course, adequate funds.

Can You Afford to Invest?   Whether you can afford to begin investing is a personal decision. However, there are some general guidelines that can help you in your decision. (1) Do you have enough money to cover living expenses? (2) Do you have money in the bank to cover family emergencies (usually 2 months take-home pay is considered enough)? (3) Do you have adequate insurance coverage? Although these guidelines are somewhat subjective, they do alert you to matters that you need to consider. But if everyone were to follow these rules to the letter, few small investors would ever invest. They are general rules only.

Occasionally, a person wants to invest only a small amount in some common stocks, just for the "experience of it." In such a case, the person must treat this invested money as an "extra," not needed for either usual expenses or emergencies. Otherwise, he or she may find out too late that when the money is needed, it is not readily available. Or the value of a stock may have dropped greatly and selling would result in a considerable loss.

Comparing Investments.   The investor should ask several questions before deciding on the type of investment. What is the minimum amount needed for my investment? What can I expect to get as a return? Is it an income or a growth stock? How much dividends have been paid in the past? Is a return guaranteed? How *liquid* (quickly convertible to cash) is my investment? How much risk is there if I invest in a particular type of security? Are bonds a better investment than stock? Is there greater security in mutual funds? What specific measures can I apply to evaluate a particular security?

A fairly specific tool one can use to analyze and compare stocks is the *price-earnings ratio* (P/E). This ratio is the market price of the stock divided by the company's annual net earnings per share. For example, a stock valued at $100 earning $5 a share would have a P/E ratio of 20 (100 divided by 5). Buyers may be anticipating higher expected dividends, and the P/E ratio trends can help you spot such events. However, since the P/E ratio is open to varied interpretation, it is a good idea to look at it and then get the help of an experienced stockbroker for full interpretation.

When comparing types of investments, look at the advantages and disadvantages of each. If you choose common stock, you must choose both an industry and a specific stock. If you choose bonds, you must decide whether to buy corporate, municipal, or government. No hard and fast rule will fit all cases. Each investment must be looked at individually.

Guidelines for Investing.   Most novice investors need help—some particular path to follow. One such path is found in the guidelines of A. Vere Shaw, who first wrote them in 1925. They have since been revised and are widely followed today. These ten rules for investors, published by Dow Jones, include:

1. Own only bonds and stock of leading companies in sound and essential industries.
2. Own only stocks which are listed on a registered Securities Exchange, or which conform to Exchange requirements.
3. Own only stocks which can boast an earnings or a dividend record—or both—unbroken for at least ten years.
4. Own stocks in at least five different industries.

5. Own stocks in fairly equal amounts in at least eight or ten different companies.
6. Own a few low-yield stocks as a means of building up capital and future income.
7. Buy bonds below par or slightly above to reduce the likelihood of spending capital.
8. Once a year sell at least one stock, choosing the weakest on the list with no consideration whatever for its original cost. Replace it with a more attractive stock.
9. Do not be disturbed by losses on individual risks, but keep an eye out for a gain or loss on the aggregate.
10. Subscribe to at least one high-grade financial publication and read it regularly and thoroughly.

Although these guidelines seem more appropriate for the more advanced investor, they also have value for the beginner.

APPROACH TO INVESTING

Effective investing cannot be done spontaneously. It requires knowledge about investing and careful planning. And help can be had from professional investment counselors or brokers.

To invest capably, a person must have a purpose or a philosophy of investing. Facts about business operations and cycles, including appropriate charts, graphs, other factual data, and various types of investment plans are helpful guides. These, along with a well-thought-out philosophy of investing, will aid in investing soundly rather than speculating foolishly.

Philosophy of Investing during One's Life Cycle

Most people would like to do some type of investing during their lifetime. Naturally, the investments would vary in amount, type, purpose, and duration. Essentially, investing depends on one's philosophy about life and investments. Moreover, as one gets older, takes on greater responsibilities, and becomes more knowledgeable about investments, one is

likely to alter investment ideas. Let's look at some phases of the life cycle and how they could affect one's investment philosophy.

Young Singles. Jose Lupio of Denver landed his first fulltime job since graduating from college. He had a general knowledge of investments, but was not a student as such. He was willing, however, to talk with investment experts if necessary.

Jose had been bombarded with literature and other investment information recently and just hadn't known how to react. He decided to contact an investment counselor, who asked him why he wanted to invest. Jose said that he had saved several hundred dollars for emergencies and now wanted to use his extra income to invest for the future. The counselor advised him to think in terms of *growth* (increasing in value over time) and long-term investments, particularly since he did not need short-run income-producing investments at the present time. Furthermore, the counselor advised Jose to consider making regular investments every 3 months himself or perhaps join a *monthly investment plan* (MIP) and invest a set amount each month through a broker. By doing so he could get into the habit of investing regularly. It was not important to invest too much at one time, but to continue to invest however much he wanted on a regular basis.

This type of steady, long-range investment would allow Jose to meet his objective—growth. Then he would have funds available for retirement or other purposes later in life.

Young Married Persons. Lorna and Jose were married, and now there were two incomes from fulltime positions. Lorna taught high-school special education, and Jose worked as an assistant manager of a small department store. Their salaries were not large, but they were more than enough for two to live on comfortably.

Lorna and Jose continued to invest as Jose had before. Only now the purpose had changed. They wanted their investments to be easily convertible to cash when their children were old enough to attend college. They were convinced that investing would meet this objective. Also, they wanted some short-term investments, which would give them more income and could be used to help pay for a house later. Thus, they kept their growth stocks and sought out a few low-risk investments for income purposes.

Jose and Lorna conferred with their investment counselor about their altered investment philosophy. Again the counselor suggested steady investments for long-term growth. The counselor also advised them to buy government securities—municipal bonds, treasury bills, or notes—which had lower risk and which would cover their short-term investment goal. Although their investments were not directed at producing a periodic income, these short-run government securities could provide some.

After a few years Jose and Lorna decided to buy a house. They changed from paying rent to investing in a house. They redeemed their short-term government securities and used them as a down payment on the house they purchased. Yet they continued making their long-term investments on a regular basis.

Middle-aged Persons. About this time in the life cycle, the children (if there are any) have grown and finished school; they have left home and are on their own, or they are providing for themselves at home.

Jose and Lorna put their children through college with the money they got from the investments they had made for that purpose. Any additional money required came from their regular income. Soon the children were working and were self-sufficient. The Lupios continued to earn—Lorna had resumed her teaching, after several years off, when the children had started school. They also continued to invest.

They consulted further with their investment counselor, who advised them to invest with a goal of producing retirement income,

since retirement was only about 10 to 15 years away. Although there would be Social Security, Lorna's teacher's retirement pension, Jose's employer's pension, and some earlier investment earnings to help provide needed income, more investment income would certainly help. The Lupios followed this advice and invested accordingly. But now their philosophy had changed to one of investing for income for retirement rather than long-term growth.

Retired Persons. The benefits of the Lupios wise investments would now be returned once more. Their careful, thoughtful investing would begin to pay them the income they needed now that they have retired.

What with the various amounts and sources of income received by the Lupios, they found that they had more than they needed to meet their day-to-day expenses. So they sought the help of their investment counselor again. This time the purpose was different. They had a change in their investment philosophy now that they were living, not elaborately, but comfortably.

Jose and Lorna Lupio wanted to invest their extra earnings to provide something for their children, something to leave them when they passed on. Low-risk stock of a well-established company, mutual funds for long-term growth, or long-term certificates of deposits (5 to 7 years) were recommended to the Lupois. Income-producing investments were not the objective at this time. They chose a sound mutual fund for long-term growth which would provide more for their children.

This example explains how over the years, the Lupios modified their investment goals and philosophy. These changes came about as their lifestyle changed. The purposes and goals of living as a family unit influenced their investment goals and purposes. In the final analysis, it was careful planning and relying on sound investment counseling that helped the Lupios achieve these lifestyle and investment goals.

Dollar Averaging Approach

Dollar averaging is using the *average* cost of all shares of stock bought over a period of time regardless of cost at the time of purchase. When using dollar averaging, you invest a selected dollar amount regularly into the same stock or stocks, and you buy these securities regardless of the current price. Simply put, your regular investment buys more shares when the stock price is low, and fewer shares when the stock price is high. Over the years dollar averaging will result in the average cost of *all* shares purchased being lower than the average price at which the shares were bought. Most importantly, you must stick to your schedule of buying even though the price declines. This will bring the average cost down, and any future increase in stock value will yield a nice profit.

Let's look at an example of how dollar averaging works. Assume that $150 is invested at intervals in a certain stock and that the first four purchases are made at prices of $12.50, $15.00, $10.00 and $5.00, as shown in Table 14-1. Note that the average cost is only $8.96. More shares were bought at $5.00, and as a result the average cost is lower than the average price paid ($12.50 + 15.00 + 10.00 + 5.00/4 = $10.63) when purchased.

Regardless of the market changes, decline or rise, any selling price above the dollar

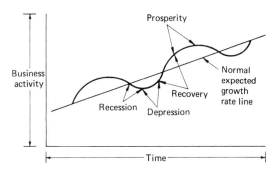

FIGURE 14-3   Business cycle phases

average per share will result in a profit for the investor when the stocks are sold. Moreover, dollar averaging is a worthwhile practice to follow, even for the novice investor.

A Business-cycle Approach

An approach to investing followed by many is that of using business cycles as a monitor of the investment marketplace. A *business cycle* is a regular yet uneven fluctuation of business activity (from a high point of activity, or prosperity, to a low point of activity, or depression). Figure 14-3 illustrates these fluctuations and identifies the phases of the business cycle. Thousands of bankers, investment specialists, and other experts devote a major portion of their time to studying the business cycle, since it reflects employment, the prosperity of busi-

TABLE 14-1

Illustration of Dollar Averaging

| | Periods of Purchases | | | |
	1	2	3	4
a. Amount invested	$150.00	$150.00	$150.00	$150.00
b. Share price	$ 12.50	$ 15.00	$ 10.00	$ 5.00
c. Shares purchased	12	10	15	30
d. Total shares owned	12	22	37	67
e. Total dollars invested	$150.00	$300.00	$450.00	$600.00
f. Average dollar cost per share*	$ 12.50	$ 13.64	$ 12.16	$ 8.96

* Line e ÷ d

ness firms, individual incomes, and spending patterns.

Financial experts generally associate business-cycle movements with the unsteady flow of money and credit, the changing rates of savings and investments, and the shift of business and consumer confidence from one extreme to another. Regardless of the causes, the business cycle changes from a period of business expansion to a period of business contraction and back again often. These cyclical changes can never be eliminated, so everyone must learn to live within their framework.

An obvious impact of the business cycle is the change in personal income, business earnings, government revenues, and the fluctuation in the investment market. For example, in times of business recession, unemployment affects about 7, 8, or even 10 percent of the labor force, and paychecks reflect little or no overtime work. Also, statistics show that average personal income declines about 6 percent during mild recessions. During recessions, prices level off and business volume declines. Later, when labor is at full employment and business is good, prices tend to rise.

Real and personal property values and common stock prices reflect the fluctuations of the business cycle. Sales and frequent discounts to sell houses, automobiles, and appliances during recessions is a typical pattern. In prosperous years, the prices of these items hold firm and tend to rise. Stock market prices similarly rise and fall with the business cycle. The uncertain and irregular movement of these prices, however, places doubt on the current value of any one individual's investments and assets.

For those persons using the business-cycle approach to investments, there are certain ways to gain during inflationary periods. One way would be to place surplus income immediately into certain speculative investments. The gain, however, is apt to be short-run, as this may extend the price spiral. Funds are likely to flow into those activities that offer the highest return to the investor.

At the end of a period of prosperity, just as the cycle begins heading downward toward a recession, investors should buy bonds or countercyclical securities; if a bond continues to pay $4 a year, for example, and prices are falling, the investor receives a higher real return as time goes on. Countercyclical or "recession-proof" stocks are those that usually do not drop in value during a recession. "Habit" products like tobacco, soft drinks, and gum rarely drop in such periods. Also, neither do utility or gold stocks as a rule. Prices as a whole do fall during a recession. So those investors who can get quick cash can take advantage of bargains by investing in stocks such as automobiles and steel, which will definitely rise in value as the business cycle returns to prosperity.

All in all, investors using the business-cycle approach need to become knowledgeable about the cycle variations and their implications. It is quite an exacting process and requires skill to make it work as an investing tool. For the beginner, it is an excellent technique, but other approaches need to be investigated too.

A Charting Approach

For those persons who prefer to use charts as a source of investment information and decision making, there are a number of chart services available in the country. Four companies that offer excellent investment charting services are: M. C. Horsey and Company, ChartCraft, Inc., Trend Line, and Dines Chart Corporation. There are a variety of chart books that graphically portray the periodic movement of prices and sales volume for stocks over several years. For example, Horsey publishes a book *The Stock Picture*, showing well over 1500 charts. Over 2500 point-and-figure charts are shown in a monthly chart book published by ChartCraft, Inc.

A book of charts, *Current Market Perspectives*, on nearly 1000 listed issues showing weekly high, low, and close prices, and the *OTC Chart Manual* covering over 8000 OTC stocks are published by Trend Line. (*Over-the-*

counter or OTC is a market for securities not traded on an exchange made up of dealers who may or may not be members of a securities exchange.) The *Dines Cross Chart Book,* for example, shows point-and-figure charts for selected OTC stocks.

If you are an investor who prefers a charting approach to investment decisions, many published sources are readily available to broaden your knowledge. How you use the charting information will depend on you, the investor.

Monthly Investment Plan Approach

A way to invest that is popular with the novice small investor is through a *monthly investment plan* (MIP). Usually one can pay in as little as $40 every month to an *investment broker.* The investment broker is a person licensed to handle the buying and selling of securities for others, and is often a member of a stock exchange such as the New York Stock Exchange. The purpose of the MIP is to invest an amount you can afford regularly, and then have stock—in even and partial shares—purchased for you by an experienced broker. Several types of investments are sought, as some stocks may decrease in value and others may increase, but as long as the "average" increases or remains fairly constant, the investments should be regarded as sound if the return is satisfactory.

The monthly investment plan is designed for long-term rather than short-term investing, although some do short-term investing this way. The MIP was very popular a few years ago, but the development and selling of mutual funds, declines in the stock market from time to time, and relatively high broker commissions has caused them to be less popular today. However, those who still prefer this approach will find that it is available through most investment firms.

Investment-club Approach

An investment club is a group of small investors, often with 8 to 20 members, with the purpose of being able to pool monies in order to both learn more about investing and increase their potential for profits by investment. The number of clubs in the country is in excess of 20,000. Many of the people who belong to a club are small investors and are beginners in the investment business. Essentially, the newcomer leans on the experience and know-how of the other members of the club but is also reading and learning at the same time. The major objective is generally long-term investing, but purposes of different clubs vary. Dollar averaging is a primary practice of club investments rather than trying to "out-expert" the market.

Since investment clubs serve a splendid purpose for the small inexperienced investor, they have been becoming more popular. Clubs gain popularity as the market advances and lose it during declines. They, however, are used by many colleges and universities as a way of teaching students about investments and trading in the stock market as part of a business program.

THE BUYING AND SELLING OF SECURITIES

Once a person decides to invest in common stock or bonds of various types, certain established procedures must be followed. But before giving an order to buy, a quick check in the financial section of the newspaper will give one an idea of how the stock or bond is doing at the moment.

Price Quotations

Most large city newspapers, and the *Wall Street Journal* in particular, print daily stock quotations; some print bond and mutual fund prices, too. These quotations are taken from the day's buying and selling activities on stock exchanges throughout the country. The New York and the American Stock Exchanges are the largest, but altogether there are more than twenty.

To benefit from these quotations, obviously the investor must understand them. Figure 14-4 shows a section of a newspaper stock quotation with one stock highlighted to illustrate specific figures. The column headings are standard. Only the figures will change from one stock to another. The price listed is not necessarily that at which one can buy the stock the next day, although it should be reasonably close. The official price will not be known until the actual sale takes place at the exchange. Bond quotations are different. If one is buying a new issue of a bond, it may sell at par value, say $1000. But often it is higher or lower. The same is true for existing bonds that people want to sell on the bond market because they are not redeemable yet. The price varies primarily because of current interest rates, the rate stated on the face of the bond, and the risk involved. If an old bond pays 6 percent interest but because of market forces the cost of money is about 7 percent, to sell the bond the price must be lowered so that the yield for the potential buyer is increased to current levels. Thus, a $1000, 6 percent bond in this case might be quoted in the newspaper for sale (the "asking price") for $925.

Reprinted with permission from CHANGING TIMES Magazine, © Kiplinger Washington Editors, Inc.

"Well, you did *not* buy any eight years ago when it was $3 a share so kindly keep quiet about it."

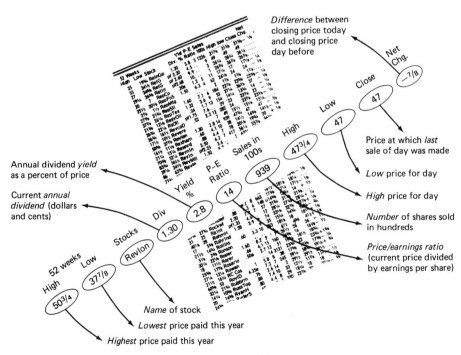

FIGURE 14-4 Newspaper stock market quotations

Buying and Selling Processes

A consumer who wants to buy a new television set goes to a store that sells television sets. Similarly, to buy securities, the consumer must go to where securities are sold. In practice, the consumer will almost certainly deal with a broker, who is a person licensed to buy and sell securities through the exchanges. A typical procedure followed when buying and selling through the New York Stock Exchange is illustrated in Figure 14-5.

The transaction illustrated is just one of thousands that take place daily at the various exchanges. In one day these transactions can result in the trading of over 30 million shares of stock at the New York Stock Exchange alone. For each share traded, there must, obviously, be an agreement between two parties—buyer and seller—on the price. The *bid* price is the highest that anyone is willing to pay per share. The *ask* price is the lowest for which the seller is willing to sell. The compromise sale price is decided on the floor of the stock exchange.

In addition to the price of the stock, the buyer must pay a broker's commission, which is a fee for the broker's services. Generally, the fees range from 1½ to 6 percent of the purchase value, often with a minimum charge of perhaps $20. However, it will vary a little with brokers. Also, with large stock purchases, 100,000 shares, for example, the broker's fee would usually be negotiated.

Diversification

"Do not put all your eggs in one basket" is an oft-quoted phrase to warn persons of possible high risk or losses in investments. Diversification means to put your money into several types of investments. This may mean several

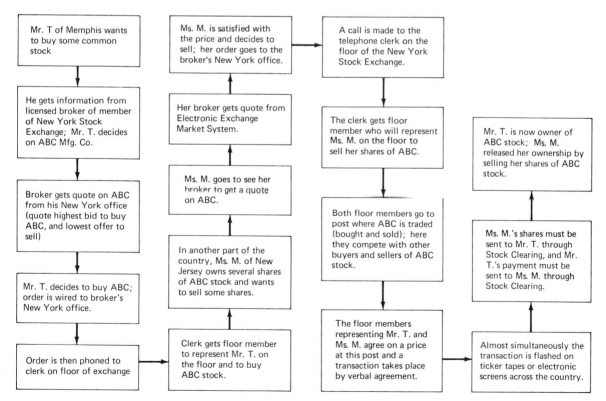

FIGURE 14-5   Buying and selling stock

different stocks, or stocks from different industries, or a combination of stocks, bonds, and mutual funds. In other words, spread around (diversify) your investments so if one type of investment does not work out, you will not lose all your money.

The principle behind diversification, according to the investment experts, is that it is highly unlikely that all types of investments will go bad at any one time. If one stock drops greatly in value, another will rise; if some bonds increase in value, some stocks will fall in value, and so forth.

For the novice investor diversification is quite important. In fact, the inexperienced investor can get diversification quite easily by investing in mutual funds (discussed earlier in the chapter). By design, most mutual funds guarantee diversification. But you've got to know enough to choose the proper type of high-quality fund.

Leverage

In order to improve his or her financial position and/or potential investments, an investor may want to use leverage. *Leverage* in financial dealings is the practice of using someone else's money in order to realize an improved financial position for yourself.

There are varying degrees of leverage for each investment transaction. For example, if one purchases a $60,000 home with a $20,000 down payment and sells it 1 year later for $65,000, a $5000 profit was made (excluding expenses). It "cost" a $20,000 down payment to "make a profit" of $5000—a return of 25 percent on the investment. The leverage here is gained because of the amount of credit used. If, in the same illustration, a down payment of only $10,000 had been made, the leverage would have been even better—a return of 50 percent. Moreover, if one can use someone else's money over a period of time and get a greater return than what the money is costing in interest, the use of leverage is effective.

When an individual is getting funds together for investments of various kinds, the leverage used can enhance or reduce the potential financial position. The more knowledgeable and experienced the investor becomes in the use of leverage, and the more efficiently it is used, the better the results will be in the investment program.

POINTS OF VIEW AND PROBLEMS TO THINK ABOUT

Many consumers have a misconception that businesses typically operate with a 20 to 25 percent profit rate. In reality, however, the profit rate is less than 5 percent for most businesses. Investing by many consumers in the American free enterprise system may help to eliminate this misconception. Investment is good because, among other things, it gets people involved in and helps them understand the economic system. Unfortunately, some restrictions have been placed on the small investors. For example, they cannot buy certain securities simply because of the large amount of money needed. Typical of such securities are bonds issued by corporations, municipalities, and the federal government. Usually a minimum purchase price for these bonds is $1000, but some cost $10,000. What would be wrong with having $100 or $500 minimums on these bonds, thus putting them within the reach of the small investor?

Of course, lower-income persons can invest in government savings bonds, Series E and H, but the return on their investment is not as great. Usually the regular long-term government or corporate bonds provide a greater return. Furthermore, the average-income investor cannot equally enjoy the tax-exemption benefits of municipal bonds because the real benefits do not begin until one's income is more than $30,000.

Recently the director of enforcement for the Securities and Exchange Commission, Mr. Stanley Sporkin, proposed a small investors "bill of rights." His proposal was a direct result of deception and dishonesty practiced by publicly owned corporations to drive the "little guys" from the market. He suggests that there is not enough legal protection to offset these unfair tactics and to protect the millions of American stockholders who are classified as small investors.

Sporkin's proposal is directed generally at combatting illegal and hidden corporate political payments, bribery to maintain sales, compensation to top executives beyond that which is publicly disclosed, and the technique of taking away the small investors' ownership without them having any say whatever except for getting a higher value for their shares. One case is recorded where a company offered a small percentage of investors (not all of them) well over the apparent current market value for stock, thus "forcing" them to sell. Redress in the courts for this intimidation could not be sought because a class action lawsuit was prohibitively expensive. Moreover, the company had a formal asset-appraisal report which showed that the stock being purchased for $150 had a value of $250. The small investor was being fleeced, intimidated, ripped-off, and openly deceived with those corporate tactics.

The "bill of rights" would provide for the investor:

1. The *right to know* all critical facts concerning an investment.
2. The *right to be represented* by directors who look out for *all* investors' interests as well as the company's.
3. The *right to be treated fairly* by corporate management.
4. The *right to a guarantee* that lawyers and independent auditors engaged by the corporation will act in the interest of the entire company and not give preference to a special interest group of stockholders.
5. The *right to redress* in the federal courts.

It remains to be seen whether any or all of these "small-investor rights" will be enacted into law. But open deception, small-investor discrimination, and dishonesty practiced by corporate managers must be stopped.

Continued vigilance must be maintained by the Securities and Exchange Commission to keep the investment business honest. As more businesses enter the marketplace, as corporations grow to gigantic sizes, and as more securities are traded, the role of the SEC will take on greater importance, and consumers must support it.

CHAPTER ACTIVITIES ━━━━━━

Checkup on Consumer Terms and Concepts

Investing	Municipal bonds
Stockholder	Tax-exempt bonds
Stocks	Mutual funds
Share	No-load
Par value	Broker
Market value	Open-end funds
Common stock	REIT
Stock split	OTC
Dividends	MIP
Preferred stock	Price quotations
Cumulative preferred stock	Diversification
	Leverage
Bonds	

Review of Essentials

1. What are some of the problems involved in investing money in securities?
2. What are two reasons why people might want to invest in securities rather than put money in a savings account?
3. For what reason might a small investor want to invest in government bonds rather than in common stock?
4. How are investments important to businesses and governments?
5. What are the basic differences between common stock and preferred stock?
6. What advantage is there is owning cumulative, participating preferred stock instead of regular preferred stock?
7. Distinguish between bonds and stocks issued by the same corporation.
8. What is one attractive characteristic of municipal bonds to the person who falls in a high income-tax bracket?
9. Explain the basic operating format of a mutual fund.
10. What are some reasons why a person

would invest in a mutual fund rather than in other types of common stock?

11. Distinguish between no-load and load mutual funds.

12. What are the similarities between a mutual fund and a real estate investment trust? The differences?

13. Name one way in which investments are important to the individual investor.

14. Give some ways in which a person's philosophy of investing can change as he or she grows older. Also, indicate some purposes for this change.

15. Explain why a person would want to use the MIP approach when investing.

Issues for Analysis

1. Should the various government agencies be given more regulatory powers than they have to fight unethical securities industry practices? Why or why not?

2. Should the minimum investment amount for government and municipal bonds be lowered to $100 to let the small investor benefit from such investments? Why or why not?

15

Life Insurance

PROBLEMS

Life insurance is something that most Americans feel they need. After all, when a person dies, there will be bills to pay, funeral expenses, and maybe house or other continuing payments for the survivors. As a consequence, about 150 million Americans have some type of life insurance; the average family has just over $30,000 in life insurance coverage. Basically, *life insurance* is a contract between the company and the person insured stating that if the insured dies while the policy is in force, someone (the *beneficiaries*) will receive a specified amount of money. It sounds simple enough, but for consumers it gets to be very confusing.

Many types of policies are available. The dollar cost, or premium, for one policy that will pay your survivors perhaps $20,000 when you die may be ten times as high as that for another policy with the same death benefit. It depends upon the policy and the company selling the policy. And more than 1800 companies are trying to sell life insurance to consumers.

The thousands of salespersons knocking on doors may be equally sincere in trying to do their best for you, yet often the salesperson from the company with the lowest annual dollar premium is selling the most expensive policy when *all* factors are considered. And rates for the same coverage may vary by 200 percent or more!

The Federal Trade Commission (FTC) is investigating whether or not life insurance companies are telling their customers enough about the cost of the policies. Margery W. Smith, the acting director of the FTC's Consumer Protection Bureau, reports that "There's great potential for consumer savings if consumers could compare the cost of life insurance policies. We found one instance where the amount of profit or overhead retained by insurance companies ranged from $894 to $2291 on a comparable insurance policy." This was for a $25,000 policy maturing in 20 years purchased by a 35-year-old man.

Overpricing and buying something you don't need cannot be better demonstrated than with *industrial* life insurance. These are policies with coverage of less than $1000; the premiums are collected at the person's home by an agent of the company on a weekly basis. Sending someone out once a week to collect $0.50 to $4 is obviously an expensive way to sell anything; thus the price for industrial insurance is easily ten times higher than other policies. Yet, in spite of these costs, the industry still promotes this form of selling. Over one-third of all the individual life policies sold annually are on a weekly premium payment basis.

Problems for consumers abound in the world of life insurance. It seems almost impossible for consumers to determine just how much protection they have and how much they are paying for it. The vocabulary, sales techniques used, choices of policies, options available, varying dollar costs, grossly misleading ratings of the financial integrity of the companies, weak and ineffective state regulation, and attempts to determine one's own insurance needs are perplexing problems facing consumers.

WHY HAVE LIFE INSURANCE?

We all die, and when we do even our deaths cost money. We leave behind us some financial obligations for our survivors. Early death creates even greater problems. The financial protection provided by life insurance may or may not be enough to pay for burial expenses, for some immediate cash for the survivors' living expenses, for monthly checks for them to make up for the loss of the breadwinner's income, for cash to pay off a mortgage, and for the post-high school education of children. Having some life insurance reduces these problems, since death creates an "instant estate." If your heirs are named as beneficiaries, there is no income tax on the proceeds if they are taken as a lump sum; if they are taken in payments, only the interest is taxed. With life insurance the named beneficiaries are mailed a check immediately with no delays about wills or probate court and the like. Life insurance supplements the minimum protections provided by Social Security or a small employer-provided group life insurance plan. Thus, life

insurance protects against loss of earnings, which is an unintended and unforeseen event.

Life insurance is usually thought of as *death* benefits, such as cash for survivors. But *living* benefits are available too. They are mainly associated with policies that pay back income after one retires, such as a family income policy. Another living benefit is that with some types of policies you can later borrow against the built-up "cash value" at very low interest rates—lower than at a credit union or bank—should you ever need the money.

Life insurance, when you finally get down to the bottom line, is really a bet. The insurance company bets that the buyer will live long enough to pay in a lot of premiums. The buyer bets that he or she will die early. If a person were to be accidentally killed 1 week after buying a policy, the company would lose its bet, and even if the insured had paid only a $100 premium on a $20,000 policy, the company would still have to pay.

The probability of death is based on average mortality rates among large groups of people. Various organizations publish different mortality tables; one is shown in Table 15-1. Note that the lowest mortality rate, 1.21 per 1000 people, is for children aged 9 and 10. From that age on, the probability of death (the death rate) steadily increases. For example, of every 1000 people who are aged 22, approximately 2 will die this year (actually 1.86). Of every 1000 who are aged 40, 3.53 will die. The statistical averages of the different mortality tables are accurate for the population as a whole, although they are somewhat conservative to provide a "cushion" for the insurance companies.

Obviously, a certain number of people are going to die every year, and the probability of death increases with age. People realize this, and many try to get some financial protection by buying life insurance. The main reason for buying life insurance is security—to pay for one's final expenses and to protect the finances of the survivors. Many people are under the mistaken notion that they will die by accident, in an auto wreck, for example. Quite the

TABLE 15-1

Commissioners 1958 Standard Ordinary Mortality Table

Age	Number Living, Beginning of Year	Number Dying during the Year	Death Rate per 1000	Age	Number Living, Beginning of Year	Number Dying during the Year	Death Rate per 1000
0	10,000,000	70,800	7.08	36	9,350,279	24,685	2.64
1	9,929,200	17,475	1.76	37	9,325,594	26,112	2.80
2	9,911,725	15,066	1.52	38	9,299,482	27,991	3.01
3	9,896,659	14,449	1.46	39	9,271,491	30,132	3.25
4	9,882,210	13,835	1.40	40	9,241,359	32,622	3.53
5	9,868,375	13,322	1.35	41	9,208,737	35,362	3.84
6	9,855,053	12,812	1.30	42	9,173,375	38,253	4.17
7	9,842,241	12,401	1.26	43	9,135,122	41,382	4.53
8	9,829,840	12,091	1.23	44	9,093,740	44,741	4.92
9	9,817,749	11,879	1.21	45	9,048,999	48,412	5.35
10	9,805,870	11,865	1.21	46	9,000,587	52,473	5.83
11	9,794,005	12,047	1.23	47	8,948,114	56,910	6.36
12	9,781,958	12,325	1.26	48	8,891,204	61,794	6.95
13	9,769,633	12,896	1.32	49	8,829,410	67,104	7.60
14	9,756,737	13,562	1.39	50	8,762,306	72,902	8.32
15	9,743,175	14,225	1.46	51	8,689,404	79,160	9.11
16	9,728,950	14,983	1.54	52	8,610,244	85,758	9.96
17	9,713,967	15,737	1.62	53	8,524,486	92,832	10.89
18	9,698,230	16,390	1.69	54	8,431,654	100,337	11.90
19	9,681,840	16,846	1.74	55	8,331,317	108,307	13.00
20	9,664,994	17,300	1.79	56	8,223,010	116,849	14.21
21	9,647,694	17,655	1.83	57	8,106,161	125,970	15.54
22	9,630,039	17,912	1.86	58	7,980,191	135,663	17.00
23	9,612,127	18,167	1.89	59	7,844,528	145,830	18.59
24	9,593,960	18,324	1.91	60	7,698,698	156,592	20.34
25	9,575,636	18,481	1.93	61	7,542,106	167,736	22.24
26	9,557,155	18,732	1.96	62	7,374,370	179,271	24.31
27	9,538,423	18,981	1.99	63	7,195,099	191,174	26.57
28	9,519,442	19,324	2.03	64	7,033,925	203,394	29.04
29	9,500,118	19,760	2.08	65	6,800,531	215,917	31.75
30	9,480,358	20,193	2.13	.	.	.	.
31	9,460,165	20,718	2.19	.	.	.	.
32	9,439,447	21,239	2.25	96	63,037	25,250	400.56
33	9,418,208	21,850	2.32	97	37,787	18,456	488.42
34	9,396,358	22,551	2.40	98	19,331	12,916	668.15
35	9,373,807	23,528	2.51	99	6,415	6,415	1,000.00

contrary is true. Life insurance data shows that 91.2 percent of deaths are from natural causes, 3.0 percent from motor vehicle accidents, 3.1 percent from other accidents, and 2.7 percent from suicides and homicides. Of all deaths, 49.8 percent are from cardiovascular-renal diseases, with another 21.4 percent caused by cancer.

COSTS AND TYPES OF LIFE INSURANCE

The cost of life insurance varies widely. It depends upon how much insurance is bought, the type of policy, the options within the policy, the company, and the age of the person buying the insurance.

Mortality Rates and Premium Costs

Americans are living longer than ever, and more than 220 million of them are alive today. Yet a number of them are going to die each year. Therefore, one main factor in determining the cost of a policy is how old the person is at the time of buying a policy, because that is a good indication of how much longer the person is likely to live.

Let us assume that there are 100,000 people, all 27 years old, who wish to take out policies of $1000 each at about the same time. The mortality table shows that, statistically, 199 of them will die during the coming year. To pay their survivors $1000 each will require a total of $199,000. So, to get that amount, all 100,000 people will have to pay in $1.99 at the beginning of the year. If the surviving 99,801 people want to insure themselves again the following year, they will each have to pay $2.04 in order to pay the survivors of the 203 people who will probably die. The cost is now $2.04 because there are only 99,801, not 100,000, people to pay in the amount needed.

Does this mean that a person aged 27 pays only $1.99 for $1000 of life insurance for that year? Certainly not. There are other factors involved. Most of the 100,000 people have to be sold insurance through a salesperson. Who is going to collect the premiums? Will bills have to be mailed out? Who will invest the

premiums so that the funds earn a fair return until needed? Will a checking account have to be opened to pay survivors' benefits? Obviously there are many administrative costs involved. So a life insurance firm must charge premiums that are high enough to cover its costs and leave a little extra for profit. Perhaps a really efficient business could provide all those $1000 policies for $3.10 per person. A less efficient company might have to charge $3.30.

But all companies are working from the same mortality tables, so the premium cost for each $1000 of life insurance should be at least similar. This sounds reasonable, but it is nowhere near accurate. Prices vary for a lot of reasons, and a major factor in determining cost is the *type* of policy sold.

Basic Types of Life Insurance

There are two basic types of life insurance policies: term and permanent. And the permanent type has three popular plans—straight life, limited payment, and endowment.

Term Life Insurance. A term insurance policyholder buys protection for only a certain number of years—perhaps a term of 1, 5, 10, or 20 years. The policy pays off only if the insured dies during the time period covered by the policy. If a person aged 25 buys $10,000 in term insurance for 1 year, the premium might be $38.10, or $3.81 per thousand. For the same coverage for a second year, the premium might be $39.55—it goes up because the probability of death increases. However, to help average these rising costs, most term policies are sold for periods of 5 or 10 years and the premiums are level—set at the "average cost"—during the time period. This is why many term policyholders buy 10- or 20-year contracts: they want to reduce the jolt of paying sharply increased rates. Therefore, if our 25-year-old buys a 5-year term policy, the premium might be $41 each year for $10,000 of insurance for a period of 5 years.

If the health of the insured declines, however, it may be hard to get any type of life insurance after the current contract expires. Therefore, an important clause to have in *any* policy is *guaranteed renewable*. This means that you can renew your present policy regardless of your health with no further medical examination. Of course, the premiums for term insurance will be higher with each renewal because of age and the greater probability of death. But the rates will not be higher than for anyone else buying the same coverage. For a 25-year-old, a 10-year policy may cost $48.20 per year; with the guaranteed renewable clause, the rate may be $49.50.

Term insurance is the least expensive of all the basic types of life insurance. This is because the policyholder is *only* buying protection against death. Thus, it is quite suitable for young families who want the most protection for the least cost. The other basic types of life insurance—called *permanent* types—have some variation of "savings" included in addition to the pure protection and therefore cost more.

Term policies often have a *convertible* clause that lets the policyholder convert to another type of policy without a medical examination should he or she want to do so. This may be desirable, since one's economic position might become such that one could afford a higher-priced permanent policy.

Straight Life Insurance.   Straight life insurance is also known as *whole life* or *ordinary life*. The policyholder agrees to pay the same rates—fixed level premiums—until he or she dies, at which time the *face value*, the amount of the insurance policy, is paid to the survivors. This kind of permanent insurance costs about twice as much as term coverage because the premium rate remains level, or is fixed forever, *and* the contract has a built-in savings feature. All permanent insurance has some extra charge that permits building up savings within the policy. A 25-year-old paying $49.50 for $10,000 worth of term insurance must pay more for straight life insurance. The premium would perhaps be $127.50 per year. Thus, straight life insurance is a form of *forced*

savings. Perhaps not surprisingly, about half those buying life insurance take this approach.

The major advantages of straight life insurance are that the premiums remain level and that a cash value builds up. The cash value (often called a *cash surrender value*) is the savings. With straight life, any cash value built up must be "surrendered" to the policyholder if the policy is cancelled. As with all insurance policies, the insured can cancel at any time simply by not paying the premiums. State laws protect all policyholders by requiring the policies to remain in effect for 30 days after a premium is due. This, for example, protects against late payments because of hospitalization.

While the straight life policy remains in effect, the policyholder can borrow against the cash value—rather like withdrawing from a savings account. By the time a policyholder is aged 65, the accumulated cash value normally amounts to close to half the face value of the policy. Usually the rate of interest for a loan is extremely low (an annual percentage rate of 6 to 8 percent), and the insured can borrow up to 95 percent of the accumulated cash value. This is a very inexpensive source for borrowing money, even if you are actually borrowing your own funds. But the temptation not to repay is quite real. If you do not repay, and the insurance company will not insist upon it, when you die your survivors will receive the face value of the insurance *less* the unpaid loan and interest.

Other options are also available with most straight life policies. One, for example, lets the policyholder convert to a paid-up policy. That means that, say, a 45-year-old person with 20 years of accumulated cash value on a $30,000 life insurance policy could convert the cash surrender value to another policy that might have a $20,000 face value and be fully paid up. This option lets the policyholder with large accumulated cash values change policies and not worry about paying premiums after reaching retirement. Another *conversion* option lets the policyholder change the contract to some kind of term insurance, the total insurance amount depending upon the cash surrender value of the first policy. Then again, one might cancel the policy and receive the cash surrender value either in a lump sum or in a number of payments for a limited period of time. Different types of conversion privileges are available with most life insurance policies.

Limited-payment Life Insurance. With limited-payment life insurance (another type of permanent insurance), premiums are paid for only a certain period of time. Usually level premiums are paid for 20 years, or until the insured reaches the age of 65—hence the terms "twenty-pay-life" and "paid-up-at-65." The basic idea is for the policyholder to pay the premiums during the years of greatest earnings and not have to make any premium payments later in life. The premiums are higher than those for straight life insurance, since there are fewer years in which to pay them. Since the probability of death remains constant for any one age group, the policyholder is in effect simply advancing the payments.

A 25-year-old buying a $10,000, 20-year, limited-payment policy might pay $233.60 per year—about double the premium for straight life insurance or four times the cost of term coverage. Paid-up-at-65 premiums for the same age and coverage might be $144.10 per year—slightly more than for straight life, but with no payments due after the person reaches the age of 65 even though the insurance remains in effect until death. Also, with limited-payment policies, the cash value builds up more quickly than with straight life policies.

Endowment Life Insurance. A policyholder of endowment life insurance pays a fixed-level premium for a specific time and can receive the face amount of the policy *himself or herself* at the end of the endowment period. During the term of the policy he or she is also fully insured for the face value. For example, a 20-year endowment policy for $10,000 issued when the policyholder is aged 25 will pay

$10,000 if the person is alive at the age of 45. Of course, the premiums are much higher for this special type of forced-savings life insurance. For a 25-year-old person, the premium might be $394 per year.

The primary advantages of endowment insurance are the rapidly growing cash surrender value and the fact that if the policyholder does live to the end of the endowment period, he or she will receive the face value amount of the policy. People who want a retirement income sometimes buy endowment policies.

All the basic types of life insurance provide cash benefits if the policyholder dies. Depending partly upon the cash surrender value that builds up (there can be none with term insurance), the premium costs vary. Examples of comparative costs of various basic policies at different ages are shown in Table 15-2.

Other factors also affect the premium cost. A *double-indemnity* clause (or even triple-indemnity) can be included for a little extra premium; the company will then pay double the face value of the policy in the event of an accidental death—only 6 out of every 100 deaths are by accident. For another small fee, a rider can be purchased to waive the premiums in the event of permanent disability. Special types of policies are available too which may cost more or less than others.

TABLE 15-2

What Basic Policies Cost: per $1000 of Coverage

| Type of Policy | Age at Issue | | |
	25	35	45
Term			
10-year renewable term	$ 4.95	$ 6.88	$12.93
Straight Life			
Straight life	12.75	17.15	25.28
Limited Payment			
Paid-up-at-65	14.41	20.82	35.35
20-payment-life	23.36	28.02	35.35
Endowment			
20-year endowment	39.40	39.81	42.71

* Rates based on those of a large mutual company.

Other Policy Values, Benefits, and Options

In addition to the general values associated with most life insurance policies, there are particular values associated with each basic type of life insurance policy. You get high protection with term insurance, for example, in contrast to the rapid buildup of cash values with limited-payment policies. Various benefits and options permit flexibility in meeting the needs of each consumer who wants life insurance.

When you buy life insurance, you will receive a policy and a copy of the application form. A medical examination is normally required. The company has 2 years to check the truthfulness of what is reported on the application; after that time what is on the application is considered by law to be incontestable. An *incontestability* clause is especially valuable if, for example, you had a disease that was not discovered during the medical exam but did show up later as the cause of death. The survivors would still receive benefits. One exception exists and that is age. Benefits from policies that provide them will be paid on the correct age if the age on the application is determined later to be incorrect.

Something called *nonforfeiture values* are also included in cash-value policies. These are choices that are available to you if you stop paying premiums. With permanent policies, after a few years there may be some cash value built up which you could ask for and receive. Depending upon the policy, other nonforfeiture clauses include giving you full face-value protection for a limited amount of time, allowing you to convert to a paid-up policy, with a lower face value than the present one, and providing you with an automatic premium loan that takes the cash value for the loaned premiums until the cash value is used up.

Another important option to look for is the right to change the *beneficiary*, the person(s) to whom the proceeds of the policy are to go. Most policies permit changing, but some companies require notification of the beneficiary and their permission. You also have various choices as to the *settlement options*, or how the proceeds will be paid. You may want the beneficiaries to get a lump-sum payment, installment payments for a certain amount of time, or a lifetime income.

Special Types of Life Insurance Policies

There are many special types of life insurance policies. Each has its own purposes, but all are based upon some variation of one or more of the two basic types of life insurance. Many include some term insurance (pure protection) to keep the premium cost lower than that of basic permanent policies.

Modified Life Policies. This type of policy is actually a combination of straight life and term insurance designed to keep the premium costs down during the first few years. It does this by combining, for example, $25,000 of straight life coverage with $10,000 of term insurance (which is convertible). After 4 or 5 years the lower-premium term insurance portion is automatically converted to straight life coverage. The same face amount of insurance is maintained throughout, but since term provided some of the protection during the early years, the premium cost is lower.

All Family Policies. A package insurance plan for the entire family is available and sold as an all family policy. Again, straight life and term insurance are combined. Frequently, the husband is insured for $10,000 with straight life coverage, the wife for $5000 of term insurance, and each child for $2000 of term coverage (and any subsequent children born are covered automatically). In this way one policy can protect the main wage earner (if it is the husband) and other members of the family.

Family Income Policies. Another combination of term and straight life insurance is a family income policy. This provides that should the insured die, a specific monthly income would go to the survivors for the remainder of the term of the policy. For example, suppose the policyholder buys a 20-year policy and then dies after 15 years. The family would receive the agreed-upon income for the remaining 5 years. A *family maintenance* policy is similar but more costly because the benefits last longer. If a 20-year family maintenance policyholder dies at any time within the life of the policy, the agreed-upon monthly payments go to the heirs for 20 years from that point forward. With family income and family maintenance policies, the monthly income for the beneficiaries is usually $7 for every $1000 of coverage.

Decreasing Term Policies. Preplanned decreasing term policies are available to meet the needs of many people. These policies are especially for those who believe that in later years they will have acquired so many assets that they will have little need for insurance. What they usually want is lots of protection now and less later on. The premiums remain level while the face amount of the insurance uniformly decreases to zero over the life of the policy. A 25-year decreasing term policy for a man aged 25 could begin with protection in the amount of $75,000. Each year the face value of the policy will decline by $3000. Therefore, after 10 years the policy would pay only $45,000 in the event of death. After 19 years it would pay $18,000.

A similar type of policy is *mortgage decreasing term*. Such a policy is designed to pay off the amount of the mortgage loan on the house of the insured in the event of death. Here too the coverage declines, but in uneven dollar amounts, since the face amount of the policy is the same as the principal owed on the mortgage loan. This declines slowly during the early years and rapidly toward the end of the mortgage loan (this is discussed in Chapter 11). A family person with small children and a large home-mortgage loan may decide that a great deal of life insurance protection is needed while the children are young and less as they grow up and the mortgage is paid off. Since the coverage in decreasing term policies "declines," it is less costly than regular term coverage.

Credit Life Policies. This coverage is decreasing term also. It is often offered as an option and is sometimes required by lending agencies when they make consumer loans. The *beneficiary*—the person(s) named in the policy to receive the financial benefits if the insured dies—in this plan is the lending agency. This means that the lending agency is rather certain to be paid back the amount loaned regardless of what happens to the policyholder. Credit life coverage duplicates any existing policy the person might already have, and this makes such a policy totally unnecessary. Most distressing is the high cost of coverage. A dollar a month to cover a 12-month $1000 loan may not sound like much, but it is at least six times the cost of a comparable regular term policy available from any other company.

Jumping Juvenile Policies. These are frequently term insurance policies in amounts of $2000 that increase to five times the face amount when the child reaches age 21. The level premium does not increase at that time or later if the policy remains in force. Also, there is no medical examination required.

Veteran's Policies. Servicemen's Group Life Insurance is a very low-cost program which provides up to $20,000 in term coverage while a person is on active duty. The annual cost for a $20,000 policy is $2.04 per $1000. After discharge, service personnel have only 120 days to convert to another policy, since the extremely low subsidized rates are no longer available. One choice is to convert to a still quite low cost term program called Veterans Group Life Insurance. Policyholders have up to 5 years to convert to a straight life policy sold by a commercial company at traditional rates. One good point is that when buying the straight life policy no medical examination is required; this government program guarantees the availability of coverage for veterans through private insurance companies.

Retirement Income and Annuity Policies. A retirement policy is similar to endowment insurance in that it provides relatively little insurance coverage but a large amount of savings (or investment). The savings here are even greater since the object of the retirement income policyholder is to have income from the policy when it matures. If a retirement income policy is paid in full after 20 years, the life insurance stops while the cash value goes to the policyholder or the survivors in the manner requested. At that point there are several *settlement options* available. The cash value can be taken in a single sum; it will be greater than the proceeds from an endowment policy because the premiums for a retirement income policy are higher. Or it can be taken in installments—a specified sum each month to supplement other income until the insurance funds are exhausted. These policies usually provide about $7 per month for each $1000 of face value.

An annuity is *not* a life insurance policy, but the objectives are similar to those of a retirement income policy. Life insurance always pays the beneficiary upon the death of the policyholder. An annuity investment program always pays the owner if he or she lives and often the heirs if the owner dies. Most annuities are bought just before retirement. A person may pay the company $14,000 in cash and then receive $100 a month until death. Another may buy a $14,000 annuity over a 10-year period before retirement and then begin to receive benefits at a rate of $200 a month but guaranteed only for 10 years. What you pay in is based upon statistical averages. If you die young, the company saves payments. If you die very old, it loses since it must pay longer. If you die at the average age, the company "breaks even"—that is, it makes the average number of payments and also makes a reasonable profit.

Different kinds of annuities are available to suit the needs of the individuals involved; these are sold by licensed investment persons. The company makes its profit in retirement income life insurance policies and in investment annuities by using the funds for investment purposes and making earnings higher than the total benefits paid out.

Variable Life Policies. These policies are special combinations of permanent life insurance and investment in common stocks. Part of the premiums are used for life insurance coverage and part for investment. Recent changes in regulations by the Securities and Exchange Commission (SEC) permit life insurance companies to sell this type of policy. Besides being life insurance, the SEC considers it to be a security, and thus it is regulated accordingly. The prospective buyer must be given a prospectus just as if he or she were purchasing a share of common stock.

Variable life policies work like this: If the value of the stocks (chosen by the company) rises and returns an after-tax profit of perhaps 7 percent or more, the benefits of the policy also rise. For example, a profitable group of stocks might, over 10 years, raise the value of a $10,000 policy to $14,500. Thus, higher cash values accumulate and the death benefit is greater. A poor combination of stocks or a temporarily depressed stock market might lower the cash value to $3720 at that point in time. But by law, the death benefit *cannot* drop below the original face amount. The buyer hopes, of course, to gain additional cash values and to increase the total value of the policy through investing. This would help to offset the effects of inflation and the declining purchasing power of the dollar. The main risk lies in the possibility of losing cash value during the life of the policy. The premiums for variable life policies are higher because the company is guaranteeing the death benefit to be the face amount of the policy in addition to providing a greater death benefit if the investments do well.

Industrial Policies. Some insurance companies have dropped industrial life policies from their line of policies, but most have not. Industrial policies are those that provide coverage of less than $1000 and where the

Reprinted with permission from CHANGING TIMES Magazine, © Kiplinger Washington Editors, Inc.

premiums for each policy, amounting to a dime, a quarter, or fifty cents, are collected at the person's home by an agent of the company on a weekly basis. Even though industrial policies amount to only 4 percent of the total annual dollar volume of life insurance sold (just over $8 billion out of nearly $200 billion total), almost one-third of the *individual* life policies are industrial insurance. This means that about two-thirds of the life insurance customers each year who purchase individual policies buy the traditional ones like term, straight life, or a combination plan, while the remaining one-third buy an extremely expensive product.

Industrial policies are issued without medical examinations, and customers usually have more than one policy. Many purchasers have ten, twenty or even more than thirty separate industrial policies upon which they pay weekly premiums. It is not only expensive to send out a collector weekly—which pushes the basic cost of such protection up to ten times more than traditional policies—but it is also "expensive" to the customers, since they often buy "another policy for another purpose" when the ever-present salesperson is there ready to sell. As James R. Young points out in an article in the *Journal of Consumer Affairs*, "The continued writing of weekly premium insurance does not represent a crisis in the over-all private insurance industry today, but it is an unsightly blot on the picture. Economic and social forces are slowly phasing it out but not fast enough to prevent the victimizing of thousands of families who can least afford it.''

Group Insurance Policies. Group insurance is usually basic term coverage written under a blanket policy and made available to all members of an organization, employees of a company, or members of some other sponsoring association. Since the groups are large—often thousands of consumers—selling costs are dramatically reduced, as each prospect need not be contacted, persuaded, have an individual policy written, and sold. Employers, for example, often do most of the bookkeeping to further reduce the cost per thousand. Therefore, the costs can be better controlled, while at the same time risks for each particular group of consumers can be better estimated. Premium costs for a group policy are 15 to 40 percent lower than the same coverage made available through an individual plan.

One very common and important feature is that a medical examination is *not* required for the person to obtain minimum amounts of coverage. Thus, people with special health problems can purchase $20,000 or perhaps $40,000 in coverage without a medical examination. Employers often pay part of the premium as a fringe benefit, which further reduces the net cost to the consumer. If one leaves the organization, because of a new job or retirement, for example, conversion privileges are normally available that permit purchasing a similar or lower amount of coverage (at traditional rates), again without a medical examination. Thus, it seems clear that if one needs life insurance, the best coverage for your money can be obtained through group life policies. Nearly 40 percent of all life insurance is sold through group plans.

What You Are Really Paying For

Premiums paid by the policyholder pay for far more than simple life insurance protection. The final price tag depends upon the company, the type of policy, various options available, the salesperson's commission, dividends, and the cash value that may be built up. Let us consider a few of these factors in greater detail.

Premium. The amount of the periodic payment, or premium, that the policyholder must pay is determined by the company from which he or she buys insurance. The company bases this amount on the type of policy and the age of the insured, but also, and this is very important, on the reserves that it has on hand. The *reserves* are the surplus funds—those remaining after all death claims have been paid. Technically these are funds that must by law be set aside to meet the company's future obligations to policyholders and beneficiaries. During its early years, a company accumulates reserves quickly; there are not too many claims, and the reserves are invested to earn profits. Later, after profitable investing, claims can be met even though the amount paid out in claims may be more than the amount coming in through premiums. And, of course, most companies continue selling new insurance policies, which helps build up reserves for further investment. Companies that earn high yields on these investments—5 or 6 percent—are then in a better position to offer lower premiums than their competitors.

The amount of commission that a company pays its salespersons also affects the cost of the premium. The commission depends primarily upon the type and amount of the policy. First-year commissions vary, but here are some sample estimates on policies written for $5000 or more: term insurance, 35 percent of the premium; straight life, 55 percent; limited payment, 50 percent; and endowment, 45 percent. Commissions are paid every year the policy is in force, but commissions in the second and succeeding years drop steadily. The second-year commission usually drops to about 15 percent of the premium; the third year to 10 percent; the fourth year to 7 percent; the fifth year to 5 percent; and the remaining years to somewhere between 3 and 5 percent. Now you may understand the major reason why insurance salespersons are persistent and attentive (continually sending birthday and Christmas cards), and welcome an opportunity to "reevaluate your insurance needs." If you buy a new policy, the salesperson earns that steep first year's commission again, as shown in Table 15-3.

Other expenses of the company also contribute to the premium cost. If a company is efficient in its use of resources and not wasteful or lavish, it should be in a more competitive position regarding premiums. An insurance company must be accurate in its work, too, since misjudgment on mortality estimates results in losses which can only be made up through price increases on newer policies—the ones you might buy from the same salesperson who sold you your first policy.

Options of many kinds are available with life insurance, and each affects the premium cost. If a policy is *guaranteed renewable*, regardless of the health of the policyholder, the company is taking an added risk, and therefore the cost rises a little. *Guaranteed insurability* means the same thing. This option is extremely important because one does not want to buy life insurance and then later find out that because of one's health problems it is no longer available. A *convertibility* provision raises the cost slightly too. Guaranteed convertibility is an important option, since one's need for particular types of policies may

change. For example, a person aged 50 might decide to convert an expensive straight life policy to term insurance; the built-up cash value is likely to be enough to pay all the remaining premiums for life.

Settlement options—giving the insured a choice of ways of having the policy benefits paid—are important to the person planning the insurance program as well as to the beneficiaries. The choice has a slight effect on premiums but a dramatic impact on how much the survivors may actually get. For example, paying the total face value of the policy in a lump sum is one type of settlement, but since with this method the company must pay out a lot of money at one time, this option makes the premium higher. If the company can keep most of the face amount while making installment payments to beneficiaries, it can invest and earn profits on such funds, which lowers the cost of the policy.

Other options for settlement are also available; each permits the company to retain part of the funds for a period of time, thus somewhat reducing the premium costs. One option allows the company to hold the principal sum while paying only interest (usually 3½ to 4½ percent) to the beneficiary for a specified number of years or for life; the total principal is finally given later to those specified in the contract. Another option permits larger regular payments to the beneficiary until the face amount of the policy has been paid out in full.

A *disability clause*, available in most policies, also adds to premium cost. This option provides for the payment of all remaining premiums if the policyholder becomes so ill or disabled that he or she cannot work. It usually begins after one has been disabled for 6 months. Another option available is *double* or *triple indemnity*. This means that a policy with a face value of $25,000 will pay the beneficiaries twice or three times that amount should the insured die from an accident. An *incontestability* clause guarantees payment to the beneficiaries regardless of the cause of death, including suicide, after 2 years. Many other options are available, and such individ-

TABLE 15-3

First-year Commissions for Different Policies $40,000 in Coverage (Male Aged 25)

Type of Policy	Premium	Commission Rate	Commission
Term (10-year renewable)	$ 198.00	35%	$ 69.30
Straight life	510.00	55	280.50
Limited payment (20 years)	934.40	50	467.20
Endowment (20 years)	1576.00	45	709.20

ual tailoring means some increase (or decrease) in the cost of the premium.

Dividends. Like common stockholders in a large manufacturing corporation, many policyholders of permanent policies share in the profits of a company by receiving dividends. This can occur only if the policy is sold by a mutual company rather than a stock company. A *stock company* is owned by the stockholders, and any profits belong to them. A *mutual company* is similar to a cooperative in that any profits theoretically belong to the policyholders. When one buys insurance from a mutual company, the insured usually has the option of being classified as *participating* or *nonparticipating*. Participating policyholders are entitled to receive dividends, and these reflect the difference between the premium originally charged and the company's experience. The initial premium cost for a nonparticipating policyholder is lower than for a participating. This is a false picture, however, since the participating policyholder is eligible to receive dividends at the end of each year if the company is profitable (usually one is not eligible for dividends for the first and second years). This, of course, reduces the net cost of the insurance. The dividends can be paid in cash, in credit toward the next year's premium, or in the automatic purchase of more life insurance. In effect, the mutual company is refunding an "overcharge" to the policyholders when it gives them a dividend. Stock companies usually offer only nonparticipating policies, and in general the net cost of life insurance purchased from mutual companies is less than that purchased from stock companies.

Cash Value. A final factor affecting the total premium for life insurance is cash value. Except for term insurance, all policies have some built-in cash surrender value. Obviously, if you cancel your coverage and have the cash value returned to you, the net cost of your insurance coverage over those years will have been less. For example, suppose you paid in $3000 for a permanent type of life insurance

that now has a cash value of $700, while the remaining $2300 went for pure protection. If you now request your cash surrender value by giving up the policy, the net cost of the insurance will have been only $2300 rather than $3000. If on the other hand you remain with the company and do not cancel and pull out your cash values, the net cost by necessity must be higher.

Calculating the Real Cost of Life Insurance

For the consumer, shopping for life insurance is extremely difficult. Perhaps that is why approximately three-fourths of the purchasers of life insurance see only one salesperson! There are so many types of policies, options, clauses, and special-benefit provisions that comparisons are confusing. Your task, once you have decided upon how much insurance you need and can afford, is to use a method of calculation that will show you the true real costs of buying. Two methods are described below which address the topic of "real cost."

The Net-cost Method. The most popular method of showing a prospective buyer how much a life insurance policy will cost is the net-cost method. The reason is that it shows an appealing picture, but it is also a false picture. For example, let us assume that the XYZ Life Insurance Company charges a premium of $233.20 for a 35-year-old female for a $10,000 straight life policy. She participates in dividends averaging $72.79 per year. Over a 20-year period she would pay out $3208.20. Meanwhile, the cash value of the policy will build up to $3570. The salesperson says that at that point in time the policy can be cancelled and the cash value will be surrendered. So the net-cost method shows a negative cost of $361.80 for the buyer ($3208.20 minus $3570.00 equals a negative $361.80). Not surprisingly, most life insurance policies show up with a negative *net* cost, but that does not show the *real* cost of the policy.

Cost, of course, is only one of many factors to consider in buying life insurance, but it is an important one. If a person wants pure protection, term insurance is best. If a person wants to build some savings through a life insurance program, then some type of permanent policy is indicated. But the true real cost for any type of permanent insurance may be higher, lower, or even the same as term coverage. Since one is not usually comparing identical policies when considering life insurance, it is virtually impossible to make the best choice with the information most often given with permanent types of insurance. For the *real* cost of life insurance, one should consider the cost of the premiums less any dividends, the cash value accumulated, *and* the interest that the funds could have safely earned (perhaps 4 percent) if invested elsewhere, and some other factors too.

The Interest-adjusted Method. The interest-adjusted method takes into consideration numerous variables and results in an interest-adjusted index. This is a sophisticated attempt to determine the real cost of life insurance. The index can be converted into dollars to show the various costs of the different policies. One important thing it considers is what a person could have earned on the premium money if it had been invested elsewhere. This opportunity cost is now recognized even by the insurance industry (officially through the National Association of Insurance Commissioners) as an important factor in comparing policies. What if the premium money were placed instead in a savings and loan association, in government bonds, or in a similar safe investment?

The American Institute for Economic Research made a clear analysis of this method and showed why it is extremely important to consider the opportunity cost of the interest factor; it was published in the *Economic Education Bulletin*.

> Neglect of the interest factor would create at least one misleading impression. By disregarding interest on the premiums, for some endowment and limited life policies the return to the

policyholder can be made to appear more than he has actually paid. For example, a low annual premium per $1,000 face amount for a nonparticipating 20-year endowment policy issued today at the age of 25 is $41.76. After 20 years the policyholder will have paid $835.20 in premiums and will receive $1,000. If the interest that the annual premiums could have otherwise earned is disregarded, the impression is that the insurance company is giving the policyholder $164.80 more than he paid. That this impression is erroneous can be seen if we take into account the interest that the premiums would have earned if invested otherwise. $41.76 invested annually at 3½ percent interest will amount to $1,222.20 at the end of 20 years. Therefore, instead of the company's giving the policyholder $164.80, the policyholder will have paid the insurance company $222.20 for the insurance protection he has received while the policy was in force.

Also considered in the interest-adjusted method is what would happen if the policy were turned in and cancelled after a certain number of years. The returned cash value would have an effect. The factors of dividends, premiums, cash value, mortality tables, interest rates, policy-lapse rates, and others are all considered in calculating such an index. Of course, it takes a computer to make such an analysis. The individual responsible for this breakthrough in policy comparison is Dr. Joseph M. Belth, professor of insurance at Indiana University, who conducted many studies to perfect the techniques.

Controversy erupted in the insurance industry when the then Commissioner of Insurance of Pennsylvania, Herbert S. Denenberg, published *A Shopper's Guide to Life Insurance*. Using all the factors noted above, the study calculated the real cost of straight life insurance policies sold in that state. The formula used assumes that the policyholder will live and that the policy itself will be surrendered for its cash value after a certain number of years. The interest-adjusted method, which is by far the most accurate method of comparing permanent policies, was used to calculate an interest-adjusted index for each policy. This was then converted into the *average yearly cost* of life insurance. Straight life policies were chosen because they are the most often bought and are also the most confusing to compare.

The findings of Commissioner Denenberg showed a cost variation of as high as 170 per-cent. Table 15-4 shows the average yearly costs of the ten lowest-cost policies of 166 companies selling insurance in Pennsylvania at that time. Table 15-5 gives the same information for the ten highest-cost companies. Both tables use as a base a $10,000 straight life cash-value insurance policy. Note that since women live longer than men, the premium costs are adjusted accordingly.

The best and the worst buys for certain age groups can easily be seen. National Life Insurance Company, for example, charges an annual premium of $152.70 (Table 15-4) for a

TABLE 15-4

Premiums and Insurance Cost for the 10 Lowest Cost $10,000 Straight Life Cash-value Insurance Policies[2]

Company[4]	Male Age 20 or Female Age 23[3]			Male Age 35 or Female Age 38[3]			Male Age 50 or Female Age 53[3]		
	Annual Premium	Average Yearly Cost of Insurance	Rank-ing[5] at Age 20/23	Annual Premium	Average Yearly Cost of Insurance	Rank-ing[5] at Age 35/38	Annual Premium	Average Yearly Cost of Insurance	Rank-ing[5] at Age 50/53
1. Bankers Life Company (Iowa)	$149.70	$24.70	4	$229.10	$42.00	1	$400.30	$119.20	2
2. Home Life Ins. Co. (NY)	150.70	23.10	3	228.40	43.10	2	405.10	125.90	5
3. National Life Ins. Co. (VT)	152.70	28.30	10	230.30	46.30	5	389.80	125.80	4
4. Connecticut Mutual Life Ins. Co.	135.00	22.40	1	218.50	46.70	6	397.70	132.70	11
5. Phoenix Mutual Life Ins. Co.	157.00	26.60	7	233.60	48.60	7	392.50	127.70	6
6. Northwestern Mutual Life Ins. Co.	157.40	28.70	11	234.80	45.50	3	405.40	129.40	8
7. Central Life Assurance Co. (Iowa)	155.10	22.90	2	235.70	46.10	4	404.00	136.00	15
8. State Mutual Life Assurance Co. of America (Mass.)	149.50	28.80	12	231.60	49.00	9	408.30	132.70	11
9. Modern Woodmen of America[1]	138.80	27.50	9	214.10	48.90	8	377.80	134.80	13
10. Lutheran Mutual Life Ins. Co.	144.80	27.30	8	226.10	49.50	10	394.90	135.00	14

[1] Fraternal organization; policy available only to members.

[2] The ten lowest cost policies of those sold by 166 larger companies licensed in Pennsylvania.

[3] Usual premiums for a female are the same as those for a male three years younger.

[4] Listed according to the average of the interest-adjusted costs at the three ages.

[5] Ranked at each age according to the average yearly cost of insurance over a twenty-year period.

Note. All are participating policies.

Source: Herbert S. Denenberg, *A Shopper's Guide To Life Insurance* (Harrisburg: Pennsylvania Insurance Department)

male aged 20 or a female aged 23. In contrast, Georgia International Life Insurance Company charges $119.20 (Table 15-5). But comparing the policies solely on premium costs is very deceptive. Most revealing is that the average yearly cost of the Georgia policy was $61 (the highest in the study), while the National policy cost $28.30 (the tenth lowest in the study).

Premiums and policies change, of course, but the wise shopper can use these tables as a good starting point. Be sure in your shopping that the insurance agents show you interest-adjusted cost index figures for the policies in which you might be interested over 10-, 20-, and 30-year time periods. The agents should also show you figures on comparable policies given by other companies, which are found in insurance industry manuals. If the agent or company cannot give you such information, don't let them waste your time—shop elsewhere. It is possible that the insurance commissioner in your state may have recently conducted an interest-adjusted method study of all the companies doing business there. You might ask.

Fallacies in the Interest-adjusted Method. The pressure to look better in the interest-adjusted costs being published in many states has encouraged companies to come up with ways to tinker with the figures in order to improve

TABLE 15-5

Premiums and Insurance Cost for the 10 Highest Cost $10,000 Straight Life Cash-value Insurance Policies[3]

Company[5]	Male Age 20 or Female Age 23[4]			Male Age 35 or Female Age 38[4]			Male Age 50 or Female Age 53[4]		
	Annual Premium	Average Yearly Cost of Insurance	Ranking[6] at Age 20/23	Annual Premium	Average Yearly Cost of Insurance	Ranking[6] at Age 35/38	Annual Premium	Average Yearly Cost of Insurance	Ranking[6] at Age 50/53
1. Georgia International Life Ins. Co.[1]	$119.20	$61.00	166	$192.20	$94.50	166	$344.90	$202.40	165
2. The State Life Ins. Co. (Ind.)	155.70	55.70	165	237.00	88.70	165	410.60	199.60	162
3. Valley Forge Life Ins. Co.[1]	120.20	51.80	154	195.70	87.80	163	354.00	201.70	164
4. The Employers Life Ins. Co. of America (Del.)[1,2]	119.60	50.70	145	194.00	84.30	150	361.00	205.20	166
5. Old Republic Life Ins. Co. (Ill.)[1]	122.00	52.30	158	196.30	85.90	157	357.90	201.00	163
6. Wabash Life Ins. Co.[1]	120.30	52.80	159	192.90	86.70	159	348.70	199.30	161
7. Pennsylvania Life Ins. Co.[1]	110.40	53.60	162	183.60	86.40	158	340.40	198.30	160
8. Puritan Life Ins. Co.[1]	114.60	53.00	160	188.00	86.90	160	338.70	193.50	152
9. Security Life and Accident Co. (Colo.)	164.50	49.50	140	250.40	88.30	164	417.30	194.60	155
10. Travelers Ins. Co.[1]	118.00	53.10	161	190.90	84.70	154	348.10	194.40	154

[1] Non-participating policy—no dividends, guaranteed costs. All others are participating.

[2] Policy includes Waiver of Premium for disability at no extra cost. Costs have been adjusted to remove the estimated charge for this benefit.

[3] The ten highest cost policies of those sold by 166 larger companies licensed in Pennsylvania.

[4] Usual premiums for a female are the same as those for a male three years younger.

[5] Listed according to the average of the interest-adjusted costs at the three ages.

[6] Ranked at each age according to the average yearly cost of insurance over a twenty-year period.

Source: Herbert S. Denenberg, *A Shopper's Guide To Life Insurance* (Harrisburg: Pennsylvania Insurance Department).

their standing. Wouldn't you know it—just as soon as the industry had a formula that could be used consistently to compare policies, things would happen to muddle the works. Some culprits causing confusion are those which illustrate very high dividends during the first 10 or 20 years and very low dividends in future years. If you are comparing one company's policy with another, be certain to request interest-adjusted figures for 10, 20, *and* 30 years. The fairest comparisons are among those with rather consistent estimates of dividends. Say "goodbye" to any company that shows dividends dropping off dramatically after 20 years, because the comparisons at 10 and 20 years are gimmick figures rigged up to make the policy look better.

Even worse are companies that use a new method of determining dividends. The situation is such that comparisons are again virtually useless unless one of two things occurs: (1) You find out if the companies use the *investment-year method* of determining dividends (then scratch those companies out of the comparisons, since they are not valid), or (2) all companies in the industry decide not to use the investment-year method of paying dividends.

This *investment-year method* of determining dividends is simply to pay higher dividends to newer policyholders instead of giving all policyholders the same dividend. Thus, policyholders of certain years are paid lower dividends, partially based on the argument that those funds are tied up in long-term bonds and mortgages at rates earning considerably less than today's rates. The Equitable Life Assurance Society of the United States, the only company to publicly announce that they are using this method (others like Pan American Life Insurance Company and American United Life Insurance Company are doing it too but won't admit it—even to their own policyholders, according to Joseph M. Belth) is calculating dividends estimated by Belth to be 5.15 percent for its most recent policyholders and 4.65 percent for its oldest.

The results: (1) Old policyholders have had

the rules changed on them many years after they bought in, and they are losing money because of it, and (2) interest-adjusted cost figures are gimmicked to the point of deception. You see, what is also important is that the formula considers what the company assumes will be its projected dividends in future years. By reporting that the company may earn high dividends, it makes it look better in cost comparisons. Many industry experts say that the estimated dividends of these companies simply cannot be obtained. For example, Equitable's new formula dropped the interest-adjusted cost figure from $176.50 a year to $133 for a $50,000 policy on a 35-year-old man. *Money* magazine reported that "A few years ago, Equitable's whole life policies ranked middle to high in cost. Now they rank among the cheapest."

So consumers trying to compare permanent types of life insurance are back in the dark again. To escape the whole dilemma, one could buy nonparticipating policies, since the interest-adjusted figures are accurate for them. However, in the long run the best participating policies are less costly than nonparticipating.

Information Disclosure. From the above discussion it should be apparent that consumers do in fact have a difficult time understanding life insurance, and that even when they want to know more, they are unable to because of various aspects of the insurance industry. Thus, there is talk about the need for "truth-in-life-insurance" regulations. Just a year before he died, Senator Phillip A. Hart introduced a bill known as the "Consumer Insurance Information and Fairness Act."

Proponents of insurance information disclosure have seen several states pass legislation requiring limited degrees of disclosure. Some other helpful informational booklets must be made available to consumers, too. Proponents feel that point-of-sale disclosure should be stronger and should include yearly information on premiums; amounts payable on death and on surrender; dividends, illustrated using a consistent approach; amounts of protection; yearly prices for various components of the policy; and rates of return on the portion retained as the savings element of the policy. Also, as Joseph M. Belth proposes, summary information should be provided which would show the breakdown of the premium into its particular components: the protection element, the savings element, the illustrated dividends, and the amount retained by the company. Periodic disclosure *after* the policy is sold is needed, too. Here the policyholder could benefit by knowing yearly price information and rate of return data concerning the dividend. Comparing policies is a complex and difficult task indeed, and as more information *of value* is provided, consumers will make better decisions.

SOCIAL SECURITY PROVIDES LIFE INSURANCE BENEFITS

Much of the security people want from life insurance is already provided under our present Social Security system. Social Security protection is sometimes limited but quite valuable. Realize, of course, that it was never intended to be more than a form of minimum protection. Since most people are covered by Social Security, it is important that life insurance be considered together with what one might expect from Social Security.

About nine out of every ten workers have some degree of protection through the Social Security program. And one out of seven Americans is receiving cash benefits. The retirement, survivor, and lump-sum death benefits need to be better understood, since they are in many ways similar to benefits received from life insurance.

To obtain any Social Security benefits, one must apply; the recipient must ask for the benefits, since the government does not actively seek out those who should be receiving assistance. To be covered under Social Security, you have to have worked and paid Social Security taxes for at least 1½ years. Even young workers have usually worked that long, and at

Reprinted with permission from Life Insurance Selling, June 1975. Copyright © 1975 by Commerce Publishing Company.

"Our policies are the easiest to understand in the whole business. There isn't a letter in this policy that's less than one inch high."

that point people are classified as *currently insured*. Older earners become *fully insured* (permanently insured) after working for 10 years. Social Security credit is measured by "quarters of coverage" with four quarters per year. If one pays Social Security taxes on $300 or $400 earned in a quarter, it counts. Therefore, 6 quarters equals 1½ years, and 40 quarters is the same as 10 years.

Benefits are directly related to the amount of income a person has earned upon which Social Security taxes were paid. You can easily get a record of your earnings from the Social Security Administration (P.O. Box 57, Baltimore, MD 21203). They will also tell you what benefits you are entitled to in a series of little booklets. You can also consult your local Social Security Office for more information.

For survivors benefits to widows, widowers, and children, there is a variable basis for qualifications. Children of a retired parent or who are survivors qualify for benefits when they are young and then continue to receive benefits between the ages of 18 and 22 if they remain in school full time and are unmarried. More than 700,000 college students are receiving benefits. To qualify for retirement benefits, the worker or the spouse of the worker must have earned 10 years of credits. Examples of monthly benefits are shown in Table 15-6. These figures are examples and are based upon *maximum* contributions. Determining benefits, which are almost always substantially *less* than the amounts shown, requires a visit to your local Social Security office. Since the government keeps on raising the amount necessary for maximum contributions (by law, as the cost of living goes up, the wage base also must rise), the benefits in the last few columns on the right will not be payable until later.

As an example of Social Security benefits, let us consider a young worker with dependents, who dies unexpectedly. John Jensen died this year at age 30, after working full time for 8 years. The benefits for his widow and two small children would be somewhat as follows. There would first be a lump-sum death benefit of $255, which may be used for burial expenses. (Given the high cost of dying, perhaps someone ought to raise this amount one of these days.) Assuming that Jensen's average earnings were $10,000, upon which he paid Social Security tax, the maximum possible benefit would be $829.50 Since his tax payments were not always based on $10,000 (see footnote to Table 15-6),

TABLE 15-6

Examples of Monthly Social Security Payments

| Benefits Can Be Paid To A: | Average Yearly Earnings After 1950 | | | | | | |
	$923 or Less	$3000	$4000	$5000	$6000	$8000*	$10,000*
Retired worker at 65	107.90	223.20	262.60	304.50	344.10	427.80	474.00
Worker under 65 and disabled	107.90	223.20	262.60	304.50	344.10	427.80	474.00
Retired worker at 62	86.40	178.60	210.10	243.60	275.30	342.30	379.20
Wife or dependent husband at 65	54.00	111.60	131.30	152.30	172.10	213.90	237.00
Wife or dependent husband at 62	40.50	83.70	98.50	114.30	129.10	160.50	177.80
Wife under 65 and one child in her care	54.00	118.00	186.20	257.40	287.20	321.00	355.60
Widow or dependent widower at 65 (if worker never received reduced benefits)	107.90	223.20	262.60	304.50	344.10	427.80	474.00
Widow or dependent widower at 60 (if sole survivor)	77.20	159.60	187.80	217.80	246.10	305.90	339.00
Widow or dependent widower at 50 and disabled (if sole survivor)	56.80	111.70	131.40	152.40	172.20	214.00	237.10
Widow or widower caring for one child	161.90	334.80	394.00	456.80	516.20	641.80	711.00
Maximum family payment	161.90	341.20	448.80	561.90	631.30	748.70	829.50

* Maximum earnings covered by Social Security were lower in past years and must be included in figuring your average earnings. This average determines your payment amount. Because of this, amounts shown in the last two columns generally won't be payable until future years. The maximum retirement benefit payable to a worker who was 65 in 1977 was $412.70.

the family would receive less than the maximum—perhaps $620. These benefits would go to his widow to help care for the children. They would continue until the children were aged 18, or 22 if they continued their schooling, whereupon they would stop. At that point the widow would have no further income from the Social Security Administration because the children are grown. This is commonly called the "blackout" or "Social Security gap." If she does not work, the widow obviously needs another source of income after the children are grown, as survivors benefits for the widow herself don't begin until she reaches age 60. All of us must plan ahead, realizing that this "gap" exists.

Now let us consider an example of the value of Social Security to those who are retiring. A fully insured worker, aged 65, can retire with maximum benefits of $474.00 *if* average yearly earnings were $10,000. A retiring couple could receive a maximum monthly payment of $829.50. Or the widow, aged 60, of a working man with similar earnings could expect a pension of $339.00. Very importantly, these benefits assume that the worker has had earnings averaging $10,000. However, as noted, it is almost impossible to receive maximum benefits, since the wage base upon which one

must contribute continues to rise. Therefore, in reality many workers do not receive the maximum benefits. In 1978 the average monthly amount *received* by all retired workers was about $260.00. Moreover, it is imperative that in estimating your Social Security benefits you first secure a statement of earnings, then visit your local Social Security office for assistance.

Careful examination of your expected Social Security benefits is imperative if you are planning on buying life insurance. Since your survivors will have some income if you qualify under Social Security, buying life insurance to duplicate that would of course be unnecessary. Also, one needs to be aware of changing Social Security regulations, benefits, and cost-of-living allowances to see how they might affect your life insurance needs.

Today's workers are paying taxes for the Social Security benefits that are going to more than 35 million people. The tax *rate* in 1978 was 12.10 percent; the employee pays 6.05 percent and the employer matches it. (Actually, all consumers pay the employer's share in the form of higher prices.) Self-employed persons, by the way, must pay a higher rate: three-fourths of the total for employers and employees. In 1978, the first $17,700 of earn-

TABLE 15-7

New Social Security Increases

Year	Tax Rates Old	New	Tax Base Old	New	Maximum Tax Old	New
1972	5.20%	5.20%	$ 9,000	$ 9,000	$ 468	$ 468
1977	5.85	5.85	16,500	16,500	965	965
1978	5.85	6.05	16,500	17,700	965	1070
1979	6.05	6.13	18,900	22,900	1143	1403
1980	6.05	6.13	18,900	22,900	1143	1403
1981	6.30	6.65	21,900	29,700	1380	1975
1982	6.30	6.70	21,900	31,800	1380	2130
1983	6.30	6.70	21,900	31,800	1380	2130
1984	6.30	6.70	21,900	31,800	1380	2130
1985	6.30	7.05	27,900	38,100	1758	2686
1986	6.45	7.15	29,400	40,200	1896	2874

ings was the *base* upon which the tax rate was applied. Therefore, during that year the workers paid a maximum of $1070 in Social Security taxes in order to hopefully receive full benefits later. As you can see from Table 15-7, both the wage base and the tax rates are expected to rise in the coming years. Recent changes in the Social Security laws require that the benefits keep up with the rising cost of living, and the base must rise also.

The taxes for Social Security paid by covered persons rose eight and a half times from 1950 to 1977, yet the benefits increased only about three times. At the same time, the number of people covered under Social Security went from half the workers to over 90 percent. Obviously, today's workers are paying for the increasing numbers of people receiving Social Security benefits. As more workers retire each year, others will have to pay higher taxes for them.

WHO NEEDS LIFE INSURANCE?

Some people need little or no life insurance at all! Of course, most people in the insurance industry will disagree with this statement. Consumers must decide for themselves whether or not their lives should be insured, why, and if so, for how much. Let us look at the general life insurance needs of children, teenagers, college students, young married couples, and established families.

Children

A child is born. During the first year of life, the probability of death is as great as that of a person aged 49, but the need for life insurance is not the same. A 49-year-old man, the probable "breadwinner" in his family, is likely to have many financial responsibilities. Without adequate life insurance coverage, his death could result in a tremendous financial strain and perhaps ruin to his survivors.

A child aged 1, 5, or 10 years does not have an income to protect. Much grief accompanies the loss of a child, but often the only financial

problem parents have is burial expenses. At present, families pay an average of nearly $2000 for such traditional expenses; cremation and ceremony costs amount to less than $500. In reality the big problem with a serious illness is not the burial cost but the high medical treatment expenses. Perhaps the money spent on life insurance coverage for children might be better used to get more medical coverage. Buying life insurance for small children is probably unnecessary, although some parents do choose to protect themselves financially. In that case a $1000 or $2000 term policy is adequate. It should cost $3 to $6 per year.

Unfortunately, some parents who buy life insurance on their children make a serious error in judgment by purchasing an endowment policy. Most often, it is a policy that matures in 15 or 18 years when the child may need funds for college. Should the child die before the end of the period, the face amount is paid. Should the child live (9,698,230 of every 10,000,000 born are alive at age 18), the policy is cancelled, leaving the face amount available to be spent. But during the intervening years, the family budget must adjust to paying perhaps $60 per year per child for each $1000 in coverage—ten times the cost of term insurance with the same face value. And 15 years from now the cost of 1 year of higher education may be close to $20,000. Therefore, for those who want both insurance on the life of a child and some provision for higher education costs, most experts recommend term insurance and a regular savings or investment plan. Overpriced protection in the form of endowment policies should be avoided.

Teenagers

Teenagers, also, rarely provide a major part of family income and therefore do not usually need life insurance. On the other hand, if the teenager has accumulated debts for clothing, a music system, or an automobile, then a limited amount of insurance may be wise. Remember, however, that credit life insurance (decreasing term) may have been required by the lenders if loans were made, so that extra protection to pay off such debts may be unnecessary. For those who wish to protect the family finances against the possibility of a teenager's death, the cost per $1000 of term insurance is even less than that for small children.

One exception should be noted. If the family has an extremely poor health history, perhaps with some hereditary problems, it may be wise to buy insurance early rather than taking the chance that a teenager will be uninsurable later. Note, however, that only 3 percent of all applicants for life insurance policies, including the elderly, are refused.

Should one want a policy for a teenager, the recommended route is to buy a term policy that is both guaranteed renewable and convertible. Then, should a health problem develop later, the individual will always have some guaranteed protection. And with the convertibility provision, the policy can eventually be changed to a permanent type. Later, too, a person with a health problem often gets group insurance through an employer, and this too is frequently guaranteed renewable even if the person leaves the job. In such cases, even an "uninsurable" person can build up life insurance protection, despite the widely held belief to the contrary.

College Students

About the last thing a college student needs is life insurance. Any unnecessary expense added to the thousands of dollars spent for college is severely felt in the budget. In addition, the probability of death during those years is extremely low. Unless the student has children, there is usually no need whatsoever to buy life insurance.

Insurance people, of course, do not agree with this position. In fact, more than 400 life insurance companies have special sales programs aimed at college students. Surveys show that most students are contacted by an insurance salesperson between four and six times a year. Just what is the "pitch" that all too often makes these students buy unnecessary insurance? It is much the same as for

anyone else, but it is carefully slanted to the typical student situation.

In his article in *Life Insurance Selling,* Charles W. Alexander notes how the salespersons work. When the student prospect says, "I want to talk it over with my father," the following approach is often used: "Bill, probably the first thing your dad bought for you when you were a child was a piggy bank, to get you in the habit of saving money. All you're going to do by talking to your father is ask him if you may start a program to make you do what he has been trying to get you to do since you were a child. That's kind of silly, isn't it?" Or he might say, "Bill, this program is designed for you in a way that will enable you to start it for yourself. You will be putting your money in the program, and you will cover your wife and family with it. This is why the decision should be one that you make. Don't you agree?"

Most college sales programs have been aimed toward seniors, but with the lower age of majority in most states, the salespersons are now concentrating on freshmen and sophomores as well. Interestingly, and logically, the salespersons for college policies are often campus leaders, recently graduated star athletes, former coaches, and even faculty members and administrators. Students are more apt to identify with and trust them. Since commissions run from 50 to 75 percent of the first year's premium, many people are interested in selling these policies.

Let us examine what students are buying in a typical college life insurance program. To start with, the policy is usually a combination of term and straight life. After 4 or 5 years all the term automatically converts to straight life. Policy amounts of $10,000, $15,000 or $25,000 are most common. The amount of coverage is inadequate for those few that really need life insurance protection (as will be shown later under "How Much Insurance Is Needed"), but it is intentionally kept low so as not to make the total cost of the program seem too high. Since college students rarely have extra funds available, the company offers to "waive" the first and sometimes the second year's premium. Instead, the student signs a promissory note, usually payable in 5 years, and thus has an insurance program started and "need not worry" about becoming uninsurable. The student not only is insured now, but will be for as long as he or she continues making payments. Studies by Joseph M. Belth indicate that many students do not even realize that they are signing promissory notes when they buy such policies.

According to *Forbes* magazine, an interesting "gimmick" being used is to make it appear that the college endorses the company. The idea is to have the student make the college a partial beneficiary—perhaps for 2 or 3 percent of the proceeds—and then after the agent notifies the school, the student receives a thank-you letter from the dean. "As a result," says *Forbes*, "many students think the school is endorsing the company and its insurance policies."

Companies that specialize in selling life insurance to college students include Fidelity Union Life (more than one-half of its insurance is in this market, and one out of every twenty policies sold to college-aged students are made by this firm), National Life and Accident of Nashville, Jefferson Standard of North Carolina, Shenandoah Life of Virginia, American United Life of Indianapolis, Indianapolis Life, Lincoln National of Fort Wayne, State Life of Indiana, and Fidelity Bankers Life Insurance Company of Virginia. The big mail-order sellers of life insurance to students include Globe Life and Accident Insurance Company of Oklahoma City, Fidelity Bankers Life Insurance Company of Richmond, Virginia, and Beneficial National Life Insurance Company of New York City. Consumers Union studied the prices of the mail-order and regular college-student policies and concluded that they were in fact quite high. Even more surprising were the stiff prices of the so-called "low-cost" United States Student Association Insurance Plan.

CU wonders if the National Student Association (like the one on your campus) "has made any attempt to stay current about insurance costs, to see if the plan offers its members a bargain?"

Concerning cost, Fidelity Union deserves special attention. *Best's Review*, the insurance trade publication, does provide some cost comparisons on various policies. In a recent issue, Fidelity Union ranks as the lowest in cost. Upon closer inspection, the policy being referred to is its President's Preferred Life. But surprise! That policy is hard to get from the sales personnel. What is highly touted and sold instead is their "CollegeMaster" plan, a very gimmicky and high-cost product.

Now let us examine the primary reasons why students should *not* consider buying such college-student-oriented life insurance programs.

First, what student needs $25,000 of life insurance? Or even $10,000? Certainly not one who is single. Financial responsibilities then consist of burial expenses and perhaps an automobile loan. And frequently the parents already have a $1000 or $2000 policy on the student's life. For college students, the probability of death is low, and not only is the probability of becoming uninsurable even lower, but the "problem of uninsurability" is a myth. Overly concerned students might more wisely consider an inexpensive guaranteed renewable and convertible term policy. But most just do *not* need life insurance.

Second, if insurance is needed, why go into debt to purchase it? And why buy such an expensive insurance policy—straight life? (Fidelity Union's CollegeMaster policy doesn't even bother with a term plan converting to straight life to help keep the total cost down; they just sell straight life.) Signing a promissory note for 5 years means interest due and payable, along with the principal, in the years to follow, and interest rates are commonly around 8 percent. And, of course, the interest is compounded until one begins to pay off the note. This adds to the already high cost. A first-year premium loan of $151 on a $10,000 policy sold by Fidelity Union had an annual interest rate of 8.5 percent. Compounded, the finance charge comes to $76.07. That is an awfully high cost.

Third, the typical contract loan requires the policyholder to sign a *policy-assignment* form. This guarantees that, should the insured die, the insurance company is the first beneficiary. It collects the unpaid premium and interest before paying parents or other beneficiaries the remaining proceeds. This is another reason why selling such a program to college students is financially such a safe business—for the insurance company!

Fourth, a common built-in feature of such policies is the savings aspect of any permanent insurance policy. After the first year, part of the premium goes to build up cash values. Depending upon the length of the loan contract, the amount of the savings portion of the policy grows. A clause in the contract permits the company to take possession of those cash values if the student defaults, thus further guaranteeing repayment of the loan and interest to cover the first year's premium. This is sort of an overpriced "miniature endowment policy" with the insurer as the beneficiary.

Fifth, like many credit agreements, the promissory note contains an *acceleration clause*. Should the student not make a payment on time, the lender (the insurance company) can demand payment in full immediately. A court judgment is issued against the student ordering him or her to pay. Something like that stays on one's credit record for seven years.

Sixth, such promissory notes and the life insurance are almost impossible to cancel. With *all* other life insurance policies, a person who stops paying has a *grace* period of 30 days before the insurance is officially cancelled by the company. After that, the coverage no longer exists and consumers are not billed for something they are not buying. With a college life insurance program, there is a promissory note. It is the note the student is paying on, *not* the life insurance. Therefore, without a clause

stating that the *note* can be cancelled, the student cannot get out of the contract. If the salesperson says that the student can cancel, this is pure "sales talk," will not hold up in court, and is worthless. To date, *no* college-aimed contract has been seen with such a clause, and until (if ever) there is such a cancellation clause, this is a contract the buyer legally just cannot get out of. The buyer is stuck!

To summarize, why buy too much of something you do not need? Why go into debt to get it? And why sign a contract that legally you cannot get out of should you change your mind? If you really need an insurance policy, choose one carefully. Do not let yourself be sold more than you need, at more than you can afford, when you might not need it in the first place. *Consumer Reports*, the most respected and objective publication in the consumer field, comes to these conclusions about campus life insurance policies: "The last thing most college students need is life insurance. We strongly advise against buying life insurance from Fidelity Union Life Insurance Company. And we suggest thinking twice before buying any policy designed primarily for sale to college students. Many of the term policies and whole life policies offered in the general marketplace are, in our judgment, far better deals."

Young Married Couples

If a young married couple has no debts or children, then they probably need only a limited amount of coverage, if any at all. They may want a term policy to cover burial expenses in case either of them should unexpectedly die. Even if they are acquiring debts—perhaps for an automobile and some furniture—their need for coverage is still quite low. If they are buying a house, then they might well reconsider and perhaps start a well-thought-out insurance program to meet their needs. They should consider both future financial plans and present income. A term or straight life policy may be their best course of action, or some combination of both. Such an insurance plan should definitely take into consideration the earning potential of both spouses, especially if one stays home and remains out of the job market. If it is the wife who stays home and she has a marketable skill (and certainly most women today do; 46 percent of the U.S. labor force is made up of women), then the need for insurance on the husband need not be as great as was first suspected. Both spouses employed or employable is the best "insurance" a young couple can have.

A couple with children has additional responsibilities. The possibility of the loss of either parent or both must be considered. The long-range goals of the parents, the need for income for the years while the children are growing up, the possible Social Security benefits, and the current family income will to a large extent determine the amount of protection they might need.

The Established Family

More children, more debts, a mortgage on a home, and possibly the need to pay for higher education costs in a few years—all these face a growing family. Most are financial problems, and the need for life insurance protection, perhaps with a savings feature, becomes apparent. Straight life insurance on the breadwinner might be best, with additional term insurance for the time when his or her loss might most hurt the family financially, and with some term insurance on the spouse. Group life insurance is often available through employers. It can supplement a basic insurance program and include limited amounts of coverage on the children.

As the children grow up and leave home, responsibilities lessen and the need for insurance diminishes. The death of the breadwinner may no longer be such a financial strain on the survivors. Specific term insurance policies may then be dropped. And during later years the couple may want to convert their permanent life insurance into paid-up term insurance. This way they will no longer have to pay premiums when they retire, but they will still

have some life insurance coverage. Their needs will have been met by effective financial planning while using life insurance to help accomplish their goals.

ACHIEVING YOUR LIFE INSURANCE GOALS

By now you have an idea of whether or not you need life insurance. Whether you do or do not, you need to understand and avoid the deceptive sales practices that occur in the life insurance business. If you need life insurance, you have to determine how much you might need for adequate protection (taking into consideration Social Security benefits), decide what type(s) of life insurance will best serve your needs, and discover how to get the best buy in life insurance and how to choose a good insurance agent.

Deceptive Sales Practices

The term *deceptive* in this context refers to aspects of a sales presentation that tend to either give the consumer an erroneous impression or perpetuate incorrect myths. Such deceptive sales practices may or may not be intended by the company or salesperson, but the result is the same.

One myth, for example, is that "as you get older the cost of life insurance rises, so you better buy now while you are young." In every life insurance contract, say for $10,000 of coverage, the wager is the same. You are betting a certain amount of dollars in premiums that you will die; the company bets that you will live. The only difference in buying at different ages is that the *length* of time of the "bet" changes. A 20-year-old person who buys a policy has more years during which to pay premiums. An older person has fewer years in which to pay premiums and thus pays a higher dollar premium each year—but by paying premiums over more years the younger person loses the earning power of that money. Thus, the true cost of coverage is about the same no matter when you buy.

The "uninsurability myth" was noted earlier but needs to be repeated here. In a survey conducted by the Institute of Life Insurance, a public relations organization for insurance companies, it was shown that very few people become uninsurable when it comes to buying coverage in the open market. Only 3 percent of the applicants for life insurance are rejected, and this includes people of all ages and in all conditions of health. The study showed that 92 percent of the people are accepted, while another 5 percent are accepted but at extra-risk rates. Even then, a person can almost always get some type of group insurance through an employer, professional or social organization, or credit union. Group plans take all applicants regardless of health.

Another myth, especially being pushed in recent years, is that "women should have lots of insurance on themselves just like men do." No one disagrees that more women should be insured, but the amount should be in proportion to the financial contribution of each spouse. The Equitable Life Assurance Society of the United States put out a brochure quoting a woman as saying, "If I were married, I would make sure I had a policy equal to my husband's. I do feel the woman's role, the mother's role, is as important as the husband's." As observed most accurately by columnist Jane Bryant Quinn, this feminist-sounding approach could be harmful. She notes, "When a woman doesn't work, she and the children are entirely dependent on the husband for support. If half of the money available for insurance premiums is spent insuring the wife, it reduces the amount that the husband can afford to carry. If the wife dies, the husband gets an insurance payoff that he doesn't really need. But if the husband dies, the wife and children are up the creek."

The president of Kemper Life Insurance Company, Richard E. Sauder, commented recently that "Until now . . . the products and services delivered to the buyer have been dictated by the whims, ineptness, attitudes, and avarice of the people doing the so-called selling, rather than by the desires and needs of the consumer. Some life insurance sales people and companies have been prostituting the needs and desires of the consumer in their anxiety to get the commission dollars and the business on the books." The "until now" part can only be interpreted to mean that consumers are becoming more knowledgeable and demanding the right type of product to meet their needs. To do this, however, takes even more understanding of some of the deceptive sales practices of the life insurance industry.

When a prospective customer is shown the dividends the participating straight life policy is expected to earn over the next 10 or 20 years, the chance for inaccurate conclusions is quite high. The dividends shown are based upon estimates using today's earnings. Will the high interest and earnings rates this year be true in 20 years?

Also, in permanent types of policies, the costs are often broken down into so many dollars for protection and so many for savings. It is easy to overstate the rate of return on the savings element or understate the price of the protection element. Understating the protection cost can occur, for example, in this way: For a $5000 participating straight life policy in its twenty-seventh year, an advertisement might say that "the *increase* in value from 1978 to 1979 amounted to $85.90, which grew out of the payment, just made, of an annual premium less dividend of only $60.26 . . . which means that my cash value this year increased at the rate of $142.54 for each $100 deposited!" The deception is in attributing the entire cash-value increase of $85.90 to the payment of $60.26 in that year, when most of the $85.90 increase came from interest on the savings element developed during the earlier years. The implication is that the price of protection that year was a minus $25.64. If one reasonably allocates the interest factor, the price for protection in that year is $90.97 rather than minus $25.64, as calculated by Joseph M. Belth.

Similar misallocations of the interest factor result in increasingly larger minus figures for the cost of protection as the policy gets older.

In participating policies the rate of return on the savings element can be overstated. This shows a higher cost for the protection element but also shows impressive figures for building up cash values.

Further understatements of the price of protection occurs with the widespread use of the net-cost method. Frequently, a 20-year time period is used. One simply adds all the annual premiums over 20 years, say $2448 per year on a $100,000 policy for a total of $48,960. Then, one adds the total dividends over the 20 years, perhaps $8441, and the final cash value of the policy at the end of the 20 years, perhaps $39,500, for a total of $47,941. The 20-year average net cost takes the $47,941 from the $48,960 leaving $1019 divided by 20 resulting in $50.95, or 51 cents per $1000 of the face amount of the policy. Obviously, the method does not consider the timing of the amounts paid in premiums by the policyholder nor the timing of the amounts received in dividends. Although this is the most widely used technique for illustrating the cost of insurance, it was defined more than 5 years ago by the National Association of Insurance Commissioners in a model regulation as a "deceptive sales practice."

Manipulation of the cash value of the policy at certain dates seriously alters the interest-adjusted cost index. This can occur simply by having the increases in cash value drop sharply after the 20-year illustration. This forces the cash values up at earlier points and makes the policy look especially good—low cost, as indicated by a low index—when in reality it is not. Another manipulation of the cash-value figures can similarly mess up any correct interpretation of the interest-adjusted cost index. This occurs when the cash values vary within the illustration, but you cannot see this because the example is shown in summary form. If, for example, the illustration shows cash values accumulated at the tenth and twentieth years, it could be that they are inflated figures and the first through ninth, eleventh through nineteenth, and those after the twentieth are purposely deflated.

Best's Insurance Reports are authoritative and widely used publications designed to show the financial strength of the companies. To one not familiar with the reports, misconceptions are rampant. If a salesperson shows the consumer/prospect a reprint from *Best's* saying that the company had achieved "satisfactory" results, had "considerable" margins to cover contingencies, that its mortality experience had been "favorable," that its executives were "capable and experienced," and that *Best's* recommends "this company," ordinary people all across America would think that it was a financially strong company. False! Less than 3 months after such phrases sprinkled the reports on the Underwriters National Assurance Company of Indianapolis and the Century Life Insurance Company of Fort Worth, one went into conservatorship under the state insurance commissioner and the other into receivership. They were both on the edge of bankruptcy.

The fallacies of *Best's* reports continue unabated, however. The reports do not mention any year-to-year changes in ratings. And that assumes you can tell which words are *not* positive. "Considerable" financial margins and "satisfactory" results are the weakest ratings *Best's* gives. In addition, *Best's* maintains a general practice of silence when "we might have to say something derogatory," according to a *Best's* vice president. In a recent year, the bond portfolios of 618 life insurance companies were rated by *Best's*. 402 received a rating of "excellent," 157 "very good," and 30 "good." One wonders how almost *all* the companies could be better than average. Most insurance experts recommend that you avoid a company whose financial status is not given one of the top two ratings: "most substantial" or "very substantial."

Evidence of high-pressure sales tactics is occasionally documented, but is perhaps most evident in the amazingly high *lapse* or *dropout rates* of policies. A Senate subcommittee on monopolies revealed statistics showing that one-fourth and sometimes as many as one-half of the best-selling permanent insurance policies of the leading companies in the industry are dropped by the buyers *within* 1 year. Almost one-half of all policies are cancelled within 10 years and three-fifths within 20 years. Only about one-third of the policyholders of these "permanent" types of policies keep them into old age.

The buyers lose heavily because no cash value accrues during the first year. Dean E. Sharp, counsel to the Senate subcommittee, comments that "If any other industry found a quarter to a half of the public rejecting its supposedly 'lifetime' products within a few months or a year, it would begin to wonder whether it was selling the right product. But not the insurance industry. It keeps on forcefeeding the public the same products in the same way, in spite of these tremendous dropout rates."

How Much Insurance Is Needed?

Whether you are single or married, if no one but you depends on your income, then you probably need little or no life insurance. Perhaps enough to cover burial costs, medical expenses above your health insurance coverage, payments of any debts, and maybe a little for relatives will meet your needs. Renewable and convertible term insurance may be your best bet, since your needs may change later.

One way of deciding how much insurance you need is shown in Figure 15-1, in which the financial status of the Jackson family is calculated. Henry Jackson is a 27-year-old middle-management employee of a large company. His wife, Charlotte, is 26. They have a son, aged 3, and a daughter, aged 2.

Henry's after-tax income is about $12,000; he has $1000 in savings and $2000 invested in

Cash Fund

1. Hospital expense, burial, probate, death taxes $ __3,000__ (1)

2. Cleanup expenses and emergency fund $ __4,000__ (2)

3. Family readjustment expense $ __2,000__ (3)

Income Fund

4. __75__ % of annual after-tax income to family $ __9,000__ (4)

5. Subtract annual Social Security benefits plus pension benefits from any source $ __7,280__ (5)

6-7. Divide by effective interest rate $ __1,720__ (6) ÷ __.04__ % = $ __43,000__ (7)

8. Add items 1, 2, 3, and 7 $ __52,000__ (8)

9. Subtract all convertible assets other than occupied real estate (savings, investments, amount payable under existing life insurance, and lump-sum death benefits) $ __13,000__ (9)

10. Life insurance required (additional) $ __39,000__ (10)

Source: Adapted from a method developed by the editors of *Changing Times* magazine.

FIGURE 15-1   Calculating your insurance needs

mutual funds. Charlotte does not work. The only insurance Henry has is a group family term policy that provides $10,000 on his life, $5000 on his wife's, and $2000 on each of the children. The Jacksons are still making payments on their 1-year-old automobile, as well as on some furniture and clothing. They are now renting an apartment, but they hope to be able to buy a house within the next 2 or 3 years.

If Henry died tomorrow, the surviving Jackson family would soon be in financial trouble. That $10,000 group policy would probably not last Charlotte and the children a year. She did finish college and also has good accounting skills, but getting a job would mean leaving the children and paying for their care. Henry and Charlotte discussed all this and made up their minds to find out just how much insurance they needed, assuming Charlotte did not go to work.

They decided together that item 1 in Figure 15-1 would probably amount to about $3000. They have so few assets that death taxes would not affect them, and both preferred the idea of a not-too-expensive funeral or a cremation. The emergency fund, item 2, was estimated at $4000. This, they figured, could cover any automobile breakdowns, health problems, or similar emergencies. Readjustment expenses, item 3, they set at $2000, feeling that the family would probably need a higher income for a few months until Charlotte could manage effectively on her own.

The income fund, item 4, was more difficult to figure. With Henry gone, how much would it take "after taxes" to support the family? Expenses attributable to him would not exist, and income taxes would drop sharply because most income would be tax-free Social Security benefits. Thus, they finally decided that 75 percent of their current after-tax income, or $9000, was appropriate. A short visit to the local Social Security office gave them the information they needed for item 5, survivors' benefits. Charlotte's estimated tax-free income with two dependents was $7280. Sub-

tracting the $7280 from $9000 left $1720 still needed to maintain their level of living, item 6. But that $1720 was for just 1 year. What about the following years, inflation, and the rising costs of raising children?

The first part of item 7 shows the effective interest rate that Charlotte could get if she received a large sum of money from an insurance policy. They decided that she could easily get a return of 5½ percent or more if she put the money in a savings and loan association. But they reduced this to 4 percent to allow a margin of safety and to consider that some taxes would have to be paid on that interest income. They put 0.04 in the blank. Dividing the $1720 by 0.04 resulted in $43,000 the second part of item 7. Adding up all the income and needed cash totaled $52,000, item 8. Item 9 revealed that savings, investments, and the group insurance policy on Henry totaled $13,000. The subtraction in item 10 suggested that they needed an additional $39,000 in life insurance.

The minimum extra insurance they needed was $39,000! But what about the years after Social Security stops? What about the costs of possible higher education for the children? Was even more insurance needed, or could Charlotte squeeze by?

Further investigation showed that cost-of-living increases are automatic with Social Security payments. So, they concluded that those benefits would offset most inflation problems. Careful analysis revealed that if Henry died, the assets of $43,000 in the form of life insurance proceeds could earn $2365 annually at 5 percent. That would yield a total of $645 more than the $9000 annually that Charlotte would need ($2365 minus $1720). If she saved these funds, she could create a college fund for the children. After Social Security benefits stopped, 20 years from now if the youngest went through 4 years of college, Charlotte would still be only 46 years old. She would have 14 years before she could begin to collect retirement benefits from Social Security. But if she still chose not to work, she could invest some of the intact $39,000 in higher-paying securities, use some of it to supplement her income, and perhaps use some of it to buy an annuity that would guarantee her 14 years of income. All these efforts could give her income during those years and carry her into her retirement years when Social Security benefits would begin again. So the Jacksons concluded

TABLE 15-8

Estate Buildup of Term Insurance if the Difference Is Invested*

Age	Premium for Term	Difference	Invested at 5%†	Total Estate
30	$ 325	$ 1152	$ 1,210	$101,210
31	331	1146	2,484	102,484
32	338	1139	3,804	103,804
33	346	1131	5,182	105,182
34	356	1121	6,618	106,618
35	371	1106	8,110	108,110
36	391	1086	9,656	109,656
37	414	1063	11,255	111,255
38	441	1036	12,906	112,906
39	472	1005	14,607	114,607
40	504	973	16,359	116,359
41	540	937	18,161	118,161
42	577	900	20,014	120,014
43	616	861	21,919	121,919
44	661	816	23,872	123,872
45	708	769	25,873	125,873
46	762	715	27,917	127,917
47	821	656	30,002	130,002
48	884	593	32,125	132,125
49	954	523	34,280	134,280
50	1028	449	36,465	136,465
51	1108	369	38,675	138,675
52	1194	283	40,906	140,906
53	1285	192	43,153	143,153
54	1385	92	45,407	145,407
55	1492	− 15	47,662	147,662
56	1610	− 133	49,905	149,905
57	1739	− 262	52,125	152,125
58	1882	− 405	54,306	154,306
59	2037	− 560	56,433	156,443
60	2202	− 725	58,498	158,498
61	2378	− 901	60,472	160,472
62	2581	−1104	62,336	162,336
63	2813	−1336	64,050	164,050
64	3081	−1604	65,568	165,568

* The straight life policy premium for the same $100,000 in coverage is assumed to be $1477.

† Savings compounded annually.

that Charlotte and the children could get by if they bought $39,000 more life insurance. Guaranteed renewable and convertible term would cost about $217 for the first year of coverage, and straight life would cost a level premium of about $558.

What Type of Life Insurance to Buy

No matter how much insurance you need, you must also consider what type to buy because they differ in purpose as well as cost. Your values and goals may be very different from the Jacksons', even though your personal situation may be very similar. If you have no children, the amount of insurance needed could be substantially reduced. If the surviving spouse gets a job, the need would be reduced even further. If you have no dependents, you may not need life insurance at all. You yourself must therefore put your own figures on such a form to determine how much insurance you might need. Also, circumstances change, and thus it is wise to reevaluate your life insurance needs every few years.

Basically, the decision of what type of life insurance to buy falls between two choices: (1) Buy term and invest the rest, or (2) buy permanent insurance.

Buy Term and Invest the Rest. A man aged 30 could buy $100,000 in term insurance for about $325 per year, assuming he had a guaranteed renewable policy. A straight life policy for the same person would cost about $1477. The principle underlying "buy term and invest the rest" is simple: If you save or conservatively invest the difference between the cost of term insurance and that of another type of policy, you will *always* be ahead.

For example, look at the first year of the estate build-up as shown in Table 15-8. John buys $100,000 of term insurance for $325 and puts $1152 in the bank, which pays 5 percent interest. Max buys $100,000 of straight life insurance for $1477. If both die at the end of the year, Max's estate is $100,000, and John's is $101,210 because he earned interest on his savings.

If both live, the premium costs of John's term policy go up every year that he renews, while Max's premiums remain level forever. In addition, the permanent insurance builds up cash values, while the term insurance does not. If a financial emergency should arise, John could go to his bank and take out some of the money he has been depositing, while Max could borrow against his cash value (really his own money). Furthermore, at no time between now and the time at which both men are aged 65 will the permanent insurance estate be higher than the one created by purchasing term and investing the rest. As shown in Table 15-8, if John died at age 48, his total estate would be $132,125: $100,000 in life insurance proceeds and $32,125 in savings. Max's death at that age would result in payment of the face amount of the policy, only $100,000.

The *Report on Life Insurance* by Consumers Union shows, in Table 15-9, how the term insurance buyer consistently stays ahead even when the coverage is reduced, since the savings offsets the need for $50,000 in coverage through the years. Calculations are based on

TABLE 15-9

Insurance Cash Values versus Separate Savings at 4 Percent Net* (from Age 25)

Age	Straight Life Policy Cash Value	Separate Savings of Term Policyholder
25	$ 00	$ 429
30	1,200	2,853
35	4,250	5,820
40	8,250	9,265
45	12,800	13,206
50	16,650	17,599
55	20,650	22,443
60	23,700	27,686
65	28,650	33,308

* Both estates kept at $50,000 as the term policyholder kept reducing his coverage.

Source: Report on Life Insurance, rev. ed. (Mt. Vernon, N.Y.: Consumers Union).

premiums for two $50,000 policies from Connecticut General. The cash value built up is based on a straight life nonparticipating policy with an annual outlay of $623.50 bought at age 25. The cost of the 5-year renewable convertible term for the first year was $195.00. The important point here is that the term policyholder kept *reducing* the coverage to maintain an estate balance of $50,000.

If at any point the two policyholders die, the estates are both $50,000. Should they live and cancel the policies at age 65, the cash surrender value would amount to $28,650 for the straight life policyholder compared with $33,308 in cash savings of the term policyholder. Clearly, even with a conservative net return (4 percent on the invested savings, which also allows a cushion to pay income taxes), the term policyholder remains ahead.

All it takes is the self-discipline to save or invest the difference. This can be done by using payroll deductions for savings bonds, automatic transfer from a checking to a savings account, or conservative investments on a regular basis. Mutual funds or more speculative investments may bring an even greater return.

For the term insurance buyer, it is wise to purchase several policies of small denominations. This provides greater flexibility. For example, if children marry and leave home early, or if investments or savings do better than anticipated, the term buyer may want to drop one or more policies.

Buy Permanent Insurance. All types of permanent life insurance—straight life, limited payment, and endowment—have a built-in savings feature. The premiums are two to ten times higher than term insurance, but a cash value begins to accumulate after the first or second year. For those people who find it difficult to invest or save, a permanent type of life insurance policy might be a better alternative. Also, the amount of the premium remains level through the years. Inflation may come, salaries may rise or not, but the premium cost

remains the same. The permanent policy provides coverage forever, while term insurance is usually unavailable after age 65.

Straight life policies have many options available, such as for disability or possible conversion to another form of insurance. Term buyers with a disability waiver of premium clause have the same benefit, but with a cash-value policy the premiums can continue to be paid from the built-up cash value should the policyholder prefer. Furthermore, permanent insurance with a participating feature permits sharing in the company's profits, which can reduce the average year's premium cost. Critics call this a refund for overcharging in the first place, but through years of profitable investments many companies have been able to return considerable dividends to their participating policyholders.

Getting the Best Buy in Life Insurance

Deciding on what you want in life insurance is similar to deciding on what you want in an automobile. Do you buy the big one and get low gas mileage? Do you get the one with the most options? Do you get the one with later high trade-in value? The questions are similar, although the purchases differ. And note that buying the wrong type of life insurance could hurt you financially during your life and provide inadequately for your survivors after you die. The selection process, therefore, must be undertaken carefully.

The convincing conclusions of the Pennsylvania study and of the American Institute for Economic Research show that comparing permanent life insurance policies is very difficult. One could do better financially by purchasing a straight life policy from a highly rated company with a good interest-adjusted cost calculation than by buying an overpriced term policy—that is, if the calculation is valid and not deceptively manipulated.

Consumers living in Massachusetts, New York, and Connecticut can buy limited amounts of extremely low-cost life insurance from mutual savings banks. Savings Bank Life

Insurance (SBLI) is sold only in these states, and the cost is lower mainly because there are no salesperson's commissions to pay.

Other ways to save money in buying the type and amount of insurance to meet your needs include buying group insurance through an employer or through professional and fraternal associations and, if you qualify, buying veteran's insurance. The cost is generally quite low. Finally, there is a best buy for the consumer who wants to *supplement* an insurance program with an accidental life insurance policy. This type of term insurance is extremely inexpensive and also extremely limited, as it pays only if the policyholder dies in an accident (6 percent of all deaths). Keep in mind that if you cancel and surrender a policy during the first few years, particularly a permanent policy, much of the premium has gone for company expenses, and the real cost to you in relationship to the benefits is extremely high. Moreover, you are the only one who can decide on your own personal best buy. Policies that are too expensive, companies that charge high premiums, and policies that have a low true cost can be identified. The rest is up to you.

Choosing a Good Insurance Agent
If you are going to buy life insurance, go with a good agent and company. This is easier said than done, as Herbert S. Denenberg notes in *The Shopper's Guidebook*: "There simply are not enough competent insurance agents to go around." To truly make a best buy in life insurance, you will need the services of more than one competent salesperson in order to assess their competence and the specific policies they are offering.

The agent can help you decide how much insurance you realistically need and can afford, help you decide what kind(s) of policies are best for your circumstances, and provide guidance in selecting beneficiaries and deciding how the proceeds might later accrue to them. The agent should be informed, patient, and willing to answer your questions fully.

A good life insurance agent can help you decide how much insurance you need and can afford and what kinds of policies are best for you. (*Kenneth Karp*)

A list of guidelines for choosing a good insurance agent follows, adapted in part from *The Shopper's Guidebook*.[1] The more "positive" answers, the more likely it is that you are dealing with a good agent.

1. Get a full-time agent with experience, perhaps one with at least 4 years of full-time sales experience in the field. Avoid part-timers who sell insurance as a sideline and "incompetent brothers-in-law" who sell it.
2. Try to get suggestions from people with experience in dealing with insurance agents. Good recommendations might be available from your banker, your lawyer, a businessperson, or an insurance-wise personal friend.

[1] Herbert S. Denenberg, *The Shopper's Guidebook to Life Insurance, Health Insurance, Auto Insurance, Homeowner's Insurance, Doctors, Dentists, Lawyers, Pensions, Etc.* rev. ed. (Washington, D.C.: Consumer News Inc.), pp. 6, 7, 9, 10, 61.

3. Look for agents with special educational and professional qualifications. In particular, look for the initials CLU. They refer to a Chartered Life Underwriter, which is a designation that is supposed to certify that the agent is especially qualified, just like the certification CPA (Certified Public Accountant) is supposed to certify that an accountant is especially qualified. Another but less rigorous schooling program is provided by the Life Underwriter Training Council (LUTC). The National Quality Award (NQA) is given to agents 90 percent of whose policies sold during the second preceding year continue to remain in force. This strongly suggests that the agent very frequently sells contracts of the "right type in the right amount" to customers, or the lapse rate would be much higher.

4. Is the agent connected with a well-established agency?

5. Does the agent (if you have one already) do more each year than just send you a bill? For example, does your agent contact you once a year to see if your insurance program needs to be changed? Keep in mind that this contact should *not* be designed to sell more insurance, but rather to be sure that your insurance needs are still being properly taken care of.

6. Does the agent explain the policies and what they cover?

7. Do you understand what the agent says about the policies and your total insurance program?

8. Does the agent come to you to explain new insurance developments without being asked?

9. Does the agent take the time to carefully consider your overall insurance picture before selling you individual policies? Be aware that it is rarely advantageous to switch policies after they have been in force several years. Regulations in some states require that before you switch

policies, you get an expert opinion in writing from the insurance agent involved that the switch will, in fact, be advantageous. The state insurance commissioner's office then examines these statements for accuracy, and can take disciplinary action if necessary.

10. Does the agent return your calls and answer your correspondence and questions promptly?

11. Does the agent have someone to answer your calls and questions when he or she is not there rather than merely using an answering service or simply letting the telephone ring unanswered?

12. Does the agent explain the difference between the premiums you pay and the actual cost of your life insurance? For example, are you shown the interest-adjusted cost of life insurance that the agent wants to sell you in comparison to that of other policies?

13. Does the agent explain the cost and coverage differences between companies?

14. Does the agent suggest you buy from insurance companies that are strong financially and show you the company's financial rating to prove it? Looking at *Best's Insurance Reports, Life-Health Edition* will show the financial rating of the company. Most experts recommend not buying from any company that is not given one of the two highest of *Best's* four ratings: "most substantial" or "very substantial."

15. Is the agent a member of a professional trade association that can help agents stay up to date on developments and subject them to higher standards of performance? An example is the National Association of Life Underwriters (NALU).

16. Does the agent participate in some of the continuing education activities for agents?

17. Test the agents yourself. If they cannot communicate well with you and answer questions to your satisfaction, shop elsewhere.

CONSUMER RIGHTS AND RESPONSIBILITIES

Consumers' responsibilities in buying life insurance are much the same as in other consumer purchases. With life insurance in particular, however, one needs to carefully assess the Social Security benefits with the help of the Social Security Administration, not just of a life insurance company which might understate benefits. Also, it is imperative that beneficiaries be notified that they are indeed beneficiaries. Many millions of dollars each year never reach the intended beneficiaries because of difficulties in locating and contacting them. Moreover, the responsibilities of consumers in life insurance in general run parallel in that every right carries with it some responsibilities.

Several rights of consumers are noted below as adapted from Denenberg's *The Shopper's Guidebook*:

1. Policyholders have the right to competitive pricing practices and to marketing methods that let them determine the best value among comparable policies.
2. Policyholders have the right to fair access to insurance coverage they need and want.
3. Policyholders, and women in particular, have the right to premiums that reflect risks fairly and that are not based on sex.
4. Policyholders have the right to obtain comprehensive coverage with a minimum of gimmicks and exclusions.
5. Policyholders who are women have the right to fair and nonsexist treatment by agents, brokers, and claims representatives in their right to buy insurance and qualify for coverage regardless of marital status, and in settlement of claims.
6. Policyholders have the right to insurance advertising and other selling approaches that give accurate and balanced information on the benefits and limitations of a policy.
7. Policyholders have a right to an insurance company that is financially stable and efficiently and honestly managed.
8. Policyholders have the right to be serviced by a competent, honest insurance agent or broker.
9. Policyholders have a right to privacy in the claims process, the underwriting process, and other aspects of insurance-industry operations.
10. Policyholders have the right to insurance policies that they can read and understand.
11. Policyholders have the right to insurance laws that are written by the legislature for the people, not for the insurance industry.
12. Policyholders have the right to government regulation that serves policyholders first instead of insurance companies and that tries to bring about all these other rights.

POINTS OF VIEW AND PROBLEMS TO THINK ABOUT

Why not rename this whole *life* insurance industry the *death* insurance industry? Let us put the proper label on the product—the companies sell death insurance.

More seriously, however, a question of primary importance is, "Why must insurance policies be so hard to compare?" Much can be done to simplify comparison shopping, but the industry discourages such efforts. For example, the industry stopped many states from selling Savings Bank Life Insurance (SBLI). SBLI was created more than 70 years ago for the express purpose of providing low-cost insurance. After Massachusetts, New York, and Connecticut passed such programs, the insurance lobby successfully discouraged other states from legislating similar plans. More recently, life insurance cost-disclosure regulations for consumers have been watered down through industry pressures so that the state regulations (like in New Jersey and in Iowa) really have little value for the consumer who needs to compare policies or companies.

State insurance regulations are woefully inadequate across the nation with but a few exceptions like California and New York. In the past decade more than 100 companies went bankrupt. The Equity Funding Life Insurance Company, described by *Best's* as "composed of capable and experienced insurance executives," was revealed to have been writing billions of dollars of fictitious insurance policies (over 60,000) before being discovered and going under. It was a paper empire created by the company with phony policyholders.

Most state insurance commissions lack the authority to get information from the companies in order to make more informed judgments; they also very frequently lack careful regulatory authority. For example, old policyholders too often get the short end of the stick when it comes to premium changes that are permitted or not regulated by state insurance commissions. Giving premium discounts to new policyholders, as noted earlier, keeps the older policyholders from sharing in present-day higher investment yields. Perhaps regulators should consider a ban on the use of the investment-year method of calculating dividends. This technique, as well as some others, are effectively eliminating the value of the interest-adjusted index method of comparing policies. Even more unfortunate among older policyholders are those receiving premium increases of up to 300 percent! This sometimes occurs when one firm, like First Republic Life Insurance Company, buys out another company, such as National American Life Insurance Company. Older policyholders have too much invested (in cash value and/or insurability) to be forced to drop their coverage, so they must pay the increases.

States with reputations for particularly weak insurance supervision, as noted by John F. Berry, a *Washington Post* staff writer, include Arizona, Texas, Oklahoma, Mississippi, Florida, and Louisiana. In Oklahoma, and in several other states, all it takes to begin an insurance company is money. With $500,000 down you can start selling insurance policies.

"The fact you don't know anything about insurance doesn't make any difference," according to the general counsel of the Oklahoma Insurance Department, Mark Hain. An expensive outcome is that when one company goes bankrupt, it has a ripple effect throughout the industry because of the reinsurance treaties among companies; they share the risks further by buying the policies of other companies. And since most states have laws that require financially healthy companies to pay the claims of those going bankrupt, the costs are always passed on in the form of increased premiums. A management consulting firm, McKinsey & Company, noted in a report that "77 percent of the life insurance companies that became insolvent during the past decade got that way because of dishonesty by management." Surely some improved regulatory apparatus, either state or federal, could be developed to root out some of these problems.

The mortality tables used to set rates are extremely old, and they are somewhat inflated to cover for losses. Yet these are the tables from which the companies begin the process of establishing their premiums. At the same time, conclusive evidence shows that nonsmokers live longer than others. Why don't special policies and premium costs reflect these mortality rates?

One costly and almost useless insurance-industry process is that of investigative reports. When someone applies for life insurance, the insurance company frequently hires an investigative firm to find out more about that person. Presumably this helps them avoid the "worst risks." By law, the company must notify you of the existence of such an investigation. Under the Fair Credit Reporting Act, you have the right to find out the "substance" of the investigative report and request reverification of findings you believe questionable. You do not, however, have the right to know the source of any particular negative comments. And even though the act requires that life insurance companies inform consumers of such reports, one Federal Trade Commission study showed that 40 percent of the industry did not do so.

The investigators question neighbors, friends, acquaintances, and business associates. The validity of the information, as you might suspect, is sometimes questionable. Another important point is that many dollars are spent on thousands of these useless investigations. A consumer who has some kind of "bad mark" in private life and cannot be insured by one company must turn to another. In the field of automobile insurance, the consumer may wind up paying higher rates; in the field of life insurance, the consumer may not be able to be insured at all, or will have to pay higher than normal rates. Thus, this consumer is often forced out of the traditional market and must seek a limited amount of group coverage elsewhere. All insurance buyers pay for these investigations through higher premiums.

As originally conceived, the Social Security system was intended to provide low-cost government insurance for workers in their old age. Now the tax has turned out to be highly regressive. It takes a disproportionate amount of the paycheck of low- and middle-income workers. A person earning $17,700 this year pays the same Social Security tax as does the person earning $75,000. And further inequities occur. The part-time retired worker can earn a maximum of up to $3000 in 1982 to supplement the meager Social Security payments; after that point benefits are reduced. Yet the person who has income from savings interest, investment dividends, and private insurance proceeds totaling perhaps thousands of dollars still receives the full retirement benefits. The system today reflects many of the inequities it was designed to get rid of. It relies heavily upon the middle-income worker for funding, and provides benefits that are insufficient for some yet perhaps too ample for others.

Furthermore, the spiraling costs of programs under Social Security place the responsibility of funding upon today's *and* tomorrow's workers. When they eventually retire, hopefully there will be other workers paying for *their* retirement, or perhaps the system itself will be changed. The Social Security program is basically solvent, but not enough people realize that forecasts of upcoming expenditures are far beyond anticipated tax revenues. Under present law, the tax on annual earnings can creep up to $85,200 by the year 2014, meaning a payroll tax of $5581 for each employee! Who is going to pay the bill? Responsible consumers must ask their congressional representatives why Social Security taxes are rising so fast. And what can be done about them?

CHAPTER ACTIVITIES

Checkup on Consumer Terms and Concepts

Premium cost	Annuity
Life insurance	Group insurance
Mortality rate	Settlement options
Term life insurance	Participating
Straight life	policyholder
insurance	Net cost of insurance
Limited-payment life	Interest-adjusted
insurance	index method
Endowment life	Currently insured
insurance	(Social Security)
Guaranteed	Policy assignment
renewable	Promissory note
Permanent life	SBLI
insurance	Social Security
Convertible	inequities
Face value	

Review of Essentials

1. Give some reasons why many people consider life insurance a necessity.
2. Explain what "probability of life" means, using the mortality table for examples.
3. Give an example of how decreasing term insurance works if the insured is aged 20.
4. Explain why the two basic types of life insurance charge different premiums.

5. Differentiate between a retirement income life insurance policy and an annuity.

6. What are the primary disadvantages of family-income and family-maintenance policies?

7. Explain and give examples of the types of items that go into setting the premium cost for a permanent insurance policy.

8. Contrast the value to the consumer of the net-cost and the interest-adjusted index methods of calculating the real cost of life insurance.

9. What kind of Social Security benefits might a young worker expect should he die prematurely, leaving behind a wife and a child? How much might his survivors expect to get?

10. Generally, what kinds of people probably need little or no life insurance?

11. Describe three examples of deceptive sales practices in the life insurance industry.

12. What type(s) of life insurance amounting to $39,000 would you recommend for the Henry Jackson family? Why?

13. Do you think it advisable for people to "buy term and invest the rest"? Why or why not?

14. List some sources that might be available to help you decide your best buy in life insurance.

Issues for Analysis

1. Develop an argument for or against prohibiting stock insurance companies from selling life insurance. Remember, stock companies are like any profit-making corporation where the profits go the stockholders, but mutual companies are run for the benefit of policyholders.

2. What are your views on the aspects of the present Social Security system that are similar to life insurance? Should any changes be made? If so, what do you suggest?

3. React to insurance expert Jean M. Vogel's statement that "In the absence of federal authority in life insurance regulation, state insurance commissioners have been conspicuously negligent in noticing the mounting evidence that consumers were choosing policies in a vacuum of information."

16

Local, State, and Federal Taxes

THE PROBLEMS

Taxes take about 37 cents of every dollar of the consumer's income, and the federal government receives approximately two-thirds of that. The remaining one-third goes to the states and the more than 80,000 local taxing agencies. An employed person works 2 hours and 42 minutes of an 8-hour day to pay for taxes. On a calendar basis, people work from January 1 to May 4 to pay federal, state, and local taxes. While the cost of living has been steadily increasing, the typical family's total tax bill has been rising approximately 50 percent faster than prices in general. And taxes are still rising!

Many factors are behind the increases in taxes. There has been a steady growth in the demand for more government services. Elected officials who depend on public support for reelection often press for programs their constituents want. And many vested-interest groups seek special consideration and lobby to protect themselves when tax laws are drafted.

The end result is an extremely complex set of systems of taxation riddled with inequities. The U.S. Tax Code alone is 6000 pages of very small print, not to mention the laws and regulations of the many state and local taxing jurisdictions. Another result is waste and inefficiency.

The "overburdened" taxpayer—the consumer—is more and more voicing concern about our tax systems. Questions are being asked. Are we getting a fair return on our tax dollar? What are our priority needs for government services? Do we really need more than 1000 different federal programs aimed at shifting income from some people to benefits for others? How can we control the tremendous growth in government employees? (One out of every six working Americans is employed at some level of government.) How can governments budget more wisely for authorized programs? How can we get rid of the inequities in different taxing systems? What can be done to eliminate ineffective government services? What can be done to slow the steady rise in taxes? What can be done to simplify the filling out of tax forms?

Elected officials, businesspersons, and consumers will be confronted with questions such as these from now on. To deal with them effectively, all parties, especially consumers, must become more informed about the issues.

THE NEED FOR TAXES

Oliver Wendell Holmes once said, "Taxes are what we pay for civilized society." In other words, we "buy" civilization when we pay taxes. Obviously, without taxes we could not have the educational, economic, and social programs that have the potential to deal with problems that could not be handled otherwise.

Taxes are compulsory charges imposed by elected officials upon citizens and/or their property for public purposes. The early settlers paid taxes based upon their occupation. The English Stamp Act and the Tea Act that followed are examples of early customs taxes that were levied without representation—the taxes were paid to the British. After the American Revolution, the democratic system of government emerged; the people wanted a representative government solely to serve the people. Few federal taxes were imposed during those formative years. Customs taxes on imported goods provided enough funds. Local taxes remained quite low, as the early consumers did not expect or get much in the way of public services.

By 1895, several federal excise taxes and fees were being imposed. A direct income tax was legislated in both 1861 and 1894, only to be declared unconstitutional by the U.S. Supreme Court. In 1913, the sixteenth amendment to the Constitution was ratified by the states. It contained the significant words, "The Congress shall have power to lay and collect taxes on incomes, from whatever source derived, without apportionment among the several states, and without regard to any census or enumeration." These few words authorized the federal government to fund the expenses of wars and the extraordinary costs of the social programs that were to follow.

Political planners and decision makers discovered that taxes influenced the health of the economy. Raising taxes on the local or national level "dampened down" personal and corporate spending and raised the cost of borrowing money. Conversely, reducing taxes spurred on or "heated up" the economy and increased the money in circulation. More spending occurs especially when reduced taxes are accompanied by consumer confidence in the economy. Thus, increasing or decreasing taxes plays a strong role in the regulation of the economy.

TYPES OF TAXATION

Local, state, and federal taxes are classified according to how they are levied, or paid, and by the relationship of the tax to the taxpayer's income or ability to pay. Let us consider some of these points, as illustrated in Table 16-1.

Direct and Indirect Taxation

Taxes are paid either directly or indirectly. A *direct* tax is paid directly to the government agency that levies it. When you report your annual income and settle with the Internal Revenue Service, for example, you are paying a direct tax. An *indirect* tax is collected by someone other than a government agency. A sales tax is indirect. It is added to the cost of goods and services and is later returned to the appropriate government agency by the business making the sale.

Progressive and Regressive Taxation

The relationship of the tax to the taxpayer's income or ability to pay is called progressive or regressive. A *progressive* tax is one in which the rate increases with the ability to pay. The federal income tax is a progressive tax. A person earning $14,000 may pay a tax rate of 17 percent after allowable deductions, exemptions and exclusions. Another person earning $30,000 may pay a rate of 22 percent. The rate is progressively higher for those with higher incomes.

A *regressive* tax is one in which the rate decreases or remains constant as the ability to pay increases. Obviously, such a tax tends to take proportionately more from those with lower incomes. The state sales tax is an exam-

Drawing by H. Martin; © 1969 The New Yorker Magazine, Inc.

"For want of a better word, I call my idea 'taxes.' And here's the way it works."

TABLE 16-1

Classifications and General Characteristics of Taxes

Progressive Direct	Regressive Direct	Regressive Indirect
Federal	State	Federal
Personal income	Personal property	Import duties
Estate and gift	Real property	Excise taxes
Corporate	Motor vehicle licenses	Business taxes
State	Business licenses	Value-added taxes
Personal income	Business permits	Social Security
Estate and gift	Local	Unemployment
Corporate	Personal property	State
Local	Real property	Excise taxes
Personal income	Business licenses	Sales taxes
	Business permits	Value-added taxes
	Home alteration or addition permit	Unemployment
	Personal licenses (dogs and marriage)	Local
	Motor vehicle stickers	Sales taxes
	Mobile home tax	Value-added taxes

ple. Each consumer pays the same rate, regardless of ability to pay. Whether a person has a monthly income of $1000 or $600, if a $300 stereo is purchased and the sales tax is 5 percent, the amount will be $15. While the actual tax dollars are the same, the person earning $1000 monthly pays 1.5 percent of that income, while the person with the $600 income pays 2.5 percent—almost twice as much. With this type of tax, it is the less affluent consumer who must spend the greater percentage of income for the same fairly standard items bought by much of the population.

SOURCES AND USES OF TAX DOLLARS

Federal, state, and local governments require a wide range of taxes for their needed revenue. In the main, federal revenue comes from income taxes. Most state revenue comes from sales taxes, and most local revenue comes from federal and state aid and from property taxes. For a better understanding of the financial problems facing the several levels of government, let us examine the sources and uses of tax dollars and the resulting benefits.

Federal Taxes

Federal taxes have increased dramatically in recent decades. In 1940, the federal government collected $8.4 billion, or about 10 percent of the national income. In 1950, it rose to $49 billion, or about 20 percent; in 1960, it collected $94 billion, or about 23 percent; in 1970, about $189 billion, or 24 percent; and in 1980 it is expected to amount to $500 billion, or 25 percent. Projections indicate that the percentage in future years will not exceed 25 percent. This is based on the expectation that national income itself will rise, and that state and local taxes will increase as more and more services are administered at those levels.

The sources and uses of federal tax dollars for a recent year can be seen in Figure 16-1. Sixty-six cents of each tax dollar comes from the people through individual income taxes, social insurances taxes and contributions, and

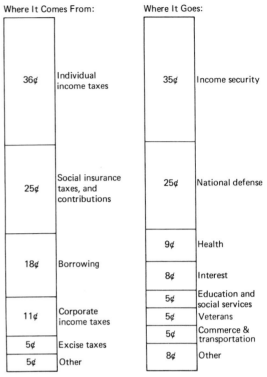

Where It Comes From:

36¢	Individual income taxes
25¢	Social insurance taxes, and contributions
18¢	Borrowing
11¢	Corporate income taxes
5¢	Excise taxes
5¢	Other

Where It Goes:

35¢	Income security
25¢	National defense
9¢	Health
8¢	Interest
5¢	Education and social services
5¢	Veterans
5¢	Commerce & transportation
8¢	Other

Source: Internal Revenue Service

FIGURE 16-1   Sources and uses of federal tax dollars

excise taxes. Fifty-four percent of the expenditures are for "human resources," including income security (welfare), health, education and social services, and benefits for veterans.

More often than not the federal government spends more money than it takes in; this is called *deficit spending*. This means that the government borrows money, just as consumers do when they are short of cash. It does this by selling bonds—to businesses, other governments, and individuals. Large deficits of $30 or $60 billion occur when the federal government chooses to meet its needs through borrowing as a source of revenue (18 percent in Figure 16-2) instead of increasing taxes. The *national debt,* the total amount of authorized federal borrowing, is approaching $1 trillion and is the result of deficit spending. Of course,

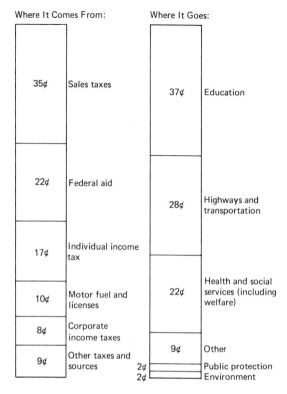

Where It Comes From:

35¢ Sales taxes

22¢ Federal aid

17¢ Individual income tax

10¢ Motor fuel and licenses

8¢ Corporate income taxes

9¢ Other taxes and sources

Where It Goes:

37¢ Education

28¢ Highways and transportation

22¢ Health and social services (including welfare)

9¢ Other

2¢ Public protection

2¢ Environment

Amounts are generalized for a "typical" state

FIGURE 16-2   Sources and uses of state tax dollars

the government must pay interest on the debt (8 percent of all expenditures in Figure 16-1).

State Taxes

State and local governments combined receive about one-third of all tax dollars. And over the past decade, state and local revenues have doubled as a percentage of the gross national product (GNP), reflecting a greater influence of these governments in almost all expenditure areas.

The sources and uses of state tax dollars differ from state to state. Historically, the sales tax has usually been the largest source of revenue, although the state income tax has been growing in importance. Together, the two forms of taxes amount to about one-half of the typical state's revenue, as shown in Figure 16-2.

Federal funds amount to nearly one-fourth of the revenue of most states. Federal *grants-in-aid* are monies for special programs and projects, frequently in the form of joint state and federal financing of such specific programs as rapid transit systems, highway construction, unemployment benefits, welfare, and education. Other federal funds come as *revenue sharing,* which is basically a "no strings attached" program where the states can spend the funds on just about any project they feel is worthy. These latter funds are often used to reduce other taxes on the residents of the states. Other sources of state revenue include taxes on gasoline, liquor, cigarettes, estates, personal property, and gifts. Money also comes from state-owned or state-regulated industries, licenses, and lotteries.

Expenditures are increasing annually because of demands for greater financial assistance, particularly for education, welfare, and transportation. Figure 16-2 shows that 87 percent of a typical state's tax dollar is spent on education, highways and transportation, and health and social services (including welfare).

Local Taxes

About one-sixth of all taxes paid by consumers go to their local governments. These commonly include cities, counties, townships, and numerous special agencies such as junior colleges, regional libraries, bridges, and sanitary landfills. As local governments provide more and more services, it is no wonder that local taxes have increased more than 150 percent over the past decade. The typical family of four pays more than $1000 a year in local taxes.

The largest single source of local revenue is money from the federal and state governments, as shown in Figure 16-3. Funds to help build roads and pay for social services often come to local governments. The next biggest source of revenue is the real estate property tax, which is based on an assessment of the value of buildings and land. Because property taxes are especially regressive, communities are increasingly seeking out

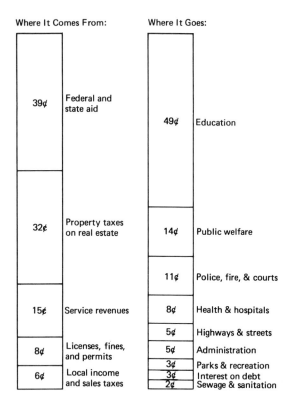

Where It Comes From:

39¢ Federal and state aid

32¢ Property taxes on real estate

15¢ Service revenues

8¢ Licenses, fines, and permits

6¢ Local income and sales taxes

Where It Goes:

49¢ Education

14¢ Public welfare

11¢ Police, fire, & courts

8¢ Health & hospitals

5¢ Highways & streets

5¢ Administration

3¢ Parks & recreation

3¢ Interest on debt

2¢ Sewage & sanitation

*Amounts are generalized for a "typical" local municipality or city.

FIGURE 16-3 Sources and uses of local tax dollars

other sources of revenue, such as local income and sales taxes. More than 6000 cities and towns have some form of income tax that is their most important source of revenue. New York City, Philadelphia, Columbus, Toledo, and Louisville, for example have a city income tax.

The major share of local funds goes for education. New equipment, increased pay for teachers and other school personnel, and a demand for more effective education has placed an increasingly heavy financial burden on local officials. It is no wonder that communities are looking to state and federal governments to share this expense. State supreme courts, such as those in California and New Jersey, are ruling that *all* students must be given equal-dollar-value education, regardless

of the ability of the local community to pay. Historically, it has not been uncommon to find one school district spending $860 per pupil per year, while another, more affluent district nearby spent $3800. Thus, the states are developing systems to equalize the amounts spent to educate young people in all communities, regardless of the local tax base.

Public welfare is an increasingly larger share of local expenditures, and growing rapidly. New York City, teetering on the edge of bankruptcy, spends more than 22 percent of its local revenues for welfare.

Services Rendered by Government Taxes

Living in a society with more than 220 million people is expensive. The Organization for Economic Co-operation and Development (OECD), in Paris, reports that all taxes take 28.9 cents out of each dollar of the gross national product in the United States. They take even more from our counterparts in most other industrial countries: Sweden, 50.9 cents; Netherlands, 46.4 cents; Norway, 45.3 cents; France, 39.1 cents; West Germany, 36.0 cents; and Canada, 35.4 cents. Citizens of Japan (21.3 cents) and Spain (20.3 cents) pay less. Frequently, in the countries where a higher percentage of tax is collected, the governments provide more services, such as the nearly free health care in most Western European countries. However, this information does not mean much to American consumers who see their tax bills rising year after year. This brings up the question, "What are we getting for our tax dollars?"

Imagine what life would be like without taxes. You would certainly have more money, but your real income and your quality of life would drop drastically! Without tax money, government workers would not be paid and the country would be faced with an unemployment problem of gigantic proportions, since one out of every six workers is a government employee. Without tax funds, there would not be public schools or colleges. There would not be police or fire protection or even a postal service. Streets and highways would fall into disrepair. The subsidized railroads and airlines would go out of business or else increase fares to the point where few could afford them. Parks and recreation areas would go untended. All water, food, drug, health, and safety regulations would cease to be enforced. Street lights and electric power in many areas would be discontinued. Sewers would block up from lack of maintenance. Some pension plans and the Social Security benefits of millions of Americans would no longer exist. Many hospitals would close, and only a few consumers could afford those that managed to stay open. The welfare system would disappear, leaving one out of every ten households with no income. Day-care centers for young children and food programs for the elderly would cease to exist. The court and prison systems would break down, and crime would go unchecked. Government-sponsored and government-funded programs for energy research, the preservation of natural resources, soil conservation, community development, housing facilities, and national defense would all be discontinued.

It is safe to conclude that life in America would not be acceptable without taxes. Obviously, the consumer gets quite a bit from those tax dollars.

NEW SOURCES OF REVENUE

The increasing needs of a growing population are being met by ever-greater government spending. At all levels of government, most conventional methods of taxing appear to be reaching a danger point—there is some fear of a "taxpayer revolt." When taxes rise faster than personal incomes, for example, consumers have less to spend, and this can cause severe trouble in the economy as well as in consumer confidence. To offset potential problems, consumers, businesspersons, and elected officials must jointly analyze existing tax programs and find more acceptable ways of getting needed revenues, such as those discussed below.

Among the many services paid for by taxes are public schools, police and fire protection, enforcement of traffic laws, and street and highway maintenance. (*Guy Debaud*)

Grants-in-Aid

Grants-in-aid are joint financial ventures of the federal government and individual states and localities. Monies granted are restricted. For example, if a state wants to build a 20-mile, four-lane highway, the federal government may pay 90 percent of the cost and the state the remaining 10 percent. But a grant received from a federal agency for such a project must be spent on that project and nothing else.

There have been more grants-in-aid in recent years, owing to the efforts of Congress to deal with problems that extend beyond the boundaries of any one state or locality and that exceed local resources. The federal government appropriates billions of dollars for these programs. Funds in a recent year (in descending amounts of dollars given) went to programs for the aged, the disabled, welfare families, highways, food stamps, elementary and secondary school education, poverty programs, urban renewal, water-treatment facilities, job training, unemployment pay, school lunches and milk, low-rent housing, vocational rehabilitation, school aid in federally affected areas, vocational education, hospital and health research, and the distribution of farm surpluses.

Revenue Sharing

Federal revenue sharing means returning tax revenue to the states and localities without imposing restrictions on how the money must be spent. Thus, revenue sharing has basically "no strings attached," and this lets the receivers spend the money where it is needed most—according to their own priorities. Congress authorizes about $6 billion in such funds annually.

Complex formulas are used to decide how much each state and locality receives. States and localities with relatively low levels of personal income need more federal revenue than others. However, places with relatively high tax burdens suggest that they are already vigorously trying to finance their own public programs. Hence, the largest share of the money is channeled into heavily populated industrial states and large cities. Therefore, those states and localities with high personal incomes and low tax levels in relation to their income are subsidizing other areas of the country.

Tax Loopholes

Every year or two, Congress passes a new "tax reform act" which is intended to make tax laws more fair and less complicated, and reduce waste. To be sure, some of these ends are approached, but only slightly. Tax loopholes probably receive the most attention, perhaps undeservingly. Tax loopholes such as individuals being able to deduct interest and taxes on their real estate property from their federal tax liability were put there deliberately. They serve specific purposes, either encouraging some types of activities or permitting relief to groups of taxpayers. In this example, the purpose is to encourage home ownership.

No doubt there are many good reasons for the tax loopholes or expenditures, but there are two areas in particular that seem to get plenty of attention: wealthy individuals and some corporations. In a recent year, 244 people who reported gross incomes of more than $200,000 paid no federal income taxes; 13 of them earned more than $1,000,000. Corporations are sometimes good at escaping taxes, too. Representative Charles Vanik reports annually on which corporations paid little or no income taxes to the federal government. In a recent year, 11 major corporations with earnings in excess of $1 billion paid no federal taxes: Ford Motor Company, Delta Air Lines, Northwest Airlines, Chemical New York Corporation, Manufacturer's Hanover Corporation, Western Electric Company, Bethlehem Steel Corporation, Lockheed Aircraft Corporation, National Steel Corporation, Phelps-Dodge, and Freeport Minerals. And 27 other firms paid less than 10 percent in taxes, including American Telephone & Telegraph (2.4 percent), Mobil Oil Corporation (1.8 percent), Gulf Oil Company (6.0 percent), Texaco, Incorporated (9.2 percent), and Citibank (6.7 percent, and it is the second largest bank in the country).

Corporations, by law, pay a maximum federal tax rate of 48 percent on their earnings, but many avoid taxes through legal loopholes, or as Vanik says, "the myriad of exemptions, deductions and credits that have turned the tax code into a paradise of loopholes." These revelations may be shocking, but whether they are unfair is another question.

Most state and city income taxes have been patterned after the federal regulations. Mrs. Donna Heim, a Californian, wrote to her governor and complained that her taxes were too low. She paid a federal tax of $967, but after taking advantage of the exemptions, deductions, and exclusions available in California, her state tax came to $4. "This I consider an outrage," wrote Mrs. Heim. "And if our federal tax is that high, there's something terribly wrong about paying only $4 to the state, which provides me with all kinds of services and is in such terrible shape financially." Do you believe her point is good?

A National Value-Added Tax

A proposed source of new tax revenue has been labeled VAT, for value-added tax. It would be a national sales tax, and regressive. Unfortunately, the sales tax feature of the value-added tax would also be hidden. A flat amount would be added to the cost of a product at every stage of its production or distribution, and each processor would pay a tax directly to the government for the value added. The end result would be multiple taxes paid all along the production route, with the consumer repaying the entire tax in the form of a higher list price. And state and local sales taxes, of course, would then be added to the final price of the item.

The concept of a value-added tax is not new. Several European countries have used it for many years. And in this country, it is common to pass on the cost of business taxes to consumers in the form of higher prices.

Proponents of the value-added tax suggest that some products and services be excluded from the VAT, making it less regressive. Tax credits or cash refunds at the end of the year have also been proposed to reduce its regressiveness. Some surveys indicate that 30 percent of the people would prefer this method of increasing taxes. Politicians in favor of such a tax argue that it will be painless and easy to collect.

Critics suggest that if the government wants a national sales tax, it should simply add one. While it would still be regressive, it would be more efficient, and the objectionable concealment feature could be eliminated.

Lotteries

Gambling in general and lotteries in particular are another form of revenue for states and cities. More than two-thirds of the states permit some form of legalized gambling, ranging from the slot-machine "one-armed bandits" to bingo to off-track betting. Sixteen states have lotteries which gross over $2 billion annually. In each instance, the state gets a share of the revenue, through licensing and/or a percentage of the sales. Earmarking the revenues

from such sources for a specific purpose, such as education, roads, or the elderly, usually pushes the moral issue of gambling aside in the minds of the public. Unfortunately, this source of revenue is regressive, since low- and middle-income consumers are most likely to gamble.

Generally, about 40 percent of the lottery revenue goes for prizes, 15 percent for operating expenses, and 45 percent for the state. The New York lottery accounts for only one-half of 1 percent of that state's total revenues. The Federal Commission on the Review of National Policy Toward Gambling concluded in part that even if all states legalized all the various types of gambling, the net take from legalized gambling would amount to only 4 percent of total revenues.

Apparently lotteries can raise some money, and part of the reason is that two out of every three Americans gamble each year. It was once thought that legalizing gambling would suppress illegal gambling, but studies have shown just the opposite. The University of Michigan Survey Research Center conducted a national study on gambling and found that legalized gambling stimulates illegal gambling. The legal wagering in New York at an off-track betting parlor, for example, attracts *new* gamblers. Many of them then wind up placing bets with the neighborhood bookie who offers more pleasant surroundings in which to wager, accepts telephone bets, and offers wagering on other sporting events, easy credit, and tax-free payoffs.

Putting People to Work

One very important source of revenue is having people working and paying taxes. A person who is unemployed and receiving public assistance is a drain on the taxing agencies. A person who is employed can pay in taxes. Hence, getting people off the unemployment rolls and into jobs is a priority item in raising revenues.

Until recently, a greatly overlooked segment of our population in terms of employment has been the disabled. More than 50 million Americans have some physical impairment, with one out of every eleven adults having either total or partial work disabilities. The federally funded Rehabilitation Services Administration places high priority on helping the disabled become productive, tax-paying members of society.

Besides the humane values involved, it's good economics. Putting $1000 into rehabilitative medical care for the disabled returns $9000 to the economy. This 9 to 1 return reflects the taxes paid by the disabled person returning to the work force, the halt of social welfare assistance, and, of course, the multiplier effect of the dollars in the economy earned and spent by the individual.

PROBLEMS OF WASTE AND INEFFICIENCY

Inefficiency in government management of tax revenue is evident in many areas, such as direct subsidies, general waste, corruption, and tax evasion.

Direct Subsidies

Americans receive over $120 billion annually in direct subsidies, according to a staff report of the Congressional Joint Economic Committee. Such subsidies are sometimes referred to as "assistance," "incentive," or "expenditures in the national interest." Examples are cited below:

- *Cash subsidies* to build and operate ships; encourage farmers to produce or not produce crops; urge students to go to college; persuade businesses to hire certain kinds of workers. The cost to taxpayers is $20 billion a year.
- *Tax subsidies* are provided to encourage persons to stay in the military; to promote the use of certain natural resources; to stimulate the purchase of heavy machinery; to encourage home ownership. The cost to taxpayers is $76 billion a year.
- *Credit subsidies* are provided to farmers; to facilitate rural electrical service; to aid small businesspersons; to research

weapons systems; and other such ventures. The cost to taxpayers is $10 billion a year.
- *Benefit in kind subsidies* provide goods and services at reduced prices, such as postal services, airport and airway facilities, railroads, public housing, and food. The cost to the taxpayer is $20 billion a year.

These subsidies are controversial, especially in times of taxpayer resistance to increased taxes. Subsidies of this magnitude are a problem area for the government, particularly when the real value or true economic impact is frequently not substantiated. The government has not fully applied its facilities to instigate cost-benefit analyses and to report on the merits and demerits of its subsidies. To counter this lack, consumers need to ask themselves and their elected representatives how much value they are getting for each subsidy dollar.

General Waste

There are many cases of government waste and inefficiency. Roads, sewers, and public parks often suffer from lack of maintenance because of nonproductive work crews. Fraudulent welfare claims are uncovered daily, and it is estimated that as much as 10 to 40 percent of such funds goes to unqualified people. Productivity is low at city, township, county, state, and federal levels, owing, in part, to duplication of effort and responsibilities.

Patronage appointments and *double-dipping* are other wasteful practices. Patronage workers are generally those who campaigned for an elected official; they are rewarded with a job for which they are unqualified or which they simply do not perform. In the Chicago Parks and Recreation Department, a study by the independent Better Government Association revealed that about three-fourths of the play areas for children were locked up because those responsible for their operation were never there.

Double-dipping is receiving two government paychecks at the same time. One flagrant example of this practice is the case of an Illinois representative who drew $20,000 a year as a Chicago vehicle inspector and $17,500 a year for his legislative position. Such practices are *not* outlawed in most states. Another form of double-dipping involves those who are retired and drawing a pension from one federal job, but who work for another government agency. One patrol officer–dispatcher for the District of Columbia retired as a patrol officer after 20 years. His earlier income was $18,562, and he retired with a pension of $10,764. Shortly after retirement, he was hired back as a civilian dispatcher at a salary of $14,431—including retirement, a 22 percent increase over his original salary. Civil Service Commission study showed that more than 150,000 federal workers were retired from the military. No one is sure how many nonmilitary government retirees are working for other government agencies at the local, state, and federal levels.

Another practice of many government agencies is to deposit money in banks that do not pay interest. Such waste—a loss of interest income. Laws normally do not tell officials how and where public money is to be managed and safeguarded. Yet a bank holding $30 million in collected taxes for 3 months can earn $450,000 simply by reinvesting the money in government bonds paying 6 percent interest. It is no wonder that some allege that this sometimes happens because of political favors owed bankers by certain public officials.

Corruption

Exposure of corruption by officeholders is on the rise, and every conviction both shatters and restores faith in government. More than one incumbent politician has used public funds for printing reelection posters, for mailing reelection literature, and for travel and entertainment expenses not related to official duties. Rigged bidding on state contracts is another corrupt practice. Collusion between a government representative and a businessperson involving contract specifica-tions or the cost of goods or services results in budget overruns and reduced government efficiency.

Underassessment of land and building values is perhaps the most flagrant type of corruption practiced by local officials. Through undercover arrangement, many properties are grossly underassessed. The resulting lost tax revenue must be made up by higher tax rates somewhere else. The Chicago O'Hare Hilton, connected to the airport, was under construction for 2 years "before anyone noticed that it was not being assessed property taxes." In the same city, pressure from investigative news reporters caused a threefold increase in the tax assessment of the 110-story-tall John Hancock Center.

More than 1000 officials ranging from former Vice President Spiro Agnew to county sheriffs have been convicted of violating the public trust in the past 10 years. Bribery, kickbacks, extortion, and similar schemes often seem too common. Illinois and New Jersey seem particularly vulnerable, as federal prosecutions in those states have been quite high. Convicted in New Jersey recently: ten mayors, two state treasurers, a secretary of state, a former state party chairperson, a member of Congress, a speaker of the state assembly, two judges, and several other political leaders. No fewer than thirteen members of Congress have been convicted of violating federal laws in recent years. Maryland's former governor, Marvin Mandel, was convicted on mail fraud and racketeering charges while still in office. Former federal Appeals Court Judge Otto Kerner was convicted of mail fraud and tax evasion in a race-track scandal which occurred while he was the governor of Illinois.

The conviction rate of the federal prosecutors is above 80 percent, and with the rise in the number of investigations, this should serve as a stiff warning to those in or seeking public office. The American people want and demand honesty in their public officials. To accept anything less would waste taxpayers' dollars and reflect declining moral values.

the small society

WHAT'S THE STANDARD AMOUNT TO GIVE?

FIGHT CANCER

THE SAME AMOUNT YOU DEDUCT—

© Washington Star Syndicate, permission granted by King Features Syndicate, Inc. 1971–72.

Tax Evasion by Business

The IRS has uncovered many schemes involving illegal kickbacks and payoffs. Former IRS head Johnnie M. Walters summarized the concern by noting that, "It is astounding that large publicly held corporations engage in such schemes." Tax evasion and illegal slush funds for political contributions by corporations have been too well documented in recent years.

In the 1970s it was revealed that more than 200 corporations had made illegal contributions to various political campaigns. Former Gulf Oil Corporation lobbyist Claude C. Wild, Jr., for example, pleaded guilty to making an illegal contribution to Senator Sam Nunn; he also pleaded guilty to giving vacation trips to an IRS auditor. And according to papers recently filed in the U.S. District Court in Los Angeles, William Keeler, the ex-president of Phillips Petroleum Company, said that he "personally handed $50,000 to Richard Nixon in Nixon's New York City apartment in 1968." Phillips was fined $30,000 for pleading guilty to one count involving a $3 million political slush fund. Other organizations admitting guilt in making illegal political contributions include the International Seafarers Union, Lockheed Aircraft, International Telephone and Telegraph (ITT), R. J. Reynolds Industries, and U.S. Steel.

Such contributions are made to buy favors, to maintain favorable weak legislation and/or regulations, and to keep stronger proposed regulations from becoming law. What is additionally so frustrating is that there are not enough investigators to audit the books of the thousands of corporations. Only limited auditing of the 1200 largest corporations can be carried out because of budgetary restraints. Makes one wonder about priorities, doesn't it?

Tax Evasion by Consumers

Most Americans fill out their tax forms accurately each year, and less than 8 percent are delinquent in paying. This is characteristic of the basic honesty and faithfulness of Americans in obeying the laws and supporting their government. Computers check the arithmetic on all individual returns, and amazingly enough, the IRS finds more errors in favor of taxpayers than of the government. Computers also subject all returns to *reasonableness tests,* and this is where an increasing number of consumers are being questioned: Forms with any deduction that exceeds the national average are sorted out for possible auditing.

The IRS cannot audit as many forms as it would like to. Presently, just over 2 million of the more than 80 million returns are audited each year; this amounts to less than 3 percent. And four out of five of those investigated are first scanned by computerized reasonableness tests. The audits return an additional $5 billion in taxes and penalties each year, which are partially offset by about $300 million worth of refunds for people and companies that overpaid. For the benefit of nonbelievers, in a recent year, there were 1145 tax-evasion prosecutions, 885 convictions, and 291 jail sentences. Although the IRS is mainly interested in having taxpayers report their incomes accurately, in cases of fraud they do prosecute.

CONSUMER TAX INEQUITIES

There are many consumer tax inequities, and some will always exist since many are to a great extent subjective. However, many inequities can be modified. One can help by becoming informed. Perhaps you can join a tax reform citizen's lobby (see the Appendix), write legislators, and appeal unfair tax rulings on your own. These are just a few of the responsible actions you can take.

Real Property Taxes

Between 30 and 80 percent of total community revenues come from property taxes on real estate. No two communities assess and tax real property in the same way, but there are similarities. To determine the final amount of tax due, the following process is used:

1. The *fair market value* of the property is determined. That is, the local tax assessor arrives at a figure that theoretically is what "a willing buyer would pay a willing seller." Sometimes the replacement cost of the property is used as the fair market value. With business property, the assessor might use the income approach to determine the fair market value, although this method requires a professional appraiser and often an economist as well.

2. The *assessed* or *taxable value* of the property is also figured. This is usually supposed to be a fixed percentage, set by law, of the fair market value. The figure itself is determined by the local assessor. A structure with a fair market value of $60,000 and a set valuation rate of 50 percent is likely to have an assessed or taxable value of $30,000.

3. The *tax rate* is established by the local body that has the authority to levy taxes. It is frequently levied in mills, with each mill equal to one-tenth of a cent ($0.001); a mill is 1/1000th of a dollar or $1 for each

$1000 of taxable value. Property with a taxable value of $30,000 and a tax rate of 65 mills would be taxed $1950 (0.065 × 30,000) for that year.

The process is rarely as smooth and without challenge as it may sound. Problems first arise when the assessor tries to determine "a fair market value." Ralph Nader says of the situation, in an issue of *Property Tax Newsletter,* "Property tax administration and assessment is nothing short of scandalous. Unprofessional assessments done by assessors [who are] subject to enormous political and economic pressures [too often] results in a system that favors large economic interests at the expense of the small homeowner and businessperson." The accuracy of Nader's statement is evidenced in part by the fact that only a small minority of property assessors have professional qualifications.

The process is shrouded in secrecy and tends to confuse even the interested consumer. A fair market value can be just about anything that the tax assessor wants it to be, but most often it is somewhat *lower* than a realistic fair market value. A curious homeowner who "knows" that a home is worth $65,000 is not likely to complain if the assessor states that the fair market value of the home is $55,000.

Another problem area is that of *equalization factors*. These are attempts to rate properties that are different. In many communities, there are several classification of properties, such as agricultural, business (income-producing), business (non-income-producing), apartments, and single-family dwellings. In other communities, many little factors are identified which theoretically try to "equalize" the tax assessment. The imprecise methods of determining increases and decreases in the assessed valuation of properties invite criticism of the system.

One should approach the purchase of real property intelligently. You need to know *much* more than just what the tax rate is if you are to choose wisely. To illustrate, look at the calculations in Table 16-2 for two homes with an honest fair market value of $60,000. The community with the lower tax rate has a higher tax bill than the other.

Do not rely on tax information given by people trying to sell property or received in casual conversation with those who seem to be informed. A visit to the local assessor's office, usually located in the county courthouse, allows you to look at any of the records. These are maintained by parcels or neighborhoods, and a clerk can assist you.

When a tax bill is received, it will often list the valuation, the names of the taxing bodies, the tax rates, and the amount of the tax. Most local taxing agencies automatically provide itemized data for the taxpayer on the bill. Other communities, however, just send a total bill without itemization. Would you pay a department store bill if it were not itemized?

Property taxes across the country vary greatly, as revealed by figures from the U.S. Department of Housing and Urban Development on new FHA-financed homes. Comparable homes with a fair market value of $50,000 in selected cities were taxed as follows: Albuquerque, $986; Birmingham, $466; Denver, $1326; Fort Worth, $1060; Jackson (Miss.), $386; Minneapolis, $1526; New York, $1590; Salt Lake City, $740; and San Jose, $1190. However, one cannot interpret these differences without knowing what other local taxes are imposed. If one community has a low

TABLE 16-2

Tax Bills in Two Communities

	Community One	Community Two
Fair market value	$60,000	$60,000
Assessed valuation rate	30%	50%
Dollar assessed valuation	$18,000	$30,000
Tax rate	63 mills	40 mills
Final tax bill	$1134	$1200

property tax but also has an income tax, for example, the *real tax cost of living* may be higher than it is in another community that has a high property tax but no income tax.

Additionally, about one-third of all the real property in the United States is exempt from taxation. In New York City, the tax-exempt percentage is about 40 percent; in Washington, D.C., about 55 percent of the land and buildings are untaxed. Alfred Balk, in his book *The Free List: Property without Taxes,* calculates the cost of $600 billion of exempt properties to be about $310 per family per year. About 70 percent of the tax-exempt property is owned by governments, and the remaining 30 percent is owned by religious and educational groups. A few states, including Oregon and Kansas, tax some church-owned land. There is, of course, much debate over whether government- or church-owned property operated for profit should be taxed, especially since they receive the same services as taxed properties. Balk suggests that such property holders should have to pay for such services as water, sewage treatment, sanitation, and perhaps police and fire protection.

Since so much property is untaxed, someone else must foot the bill—other consumers. Paula Kellerhouse of the United Organizations of Tax Payers, Inc., in Los Angeles reports, "My property taxes went from $1100 to $2017 in one year. I didn't pay my tax bill in December. Somebody has to show them." Kellerhouse claims that a person who does not have to make monthly payments on a home can skip the taxes for 5 or 6 years without facing eviction. This is radical action to be sure—but perhaps someone will notice her situation.

In Michigan, as well as in other states, a *circuit breaker* type of reform in real property taxes exists. In that state, those over age 65 receive a rebate on the portion of the tax that exceeds 3.5 percent of household income. The refund amounts to 60 percent of the excess up to $1200. Also, special property tax relief programs are being passed in other states to protect the elderly from losing their homes because taxes go up while their incomes remain rather fixed.

More and more consumers are taking their rising tax bills down to city hall and fighting for reductions. The Pennsylvania TEA Party, a tax justice group, conducted studies throughout the state and found that in some areas, about 90 percent of all properties were inaccurately assessed. A study for the Department of Housing and Urban Development revealed that 50 percent of the assessments on commercial properties were appealed, but only 4.4 percent of assessments on single-family dwellings. That latter figure is expected to rise because of increased taxpayer resistance to rising real estate taxes. Taxpayers in California, Colorado, and many other states have refused to vote for tax increases for schools, forcing many of them to close down for indeterminate lengths of time and cut back on the quality of education.

Workable solutions to such problems are not easily found. Major efforts are being made to upgrade the quality of assessors, to establish more precise equalization factors for property in special circumstances, and to tax business properties more fairly. And in many communities, there has been an attempt to reduce real property taxes and instead rely upon sales taxes, local income taxes, and/or revenue-sharing funds for revenue.

The responsible consumer who wishes to appeal a tax assessment notice needs to become carefully aware of the local rules concerning how to complain. The process is basically simple, and assessors often go along with a proposed reduction if it seems logical and is presented in a nonantagonistic manner. Begin by determining the fair market value of your home; either get a professional appraisal from a real-estate appraiser or real-estate agent or find out the selling prices of similar houses in your neighborhood (and maybe similar neighborhoods, too). Then determine the reasons for your appeal. They could include that the house was assessed at more than its correct fair market value, the official appraisal was too high, the assessment is higher than

similar houses, or the assessor made an error when inspecting the house. One must appeal within the given number of days after getting notice of the tax, or the chance to appeal is lost. An informal appeal to the local assessor might result in a change in your favor. If not, determine the proper appeals agency, timing, and method for the formal appeal. The cost is usually nothing but the time you put in. If you are not satisfied with the decision of the local appeals agency, you can take your case further to a higher appeals agency.

Personal Property Taxes

Probably the most objectionable of all taxes is the personal property tax, which is a tax on your movable property. Many states and localities mail forms to all residents requiring them to list their assets for tax purposes. One must then itemize automobiles, boats, household furniture, and jewelry, for example. You estimate the value of such assets and pay the appropriate tax according to the rate on the form.

The rates can vary widely, too. A 1-year-old Datsun registered in Arlington County, Virginia, is taxed $146.80, but it is taxed only $27.60 in Montgomery County, Virginia. Corporations are also taxed, but usually at different rates. Often, this type of regressive assessment degenerates into a pathetic game of "hide your property." Because the local tax assessor has the right to come to your residence and "look around," individuals frequently take easily movable assets to another location or hide them at home. Corporations have been known to move assets across state lines to avoid the taxes, too. As a result, personal property taxes are not very productive. In some areas, as few as 10 percent of the property owners bother to pay the tax. Pressures to eliminate personal property taxes are on the increase.

State Sales, Cigarette, and Gasoline Taxes

Sales taxes are the most prevalent of all regressive taxes. To reduce consumer objections, such necessary goods as clothing, drugs, and food are sometimes exempted from taxation. Where drugs are still taxed, it is obvious that the elderly pay much more than their fair share of sales taxes, since they purchase more than twice as many drugs as younger families. A study by *Better Homes and Gardens* showed that 66 percent of 70,000 questionnaires returned supported the position that "since lower-income groups spend a high proportion of their income on basic necessities—such as food and clothing—a sales tax on these items is unfair." In spite of such findings, several states still tax those items.

User taxes, such as those on cigarettes and gasoline, in combination with state sales taxes, account for close to one-half of all state revenues. Both types of taxes are widely used, and there are extremely wide variations in gasoline, cigarette, and sales taxes among the states.

Sometimes there is the effect of a double or even triple tax. On a gallon of gasoline, for example, one pays a state gasoline tax, a federal gasoline tax for the Highway Trust Fund, and a state sales tax. On cigarettes, the taxes are similar: The federal government gets 8 cents on every pack of cigarettes sold, and the states add on sales taxes. Although user taxes are expensive for the states to collect, consumers often accept them because they pay such relatively small amounts each time they buy something. One wonders, however, how acceptable the 7 percent sales tax is in Connecticut.

Income Tax Exemptions and Deductions
Income tax regulations on exemptions and deductions are a mix of contradictions and inequities. A blind person can claim two exemptions for the handicap, but a deaf person, an amputee, and a mentally retarded person are denied the same benefit. Interest and taxes are deductible for homeowners and reduce their final tax liability, but the part of the rent that is "equivalent" to interest and taxes for renters is not deductible.

You can spend more than $2000 annually to support a dependent parent, but if the parent's taxable income is more than $750, you might not be able to claim that person as a dependent. Unemployment benefits are exempt from taxation. To benefit financially, therefore, an unemployed person must find a job that pays more than the unemployment benefits in order to compensate for the tax that will be deducted from job earnings.

Tax Table Quirks
Tax law revisions cost uncounted numbers of Americans as much as $23 more in income taxes simply because they earned $1 too much the previous year. Since about 90 percent of the taxpayers use the Tax Table to find the final amount due, most are affected. For example, a married couple earning $16,050 and filing a joint return will find they owe a tax of $3267. Another couple earning $16,051 will have to pay $3281, or $14 more. A married person filing a separate return with an income of $18,050 will find the tax to be $5181; if the person earns $1 more, the income tax liability goes up $23 to $5204.

Only those earning above $20,000 avoid the discriminatory extra tax. For these people, the rate formulas (schedules X, Y, and Z) apply and the mathematics involved does not result in a sudden increase in taxes.

Marital Inequities
Before the Tax Reform Act of 1976, single people paid as much as 42 percent more in federal income taxes than married couples. Still, about 30 million single people, including the never-married, widowed, and divorced, pay as much as 20 percent more than married couples.

There is also a marriage penalty for about 13 million married two-earner couples. This inequity is particularly clear when two people earn about the same income. If each has an income of $16,000, the combined tax is $8660 on a joint return. On two separate single returns, they each would pay $3830 for a total of $7660—or an extra $1000 because they are married.

No wonder we're always short of money—we keep squandering it on taxes.

Courtesy of Edd Uluschak.

Realizing that tax dilemma, some people are still coming out ahead. In particular, we are talking about those married couples where one person has considerably more income than the other. When a person with an income of $16,000 marries someone with no income, the combined tax is $570 less than for a single person earning $16,000. The advantage lessens as the incomes of the two persons comes closer; then the disadvantageous tax tables penalize the married couple.

Several results have been apparent. More people with similar incomes are living together without getting married, in part to save on income taxes. Also, when one earns considerably more in income than the other, many who are contemplating marriage in January or February are moving up the marriage ceremony to December. Finally, for those getting divorced, splitting in December rather than January is more advantageous for tax purposes if their incomes are similar.

Distribution of Tax Payments

Everybody knows that we have a progressive federal income tax where those who earn more pay more. But in reality, in terms of the *total* taxes paid, Census Bureau figures show that most American families pay out about 30 percent of their earnings in direct, indirect, and hidden taxes. Families earning less than $2000, however, are an exception, as they pay an average of 50 percent. This includes all kinds of taxes, such as sales, excise, personal property, and real estate, as well as income taxes. The Census figures define income as "earnings only" and are shown in Table 16-3.

Taxes and Inflation

The Joint Economic Committee of Congress recently prepared a report that indicated that, "Amazingly, the biggest increases in the middle-income family's budget resulted from higher Social Security and income tax payments." During that inflationary period, food

TABLE 16-3

Earnings and Taxes

Earnings	Percent to Taxes
$ 2,000 to $ 4,000	34.6
$ 4,000 to $ 6,000	31.0
$ 6,000 to $ 8,000	30.1
$ 8,000 to $10,000	29.2
$10,000 to $15,000	29.8
$15,000 to $25,000	30.0
$25,000 to $50,000	32.8

prices rose 11.9 percent; housing, 13.5 percent; and transportation, 14.3 percent. Social Security and personal income taxes rose twice as fast. "For the family at an income level of $14,466 Social Security taxes rose 21.6 percent and personal income taxes 26.5 percent."

The less affluent suffer the greatest inequities in times of inflation, since the standard deduction and exemptions are "devalued." Inflation pushes people into higher tax brackets, and their real after-tax income frequently falls.

To illustrate, if a family with an income of $13,000 in 1979 took the standard deduction and paid $1391 in federal taxes, after-tax income would be $11,609. Let's assume that their income rose 8 percent during 1980 to $14,040, with a raise of $1101. Then, the family would be liable for $1690 in federal income taxes, and after-tax income would be $12,431. In dollar terms, the after-tax income rose 7 percent. But the diminished value of the standard deduction and the exemptions actually increases the tax burden from 10.7 percent of income to 11.5 percent. At an assumed rate of inflation of 6 percent—keep in mind that the family income increased at a higher rate of 8 percent—the family's real purchasing power drops! Inflation wipes out $842 and taxes get another $299 for a net reduction of $40, even though the family had a substantial raise in income during the year.

Social Security Taxes
One newspaper, *The Washington Post*, calls the Social Security tax "the most ruthlessly regressive tax in the country, and—inequities and all—that tax is growing at great speed." In contrast to the personal income tax, the Social Security tax has no exemptions or deductions or different rates for people with progressively higher incomes. It is simply a flat-rate tax based on income.

In fact, many people pay *more* in Social Security taxes than in federal personal income taxes. The family pays the deducted amount of Social Security tax and indirectly pays the amount the employer contributes. Remember,

if the employer did not have to make the "contribution," it would be income for the family. Thus, that half is an indirect tax.

Table 16-4 illustrates the regressiveness of the Social Security tax. Note that as a percentage of the annual wage, those earning lower incomes pay a higher tax; thus its very structure is regressive.

Recently passed increases sharply raise the burden of Social Security taxes. It is *regressive* in that it unfairly overtaxes the middle- and lower-income groups and undertaxes those with higher incomes. There had been considerable danger that the Social Security system would go broke, so new increases were passed by Congress.

What the general public doesn't realize is that the middle-income family is going to see a near *tripling* in their taxes just like the higher-income groups. Had the majority of citizens been aware of this, perhaps a fairer method of funding the Social Security system would have been devised.

The typical family of four in the United States had a median income in 1976 of $14,970, according to the Bureau of Labor Statistics. Let's see what happens if we assume that the average family has reasonable increases in income over the next several years. Assume an inflation rate of 6 percent and an income increase of 8 percent annually. This would be a typical increase in income—just keeping ahead of inflation. Thus the *income* upon which Social Security taxes for the average family would be as follows: 1976—

TABLE 16-4

Regressiveness of Social Security Taxes*

Annual Wages	Social Security Taxes	Tax as a Percentage of Annual Wage
$ 6,000	$ 367.80	6.13%
$15,000	$ 919.50	6.13%
$30,000	$1,403.00	4.68%
$45,000	$1,403.00	3.12%

* Based on rates and bases projected for 1979.

$14,970, 1977—$16,200, 1978—$17,496, 1979—$18,896, 1980—$20,408, 1981—$22,041, 1982—$23,804, 1983—$25,708, 1984—$27,765, 1985—$29,986, and 1986—$32,385, Thus, the *typical* family income in 1986 will be $32,385, upon which they will pay $2316 in Social Security taxes. This figure for Social Security taxes compares with $876 in 1976—nearly three times the amount paid a decade earlier.

Economist Martin S. Feldman of Harvard projects conservatively that with the current demographic structure of the population, "the Social Security tax rate will have to eventually rise to 18.4 percent. In short, because of the long-run demographic trends, we are now asking that the next generation pay more than twice the rate of Social Security tax that we are now paying."

These inequities have been present in the Social Security tax structure for many years, but only recently have they been emphasized. The reason is simple: With rising benefits for an increasing number of Social Security recipients, the pay-as-you-go system will go bankrupt unless more income is generated. Benefits now go to more than 30 million Americans, about one out of every seven people, and projections indicate that the number will rise.

Hence, there are only three alternatives: (1) Reduce benefits, (2) require higher Social Security taxes, and (3) pay part of the cost of Social Security benefits out of revenues from other sources, such as general revenues of the government obtained through the income tax. The first alternative is not wise from a political standpoint, as too many voters would be angered by reductions in benefits. Besides, it would lower the level of living for many persons. The second alternative is already becoming a reality with the new increases. The third alternative is a lively issue and subject to continued debate. It is more a question of *how much* of the general revenues should be used to pay for some Social Security benefits, because there is considerable fear of a revolt among younger workers burdened by rising Social Security taxes that pay for benefits

largely aimed at the aged. With accurate projections possible (since most potential beneficiaries are already living), the U.S. Department of Commerce makes this projection: In 1979, 3.2 beneficiaries will be supported by 10 workers, but by 2030, 5.2 beneficiaries will be supported by 10 workers.

Double and Triple Taxation

Many consumers pay federal, state, and city income taxes on all or part of the same income. An increasing number of large cities that have an income tax are expanding it to include nonresident commuters as well. In New York City, more than 700,000 wage earners are commuters. Although tax credits or deductions are permitted, the problem of multiple taxation is evident.

What has become known as the *commuter income tax* has brought back the cry of Americans more than 200 years ago: "Taxation without representation is tyranny!" Consider Dave and Linda Haage of Newark, New Jersey. Each year they pay a federal income tax, a New Jersey state income tax, a Newark city income tax, and a New York City income tax!

Many people also pay a second tax on dividend income. Corporations pay corporate income taxes on their profits and distribute part of the after-tax earnings to shareholders. Then the owners of these shares of stock, often consumers, must pay personal income taxes on any dividends received in excess of $200. It's double taxation.

Geographical Inequities

State and local taxes vary widely throughout the country. As shown in Table 16-5, cities in the Southern states generally have lower taxes than those in the North. For a typical family of four with a $15,000 income, the average state and local taxes amount to 9.1 percent of that income. The taxes range from 3.2 percent in Jacksonville to 18.4 percent in New York.

Some cities and states are, of course, more efficient in using public funds, but the major reason for differences is usually the amount of public services provided. Other reasons include the costs of labor, special taxes (like on motels and meals) in tourist areas, and particular tax levies on selected businesses (oil company taxes in Oklahoma and Texas, for example).

Internal Revenue Service Rulings

Law firms representing clients often get private rulings from the Internal Revenue Service. Officially, only the IRS, the law firm, and the client are involved in or informed of such

TABLE 16-5

State and Local Taxes by City (Typical Family of Four)*

| | $15,000 Income | | $30,000 Income | |
	Taxes	Percentage of Income	Taxes	Percentage of Income
New York	$2755	18.4%	$5716	19.1%
Boston	$2420	16.1%	$4499	15.0%
Buffalo	$2026	13.5%	$4314	14.4%
Chicago	$1609	10.7%	$2758	9.2%
Los Angeles	$1820	12.1%	$3826	12.8%
San Francisco	$1694	11.3%	$3576	11.9%
Pittsburgh	$1566	10.4%	$2698	9.0%
Indianapolis	$1326	8.8%	$2312	7.7%
San Antonio	$1200	8.0%	$1984	6.6%
Seattle	$1072	7.1%	$1687	5.6%
St. Louis	$1316	8.8%	$2503	8.3%
Philadelphia	$1487	9.9%	$2674	8.9%
Denver	$1251	8.3%	$2505	8.4%
Dallas	$1009	6.7%	$1653	5.5%
Phoenix	$1131	7.5%	$2310	7.7%
Cincinnati	$1144	7.6%	$2248	7.5%
Washington	$1396	9.3%	$2963	9.9%
Memphis	$ 896	6.0%	$1350	4.5%
Detroit	$1534	10.2%	$3115	10.4%
Milwaukee	$2135	14.2%	$4424	14.7%
Baltimore	$1442	9.6%	$2862	9.5%
Nashville	$ 834	5.6%	$1245	4.2%
Kansas City, Mo.	$1172	7.8%	$2265	7.5%
Cleveland	$1007	6.7%	$1968	6.6%
San Diego	$1312	8.7%	$2918	9.7%
Atlanta	$1245	8.3%	$2670	8.9%
Houston	$ 868	5.8%	$1414	4.7%
Columbus, Ohio	$ 960	6.4%	$1919	6.4%
New Orleans	$1029	6.9%	$1877	6.3%
Jacksonville	$ 485	3.2%	$ 804	2.7%
30-city average	**$1371**	**9.1%**	**$2635**	**8.8%**

* It is assumed that a family has one wage earner, two school-age children, lives in own home, and owns two cars.

Source: District of Columbia government.

proceedings. Under pressure of lawsuits based upon the Freedom of Information Act, the IRS now lets the public see these rulings; however, they are not admissible as evidence to establish precedent if other taxpayers later want to make the same argument.

Tax Advocates, a public-interest law firm in Washington, D.C., is suing the government. They want the tax courts to consider such communications as evidence. And what is perhaps more important is that they are also asking that correspondence between the Treasury Department and members of Congress on tax matters be made available to the public. Ending such secrecy could result in more equity for all taxpayers.

PREPARATION OF PERSONAL INCOME TAX FORMS

More than three decades ago, the government made it clear that each citizen should pay only a fair share of income taxes. In 1945, the U.S. Supreme Court upheld the "legal right of a taxpayer to decrease the amount of what otherwise would be his taxes, or altogether to avoid them, by means which the law permits." Judge Learned Hand went even further by urging that "nobody owes any public duty to pay more than the law demands; taxes are enforced extractions, not voluntary contributions. To demand more in the name of morals is mere cant."

So that you do not pay more tax than the law demands, you need to examine the similarity of federal, state, and local income tax forms, consider the choice of itemizing deductions or using the standard deduction, determine how you can legally reduce your tax liability, and become familiar with your rights and responsibilities should you ever be audited.

Income Tax Forms
Federal, state, and local income tax forms are in many ways similar. The first federal income tax form introduced over 60 years ago amply

illustrates the major features in all income tax forms (see Figures 16-4 and 16-5).

Information such as name and address of the taxpayer comes first. *Gross income* includes all income of any sort that is not specifically exempt, even though it may later be offset by expenses and other deductions. It includes wages, salaries, bonuses, tips, commissions, interest, dividends, rents, royalties, profits, prizes, and gambling winnings. *General deductions* permit the taxpayer to subtract certain expenses from gross income. Typical nonbusiness deductions include contributions; interest on debts; nonfederal taxes; loss from destruction of property in fire, storm, or automobile accident; medical and dental expenses; and miscellaneous expenses such as union dues and fees paid to employment agencies. *Net income* is the total income after deductions. *Exempted income and exemptions* are other special deductions allowed, such as certain amounts of dividends and other income. The reporting taxpayer and his or her dependents count as so many dollars exempt from taxes. *Taxable income* is the amount remaining after all deductions and exemptions are subtracted from net income.

The determination of state and local income taxes differs widely. Sometimes the consumer pays a flat rate based upon the final adjusted taxable income as reported on the federal form. This is a pretty easy method. Sometimes one begins with adjusted gross income from the federal form and then proceeds to reduce taxable income through larger exemptions, tax credits, and other deductions. These differences in forms result from different legislators, groups, and individuals in each area.

Itemizing or Using the Zero-Bracket Amount
One of the important decisions the consumer must make is whether to take the zero-bracket amount (ZBA), which is a flat "standard deduction" that reduces adjusted gross income before tax liability is calculated, or to itemize actual deductions. Itemization would include medical and dental expenses, taxes, interest, contributions, casualty or theft loss(es), and

INCOME TAX.

THE PENALTY
FOR FAILURE TO HAVE THIS RETURN IN THE HANDS OF THE COLLECTOR OF INTERNAL REVENUE ON OR BEFORE MARCH 1 IS $20 TO $1,000.

(SEE INSTRUCTIONS ON PAGE 4.)

List No. ....

.... District of ....

Date received ....

File No. ....

Assessment List ....

Page .... Line ....

UNITED STATES INTERNAL REVENUE.

RETURN OF ANNUAL NET INCOME OF INDIVIDUALS.

(As provided by Act of Congress, approved October 3, 1913.)

RETURN OF NET INCOME RECEIVED OR ACCRUED DURING THE YEAR ENDED DECEMBER 31, 191....

(FOR THE YEAR 1913, FROM MARCH 1, TO DECEMBER 31.)

Filed by (or for) .... of ....

(Full name of individual.) (Street and No.)

in the City, Town, or Post Office of .... State of ....

(Fill in pages 2 and 3 before making entries below.)

1. GROSS INCOME (see page 2, line 12) .... $ ....

2. GENERAL DEDUCTIONS (see page 3, line 7) .... $ ....

3. NET INCOME .... $ ....

Deductions and exemptions allowed in computing income subject to the normal tax of 1 per cent.

4. Dividends and net earnings received or accrued, of corporations, etc., subject to like tax. (See page 2, line 11) .... $ ....

5. Amount of income on which the normal tax has been deducted and withheld at the source. (See page 2, line 9, column A) ....

6. Specific exemption of $3,000 or $4,000, as the case may be. (See Instructions 3 and 19) ....

Total deductions and exemptions. (Items 4, 5, and 6) .... $ ....

7. TAXABLE INCOME on which the normal tax of 1 per cent is to be calculated. (See Instruction 3). $ ....

8. When the net income shown above on line 3 exceeds $20,000, the additional tax thereon must be calculated as per schedule below:

	INCOME.	TAX.
1 per cent on amount over $20,000 and not exceeding $50,000.... $		$ ....
2 " " 50,000 " " 75,000....		
3 " " 75,000 " " 100,000....		
4 " " 100,000 " " 250,000....		
5 " " 250,000 " " 500,000....		
6 " " 500,000		
Total additional or super tax		$ ....
Total normal tax (1 per cent of amount entered on line 7).....		$ ....
Total tax liability....................		$ ....

FIGURE 16-4 Front page of the first income tax form

Form **1040** Department of the Treasury—Internal Revenue Service
U.S. Individual Income Tax Return **1977**

For the year January 1–December 31, 1977, or other taxable year beginning _____ , 1977 ending _____ , 19 ___ .

Use IRS label. Otherwise, print or type.	First name and initial (if joint return, give first names and initials of both)	Last name	Your social security number
	Present home address (Number and street, including apartment number, or rural route)	For Privacy Act Notice, see page 3 of Instructions.	Spouse's social security no.
	City, town or post office, State and ZIP code	Occu-pation	Yours ▶ / Spouse's ▶

Presidential Election Campaign Fund ▶
Do you want $1 to go to this fund? . . . . Yes [ ] No [ ]
If joint return, does your spouse want $1 to go to this fund? . Yes [ ] No [ ]

Note: Checking "Yes" will not increase your tax or reduce your refund.

Filing Status

Check Only One Box

1 [ ] Single
2 [ ] Married filing joint return (even if only one had income)
3 [ ] Married filing separately. If spouse is also filing, give spouse's social security number in the space above and enter full name here ▶ ....
4 [ ] Unmarried Head of Household. Enter qualifying name ▶ .... See page 7 of Instructions.
5 [ ] Qualifying widow(er) with dependent child (Year spouse died ▶ 19 ___). See page 7 of Instructions.

Exemptions

Always check the "Yourself" box. Check other boxes if they apply.

6a [ ] Yourself [ ] 65 or over [ ] Blind
b [ ] Spouse [ ] 65 or over [ ] Blind

Enter number of boxes checked on 6a and b ▶ [ ]

c First names of your dependent children who lived with you ▶ ....

Enter number of children listed ▶ [ ]

d Other dependents:				
(1) Name	(2) Relationship	(3) Number of months lived in your home.	(4) Did dependent have income of $750 or more?	(5) Did you provide more than one-half of dependent's support?

Enter number of other dependents ▶ [ ]

7 Total number of exemptions claimed . . . .

Add numbers entered in boxes above ▶ [ ]

Income

8	Wages, salaries, tips, and other employee compensation. (Attach Forms W-2. If unavailable, see page 5 of Instructions.)	8	
9	Interest income. (If over $400, attach Schedule B.)	9	
10a	Dividends (If over $400, attach Schedule B) ...., 10b less exclusion ...., Balance ▶ (See pages 9 and 17 of Instructions)	10c	

(If you have no other income, skip lines 11 through 20 and go to line 21.)

11	State and local income tax refunds (does not apply if refund is for year you took standard deduction) . . .	11	
12	Alimony received.	12	
13	Business income or (loss) (attach Schedule C)	13	
14	Capital gain or (loss) (attach Schedule D)	14	
15	50% of capital gain distributions not reported on Schedule D	15	
16	Net gain or (loss) from Supplemental Schedule of Gains and Losses (attach Form 4797) . .	16	
17	Fully taxable pensions and annuities not reported on Schedule E	17	
18	Pensions, annuities, rents, royalties, partnerships, estates or trusts, etc. (attach Schedule E) .	18	
19	Farm income or (loss) (attach Schedule F)	19	
20	Other (state nature and source—see page 9 of Instructions) ▶	20	
21	Total income. Add lines 8, 9, and 10c through 20 . . . . ▶	21	

Adjustments to Income *(If none, skip lines 22 through 27 and enter zero on line 28.)*

22	Moving expense (attach Form 3903)	22		
23	Employee business expenses (attach Form 2106)	23		
24	Payments to an individual retirement arrangement (from attached Form 5329, Part III)	24		
25	Payments to a Keogh (H.R. 10) retirement plan	25		
26	Forfeited interest penalty for premature withdrawal	26		
27	Alimony paid (see page 11 of Instructions)	27		
28	Total adjustments. Add lines 22 through 27 . . . . ▶		28	
29	Subtract line 28 from line 21		29	
30	Disability income exclusion (sick pay) (attach Form 2440)		30	
31	Adjusted gross income. Subtract line 30 from line 29. Enter here and on line 32. If you want IRS to figure your tax for you, see page 4 of the Instructions . . . . ▶		31	

(left margin, vertical text) Please Attach Copy B of Forms W-2 Here
(left margin, vertical text) Please Attach Check or Money Order Here

FIGURE 16-5 Individual income tax return form

miscellaneous expenses. The zero-bracket amount for married persons filing a joint return in a recent year was $3400, or $2300 for a single person. The ZBA assumes certain typical deductions, and more than one-half the taxpayers use it in calculating their income tax. But, this may not be the better course of action. Taxpayers with atypical deductions should record them and then see whether they exceed the ZBA. If these deductions come to more than the ZBA, one should itemize them on the income tax form, as this will result in a lower income tax liability.

For example, consider the case of Pam and Alan Braunig. The Braunigs' gross income was $18,351, including $140 in interest and $90 in stock dividends. Since their deductions amounted to only $2700 they chose to take the zero-bracket amount, which was $3400. The tax amount owed ($3505) came from the Tax Table, since their joint income was less than $20,000.

Reducing the Tax Liability

Effective use of tax regulations can help reduce one's tax liability. Reducing taxable income especially involves (1) proper use of authorized adjustments, and (2) identification and use of every possible deduction and credit. For thorough basic guidance and directions, use *Your Federal Income Tax, Publication Number 17,* which is available at a nominal fee at any post office. A brief overview of how to reduce one's tax liability follows.

Adjustments to Income. Certain kinds of income and expenses may be used to reduce gross income *whether or not* you itemize your deductions later or take the zero-bracket amount. Adjustments to income are in effect *exclusions,* since they immediately reduce gross income by excluding certain items from consideration.

Certain *moving expenses* qualify as adjustments to income. New and transferred employees, self-employed persons, and partners who move 35 miles or more from their previ-

ous home and place of employment qualify for this adjustment. There are very liberal adjustments to lower gross income when an employee remains employed for 39 weeks of the 12-month period following a move. Income can be adjusted downward by a maximum of $3000 for the transportation of household goods, personal effects, and members of the family—including meals and lodging for pre-move househunting trips, for meals and lodging in temporary quarters for up to 30 days after employment, and for some expenses incurred in selling the old home and buying or renting a new one or settling the lease for renters.

Employees may exclude certain *business expenses* from gross income and report them as an adjustment to gross income if they are not paid for by an employer. Surprisingly, many business expenses are acceptable as adjustments to income whether you itemize or use the zero-bracket amount. A few business expenses may be allowable only as a deduction, however. Adjustments to income include ordinary and necessary travel expenses if they are for business or professional purposes and you were away from home overnight. These would include air, rail, and bus fares; auto expenses; taxi charges, meals and lodging; telephone; tips; and the like. If you are not away overnight, usually only the transportation expenses are considered an adjustment to income. Entertainment and gift expenses that meet the guidelines are also adjustments. Business expenses incurred and not reimbursed that are not eligible as an adjustment to income can usually be reported later as a deduction if one itemizes. Business travelers should therefore keep the records necessary to back up any expenses claimed. Receipts and an expense log are usually enough. One should record specific amounts spent, the nature of the expenditure, the names of places and people involved, business discussed, and the days spent away from home.

Educational expenses are adjustments to income also *if* one qualifies. Should the educational expenses be required of you in order to meet the minimum educational requirements for qualification in your employment or other trade or business, or if the program of study will lead to qualifying you in a new trade or business, the expenses are *not* allowable. On the other hand, if you incur such expenses to meet the requirements of your employer or to help you maintain or improve skills you need to perform your present job, they may well be allowable. Since many expenses may be involved, such as travel, lodging, meals, tuition, and books, investigation of the tax regulations might be revealing and helpful.

Other adjustments to income include disability income up to certain maximums, depreciation of business property if one qualifies, alimony or separate maintenance agreement payments, and contributions to qualified retirement plans (such as Keogh plans or Individual Retirement Accounts).

In addition, deductions (recorded elsewhere on the form) such as medical expenses depend on the amount of adjusted gross income. When gross income is reduced through adjustments, the amounts of allowable deductions are likely to increase. Also, since many state and local income tax regulations base their taxes on the adjusted gross income figure from the federal form, a reduction on the federal form may reduce these other taxes, too. Taking advantage of adjustments to income will therefore always have the obvious benefit of lowering one's tax liability.

Authorized Deductions. Deductions from adjusted gross income are authorized in six categories: (1) medical and dental, (2) taxes, (3) interest expenses, (4) contributions, (5) casualty or theft loss(es), and (6) miscellaneous deductions. *Publication 17* gives specific examples and the procedures for reporting these deductions. One can also get help from other government and private publications, tax preparation specialists, and the IRS itself.

Itemizing deductions may save a great deal, however, so the responsible taxpayer must examine the alternatives. To do so, one must become thoroughly familiar with the allowed categories. Expenditures that fall in the six mentioned categories are deductions. The categories and examples of legal deductions are listed below:

- *Medical and Dental Expenses*

  Hospital and doctors' services.

  Portion of automobile insurance policy covering medical payments.

  Cost of health insurance premiums (the first half, up to $150, is deducted without limitation; any excess is subject to a limitation of 3 percent of your adjusted gross income).

  Cost of getting to and from the doctor or hospital (7 cents per mile) plus tolls and parking fees.

  Cost of travel to accompany a person who is sick when such assistance is needed.

  Nonprescription medicines (including first-aid supplies, tonics, vitamins, and special food and beverage supplements) when prescribed by a doctor (must be in excess of 1 percent of your adjusted gross income).

  Special foods and beverages prescribed solely for treatment of an illness.

  Cost of appliances such as eyeglasses, air conditioners, humidifiers, and air-cleaning units when prescribed by a doctor.

  Cost of medical supplies, equipment, and appliances, including dentures, elastic hosiery, braces, crutches, and orthopedic shoes.

- *Taxes*

  General state and local sales taxes.

  Real property taxes (such as on buildings and land)

  Personal property taxes (which, in some states, includes a portion of your automobile registration); only an *ad valorem* tax qualifies (based on the value of the property).

Sales taxes on unusual purchases, such as an automobile or mobile homes, or taxes on utilities not included in estimated sales tax tables.

State, local, and foreign income taxes.

- *Interest Expenses*

    Interest on a personal note to a bank or other financial institution.

    Interest on a mortgage loan.

    Mortgage prepayment penalties.

    Interest on a life insurance loan.

    "Late payment" charges on utility bills are considered to be interest.

    The mortgage "points" assessed in buying a house.

    Finance charges (the actual interest paid in dollars) for bank, local, and other credit-card installment purchases.

    Interest charges paid the IRS for late taxes.

- *Contributions*

    Cash donations to religious, charitable, educational, scientific, literacy, and prevention-of-cruelty organizations.

    Mileage to and from any charitable work performed (7 cents per mile).

    Portion of the price of a benefit-entertainment show or dinner.

    New or used merchandise donations, including clothing, old television sets, and furniture (according to the fair market value).

    Estimates for out-of-pocket donations and contributions. (It is not imperative that you have receipts for every expenditure if you have a written notation of the amount.)

- *Casualty or Theft Losses(es)*

    Casualty losses (such as from a fire, storm, auto accident, vandalism, or theft) above $100.

- *Miscellaneous Deductions*

    Union dues.

    Membership fees in job-related professional organizations.

    Subscription costs to professional publications related to your job.

    Purchase and cleaning of uniforms.

Special work clothes and safety equipment.

Wage deductions for damages to an employer's property.

Certain employment agency fees for help in finding a job.

Certain job-hunting expenses in your present line of work whether or not you actually find a job.

Rental fees for a safe-deposit box, if it contains income-related papers.

Charges for professional counsel and preparation of income tax returns.

Materials purchased to help in preparing income tax returns.

Travel to and from military reserve meetings if they are outside the immediate area of employment.

Travel expenses for a second job (mileage must be more than it would be if the taxpayer returned directly home from the first job).

Portion of the expenses of trips taken for both business and pleasure (cost of transportation and meals may be deductible).

Business-related entertainment both in and away from place of residence (who was present, when, where, and what was discussed must be shown).

Business gifts up to a maximum of $25 per person.

Expenses of an income-producing hobby.

Another way to reduce tax liability is to prepay and shift as many deductions as possible to one year and claim the zero-bracket amount the following year. For example, if possible, plan big purchases and pay medical expenses—or even increase your contributions—toward the end of one year.

Tax Computation

To compute your final tax liability, first begin by reducing it to a lower adjusted gross income. Then either itemize deductions or take

"Ah, the sounds of spring—people cursing while they work on their tax forms."

Courtesy of Edd Uluschak.

the zero-bracket amount. If you itemize, you subtract the deductions above the ZBA from taxable income (also called tax-table income), then look up the tax due on the proper tax tables. Of course, if you find that it is not to your advantage to complete the traditional long tax form, check to see if you can use the simplified 1040-A return without giving up any tax privileges. The form can be filled out in just a few minutes.

Before computing your tax liability, consider these additional methods of reducing taxes.

Income Averaging. Sometimes it might be to your advantage to use the "income averaging method" of determining tax liability. Income averaging is permitted when your income rises and exceeds 120 percent of your average income for the previous 4 years by more than $3000. Of course, you must have had income during those years. You can often save substantially—$100 to $500—by using this method. For example, if over the past 5 years a couple had earned $8000, $10,000, $12,000,

$14,000, and $20,000, the regular tax this year might amount to $4380. If they averaged income, it could amount to $4260, which would be a savings of $120. A special form, Schedule G, must be used by those filing under this method.

Credits. Tax credits are special payments that are subtracted directly from the final tax liability calculated. Taxes paid to foreign governments can be subtracted. Canadian income taxes withheld and paid for work performed in Canada, for example, would qualify for credit.

Low-income families with dependent children and a household income of less than $8000 may receive a special tax credit. On incomes less than $4000, the credit can be as much as 10 percent of the amount due. The credit is gradually phased out for incomes up to $8000. The maximum special credit is $400.

A child-care credit is available, too. This credit is available for those paying for the care of children or incapacitated dependents other than children. The credit is 20 percent of the expenses of care with a maximum of $400 for one dependent and $800 for two or more dependents.

Errors and Refunds.   Sometimes people make mistakes in previous returns and realize them later. Approximately 5 to 8 percent of all returns filed have math errors, and slightly more than 1 percent use information from the wrong table. If you find such an error—for example, you did not take enough deductions on last year's income tax form—simply file an amended return, Form 1040-X, or a Claim for Refund, Form 843, with all necessary information.

Auditing

Auditing of all types by the IRS occurs in about one out of every forty returns. For those in the $50,000-plus income bracket, the odds rise to about one in eight. With the many complications and the difficulties in filling out the forms, it is no wonder that errors are made. Studies have shown that private tax-preparation specialists and even CPAs (Certified Public Accountants) often make errors in completing the income tax forms of others. In one study, the Student Public Interest Research Groups across the country came to a similar conclusion—but about the IRS itself. They took the same set of facts to twenty-two IRS offices in seven states asking for help in filling out the return. They came away with twenty-two different tax computations. And the IRS is not bound by its own advice—an auditor can reject a deduction someone else at the IRS office told you was all right. The courts make the final interpretations of the IRS code.

There are several types of audits. Sometimes the IRS sends you a letter telling you of an error you made. It could be a math error or an unallowable deduction. In such cases, the IRS tells you how much extra to pay. Another type is the *correspondence* audit, which is relatively easy also. It simply involves providing substantiation of a single tax issue that the IRS is interested in, such as a large medical deduc-

tion. Mailing in proper substantiation usually resolves such matters quickly. The *office audit* is the one people worry about. And an office audit can be for just one or two sections of your income tax form or a complete audit of the whole thing.

In any event, take all your records with you to be fully prepared. Some good advice is to not offer *any* extra information, just answer questions. Although the IRS denies that it has a "quota" on how much revenue each audit must bring in, it is well known that each office audit costs about $90 in personnel costs alone. So, don't create questions about other sections of your form in the auditor's mind or he or she might go searching. One always should be prepared to substantiate calculations and deductions for the past 3 years.

Disagreements can arise between you and the auditor. This is natural, since you may not have a receipt for everything and are probably trying to take advantage of every legal deduction. The burden of proof lies with the taxpayer, but compromise is generally the objective. You obviously don't need receipts for everything. But if you are obstinate, the auditor may become less compromising. If you keep your emotions under control, it is more likely that you can work out little disagreements. If you are unhappy with an auditor's decision, appeal the ruling. It is your responsibility to consult the superior in the office and try to have the difference resolved. If that does not work out satisfactorily, ask for a district conference. This is an informal sit-down situation with people who have more decision authority. Most disputed cases are decided here. However, if you are still unhappy, you can ask for a review by the IRS's appellate division. A review higher than that will require a lawyer's help, since such matters must go to a federal court.

Such extreme steps are seldom necessary for the ordinary taxpayer because of the U.S. Tax Court. It was established to hear and decide cases involving less than $5000 of questioned extra tax liability. By filing a petition with a $10 fee, you can have your day in court without a lawyer and before a sympathetic judge. About one in four of the petitioners emerges from court as the winner on the major issue or on at least half the amount of disputed taxes. This is possibly because none of the decisions are binding upon any other taxpayers, and therefore none sets a precedent for other cases. A much larger percentage are settled in favor of the taxpayer before going to court. Pretrial negotiations result in seven out of eight cases docketed for hearing being cancelled before coming to trial. As a result, it is good public relations for the IRS to be lenient with the few consumers who appear before this unique "small claims" tax court.

QUALITIES OF A GOOD TAX SYSTEM

Economists, tax specialists, educators, government officials, and consumers unanimously agree that a good tax system should have five fundamental characteristics:

1. *The tax should be fair.* A fair tax is determined according to the ability of the person or the business to pay. The tax should consider both income and assets and should be equitably assessed.
2. *The tax should be easy to calculate, collect, and enforce.* It should be easy for taxpayers to calculate their tax, easy to identify those who would avoid their tax obligations, and easy to force them to pay.
3. *The tax should be economical to collect.* Expenses for collecting the tax should be kept low. Currently it costs 54 cents to collect every $100 of federal income tax, but over $5 to collect $100 of personal property tax.
4. *The tax should be direct.* Taxes should be paid directly. When they are indirect or hidden, they are regressive and are difficult to administer and control.
5. *The tax should have positive economic benefits.* A tax should not impair economic vitality or negate the efforts of government to help stabilize the economy. It should be for improvements wanted by,

helpful to or needed by, and visible to businesses and consumers.

Based upon these criteria, our present tax systems are not too good. Many recognize this and are making efforts to improve things. And the tax that receives perhaps the most attention is the federal income tax. This is such a popular topic that we have had a "tax reform act" passed just about *every* 2 years since 1969.

Many suggestions will be made in future years, too. Congress will meditate on each idea, and lobbyists for each side will make their arguments. The Carter proposals attempt on a large scale to overhaul, reform, and simplify the entire U.S. tax system with four basic goals: (1) All income would be treated the same, (2) the tax rate would be made much more progressive in a realistic manner, (3) income would not be taxed more than once, and (4) many of the hundreds of "tax incentives"—especially deductions—would be wiped out.

POINTS OF VIEW AND PROBLEMS TO THINK ABOUT

Since 1948, federal spending has doubled about every 10 years. On the state and local level, the rise in spending has been even greater. It is possible, surmised Vermont Royster, writing in the *Wall Street Journal*, that within the next generation taxes will cease to exist because we will all be working for the government. Government spending now totals about one-third of all spending, and the projection is that it will increase. On the other hand, perhaps the trend can be reversed, although that would require that people start doing things for themselves they now expect to have done by government. Royster asks, "Which will it be?"

Tax reform, suggests Ralph Nader, should begin with the House Ways and Means Committee. It is here that most "special-interest tax legislation and loopholes" originate. Bills from that committee sometimes come to the floor of the House of Representatives with a "closed rule." This means that the 435 representatives cannot amend the bill, no matter how outrageous or inequitable a small part of it may be. Tax reformers in Congress have had some successes in cutting back on this source of special-interest tax legislation. Attorney Harry Margolius of California, after being acquitted on twenty-four counts of alleged tax fraud, told the jury after the trial that, "There is nothing more corrupting to our society than the system of taxation." His specialty is helping wealthy clients avoid taxes, and he openly challenges and encourages the government to put him out of business by "passing better laws."

Serious tax reform, such as a tax on gross income (including many fringe benefits), for example, would be fought vigorously by many. Lawyers, accountants, tax specialists, businesses, homeowners, stockholders, and many consumers actually prefer the system as it is, or without any significant changes. Major change could save billions of hours in preparing forms, and so-called "inequitable" loopholes could be closed, but the resulting tax might then be inequitable to some who now benefit from authorized deductions.

From the point of view of the consumer, tax reform is important, but what is especially needed is *tax indexing*. This is a method of offsetting the impact of inflation by indexing the tax rates, that is, automatically reducing the rates to compensate for inflation, which otherwise pushes taxpayers into higher brackets.

Meaningful tax reform will require much more than adding patches to the ailing systems. Senator Frank Church perhaps best summarizes how we can obtain effective tax reform to provide equity for all:

When the majority of our citizenry really wants budgets balanced and inflation stopped, wants to protect the American dollar and the industries that support it, and wants to move toward equity and balance in our tax system, they can have

it and quick. But so long as every group seeks its own advantage first, politicians will respond and we will be able to do little more than to continue to tinker and fumble with the tax laws. We are not your bosses, you are ours. The citizen is sovereign. The customer is king. When you are ready to command with a clear voice and a firm will, we will give you true tax reform, but not until.

It is safe to conclude that changes in taxes, or any other changes in the consumer's world, can come only from those who have the power—the more than 220 million consumers!

CHAPTER ACTIVITIES

Checkup on Consumer Terms and Concepts

Built-in inequities	Real property taxes
Sixteenth Amendment	Assessed valuation
Direct taxation	Personal property taxes
Indirect taxation	Exemptions
Progressive taxation	Secret IRS rulings
Regressive taxation	Adjustments to income
Deficit spending	Zero-bracket amount
Direct subsidies	Deductions
Double-dipping	U.S. Tax Court
Corporate tax evasion	Tax indexing

Review of Essentials

1. Historically, why do we need taxes?
2. Discuss the two classifications of taxation, and give examples of each.
3. What are the major sources and uses of federal monies?
4. Discuss the differences in sources of funds for state and local governments.
5. Cite various types of waste in local, state, and federal government operations.
6. Discuss the inequities in the taxing of married and single people.
7. Contrast the "real" tax rates paid by the poor and the rich.
8. List ten examples of available deductions

that you may not have been fully aware of earlier.

9. Briefly trace your paths of recourse as a consumer who is being audited by the IRS.

Issues for Analysis

1. Discuss this statement: When a nation takes a substantially larger portion of its national income for taxes (more than 35 to 37 percent), that nation loses its character as a free private-enterprise economy and turns over and becomes primarily a state-controlled and state-oriented economy.

2. Take a point of view and defend your position on the following statement: Do we really need so many layers of bureaucracy to support 50 states, 3000 counties, and 80,000 local taxing agencies?

3. React to the conclusion that the burden of taxation in recent years has been moving more heavily toward low- and middle-income consumers.

Places to Seek Redress

Names, addresses, and organizations for consumers to seek redress are arranged according to (1) national organizations, (2) federal government agencies, and (3) Consumer Action Panels.

NATIONAL ORGANIZATIONS

American Council on Consumer
Interests
Stanley Hall
University of Missouri
Columbia, MO 65201

Association of Home Appliance
Manufacturers
Public Affairs Department
20 North Wacker Drive
Chicago, IL 60606

Call for Action
1211 Connecticut Avenue, N.W.
Washington, DC 20036

Center for the Study of
Responsive Law
Box 19367
Washington, DC 20036

Common Cause
2030 Main Street, N.W.
Washington, DC 20036

Consumer Federation of America
1012 Fourteenth Street, N.W.
Washington, DC 20036

Consumers Union of the United
States, Incorporated
256 Washington Street
Mount Vernon, NY 10550

Cooperative League of the USA
1828 L Street, N.W.
Washington, DC 20036

Council of Better Bureaus,
Incorporated
1150 Seventeenth Street, N.W.
Washington, DC 20036

Credit Union National
Association, Incorporated
1617 Sherman Avenue, Box 431
Madison, WI 53701

Direct Mail Advertising
Association, Incorporated
230 Park Avenue
New York, NY 10017

Direct Selling Association
1730 M Street, N.W.
Washington, DC 20036

Electronic Industries Association
Consumer Electronics Group
2001 Eye Street, N.W.
Washington, DC 20006

Mobile Home Manufacturers
Association
Consumer Education Division
Box 32
Chantilly, VA 22021

National Alliance of Television
and Electronics Service
Association
5906 South Troy Street
Chicago, IL 60629

National Automobile Dealers
Association
2000 K Street, N.W.
Washington, DC 20006

National Advertising Review
Board
850 Third Avenue
New York, NY 10022

National Consumers League
1029 Vermont Avenue, N.W.
Washington, DC 20005

National Tenants Association
1742 North Street, N.W.
Washington, DC 20036

Tax Analysts and Advocates
2369 North Taylor Street
Arlington, VA 22207

Tax Reform Research Group
P. O. Box 14198
Washington, DC 20044

Taxation With Representation
2369 North Taylor Street
Arlington, VA 22207

FEDERAL GOVERNMENT AGENCIES

Civil Aeronautics Board
Office of the Consumer Advocate
Washington, DC 20428

Department of Commerce
Consumer Affairs Division
Office of Ombardsman
Washington, DC 20230

Consumer Product Safety
Commission
Director of Communications
Washington, DC 20207

Department of Agriculture
Office of Communication
Washington, DC 20250

Department of Energy
Washington, DC 20460

Department of Health, Education
and Welfare
Office of Consumer Affairs
621 Reporter's Building
Washington, DC 20201

Department of Housing and
Urban Development
Division of Consumer
Complaints
Washington, DC 20410

Department of Transportation
Office of Public and Consumer
Affairs
Washington, DC 20590

Environmental Protection
Agency
Public Information Center
Washington, DC 20460

Federal Energy Administration
Office of Consumer
Affairs/Special Impact
Washington, DC 20461

Federal Home Loan Bank Board
Office of Housing and Urban
Affairs
Washington, DC 20552

Federal Reserve System
Office of Saver and Consumer
Affairs
Washington, DC 20551

Federal Trade Commission
Bureau of Consumer Protection
Pennsylvania Avenue at 6th
Street, N.W.
Washington, DC 20580

Food and Drug Administration
Office of Consumer Inquiries
5600 Fishers Lane
Rockville, MD 20852

Department of the Treasury
Special Assistant to the
Secretary for Consumer Affairs
Washington, DC 20220

Interstate Commerce
Commission
Public and Consumer
Information Office
Washington, DC 20423

National Highway Traffic Safety
Administration
400 Seventh Street, S.W.
Washington, DC 20590

Nuclear Regulatory Commission
Washington, DC 20555

Securities and Exchange
Commission
Office of Consumer Affairs
Washington, DC 20549

Social Security Administration
Division of Public Inquiries
6401 Security Boulevard
Baltimore, MD 21235

U.S. Commission on Civil Rights
Washington, DC 20036

U.S. Postal Service
Washington, DC 20260

Veterans Administration
Washington, DC 20420

CONSUMER ACTION PANELS

Auto Consumer Action Program
(AutoCAPS)
2000 K Street, N.W.
Washington, DC 20006

Aviation Consumer Action Panel
(ACAP)
1345 Connecticut Avenue
Washington, DC 20036

Furniture Industry Consumer
Action Panel (FICAP)
Box 851
High Point, NC 27161

Insurance Consumer Action
Panel (ICAP)
1511 K Street, N.W.
Washington, DC 20005

Major Appliance Consumer
Action Panel (MACAP)
Complaint Exchange
200 North Wacker Drive, Room
1514
Chicago, IL 60606

Index